The Hidden Church of the Holy Grail

Its Legends and Symbolism

Considered in their Affinity with Certain Mysteries
of Initiation and other Traces of a Secret
Tradition in Christian Times

BY

ARTHUR EDWARD WAITE

Vel sanctum invenit, vel sanctum facit

Fredonia Books
Amsterdam, The Netherlands

The Hidden Church of the Holy Grail:
Its Legends and Symbolism

by
Arthur Edward Waite

ISBN: 1-58963-905-7

Copyright © 2002 by Fredonia Books

Reprinted from the 1909 edition

Fredonia Books
Amsterdam, The Netherlands
http://www.fredoniabooks.com

In order to make original editions of historical works
available to scholars at an economical price, this
facsimile of the original edition of 1909 is
reproduced from the best available copy and has
been digitally enhanced to improve legibility, but the
text remains unaltered to retain historical
authenticity.

The Hidden Church of the Holy Graal

PREFACE

If deeper pitfalls are laid by anything more than by the facts of coincidence, it is perhaps by the intimations and suggestions of writings which bear, or are held to bear, on their surface the seals of allegory and, still more, of dual allusion; as in the cases of coincidence, so in these, it is necessary for the historical student to stand zealously on his guard and not to acknowledge second meaning or claims implied, however plausible, unless they are controlled and strengthened by independent evidence. Even with this precaution, his work will remain anxious, for the lineal path is difficult to find and follow. Perhaps there is one consolation offered by the gentle life of letters. In matters of interpretation, if always to succeed is denied us, to have deserved it is at least something.

Among our aids there is one aid which arises from the correspondences between distinct systems of allegory and symbolism. They are important within their own sphere; and it is by subsidiary lights of this nature that research can be directed occasionally into new tracks, from which unexpected and perhaps indubitable results may be derived ultimately. When the existence of a secondary and concealed meaning seems therefore inferentially certain in a given department of literature—if ordinary processes, depending on evidence of the external kind, have been found wanting—its purpose and intention may be ascertained by a comparison with other secret literatures, which is equivalent to saying that the firmest hermeneutical ground in such cases must be sought in evidence which inheres and is common to several departments of cryptic writing. It is in this way that the prepared mind moves through the world of criticism as through outward worlds of discovery.

I am about to set forth after a new manner, and chiefly for the use of English mystics, the nature of the mystery which is enshrined in the old romance-literature of the Holy Graal. As a literature it can be approached from several standpoints; and at the root it has a direct consanguinity with other mysteries, belonging to the more secret life of the soul. I propose to give a very full account of all the considerations which it involves, the imperfect speculations included of some who have preceded me in the same path—writers whose interests at a far distance are not utterly dissimilar to my own, though their equipment has been all too slight. I shall endeavour to establish at the end that there are certain things in transcendence which must not be sought in the literature, and yet they arise out of it. The task will serve, among several objects, two which may be put on record at the moment—on the one hand, and quite obviously, to illustrate the deeper intimations of Graal literature, and, on the other, certain collateral intimations which lie behind the teachings of the great churches and are, in the official sense, as if beyond their ken. Of such intimations is all high seership. The task itself has been undertaken as the initial consequence of several first-hand considerations. If I note this fact at so early a stage as the preface, it is because of the opportunity which it gives me to make plain, even from the beginning, that I hold no warrant to impugn preconceived judgments, as such, or, as such, to set out in search of novelties. In my own defence it will be desirable to add that I have not written either as an enthusiast or a partisan, though in honour to my school there are great dedications to which I must confess with my heart. On the historical side there is much and very much in which some issues of the evidence, on production, will be found to fall short of demonstration, and, so far as this part is concerned, I offer it at its proper worth. On the symbolical side, and on that of certain implicits, it is otherwise, and my thesis to those of my school will, I think, come not only with a strong appeal, but as something which is conclusive within its own lines. I should add that, rather than sought out, the undertaking has been imposed through a familiarity with analogical fields of symbolism, the correspondences of which must be unknown almost of necessity to students who have not passed through the secret schools of thought.

It will be intelligible from these statements that it has not been my purpose to put forward the analogies which I have established as a thesis for the instruction of scholarship, firstly, because it is concerned with other matters which are important after their own kind, and, secondly, as I have already intimated, because I am aware that a particular equipment is necessary for their full appreciation, and this, for obvious reasons, is not found in the constituted or authorised academies of official research. My own investigation is designed rather for those who are already acquainted with some part at least of the hidden knowledge, who have been concerned with the study of its traces through an interest proper to themselves—in other words, for those who have taken their place within the sanctuary of the mystic life, or at least in its outer circles.

In so far as I have put forward my thesis under the guidance of the sovereign reason, I look for the recognition of scholarship, which in its study of the literature has loved the truth above all things, though its particular form of appreciation has led it rather to dedicate especial zeal to a mere demonstration that the literature of the Graal has its basis in a cycle of legend wherein there is neither a Sacred Vessel nor a Holy Mystery. This notwithstanding, there is no scholar now living in England whose conditional sympathy at least I may not expect to command from the beginning, even though I deal ultimately with subjects that are beyond the province in which folk-lore societies can adjudicate, and in which they have earned such high titles of honour.

After accepting every explanation of modern erudition as to the origin of the Graal elements, there remain various features of the romances as things outside the general horizon of research, and they are those which, from my standpoint, are of the last and most real importance. A scheme of criticism which fails to account for the claim to a super-valid formula of Eucharistic consecration and to a super-apostolical succession accounts for very little that matters finally. I have therefore taken up the subject at the point where it has been left by the students of folk-lore and all that which might term itself authorised scholarship. *Ut adeptis appareat me illis parem et fratrem*, I have made myself acquainted with the chief criticism of the cycle, and I have explored more than one curious tract which is adjacent to the cycle itself. It is with the texts, however, that I am concerned only, and I approach them from a new standpoint. As to this, it will be better to specify from the outset some divisions of my scheme as follows : (1) The appropriation of certain myths and legends which are held to be pre-Christian in the origin thereof, and their penetration by an advanced form of Christian Symbolism carried to a particular term ; (2) the evidence of three fairly distinct sections or schools, the diversity of which is not, however, in the fundamental part of their subject, but more properly in the extent and mode of its development ; (3) the connection of this mode and of that part with other schools of symbolism, the evolution of which was beginning at the same period as that of the Graal literature or followed thereon ; (4) the close analogy, in respect of the root-matter, between the catholic literature of the Holy Graal and that which is connoted in the term mysticism ; (5) the traces through Graal romance and other coincident literatures of a hidden school in Christianity. The Graal romances are not documents of this school put forward by the external way, but are its rumours at a far distance. They are not authorised, nor are they stolen; they have arisen, or the consideration of that which I understand with reserves, and for want of a better title, as the Hidden Church of Sacramental Mystery follows from their consideration as something in the intellectual order connected therewith. The offices of romance are one thing, and of another order are the high mysteries of religion—if a statement so obvious can be tolerated. There are, of course, religious romances, and the Spanish literature of chivalry furnishes a notable instance of a sacred allegorical intention which reposes on the surface of the sense, as in the *Pilgrim's Progress.* Except in some isolated sections, as, for example, in the *Galahad Quest* and the *Longer Prose Perceval,* the cycle of the Holy Graal does not move in the region of allegory, but in that of concealed intention, and it is out of this fact that there arises my whole inquiry, with the justification for the title which I have chosen. The existence of a concealed sanctuary, of a Hidden Church, is perhaps the one thing which seems plain on the face of the literature, and the next fact is that it was pre-eminent, *ex hypothesi,* in its possession of the most sacred memorials connected with the passion of Christ. It was from the manner in which these were derived that the other claims followed. The idea of a Graal Church has been faintly recognised by official scholarship, and seeing, therefore, that there is a certain common ground, the question which transpires for consideration is whether there is not a deeper significance in the claim, and whether we are dealing with mere legend or with the rumours at a distance of that which " once in time and somewhere in the world " was actually existent, under whatever veils of mystery. Following this point of view, it is possible to collect out of the general body of the literature what I should term its intimations of sub-surface meaning into a brief schedule as follows: (*a*) The existence of a clouded sanctuary; (*b*) a great mystery; (*c*) a desirable communication which, except under certain circumstances, cannot take place; (*d*) suffering within and sorcery without, being pageants of the mystery; (*e*) supernatural grace which does not possess efficacy on the external side; (*f*) healing which comes from without, sometimes carrying all the signs of insufficiency and even of inhibition; (*g*) in fine, that which is without enters and takes over the charge of the mystery, but it is either removed altogether or goes into deeper concealment—the outer world profits only by the abrogation of a vague enchantment.

The unversed reader may not at the moment follow the specifics of this schedule, yet if the allusions awaken his interest I can promise that they shall be made plain in proceeding. But as there is no one towards whom I shall wish to exercise more frankness than the readers to whom I appeal, it will be a counsel of courtesy to inform them that scholarship has already commented upon the amount of mystic nonsense which has been written on the subject of the Graal. Who are the mystic people and what is the quality of their nonsense does not appear from the statement, and as entirely outside mysticism there has been assuredly an abundance of unwise speculation, including much of the heretical and occult order, I incline to think that the one has been taken for the other by certain learned people who have not been too careful about the limits of the particular term to which they have had recourse so lightly. After precisely the same manner, scholarship speaks of the ascetic element in the Graal literature almost as if it were applying a term of reproach, and, again, it is not justified by reasonable exactitude in the use of words. Both impeachments, the indirect equally with the overt, stand for what they are worth, which is less than the solar mythology applied to the interpretation of the literature. My object in mentioning these grave trifles is that no one at a later stage may say that he has been entrapped.

It is indubitable that some slight acquaintance with the legends of the Holy Graal can be presupposed in my readers, but in many it may be so unsubstantial that

Preface

I have concluded to assume nothing, except that, as indicated already, I am addressing those who are concerned with the Great Quest in one of its departments. There is no reason why they should extend their dedicated field of thought by entering into any technical issues of subjects outside those with which they may be concerned already. I have returned from investigations of my own, with a synopsis of the results attained, to show them that the literature of the Holy Graal is of kinship with our purpose and that this also is ours. The Graal is, therefore, a rumour of the Mystic Quest, but there were other rumours.

In order to simplify the issues, all the essential materials have been so grouped that those for whom the bulk of the original works is, by one or other reason, either partially or wholly sealed, may attain, in the first place, an accurate and sufficing knowledge of that which the several writers of the great cycles understood by the Graal itself, and that also which was involved in the quests thereof according to the mind of each successive expositor. I have sought, in the second place, to furnish an adequate conversance with the intention, whether manifest or concealed, which has been attributed to the makers of the romances by numerous students of these in various countries and times. In the third place there is presented, practically for the first time—*pace* all strictures of scholiasts —the mystic side of the legend, and with this object it has been considered necessary to enter at some length into several issues, some of which may seem at first sight extrinsic. In pursuance of my general plan I have endeavoured in various summaries: (*a*) To compare the implied claim of the Graal legends with the Eucharistic doctrine at the period of the romances; (*b*) to make it clear, by the evidence of the literature, that the Graal Mystery, in the highest sense of its literature, was one of supernatural life and a quest of high perfection; (*c*) to show, in a word, that, considered as a mystery of illumination and even of ecstasy, the Graal does not differ from the great traditions of initiation. Whatever, therefore, be the first beginnings of the literature, in the final development it is mystic rather than ascetic, because it does not deal with the path of detachment so much as with the path of union.

It must be acknowledged assuredly that the first matter of the legend is found in folk-lore, antecedent, for the most part, to Christianity in the West, exactly as the first matter of the cosmos was in the TOHU, BOHU of chaos; but my purpose is to show that its elements were taken over in the interest of a particular form of Christian religious symbolism. That advancement notwithstanding, the symbolism at this day needs re-expression as well as the informing virtue of a catholic interpretation, showing how the Graal and all other traditions which have become part of the soul's legends can be construed in the true light of mystic knowledge.

I have demonstrated at the same time that among the romancers, and especially the poets, some spoke from very far away of things whereof they had heard only, and this darkly, so that the characteristic of the Graal legend is, for this reason, as on other accounts, one of insufficiency. Yet its writers testify by reflection, even when they accept the sign for the thing signified and confuse the flesh with the spirit, to a certain measure of knowledge and a certain realisation. It is only in its mystic sense that the Graal literature can repay study. All great subjects bring us back to the one subject which is alone great; all high quests end in the spiritual city; scholarly criticisms, folk-lore and learned researches are little less than useless if they fall short of directing us to our true end—and this is the attainment of that centre which is about us everywhere. It is in such a way, and so only, that either authorised scholar or graduating student can reach those things which will recompense knowledge concerning the vision and the end in Graal literature, as it remains to us in the forms which survive—in which forms the mystery of the Holy Cup has been passed through the mind of romance and has been deflected like a staff in a pool.

I conclude, therefore, that the spirit of the Holy Quest may be as much with us in the study of the literature of the Quest as if we were ourselves adventuring forth in search of the Graal Castle, the Chalice, the Sword and the Lance. Herein is the consecrating motive which moves through the whole inquiry. So also the mystery of quest does not differ in its root-matter, nor considerably in its external forms, wherever we meet it; there are always certain signs by which we may recognise it and may know its kinship. It is for this reason that the school of Graal mysticism enters, and that of necessity, into the great sequence of grades which constitute the unified Mystic Rite.

If there was a time when the *chaos magna et infirmata* of the old un-Christian myths was transformed and assumed into a heaven of the most holy mysteries, there comes a time also when the criticism of the literature which enshrines the secret of the Graal has with great deference to be taken into other sanctuaries than those of official scholarship; when some independent watcher, having stood by the troubled waters of speculation, must either say : " Peace, be still "; or, indifferently, " Let them rave "—and, putting up a certain beacon in the darkness, must signal to those who here and there are either acquainted with his warrants by certain signs, which they recognise, or can divine concerning them, and must say to them : "Of this is also our inheritance."

So much as I have here advanced will justify, I think, one further act of sincerity. I have no use for any audience outside my consanguinities in the spirit. As Newton's *Principia* is of necessity a closed book to those who have fallen into waters of confusion at the *pons asinorum* of children—and as this is not an impeachment of the *Principia*—so my construction of the Graal literature will not be intelligible, or scarcely, to those who have not graduated in some one or other of the academies of the soul; it is not for children in the elementary classes of thought, but in saying this I do not impeach the construction. The *Principia* did not make void the elements of Euclid. I invite them only for their personal relief to close the book at this point before it closes itself against them.

I conclude by saying that the glory of God is the purpose of all my study, and that in His Name I undertake this quest as a part of the Great Work.

CONTENTS

Contents

BOOK III

THE EARLY EPOCHS OF THE QUEST

BOOK IV

THE LESSER CHRONICLES OF THE HOLY GRAAL

BOOK V

THE GREATER CHRONICLES OF THE HOLY GRAAL

Contents

BOOK VI

THE GERMAN CYCLE OF THE HOLY GRAAL

BOOK VII

THE HOLY GRAAL IN THE LIGHT OF THE CELTIC CHURCH

Contents

BOOK VIII

MYSTIC ASPECTS OF THE GRAAL LEGEND

BOOK IX

SECRET TRADITION IN CHRISTIAN TIMES

BOOK X

THE SECRET CHURCH

Contents

APPENDIX

THE BIBLIOGRAPHY OF THE HOLY GRAAL

PART I

THE TEXTS

PART II

SOME CRITICAL WORKS

PART III

PHASES OF INTERPRETATION

BOOK I

THE ROOTS OF THE HOUSE OF MEANING

THE ARGUMENT

Heads of a General Summary of the whole subject, with the analysis thereof, including :—I. SOME ASPECTS OF THE GRAAL LEGEND.—*The word which came forth out of Galilee—The sacramental vessel—Its history and the quests thereof—The Graal in the books of chivalry—The Graal in modern poetry—The composite elements of the Legend—The Graal as a reliquary.* II. EPOCHS OF THE LEGEND.—*The higher understanding of the Quest—The outlook of romanticism—The attitude of poetry—The direction of archæology—The prospect which is called spiritual—The consideration of the present thesis—The hidden motives of the literature—Its critical difficulties—Concerning the interpretation of Books.* III. THE ENVIRONMENT OF THE GRAAL LITERATURE.—*The Catholic Doctrine of the Eucharist—The passage of Transubstantiation into Dogma—The Cultus of the Precious Blood—Relics of the Passion, and, in the first place, concerning those of the Precious Blood—The discovery of the Sacro Catino—The invention of the Lance at Antioch—The Sword of St. John the Baptist—The state of the Official Church—The Church in Britain—The Holy Wars of Palestine—The higher life of Sanctity and its annals in the Graal period—The sects of the period.* IV. THE LITERATURE OF THE CYCLE.—*Its various modes of classification and that mode which is most proper to the present inquiry—The places of the Graal Legend—The Welsh Peredur and the English Syr Percyvelle—The Conte del Graal—The Lesser Chronicles of the Holy Graal—The*

3

The Hidden Church of the Holy Graal

*Greater Chronicles of the Holy Graal—The German cycle—
The question which is posed for consideration.* V. THE
IMPLICITS OF THE GRAAL MYSTERY.—*The first consideration concerning a concealed sense of the literature—The Secret
Words of Consecration and what follows therefrom, namely,
that a true Mass has never been said in the world since the
Graal was taken away—The super-apostolical succession, the
peculiar Divine Warrant and ecclesiastical pre-eminence
claimed for the Graal Keepers—That these claims must be
distinguished from errors of doctrinal confusion and theological ignorance, of which there is evidence otherwise—
That any concealed sense must be held to co-exist with
manifest insufficiency, even within its own province, and
more especially regarding the Eucharist—That there is no
intention to present the Graal Mystery as that of a secret
process at work outside the Church—The Lesser Implicits
of the literature.*

BOOK I

THE ROOTS OF THE HOUSE OF MEANING

I

SOME ASPECTS OF THE GRAAL LEGEND

THE study of a great literature should begin like the preparation for a royal banquet, not without some solicitude for right conduct in the King's palace—which is the consecration of motive—and not without recollection of that source from which the most excellent gifts derive in their season to us all. We may, therefore, in approaching it say : *Benedic, Domine, nos et hæc tua dona, quæ de tua largitate sumus sumpturi.*

But in respect of the subject which concerns us we may demand even more appropriately : *Mensæ cælestis participes faciat nos, Rex æternæ gloriæ.* In this way we shall understand not only the higher meaning of the Feeding-Dish, but the gift of the discernment of spirits, the place and office of the supersubstantial bread, and other curious things of the worlds within and without of which we shall hear in their order. Surely the things of earth are profitable to us only in so far as they assist us towards the things which are eternal. In this respect there are many helpers, even as the sands of the sea. The old books help us, perhaps above all things, and among them the old chronicles and the great antique legends. If the hand of God is in history, it is also in folk-lore. We can scarcely fail of our term, since lights, both close at hand and in the unlooked-for places, kindle everywhere about us. It is difficult to say any longer that we walk in the shadow of death when the darkness is sown with stars.

Now there are a few legends which may be said to stand forth among the innumerable traditions of humanity, wearing the external signs and characters of some inward secret or mystery which belongs rather to eternity than to time. They are in no sense connected one with another—unless, indeed, by certain roots which are scarcely in time and place—and yet by a suggestion which is deeper than any message of the senses each seems appealing to each, one bearing testimony to another, and all recalling all. They kindle strange lights, they awaken dim memories, in the antecedence of an immemorial past. They might be the broken fragments of some primitive revelation which, except in these memorials, has passed out of written records and from even the horizon of the mind. There are also other legends—strange, melancholy and long haunting—which seem to have issued from the depths of aboriginal humanity, below all horizons of history, pointing, as we might think, to terrible periods of a past which is of the body only, not of the soul of man, and hinting that once upon a time there was a soulless age of our race, when minds were formless as the mammoths of geological epochs. To the latter class belongs part of what remains to us from the folk-lore of the cave-dwellers, the traditions of the pre-Aryan races of Europe. To the former, among many others, belongs the Graal legend, which in all its higher aspects is to be classed among the legends of the soul. Perhaps I should more worthily say that when it is properly understood, and when it is regarded at the highest, the Graal is not a legend, but an episode in the æonian life of that which "cometh from afar"; it is a personal history.

The mystery of the Graal is a word which came forth out of Galilee. The literature which enshrines this mystery, setting forth the circumstances of its origin, the several quests which were instituted on account of it, the circumstances under which it was from time to time discovered, and, in fine, its imputed removal, with all involved thereby, is one of such considerable dimensions that it may be properly described as large. This notwithstanding, there is no difficulty in presenting its broad outlines, as they are found in the texts which remain, so briefly that if there be any one who is new to the subject, he can be instructed sufficiently for my purpose even from the beginning. It is to be understood, therefore, that the Holy Graal, considered in its Christian aspects and apart from those of folk-lore, is represented invariably, excepting in one German version of the legend, as that vessel in which Christ celebrated the Last Supper or consecrated for the first time the elements of the Eucharist. It is, therefore, a sacramental vessel, and, according to the legend, its next use was to receive the blood from the wounds of Christ when His body was taken down from the Cross, or, alternatively, from the side which was pierced by the spear of Longinus. Under circumstances which are variously recounted, this vessel, its content included, was carried westward in safe guardianship—coming, in fine, to Britain and there remaining in the hands of successive keepers, or, this failing, in the hands of a single keeper, whose life was prolonged through the centuries. In the days of King Arthur, the prophet and magician Merlin assumed the responsibility of carrying the legend to its term, with which object he brought about the institution of the Round Table, and the flower of Arthurian chivalry set out to find the Sacred Vessel. In some of the quests which followed, the knighthood depicted in the greater romances has become a mystery of ideality, and nothing save its feeble reflection could have been found on earth. The quests were to some extent preconceived in the mind of the legend, and, although a few of them were successful, that which followed was the removal of the Holy Graal. The Companions of the Quest asked, as one may say, for bread, and to those who were unworthy there was given the stone of their proper offence, but to others the spiritual meat which passes all understanding. That this account instructs the uninitiated person most imperfectly will be obvious to any one who is acquainted with the great body of the literature, but, within the limits to which I have restricted it intentionally, I do not know that if it were put differently it would be put better or more in harmony with the general sense of the romances.

It might appear at first sight almost a superfluous precaution, even in an introductory part, to reply so fully as I have now done to the assumed question: What, then, was the Holy Graal? Those who are unacquainted with its literature in the old books of chivalry, through which it first entered into the romance of Europe, will know it by the *Idylls of the King*. But it is not so superfluous as it seems, more especially with the class which I am addressing, since nominally this has other concerns, like folk-lore scholarship, and many answers to the question made from distinct points of view would differ from that which is given by the Knight Perceval to his fellow-monk in the poem of Tennyson:—

> "What is it?
> The phantom of a cup which comes and goes?—
> Nay, monk! What phantom? answered Perceval.
> The cup, the cup itself, from which our Lord
> Drank at the last sad supper with his own.
> This, from the blessed land of Aromat . . .
> Arimathæan Joseph, journeying brought
> To Glastonbury. . . .
> And there awhile it bode; and if a man
> Could touch or see it, he was heal'd at once,
> By faith, of all his ills. But then the times
> Grew to such evil that the holy cup
> Was caught away to Heaven and disappear'd."

This is the answer with which, in one or another of its forms, poetic or chivalrous, every one is expected

8

to be familiar, or he must be classed as too unlettered for consideration, even in such a slight sketch as these introductory words. But it is so little the only answer, and it is so little full or exhaustive, that no person acquainted with the archaic literature would accept it otherwise than as one of its aspects, and even the enchanting gift of Tennyson's poetic faculty leaves—and that of necessity—something to be desired in the summary of the Knight's reply to the direct question of Ambrosius. Those even who at the present day discourse of chivalry are not infrequently like those who say: "Lord, Lord!"—but for all that they do not enter into the Kingdom of Heaven or the more secret realms of literature. And this obtains still more respecting the chivalry of the Graal. In the present case something of the quintessential spirit has in an obscure manner evaporated. There is an allusiveness, a pregnancy, a suggestion about the old legend in its highest forms: it is met with in the old romances, and among others in the longer prose chronicle of Perceval le Gallois, but more fully in the great prose Quest, which is of Galahad, the *haut prince*. A touch of it is found later in Tennyson's own poem, when Perceval's sister, the nun of "utter whiteness," describes her vision:—

> " I heard a sound
> As of a silver horn from o'er the hills. . .
> The slender sound
> As from a distance beyond distance grew
> Coming upon me. . . .
> And then
> Stream'd thro' my cell a cold and silver beam,
> And down the long beam stole the Holy Grail,
> Rose-red with beatings in it."

And again :—

> " I saw the spiritual city and all her spires
> And gateways in a glory like one pearl. . . .
> Strike from the sea; and from the star there shot
> A rose-red sparkle to the city, and there
> Dwelt, and I knew it was the Holy Grail."

9

So also in the chivalry books the legend is treated with an aloofness, and yet with a directness of circumstance and a manifoldness of detail, awakening a sense of reality amidst enchantment which is scarcely heightened when the makers of the chronicles testify to the truth of their story. The explanation is, according to one version of the legend, that it was written by Christ Himself after the Resurrection, and that there is no clerk, however hardy, who will dare to suggest that any later scripture is referable to the same hand. Sir Thomas Malory, the last and greatest compiler of the Arthurian legend, suppresses this hazardous ascription, and in the colophon of his seventeenth book is contented with adding that it is "a story chronicled for one of the truest and the holyest that is in thys world."

But there is ample evidence no further afield than Sir Thomas Malory's own book, the *Morte d'Arthur*, that the Graal legend was derived into his glorious codification from various sources, and that some elements entered into it which are quite excluded by the description of Sir Perceval in the *Idylls* or by the colophon of Malory's own twelfth book, which reads: "And here foloweth the noble tale of the Sancgreal, that called is the hooly vessel, and the sygnefycacyon of the blessid blood of our Lord Jhesu Cryste, blessid mote it be, the whiche was brought in to this land by Joseph of Armathye, therefor, on al synful souls blessid Lord haue thou mercy."

As an equipoise to the religious or sentimental side of the legend, it is known, and we shall see in its place, that the Graal cycle took over something from Irish and Welsh folk-lore of the pagan period concerning a mysterious magical vessel full of miraculous food. This is illustrated by the *Morte d'Arthur*, in the memorable episode of the high festival held by King Arthur at Pentecost: in the midst of the supper "there entred in to the halle the Holy Graal couered with whyte samyte, but ther was none mighte see hit nor who bare hit. And there was al the halle fulfylled with good odoures, and euery knyzt had suche metes and drynkes as he loved best in this world." That is a state of the legend which has at first sight little connection with the mystic vessel carried out of Palestine, whether by Joseph or another, but either the simple-minded chroniclers of the past did not observe the anachronism when they married a Christian mystery to a cycle of antecedent fable, or there is an explanation of a deeper kind, in which case we shall meet with it at a later stage of our studies. For the moment, and as an intimation only, let me say that the study of folk-lore may itself become a reverence of high research when it is actuated by a condign motive.

We shall make acquaintance successively with the various entanglements which render the Graal legend perhaps the most embedded of all cycles. I have said that the Sacred Vessel is sacramental in a high degree; it connects intimately with the Eucharist; it is the most precious of all relics for all Christendom indifferently, for, supposing that it were manifested at this day, I doubt whether the most rigid of the Protestant sects could do otherwise than bow down before it. And yet, at the same time, the roots of it lie deep in folklore of the pre-Christian period, and in this sense it is a dish of plenty, with abundance for an eternal festival. So also, from another point of view, it is not a cup but a stone, and it would have come never to this earth if it had not been for the fall of the angels. It is brought to the West; it is carried to the East again; it is assumed into heaven; it is given to a company of hermits; for all that we know to the contrary, it is at this day in Northumbria; it is in the secret temple of a knightly company among the high Pyrenees; and it is in the land of Presbyter Johannes. It is like the cup of the elixir and the stone of transmutation in alchemy —described in numberless ways and seldom after the same manner; but it seems to be one thing under its various ways, and blessed are those who find it. We shall learn, in fine, that the Graal was either a monastic legend or at least that it was super-monastic—and this certainly.

II

EPOCHS OF THE LEGEND

A minute inquiry into the materials, and their sources, of a moving and stately legend is opposed to the purposes and interests of the general reader, though to him I speak accidentally, and apart from any sense of election I must in honesty commend him to abstain, resting satisfied that for him and his consanguinities the Graal has two epochs only in literature—those of Sir Thomas Malory and the *Idylls of the King*. As Tennyson was indebted to Malory, except for things of his own invention, so it is through his gracious poems that many people have been sent back to the old book of chivalry from which he reproduced his motives and sometimes derived his words. But without entering into the domain of archæology, even some ordinary persons, and certainly the literate reader, will know well enough that there are branches of the legend, both old and new, outside these two palmary names, and that some of them are close enough to their hands. They will be familiar with the Cornish poet Robert Stephen Hawker, whose " Quest of the San Graal " has, as Madame de Staël once said of Saint-Martin, " some sublime gleams." They will have realised that the old French romance of Perceval le Gallois, as translated into English of an archaic kind, ever beautiful and stately, by Dr. Sebastian Evans, is a gorgeous chronicle, full of richly painted pictures and endless pageants. They will know also more dimly that there is a German cycle of the Graal traditions—that Titurel, Parsifal, Lohengrin, to whom a strange and wonderful life beyond all common teachings of Nature, all common conventions of art, has been given by Wagner, are also legendary heroes of the Holy Graal. In their transmuted presence something may have hinted to the heart that the Quest is not pursued with horses or clothed in outward armour, but in the spirit along the *via mystica*.

There are therefore, broadly speaking, three points of view, outside all expert evidence, as regards the whole subject, and these are :—

(1) The Romantic, and the reversion of literary sentiment at the present day towards romanticism will make it unnecessary to mention that this is now a very strong point. It is exemplified by the editions of the *Morte d'Arthur* produced for students, nor less indeed by those which have been modified in the interests of children, and in which a large space is given always to the Graal legend. Andrew Lang's *Book of Romance* and Mary McLeod's *Book of King Arthur and his Noble Knights* are instances which will occur to several people, but there are yet others, and they follow one another, even to this moment, a shadowy masque, not excepting, at a far distance, certain obscure and truly illiterate versions in dim byways of periodical literature.

(2) The Poetic, and having regard to what has been said already, I need only for my present purpose affirm that it has done much to exalt and spiritualise the legend without removing the romantic element; but I speak here of modern invention. In the case of Tennyson it has certainly added the elevated emotion which belongs essentially to the spirit of romance, and this saved English literature during the second half of the nineteenth century. But taking the work at its highest, it may still be that the Graal legend must wait to receive its treatment more fully by some poet who is to come. The literary form assumed by the Graal *Idyll of the King* —a tale within a tale twice-told—leaves something to be desired. Many stars rise over many horizons, including those of literature, but there is one star of the morning,

and this in most cycles of books is rather an expected glory than a dawn now visible

(3) The Archæological, and this includes naturally many branches, each of which has the character of a learned inquiry calling for special knowledge, and, in several instances, it is only of limited interest beyond the field of scholarship.

Outside these admitted branches of presentation and research, which lie, so to speak, upon the surface of current literature, there is perhaps a fourth point of view which is now in course of emerging, though scarcely into public view, as it is only in an accidental and a sporadic fashion that it has entered as yet into the written word. For want of a better term it must be called spiritual. It cares little for the archæology of the subject, little for its romantic aspects, and possibly something less than little for the poetic side. It would scarcely know of Hawker's *Quest*—not that it signifies vitally—and would probably regard the Graal symbol as I have otherwise characterised it—as one of the legends of the soul—I should have said again, sacramental legends, but this point of view is not usual, nor is it indeed found to any important extent, among those who hold extreme or any Eucharistic views. In other words, it is not specially a high Anglican or a Latin interest ; it characterises rather those who regard religious doctrine, institute and ritual, as things typical or analogical, without realising that as such they are to be ranked among channels of grace. So far as their conception has been put clearly to themselves, for them the Graal is an early recognition of the fact that doctrinal teachings are symbols and are no more meant for literal acceptance than any express fables. It is also a hazardous inquiry into obscure migrations of doctrine from East to West, outside the Christian aspects of Graal literature. This view appreciates, perhaps, only in an ordinary degree the evidence of history, nor can history be said to endorse it in its existing forms of presentation. At the same time it is much too loose and indeterminate to be classed as a philosophical construction of certain facts manifested in the life of a literature. It is a consideration of several serious but not fully equipped minds, and in some cases it has been impeded by its sentimental aspects; but the reference which I have made to it enables me to add that it should have reached a better term in stronger and surer hands. No one, however indifferent—or, indeed, of all unobservant—can read the available romances without seeing that the legend has its spiritual side, but it has also, at the fact's value, that side which connects it with folk-lore. No further afield than the *Morte d'Arthur*, which here follows the great French Quest among many antecedents, it is treated openly as an allegory, and the chivalry of King Arthur's Court passes explicitly during the Graal adventures into a region of similitude, where every episode has a supernatural meaning, which is explained sometimes in rather a tiresome manner. I say this under the proper reserves, because that which appears conventional and to some extent even trivial in these non-metaphrastic portions might prove, under the light of interpretation, of all truth and the grace thereto belonging.

Superfluities and interpretations notwithstanding, it is directly, or indirectly, out of the recent view, thus tentatively designated, that the consideration of the present thesis emerges as its final term, though out of all knowledge thereof.

It has been my object to remove a great possibility from hands which are worthy, and that certainly, but unconsecrated by special knowledge, and it is my intention to return it thereto by a gift of grace after changing the substance thereof.

In searching out mysteries of this order, it must be confessed that we are like Manfred in the course of an evocation, for, in truth, many things answer us; amidst the confusion of tongues it is therefore no light task to distinguish that which, for my part, I recognise as the true voice. The literature does, however, carry on its surface the proof rather than the suggestion of a hidden motive as well as a hidden meaning, and three sources of evidence can be cited on the authority of the texts: (*a*) Confessed allegory, but this would be excluded, except for one strong consideration. The mind which confesses to allegory confesses also to mysticism, this being the mode of allegory carried to the *ne plus ultra* degree. (*b*) Ideological metathesis, the presence of which is not to be confused with allegory. (*c*) Certain traces and almost inferential claims which tend to set the custodians of the Holy Graal in a position superior to that of the orthodox church, though the cycle is not otherwise hostile to the orthodox church.

It must be understood that the critical difficulties of the Graal literature are grave within their own lines, and the authorities thereon are in conflict over issues which from their own standpoint may be occasionally not less than vital. This notwithstanding, the elements of the Graal problem really lie within a comparatively small compass, though they are scattered through a literature which is in no sense readily accessible, while it is, for the most part, in a language that is not exactly familiar to the reader of modern French. It has so far been in the hands of those who, whatever their claims, have no horizon outside the issues of folk-lore, and who, like other specialists, have been a little disposed to create, on the basis of their common agreement, a certain orthodoxy among themselves, recognising nothing beyond their particular canons of criticism and the circle of their actual interests. To these canons there is no reason that we should ourselves take exception; they are more than excellent in their way, only they do not happen to signify, except antecedently and provisionally, for the higher consequence with which we are here concerned. The sincerity of scholarship imputes to it a certain sanctity, but in respect of this consequence most scholarship has its eyes bandaged.

The Roots of the House of Meaning

The interpretation of books is often an essay in enchantment, a rite of evocation which calls, and the souls of the dead speak in response in strange voices. To those who are acquainted with the mysteries, perhaps there are no books which respond in the same manner as these old sacraments of mystic chivalry. They speak at the very least our own language. I conclude, therefore, that the most decorative of quests in literature is that of the things that are eternal; God is the proper quest of the romantic spirit, and of God moveth not only the *High History of the Holy Graal*, but the book of enchantment which I have proposed to myself thereon.

And even now, as if amidst bells and Hosannahs, a clear voice utters the *Sanctus, Sanctus, Sanctus*—because by this undertaking we have declared ourselves on God's side.

III

THE ENVIRONMENT OF THE GRAAL LITERATURE

It is useless to approach the literature of the Holy Graal for any purpose of special consideration, in the absence of a working acquaintance with that which encompassed it externally in history, in church doctrine, in popular devotion and in ecclesiastical legend. As an acquaintance of this kind must not be assumed in my readers, I will take the chief points involved as follows : (*a*) The doctrinal position of the Church in respect of the Holy Eucharist ; (*b*) the passage of transubstantiation into dogma, and other circumstances which led up to the institution of the feast of Corpus Christi in 1264 ; (*c*) the cultus of the Precious Blood ; (*d*) the mind exhibited by the higher life and the mystical literature of sanctity ; (*e*) the standing of minstrelsy ; (*f*) the horizon filled by coincident schools of thought within and without the Church; (*g*) the state of the official Church itself, and more especially (*h*) the position of the Church in Britain, including its connection with the ambition of the English king; (*i*) the legendary history of certain relics; (*k*) the voice of Catholic tradition regarding Joseph of Arimathæa; (*l*) the true attitude of coincident heresies which have been connected with Graal literature; (*m*) the discovery of the *Sacro Catino* in 1101; (*n*) the invention of the Sacred Lance at Antioch; (*o*) the traditional history of certain imputed relics of St. John the Baptist.

The consideration of some of these points must remain over till we approach the term of our quest, but for the working acquaintance which I have mentioned the particulars hereinafter following will serve a temporary purpose, and will enable the unversed reader to approach the literature of the Holy Graal with a knowledge of several elements which entered into its creation and were concerned in its development.

Man does not live by bread alone, because it is certain that there is the supernatural bread, and although a great literature may arise in part out of folk-lore, primeval fable and legend; though in this sense it will have its antecedents in that which was at first oral but afterwards passed into writing, some records of which may remain after generations and ages; it does not come about that the development can proceed without taking over other elements. That these elements were assumed in the case of the literature of the Holy Graal is so obvious that there could and would be no call to recite the bare fact if a particular motive were not very clearly in view. As regards this, I desire to establish that every student, and indeed many and any who are simple readers in passing, will be aware that the first matter of the literature was, as I have said, folk-lore, as if broken meat and garlic, standing for the daily bread of my first illustration. We shall see, in its proper place, that Celtic folk-lore—Welsh, Irish and what not—had wonder-stories of cauldrons, dishes and goblets, as it had also of swords and lances. Those who in the later twelfth and the early thirteenth century instituted the literature of the Holy Graal—being, as they were, makers of songs and endless tellers of stories—knew well enough of these earlier traditions; they were the heritage of the minstrel from long antecedent generations of Druids and Scalds and Bards. But there had come over them another and a higher knowledge—a tradition, a legend, the hint of a secret perpetuated; above all and more than all, there had come over them the divine oppression, the secret sense of the mystery which lies behind the surface declaration of the specifics of Christian doctrine. There was the power and the portent of the great orthodox Church, there was the abiding presence of the sacraments, there was the unfailing growth of doctrine, there was the generation of new doctrine, not indeed out of no elements, not indeed by the *fiat lux* of the Seat of Peter, but in the western countries of Europe—at so great a distance from the centre—the growth was unsuspected sometimes and often seemingly unprefaced, as if there had been spontaneous generation. Ever magnified and manifold in its resource, there was the popular devotion, centred about a particular locality, an especial holy person, and this or that individual holy object. Under what circumstances and with what motives actuating, we have to learn if we can in the sequel, but we can understand in the lesser sense, and perhaps too easily almost, how far the singers and the song which they knew from the past underwent a great transformation; how the Bowl of Plenty became the Cup or Chalice of the Eucharist; how the spear of many battles and the sword of destruction became the Lance which pierced our Saviour and the weapon used at the martyrdom of His precursor. I set it down that these things might have intervened naturally as a simple work of causation which we can trace with comparative ease ; but they would not for this reason have assumed the particular complexion which we shall find to characterise the cycle ; we should not have its implicits, its air and accent of mystery, its peculiar manifestation of sacred objects, or its insistence on their final removal. For the explanation of these things we shall have to go further afield, but for the moment I need note only that the writers of the literature have almost without exception certified that they followed a book which had either come into their hands or of which they had received an account from some one who had seen or possessed a copy. We can trace in the later texts and can sometimes identify the particular book which they followed, but we come in fine to the alleged document which preceded all and which for us is as a centre of research.

Amidst the remanents of mythic elements and the phantasmagoria of popular devotion, the veneration of relics included, there stands forth that which from Christian time immemorial has been termed the Mystery of Faith, the grace not less visible because it is veiled so closely, and this is the Real Presence of Christ in the material symbols of the Eucharist. Seeing that the literature of the Holy Graal is, by the hypothesis of its hallow-in-chief, most intimately connected with this doctrine and the manifestation thereto belonging, it is desirable and essential before all things to understand the Eucharistic position at the period of the development of the literature. We have the traces therein of two schools of thought, though the evidence of the one is clearer than that of the other; they are respectively the school of transubstantiation and that which is alternative thereto, but not in a sectarian sense, namely, the spiritual interpretation of the grace communicated in the palmary sacrament of the altar.

The means of grace are infinite, but the recognised Sacraments are seven, and to each of them is allocated a *locus* which is symbolical of its position in the system. Baptism is conferred at the West in the *pronaos* of the temple, because it is the rite of entrance and the reception of the postulant. Confirmation takes place within the sanctuary itself, on the steps of the altar, because those who have been received in the body by the mediation of sponsors are entitled, if they are properly prepared, to their inheritance in the gifts of the Spirit. The place of Penance is in the sideways, because those who have fallen from righteousness have become thereby extra-lineal, having deviated from the straight path which leads to the Holy of Holies, and their rectification is to come. The Eucharist is administered at the steps of the chancel because it is taken from the hands of him who has received it from the altar itself, and thus he comes like Melchisedech carrying bread and wine, or in the signs and symbols of the Mediator. It is symbolical of the act of Christ in offering Himself for the redemption of mankind ; He comes therefore half-way to the communicant, because He was manifested in the flesh. This is the material sign of the union which is consummated within, and its correspondence in the Sacraments is Matrimony, which is celebrated in the same place and is another sign of the union, even of the new and eternal covenant. It is the work of Nature sanctified and Love, under its proper warrants, declared holy on all planes. The Sacrament of Holy Orders is conferred on the steps of the altar, and it has more than this external correspondence with that of Confirmation, of which it is the higher form ; the latter is the rite of betrothal by which on the threshold of life the candidate is dedicated to the union and the spouse of the union descends for a moment upon him, with the sign and seal of possession ; the former is the spiritual marriage of the priest, by which he espouses the Church militant on earth that the Church triumphant in Heaven may at a proper season intervene for the consummation of the higher conjugal rights. The sacrament of Extreme Unction is the last act and the last consolation which the Church can offer to the faithful, and it is performed outside the temple because the Church follows its children, even to the gate of death, that their eyes may behold His salvation, Who has fulfilled according to His Word.

It is only at first sight that this brief interpretation will seem out of place in the section; its design is to show, by the ritual position in which the sacraments are administered, that the Holy Eucharist, which has its place of repose and exposition at the far East on the Altar, is the great *palladium* of the Christian mystery, that the Orient comes from on high, moving to meet the communicant, because God is and He recompenses those who seek Him out. The correspondences hereof in the romances are (*a*) the rumours of the Graal which went before the Holy Quests, and (*b*) the going about of the Graal, so that it was beheld in chapels and hermitages—yes, even in the palace of the King.

The great doctrinal debate of the closing twelfth and the early thirteenth century was that which concerned the mystery of the Eucharist, and in matters of doctrine there was no other which could be called second in respect of it. It filled all men's ears, and there can be no question that the vast sodality of minstrelsy was scarcely less versed than the outer section of the priesthood in its palmary elements. Of this debate France was a particular centre, and Languedoc, in the persons of the Albigenses, was a place of holocaust, the denial of the Eucharist being one of the charges against them. As regards the question itself, I suppose it will be true to say that it turned upon the doctrine of transubstantiation, which was decreed by the Council of Lateran in 1215, under Pope Innocent III. The words of the definition are: "The Body and Blood of Jesus Christ are really contained under the species of bread and wine in the Sacrament of the Altar, the bread being transubstantiated into the Body and the Wine into the Blood." Long anterior to this promulgation, there can be no doubt that the doctrine represented the mind of the Church at the seat of its power. In contradistinction thereto were the opinions of the protesting sects, while external to both was the feeling of a minority which did not object openly, yet did not less strongly hold to a spiritual interpretation of the Real Presence. The external devotion to the Eucharist which was manifested more and more by the extremists on the side of the Church would scarcely be checked by the exponents of the middle way, and indeed it might well have been encouraged, though not with an intention which could be termed the same specifically. In the thirteenth century the elements were beginning to be elevated for the adoration of the people ; the evidence is regarded as doubtful in respect of any earlier period. It must have become a general custom in 1216, for a constitution of Honorius III. speaks of it as of something which had been done always. In 1229 Gregory IX. devised the ringing of a bell before consecration as a warning for the faithful to fall on their knees and worship Christ in the Eucharist. Still earlier in the thirteenth century Odo, Bishop of Paris, regulated the forms of veneration, more especially when the Sacred Elements were carried in procession. Hubert, Archbishop of Canterbury, had taken similar precautions at the end of the twelfth century. It seems to follow from the constitutions of Odo that some kind of reservation was practised at his period, and I believe that the custom had descended from primitive times. There is nothing, however, in the romances to show that this usage was familiar ; the perpetual presence was for them in the Holy Graal, and apparently in that only. Church and chapel and hermitage resounded daily with the celebration of the Mass. In one instance we hear of a tabernacle on the Altar, or some kind of receptacle in which the Consecrated Elements reposed. The most usual mediæval practice was to reserve in a dove-shaped repository which hung before the Table of the Lord. The

Book of the Holy Graal has, as we shall see, a very curious example of reservation, for it represents a Sacred Host delivered to the custody of a convert, one also who was a woman and not in the vows of religion. It was kept by her in a box, and the inference of the writer is that Christ was, for this reason, always with her. The reader who is dedicated in his heart to the *magnum mysterium* of faith will be disposed to regard this as something approaching sacrilege, and I confess to the same feeling, but it was a frequent practice in the early church, and not, as it might well be concluded, a device of romance.

As regards transubstantiation, the voice of the literature in the absence of an express statement on either side seems to represent both views. The Greater Chronicles of the Graal are as text-books for the illustration of the doctrine, but it is absent from the Lesser Chronicles, and outside this negative evidence of simple silence there are other grounds for believing that it was unacceptable to their writers, who seem to represent what I have called already the spiritual interpretation of the Real Presence, corresponding to what ecclesiologists have termed a body of Low Doctrine within the Church.

There was another question exercising the Church at the same period, though some centuries were to elapse before it was to be decided by the central authority. It was that of communion in both kinds, which was finally abolished by the Council of Constance in 1415, the decision then reached being confirmed at Trent in 1562. The ordination of communion in one kind was preceded by an intermediate period when ecclesiastical feeling was moving in that direction, but there was another and an earlier period—that is to say, in the fifth century—when communion under one kind was prohibited expressly on the ground that the division of the one mystery could not take place without sacrilege. As a species of middle way, there was the practice of the intincted or steeped Host which seems to have been coming into use at the

beginning of the tenth century, although it was prohibited at the Council of Brago in Galicia, except
possibly in the case of the sick and of children. The
custom of mixing the elements was defended by
Emulphus, Bishop of Rochester, in 1120, and Archbishop Richard referred to the intincted Host in 1175.
All these problems of practice and doctrine were the
religious atmosphere in which the literature of the
Graal was developed. There were great names on all
sides; on that of transubstantiation there was the name
of Peter Lombard, the Master of Sentences, though he
did not dare to determine the nature of the conversion
—whether, that is to say, it was "formal, substantial, or
of some other kind"; on the side of communion under
one element there was that of St. Thomas Aquinas, the
Angel of the Schools.

With an environment of this kind it was inevitable
that poetry and legend should take over the mystery
of the Eucharist, and should exalt it and dwell thereon.
We shall see very shortly that the assumption was not
so simple as might appear from this suggestion, and that
something which has the appearance of a secret within
the sanctuary had been heard of in connection with the
central institution of official Christianity. In any case,
from the moment that the Eucharist entered into the
life of romantic literature, that literature entered after a
new manner into the heart of the western peoples. Very
soon, it has been said, the Graal came to be regarded as
the material symbol of the Catholic and Christian faith,
but it was really the most spiritual symbol; I believe that
it was so considered, and the statement does little more
than put into English the inspired words of the Ordinary
of the Mass. In the middle of the mistaken passion
for holy wars in Palestine; through the monstrous
iniquity of Albigensian Crusades; the ever-changing
struggle notwithstanding between Pope and King and
Emperor; within the recurring darkness of interdict,
when the Sacraments were hidden like the Graal; the

Legend of the Holy Graal grew and brightened, till the most stressful of times adventurous, the most baleful of all enchantments, shone, as it seemed, in its shining, and a light which had been never previously on the land or sea of literature glorified the spirit of romance. It was truly as if the great company of singers and chroniclers had gathered at the high altar to partake of the Blessed Sacrament, and had communicated not only in both kinds, but in elements of extra-valid consecration.

The thesis of this section is that God's immanence was declared at the time of the literature, through all Christendom, by the Mystery of Faith and that the development of Eucharistic doctrine into that of transubstantiation was a peculiar recognition of the corporate union between Christ and His people. That immanence also was declared by the high branches of Graal romance, even as by the quests of the mind in philosophy—in which manner romance, in fine, became the mirror of religion, and the literature testified, under certain veils, to a mystery of Divine experience which once at least was manifested in Christendom.

So I who am about to speak offer a loving salutation to the learned and admirable souls who have preceded me in the way of research. It is because I have ascended an untrodden peak in Darien to survey the prospect of the Quest, and have found that there is another point of view, that I come forward in these pages carrying strange tidings, but leaving to all my precursors the crowns and bays and laurels which they have deserved so well, and offering no contradiction to anything which they have attained truly. How admirable is the life of the scholar—how unselfish are the motives which inspire him—and how earnestly we who, past all revocation, are dedicated to the one subject desire that those paths which he travels—when even they seem far from the goal—may lead him to that term which is his as well as ours, for assuredly he seeks only the truth as he conceives thereof.

As the theory of transubstantiation did not pass into

dogma till a late period in the development of the canon of the Graal, so it can be said that romantic texts like the *Book of the Holy Graal*, the *Longer Prose Perceval* and the *Galahad Quest*, but the last especially, which contains the higher code of chivalry, were instrumental in promoting that dogma by the proclamation of a sacrosaintly feast of *Corpus Christi* maintained for ever in the Hidden House of the Graal, till the time came when the great feast of exaltation and the assumption into heaven of the sacred emblems was held in fine at Sarras. There was, therefore, a correlation of activity between the two sides of the work, for it was out of the growing dogma that the Graal legend in the Greater Chronicles assumes its particular sacramental complexion.

When all has been granted and, after granting, has been exalted even, it remains that the Eucharistic symbol is so much the greatest of all that we can say that there is a second scarcely, because this is the palmary channel of grace, and—in the last resource—we do not need another. If it were not that the literature of the Holy Graal offers intimations of still more glorious things behind this mystery than we are accustomed to find in theological and devotional handbooks, I suppose that the old books would have never concerned my thoughts. Now therefore, God willing, I speak to no one, in or out of churches, sects and learned societies, who does not realise in his heart that the path of the life everlasting lies, mystically speaking, within the consecrated elements of bread and wine, beyond which veils all the high Quests are followed.

Passing from the doctrinal matters expressed and implied in the Graal literature to the sacred palladia with which it is concerned more especially, we enter into another species of environment. Out of the doctrine of transubstantiation, and perhaps more especially out of the particular congeries of devotional feelings connected therewith, there originated what may be termed a cultus of the body of God and of His blood, understood in the mystery of the Incarnation, and the instinct which lies behind the veneration of relics came into a marked degree of operation. Such veneration is instinctive, as I have just said, and representing on the external side, invalidly or not, the substance of things unseen in religion, it is so rooted in our natural humanity that it would be difficult to regard its manifestation in Christendom as characteristic more especially of Christianity than of some other phases of belief. The devotion which, because of its excesses, is by a hasty and unrooted philosophy termed superstition —which no instinct can ever be—manifested early enough and never wanted its objects. There can be scarcely any call to point out that in the considerations which here follow I am concerned with questions of fact and not with adjudication thereon. The veneration of relics and cognate objects, to which some kind of sanctity was imputed, became not only an environment of Christianity at a very early period, but it so remains to the present day for more than half of Christendom. It may be one of the grievous burdens of those ecclesiastical systems about which it prevails and in which it is still promoted, but having said what the sense of intellectual justice seems to require, that it may be exonerated from the false charge of superstition, I have only to add—and this is to lift the Graal literature out of the common judgment which might be passed upon memorials of relic worship—that the instinct of such devotions, as seen at their best in the official churches, has always an arch-natural implicit; it works upon the simple principle that God is not the God of the dead but of the living, and the reverence, by example, for the Precious Blood of Christ depends from the doctrine of His immanence in any memorials which He has left. I need not add that, on the hypothesis of the Church itself, the sense of devotion would be better directed, among external objects, towards the Real Presence in the symbols of the Eucharist; but in the Graal literature it was round about the Sacramental Mystery

28

that the Relics of the Passion were collected, operating and shining in that light.

We know already that the Sacred Vessel of the legends was in the root-idea a Reliquary, and as such that it was the container and preserver of the Precious Blood of Christ. The romantic passion which brought this Reliquary into connection with the idea of that sacrament which communicated the life of Christ's blood to the believing soul, and the doctrinal passion which led to the definition concerning transubstantiation interacted one upon another. John Damascene had said in the eighth century that the elements of bread and wine were assumed and united to the Divinity—which took place by the invocation of the Holy Ghost, for the Spirit descends and changes. The Venerable Bede had said that the Lord gave us the sacrament of His flesh and blood in the figure of bread and wine. And again: "Christ is absent as to His Body, but is present as to His Divinity." And yet further: "The Body and Blood of Jesus Christ are received in the mouth of believers for their salvation." I do not know whether the implicits of this presentation have been realised in any school of interpreters, but there is one of them which covers all phases of sacramental exegesis, however variant from each other, and however in conflict with high Roman doctrine concerning the Eucharist. I state it as one who after long searchings has found a hidden jewel of the sacrament which might be an eirenicon for all the sects alive. It has also the simplicity which Khunrath, in expounding the Hermetic side of Eternal Wisdom, has said to be the seal of Nature and Art. I testify, therefore, that the true mystery of the Eucharist resides in the assumption by the Divine Life of the veils of Bread and Wine, and that even as once in time and somewhere in the world that life assumed the veils of flesh and blood, which became the Body of the Lord, so here and now—daily on every worshipful and authorised altar over the wide, wide world—do those unspotted elements become again that sacred vehicle, so that he who communicates in the faith of spirit and of truth, receives that which is not less truly the Divine Body than the especial polarisation of elements which was born in Nazareth of the sacred and glorious Virgin. Moreover, I am very certain that the one mystery was operated as if in the terms and valid forms of the other by the invocation of the Holy Spirit and the utter consecration of the elements. The reason is that given by Leo the Great, or another, so long and long ago—that Mary conceived in her heart before she conceived in her body. But having so conceived, the elements within her were transubstantiated into the Divine Body. I desire to add with all veneration and homage that this root-mystery of redemption is that which lies behind the devotion to the Mother of God, which has ascended to such heights in the Latin Church. This Church is the one witness through the ages whose instinct on the great subjects has never erred, however long and urgently the powers of the deep and the powers of perdition have hammered at the outer gates. Among other things, she has always recognised in the withdrawn and most holy part of her consciousness that she who conceived Christ—by the desire of the mystery of God satisfied out of all measure in a consummated marriage of the mind—had entered through her humanity into assumption with the Divine, and was to be counted no longer merely among the elected daughters of Zion.

To return therefore, those who say that the Eucharist is flesh and blood are speaking God's truth, and I ask *in examine mortis*—

"In life's delight, in death's dismay"—

that I may never receive otherwise. And those who say that such things are understood spiritually say also the truth which is eternal after their own manner, whence I look to communicate with them when "the dedely flesh" begins "to beholde the spyrytuel thynges"—or ever I set forth in that ship of mystic faith which was built from the beginning of this external order that it may carry us in fine to Sarras, though it is known that we shall go further.

Well, *fratres carissimi, sorores ex omnibus dilectissimæ*, to whom I speak the wisdom of the other world in a mystery—those who out of all expectation translated the deep things of doctrine, as they best could, into the language of romance—out of the Latin, as they said in their cryptic fashion—the Palladium of all research was that Vessel of Singular Election which contained, in their ingenuous symbolism, the Blood of Christ; but seeing that they were in a hurry to show how those who were worthy to receive the arch-natural sacraments did after some undeclared manner partake at the Graal Mass of corporeal and incorporeal elements which were fit to sustain both body and soul, so did the Reliquary become the Chalice, or alternatively it was elevated and the Christ came down to distribute His own life with the *osculum fraternitatis* and the *consolamentum* of all consolation. They collected, also, under the ecclesiastical and monastic ægis, certain other relics about the relic-in-chief. Now, the point concerning all is that most of the minor Hallows were known already as local objects of sanctity no less than the palmary Hallow, but the sanctity ascribed to the latter and the devotion thereto belonging were beginning to prevail generally. It is difficult to trace the growth of this kind of cultus; but as to the worship of spiritual devotion there was offered everywhere in Christendom the Body and Blood of Christ in the Sacrament of the Altar, so at many shrines—as if the more visible symbol carried with it a validity of its own, a more direct and material appeal—there was the reputed *sang real* of Christ preserved in a reliquary. Some of these local devotions were established and well known before the appearance of any text of the Holy Graal with which we are acquainted—probably before those texts which we can discern behind the extant literature.

We have at the present day the Feast of the Precious

31

Blood, which is a modern invention, and perhaps for some even who are within the fold of the Latin Church, it is classed among the unhappy memorials of the pontificate of Pius IX. This notwithstanding, it is what may be termed popular, and has in England its confraternities and other systems to maintain it in the mind of the laity. It has the London Oratory as its more particular centre, and it is described as an union and an apostolate of intercessory prayer. Without such assistance in the Middle Ages we can understand that the cultus had its appeal to the devotional side of the material mind, for which flesh and blood profited a good deal, in spite of asceticism and the complication of implicits behind the counsels of perfection in the religious life of the age.

The historical antiquity of the local sanctities which centre about certain relics is shrouded like some Masonic events in the vague grandeur of time immemorial, and a defined date is impossible. Because the legends of the Graal are connected with the powers and wonders of several hallowed objects belonging to the Passion of Christ, it is essential rather than desirable to ascertain whether at the period when the literature arose —and antedating it, if that be possible — there were such objects already in existence and sufficiently well known to respond as a *terminus a quo* in respect of the development of the legends. The places which appear as claimants to the possession of relics of the Precious Blood are, comparatively speaking, numerous ; among others there are Bruges, Mantua, Saintes, the Imperial Monastery at Weingarten, and even Beyrout. According to the story of Mantua, the relic was preserved by Longinus, the Roman soldier who pierced the side of Christ. Within the historical period, it is said to have been divided, and some part of it was secured by the monastery of Weingarten, already mentioned. This portion was again subdivided and brought from Germany by Richard of Cornwall, the brother of Henry III. Fractional as the portion was, it is affirmed to have been a large relic, and the fortunate possessor founded a religious congregation to guard and venerate it. Later on it was, however, divided again into three parts, of which one was retained by the congregation, one was deposited in a monastery built for the purpose at Ashted, near Berkhampstead, and the third in a third monastery erected at Hailes in Gloucestershire. All these were foundations by Richard of Cornwall; and to explain such continual division, it must be remembered that this was a period when the building of churches and religious houses was prohibited without relics to sanctify them. Now, the story of Richard himself may be accepted as tolerably well founded, but there is much doubt concerning the relics at Weingarten and at Mantua itself. The alternative statements are (1) that in 1247 the Templars sent to King Henry III. a *vas vetustissimum*, having the appearance of crystal and reputed to contain the Precious Blood; (2) that in the same year, and to the same King, there was remitted by the Patriarch of Jerusalem a Reliquary termed the Sangreal, which had once belonged to Nicodemus and Joseph of Arimathæa. Now it is obvious that at the period of Henry III. the canon of the Graal literature was almost closed; the last of these stories is obviously a reflection of that literature; it was also the time when (*a*) the *Sacro Catino* of Geneva may have begun to be regarded as the Graal, and when (*b*) a similar attribution was given to a sacred vessel which had been long preserved at Constantinople; but these objects, whether dishes or chalices, were not reliquaries. It will be seen that the claim of Mantua remains over with nothing to account for its origin. Of Beyrout I have heard only, and have no details to offer. But the relic of Bruges has a clear and methodical history, passing from legend into a domain which may be that of fact. The legend is that Joseph of Arimathæa having collected the Blood from the wounds of Christ, as the literature of the Graal tells us, placed it in a phial, which was taken to Antioch by St. James the Less, who was the first bishop of that city. The possible historical fact is that the Patriarch of Antioch gave the Reliquary about 1130 to a knight of Bruges who had rendered signal services to the church in Antioch. It was brought back by the knight to his native place, and there it has remained to this day. The dubious element in the story is the gift of such a relic under any circumstances whatever; the point in its favour is that the phial has the character of oriental work, which is referred by experts in ancient glass to the seventh or eighth century.

Against, or rather in competition with, this simple and consistent claim, there is the monstrous invention connected with the monastery of the Holy Trinity at Fécamp in Normandy. Here there is—or there was at least in the year 1840—a tabernacle of white marble, decorated with sculptured figures and inscribed : "Hic Sanguis D.N., I.H.V., X.P.I." It is therefore called the Tabernacle of the Precious Blood.

The story is that Joseph of Arimathæa removed the blood from the wounds of Christ, after the body had been taken down from the Cross, using his knife for the purpose, and collecting the sacred fluid in his gauntlet. The gauntlet he placed in a coffer, and this he concealed in his house. The years passed away, and on his deathbed he bequeathed the uncouth reliquary to his nephew Isaac, telling him that if he preserved it the Lord would bless him in all his ways. Isaac and his wife began to enjoy every manner of wealth and prosperity ; but she was an unconverted Jewess, and seeing her husband performing his devotions before the coffer, she concluded that he had dealings with an evil spirit, and she denounced him to the high priest. The story says that he was acquitted, but he removed with the reliquary to Sidon, where the approaching siege of Jerusalem was made known to him in a vision. He therefore concealed the reliquary in a double tube of lead, with the knife and the head of the Lance which had pierced the side of Christ. The tube itself he concealed in the trunk of a fig-tree,

the bark of which closed over its contents, so that no
fissure was visible. A second vision on the same subject
caused him to cut down the tree, and he was inspired to
commit it to the waves. In the desolation which he felt
thereafter an angel told him that his treasure had reached
shore in Gaul, and was hidden in the sand near the valley
of Fécamp.

I do not propose to recount the various devices by
which the history of the fig-tree is brought up to the
period when the monastery was founded at the end of
the tenth century. The important points in addition
are (*a*) that the nature of the Reliquary did not satisfy
the custodians, and, like the makers of Graal books, they
wanted an arch-natural chalice to help out their central
Hallow ; (*b*) that they secured this from the priest of
a neighbouring church who had celebrated Mass on a
certain occasion, and had seen the consecrated elements
converted into flesh and blood ; (*c*) that a second knife
was brought, later on, by an angel ; (*d*) that a general
exposition of all the imputed relics took place on the
high altar in 1171 ; (*e*) that their praises and wonders
were celebrated by a guild of jongleurs attached to the
monastery, which guild is said to have originated early in
the eleventh century, and was perpetuated for over four
hundred years ; (*f*) that the story is told in a mediæval
romance of the thirteenth century, though in place of
Joseph the character in chief is there said to be Nicodemus;
(*g*) that there are other documents in French and in
Latin belonging to different and some of them to simi-
larly early periods ; (*h*) that there is also a Mass of the
Precious Blood, which was published together with the
poem in 1840, and this is, exoterically speaking, a kind
of Mass of the Graal, but I fear that a careful examination might create some doubt of its antiquity, and,
speaking generally, I do not see (1) that any of the
documents have been subjected to critical study ; or (2)
that Fécamp is likely to have been more disdainful
about the law of great inventions than other places with

Hallows to maintain in Christian—or indeed in any other —times.

So far as regards the depositions which it might be possible to take in the Monastery concerning its Tabernacle; and there is only one thing more which need be mentioned at this stage. It has been proved by very careful and exhaustive research into the extant codices of the *Conte del Graal* that some copies of the continuation by Gautier de Doulens state that the episode of Mont Douloureux was derived from a book written at Fécamp. It follows that one early text at least in the literature of the Holy Graal draws something from the Monastery of the Holy Trinity, but, lest too much importance should be attributed to this fact, I desire to note for my conclusion : (*a*) that the episode in question has no integral connection with the Graal itself ; (*b*) that the tradition of Fécamp, which I have characterised as monstrous, by which I mean in comparison with the worst side of the general legends of the Precious Blood, is utterly distinct from that of the Holy Graal in the texts which constitute the literature ; and (*c*) that this literature passed, as we shall find, out of legend into the annunciation of a mystic claim. It is the nature of this claim, the mystery of sanctity which lies behind it, and the quality of perpetuation by which the mystery was handed on, that is the whole term of my quest, and here it stands declared.

We have seen how at Fécamp there occurred a very curious intervention on the part of an arch-natural chalice, being that vessel into which the Graal passes by a kind of superincession, if it does not begin and end therein. But there are other legends of chalices and dishes in the wide world of reliquaries, and in order to clear the issues I may state in the first place that the Table of the Last Supper is said to be preserved at St. John Lateran, with no history of its migration attached thereto. The Church of Savillac in the diocese of Montauban has also, or once had, a *Tabula Cœnæ Domini* and the Bread used at that Table. As regards the chalice itself, there is one of silver at Valencia which the Catholic mind of Spain has long regarded as that of the Last Supper; but I have no records of its history. There is one other which is world-wide in its repute, and this I have mentioned already, as if by an accidental reference. The *Sacro Catino* is preserved in the Church of St. Laurence at Genoa, and it is pictured in the book which Fra Gaetano di San Teresa dedicated to the subject in 1726. It corresponds by its general appearance—which recalls, broadly speaking, the calix of an enormous flower—more closely to the form which might, in the absence of expert knowledge, be attributed to a decorative Paschal Dish than a wine-cup; but there is no need to say that it is not an archaic glass vessel of Jewry. The history of so well known an object is rather one of weariness in recital, but at the crusading sack of Cæsarea in 1101 the Genoese received as their share of the booty, or in part consideration thereof, what they believed to be a great cup or dish carved out of a single emerald; it was about forty centimetres in height, and a little more than one metre in circumference; the form was hexagonal, and it was furnished with two handles, polished and rough respectively. Now, Cæsarea was near enough to the Holy Fields for the purposes of a sacred identification in the hearts of crusaders, and moreover the vessel had been found in the mosque of Antioch, which might have helped to confuse their minds by suggesting that it was a stolen relic of Christian sanctity. But at the time when the city was pillaged there is no evidence that the notion occurred to the Genoese, unless it was on some vague ground of the kind that at the return of some of them it was deposited in their church as a gift. It may well have been a thank-offering, and this only, but I confess to a certain suspicion that, vaguely or otherwise, they had assumed its sacred character, and that its identification, not certainly with the Holy Graal, but with the dish or chalice of the Last Supper, may have begun earlier than has been so far supposed—antedating, that is to say, the first record in history. This record is connected with the name of the author of the *Golden Legend*, Jacobus de Voragine, at the end of the thirteenth century. There is, however, some reason to believe that the attribution was common already in Genoa prior to the period in question. The point which is posed for consideration is whether the wide diffusion of the Graal literature caused such a claim to be put forward by the wardens of the *Sacro Catino*. The materials for a decision are unfortunately not in our hands. With the Graal itself it could not have been connected properly, seeing that the vessel was empty ; but perversions of this kind are not outside the field of possibility. Whatever the ultimate value of an empirical consideration like this, the heaviest fines, and even death itself, were threatened against those who should touch the vessel with any hard object. A cruel but belated disillusion, however, awaited its wardens when it was taken to Paris in 1816, and was not only broken on the way back, but, having been subjected to testing, was proved to be only glass.

Second in importance only to the vessel of the Holy Graal was the Sacred Lance of the Legend, and as in the majority of texts this is also a relic of the Passion, our next task is to ascertain its antecedent or concurrent history in the life of popular devotion. We know already of the thesis issued at Fécamp, but the claims are so many that no one has cared especially. The shaft of the spear used by Longinus when he pierced the side of Christ is preserved in the Basilica of St. Peter. According to the Roman Martyrology, the Deicide was suffering from ophthalmia when he inflicted the wound, and some of the Precious Blood overflowing his face, he was healed immediately—which miracle led, it is declared, to his conversion. Cassiodorus, who belongs to the fifth century, says that the Lance was in his days at Jerusalem, but this was the head and the imbedded part of the shaft, the rest being missing. He does not account for its preservation from the time of Christ to his own. Gregory of Tours speaks of its removal to Constantinople, which notwithstanding it was discovered once more at Antioch for the encouragement of Crusaders, under circumstances of particular suspicion, even in the history of relics. This was in 1098. There is also a long story of its being pledged by Baldwin II. to Venice, and of its redemption by St. Louis, which event brought it to Paris; but this is too late for our subject. A Holy Lance with an exceedingly confused history—but identical as to its imputed connection with the Passion—came also into the possession of Charlemagne. That any history of such a hallow is worthless does not make it less important when the object is to exhibit the simple fact that it was well known in this world before Graal literature, as we find it, had as yet come into existence. According to St. Andrew of Crete, the head of the Lance was buried with the True Cross, but it does not seem to have been disinterred therewith. It is just to add that some who have investigated the question bear witness that the history of the Hallow is reasonably satisfactory in the sixth century and thence onwards.

The next relic which may be taken to follow on our list is the Crown of Thorns; it figures only in one romance of the Graal, but has an important position therein. The possession of single or several Sacred Thorns has been claimed by more than one hundred churches, without prejudice to which there are those which have the Crown itself, less or more intact. This also is not included among the discoveries of St. Helena in connection with the True Cross, and there is no early record concerning it; but it is mentioned as extant by St. Paulin de Nole at the beginning of the fifth century. One hundred years later, Cassiodorus said that it was at Jerusalem; Gregory of Tours also bears testimony to its existence. In the tenth century part of it was at Constantinople, which was a general centre, if not a forcing-house, of desirable sacred objects. St. Germain, Bishop of Paris, was in that city and received part of it as a present from the Emperor Justinian. Much earlier the patriarch of Jerusalem is supposed to have sent another portion to Charlemagne. In 1106 the treasure at Constantinople is mentioned by Alexis Comnenus. Another Crown of Thorns is preserved in *Santa Maria della Spina* of Pisa.

The Sacred Nails of the Passion appear once in the *Book of the Holy Graal*, and these also have an early history in relics. Some or all of them were discovered by St. Helena with the True Cross, and, according to St. Ambrose, one of them was placed by her in the diadem of Constantine, or alternatively in his helmet, and a second in the bit of his horse. In the sixth century St. Gregory of Tours speaks of four nails, and it seems to follow from St. Chrysostom that the bit of Constantine's charger was coupled with the Lance as an object of veneration in his days. As regards the diadem fashioned by St. Helena this was welded of iron and became the Iron Crown of Lombardy, being given by Gregory I. to Theodolinde in recognition of her zeal for the conversion of the Lombard people. Charlemagne, Sigismund, Charles V. and Napoleon I. were crowned therewith. Muratori and others say that the Nail which hallowed it was not heard of in this connection till the end of the sixteenth century, and the Crown itself has been challenged. Twenty-nine places in all have laid claim to the possession of one or other of the four nails, and there are some commendable devices of subtlety to remove the sting of this anomaly. It is sufficient for our own clear purpose to realise that the relics, if not everywhere, were in "right great plenty."

It is also in the *Book of the Holy Graal*, and there only, that we see for a moment, in the high pageant of all, a vision of an ensanguined Cross, a blood-stained Cincture and a bended rod, also dyed with blood. Of the *Crux vera* and its invention I need say nothing, because its relics, imputed and otherwise, are treasured everywhere, and I suppose that their multiplicity, even at the earliest Graal period, made it impossible to introduce the Cross as an exclusive

Hallow in the Sacred House of Relics. By the Cincture there was understood probably that bandage with which the eyes of Christ were blindfolded, and this, or its substitute, had been in the possession of Charlemagne and was by him given to St. Namphasus, who built the Abbey of Marcillac and there deposited the relic. It is now in a little country church called St. Julian of Lunegarde. According to St. Gregory of Tours, the reed and the sponge, which had once been filled with vinegar, were objects of veneration at his day in Jerusalem. They are supposed to have been taken to Constantinople, which notwithstanding an informant of the Venerable Bede saw the sponge with his own eyes, deposited in a silver cup at the Holy City. He saw also the shorter reed, which served as the derisive symbol of the Lord's royalty.

The last relic of the Passion of which we hear in the books of the Graal is the *Volto Santo*, which all men know and venerate in connection with the piteous legend of Veronica. The memorials of this tradition are, on a moderate computation, as old as the eighth century, but the course of time has separated it into four distinct branches. The first and the oldest of these is preserved in a Vatican manuscript, which says that Veronica was the woman whose issue of blood was healed by Christ, and she herself was the artist who painted the likeness. She was carried to Rome with the picture for the healing of the Emperor Tiberius. The second branch is contained in an Anglo-Saxon manuscript of the eleventh century, and this says that the relic was a piece of Christ's garment which received in a miraculous manner the impression of His countenance. The origin of the third tradition seems to have been in Germany, but it is preserved in some metrical and other Latin narrative versions. The likeness of Christ is said to be very large, apparently full length. It was in the possession of Veronica, but without particulars of the way in which it was acquired. In another story—this is perhaps of the twelfth century—the Emperor who was healed is Vespasian, and

Christ Himself impressed His picture on the face-cloth which He used when He washed before supper at the house of Veronica. She had asked St. Luke, whom tradition represents as an artist, for a copy of the Master's likeness. The fourth and last variant is the familiar Calvary legend, wherein the holy woman offers in His service the cloth which she has on her arm when Christ is carrying the Cross, and she is rewarded by the impress of His countenance thereon. The noticeable point is that the story of Veronica, of the *Volto Santo,* and of the healing of a Roman Emperor is the root-matter of the earliest historical account of the Holy Graal, and this fact has led certain scholars to infer that the entire literature has been developed out of the Veronica legend, as a part of the conversion legend of Gaul, according to which the holy woman, in the company of the three Maries and of Lazarus, took ship to Marseilles and preached the Gospel therein. They carried the *Volto Santo* and other Hallows.

I approach now the term of this inquiry, and there remains for consideration the Sword of the Graal legends, which is accounted for variously in respect of its history and is also described variously, but it is not under any circumstances a Hallow of the Passion. A romance which stands late in the cycle, so far as chronology is concerned, connects it with the martyrdom of St. John the Baptist. I have found no story in the world of relics to help us in accounting for this invention, though there are traces of a sword of St. Michael. In this respect, as indeed in other ways, the Hallow is complicated in the literature. It embodies (*a*) matter brought over from folk-lore; (*b*) deliberate invention, as when one story affirms it to be the sword of David, and another that of Judas Maccabæus; and (*c*) the semi-devotional fable to which I have referred above, and this must be taken in connection with the legends of the head of St. John, served to Herodias on a charger to satiate her desire for revenge on the precursor of Christ, he seeming to have reproached her concerning her manner of life. It will be plain from the enumeration subjoined that the relics of St. John are comprehensive as to the person of his body. (1) A martyrology tells us that some of his blood was collected by a holy woman at the time of his decapitation, was put into a vessel of silver, and was carried into her country of Guienne; there it was placed in a temple which she erected to his honour. (2) The body was, according to one account, placed in a temple at Alexandria, which was dedicated to the Saint. Another says that the head was first interred in the sepulchre of Eliseus at Samaria. During the reign of Julian the Apostate it was redeemed from possible profanation, and sent to St. Athanasius, who concealed it in a wall of his church. At the end of the fourth century the same remains were removed to a new church, built on the site of a temple of Serapis. Subsequently they were divided and distributed. (3) The *Caput Johannis* was carried to Antioch by St. Luke, or alternatively to Cæsarea. From whichever place, it was afterwards removed to Constantinople and brought finally into France, where it was divided into three parts, one of which is at Amiens, another at Angély in the diocese of Nantes, and the third at Nemours in the diocese of Sens. A distinct account states that the head was found in Syria in the year 453, and that the removal to Constantinople took place five centuries later. When that city was taken by the French in 1204, a canon of Amiens, who was present, transported it into France, where it was divided, but into two portions apparently, one being deposited at Amiens and the other sent to the Church of St. Sylvester in Rome. I have also seen a report of two heads, but without particulars of their whereabouts.

So much concerning the *Caput Johannis*, but I should not have had occasion to furnish these instances were it not for the apparition of an angel carrying a head upon a salver when the wonders of the Holy Graal were first manifested at Sarras. But this vision is not found in the story which connects the Hallowed Sword with the head

43

of St. John the Baptist. The Dish, with its content, is supposed to be a complication occasioned by the intervention of folk-lore elements concerning the head of the Blessed Bran. The Dish, apart from the head, is almost always the fourth Hallow in the legends of the Graal—perhaps, as I shall indicate later, because the Sacred Vessel, which is the central object of all, is sometimes identified with the Paschal Dish of the Last Supper and sometimes with the Chalice of the First Eucharist.

It follows from the considerations of this section that although there has been a passage of folk-lore materials through the channel of Graal literature—which passage has less or more involved their conversion—its real importation into romance has been various elements of Christian symbolism, doctrine and legend; it is these, above all, that we are in a position to know and account for, and I have made a beginning here. We have, therefore, certain lines laid down already for our inquiry which assure that it will have the aspect of a religious and even of an ecclesiastical quest.

There is nothing on our part which can be added to the discoveries of folk-lore scholars, nor have we—except in a most elementary manner, and for the better understanding of our own subject—any need to summarise the result even of such researches—as these now stand. This work has been done too well already. We are entering a new region, and we carry our own warrants. I need not add that in assuming Celtic or any other legends, the Church took over its own, because she had come into possession, by right and by fact, of all the patrimonies of the Western world.

I want it to be understood, in conclusion as to this side of the Hallows of the Holy Graal, that the literature is not to be regarded as a particular extension of the history of relics, nor should my own design in presenting the external history of certain sacred objects suffer misconstruction of this or an allied kind. The compilers of encyclopædic dictionaries and handbooks have sometimes treated the value of such legends, and of the claims which lie behind them, in a spirit which has been so far serious that they have pointed out how the multiplicity of claims in respect of a single object must be held to militate against the genuineness of any. One Juggernaut effigy of all that is virulent in heresy took the trouble, centuries ago, to calculate how many crosses might be formed full-size from the relics of the one true Cross which were then extant in the world, and an opponent not less grave took the further trouble of recalculating to prove that he was wrong. So also Luther, accepting a caution from Judas, lamented that so much gold had gone to enshrine the imputed relics of the Cross when it might have been given to the poor. The truth is that the veneration of relics is open to every kind of charge save that which Protestantism has preferred, and this an enlightened sense of doctrine and practice enables us to rule out of court on every count.

It is desirable now to notice a few points which are likely to be overlooked by the informed student even, while the unversed reader should know of them that he may be on his guard hereafter. (1) The German cycle of the Holy Graal has the least possible connection with Christian relics; speaking of the important branches, it is so much *sui generis* in its symbolical elements that it enters scarcely into the same category as the Northern French romances, with which we shall be dealing chiefly. (2) No existing reliquary and no story concerning one did more than provide the great makers of romance with raw materials and pretexts; the stories they abandoned in all cases nearly, and the symbols they exalted by their genius. (3) As I have once already indicated, but not so expressly, the knowledge or the rumour of some unknown book had come to them in an unknown manner, and of this book neither Fécamp nor its competitive monasteries, abbeys and holy houses had ever heard a syllable. The general conclusion of this part is therefore that the growing literature of the Holy Graal drew from the life of devotion in its application to the Mystery of the Eucharist and to the secondary veneration of relics at the period; but, on the other hand, it contributed something of its own life to stimulate and extend the great doctrine of the mystery, and the devotion also. The elucidations which have been here afforded represent but a part of the schedule with which this section opened; it is that, however, which is most needed at the moment, and all that remains will find its proper place in the later stages of research.

About that mystery in chief of the faith in Christ which is the only real concern of the Holy Graal, there are other environments which will appeal to us, though their time is not yet in our methodical scheme of progress. There is (*a*) the state of the official church, so glorious in some respects, so clouded in others, like a keeper of sacred things who has been wounded for his own sins, or like a House of Doctrine against which he who sold God for money has warred, and not in vain, for at times he has invaded the precincts and entered even the sanctuary, though the holy deposit has not been affected thereby, because by its nature and essence it is at once removed from his grasp. There is (*b*) the Church in Britain and its connections of the Celtic world, having aspirations of its own, as there is no question—having a legitimacy of its own, as none can dare to deny—but with only a local horizon, a local mission, and used, for the rest, as a tool for ambitious kings, much as the orthodox claim of the Church at large was the tool of the popes at need. There is (*c*) the resounding rumour and there is the universal wonder of the high impossible quest of holy wars in Palestine, without which we might have never had the Graal literature, the romances of chivalry, or the secret treasures of the disdainful East brought to the intellectual marts and houses of exchange in the restless, roving, ever-curious kingdoms of the West—kingdoms in travail towards their puberty. There is (*d*)—and of five things to be enumerated, I count this the head and crown—there is the higher life of sanctity and its annals at the Graal period, as the outcome of which the West went to the East, carrying what it believed to be the missing talent of gold, without which, as the standard of all values, all other talents were either debased or spurious. It was the age of a thousand reflections, at centuries sometimes of distance, from Dionysius, Augustine, and the first great lights of Christendom; it was the age of Hugo de St. Victor, of Bernard, of Bonaventura; it was the age which Thomas of Aquinas had taken up as plastic matter in his hands, and he shaped the mind of the world after the image and the likeness of his own mind in the high places of the schools; it was the age of many doctors, who would have known in their heart of hearts what was the real message of the Graal literature, and where its key was to be sought. There is in fine (*e*) my fifth branch, but this is the sects of the period, because more than one division of the Christian world was quaking and working towards the emancipation which begins by departing from orthodox doctrine in official religion, but seeing that it begins wrongly and takes turnings' which are the fatalities of true direction, so it ends far from God. As to all this, it is needful to say at this moment, because it is almost from the beginning, that the Books of the Holy Graal are among the most catholic of literature, and that reformations have nothing therein. I say, therefore, that the vessels are many but the good is one, of which Galahad beheld the vision.

IV

THE LITERATURE OF THE CYCLE

The cycle of the Holy Graal is put into our hands like counters which can be arranged after more than one manner, but that which will obtain reasonably for a specific purpose may not of necessity conform to the chronological order which by other considerations would be recommended to archeological research. It will be pertinent, therefore, to say a few words about the classification which I have adopted for these studies, and this is the more important because at first sight it may seem calculated to incur those strictures on the part of recognised learning which, on the whole, I rather think that I should prefer to disarm. I must in any case justify myself, and towards this, in the first place, it should be indicated that my arrangement depends solely from the indubitable sequence of the texts, as they now stand, and secondly, by an exercise of implicit faith, from several palmary findings of scholarship itself. It follows that the disposition of the literature which has been adopted for my own purpose is, on the evidence of the texts, a legitimate way in which to treat that literature. There are certain texts which arise out of one another, and it is a matter of logic to group them under their proper sections. Comparatively few documents of the whole cycle have reached us in their original form, even subsequently to that period at which the legends were taken over in a Christian interest, while many of them have been unified and harmonised so that they can stand together in a series. It is the relation which has been thus instituted that I have sought to preserve, because among the questions which are posed for our consideration there is that of the motive which actuated successive writers to create texts in succession which, although in many cases of distinct authorship, are designed to follow from one another; as also to re-edit old texts; and to adjust works to one another with the object of presenting in a long series of narratives the Mystery of the Holy Graal manifested in Britain. The bulk of the texts as they stand represents the acquisition completed and certain intentions exhibited to their highest degree. Hence a disposition which shows this the most plainly is for my object the reasonable grouping of all, that object depending from almost the last state of the literature and differing to this extent from ordinary textual criticism, to which the first state is not only important but vital.

The Graal cycle, as it is understood and as it will be set forth in these pages, belongs chiefly to France and Germany. Within these limits in respect of place and language, there is also a limit of time, for textual criticism has assigned, under specific reserves, the production of the chief works to the fifty years intervening between the year 1170 and the year 1220. As regards the reserves, I need only mention here that the romantic histories of Merlin subsequent to the coronation of Arthur have not so far been regarded by scholarship as an integral part of the Graal literature, while one later German text has been ignored practically in England. Seeing that within the stated period and perhaps later, many of the texts were subjected, as I have just indicated, to editing and even to re-editing, it seems to follow that approximate dates of composition would be the most precarious of all arrangements for my special design. As regards that course which I have chosen, I have found that the French romances fall into three divisions and that they cannot be classified otherwise. The elaborate analysis of contents which I have prefixed to each division will of itself convey the general scheme, but I must speak of it more expressly in the present case because of the implicits with which we shall be concerned presently.

We may assume, and this is correct probably, that the earliest extant romances of the Holy Graal—the speculative versions which have been supposed in the interests of folk-lore being, of course, set apart—are the first part of the *Conte del Graal* written by Chrétien de Troyes, and the metrical *Joseph of Arimathæa* by Robert de Borron—in the original draft thereof. In the earlier records of criticism the preference was given to the latter, but it is exercised now in respect of the former text.

Besides the folk-lore and non-Christian legends of Peredur and the Bowl of Plenty—which shall be considered in their proper place—there was another class of traditions taken over in the interests of the Holy Graal. That the Arthurian legend had pre-existed in another form is not only shown by the early metrical literature of northern and southern France but by isolated English texts, such as the fifteenth-century *Morte d'Arthur*, which suggest older prototypes that are not now extant. It is shown otherwise by the Welsh *Mabinogion*, which, much or little as they have borrowed in their subsisting form from French sources, point clearly to indigenous traditions. The North-French romances were re-founded in the interest—whatever that was—of the Graal sub-surface design. The most notable example in another sense was perhaps the Merlin cycle, which took over the floating traditions concerning the prophet and enchanter and created two divergent romances, each having the object of connecting Merlin with the Graal. The general process was something after the manner following: (1) Lays innumerable, originally oral but drifting into the written form; (2) the same lays re-edited in the Arthurian interest; (3) the Graal mystery at first independent of Arthurian legend, or such at least is the strong inference concerning it; (4) the Graal legend married to Arthurian romance, the connection being at first incidental; (5) the Arthurian tradition after it had been assumed entirely in the interests of the Holy Graal.

I recur, therefore, to my original thesis, that there is one aspect at least in which for my purpose the superior importance resides not in the primordial elements of the literature but in their final and unified form. As a typical example, it is customary to recognise that there was an early state of the *Book of the Holy Graal* which is not now extant. The text, as we have it, is later than most of the cycle to which it belongs properly, yet it poses as the introduction thereto. Now the early draft may or may not have preceded, chronologically speaking, the corresponding first versions of some of the connecting texts, and in either case when the time came for the whole literature to be harmonised it was and remains entitled to the priority which it claimed, but that priority is in respect of its place in the series and not in respect of time. The re-editing of the romances in the Graal interest must be, however, distinguished carefully from the innumerable alterations which have been made otherwise but to which no ulterior motive can be attributed. There is further no difficulty in assuming (1) that the passage of folk-lore into Christian symbolical literature may have followed a fixed plan; (2) that when late editing exhibits throughout a number of texts some defined scheme of instituted correlation, there may have been again a design in view, and it is this design which is the concern of my whole research.

The places of the Graal legend, its reflections and its rumours, are France, Germany, Holland, Italy, Spain, Portugal, England and Wales.

In matters of literature France and England were united during the Anglo-Norman period, and when this period was over England produced nothing except renderings of French texts and one compilation therefrom. Germany had an independent version of the legend derived by its own evidence from a French source which is now unknown. The German cycle therefore differs in important respects from the French cycle; the central figure is a characteristic hero in each, but the central sacred object is different, the subsidiary persons are different in certain cases—or have at least undergone transformation—and, within limits, the purpose is apparently diverse. The Dutch version is comparatively an old compilation from French sources, some of which either cannot be identified or in the hands of the poet who translated them they have passed out of recognition. Italy is represented only by translations from the French and one of these was the work of Rusticien de Pise, who has been idly accredited with the production of sources rather than derivatives of the legend, and this in the Latin tongue. There is also another compilation, the

Tavola Ritonda, but in both instances more than the names of the MSS. seems unknown to scholars. The Italian cycle is not of importance to any issue of the literature, either directly or otherwise, and so far as familiarity is concerned it is almost ignored by modern students. The inclusion of Spain in the present schedule of places might seem merely a question of liberality, for the Spanish version of the Graal legend exists only in (1) the inferred allusions of a certain romance of Merlin, printed at Burgos in 1498, and (2) in a romance of Merlin and the *Quest of the Holy Graal*, printed at Seville in the year 1500. Of the first work only a single copy is known to exist, and no French or English scholar seems to have seen it; the second has so far escaped the attention of scholarship, outside the bare record of its existence. This notwithstanding, according to the German cycle, the source of the legend and its true presentation in at least one department thereof, are to be looked for in Spain, and the first account concerning it was received by a Spanish Jew. Portugal, so far as I am aware, is responsible only for a single printed text, but it represents a French original which is otherwise lost; it is therefore important and it should receive full consideration at a later stage. As regards Wales, it is very difficult and fortunately unnecessary to speak at this initial stage. Of the Graal, as we find it in France, there is no indigenous Welsh literature, but there are certain primeval traditions and bardic remanents which are held to be fundamental elements of the cycle, and more than one of the questing knights are found among the *Mabinogion* heroes. In the thirteenth century and later, the legend, as we now have it, was carried across the marches, but it is represented only by translations.

For the purpose of the classification which follows, we must set aside for the moment all whatsoever that has come down to us concerning quests, missions and heroes in which the central object known as the Holy Graal does not appear. We shall deal with these fully when we come to the study of the texts severally; we are now dealing generally, and there is nothing to our purpose in the Welsh *Peredur* or in the English *Syr Percyvelle*. Whatever its importance to folk-lore, the Welsh *Peredur*, in respect of its literary history, is a tangled skein which it will not repay us to unravel more than is necessary absolutely. It has been compared, and no doubt rightly enough, to the *Lay of the Great Fool*, but, whether we have regard to his foolishness or to the nature of his mission, Peredur never interests and also never signifies. His mission is confined to the extermination of sorceresses, and among these of such sorceresses as those of Gloucester. On the other hand, the English metrical romance is entitled to less consideration except for its claims as literature, and it is only in its speculative attribution to a lost prototype that it has concerned scholarship. It must be understood at the same time that both texts are essential to the literary history of the whole subject from the standpoint of folk-lore. The remaining works may be classified into cycles, according either to affinities of intention or to the seat of their origin, and among these the Northern French texts fall into three divisions, the distribution of two being, within their own lines, a chronological arrangement strictly.

The *Conte del Graal* is allocated properly after the cycle of folk-lore—as it is reflected at a far distance in the non-Graal texts that survive. The fact that the Lesser Chronicles are given a priority of place in respect of the Greater Chronicles does not for that reason mean that all their parts are assumed to be older than all the documents contained in the third division. In the third division itself the chronological arrangement has been abandoned, as it is more important for my purpose to show the codification of the documents by which they have been harmonised into a series rather than to place them in an order of dates which would at best be approximate only and would represent the first drafts rather than the texts as they remain. The divisions are therefore as follows:—

The Hidden Church of the Holy Graal

A. The *Conte del Graal*. Let me say, in the first place, that our problems are not the authorship of an individual prose or metrical romance, not even the comparative dates of certain documents as they now stand actually, but whether we, who as mystics have come to know the significance and value of the hidden life of doctrine, can determine by research the extent to which the intimations of such doctrine found in the Graal literature are true or false lights. Now, I suppose that there is no very serious question as to the literary greatness of Chrétien de Troyes, while some of the sequels and alternatives added to his unfinished poem are not perhaps unworthy to rank with his own work ; the collection, however, as a whole, offers very little to our purpose. So far as Chrétien himself carried the story, we are not only unable to gather clearly what he intended by the Graal, but why he had adventured so far from his proper path as to plan and even to begin such a story. If he had gone further, as I believe personally, we should have found that the Sacred Vessel, Telesma, or Wonder-Working Palladium carried with it the same legend as it carried for most other writers ; but we do not know and it matters less than little, for the *Conte del Graal* at its best is Nature in the pronaos of the temple testifying that she is properly prepared. If we grant this claim, we know that in Chrétien at least, however she may have been prepared conventionally, she has not been sanctified. The alternative termination of Gerbert carries the story up to a higher level, moving it in the direction of Wolfram's *Parsifal*, yet not attaining its height. So far as any mystic term is concerned, the great *Conte* is rather after the manner of a hindrance which calls to be taken out of the way ; it is useless for the higher issues, and even for the business of scholarship it seems of late days to have lapsed from its first importance.

The chief *additamentum* of this cycle is the unprinted metrical *Perceval*, which is preserved in the library at Berne. The desire of the eyes of students is a certain lost Provençal poem, connected by the hypothesis with Perceval, as to which we shall hear more fully in connection with the German cycle of the Holy Graal.

The Chrétien portion of the *Conte del Graal* was written not later than 1189, and the most recent views assign it somewhere between that year and 1175. Manessier and Gerbert are believed to have produced their rival conclusions between 1216 and 1225. As regards the Chrétien portion, it has been recognised, and may be called obvious, that it " presupposes an early history." This being so, it does not seem unreasonable to infer that the first form of the early history was either (*a*) the first draft of De Borron's poem, or (*b*) it corresponded to the book from which De Borron drew and of which, Chrétien notwithstanding, he is probably the most faithful, perhaps even the only representative. On the other hand, if the particular quest does not draw directly or indirectly from the particular history, then my own view is that in the question of date but little can be held to depend from the priority of Chrétien's poem—which is a quest—or that of De Borron—which is a history. I have therefore no call to indicate a special persuasion. For what it is worth, the inferences from admitted opinion seem to leave the priority of De Borron still tenable in the first form of his poem, and for the rest I hold it as certain that my classification, although a novelty, is justified and even necessary; but exact chronological arrangement, in so tinkered a cycle of literature as that of the Holy Graal, is perhaps scarcely possible, nor is it my concern exactly.

B. The cycle of Robert de Borron, being that which is connected more especially and accurately with his name, and herein is comprised :—

1. The metrical romance of Joseph of Arimathæa, in which we learn the origin, early history and migration of the Graal westward, though it does not show that the Sacred Vessel came actually into Britain.

2. The Lesser Holy Graal, called usually *Le Petit St. Graal.* We have here a prose version of the poem by Robert de Borron, which accounts for its missing portions, but the two documents are not entirely coincident.

3. The *Early History of Merlin*, and this represents in full another metrical romance of the same authorship but of which the first 500 lines are alone extant.

4. The *Didot Perceval*, but this text is regarded as a later composition, though it seems to contain some primitive elements of the quest. Its designation is explained by the fact that it was at one time in the possession of M. Firmin Didot, the well-known Parisian bookseller. Its analogies with the poem of Chrétien de Troyes are thought to indicate a common source of knowledge rather than a reflection or derivation from one to another. This romance has been also somewhat generally regarded as the prose version of another lost poem by Robert de Borron. The *additamentum* of this cycle is the fuller unprinted codex of the *Didot Perceval* preserved in the library at Modena.

These documents constitute what may be termed the Lesser Histories or Chronicles of the Holy Graal. Their characteristics in common, by which they are grouped into a cycle, are (1) the idea that certain secret and sacramental words were transmitted from apostolic times and were taken from East to West ; (2) the succession of Brons as Keeper of the Holy Graal immediately after Joseph of Arimathæa.

The metrical *Joseph* may have been written soon after 1170, but the balance of opinion favours the last years of the twelfth century. Criticism supposes that there were two drafts, of which only the second is extant. It was succeeded by the early *Merlin*. As regards the *Didot Perceval*, this is known chiefly by a manuscript ascribed to the end of the thirteenth century.

C. The Cycle of the Greater Holy Graal and the Great Quest, comprising :—

The Roots of the House of Meaning

1. *The Saint Graal*, that is, *The Book of the Holy Graal*, or *Joseph of Arimathæa*, called also the *First Branch of the Romances of the Round Table* and the *Grand Saint Graal*. The last designation is due perhaps to its dimensions; but it may be held to deserve the title on higher considerations, as the most important development of the legend in its so-called historical aspects, by which I mean apart from the heroes of the various quests. The work has been widely attributed to Walter Map, sometime archdeacon of Oxford and Chaplain to Henry II. of England. While the trend of present opinion is to regard it as of unknown authorship, I think that the ascription is not untenderly regarded by scholarship, and recognising, as we must, that evidence is wanting to support the traditional view, no personage of the period is perhaps antecedently more likely. Unfortunately more than one other romance, which seems distinct generically in respect of its style, has received the same attribution. The Greater Holy Graal was intended to create a complete sequence and harmony between those parts of the cycle with which it was more especially concerned, and the Galahad Quest, as we have it, may represent the form of one document which it intended to harmonise. The alternative is that there was another version of the Quest which arose out of the later Merlin, or that such a version was intended. I believe in fine that my order is true and right.

2. The later Merlin romances, and because the *Vulgate Merlin* is in certain respects, though not perhaps expressly, a harmony of De Borron's cycle and that of the *Book of the Holy Graal*, drawing something from both sources, I refer here more especially to the *Huth Merlin* and the secret archives of the Graal from which it claims to derive. The history of Merlin is taken by the first text up to his final enchantment in the forest of Broceliande, and in particular to that point when the knight Gawain hears the last utterance of the prophet. An analogous term is reached by the *Huth Merlin* in

57

respect of Bademagus, through a long series of entirely distinct episodes; it should be stated that the references to the Holy Graal are few in both romances, but they are pregnant with meaning.

As an addendum to these branches, there is the late text called *The Prophecies of Merlin*, which I know only by the printed edition of Rouen. It has wide variations from the texts mentioned previously in so far as it covers their ground, but it has also its Graal references. It has been regarded as a continuation of the early prose *Merlin*, and in this sense it is alternative to the Vulgate and the Huth texts.

3. The great prose *Lancelot*, which in spite of its subject-matter is, properly understood, a book of high sanctity, or it lies at least on the fringe of this description, and towards the close passes therein.

4. The *Longer Prose Perceval le Gallois*, or *High History of the Holy Graal*, which offers a term and conclusion of the Graal mystery by way of alternative to or substitute for that of the Galahad quest. It is like a rite which has narrowly escaped perfection; it holds certain keys, but the doors which they open are not doors which give entrance to the greatest mysteries. Herein the king is dead, and with all the claims of Perceval it is a little difficult to say of him: Long live the king! The romance does not harmonise with the other histories of Perceval; it has elements which are particular to itself and the air of an independent creation. It should be added that it draws also from sources to us unknown and has haunting suggestions of familiarity with the source of Wolfram. So far as there has been any critical opinion expressed concerning it in England, it must be said that it has missed the mark.

5. *The Quest of the Holy Graal*, called also *The Last Book of the Round Table*, containing the term of the mystery as given in the Chronicle concerning Galahad the *haut prince*, and this is the quest *par excellence*, the head and crown of the Graal legend. I know that this

statement will be challenged in certain high quarters of special research, but before any one speaks of human interest he should say, or at least in his heart: The Life Everlasting ; and this stated, it must be added that all which is commonly understood by human interest, all which has been sometimes regarded as characterising the chief quests and one of them in particular, is excluded by the Great Prose Quest. We have in place thereof a spiritual romance, setting forth under this guise a mystery of the soul in its progress. It is only the books of perfection which make at once for high rites and gorgeous pageants of literature. Hereof is the Galahad Quest.

These five romances constitute what I have termed the Greater Chronicles of the Holy Graal. It will have been understood that the *Longer Prose Perceval* and the Great Prose Quest exclude one another ; they stand as alternatives in the tabulation. The characteristics of this cycle are (1) the succession of Joseph II. as keeper of the Holy Graal immediately after his father and during the latter's lifetime, this dignity not being conferred upon Brons, either then or later; (2) the substitution of a claim in respect of apostolical succession—which placed the Graal keepers in a superior position to any priesthood holding from the apostles—for that of a secret verbal formula applied in respect of the Eucharist.

The dates of the texts which are included in the Greater Chronicles differ widely so far as the extant manuscripts are concerned. The canon of the Graal literature was not in reality closed till the end of the thirteenth century if these manuscripts are to be regarded as the final drafts. The lost antecedent documents cannot, of course, be assigned. It is suggested, for example, that the prototype of the *Book of the Holy Graal* and the *Quest of Galahad* preceded the continuations of Chrétien. The unique text comprised in the *Huth Merlin* has been dated about 1225 or 1230, the MS. itself belonging to the last quarter of the thirteenth

century. There was a fourth part which is now wanting;
it contained a version of the Galahad quest, and though
it has been concluded that it corresponds to the extant
text, the *Huth Merlin* embodies allusions to episodes in
the lost part which are not to be met with in the Galahad
romance as it now stands.

The *additamenta* of this cycle are the quests of the
Holy Graal in the Spanish and Portuguese versions, and
one rendering into Welsh. There is also material of
importance in the draft of the Great Quest printed at
Rouen in 1488 together with the *Lancelot* and the
Morte d'Arthur, as also in the Paris edition of 1533.
Finally, the English metrical chronicle of Hardyng contains a version of the Galahad legend which differs in
some express particulars from anything with which we
are acquainted in the original romance texts.

D. The German Cycle. The *Parsifal* of Wolfram
is the high moral sense saying that it has received the
light, and I know not how we could accept the testimony even if that which uttered it had risen from the
dead. I am speaking, however, of the German legend
only in one of its phases, and at a later stage I shall
exhibit every material which will enable us to judge
of its importance. The *Conte del Graal*, except in its
latest portions, and then by chance allusions or derivations at a far distance, has nothing to tell us of secret
words, Eucharistic or otherwise; it has also no hint
of any super-apostolical succession. It is the same with
Wolfram's *Parsifal;* the legend, as it stands therein,
is in fact revolutionised, or rather it is distinct generically, and the quest, though it follows the broad lines
of the other Percevals, has gone under I know not what
greatness of alteration. If the Northern French stories
concerning the widow's son could be likened to a high
grade in Masonry, then assuredly the German version
would be that rite rectified. The *Titurel* of Albrecht
von Scharfenberg, which deserves a notice which it has
never received in England, seems to suggest that there

is a greater light in the East than has been found as an abiding presence in the West, and except in a very high mystic sense, a sense much higher than is to be found in any of the romances, this suggestion offers the token of illusion. In fine, to dispose of this cycle, let me say that the metrical romance of *Diu Crône* by Heinrich von dem Turlin has no secret message, even in the order of phantasy. At this day we rest assured, or those at least whose opinion matters anything, that the most hopeless of all worlds to enter in search of wisdom is the world of ghosts. It happens, however, that in Heinrich's poem ghosts, or the dead alive, are the custodians of the mysteries. At the same time they may hold the kind of office which it is possible to confer on Sir Gawain, who is the hero of this voided quest. I speak, of course, in comparison with the palmary texts by which the Quest itself has entered into the holy places of literature.

It will follow from the above tabulation that while the Graal literature is divisible into several cycles there are three only which belong to our particular concern. The classification which I have made is serviceable therefore in yet another way, since it enables us, firstly, to set apart that which is *nihil ad rem nostram catholicam et sanctam*, and, secondly, to come into our own.

V

THE IMPLICITS OF THE GRAAL MYSTERY

There are several literatures which exhibit with various degrees of plainness the presence of that sub-surface meaning to which I have referred in respect of the Graal legend; but there, as here, so far as the outward sense is concerned, it is nearly always suggested rather than affirmed. This additional sense may underlie the entire body of a literature, or it may be merely some concealed intention or a claim put forward evasively. The subsurface significance of the Graal literature belongs mainly to the second class. It is from this point of view that my departure is here made, and if it is a warrantable assumption, some portion at least of the literature will prove, explicitly or otherwise, to contain these elements in no uncertain manner. As a matter of fact, we shall find them, though, as I have indicated, it is rather by the way of things which are implied, or which follow as inferences, but they are not for this reason less clear or less demonstrable. The implicits of the Graal literature are, indeed, more numerous than we should expect to meet with at the period in books of the western world. They may almost exceed, for example, those which are imbedded in the alchemic writings of the late twelfth or early thirteenth century, though antecedently we should be prepared to find them more numerous in the avowedly secret books of Hermetic adepts.

The most important of the Graal implicits are those from which my study depends in its entirety, but there are others which in the present place need only be specified, as they belong more properly to the consideration of individual texts. There is, in fine, one implicit which is reserved to the end, because it is that upon which the debate centres.

The implicit in chief of that cycle which I have termed the Lesser Histories, or Chronicles of the Holy Graal, is that certain secret words, having an attributed application to the Sacrament in chief of the Altar, and to certain powers of judgment, were communicated to Joseph of Arimathæa by Christ Himself, and that these remained in reserve, being committed from keeper to keeper by the oral method only.

It must be noted, though more especially for consideration at a later stage, that the secret words are also represented in the poem of Robert de Borron as words of power on the material plane; that is to say, outside any efficacy which they may be assumed to possess in consecrating the elements at the Mass. They are "sweet, precious and holy words." It is these qualities which stand out more strongly in the metrical romance than the Eucharistic side of the formula, and there seems, therefore, a certain doubt as to De Borron's chief intention respecting their office. But in the *Lesser Holy Graal* the implicit of the metrical romance passes into actual expression, and it becomes more clear in consequence that the secret words were those used, *ex hypothesi*, by the custodians of the Holy Graal in the consecration of the elements of the Eucharist.

Let it be understood that I am not seeking to press this inference, but am stating an aspect only. If the references to the secret words in the metrical *Joseph* do not offer a sacramental connection with full clearness —because they are also talismanic and protective— their operation in the latter respects must be regarded as subsidiary and apart from the real concern of the Holy Graal. When all possible issues have been exhausted, the matter remains Eucharistic in the final terms of its appearance, and behind it there is that which lies wholly *perdu* for the simple senses in sources that are concealed utterly. It is further to be noted that any Eucharistic appearance has nothing to do with transubstantiation, of which there is no trace in the Lesser Chronicles. Finally, the sole custodian of the Sacred Vessel through a period of many centuries lived in utter seclusion, and after the words were imparted to Perceval he was interned apparently for ever. The message of the Lesser Chronicles seems to be that something was brought into Britain which it was intended to manifest, but no manifestation took place.

When the *Book of the Holy Graal* was produced as an imputed branch of Arthurian literature, there is no need to say that the Roman Pontiff was then as now, at least in respect of his claim, the first bishop of Christendom, and, by the evidence of the traditional claim, he derived from St. Peter, who was *episcopus primus et pontifex primordialis*. This notwithstanding, the romance attributes the same title to a son of Joseph of Arimathæa, who is called the Second Joseph, and here is the first suggestion of a concealed motive therein. The *Book of the Holy Graal* and the metrical romance of De Borron are the historical texts in chief of their particular cycles, and it does not follow, or at least in all cases, that their several continuations or derivatives are extensions of the implicits which I have mentioned. In the first case, the early prose *Merlin* has an implied motive of its own which need not at the moment detain us, and the *Didot Perceval* is of dubious authenticity as a sequel, by which I mean that it does not fully represent the mind of the earlier texts, though it has an importance of its own and also its own implicits. On the other hand, in what I have termed the Greater Chronicles of the Holy Graal there is, if possible, a more complete divergence in respect of the final document, and I can best explain it by saying that if we could suppose for a moment that the *Book of the Holy Graal* was produced in the interests of a pan-Britannic Church, or alternatively of some secret school of religion, then the *Great Prose Quest*, or *Chronicle of Galahad*, might represent an interposition on the part of the orthodox Church to take over the literature. At the same time the several parts of each cycle under consideration belong thereto and cannot be located otherwise.

The further divisions under which I have scheduled the body-general of the literature, and especially the German cycle, will be considered at some length in their proper place, when their explicit and implied motives will be specified; for the present it will be sufficient to say that the German poems do not put forward the claims with which I am now dealing, namely, the secret formula in respect of the De Borron cycle and a super-apostolical succession in respect of the *Book of the Holy Graal*, and that which is classed therewith. We do not know, at least here in England, that Wolfram had prototypes to follow outside those to which he himself confesses. As to these, he rejected one of them, and we have means only by inference of ascertaining what he derived from the other. It may seem certain, however, for many that his acknowledged exemplar could not have originated all those generic distinctions which characterise the German *Parsifal*, and the fact of what Wolfram borrowed throws perhaps into clearer light all that which he created, or alternatively it indicates an unknown source the nature of which we can determine only by reference to schools of symbolism which cannot be properly discussed except towards the close of our inquiry.

I have adopted what I consider to be the best way of treating the whole cycle for the purpose in view. I have said already that it is not an instruction to scholarship, nor is it an appeal thereto, except for reasonable tolerance regarding an issue external to its own, and then even only in the sense of that forbearance which I should be expected to extend on my own part to the probability of a speculative date, or the existence of a lost text, which scholars may favour in a particular case.

If certain mystic sects took over at a given period the hypothesis and symbolism of alchemy, if they used them as a secret language to enshrine their researches and discoveries in a wholly different region, it is obviously useless for any one to have recourse to the physical alchemists—otherwise than as a light on method and especially on the antithetical use of terms—for an explanation of the later mode and intention. If also some other or any mystic sect appropriated certain crude legends, prehistoric or what not, which they magnified, developed and transformed, designing to use them for the furtherance of a particular scheme to which they were themselves dedicated; it is not then less obvious that the original form of such legends will in no wise help us to understand the later position to which they have been assigned by that school. In these few words the whole thesis of scholarship concerning the sources of the Graal elements is disposed of for our purpose, though with many titles of honour, and the alternative with which we are concerned can be put no less shortly.

As regards both the claims with which I am at the present moment more especially concerned, we must remember that although we are dealing with a department of romantic literature, their content does not belong to romance ; the faculty of invention in stories is one thing, and I think that modern criticism has sometimes made insufficient allowance for its spontaneity, yet through all the tales of chivalry it worked within certain lines. It would not devise secret Eucharistic words or put forward strange claims which almost make void the Christian apostolate in favour of some unheard-of succession communicated directly from Christ after Pentecost. We know absolutely that this kind of machinery belongs to another order. If it does not, then the apocryphal gospels were imbued with the romantic spirit, and the explanation of Manichean heresy may be sought in a flight of verse. In particular, the higher understanding of secret consecration is not a question of literature, but of the communication to the human soul of the Divine Nature. It lies behind the Eucharistic doctrine of the Latin Church, but on the external side that doctrine—and of necessity—by the hypothesis of transubstantiation, communicates the Divine Humanity rather than the Eternal and Divine Substance.

I suppose that what follows from the claims has not entered into the consciousness of official scholarship, because it is otherwise concerned, but it may have entered already into the thought of those among my readers whose preoccupations are similar to my own, and I will now state it in a summary manner. As the secret words of consecration, the extra-efficacious words which must be pronounced over the sacramental elements so that they may be converted into the arch-natural Eucharist, have, by the hypothesis, never been expressed in writing, or alternatively have been enshrined only in a lost or hypothetical book, it follows that since the Graal was withdrawn from the world, together with its custodians, the Christian Church has had to be content with what it has, namely, a substituted sacrament. And as the super-apostolical succession, also by the hypothesis, must have ceased from the world when the last keeper of the Graal followed his vessel into heaven, the Christian Church has again been reduced to the ministration of some other and apparently lesser ordination. It follows, therefore, that the Graal literature is not only a cycle of romance originating from many traditions, but is also, in respect of those claims — and even in a marked manner — a departure from tradition.

If I were asked to adjudicate on the value of such claims, I should say that the doctrine is the body of the Lord and its right understanding is the spirit. Whoso-ever therefore puts forward a claim on behalf of secret formulæ in connection with the Eucharistic Rite may appear in the higher hermeneutics to have forgotten one thing which is needful—that there are efficacious consecrations everywhere. The question of apostolical succession would seem also in the same position, because the truly valid transmissions are those of grace itself, which communicates from the source of grace direct to the soul; and the essence of the sacerdotal office is that those who have received supernatural life should assist others so to prepare their ground that they may also in due season, but always from the same source, become spiritually alive. If there is another and higher understanding of any apostolical warrant, I do not know what it is. It remains, however, that the implicits with which I have been dealing are actually the implicits in chief of the Graal books, and that they do not make for harmony with the teaching of the orthodox churches does not need stating. From whence therefore and with what intention were they imported into the body of romance? Before this question can be answered we shall have to proceed much further in the consideration of the literature.

The few people who have approached the Graal legend

with any idea of its significance—I will not say from the mystic standpoint, but from that of a secret tradition perpetuated through Christian times, or a certain remanent thereof—have been wholly unequipped in respect of textual knowledge and in a manner of official religious training. They have, therefore, missed the points. Scholarship, on the other hand, has been well trained in its proper groove, but it has had no eyes for another and more especially for any mystic aspect. I am about to tabulate a few facts and to draw from them several inferences which have not been noted previously.

The Graal in the Graal Castle appeared on certain occasions in connection with the Mass, but it was, for the most part, manifested only at a feast. There it operated sometimes in relation to the idea of sustenance, but seemingly by way of transmutation. Subject to a single exception, it was not itself eaten or drunk, but it was passed over food and wine when these were available. When they were not forthcoming, it produced the notion of rare refection. The particular vessel—understood usually as a cup or chalice—which, as we shall see, was, under the distinctive name of Graal, the chief Hallow of the Castle, contained, however, blood and water, without increase, of which there is no record, or diminution, of which there is also no record, though on one occasion which passes all understanding it might have been supposed to occur. It was therefore solely a relic of great virtue and miraculous efficacy. We shall see in what manner, at the end of various quests, it was taken to heaven, or at least into deeper seclusion; but this, in spite of the Eucharistic implicit, did not mean, in the minds of the makers of romance, any sacramental decrease, because it is obvious from all the texts that Mass was said independently in church and hermitage whiie the Graal was still in the castle. The indubitable inference from the *Book of the Holy Graal*, and indeed from De Borron's poem, is that Britain was entirely heathen when Joseph came thereto, and it might therefore follow that its priesthood held subsequently from him. In the later and longer text the claim of Robert de Borron is voided, or rather has undergone substitution ; there are no secret words, of consecration or otherwise ; the Eucharistic formula is given in full, and its variations, such as they are, from that of the Latin rite, bear traces of oriental influence derived through a Gallican channel and offer nothing to our purpose. In this case, and so far certainly as England was concerned, when the time came for the Graal to be taken away, that removal signified at most the loss of a great hallow, a precious relic, and, this granted, things remained as they were for all ecclesiastical purposes. In connection with the recession, a period was put to certain times of adventure, aspects of enchantment, inhibition and disaster, much as if a sovereign pontiff had laid the city or land of Logres under a long interdict and had at length removed it, one only sanctuary, during the whole period, remaining free from suspension.

The question therefore arises as to what was the nature of the pre-eminence ascribed to Joseph and his line. I speak here so far as its object and intention were concerned, and, of course, the readiest answer will be sought in the secret aspirations of the Celtic Church ; but we shall see in the end that they are inadequate. There is another explanation which is not only ready to our hand, but is so plausible that it is desirable to exercise a certain caution against it. I would say, therefore, that the claims with which we are concerned must be distinguished from doctrinal confusions and errors of theological ignorance ; of these we have full evidence otherwise. They are to be accounted for in the most natural of all manners, but, whether explicit or implied, the claims of Eucharistic efficacy and supereminence in succession carry with them an evidence of set purpose which makes it impossible to enter them in any category of mere blunders. I say this with the greater certainty because every concealed sense which we can trace in the literature must be held to co-exist with manifest surface insufficiency even within its own province, and more especially regarding the Eucharist. We shall learn towards the term of our inquiry that this fact offers evidence in itself that the real mystery of the Graal was brought from a great distance—not exactly in time or place, but in the matter of connection with its source. I should add that other concealed literatures offer similar difficulties, as, for example, those which are constituted by the grossness of the Talmud, the barbarisms of the Zohar and other *Midrashim*, or the scientific fatuities of Latin alchemy. In conclusion for the moment as to this part, if I have spoken as though there were some fundamental spirit of rivalry to the external Church indicated by the fact of the romances, it is pre-eminently desirable to state that there is no intention, at least on my part, to present the Graal Mystery as a secret process at work outside the Church. It was assuredly working from within, as if in the opinion of those who held its keys they looked that it would act as a leaven and accomplish some modification in the entire mass. It would be a mistake to suppose that the Eucharistic and super-apostolical claims denied those which have their authority in the New Testament and in the outer offices of the Church. The institutions of the one remain as we know it already on sacred evidence; as to the other, its validity is in no sense diminished, but the presence of a still higher or at least of a distinct warrant is indicated, and it is of the essence thereof that it is not in competition; it is a secret thing, but it might have been manifested more openly, if the world had been worthy : the world, however, was so unworthy that the Palladium was taken still farther away. One evidence of the whole position is that the apostolate of Joseph II. is compared with that of the known apostles in other countries than Britain, and without diminution of either. This notwithstanding, there remains the irresistible suspicion of the external Church at the suggestion that one who was outside the chosen twelve is represented as the first to consecrate the Eucharist under an imprescriptible title and to receive the benefit of installation in the episcopal chair; Peter, who in the days of his Master understood so little, seems to take an inferior place. But if, as I believe, the implicits of the Graal literature are the rumour rather than the replica of secret sanctuary doctrine, there is probably a better understanding of both than can be found imbedded in the texts. The true intention may have concerned a statement of higher experience in the communication of the Divine Substance; or, in still more simple language, the external Eucharist conveys Christ symbolically, but the attainment of Christ in the higher consciousness offers a direct experience. The succession, the modes of ordination in a company of sanctity who have thus attained is *ex hypothesi* and *de facto* of a different order than that which, also *ex hypothesi* and *per doctrinam sanctam*, is conveyed from one to another by the episcopal intention. We have, however, to take things as they are offered to us in the official churches and in the glorious literatures of the soul, ascribing to them that sense in which we can understand them best, so only that it is our highest sense.

In conclusion as to the greater implicits, seeing that the import of the Secret Words in the cycle of Robert de Borron has eluded critical analysis, while that of the extra-apostolical succession was appreciated—it is sixty years since, and has occasioned scarcely a notice—by Paulin Paris, there is one thing at least obvious—that the second is more largely written on the surface of the particular texts than the first, and when we come to consider in their order the romances comprised in the cycle of the Lesser Chronicles, we shall find that there are several difficulties. It is only after their grave and full evaluation that I have put forward in this section the possession of certain secret words in relation to the Eucharist as being one of the two sovereign implicits of the Graal literature.

The lesser implicits may, for purposes of convenience, be tabulated simply as follows :—

a. The Implicits of Moses and Simeon.

b. The Implicits of the Merlin legend.

c. The Implicits of the Graal keepers.

d. The Implicits of the several Quests and the distinctions thereto belonging.

I recognise that the general subject of these and the other subsurface meanings is at this stage much too advanced for the reader, who is perhaps wholly unskilled, and hence those that are major I have sketched only in outline and those that are minor I have limited to a simple enumeration : it has been necessary to define all, so that the scope of the literature may be indicated in respect of our proper concern even from the beginning. After the problems which they offer have been studied at length in the light of the texts themselves, we shall turn for further help to certain coincident schools of symbolism.

BOOK II

MYSTERIES OF THE HOLY GRAAL IN MANIFESTATION AND REMOVAL

THE ARGUMENT

I. A Preliminary Account of certain Root-Secrets included in the Whole Subject.—*Further considerations concerning the several groups of the literature—Quest versions and versions of early history—The Suppressed Word of the Perceval Quests—The suppressed sacramental formula—The secret school of ordination—The passing of the sacraments.* II. The Institution of the Hallows, and in the First Place a General Introduction Concerning them.—*Their powers and offices—Their passage from East to West—The Hallows in Britain—An alternative division of the cycle—Texts of the sacramental claims—The implied mystery of the Hallows—The four Hallows-in-chief.* III. The Institution of the Hallows, and, secondly, the Variations of the Cup Legend.—*The Holy Vessel in the legends of Joseph of Arimathæa—The high symbolism of the Cup—Sources of information concerning the Sacred Vessel—Certain apocryphal Gospels and certain chronicles of Britain—Variations of the Conte del Graal—The Cup in the metrical romance of De Borron—Its Eucharistic character—Philology of the term* Graal—*The Cup in the Lesser Holy Graal—In the Early Prose Merlin—In the Didot Perceval—The Cup in the Book of the Holy Graal—The Chalice and the Paschal Dish—References in the later prose Merlins—The Graal in the Longer Prose Perceval—Certain visions of the Holy Vessel in the great prose Lancelot—The Graal in the Quest of*

75

Galahad—*The Hallow in the German cycle—Possible hypotheses regarding the Most Precious Vessel—The conclusion of this matter.* IV. THE GRAAL VESSEL CONSIDERED AS A BOWL OF PLENTY.—*Developments of this tradition in the Greater Chronicles—In the poem of Robert de Borron—Of spiritual refreshment—Material presentation in the Book of the Holy Graal—Two aspects of magical feeding in the German cycle.* V. THE LESSER HALLOWS OF THE LEGEND.—*The Summary of these matters—The Lance—The Broken Sword—The Dish or Salver.* VI. THE CASTLE OF THE HOLY GRAAL.—*The place of the Holy Vessel—The House of the Rich King Fisherman—The Castle in the Valley—The Castle of Eden—The Palace of Dead Men.* VII. THE KEEPERS OF THE HALLOWS. —*Variations of tradition in respect of the Graal and its Guardians—How the life of Brons was prolonged throughout the centuries—The Keepers in the Greater Chronicles.* VIII. THE PAGEANTS IN THE QUESTS.—*Order of the Ceremonial Procession in the Conte del Graal—The Pageant in the Romance of Lancelot—In the Quest of Galahad—In the Longer Prose Perceval—In the German cycle.* IX. THE ENCHANTMENTS OF BRITAIN, THE TIMES CALLED ADVENTUROUS AND THE WOUNDING OF THE KING.—*The Cloud upon the Sanctuary—The suspension of Nature—Times of peril and distress—Of sin entering the Sanctuary—Of help coming from without—The Dolorous Stroke.* X. THE SUPPRESSED WORD AND THE MYSTIC QUESTION.—*One distinction between Perceval and Galahad—Mischances of the Word in its suppression—The Word in partial manifestation—Of the causes of silence —Of the plenary demand.* XI. THE HEALING OF THE KING.—*How the burden was lifted from old age—Of*

BOOK II

MYSTERIES OF THE HOLY GRAAL IN MANIFESTATION AND REMOVAL

I

A PRELIMINARY ACCOUNT OF CERTAIN ROOT-SECRETS INCLUDED IN THE WHOLE SUBJECT

IT is a very curious heaven which stands around the infancy of romance-literature, and more than one warrant is required to constitute a full title for the interpretation of those strange signs and portents which are seen in some of its zones. The academies of official learning are consecrated places, and those who have graduated in other schools, and know well that they hold, within their own province, the higher authority, must be the first to recognise and respect the unsleeping vigilance and patience of students who are their colleagues and brothers in a different sphere. In the study of archaic literature, the external history of the texts and the criticisms thereto belonging are in the hands of a recognised college, and its authority is usually final; but the inward spirit of the literature is sometimes an essence which escapes the academical processes. At the same time, any school of criticism which should decide that some books of the Holy Graal do not put forward extraordinary claims of the evasive kind, and do not so far contain the suggestion of an inward purpose, must be held to have failed even within its own province.

Having indicated after what manner the literature

with which we are dealing falls readily into several groups of a distinct kind for the purpose of particular classification, we are now called to regard it a little differently, though without prejudice to the schedule-in-chief of my proper choice. The distinction between quest-versions and versions of early history is known to students, and though it is not absolutely definite in itself, so far as the intention of criticism is concerned solely, it is important from another point of view. The reason is that both classes have their particular mystery, which is not without its antecedents in distinct schools of symbolism. The keynotes of the historical series—to make use of the expression in a sense which is not usually or so concisely attached to it—are those which have been considered as the implicits-in-chief of the literature. They are two in number, and they are embodied in two palmary historical texts, from which they were carried forward through intermediate documents which answer, broadly speaking, to the same description, and thence through certain quest-versions by which the literature is taken to its term. I am speaking, however, only of those cycles which have been classified in the previous section as the Lesser and Greater Chronicles of the Holy Graal; but it should be understood that the same or analogous early histories are presupposed by the later sequels to the poem of Chrétien de Troyes. On the other hand, the German cycle, as represented by Wolfram von Eschenbach and the author of the later *Titurel*, has an early history which differs from all existing French sources, though the Quest of Parsifal is in close correspondence with the Perceval quests current in northern France.

We have seen, concerning the keynotes of the early histories, that they are :—

A. The suppression or concealment of a potent sacramental formula, in the absence of which the office of the Christian ministry is not indeed abrogated but is foreshortened or has become substituted, so that there seems to be something of a vital character wanting to all the sanctuaries. Whatever therefore the elements which entered into the composition of the Graal conception, several versions of the legend unite in relating it to the mystery and power of certain high consecrations or of certain unmanifested and withheld forms of speech. Those who can acquire and retain the words may exercise at will a strange power and mastery over all about them, and will possess great credit in the sight of God. They need never fear the deprivation of their proper rights, sufferings from evil judgments, or conquest in battle, so long as their cause is just. It is, however, as I have intimated, either (1) impossible to communicate these words in writing, or (2) they are recorded in one place only ; that is to say, in the secret archives, or great book of the Graal. They are too precious and holy for common utterance, and, moreover, they are the secret of the Graal itself, in which a strange power of speech also resides. Joseph was himself under singular direction in accordance with the preconceived order of the Mystery, for the fulfilment of its concealed term.

B. The removal, cessation, or assumption of a certain school of ordination, which held from heaven the highest warrants, which was perpetuated from generation to generation in one line of descent, which had the custody of the sacred mysteries, which, in fine, ordained no one ; and the substitution, both concurrently and thereafter, of some other form of succession—venerable enough in its way, and the next surviving best after the abrogation of the first, but not the highest actuality of all, not the evidence of things unseen made spiritually and materially manifest as the term of faith. To this extent did the powers of the Secret Sanctuary differ by the hypothesis concerning it from the powers of the Holy Church manifested in the world. Yet the Church manifest was also the Church Holy.

In the prologue or preamble to the *Book of the Holy Graal*, the hermit who receives the revelations and the custody of the mysterious Book of the Legend testifies that the greatest secret of the world has been confided to him, and the communication took place amidst inexpressible experiences in that third heaven to which St. Paul was translated. The description of his ecstasy is written in fervent language, but in place of an indicible formula there is a great mystery attributed to the entire text of that cryptic record which, although it is said to be translated, yet remains unknown. The form wherein we have it is a concession to human disqualification and even to the frailty of external Nature. We possess only a substitute. On the other hand, the keynotes of the French quests are also of two kinds, by which—if it were possible otherwise—they might be divided into two cycles. That of the several Percevals is the suppression of a certain word, question, or formula, which suppression, on the surface side of things, causes dire misery and postpones the advancement of the elect hero, but in the end it makes for his further recognition and ensures his more perfect calling, so that he is crowned in fine as he might not have been crowned at first. If at his initial opportunity he had asked in the Graal Castle that simple question which covers the whole adventure with so deep a cloud of mystery, he would not have been perfected in suffering, regret and exile; some of the quests would have terminated almost at their inception, and one in its present form could not have existed at all.

The withheld word of the Perceval quests takes, as I have indicated, the form of a simple question—a question, that is to say, which should have been asked but was not; as such it is, so to speak, the reverse side or antithesis of the old classical legend of the sphinx. The sphinx asked questions and devoured those who did not reply or whose answers blundered. Perceval kept silence when he should have urged his inquiries, sometimes through false modesty, sometimes because he had been cautioned against idle curiosity; but in both cases, by the working of some apparently blind destiny, the omission carried with it the long series of its disastrous consequences. There came, however, a time of joy and deliverance, and it followed a belated utterance of the word ; thereby great enchantments were determined, great wrongs were redressed, and the wounds and sufferings endured through many years were healed and annulled. It follows that there is a twofold mystery of words connected by certain texts with the Quest of Perceval. Its higher sense is that of the sacramental formula, and this was interned with Perceval according to the Lesser Chronicles. But the word alternative—that which could be reserved or uttered—had performed in the meantime, and was still fulfilling, a certain office of amelioration, so that it is not by a merely vain observance that, in a sense, it is replaced by the quests for that unknown formula which was reserved as the last mystery of the Hidden Sanctuary. In contradistinction to this, there is one quest —and it is to be noted that it is one only—which depends entirely from the second alternative of the historical implicits. This is the Galahad Quest, and the keynote hereof is separate from all mysteries of asking, all joy of answer, as if these were of the Lesser Enigmas, and it is uplifted into a great world of holiness, where no longer is there any shadow of similitude to secret claims —doctrinal or ecclesiastical ; but the heroism of human life is received into the Divine Rapture, so that the last formulary of the search after and finding of the Holy Graal is in all truth that which is expressed by the admirable doctor Ruysbroeck—*in vastissimum divinitatis pelagus navigare*. Of such is the Graal legend, and those who are acquainted with it in the most elect of its early forms will agree not only that many portions of it are singularly winning, but that it is indeed

> "A part
> Of the hunger and thirst of the heart."

It is also on the external side a very melancholy legend ; it is the passing of a great procession and a great sacrament, which, owing to the imputed stress and terror of the time, is destined never to return in the same form; it is a portion of the loss of humanity on one side of its manhood; and it is no matter for surprise that in these late days, which are so full of the hunger and the thirst, several persons have attempted to read into it the particular significance which appeals to them. This has been anything in some cases but that which could have been intended consciously by any maker of chronicles, and the question of Perceval abides therefore amongst us, but now in the reverse form, seeing that it is asked, and this often, yet it remains to this day unanswered, save in those Holy Places, beyond the external voices, of which this world, as such, knows not anything. To the glory of God and to those Holy Places, within the Great Church of the Mysteries, I dedicate this research as a sign without of the things signified within.

II

THE INSTITUTION OF THE HALLOWS, AND IN THE FIRST PLACE A GENERAL INTRODUCTION CONCERNING THEM

Having thus indicated after what manner the Graal legend and its literature is tinged with mystery and symbolism *à parte ante et à parte post*, the next matter of our inquiry is concerned with the Institution of the Hallows. In all its forms indifferently, the Legend of the Holy Graal depends upon powers and offices ascribed to certain sacred objects. Those texts which it has become customary to term the Early Histories, equally with those which present the various versions of the Quest, revolve about these Hallows, showing how they were instituted, how they came into Britain, in whose hands they were preserved at first, to whom they were transmitted successively, why and by whom they were sought, and what, in fine, became of them.

Among the general characteristics of the French cycle we shall find that there is the passage of these Hallows from East to West. They are in hereditary keeping, and in the end, according to certain versions, they are again taken East. There are, however, numerous phases of the legend, important variations in the Hallows, while claims which are manifest in certain texts are in others non-existent. The cycle in Germany took over the legend of the Swan Knight and imported the Templar interest expressly; on the other hand, the introduction of certain highly ascetic elements is thought to be characterised by the coming of Galahad into the Graal Quest. The peculiar ecclesiastical claims which are the subsurface warrant of the cycle written in Northern French were never put forward ostensibly, and in the Galahad legend there remains only the shadow of those earlier designs which might be constructed as in dissonance with the Latin rite.

The Quest of the Holy Graal and of the other Hallows which were from time to time connected therewith is followed by many knightly heroes, most of whom are unsuccessful; the preliminary conditions of attainment are purity and sanctity, but there is nothing to show that these were sufficient in themselves, and as there were other qualifications, so in some signal instances a partial success was not impossible in the absence, or at least comparatively, of those warrants which in given cases were claimed as essential. Once more, therefore, the cycle of Northern France may be regarded as falling into four divisions :—

(*a*) The Institution of the Hallows, and more especially that which concerns the origin of the Sacred Vessel.

(*b*) The circumstances under which the Hallows were carried into Britain, or alternatively were found therein, and the later circumstances of their partial manifestation.

(c) The details of the search for the Hallows, and other things within and without which led to their removal or recession.

(d) The occasion of their final departure.

The texts, therefore, purport to provide the complete History of the Graal, including whence it came, where it abode for a while, and whither it has gone. This is not to say that there are express books treating of each section only. The metrical romance of De Borron does, however, stand simply for the first part, and the same applies to its prose rendering in the *Lesser Holy Graal*. The second part is found in the *Book of the Holy Graal*, and the third in the *Didot Perceval*, the *Conte del Graal*, the *Parsifal* of Wolfram, the *Longer Prose Perceval* and the *Great Quest of Galahad*. The German *Perceval* excepted, all these stories of research give an account of the withdrawal—some at considerable length, and some briefly.

Again, the later romances may be divided into two sections : (a) those which speak of an enchantment fallen on Britain, and (b) those which are concerned with the termination of certain adventurous times. If the literature follows any set purpose, a definable importance must be attributed to the meaning of that enchantment and those adventures. In this manner, the chief questions may be summarised alternatively as follows :—

(a) The sacramental claim and its connections, so far as these appear in the Quests.

(b) The qualifications for the Quest.

(c) The Hereditary Keepers of the Graal.

(d) The King's Wounding and the King's Healing.

(e) The enchantments of Britain in connection with the Wounded Keeper.

(f) The removal of the Graal and the close of those times which the texts term adventurous, since when there has been silence on earth in respect of the Holy Graal.

The sacramental claim is introduced, among other documents, in (a) the De Borron poem; (b) the *Lesser*

Holy Graal; while its shadow is projected as a secret which cannot be told in (*c*) the proem to the *Conte del Graal.* It seems to be found by a vague and remote inference in the *Longer Prose Perceval,* and it may be gathered by brief allusions in the early prose *Merlin.* In the Great Quest it has been expunged, while it is outside the tradition as represented by Wolfram. The Quest qualifications are vague in Chrétien and exceed reason. They are perhaps what might be termed ethical —but in the high degree—in Wolfram, who presents the marriage of Perceval. The so-called ascetic element appears fully in the *Book of the Holy Graal,* in the *Longer Prose Perceval,* and in the *Quest of Galahad.* The King's Wounding is accounted for differently in every romance; the withdrawal of the Graal is also told differently; sometimes it passes simply into deeper concealment; sometimes it seems taken away utterly; in one version there is another keeper appointed, but of the realm apart from the Hallows; it is carried to the far East in another; in two texts it remains where it was.

If there is a secret intention permeating the bulk of the literature, again it must partly reside in those epochs into which the literature falls; their consideration should manifest it and should enable us to deal, at the close of the whole research, with the final problem, being that which is signified by the departure of the Sacred Vessel.

Each of the Hallows has its implied enigma, besides that which appears openly in its express nature, and as we know that the mysteries of God are mysteries of patience and compassion, we shall be prepared to find in their reflections through the Graal Legend that even some offices of judgment are formularies of concealed mercy. They are therefore both declared and un-declared—that is to say, understood; and as there are certain Hallows which only appear occasionally, so there are suggestions and inferences concerning others which do not appear at all. That which was always in evidence is that to which the distinctive name of Graal is applied in every text, but enough has been said concerning it till we come to its exhaustive consideration in the next section. The second and third Hallows are the Lance and the Sword. The Lance is that which was used by the Roman soldier Longinus to pierce the side of Christ at the Crucifixion, or it is this at least according to the more general tradition. Of the Sword there are various stories, and it is this which in some cases serves to inflict the wound from which the Enchantments of Britain follow. It is (*a*) that which served to behead St. John the Baptist, in which connection we can understand its position as a sacred object; (*b*) that of the King and Prophet David, committed by Solomon to a wonderful ship, which went voyaging, voyaging throughout the ages till it should be seen by Galahad, the last scion of the royal house of Israel; or (*c*) it is simply an instrument preserved as a token belonging to a legend of vengeance, in which relation it was brought over from folk-lore and is nothing to the purpose of the Graal.

The Dish, which is the fourth and final object included among the authorised Hallows, is more difficult to specify, because its almost invariable appearance in the pageant of the high processions is accompanied by no intelligible explanation respecting it; and although it has also its antecedents in folk-lore, its mystic explanation, if any, must be sought very far away. Like the rest of the Hallows, it is described with many variations in the different books. It may be a salver of gold and precious stones, set on a silver cloth and carried by two maidens; it may be a goodly plate of silver, or a little golden vessel, and this simply, except in the *Longer Prose Perceval*, which as it multiplies the Hallows so it divides their ministry; but here, as elsewhere, the Dish does not embody apparently the feeding properties which are one aspect of the mystery.

In summary therefore: subject to characteristic variations which are particular to each text, it will be found that the several romances follow or forecast one general process, exhibiting a general secret intention, manifested though not declared, and it is for this intention that my study has to account.

III

THE INSTITUTION OF THE HALLOWS, AND, SECONDLY, THE VARIATIONS OF THE CUP LEGEND

We have seen that the secret of the Graal, signifying the super-substantial nourishment of man, was communicated by Christ to His chosen disciple Joseph of Arimathæa, who, by preserving the body of his Master after the Crucifixion, became an instrument of the Resurrection. He laid it in the sepulchre, and thus sowed the seed whence issued the arch-natural body. On Ascension Day this was removed from the world, but there remained the Holy Vessel, into which the blood of the natural body had been received by Joseph. Strangely endued with the virtues of the risen Christ and the power of the Holy Ghost, it sustained him spiritually, and by a kind of reflection physically, during forty years of imprisonment, through which period he was in that condition of ecstasy which is said by the Christian masters of contemplation to last for half-an-hour—being that time when there is silence in heaven. We find accordingly that Joseph had no sense of duration in respect of the years; he was already in that mystery of God into which the ages pass. After his release the Holy Vessel became a sign of saving grace, instruction and all wonder to that great company which he was elected to take westward. He committed it in fine to another keeper, by whom it was brought into Britain, and there, or otherwhere, certain lesser Hallows were added to the Hallow-in-chief, and were held with it in the places of concealment. Those which are met with most frequently, as we have seen, are four in number, but the mystery is really one, since it is all assumed into that vessel which is known for the most part as the Cup of legend. It is understood that for us at least this Cup is a symbol, seeing that the most precious of all vessels are not made with hands. It is in such sense that the true soul of philosophy is a cup which contains the universe. We shall understand also the ministry of material sustenance, frequently attributed to the Holy Graal, after another manner than that which can be presumed within the offices of folk-lore. It is in this sense that the old fable concerning the Bowl of Plenty, when incorporated by the Graal Mystery, may prove to have a profound meaning. Some things are taken externally; some are received within; but the food of the body has analogies with that of the soul. So much may be said at the moment concerning certain aspects which encompass the literature of the Graal, as the hills stand round Jerusalem.

The four Hallows are therefore the Cup, the Lance, the Sword and the Dish, Paten or Patella—these four, and the greatest of these is the Cup. As regards this Hallow-in-chief, of two things one: either the Graal Vessel contained the most sacred of all relics in Christendom, or it contained the Secret Mystery of the Eucharist. Now, the first question which arises is whether the general description which obtains concerning it—as I was almost about to say, in the popular mind—reposes on the authority of the texts. Here also will be found our first difficulty. I may not be pardoned such flippancy, but the Psalmist said: *Calix meus quam inebrians est*, and this has rather a bearing on the Graal chalice; for the variety of the accounts concerning it may produce in the mind a sense of having visited some inn of strange description where those who come to ask questions are served with strong measures, and full at that.

There are three available sources of information concerning the Sacred Vessel, including those which are purely of the Eucharistic office. (1) The apocryphal legends concerning Joseph of Arimathæa which are distinct from those that have been incorporated with the romances of chivalry and with the histories leading up to these. (2) The romances themselves and their prolegomena, which are the chief bases of our knowledge, but on the understanding that there is no criterion for the distinction between that which is traditional and that which is pure invention. (3) Some archæological aspects of sacramental practice.

The apocryphal legends which connect Joseph with the cultus of the Precious Blood are late, and they lie under the suspicion of having been devised in the interests of Glastonbury, or through Glastonbury of ecclesiastical pretensions on the part of the British Church at or about the period of Henry II. Above these as a substratum of solid fact—I refer to the fact of the inventions—there has been of late years superposed an alleged dream of a pan-Britannic Church, which belongs, however, more particularly to the romance of history. The chivalrous romances themselves have so overlaid the Graal object with decorations and wonder-elements that the object itself has been obscured and its nature can, in some cases, be extricated scarcely. Eucharistic archæology remains as a source of information on which it is possible to rely implicitly, but while this can satisfy us as to the variations in the form and matter of the Sacred Vessel used in the Sacrifice of the Mass, it does not offer us, except indirectly, much or perhaps any assistance to determine the relic of legend.

The *Evangelium Nicodemi*, *Acta [vel Gesta] Pilati*, and some other oriental apocryphal documents are the authorities for the imprisonment of Joseph by the Jews because he had laid the body of Christ in the sepulchre. William of Malmesbury, John of Glastonbury and similar makers of chronicles are responsible for referring the first evangelisation of Britain to Joseph of Arimathæa. From these, however, we must except Geoffrey of Monmouth, and William of Malmesbury has nothing to tell us of the Graal, though he has the story of two phials containing the Precious Blood. The reference to relics of any kind is also late in the chronicles. An English metrical life of Joseph, belonging to the first years of the sixteenth century, but drawing from previous sources, shows how the precious blood was collected by that saint and received into two cruets, which we find figuring at a later period in the arms of Glastonbury Abbey. One of these sources, though perhaps at a far distance, may have been the lost book attributed to Melkin or Mewyn, which gives an account of these cruets. The tradition supposes (1) that they were buried at Glastonbury, (2) that they will be discovered concurrently with the coffin of Joseph, and (3) that thereafter there will be no more drought in Britain. John of Glastonbury is one of the authorities for the existence of a book of Melkin —sometimes identified with the *Chronicle* of Nennius. The more immediate antecedent of the metrical story is, however, the *Nova Legenda Angliæ* of Capgrave, and it represents Joseph as living with twelve hermits at Glastonbury, where he also died and was buried. The Oxford Vernon MS., written in verse about 1350, shows that there was a sacred vessel containing blood. The *Chronicle of Helinandus* describes the Graal as a wide and shallow vessel, wherein meats in their juice are served to wealthy persons. The *Historia Aurea*, written by John of Tynemouth, connects Joseph with the Holy Vessel, which it describes as that large dish or platter in which the Lord supped with His disciples, with which concurs one entire cycle of the legend. It may be added, for what it is worth, that the Armorican Gauls seem to have had a sacred vessel used in certain rites from a very early period. An object of this kind is thought to be depicted on Armorican coins, being semi-circular in shape, held by means of thongs and devoid of stem or base. Under Roman domination the vessel was figured with a pedestal.

We come now to the putative historical romances and

the poems and tales of chivalry which contain the developed legend of the Graal. The *Conte del Graal*, which is the first text for our consideration, has many decorative descriptions of the Sacred Vessel, but they present certain difficulties, as will be exhibited by their simple recitation in summary. (1) It was covered with the most precious stones that are found in the world, and it gave forth so great a light that the candles at the table were eclipsed, even as are the stars of heaven in the glory of the sun and moon (Chrétien de Troyes). (2) It passed to and fro quickly amidst the lights, but no hand appeared to hold it (Gautier de Doulens, or, as he is now termed, Wauchier de Denain). (3) It was borne uplifted by a beautiful maiden, who was discounselled and weeping (Montpellier MS.). (4) It was carried to and fro before the table by a maiden more beautiful than flowers in April (second account of Gautier, with which compare the similar recital of Gerbert). (5) It was carried amidst a great light by an angel, to heal Perceval (Manessier). (6) It was carried in the pageant by a maiden through the castle chamber (*ibid.*). (7) It was carried openly at the coronation of Perceval, also by a maiden (*ibid.*). (8) It was, in fine, ravished with the soul of Perceval, and has never since been seen so openly :—

> "Ne jà mais nus hommes qui soit nés
> Nel vera si apiertement."

What follows from these citations will have occurred to the reader—that in all these several sections of the *Conte del Graal* there is no intelligible description of the sacred object ; that the writers knew of it at a far distance only ; that some of their references seem to indicate a brilliant lamp rather than a chalice ; and, when they allocated it to Christian symbolism, that they may have wavered in their meaning between the idea of the Paschal Dish and the Cup in which Christ consecrated the wine of the first Eucharist ; but we cannot tell. I should add that the prologue, which is certainly the work of a later or at least of another hand, and embodies some curious material, mentions, but very briefly, the pageant of the Graal procession, saying that the Vessel appears at the Castle without sergeant or seneschal, but again there is no description of the Vessel. In conclusion of this account, the alternative ending of Gerbert retells with variations part of the story of Joseph, and although there is once again no intimation as to the form of the Graal, an account of the service performed at an altar over " the holy, spiritual thing "—the Vessel more beautiful than eye of man has seen—is there recounted, while it leaves no doubt in the mind that this service was a Mass of the Graal. It is the only suggestion of the kind which is afforded by the vast poem, though the origin and early history of the sacred object is in accordance with the received tradition.

The fuller memorials of this tradition are embodied, as we have seen, in two cycles of literature, but the text which is first in time and chief in importance is the metrical *Romance of the Graal, or Joseph of Arimathæa*, by Robert de Borron. A French and a German critic have said that this is the earliest text of the Graal literature proper, and an English writer has concluded, on the contrary, that it is not : *mais que m'importe ?* I will not even ask for the benefit of the doubt, so far as enumeration is concerned. The metrical *Joseph* says that the Graal was a passing fair vessel, wherein did Christ make His sacrament. This is vague admittedly, and assuming a certain confusion in the mind of the writer, it might have been that Dish mentioned by John of Tynemouth in which the Paschal Lamb was eaten by Christ and His disciples. In place of the words *mout gent*, which are given by the original French editor of the only text, Paulin Paris, following I know not what authority, or imagining a variant reading, substituted the words *mout grant*, which might well apply to the Paschal Dish. But Robert de Borron certifies to his own meaning when he recites an utterance of Christ in His discourse to Joseph, for it is there said that the vessel which has served as the reliquary shall be called henceforth a chalice :—

> " Cist vaisseau où men sanc méis,
> Quant de men cors le requeillis,
> Calices apelez sera."

It is impossible to read the later verses in which the Eucharistic chalice is compared with the sepulchre of Christ, the mass corporal with the grave-clothes, and the paten with the stone at the mouth of the tomb, without concluding that by the Graal was intended the first Eucharistic chalice, and the presence of this symbolism in the mind of Robert de Borron suggests a symbolical intention on his part in the whole legend which he presented. If it is said that his idea of a chalice does not correspond to a vessel the content of which is sacramental wine, it should be remembered that the *ciborium* which contains consecrated Hosts is still at this day replaced on occasion by a chalice of the ordinary form.

The idea of the devotional poet, supposing it to have been as purely mystical as he was himself deeply religious, might have embodied an attempt to shadow forth in the perpetuation of the most precious of all reliquaries the sacramental mystery of the Real Presence.

It seems certain, in any case, that when Robert de Borron speaks of the Graal as that vessel in which Christ made his sacrament, this must not be understood as referring to the Paschal Dish, though one probable derivation of the word Graal would support the latter view. In the dialect of Languedoc, *Grazal* signified a large vessel, usually of clay ; in the dialect of Provence, *Grasal* was a bowl or platter ; in Anglo-Norman, or its connections, *Graal* was a dish made of some costly material for the purpose of great feasts, which, as we have seen, is the description of Helinandus. With all this some of the later romancers were dissatisfied, and, following Robert de Borron, they exalted the vessel into a chalice, so that they might bring it into line with the Eucharistic side of the legend, with which side a paschal dish—whether that of Christ or another—offered little analogy. The material of such a chalice would have been probably glass. It follows from Tertullian that in Rome at the beginning of the third century they used glass chalices; so did the Bishop of Toulouse at the end of the fourth century; and about A.D. 550 the same custom prevailed, as appears by the life of Cesarius, Bishop of Arles. A council of Rheims in the days of Charlemagne is said to have forbidden glass chalices because they were brittle.

The *Lesser Holy Graal* does not depart from the rendering which I have here given in respect of the metrical romance, but it seems to make the assurance of the poet more certain by elucidating further the application of the secret words to the consecration and administering of the Eucharist. Where the poem says that there is a great book in which has been written the great secret called the Graal, the *Lesser Holy Graal* says: This is the secret uttered at the great sacrament performed over the Graal—that is to say, over the chalice. The vessel is otherwise described as the one in which Christ sacrificed, as if He actually celebrated the first Mass, and from the Eucharistic standpoint this seems much stronger than the corresponding *feisoit son sacrement*, which are the words of Robert de Borron. The repetition of the experience of the sacred table which is enjoined by Joseph in both texts is in both termed the service of the Graal, but in the prose version alone is it adjudged to the hour of tierce, as if the Mass of the day were celebrated, and as if certain persons, evidently in a state of grace, were sustained in the body by the sacramental nutriment of the soul. The *Early Merlin* and the *Didot Perceval* neither reduce nor increase the evidence; but it may be hazarded, for what it is worth, that the original disclosure of the secret words may have had some office in preserving the content of the great relic.

In the *Early Merlin* there is no allusion to the office

of secret words, and no Graal Hallows are mentioned excepting the Cup, as it is obvious that we cannot include the sword of Merlin, through which Arthur was chosen to be king. It does not appear that this weapon had any antecedent history. In the *Didot Perceval* the rumour and the wonder of the Graal moves pageant-like through all the pages, but it is more shorn of descriptive allusions than anything that has preceded it in the quests. When the predestined Knight visits the castle, tower, or hold in which the Hallow has been preserved through so many centuries, he sees it plainly enough at the supper-table, along which it passes, carried with no ostentation by a mere page of the chamber; but he is said only to hold a vessel wherein the blood of our Saviour reposed. This is at the first visit, and at the second, when Perceval is initiated into the whole mystery and becomes the Lord of the Graal, the description is repeated merely, as if it were a counsel of perfection to maintain and even to increase in the third text of the trilogy whatsoever could be called vague and dubious in the first.

The *Book of the Holy Graal*, even when it reproduces with several variations the prose version of Robert de Borron's poem, gives, in some of its codices, an explanation of the Sacred Vessel which is the antithesis of his own. It is described as that Dish in which the Son of God partook of the Last Supper before He gave to the disciples His own flesh and blood. It was, therefore, the Paschal Dish. Certain manuscripts, however, differ so widely that it is difficult to determine the original state of the text. Another codex follows the account of the *Lesser Holy Graal*. According to a third codex, it was the content and not the Vessel which was called the Holy Graal; but, speaking generally, most versions concur in describing it as the Holy Dish. The connection with the Eucharist is, however, sufficiently close, for he who is elected to say the first Mass and to consecrate the unspotted elements is he also to whom by Divine instruction

Joseph surrenders the vessel. But the Blessed Reliquary would seem to have been rather the outward witness to the presence within those elements. For example, in the first unveiled vision of the Holy Graal which is granted to any one outside Joseph himself, we hear of an altar, on one side of which were the nails used for the Crucifixion, together with the hallowed Lance; on the other side was the Dish; and in the centre there was an exceeding rich vessel of gold in the semblance of a goblet —obviously the chalice of consecration: it had a lid after the manner of a *ciborium*. More astonishing still, the cup of the Eucharist is placed within the Graal during a ceremony which corresponds to the Mass. In a romance so overcharged with decoration and so lavish in episodes of wonder, we should expect, and shall not be disappointed, that many pageants and ornaments would collect about the Holy Vessel, and that it should work many marvels. The Sacrament consecrated within it reveals the mysteries of Christ openly to chosen eyes, but thereon can no man look until he is cleansed from sin. It gives also on occasion the vision of an Eternal Eucharist and a great company sitting at the high table in the Paradise which is above. So far as concerns the authority of the text itself, it would appear that the Mass of the Graal is not like that of the Church without—an office which recurs daily; it is rather an arch-natural sacrifice, at which the incarnate Christ figures as the sensible oblation and subsequently as the Melchisedech of the rite, communicating Himself to the witnesses, while a thousand voices about him give thanks to God amidst a great beating of birds' wings, and

> " Young men whom no one knew went in and out
> With a far look in their eternal eyes."

The texts of the later *Merlin* have several references to the Graal, and it is the chief purpose which moves through the dual romance, leading up, as it does obviously, to a Quest of the Sacred Vessel; but what is understood thereby must be gathered chiefly from its reflections of the Joseph legend. We shall see that in certain codices the account differs from that of Robert de Borron. The *Vulgate Merlin* has one very remarkable passage, which tells how the tidings of the Holy Graal spread through the realm of King Arthur, and how the Graal was that Vessel in which Joseph of Arimathæa received the blood from the side of Jesus Christ when He hung upon the Cross. It represents, therefore, a tradition which is familiar enough not only in the literature of romance, but in that of religious legend, though it is the antithesis of the account given in the Lesser Chronicles, wherein we are told that the blood was drawn into the Vessel after Joseph and Nicodemus had taken down the Body of the Lord. Secondly, the Graal was that Holy Vessel which came from Heaven above into the city of Sarras. We have here a reflection only, and that at a far distance, of the *Book of the Holy Graal* in the form which is now extant. Thirdly, and to us most important, the Graal was that Vessel in which Christ first sacrificed His Blessed Body and His Flesh by the mediation of His bishop, the Second Joseph, whom He ordained with His own hands. According to the *Huth Merlin* the Graal was that Vessel in which Jesus and His Apostles ate the Last Supper. It was again, therefore, the Paschal Dish.

The *Longer Prose Perceval* has many descriptions of the vessel, all of which are designed to connect it with the chalice, but they are highly mystical in their nature. As one of the most express attempts to relate the Graal with the Eucharist, it must be regarded as important for the subject of the Hallow-in-chief. This romance and the great *Quest of Galahad* are both texts of transubstantiation, and they must rank also among the latest documents of the literature. The Lesser Chronicles, even in the prose version of De Borron's poem, offer no suggestion concerning this doctrine, the Graal Vessel being simply a Hallow containing a precious relic. About the period of the *Quest* and the *High History*, the tide of ecclesiastical feeling, which long previously had set towards the definition of the dogma, must have permeated the mind of the laity, prepared as it also was by the desire of things sensible and tangible in matters of religion. It was, this notwithstanding, still long to the establishment of the high, symbolical festival of Corpus Christi, which provided an external epilogue to the closed canon of the Graal, as if by a final substitution that which was taken away, or at least *ex hypothesi*, was to be in perpetuity memorialised about the precincts of the gate by the wardens thereof. In connection with transubstantiation, it may be remarked that the religious office of Knighthood was above all things to hear mass, and, next, to confess sins. There are few records in the Graal romances that the chivalry of Logres communicated, except in the *Quest of Galahad*, and then only in the case of the elect knights. All high festivals were observed, all penances fulfilled; but to participate in the Eucharistic mystery seemed apart from the life of the world and withdrawn into the sphere of sanctity. However this may be, the *Longer Prose Perceval* has two cryptic descriptions of the Graal Vessel, which, on account of their complexity, but for the moment only, I must present as they stand actually in the story. (1) It is said concerning Gawain, when he looked at the Graal in his wonder, that it seemed to him a chalice was therein, "albeit there was none at this time." It was, therefore, an ark or a tabernacle which was designed to contain a cup, but when the latter was removed it still held the shadow or semblance thereof. (2) In the course of the same episode a change was performed in the aspect of the external object, and it appeared to be "all in flesh," meaning that it was transformed into a vision of Christ crucified. Towards the close of the story, when a certain Queen Jandree relates her visions to Perceval, she sees, in one of these, an image of the crucifixion from which people collect the Blood into a most Holy Vessel, elevated for that object by one of them. There are no names mentioned, but for purposes of simplicity we may assume that they were Joseph and Nicodemus. In the castle of King Fisherman the office of the Cup was to receive the Blood which fell from the point of the Sacred Lance. The priest who officiated at the Graal service is said to begin his sacrament, with which expression we may compare the words *feisoit son sacrement*, which are those of Robert de Borron. There is indubitably reference to the Eucharist in both cases, and perhaps the Graal Mass Book was a traditional version of the Mass, supposed, *ex hypothesi*, to follow the Last Supper. Speaking generally, the historical account of the Cup follows the *Book of the Holy Graal* rather than De Borron's poem, for the blood which flowed from the wounds of Christ when He was set upon the Cross is said to have been received into the Sacred Vessel. There is no ministry in respect of material sustenance attributed to the Graal in this spiritual romance.

It is, therefore, in one sense the antithesis of the *Quest of Galahad*, which dwells with equal fulness on the food-giving properties of the Vessel and on its connection with the mystery of such a mass and such an office of the Eucharist as never before or after was said in the wide world, apart from this sacred object. When the Holy Graal enters the court of King Arthur and into the banqueting-hall it is clothed in white samite, but neither the Vessel nor the bearer are visible to human eyes. On a later occasion it manifests as a Holy Vessel on a table of silver in an old chapel. Elsewhere it is observed that the Flesh and Blood of God are present in the Graal. When it appears to Lancelot in the Castle of Corbenic, it is still upon a table of silver, but this time the object is covered with red in place of white samite, and it is surrounded by angels. In the course of the ceremony Lancelot sees three men, who represent the Trinity, exalted above the head of the officiating priest. Two of them place the youngest between the hands of the priest, who again exalts him. On another occasion a child enters visibly into the substance of the Mass-bread. A man is also elevated, bearing the signs of the Passion of Christ, and this Personage issues out of the Vessel, coming subsequently among the knights present, and causing them to communicate sacramentally. It is after this episode that the Graal is removed to the spiritual city of Sarras. There Christ appears to Galahad and his companions, and this is the last manifestation in connection with the Sacred Vessel. It is the *viaticum* of the *haut prince*, who thereafter exercises the high option which has been granted previously and demands that he should be taken away.

As the chief Hallow in the *Parsifal* of Wolfram differs from all the other romances, it will be left for more full consideration in dealing with the German cycle ; but seeing that in this cycle there are correspondences outside this great poem with the Northern French accounts, one of these may be placed here so as to illustrate the Germanic allusions to the Sacred Vessel in the general understanding thereof. *Diu Crône*, the poem of Heinrich, says that it was borne on a cloth of samite and had a base of red gold, on which a reliquary of gold and gems was superposed. It was carried by a crowned maiden. There is here, however, a fresh departure from the Graal in Christian symbolism, for as, on the one hand, it is the quest of a feigned and impossible hero, so, on the other, the content ascribed to the reliquary is not the true content. It holds the semblance of bread, as if that of the Divine Body, but the wine or royal blood, which corresponds to the second element of the Eucharist, is distilled from the Lance of the legend.

We are now approaching the term of the inquiry allocated to this section, and it will be seen on reflection that we have three possible hypotheses regarding the precious vessel : (1) that it was a cruet or phial, wherein the blood of Christ was reserved permanently—in which case we can understand the legend on the score of comparative possibility; (2) that it was an open platter or bowl, which, it is obvious, could have had no permanent content, much less the precious or indeed any other blood; (3) that it corresponded to the notion of a chalice, but probably with a cover, after the manner of a *ciborium*. It is in late texts that the vessel appears most indubitably in connection with the sacrifice of the Mass; it was and could be only that which was recognised by *Diu Crône* of Heinrich and by John of Tynemouth— namely, a reliquary; but the mystic side of the legend, reflecting in the minds of the romancers many conflicting issues, took it over to the Eucharist, influenced by the irresistible connection between the sacramental blood and the *sang réal* poured out at the Crucifixion. There is evidence that this view is almost coincident with the marriage of the legend to romance. The mind of romance connected the vessel and its office with secret words of consecration and a wonderful grade of priest-hood, the root-matter of which must have been drawn from some source wherein relics could have counted for little in the presence of the higher secrets of sanctity.

In conclusion as to this matter, the Holy Graal, accord-ing to the Greater Chronicles, was not the only Hallow which was brought into Britain by those whose mission was to preach first the gospel therein, but it was more especially the exotic of the legend, as this was developed in Northern France. In several cases the other Hallows, as we shall see, were either present in Britain or arrived some centuries later. As regards the Lesser Chronicles, it is warrantable to decide that, in the mind of Robert de Borron, the Sacred Vessel was a *ciborium* or covered chalice, and that in some manner which is not clearly declared it was connected with a sacramental service per-formed in great seclusion. As regards the Greater Chronicles, it was originally a Dish, and that Dish in which the Paschal Lamb was eaten at the Last Supper; but from the very beginning of this ascription the notion of a cup was essential to the Eucharistic office which also resided in the Vessel; in the *Book of the Holy Graal* a cup is inserted therein, but in later texts of the cycle the Dish sometimes undergoes transmutation and reappears as a chalice.

IV

THE GRAAL VESSEL CONSIDERED AS A BOWL OF PLENTY

The incidental allusions which have been made already to certain physical properties which are ascribed to the Holy Graal in several branches of the literature seem to call at this point for some further explanation, without anticipating what will be said at the close as to any higher aspects of this tradition or exhausting specifically its connections with folk-lore, which remain to be stated separately. The conception itself seems so repugnant to all that we attach to the Graal that it is at least desirable to ascertain its scope in the texts. As it is acknowledged to embody a reversion from old non-Christian fable, we should expect it to be most prominent in those texts which are nearest to the transitional stage, and more especially in the Chrétien portion of the *Conte del Graal.* It should be understood in the first place—as indeed it follows sufficiently from previous sections—that in the Perceval quests—one version excepted—and in more than one of the Gawain quests the visit to the Graal Castle is followed by a banquet or supper, at which the questing knight is treated for the most part as an honoured guest.

The exception as regards Perceval is in the longer prose romance or *High History*, the action of which is subsequent to the first visit of the hero, and he does not enter it a second time till he has taken it by force of arms out of the hands of God's enemy and the enemy of Holy Church. In other cases, where the ceremonial meal is described—sometimes at considerable length—it is nearly always at the table and before or in the midst of the festival that the Graal and the other Hallows make their processional appearance, and there are certain texts which say that the Sacred Vessel serves the high company—sometimes with rarest meats, sometimes also with wine. In these specific instances the manifestation is that which occurs first after they are seated at table. It was to be expected, as I have said, that we should hear of this material efficacy in Chrétien, but though the courses of the banquet are described fully, and are rare and precious enough, it is only a high reverence in a lordly castle of this world, and it is precisely from this text that it proves wanting. The wonder resides in the Hallows, but they dispense nothing to the body. It follows from this that the metrical romance of De Borron was not written to explain Chrétien. It follows also that Gautier had no precedent in the poet who was his precursor, and it was therefore from other antecedents that he derived his notion of the Feeding Dish and from yet others his knowledge of early Graal history which does not appear in Chrétien. When Gautier brings Gawain to the Graal Castle, he says that the Sacred Vessel served seven courses, but the wine was served by the butlers. His idea of the Sacred Vessel must therefore have corresponded rather to the Paschal Dish than to a Reliquary of the Precious Blood. On the other hand, his account of Perceval's second visit contains no allusion to this side of the festival. Manessier, in continuation of the same visit, offers no suggestion ; but when the time comes for him to tell the story of Perceval's third arrival, the Hallows appear in their order and all are filled at the table. At the fourth and final visit, and the coronation of the questing knight, Manessier recounts how the Graal feeds the whole company with costliest meats. On the other hand, Gerbert, preoccupied by far other matters, gives no indication of the kind.

Except in so far as the *Early History of Merlin* reproduces one episode from the *Lesser Holy Graal*, it has no allusion to the properties under consideration, and they have passed out of all recollection in the *Didot Perceval*. On the other hand, the Greater Chronicles, represented by the *Book of the Holy Graal* and the *Quest of Galahad*, embody a marked development of this particular tradition. Between them there is the later *Merlin* without any reference whatever, the prose *Lancelot*—to which we shall see that it is a foreign element—and the *Longer Prose Perceval* into the consciousness of whose author it has never once entered and by whom it would, I think, have been repudiated. Its recurrence, on a single occasion, in the presence of Galahad, and in connection with his story, may seem unsearchable, having regard to the claims which inhere in this romance, but in the order of the texts it is explained by the antecedents in the first form of the first document of the cycle. We must recur, therefore, to the root-matter of the early histories.

The poem of Robert de Borron narrates that among those who accompanied Joseph westward a certain number departed from grace through the sin of luxury, but the spiritual mind of the minstrel has spared us all particulars. The result was a famine in the company; it does not appear that it fell upon all without exception, for the fact that there was want among the people had to be notified to the leaders; but, these apart, good and bad seem to have suffered indifferently. An appeal was made to Brons that he should take counsel with Joseph, which was done accordingly, and Joseph invoked the Son of God on his knees in the presence of the Graal, reciting the petition of his people, who were in need of bread and meat. He was told in reply to expose the Sacred Vessel openly in the presence of the brethren, on a table similar to that of his own Last Supper,— by which means the sinners will be discovered speedily. It is Christ Himself who was speaking, and He ordained further that Brons should repair to a certain water and there angle for a fish. The first which he caught must be brought straightway to Joseph, who, on his part, should place it upon the Graal table over against the

Sacred Vessel. The people were then to be summoned and informed that if they were true believers, who had kept the commandments and followed out the teachings of Christ, as given through Joseph, so that they had trespassed in nothing, they would be welcome to sit down at the table. These instructions were followed, with the result that a part only of the company accepted this invitation. The table was arranged duly, and whosoever was seated thereat had the accomplishment of his heart's desire, and that entirely. Petrus, who was one of the recipients, asked the crowd who stood about whether they did not experience anything of the good which penetrated those at the table, and they answered that they felt nothing. Thereupon Petrus denounced them as guilty of the vile, dolorous sin, and they went forth out of the house of Joseph covered with shame. The poem says :—

> " La taule toute pleinne estoit,
> Fors le liu qui pleins ne pooit
> Estre ; "

but the experience of the sitters, thus collected together, seems to indicate that they were fed from within rather than from without. It will be seen and we must always remember that the chief necessity and often the chief privation of early quests and ventures in the voyages of romance was that of food in season, but in this case what I have called the spiritual mind of the poet could not clearly connect the idea of physical refreshment with the sacramental powers of the Relic. As regards the elect who were present, when the service was finished each of them rose up and went out among the rest, Joseph commanding that they should return day by day to partake of the grace administered. Thus was the vessel, says the poem, proved for the first time. In the speech of Petrus to the people who were rejected there is further evidence that the sustenance was more especially of the spiritual order, and it is important to establish this point from the earliest of the Graal histories. He speaks of the great delight experienced in the *Grace* and of the great joy with which the communicants were penetrated. They were filled as the Psalmist was filled and she who sang the Magnificat: *Esurientes implevit bonis.* What was filled was the heart of man, and what was refected was the entire soul. My contention is therefore that Robert de Borron had the idea of the Feeding Dish present to his mind when he made the scarcity of food for his company an opportunity for the discriminating test of the second great table of refection, but in place of bodily meat and bread, symbolised by the single fish, as something intentionally placed out of all reasonable proportion, he administered *extasis.* That question of Petrus to the unworthy crowd about him: Do you experience nothing? is so evidently impossible, in their case, as a reference to eating and drinking that there is no need to dwell thereon. It left no opportunity to the prose editors whose versions complete the trilogy, and they lose all touch with the notion.

As regards the Fish, by which we shall be brought at a later stage to another form of symbolism found in the poem, the text offers a comparison which, although a little cryptic, seems also significant. It says that in the sight of the Graal, in its company and the service thereof, true believers experience as much satisfaction as a fish, which, having been taken by a man in his hand, has contrived to escape therefrom and again go swimming in the sea. The specific fish of the story was placed before the Sacred Vessel exactly in the middle of the table, and was covered with a cloth. There is no suggestion that it was eaten, and it appears to have remained as a kind of fixed dish whenever the service was celebrated.

The noticeable point about the poem is that the material sustenance provided once only by the sacred vessel, as something *nihil ad rem*, is passed over so slightly and lightly that on the face of the text it is a matter of inference whether the Company partook (*a*) of anything physical at all, except the broken meats which remained in the stewardship of the camp; or (*b*) alternately of anything except the Eucharist, which certainly provides bodily sustenance in the most material of the sacramental texts. On the other hand, all processes of language are enlisted by Robert de Borron to show that they were sustained spiritually. Further, the palmary miracle accomplished by the vessel on this occasion was not any kind of refreshment, spiritual or corporeal, but that of discrimination between the good and evil among the people : for this kind of judgment the table of Joseph was set up and the goats were separated from the sheep. There was, I suppose, in the poet's mind no question that what could nourish the soul, which is vital, could at need refresh the body, which is accessory only. It is therefore small wonder that when the fountain text says so little, those which derive therefrom are content to leave it thereat, and they add nothing. For Joseph and his brethren it remained that the Lord was the part of my chalice, and perhaps in the last understanding the famine which fell upon the companions was the scarcity of grace in the soul rather than of food in the stomach.

Now, on the other hand, the *Book of the Holy Graal* is in one sense the legend of the Feeding Dish consecrated and exalted, and seeing that as the texts stand it is that from which the greatest of all quests and the most wonderful version of all the quests which are accessory must be supposed to derive *ex hypothesi*, it is essential that we should understand its position clearly, and I will tabulate the references as follows :—

(1) The people on their way to Britain are fed marvellously with all manner of viands, both meat and drink, as, for example, at houses by the way and at lordly castles. (2) In this primary allusion the Graal is not said to feed them. (3) They receive nourishment from the table of the Graal, but this is

the Eucharist, and it is expressly stated that the company had nothing else on that day. (4) At a later stage, a second instance is given of this super-substantial refreshment. (5) It is not till we are approaching comparatively the close of the chronicle that we reach something more definite. The company are already in Britain, and through the persecution of their heathen enemies they are hungry. Twelve loaves are obtained; they are broken by Joseph, are placed in the Dish, and they feed 500 people, more than the twelve loaves being left subsequently. (6) It does not prove food of spiritual life, for those who were filthy before are filthy still. (7) At yet a later stage, the heathens test the feeding powers of the Vessel by the imprisonment of the Christians. In Wales the Vessel again furnishes all manner of viands, and one fish is a super-abundant provision for the whole company. After a similar manner, they are fed with all possible delicacies in Scotland.

Passing over the later Merlin romances, which are neither exactly Graal histories nor quests, and offer nothing to our purpose, we find that the shadow of the Quest is projected into the prose *Lancelot*, though there is no questing intention, and the visit of Gawain to the Graal Castle is the one example of indignity offered to a guest therein. The responsibility, however, does not rest with the royal and saintly host, whose "high-erected thought" is "seated in a heart of courtesy." There is the flight of the mystical dove from casement to inmost Shrine, as if the bird went to renew the virtues of the Holy Graal; there is the apparition of the unattended damozel, bearing that which itself bore the likeness of a chalice; there is the genuflection of all knees before the Holy Vessel; and there are sweet odours with all delicacies lavished upon the great table. But in the feast which follows, the peer of the Round Table alone has an empty plate. It was the discrimination and forejudgment of the Hallow in respect of that Knight, who, in the days of Galahad, would indeed propose the Quest but would not persevere therein.

In the *Longer Prose Perceval*, after the restitution of all things, there is abundance everywhere in the Castle, "insomuch that there is nought wanting that is needful for the bodies of noble folk," even as for noble souls. But the source of all this plenty is in a river which comes from the Earthly Paradise and not in the Holy Graal. On the occasion of Gawain's visit, the table is garnished richly, but it is with game of the forest and other meats of this world; it is the same on the arrival of Lancelot; and then even the earthly food does not vary.

In the *Quest of Galahad* the manifestations of the Graal are as follows: (1) In the banqueting-hall of King Arthur, and it is the only record of its appearance in any castle of the external world, the reason being that the Graal is "going about." On this occasion—yes, even in the presence of Galahad—"every knight had such meats and drinks as he best loved in this world." As the table was dight for the festival, it seems to follow that what was otherwise provided already underwent transformation, probably in the minds of the participants. (2) At the stone cross in the forest and in the waste land, where stood the old chapel and where in the presence of Lancelot the sick knight was made whole by the Precious Vessel. (3) To Lancelot in the Graal Castle, where there was, firstly, a Mass of the Graal, and, secondly, a banquet at which all were fed by the Vessel. (4) To Galahad and his elect companions at the consummation of the Quest, but the sweet meats were those of the Eucharist exalted to the arch-natural degree. (5) In Sarras at the close of all, "when the deadly flesh began to behold the spiritual things," and Christ's transcendence was manifested in Christ's immanence. Of these five changes in the exposition of the Holy Graal, the first only and the lowest was that of earthly food; it was communicated by a special indulgence, in the palace of a lord of the world, as an encouragement to the quest of Heaven.

If we turn to the German cycle, we shall find that the feeding qualities are before all things obvious in Wolfram. At the first visit of Parsifal, what is taken from the Graal is bread, but other dishes stand before it in right great plenty, both rare and common. Some say that there are no such riches on earth, but to the poet this is a word of foolishness, since the Graal is the crown of all. The wine also was the gift of the precious object, and the cups on the table were filled by the power thereof. In the great and high festival, when the questing Knight was crowned as King and Warden of the mystery, even the ordinary fowl of the forest were taken from the Graal. I am afraid that such ministry in the *Parsifal* is comparable to the procession therein, somewhat indiscriminate in method and "like a tale of little meaning, though the words are strong." In the curious chronicle of Heinrich, the service of the table is after the manner born of this world, but the host does not partake till he is served from the sacred Reliquary with something which, by its description, bears the external semblance of the symbolical Bread of Heaven. The poem, however, has otherwise no sacramental connections, nor has the Vessel, strictly speaking, what is understood here by feeding properties.

It remains now to sum up and to ask in our hearts—though the answer is remote in our quest—what is the meaning of all this disconcerting medley, which out of the Holy Graal, as an issue in time and place, brings now the voice of an oracle, like the classical *Bætylus;* now a certain βασανος or touchstone, a criterion of judgment which separates the good from the evil; now a suspended viaticum, which keeps the sick alive and the dead in a false life, but offers no relief in suffering; now manifests the corporeal changes in the growth of the Divine Body; now shows Christ crucified; and now out of all reason—like a coarse Talmudic allegory—provides the game of the forest—all commonest and rarest meats; yet in all and through all is (*a*) the Mystery of the Eucharist, and (*b*) a simple reliquary containing *ex hypothesi* the Precious Blood of the Redeemer. At the moment let us note further—and this only—as a little curious, that two out of the three express texts of transubstantiation are texts of the Feeding Dish, but the third in the series has spiritualised all its houses and acknowledges not the flesh or its ministry except in the Eucharist. The Chrétien portion of the *Conte del Graal* is a pagan wonder-book tinctured thinly with Christianity, but it is not nearly so gross regarding the service of the Sacred Vessel as the *Book of the Holy Graal* or the Great Quest itself. There is more in Gautier than in Chrétien, and very much more in Wolfram than in the putative Walter Map. But those who continued and those who finished the *Conte* are fitful in their introduction of the feeding element, and the romance of Galahad puts the disconcerting ceremonial outside the holy places of the mystic Castle.

I think, in conclusion, that the intention of the Greater Chronicles concerning the Feeding Dish is to be taken in another sense of the *Quest of Galahad*, which says of Lancelot: "Yf ye wold aske how he lyved, he that fedde the peple of Israel with manna in deserte, soo was he fedde. For every day when he had sayd his prayers, he was susteyned with the grace of the Holy Ghoost." And, as the Welsh version has it, "so that he thought himself to be full of the best meats."

V

THE LESSER HALLOWS OF THE LEGEND

§ *A.*—THE SUMMARY OF THESE MATTERS

The Hallows of the Graal legend are the beginning of its wonders and of its meanings only; but, as I have intimated already, the greater includes the lesser, and that which is of all the highest has assumed from the beginning in its symbolism the things by which it is surrounded. As it is in the light of man's higher part that we are able to interpret the lower, as the body is explained by the soul, so even the Castle of the Graal and the great Temple, with all their allusions and all their sacred things, are resolved into the mystery of the Cup, because there is a cloud of witnesses but one true voice which is the spokesman of all. There is obviously no need in this place—as we are concerned with the greater subjects—to lay stress upon the subsidiary Hallows as if they were an integral portion of the Holy Graal regarded symbolically. They are of the accidents only, and as such they are not vital. The Lance is important to the legends, but not otherwise than from the legendary standpoint; the Sword is also important, but not in a sacramental sense; the Dish signifies nothing, or next to nothing. The explanation is that the French literature of the Holy Graal, in its form as now extant, has on the external side its roots in traditions and memorials connected with the Passion of Christ. The different cycles of the literature develop their account of these memorials with motives that vary, but they combine therewith certain sacred objects derived from other sources and not belonging logically to the scheme. They worked, for example, upon pre-existent materials which were not assimilated wholly into the matter of the romances, and it is largely these portions for which, in any scheme of interpretation, we shall be scarcely able to account unless upon divergent lines.

Speaking generally of the Lesser Hallows, the following points are clear. The German cycle, as represented by Wolfram, derived its idea of the Lance from a source in folk-lore apart from the Graal legend as we know it in Northern French. The Northern French literature is clear as to those Hallows connecting with the Passion of Christ; these are the Cup, otherwise the Paschal Dish, and the Lance. It is dubious and variable about the Sword and Dish or Platter, for which there are no antecedents in the Passion. Several texts have carried over some of the Hallows without modification from folk-lore, even when great Christian relics were ready to their hands. For example, the sword used by Peter at Gethsemane did not occur to them, though it would have been more to their purpose, the reason being that there was no official tradition concerning it in the external life of the Church. The Dish is in the same position of unmodified folk-lore; the platter on which the head of St. John the Baptist was served to Herodias is a chance missed even by the *Longer Prose Perceval*, despite its allocation of the Sword to the instrument of the Precursor's martyrdom. Other subsidiary Hallows, mentioned therein, which are by way of after-thought, increase without exhausting the possible relics of the Passion—one of them tells of the Crown of Thorns; another of the cloth with which Christ was covered when He was laid on the sepulchre; and yet another of the sacred nails used at the Crucifixion. I do not remember that the scourge has occurred to any maker of texts. The Crown of Thorns was called the Golden Circle, having been set in precious metal and jewels by the Queen of the Castle where it was preserved. We have also the pincers wherewith the nails were drawn from the limbs of Christ when He was taken down from the Cross. Finally, the shield of Judas Maccabæus is met with in one romance, where it is won in battle by Gawain. The Sword has been also referred to the same prince in Israel.

I suppose that the legend of the face-cloth, which is part of the Veronica legend, is the earliest of the Passion relics, and among the evangelisation traditions, that of Lazarus and his companions coming to the South of France, carrying the face-cloth with them, has the palm of antiquity in the West. But this relic, though it occupies an important position in the early history of the Graal, is not included among the Hallows of the Graal Castle.

The metrical romance of De Borron has one Hallow only, and this is the first extant Graal history. The first extant Quest is that portion of the *Conte del Graal* which we owe to Chrétien ; so far as his work is concerned there are four Hallows—the Vessel called Graal, the Lance, the Sword and the Dish. The Lance has been called his particular introduction. The *Didot Perceval*, which is thought to owe something to Chrétien, introduces the Lance without any explanation concerning it. The Chrétien sequels, the *Longer Prose Perceval* and the Galahad *Quest*, lay stress upon the Sacred Sword, which is usually broken, and the task of the elect hero is to re-solder the weapon. In all texts the Lance ranks next to the Cup in importance, and when the one is removed to heaven at the close of the Galahad *Quest*, it is accompanied by the other. The *Longer Prose Perceval* is a very late Quest, and it has Hallows innumerable. The *Book of the Holy Graal*, at least in its present form, is a very late history, and it introduces the Nails of the Passion ; it gives also an invented and artificial allegory to account for the Sword.

It being obvious, as I have said, that the Sword and the Dish are but little to the purpose of the Graal, it will not be difficult to understand that those who took over these objects from antecedent legends were not of one mind concerning them, more especially in respect of the Dish, which remains a superfluity in the pageant and a hindrance in the symbolism as it stands. The Sword in several instances is important especially, as I have said, to the plot of the story, but it has no reason in the symbolism.

§ B.—Legends of the Sacred Lance

In the Gautier section of the *Conte del Graal*, and in the description of Gawain's visit to the Graal Castle, he sees among the sacred objects a Lance, which bleeds into a silver cup, but it is not the Cup of the Graal. The Lance is the weapon which pierced the side of Christ, and it is said that it will bleed till Doomsday. The body of the arm was of wood. The blade was white as snow, and the weapon was at the head of the master dais ; it seems to have reposed in the vessel, and two tapers were burning before it. The stream of blood issued from the point of the Lance and ran down into the vessel, from which, as it overflowed, it poured into a channel of gold and ran without the Hall. This extravagant description is substituted for a much simpler account in Chrétien's portion of the poem ; there only a single drop of blood trickles down to the hand of the squire who bears the weapon in the pageant. The fuller historical account is found in Manessier's section, which says that the Lance is that of the Roman soldier who pierced the side of Christ. According to a Montpellier manuscript, Joseph of Arimathæa was present at the foot of the Cross, and seeing, as the spear was withdrawn, how the blood ran down, he collected it in the Holy Vessel, turning black as he did so with sorrow. The *Didot Perceval* says only that a squire in the Graal Castle carried a Lance in his two hands, that it was that of Longinus, and that a drop of blood flowed from the sacred point. I believe that this romance represents a primitive state of the Christian Quest, though it is late in its actual form, the reason being that the Hallows of the Passion are the only wonder-objects which belong properly to the Quest. The wider field of vision offered in the Greater Chronicles and the multiplication of relics are indubitable signs of lateness. In the *Book of the Holy Graal* the Hallows which are seen in the vision preceding the ordination of the younger Joseph are a great ensanguined cross, three nails from which blood seems to flow, a Lance of which the iron point is stained also with blood, an ensanguined cincture and a bended rod dyed in the same manner. It will be seen that the writer of this romance knew well enough that with the Graal itself he could connect only the things thereto belonging—namely, the other Relics of the Passion, and realising this fact in later branches of his Chronicle, while he perpetuates other objects through centuries of hidden life, he is careful not to locate them in the Graal Castle. The *Huth Merlin* is the only legend of the prophet which knows of another Hallow than the Sacred Vessel ; and this is the Lance, but the circumstances under which it is introduced and the account which is given concerning it belong to a later stage of our research. I may say, however, that it was an instrument of mystic vengeance, and as such it reappears in the great prose *Lancelot*. It is seen there by Gawain, who is smitten by its blade of fire, and afterwards is healed by the Graal. It is seen also by Sir Bors when he visits Corbenic ; an old man carries it in one hand, while he swings a censer with the other. In the romance of Galahad, as we know it, the Lance manifests twice, and this is at the end of the Quest, when it is borne in one hand by an angel, who holds in the other a box to receive the blood from its point. The *ipsissima verba* of the *Longer Prose Perceval* are that of the Hallows there are " right great plenty." Perceval's shield had in the boss thereof some of the Blood of our Lord and a piece of His garment ; they were placed therein by Joseph of Arimathæa. As regards the Lance itself, the point bleeds into the Holy Graal, and here also the weapon is one of vengeance, or rather of doom, for he who is elected to the Quest has something to perform in respect of it, and he fails therein. This notwithstanding, the Hallow in the romance under notice serves little purpose, because it does nothing. For the sake of completeness the Lesser Hallows of the German cycle may be mentioned with great brevity in this section, though their history and import must be held over for a very long time to come. In the *Parsifal* of Wolfram, the ensanguined head of a Lance is carried round a certain chamber; it has no connection with the Passion, but once more it is a memorial of vengeance, of fatality which is long and grievous. In Heinrich's *Diu Cr*ô*ne*, the Lance is held by two young men, and it sheds three great drops of blood, which are received in a salver. I should observe in conclusion, for the time being, as to this Hallow that the French cycle may be classified in three sections, of which *A* does not mention the Lance, *B* mentions but does not explain its antecedents, and *C* says that it is the Lance of Longinus used at the Crucifixion. Late or early, there is no other history concerning it.

§ C.—The Broken Sword

The Graal Cup was not so much connected with the Passion as originated therefrom, because it is clear in history that, or ever Robert de Borron spoke of secret words, the meaning of Mass chalices, and the transit of the Great Hallow from East to West, the Precious Blood had been brought already within the wonder-world of relics. So also the sacred Lance had received its justification in tradition before it was exalted in romance. The allocation of other objects within the same sphere of devotion was so natural that it was not likely to be resisted, but it must be observed that the attributions were inherited and not invented by the makers of books of chivalry. Face-cloth and loin-cloth, nails and crown of thorns had long been included among the objects provided for veneration before the *Book of the Holy Graal* or the *Longer Prose Perceval* had dreamed of registering them among the Hallows of the Graal ark, or otherwhere in their holy and marvellous shrines. That they were capable of inventing relics is shown by the history of the sacred Sword, and such relics had their imputed antecedents in Scripture; but the things of the Passion of Christ were too sacred for their interference, and they were left in the hands of the Church. The Church perhaps was not idle, and the Church did not scruple perhaps, but minstrels and weavers of stories knew their proper limits and abode therein. Their respect in the case under notice guarantees it in yet another, for which reason I hold it as certain that never did Robert de Borron tamper with Eucharistic formulæ, or, in other words, that, whether from far or near, he inherited and did not invent the sacred words of the mystery.

The Sword of the Graal is considerable under two aspects —firstly, as a derivative from folk-lore, which passes, as we have seen, through certain branches of the literature without suffering an especial change in its nature ; secondly, as a hallowed object having an imputed derivation from the history of the Church of God under one of its two covenants. In the second case, we must be prepared to find—and this is natural also—that certain reflections from folk-lore, as from the earlier state of the object, are to be found in its consecrated form. In the Chrétien portion of the *Conte del Graal* the Sword is suspended from the neck of a page or squire and is brought to the Master of the House as a present from his niece, with leave to bestow it apparently howsoever he will, so only that it shall be well used. An inscription upon it says that it will never break except in one peril, which is known only to the smith who forged it.

In his time as a craftsman he made three such weapons, and no others will follow. As regards this particular example, the belt was worth a treasure, the crosspiece was of fine gold, and the sheath was of Venetian smith's work. It is given to Perceval by the King of the Graal Castle as something to him predestined. But it is only at a later stage that he learns under what circumstances it will fly in pieces and how it may be repaired—namely, by plunging it in a certain lake which is hard by the smithy of him who wrought it. The continuation of Gautier ignores these facts and reproduces the Sword at the Castle, where it is carried by a crowned knight ; it is broken already and Gawain is asked to resolder it, in which task he fails. Perceval succeeds, on the occasion of his second visit, except for a slight crevice, thus proving that, at least in a certain measure, he is a lover of God, a true knight, and one who loves also the Church, which is the Spouse of God. The conclusion of Manessier furnishes the history of the Hallow in full, though it has been the subject of allusion previously : (*a*) one stroke was given therewith ; it destroyed the realm of Logres and the country thereto adjacent ; (*b*) this stroke was inflicted on the King's brother, in the course of a battle ; (*c*) when the King himself took up the fragments unwarily, he was pierced through the thigh, and the wound will be healed only when his brother's death has been avenged. In Chrétien, on the contrary, the wound of the Graal King is caused by a spear which passes through his two thighs. The intercalation or alternative conclusion of Gerbert sends Perceval again into exile, because certain imperfections in his life account for the fact that he cannot resolder the Sword, and the Quest must be fulfilled better. The Hallow remains in the Castle, but another sword is introduced and serves to indicate that behind the strange memorial of this unknown poet there were sources of legend which, if we could now recover them, might place yet another construction upon the root-matter of the Graal legend. In Gerbert the sword under notice is broken not in a conflict which calls for a conventional vengeance, after the worthless motives of folk-lore, but in an attempt to enforce an entrance into the Earthly Paradise.

Passing over the Lesser Chronicles, which, although in the *Didot Perceval* it is hinted on one occasion that there were many worthy relics, make no reference to the Sword, and coming to the Greater Chronicles we find that in the *Book of the Holy Graal* there is a Hallow of this kind, and it is very important from the standpoint of the romance itself and for the Quest which follows therefrom. It was the sword of David the King, and it was placed, as we have seen, by Solomon in a mysterious ship destined to sail the seas for centuries as a testimony to Galahad that his ancestor was aware of his coming at the end of the times of the Graal. During the course of its history more than one wound is inflicted therewith, and the circumstances under which it is broken are also told variously. In the *Book of the Holy Graal* there are actually two swords; to that of David the particular virtue ascribed is that no one can draw it—before the predestined hero in the days of the Quest—without being visited heavily for his rashness. The doom works automatically even to the infliction of death. It is only by a kind of accident that this sword is broken, and then it is rejoined instantly, according to one of the codices. In another there is a distinct account, which does not say how or whether the sword was resoldered in fine. As regards the second sword, it is merely an ordinary weapon with which Joseph II. is smitten by a certain seneschal when he is endeavouring to convert the prince of a certain part of Great Britain. The sword breaks when it pierces him, and the point remains in the wound. After various miracles, which result in the general conversion of the people, the sufferer places his hand on the point of the sword, which is apparently protruding from his thigh; it comes out of the wound, and the place heals up immediately. Joseph then takes the two portions of the broken sword and says: "God grant that this good weapon shall never be soldered except by him who is destined to accomplish the adventure of the Siege Perilous at the Round Table, in the time of King Arthur; and God grant also that the point shall not cease to exude blood until the two portions are so soldered."

It is reasonable to expect that these Hallows should prove a source of confusion as to their duplication and their purpose. I do not conceive that the sword which is brought out of Fairyland in the *Huth Merlin*, which is claimed by Balan, which brings about the Dolorous Stroke —though this is inflicted actually by another instrument, which in fine involves the two brothers in mutual destruction, can be connected with either of the weapons with which we have been just dealing. The alternative later *Merlin* has no mystery of swords which can be identified with the Hallow of the Graal, and the prose *Lancelot* knows nothing of that of David. It speaks, however, of a knight named Elias, who carries two swords; one of them is enclosed in a priceless sheath, and is said to be that which pierced the loins of Joseph of Arimathæa and was broken therein. It is scarcely necessary to notice that the father here is confused with the son. The *Quest of Galahad* distinguishes the two swords, except in the Welsh version, which identifies them by a natural mischance. That one of them by which Joseph was wounded is presented to Galahad for soldering, and when the elect knight has performed the task, it is given into the charge of Bors, because he was a good knight and a worthy man. After the soldering "it arose grete and marvellous, and was full of grete hete that many men felle for drede." It seems to follow that it was brought back to Logres on the return of Sir Bors from Sarras. The Sword of David was carried to Sarras, as we may infer, by Galahad, but it was not taken to heaven with the Graal and Lance, the reason being doubtless that it was not a symbol of the Passion. In the *Longer Prose Perceval* the Sword, as we know, is that with which St. John the Baptist was beheaded, and though there is, firstly, no attempt to account for the presence of this Hallow in England, nor, secondly, any reference to it in early literature, the identification helps us to understand better its place among the Hallows, as some other swords met with in the literature have scarcely a title to be included with sacred objects. The office of Gawain, before he can know anything of Graal mysteries, is to obtain this Sword from its wrongful keepers, and herein he succeeds. The scabbard is loaded with precious stones and the mountings are of silk with buttons of gold. The hilt has also precious stones, and the pommel is a holy and sacred stone set upon it by a certain Roman Emperor. When the Sword came forth from the scabbard it was covered with blood, and this seems always to have been the case at the hour of noon, which was the time of the saint's martyrdom. When noon has passed it becomes clear and green like an emerald. It is the same length as another sword, but when sheathed neither the weapon nor the scabbard seems to be of two spans length. It is said on the testimony of Josephus that the Old Law was destroyed by a stroke of this sword without recovery, and that to effect the destruction our Lord Himself suffered to be smitten in the side with the Spear. These things are not to be understood on the open sense of the text.

The Greater Chronicles of the Graal may be, as they indeed are, upon God's side, but the judgment concerning this sub-section of the Lesser Hallows must be that the Sword is an impediment before the face of the symbolism of the cycle, and often an idle wonder which we could wish to be taken out of the way. We could wish also—or at least I personally—that something of the mystery behind the ascription of Gerbert might come at this day into our hands. In the *Parsifal* of Wolfram the hero of that great Quest is refreshed as by fruits brought from the Earthly Paradise on the occasion of his first visit to the Temple of the Holy Graal. We know not how or why, but this is another reflection, probably from the source of Gerbert, and one which takes us no further, except that from time to time, by dim hints and allusions, we see that the legend of the Graal is not so far apart from the legend of Eden. In this manner we recur to the German cycle, and there we find that there is a sword of mark in the *Parsifal;* it is that which was given to the hero by Amfortas, the Graal King. Now that this, amidst any variations, is the same story as that which is told by Chrétien is rather evident than likely. Another sword broke when Parsifal was fighting with his unknown brother Feirfis, because it would not drink the blood of his kinship, and this is the far antithesis of some of the French stories. In Heinrich's *Diu Crône*, a fair youth of exalted mien carries a fair broad sword, which he lays before the King of the Castle, and this sword is given by the King to Gawain after he has asked the question which we know to be all important.

In conclusion as to this matter, the Hallow of the Sword is not unlike a corresponding weapon in some of the grades of Masonic chivalry; in the same way as the reverend Knights therein do not, in many cases, know how to use the symbolic arm, so in the Graal literature the poets and romancers have accepted the custody of something which is so little to their purpose that they know scarcely what they shall do therewith: had they only thought less of their folk-lore and hence omitted it entirely, they would have told a better—aye, even a truer—story from the standpoint of their own symbolism.

§ *D.*—The Dish

The Sacred Dish being also, as we have seen, rather an unmeaning mystery, and as although it recurs frequently the descriptions are brief and the office which it holds is doubtful, it will be only desirable to distinguish those texts in which it is found. Subject to one possibility, and this is of the speculative order, it is, as we have seen, an unmodified survival from folk-lore; we should therefore expect it to appear in the Chrétien portion of the *Conte del Graal*, and this is the case actually, but it serves therein a very practical and mundane purpose, being used by the King and his guest to wash their hands. It is a silver plate and is carried by a damsel. It reappears in one codex of the continuation by Gautier. The conclusion by Manessier describes it after a similar manner, but its purpose is not delineated; Perceval asks all the necessary questions regarding the Graal and Lance; he asks also concerning the Dish, but there is apparently nothing to ask, or at least he hears nothing. At the same time it may have had a higher significance for this poet than for all the others, since he causes the Holy Dish to follow Perceval with the other Hallows when he goes with a hermit into the wilderness, where he serves the Lord for ten years. Finally, he states in his last words that the Dish was doubtless assumed into heaven with the other sacred objects, namely, the Lance and the Sword. According to Gerbert, a lady named Philosophine, who here, as in another romance, figures as the mother of Perceval, came over with Joseph of Arimathæa bearing a certain plate; another lady carried an ever-bleeding lance, while Joseph himself bore a fairer vessel than eye had ever beheld. In the Lesser Chronicles there is only a single reference, which occurs in the *Didot Perceval;* when the Graal and the other Hallows are first manifested to Perceval, it is said that a damsel bears two silver plates, together with draperies. In the *Book of the Holy Graal*, and on the occasion that the Second Joseph is raised to the high pontificate, the Paschal Dish is seen on the altar, and in the middle place thereof is an exceedingly rich vessel of gold and precious stones. Here the reference is probably to the Sacramental Cup, but the account is confused; and elsewhere the complex romance presents a new aspect of folk-lore, for there is another Dish or Charger, bearing a great and glorious head, about which we have no explanation and of which we hear nothing subsequently, either in the text itself or in the later documents of the cycle.

The Dish also passes out of the horizon, not only in the prose *Lancelot* but also in the *Quest of Galahad.* The German cycle speaks of a Golden Salver jewelled with precious stones and carried upon a silken cloth. It is used in Heinrich's poem to receive the blood which issues from the Lance.

It seems possible that there was an early tendency on the part of Christian romancers to distinguish between the chalice—being the Cup in which Christ made His sacrament—and the Dish—being the vessel in which He and His disciples ate the Paschal Lamb. They are to some extent confused in the *Book of the Holy Graal,* and the prose *Lancelot* knows of a single vessel only, which is the Eucharistic Cup. If such an implicit was present to the mind of Manessier, we can understand why he says that the Dish was assumed into heaven.

I wonder that it has not occurred to some of those who have preceded me in the tortuous paths and among the pitfalls of interpretation, to understand the four Hallows after another and more highly symbolical manner, as follows : (1) The Chalice is the Cup of the Sacrament ; (2) The Dish is the Paten ; (3) The Sword symbolises the Body of Christ ; its fracture is the bruising for our sins and the breaking for our trespasses, while at some far distance the resoldering signifies the Resurrection ; (4) In another sense, the Spear is also the wounding for our iniquities, by which the life flowed from the body, and the issue of blood therefrom is the outgoing of the divine life for our salvation. Yet it is not after this manner that we shall come into the truth of the Graal, while it is likely enough that hereabouts is one of those pits which bring the unwary to destruction.

We shall meet with all the Hallows under a very slight modification in the most unexpected of all places, but this will be at a later stage. We shall then see that the people preserved something besides folk-lore, or that folk-lore had other meanings behind it than the recognised schools would be disposed to attribute thereto.

VI

THE CASTLE OF THE HOLY GRAAL

The true legitimacies are for the most part in exile, or otherwise with their rights in abeyance. The real canons of literature can be uttered only behind doors or in the secrecy of taverns. The secrets of the great orthodoxies are very seldom communicated, even to epopts on their advancement. The highest claims of all are not so much wanting in warrant as wanting those spokesmen who are willing to utter them. We shall not be surprised, therefore, to find that the custodians of the Holy Graal, which was a mystery of all secrecy, "there where no sinner can be," despite the kingly titles ascribed to them, sometimes abode in the utmost seclusion.

Let us seek in the first instance to realise the nature and the place of that Castle or Temple which, according to the legend, was for a period of centuries the sanctuary of the Sacred Vessel and of the other hallowed objects connected therewith. It is in the several locations of the Hallows that we shall come at a later time into a fuller understanding of their offices and of the meanings which may lie behind them. They are not to be regarded exactly as part of the mystery of the Castle; but at least this is more than a casket, and between the container and the things contained, distinct though their significance may be, there are points of correlation, so that the one throws light on the other.

We have seen that the Vessel itself was brought from Salem to Britain, and it follows from the historical texts that the transit had a special purpose, one explanation of which will be found ready to our hands when the time comes for its consideration. The Castle is described after several manners, the later romances being naturally the more specific, and we get in fine a geographical settlement and boundary. In the Chrétien portion of the

Conte del Graal, Perceval discovers the Castle in a valley, wherein it is well and beautifully situated, having a four-square tower, with a principal hall and a bridge leading up to the chief entrance. In some of the other legends the asylum is so withdrawn that it is neither named nor described. The *Early History of Merlin* speaks of it not less simply as the place where they had the Holy Vessel in keeping. According to the *Didot Perceval*, it is the house of the Rich King Fisherman; it is situated in a valley; it has a tower, and is approached by a bridge. It might be a tower merely, for the description is not less vague than many accounts of the Cup. One of the late Merlin texts says merely that the Holy Vessel is in the West—that is, in the Land of Vortigern, or that it abides in Northumbria. Another says that the Castle is Corbenic; but though we hear a good deal concerning it, there is no description whatever.

The section of the *Conte del Graal* which is referable to Gautier de Doulens says that it is situated on a causeway tormented by the sea. The building is of vast extent and is inhabited by a great folk. We hear of its ceiling, emblazoned with gold and embroidered with silver stars, of its tables of precious metal, its images and the rich gems which enlighten it. In a word, we are already in the region of imaginative development and adornment, but it is all mere decoration which carries with it no meaning beyond the heavy tokens of splendour. Manessier furnishes no special account, and Gerbert, who has other affairs at heart than solicitude about a material building or desire to exalt it into allegory, leaves it unsketched entirely.

The *Book of the Holy Graal* is the only French text which contains in a methodical account the building of the Holy House. The first wardens have passed from the land of the living, and Alain le Gros is the keeper of the Blessed Vessel. The actual builder is a certain converted king of *Terre Foraine*, and there is a covenant between him and Alain, one condition of which is that the Graal shall remain in his kingdom. The Castle on its completion is given the mystic name of Corbenic, in obedience to an inscription which is found blazoned on one of the entrance gates. The name is said to signify the Treasury of the Holy Vessel. The Graal is placed in a fair chamber of the Castle, as if on an altar of repose, but, all his munificence notwithstanding and all the sacramental visions which he sees in the Holy Place, beating of birds' wings and chanting of innumerable voices, the king is visited speedily for his mere presence and receives his death-wound at the very altar : it is the judgment of the sanctuary on those who desecrate the sanctuary by carrying, however unwittingly, an unhallowed past therein, and it recalls the traditional conclusion of the Cabiric Mysteries, wherein the candidate was destroyed by the gods. Setting aside an analogy on which I am by no means insisting, the event was the beginning of those wonders which earned for Castle Corbenic the name of the Palace Adventurous, because no one could enter therein, and no one could sleep, its lawful people excepted, without death overtaking them, or some other grievous penalty.

The prose *Lancelot* is in near correspondence with Chrétien, representing the Castle as situated at the far end of a great valley, with water encircling it. On another occasion it is named rather than described, and visited but not expounded, but we learn that it is situated in a town which has many dwellers therein. In the *Quest of Galahad* it is a rich and fair building, with a postern opening towards the sea, and this was guarded by lions, between which a man might pass only if he carried the arms of faith, since the sword availed nothing and there was no protection in harness. For the visitor who was expected or tolerated, it would seem that all doors stood open, except the door of the sanctuary. But this would unclose of itself ; the light would issue from within ; the silver table would be seen ; and thereon the Holy Vessel, covered with drapery of samite. There also on a day might be celebrated, with becoming solemnity, the Great Mass of the Supersanctified, and this even in the presence of those who were not clean in their past, so only that they had put away their sin when they entered on the Quest. It was thus beheld by Lancelot, though he lay as one dead afterwards, because of his intrusion. So also the welcome guest had reason to know that the court of King Pelles held a great fellowship in the town of Corbenic. But there were other visitors at times and seasons who saw little of all this royalty, like Hector de Marys, who—brother as he was to my lord Sir Lancelot—found the doors all barred against him and no warden to open, long as he hailed thereat.

The most decorative of all the accounts is, however, in the *Longer Prose Perceval*, where the Castle is reached by means of three bridges, which are horrible to cross. Three great waters run below them, the first bridge being a bow-shot in length and not more than a foot in width. This is the Bridge of the Eel; but it proves wide and a fair thorough-way in the act of crossing. The second bridge is of ice, feeble and thin, and it is arched high above the water. This is transformed on passing into the richest and strangest ever seen, and its abutments are full of images. The third and last bridge stands on columns of marble. Beyond it there is a sculptured gate, giving upon a flight of steps, which leads to a spacious hall painted with figures in gold. When Perceval visited the Castle a second time he found it encompassed by a river, which came from the Earthly Paradise and proceeded through the forest beyond as far as the hold of a hermit, where it found peace in the earth. To the Castle itself there were three names attributed: the Castle of Eden, the Castle of Joy and the Castle of Souls. In conclusion as to this matter, the location, in fine, is Corbenic—not as the unvaried name, but as that which may be called the accepted, representing the Temple at its highest, and corresponding in French romance to Montsalvatch in

German—which our late redaction of the *Book of the Holy Graal* mentions specifically, and which, all doubtful clouds of mystic adventure notwithstanding, looms almost as a landmark in the *Lancelot* and the *Quest of Galahad*.

I must speak very lightly of the German cycle, because, through all these branches, it is understood that I shall deal with it again. In the *Parsifal* and *Titurel* the Temple is completely spiritualised, so that it has ceased almost to be a house made with hands, though the descriptions on the external side are here and there almost severe in their simplicity. On that side it has the strength of a feudal fortress, turret by turret rising. In the master-hall of the palace there is something of Oriental splendour—carpets and couches and cushions, marble hearths burning strange fragrant woods, and a great blazing of lights. So far the *Parsifal* of Wolfram, but we must turn to other texts for the building of the Temple— which is after another manner than anything told of Corbenic in the Northern French cycle. The building was the work of Titurel, the first King of the Graal, and in answer to his prayers the High Powers of Heaven prepared the ground-plan of the Holy Place and furnished the raw material. Over the construction itself the powers of earth toiled by day and the Powers of Heaven by night. The floor was of pure onyx; at the summit of the tower there was a ruby surmounted by a cross of crystal, and carbuncles shone at the meeting-points of the great arches within. The roof was of sapphire, and a pictured starry heaven moved therein in true order.

We are on a different level when we have recourse to the poem of Heinrich, which presents several anomalies in respect of the literature as a whole. The road leading to the Graal Castle was one of harsh and hazardous enterprise—world without end ; but it brought the questing hero at some far point into a plenteous and gracious land, where rose the Palace of Desire, looking beautiful exceedingly, with a meadow before it which was set apart for joust and tournament. A great concourse of knights and gentlewomen abode in the burg, and for the Castle itself we are told that there was none so fair. Though it will be seen that there is nothing distinctive in this account, as it is here reduced into summary, the design is among many things strange, for if it is not the Castle of Souls it is that of a Living Tomb, as the story concerning it will show at the proper time.

So did the place of the mysteries, from a dim and vague allusion, become

> "A wilderness of building, sinking far
> And self-withdrawn into a wondrous depth
> Far sinking into splendour."

We can scarcely say whether that which had begun on earth was assumed into the spiritual place, or whether the powers and virtues from above descended to brood thereon.

I have left over from this consideration all reference to another spiritual place, in Sarras on the confines of Egypt, where the Graal, upon its outward journey, dwelt for a period, and whither, after generations and centuries, it also returned for a period. As this was not the point of its origin, so it was not that of its rest; it was a stage in the passage from Salem and a stage in the transit to heaven. What was meant by this infidel city, which was yet so strangely consecrated, is hard to determine, but its consideration belongs to a later stage. It is too early again to ask what are the implicits of the great prose *Perceval* when it identifies the Castle of the Graal with the Earthly Paradise and the Place of Souls; but we may note it as a sign of intention, and we shall meet with it in another connection where no one has thought to look for it.

VII

THE KEEPERS OF THE HALLOWS

Such was the Abode of the Hallows; and those who dwelt therein, the succession of Graal Keepers, belong to that Order which we should expect in such precincts. It should be noted that in the poem of Chrétien the Keeper is called the Fisher King, but his other name and his lineage are not disclosed. It is, however, the beginning only of a very long story, and though it is difficult to say how the poet would have carried it to its term, personally I do not question that he would have borne no different witness to the rest of the Graal cycle in Northern French. By this, without exception, Joseph of Arimathæa is the first guardian of the Sacred Vessel, but either he passes from the scene before it has found a sanctuary or he assumes a secondary position in his son's favour. According to the metrical romance of De Borron and the Lesser Chronicles generally, he was succeeded by his son-in-law, Brons; but according to the Greater Chronicles, as I have termed them, he was succeeded by his own son, the second Joseph, who is unknown to the other cycle. The Lesser Chronicles bridge the centuries between that generation which saw the Ascension of Christ and that which was to behold the Flower of Chivalry in Arthur, by means of a single keeper, who was to remain on earth until he had seen his grandson, Perceval, and had remitted into his hands the secrets and Hallows of which he had been in charge so long. Perceval is the third who counts in the line of election to complete the human trinity of Graal guardians, reflecting, after their own mystic manner, those Three who bear witness in heaven, namely, the Divine Trinity. To accomplish the hero's geniture, Alain, the son of Brons, although he had accepted celibacy, married in some undeclared manner, and it was as his issue that

Perceval was born in the fulness of the adventurous times. For the *Early History of Merlin* the Keepers are those who have the Holy Vessel, and the reticence in this case may seem like that of Chrétien, but it is not so exactly, because the prose romance of Merlin follows directly from the metrical romance of Joseph. We infer further that the promise of union with the Keepers is like *la joie perdurable*.

Gautier's continuation of the *Conte del Graal* offers no materials for the identification of the Fisher King, but the variants or interpolated passages in the Montpellier MS. follow the Lesser Chronicles, representing him as the father of Alain le Gros who married Enigea, the sister of Joseph. Manessier and Gerbert, on the other hand, reflect the Greater Chronicles, and apparently some early draft of the *Book of the Holy Graal*, for they know nothing concerning the younger Joseph.

From one point of view, the succession, in respect of the Greater Chronicles, involves fewer difficulties, because it exhibits a rudimentary sense of chronology and develops in consequence a long line of successive custodians. They are, however, quite shadowy, and exist only to bridge the gulf of time in the order following: (1) Joseph of Arimathæa and Joseph II.; (2) Alain, the son of Brons; (3) Eminadap, the son of Joshua, who was himself a brother of Alain; (4) Carceloys; (5) Manuiel; (6) Lambor: the last four were kings, holding from Calafas of Terre Foraine, called Alphasan in baptism; (7) the King Pelles.

So far as regards the *Book of the Holy Graal*, and it is difficult to say what version or prototype of this text was before the authors of the *Vulgate* and *Huth Merlin*, but whatever it was they seem to have drawn from the same source. The Graal Castle, as we have seen, is Corbenic; it is situated in the realm of Listenoys, and the Keeper is King Pelles. As much and no more may be said concerning the prose *Lancelot*. Enumerations of this kind serve very little purpose, and I will speak, therefore, only of the alternative keepers who were in evidence during the days of quest. On the one side, there is Brons, to whom succeeded Perceval at the close of a life of search ; on the other, there is King Pelles, of the Castle Corbenic, whose daughter, Helayne, gave Galahad as issue to Lancelot, himself the lineal descendant of the king reigning at Sarras in the days of Joseph of Arimathæa and the first flight of the Graal. Galahad was the last Keeper recognised by this cycle, except in the *Longer Prose Perceval*, and he seems to have been appointed only for the purpose of removing the Vessel. It was : *Ite, missa est*, and *est consummatum*, when he died and rose to the stars. As the *Longer Prose Perceval* is extra-lineal and thus stands by itself, though its antecedents and certain characteristics have involved its inclusion among the Greater Chronicles, I will say of it only in the present place that the King's title is that adopted by Chrétien, or the Rich King Fisherman, and that his name is not otherwise declared. His successor is Perceval, but he enters into the secret royalty after an interregnum only, and his stewardship also is with a view to the withdrawal of the mystery. As regards the German cycle, which will be dealt with elsewhere, the succession of Graal Keepers are Titurel, Frimutel and Amfortas, to whom succeeds Perceval. Titurel at the beginning was a holy hero of earthly chivalry, to whom a divine voice brought the strange tidings that he had been elected to guard the Holy Graal on Mont Salvatch. His progenitor was a man of Cappadocia who was attached to the Emperor Vespasian, and received for his services a grant of land in southern France.

The hereditary stewardship of the Holy Graal was the most secret of all mysteries, and never initiated any one outside the predestined family. There is seclusion in all cases, but that of the Brons keepership is greater beyond comparison than that of Alain and his successors. One explanation of this may be sought in the simple fact that, as regards the first case, several intermediate texts are or may be wanting, and that transparently. This is true so far as it goes, but in the most proximate pre-Arthurian period, and in the time of the king, we find still the same concealment, though it is not quite so unvaried in the records of the *Conte del Graal* as it is in the *Early History of Merlin* and in the *Didot Perceval*. The comparative position seems as another line of demarcation between the Lesser and Greater Chronicles, but always on the understanding that the allocation of the *Longer Prose Perceval* to the second series, though it cannot be placed otherwise, and apart especially, is not fully satisfactory in the nature of things. Speaking generally, the distinctions between the two branches will be appreciated most clearly by a comparison between the *Early History of Merlin* and the later *Vulgate* and *Huth* texts. The sanctuary is shrouded in the first, and we know only that those who have the Sacred Vessel are somewhere in Northumbria. In the second, the keeper, King Pelles, is in continual evidence. He is also a king in warfare, and it is by no means certain that he is always on the side of the over-lord Arthur.

It would be easy to extend this section very much further than I purpose doing, in view of all that is to follow; my intention here is a schedule, or this mainly; and the specific summary is as follows. There are two prototypes of the Early History versions, and they are represented, firstly, by the original draft of De Borron's metrical romance, which is much earlier than any other historical account; they are represented, secondly, by the speculative prototype of the *Book of the Holy Graal*. About this book there are two things certain: (*a*) that it is very much later—or at least that it is later certainly—than the first recension or transcript of the book which in some undeclared manner had come into the hands of Robert de Borron; (*b*) that it is a good deal earlier than the *Quest of Galahad* as we know it, which involves also an antecedence in some form of the prose *Lancelot* and the *Later Histories of Merlin*. We are left therefore with two claims which appear to be at the root of the Mystery of the Holy Graal, as it is manifested in the French literature of the twelfth and thirteenth centuries: these are the claim of an Eucharistic formula, the validity and efficacy of which transcended the words of institution known by the official Church, and the claim of a priesthood which did not draw from the official apostolate, though it did not question its authority. These two are one probably in their essence, and it is out of these respectively that we come to understand why Perceval is withdrawn into the innermost seclusion by the Lesser Chronicles, and why in the Greater Chronicles Galahad is assumed into heaven—both carrying their warrants.

VIII

THE PAGEANTS IN THE QUESTS

The presence of the Holy Vessel signified the Divine Presence. The Life of Life had remained in the Precious Blood. The Voice of the Angel of Great Counsel, the Voice of the Son and the Voice of the Holy Spirit abode therein, or spoke as if from behind it. The Presence was sacramental, but the Presence was also real, and through the soul it was one which sustained the body itself at need. So far as regards the Lesser Chronicles, and in those which I call Greater, there was a reservation which continued through centuries, an arch-natural Mass —said from time to time and not, as we may suppose, daily—an unfailing ministry to body and soul alike. In a word, the Last Supper was maintained for ever and ever. It was the sacramental side of the eternal festival of the followers of Bran, and those who say that the roots of the mystery are in folk-lore say only the most negligible part of the truth concerning it; for if I accomplish by a secret science the transmutation of lead into gold, it will be useless for any scholarship of science to depose that the important fact is the lead. The latter is the antecedent, and as such is, of course, indispensable, but the great fact is the conversion; and I say the same of the Graal literature.

On this and all other considerations, it will be understood that the Mystic Castle was a place of the highest reverence, and that all things concerning the Sacred Vessel were done with ceremonial solemnity, following a prescribed order. In this way it comes about that all the quests present the pageant of the Graal on its manifestation within the hall and the shrine of the Castle. There are instances in which it is exceedingly simple, and others in which it is ornate. It is the former in the Lesser Chronicles, and demands scarcely the express name of a pageant; in the Greater Chronicles it is decorative, and this term will apply to some of the manifestations which are described in the *Conte del Graal*. The section which is referable to Chrétien offers, however, nothing to detain us. The procession enters the hall in single file, and consists in succession of a page, or squire, who carries the mysterious Sword which will break in one danger only, of another squire who bears the Sacred Lance from which the blood issues, and then of two squires together, each supporting a ten-branched candlestick. Between these there walks the gentle and beautiful maiden who lifts up the Holy Graal in her two hands; she is followed by another maiden, who carries the Silver Dish. The procession passes twice before the couch on which the King of the Castle reclines, and it is to be noticed that whatever efficacy and wonder may reside in the objects which are manifested thus, the office of the bearers is as purely ceremonial as that of the acolytes and thurifers at any High Mass in the world. When the questing knight pays his first visit in the *Didot Perceval*, the offices are transposed partially and the Sword is missing from the pageant. He who up-raises the Lance enters in the prescribed manner, but he carries it with both hands and is followed by a maiden with two silver plates and a napkin on her arm, while the vessel containing the Precious Blood of our Saviour, as if it were a phial or reliquary, is in the charge of a second squire. On the occasion of the later visit, it is said, still more tersely, that the Graal and the other venerable relics come out from a chamber beyond, but we do not learn who carries them. It is a characteristic of all the versions that, even in telling the same story, it is done always with respect to a certain genius of difference and a variant intervening in the text. Gautier de Doulens recounts in two versions the visit of Gawain to the Graal Castle, in the more important case under circumstances of unexplained mystery, for no one was less on the quest. This is comparable to the reception of a neophyte who is neither introduced nor prepared, but is mistaken at first for another. The pageant is also dismembered, for the Dish does not appear, the Hallow of the Broken Sword is placed upon the breast of a dead body, which lies on a rich bier. As if it were a subsidiary Hallow, a stately clerk carries an enormous cross of jewelled silver, and the only procession described is of canons in silken copes, who celebrate the office of the dead amidst thuribles and golden candlesticks. The Graal itself does not appear till the supper is served in the hall, but it is held by no visible hand and no other sacred object is seen in connection therewith. At a later stage of the episode, the Lance manifests and the blood which distils from its point is received, as we have seen, in a silver cup; the Broken Sword, in fine, reappears at the close; it is a very curious and piecemeal pageant. When Perceval revisits the Castle, the account of Gautier is in better conformity with what may be termed the conventional or authorised ceremonial type.

Passing to this point at the term of the continuation by Gautier de Doulens, there is again a very simple pageant, in which the Graal comes first—a Holy and

Glorious Vessel—under the charge of a maiden, who issues from the secret chamber and passes before the royal table, carrying the Hallow exalted. There follows a second maiden, than whom none is fairer, clothed in white drapery, and bearing the Lance from which flows the mysterious blood. In fine, there enters the squire exposing a naked sword broken in the middle thereof. It is at this point that, abruptly enough, the continuation reaches its term and is taken up by Manessier, who causes the Graal and the Lance to pass for a second time before the King and his guest, together with the noble Silver Dish, which is carried by a third maiden— a procession of vestals only, seeing that the work of the Sword—which has been partly resoldered by Perceval— has no longer its place in the pageant. When the questing hero pays his third visit to the Graal Castle, under the auspices of the same poet, the Lance and Graal are carried by two maidens, and a squire holds the Silver Dish, enveloped in his rich amice of red samite. The sacred objects pass three times, and return as they issued into the secret chamber, the mystery of which is never disclosed fully by the makers of this romance. In fine, when Perceval is crowned—and this is his fourth visit—a gentle maiden exalts the Holy Vessel, the Lance is borne by a squire, while another maiden holds the Silver Dish. It will be seen that on each occasion there is some variation in the offices, as if these were determined by accident. The alternative of Gerbert—which seems interposed before the partial resoldering of the sword by Perceval in the Gautier version—some few verbal modifications notwithstanding, gives the same account of the Graal procession.

In the prose *Lancelot*, which prefaces the great and glorious *Quest*, the pageant has this characteristic— that it is preceded invariably by a dove which enters through a window bearing a golden censer in its beak, and the palace fills thereupon with the eternal sweetness of the Paradise which is above. The bird passes through the hall and from sight into a chamber beyond. Out of that chamber—as if at a concerted signal—almost as if the dove had suffered transformation—there issues the maiden of the Graal, carrying the Precious Vessel. The manifestation in the prose *Lancelot* is at first on the occasion of Gawain's visit, and he sees nothing of the other Hallows till the Lance at a later stage issues from the chamber beyond and smites him between the shoulders. In the middle of the night of terror which follows this episode, he beholds another pageant preceded by a choir of voices. Once more the maiden issues from the hidden chamber carrying the sacred vessel, with lights and thuribles before her, and the service of the Graal is performed on a silver table in the middle place of the hall, but there are no other Hallows. When Lancelot comes to the Castle—from which event follows the conception of Galahad—the manifestation of the Graal is identical; but because of that which must be consummated he suffers no infliction, and he does not therefore behold the avenging Lance. It can be said scarcely that there is a pageant; the dove enters and vanishes; it passes within the secret chamber that the maiden in charge of the Vessel may come out therefrom; she appears accordingly, bearing the Holy Palladium, a vessel of gold, "the richest thing that any man hath lyving." She issues from the secret chamber, and again she returns therein, but not before Lancelot—also for that which must follow—is dazzled by her surpassing beauty.

In the time of the great Quest there are, strictly speaking, no pageants in the sense of the other romances, for the Graal is going about. Its apparition at the Court of King Arthur is heralded by a sunbeam only, and it is borne by no visible hand. In Corbenic, when all things draw to the holy marvel of their close, there is a solemn procession of angels to the secret shrine of the Graal, two of them bearing wax lights, the third a cloth, and the last the Sacred Lance, because heaven has come down at the removal of that which is meant for earth no more. In Sarras, at the last scene of all, which ends the strange, eventful mystery, there is a great cohort of angels; but this is the choir above descending to witness that which must be done in fine below. There is no passing between intermediate spaces.

In the *Longer Prose Perceval* two damosels issue together from a chapel which is attached to the banqueting-hall, one of them carrying the most Holy Graal and the other the Lance, the point of which distils its blood therein. It is suggested also, but as if by a dream within a dream, that there are two angels, bearing two candlesticks of gold filled with wax lights. The damosels move through the hall and pass into another chapel; again they come forth, and it seems then that there are three maidens, with the figure of a child in the midst of the Holy Graal. They pass for a third time, and then above the Vessel there is a Vision of the Crucified King.

In the *Parsifal* of Wolfram a Squire enters hurriedly bearing the Lance, which bleeds profusely into his sleeve —an uncouth and ill-begotten symbol. Two gracious maidens, wearing chaplets on their heads, follow with flowing hair; they bear up golden candlesticks. Two other women, of whom one is described as a duchess, carry two stools of ivory, which they place before the king. Next in order are four maidens having as many tapers, and four other maidens who sustain between them an oblong slab of jacinth. There are then two princesses carrying knives of silver, and these also are preceded by four maidens. The princesses are followed by six additional maidens, holding tall glasses filled with rare perfumes. There is, in fine, the queen of all, with the Graal in the hands of her, and behind is the squire who carries the Sword of Legend. When we come at the proper time to see how much and how little on the surface sense of things follows from this cumbrous display, we shall turn with the more relief to versions that are less decorative, though we can understand and excuse also the influence of the oriental mind reflected in the *Parsifal* from the prototype of Guiot de Provence. Relief at the moment will come from the poem of Heinrich, though it is the idlest of all the quests. Here the procession is in two parts. In the first there is a beautiful youth of highest mien, holding the Sword in one hand, and followed by cupbearers who serve wine at the feast. When this is over there enter two maidens carrying golden candlesticks; behind them come two youths, who lift up the Lance between them; they are followed by other two maidens, in whose charge is a salver of jewelled gold, borne upon a silken cloth. Behind these there walks the fairest of women holding the Precious Reliquary of the Graal, and after her the last maiden of all, whose hands are empty, whose office is weeping only—a variation which will be found also in the Montpellier codex of the *Conte del Graal*.

IX

THE ENCHANTMENTS OF BRITAIN, THE TIMES CALLED ADVENTUROUS AND THE WOUNDING OF THE KING

The *Longer Prose Perceval* says that the great and secret sanctuary gives upon the Earthly Paradise, even as the visible world may be said to give upon the world unseen—a comparison which would signify for us—or at least by a suggestion to the mind—that the Temple of the Hallows and all its external splendour are the adornment of the soul which is within. Even apart from such a reading, we can understand that the manner of doctrine put forward evasively in story-books by the Graal literature, was sufficient to make the orthodox church stand aloof, but vigilant and dubious. We have now to consider how a horror fell upon the Secret House of God and a subtle work of sorcery on the world which encompassed it. All texts indifferently of the Northern French cycles say that, as a consequence of certain events connected with the Castle of the Graal, there fell an interdiction upon Logres. In the Lesser Chronicles it is termed an Enchantment, while in the Greater Chronicles it is characterised as Adventurous Times, but the distinctions dissolve into one another; there is not less adventure, nor is it less hazardous, in the texts of enchantment, while in the adventurous texts the graces and terrors of sorcery abound on every side. We can therefore consider them together, as aspects of the same subject which are scarcely so much as alternative, and, in fact, on the study of the documents it will be found that the adventurous times are almost too vague by themselves to admit of being specified separately. As regards the enchantments, they are a consequence which works outward from within—that is to say, directly or indirectly, something which has transpired within is responsible for the inhibition without. The enchantments are the result of an evil which has fallen on the keeper for the time being of the Holy Graal. They are the exteriorised sorrow of the king. The action is, however, reciprocal, for in some instances that sorrow has reached him by an intrusion of the external order, though in certain other cases it has arisen in his own house or in his own person. It remains that as enchantment fell upon Merlin, so also it has fallen about the Secret House and has entered into the Holy of Holies. Now, the places of enchantment are also places of sadness, and the nature of the horror within, abiding as a certain cloud upon the sanctuary, is described after several manners. In one story, the flesh, which at no time profits anything, has smitten deeply into the life of the Keeper, who has been a victim of earthly passion. In another, he is unable to die till he has seen the last scion of his house, and because of the protraction of the centuries, he is suffering, in the meantime, the heavy burden of his great age. He has alternatively received a dolorous stroke, reacting on him from the person of one of his relatives; and as a final explanation he is afflicted by the failure of a knight to ask the conventional question, which is at once vital and mystic. These things are reflected upon the order without, sometimes, as it would seem, only in the immediate neighbourhood of the Castle; more generally through the whole of Logres; while in rare instances the world itself is involved, at least by imputation.

The Perceval Quests turn entirely on the asking of that question which I have specified in the previous enumeration, and the pivot of the question itself is the failure to perform what is expected in this respect—namely, to ask and to receive. In the Chrétien section of the *Conte del Graal* the explanation of the king's sickness is that he was wounded by a spear in battle and hence is carried by four sergeants because he has no strength in his bones. In the *Didot Perceval* Brons, the Rich Fisherman, is said to be in great infirmity, an old man and full of maladies, nor will his health be restored until the office of the question has been fulfilled in all perfection. But this is not ordinary old age; rather—as I have just intimated—it is the oppression of many centuries. It is clear, however, that Brons was not suffering from any curse or enchantment; he cannot depart from this life until he has communicated to Perceval the secret words pronounced at the sacrament of the Graal, which he himself learned from Joseph. This and the instruction which will follow the question asked by the hero shall put a period to the enchantments of Britain. There is a failure in the first instance, as in the poem of Chrétien, and the Quest in the *Conte del Graal* is to some extent assumed by Gawain, who visits the Graal Castle in the continuation of Gautier; he does ask, and thereupon the king promises him that, subject to one other condition, he shall hear the great story of the Broken Sword and of the woe which it brought upon the kingdom of Logres—but Gawain fails and falls asleep. The failure of Perceval has worked the destruction of kingdoms, which may mean certain petty principalities of Britain passing under this name—otherwise they cannot have been of this world, as the prophecy does not come to pass here. On the occasion of Perceval's second visit, the king is seated on a couch as before, and the discourse is not closed in the section of Gautier. The conclusion of Manessier recounts how the Broken Sword dealt that stroke which, prior to the voided question, has destroyed the realm of Logres and all the surrounding country. The unfinished inquiry of Gawain, before he fell into slumber, restored verdure to the land about the Graal Castle and the waters found their course. It was not, however, the keeper but his brother who received the Dolorous Stroke, being slain treacherously in a battle. The sword, which broke in the act, was placed upon the bier when the body was brought to the Castle; it was taken up incautiously by the king and in some undeclared manner it wounded him in both thighs; this wound could not be healed till the death of his brother was avenged. For these events the late prologue to the *Conte del Graal* substitutes a desolation which fell upon Logres prior to the coming of King Arthur. There were certain maidens who kept the wells and ministered refreshment to travellers out of golden cups. So admirable as was this custom, an evil king despoiled the maidens and scattered them, after which the service ceased. The elements of the prologue stand apart from the rest of the literature, like an allegory in another tongue; and though it is very curious in itself, it connects with nothing which follows in the texts that it is supposed to introduce.

The *Book of the Holy Graal*, like the metrical romance of De Borron, antecedes the period alike of enchantments and quests; but as, in its present form, it is later in fact than the chronicles which it is supposed to precede, so, as a part of its warrants, it forestalls many of their characteristics by a kind of spurious prophecy. It tells how the younger Joseph, the second keeper of the Graal, was smitten in the thighs by an angel for aiding certain people who did not embrace Christianity, and it testifies that the avenging spear with which the wounds were inflicted will be heard of again at the beginning of those marvels that shall occur in the land of Britain. In this manner it foreshadows the particular Dolorous Stroke of which we have a full account in the *Huth Merlin* and all the sorrowful adventures which follow therein. These are destined to continue for twenty-two years, corresponding to the twenty-two days during which the head of the Lance was embedded in the flesh of Joseph.

The *Vulgate Merlin* has nothing to say concerning the enchantments of Britain, except that the prophet's skill and discretion were gifts vouchsafed by God so that he might accomplish the adventures of the Seynt Graal. That it was the rumour of the Sacred Vessel which inaugurated the time of adventure is clear from this passage, as it is also from the *Huth Merlin*, which speaks of a prophecy written by the enchanter on parchment and concerned with those marvels which would characterise the Quest, encompassing in fine the destruction of the marvellous lion—that is to say, the overthrow of King Arthur. The implicits of this statement are one *crux* of the Merlin cycle. It is also, as I have intimated, to the *Huth Merlin* that we owe our acquaintance with the beautiful story of Balyn and Balan, the two brethren born in Northumberland, who were good knights, according to Malory. Balyn was destined to inflict the Dolorous Stroke, which during the allotted period of twenty-two years would cause dire distress throughout three kingdoms, for by this stroke he would pierce the most holy man in the world, and inaugurate the marvels of the Graal in Great Britain.

There can be no doubt that the Warden of the Sacred Vessel is here the intended victim, and that the stroke is actually given in the Graal Castle, with the hallowed spear of the legend. Balyn himself nearly loses his life in the cataclysm which follows, and is informed by Merlin that he has deserved the hatred of the whole world, the obvious reason being that he has desecrated the sanctuary. The recipient of the wound is, however, said to be King Pellehan, who is the brother of King Pelles the Keeper. In any chronological tabulation this event would most likely precede the visit of Gawain to the Graal Castle and indubitably the first arrival of Lancelot therein. These occurrences are related in the prose *Lancelot*, but in this romance the Keeper of the Sacred Vessel is, as I have said, King Pelles, and he is not wounded. Pellehan reappears in the *Quest of Galahad* not only as the Maimed King, but as he who bears the title of the Rich Fisher, which is reserved to the royalty of the Graal wardens. It will be seen, therefore, that a certain confusion has arisen, owing to continuous editing, and it may follow that there was originally but one King in the Castle, that his name was Pelles, that he was wounded by the Dolorous Stroke, and was destined to be healed by Galahad at the term of the Quest. As it is, there is actually a dual healing—that of the King Pellehan and that of another personage whose sin dates back to the first times of the legend, being one of unprepared intrusion into the most secret mysteries of the Graal. In the *Quest of Galahad* the confusion which I have noticed is made greater by the story of Sir Perceval's sister concerning the maiming of King Pelles, who found the ship of Solomon towards the coast of Ireland. He entered therein and drew the sword of David about half-way from its scabbard. In punishment of this rashness a spear smote him through both thighs, and never since might he be healed, says she, "to fore we come to hym." None of this takes place actually, but it goes to show that the original intention of the story was the intention of the Perceval quests—namely, to wound the keeper of the Graal. Speaking otherwise of this great romance, the whole process of the Quest is lifted into a high spiritual region, the implicits of which will provide us at a later stage with one key of the mystery.

In the *Longer Prose Perceval* it is said that there shall be no rest in the land till the Graal has been achieved. But here the horror of the house was the failure of Perceval to ask that question the simplicity of which is the seal of the whole enigma. As a consequence, the shepherd has been smitten and the sheep have been scattered. Those who ministered in the Castle were sent out by the general fatality beyond the sacred precincts, for no other reason apparently than to act as witnesses of the woe abroad before the face of the world; and so, therefore, in place of ceremonial pageants within, there are strange processions without.

In the German cycle, the adequate consideration of which must be referred as before to a later stage, the *Parsifal* of Wolfram sets a blot on the scutcheon by showing that sin entered the sanctuary, and in this, as in other respects, the story is set apart from all else in the general pageant of the literature. On the other hand, the poem of Heinrich, though its root-matter is almost out of knowledge, conforms, as it does usually, to the more normal tradition in points of detail, saying that the doom of the king was the outcome of war between brothers. With this, in other connections and a far other sense, we have some analogy in the *Longer Prose Perceval*.

I believe that the implicits of the Graal keepers must rank among the most important of those which remain for consideration in their place. While they are connected more especially with the headship in the persons of the successive Wardens, there are also subsidiary matters which will arise in their proper order. Woe has fallen on the Wardens, though, speaking symbolically, they abide in the place of life. Not only is the hereditary custodian of the secrets that person in most of the romances on whom comes the symbolic grief, but he is dependent peculiarly on help expected from without, and although his sustenance is within his healing is beyond the sanctuary. Even such a sinner as Gawain can bring him a partial consolation. He receives a nondescript savage like Perceval, as he is depicted in the more primitive stories, within the fold of election, for doing something after a clownish failure which any child might have been expected to perform at once. All this is so out of reason on the surface that a meaning in conceal-ment seems inevitable. Its investigation is reserved of necessity, but as something consistent with the subject down the first vistas of which we are looking only, it may be said, as the characteristic of every initiation, that the candidate does not ask questions; it is he who is catechised and must answer. One key from one point of view might again be the counsel: Ask, and ye shall receive. But the Graal quester is to bestow before he receives. The suggestion seems that if we are dealing with a rite which follows a certain procedure, it is one which works rather the reverse way, so far as other mysteries are concerned. That rite has been going on for generations, inviting and accepting no candidate, for it is perpetuated by hereditary transmission, though its treasury has been a heritage of woe. There is no symbolical object in all the literature of romance to compare with the secret guardianship, whether the keeper is wounded for his own, or another's, and even for our transgressions; whether also the consideration of his mystery arises from the texts themselves or from suggestions belonging thereto and admitted from a very high standpoint. No one could find the Castle, or come into the presence of the king, except by a special warrant and sometimes by a congenital election. The Castle was hidden from the world, like the analogous House of the Holy Ghost in the Rosicrucian Mystery, and he who entered therein had somehow to awaken the oracle. The hidden life of the keepers passed in the Castle, but not in the visionary rapture of those who go into Avalon and other isles of the blessed. Now, there are two palmary mysteries connected with two divisions of the Chronicles of Quest—one is the silence of Perceval and the other is the conception of Galahad. By the way of anticipation something more will be said of the first in the next section.

X

THE SUPPRESSED WORD AND THE MYSTIC QUESTION

It is agreed that the essential and predominant characteristic of the Perceval literature is the asking and answering of a question which bears on its surface every aspect of triviality, but is yet the pivot on which the whole circle of these romances may be said to revolve. On the other hand, the question is absent from the Galahad story, and in place of it we have a stately pageant of chivalry moving through the world of Logres to find the high mystery of sanctity. But that finding is destined only to dismember the Arthurian empire and to pass, in fine, leaving no trace behind it, except the sporadic vision of a rejected knight, which is mentioned but not described, and occurs under circumstances that justify grave doubts as to its existence in the original texts.

Now, the entire critical literature of the Graal may be searched in vain for any serious explanation as to the actuating motive, in or out of folk-lore, concerning the Graal question. On the part of the folk-lore authorities there have been naturally attempts to refer it to something antecedent within the scope of their subject, but the analogies have been no analogies, and as much extravagance has resulted as we have yet heard of in the connection which some scholars have vaguely termed mysticism. The symbolical and sacramental value of the Graal Quest, outside all issues in folk-lore, is from my standpoint paramount, as it is this indeed without any reference to the opinions which are founded in folk-lore or to the speculations thereout arising; and the fact remains that the palmary importance of the mystic question lapses with the pre-eminence of the Perceval Quest. Initiation, like folk-lore, knows many offices of silence but few of asking; and after many researches I conclude—or at least tentatively—that in this respect the Graal romances stand practically alone. It is therefore useful to know that it is not the highest term of the literature.

In the *Conte del Graal* of Chrétien, the law and order of the Quest is that Perceval shall ask the meaning of those wonders which he sees in the pageant at the Castle of the Quest. The references are many in the poem, but they are merely repetitions. Perceval did not ask (1) how such things came to pass; (2) nor anything whatsoever; (3) he did not dare to ask about the Graal, *qui on en servoit*, because his teacher in chivalry had cautioned him against idle curiosity and such impertinence, for which reason he reserved his speech. It is understood that through the oppression of the centuries the keeper of the Holy Graal is, according to the *Didot Perceval*, in a state of distress, longing for his delayed release. Before he can go in peace he must pass on the divine tradition of the Secret Words, but before he can so transmit them he must be asked a question. That question is: *De quoi li Graus sert.* It will perform a twofold office, firstly, to heal the king, and, secondly, to liberate his speech. Perceval reaches the Castle, but notwithstanding that the voice of one who was invisible had announced at the Court of King Arthur, in Perceval's presence and in that of all the knights, both the nature and effect of the question, he entreats nothing for fear of offending his host. Hence he departs in disgrace, and the king remains unhealed.

Within the limits of the Gautier section of the *Conte del Graal* there are not less than three versions of the visit of Gawain to the Graal Castle, representing specific variations of different manuscripts. Without exercising any discrimination between them, but rather by a harmony of all, it may be said that he does ask concerning the Lance and Graal, but as he cannot re-solder the sword, he can learn nothing regarding the Sacred Vessel, or, if there is a sign of willingness on the part of the Keeper, he goes to sleep and so escapes the story. The result is that the enchantment is in part only removed from the land. When the same poet recounts the second visit of Perceval, the knight on beholding the Hallows does not know where to begin, but at length prays that he may hear the whole truth concerning the Graal, the Sword and the Lance. The condition of the answer, as in the case of Gawain, is that he shall re-solder the Sword, and we have seen already that in this task Perceval is successful partly, but the king's healing does not seem to be effected, though the path thereof is open, and the knight has not yet achieved the Quest. The result on external nature is not stated by Manessier.

At the beginning of the *Longer Prose Perceval* it is said that the reticence of the questing Knight at the Graal Castle caused such mischances in Greater Britain that all the lands and islands fell into sorrow. There appeared to be war everywhere, no knight meeting another in the forest without running on him and slaying him, if he could. The King Fisherman himself passed into languishment. The question which ought to have been asked was: " Unto whom one serveth of the Graal." Many penances will be ended, it is said, when he who visits the Graal Castle demands unto whom it is served ; but this event never comes to pass in the story. The desire to ask questions seems to have been rare therein, for Gawain when conversing with a wandering damsel, who was formerly the bearer of the Graal, fails to inquire why she carries her arm slung on her neck in a golden stole, or concerning the rich pillow whereon her arm reposes. He is told that he will give no greater heed at the court of King Fisherman. The King himself always dwells on the misfortune which overtook him through the failure of Perceval. When Gawain actually reaches the mystic Castle, he sees the Graal and the Lance, but he is lost in a joy of contemplation and he utters no word.

It has been said that there is a question in the Romance of Galahad, and it might have been added that there is one in the prose *Lancelot;* the second illustrates the first, and we shall find that they are both mere traces and survivals, as the prologue to the *Conte del Graal* has the shadow of the secret words, peculiar to the cycle of De Borron, when it affirms that the Graal secret must be never disclosed. I do not think that, as regards the later instance, I should be justified in assuming that he who wrote this prologue was in touch direct with the implicit of the De Borron cycle, and I do think alternatively that if people were disposed to lay stress on such remanents of the question as I am citing here, they are likely to find that it will work rather in a reverse direction. The fact remains that Lancelot saw the Graal in one episode of the great story dedicated to him, that he asked the question which is so important in some other romances, that he asked it quite naturally—as who would have failed to do? —that he was answered also naturally, and that nothing depended therefrom. He cried in his wonder : " O Jesu! what does this mean?" He was told : "This is the richest thing in the world." In the Galahad romance, when he beheld, by the Stone Cross in the wild, a sudden passage of the Graal and the healing of a certain knight, it is hinted by some texts that he ought to have asked something, despite the lesson which he had in the voiding of things previously ; but he was so far right on the fact that his imputed omission carried no consequence.

The hindrance to the question in the *Parsifal* is the same as we have found in Chrétien; at all that he saw the knight of the Quest was agaze with wonder; he thought also that if he refrained from asking he would be told eventually. That which followed herefrom was sorrow to the host, with continued suffering, and woe also to the guest. For this silence he is always represented in the romances as earning reproach and contumely from persons outside the Castle, but in the German poem there is no suggestion of an external enchantment. It is to be noted further that Parsifal has not received a prefatory warning regarding the question, as he has in the *Didot Perceval.*

In *Diu Crône* by Heinrich, when the questing knight has beheld the Reliquary and the Spear, he does the opposite exactly, for he can no longer contain himself, and so asks his host, for the sake of God, to tell him what the marvels mean and who also are the great company whom he beholds. Even as he speaks, all present spring from their seats with a loud cry and the sound of great rejoicing. The host tells them to sit down again, and then he explains to the knight that he has seen the Holy Vessel of which he may say nothing, except that joy and consolation supervene upon his saving question. Many are liberated from the bondage which they have endured so long, having little hope of acquittance. There was a time when they trusted in Perceval, as in one predestined to enter into the knowledge of the Graal, as if through everlasting portals, but he fell away like a knight of no spirit who dared and demanded nothing. Had he done otherwise, he would have released many from their toil who remain in the semblance of life and are yet dead. The woe came about through the strife of kinsmen, "when one brother smote the other for his land." For this disloyalty the judgment of God descended upon him and his consanguinities, so that doom overtook them all. The living were expatriated, and the dead, under greater disaster, remained in the shadow of life. To end their woe it was necessary that a man of their race should seek an explanation of their sad, long-enduring prodigies. It does not appear that the Graal or the Spear have any connection with the Passion of Christ, and there is no secret communicated, for the history of the Sacred Vessel is not recounted?

From the consideration of this subject we may come away therefore, confirmed in our reasonable certainty that the question with which we have been dealing is unlike anything in literature. We shall see ultimately how it is accounted for by expert knowledge of folk-lore—connected or otherwise with quests and vengeance missions —in Welsh or English literature.

XI

THE HEALING OF THE KING

It came about, therefore, at the end of the Quest, that the Suppressed Word was at last spoken, that the question was asked and answered. There are certain texts in which the asking and the answering are all that was required by the hypothesis, and then it was well in the Secret House of the Wardens. There are other texts, which connect more directly with folk-lore, in which the king's healing depended upon a dual office, of which the first part was the question itself, as a kind of interlocutory discourse, and then upon a mission of vengeance. It was fulfilled in either case. The head of the Blessed Bran does not appear in the symbolism of these branches, but the head as the sign of the accomplished sacrifice is an essential, in these branches, of the Quest fulfilled, and this is the characteristic in chief of the *Conte del Graal*. As a Rite of the Observance with Mercy, the question and its answer were held to be all-sufficient in the Lesser Chronicles, because the curse on the Keeper is like that on the Wandering Jew—it is the ages continued henceforward, and he comes at length to his rest. The Greater Chronicles offer another pageant of the Quest, the particulars of which are as follows : (1) The Building of the Ship of the Secret Faith, that at the end of a certain time it might carry into the far distance the most valid and efficacious symbols of the Mystery of Faith ; (2) the healing of a King of the East who is not to be confused with the Keeper himself, but he dates *ab initio symboli* and is doubtless the witness in chief of the mystery even to the times of the Quest : concerning him it may be said that he tried to take the mystery of faith by violence, outside which his existence is parallel to that of the Keeper Brons, having been prolonged through the centuries from the first times of the legend ; (3) the redemption of the Cain of the legend who slew his brethren ; (4) an intercalatory and voided wonder concerning the maiming of the Graal King when he drew the Sword of David.

The particulars in all branches may be collected shortly as follows : In the *Conte del Graal* Gautier presents a certain lifting of the heavy veil of enchantment, so that the desert becomes the sown, and we are enabled to compare how it was in the dry tree with that which it is in the green : Winter has passed, so to speak, and the voice of the turtle is heard again in the land. In Manessier, the keeper, who has suffered from that illogical maiming occasioned by the death of his brother, is healed at the sight of his head who committed the original act of violence. The whole business is foolish, and so unutterably. It was necessary, for some reason that derived probably its roots from folk-lore, for the king to be smitten in his thighs ; the event comes to pass under circumstances that are quite and frankly impossible; and there is also no reason why the wound which was self-inflicted unconsciously should not have been healed at once, unless death intervened as the term. Assuming that Gerbert knew nothing of Manessier's conclusion and that he regarded the last words of Gautier—in which the

Rich Fisher hails Perceval as the Lord of his house—as the term, in fine, of the story, his own intercalation was intended to account for the closing along better lines, and he did not concern himself with any explanation of the King's wounding. On the contrary, his intention was to show that the proper demand and reply exercised their proper office, and that the one thing which remained to complete the whole was for Perceval to redeem his past. The poem does not offer a termination which follows from the text, while that of Manessier, from any explanatory standpoint, is so much idle baggage. The *Conte del Graal,* considered as a Graal story, is therefore at once imperfect and piecemeal. The *Didot Perceval* is by no means entirely satisfactory as a completion of De Borron's trilogy, but as a simple term of a quest which is exceedingly simple, it leaves nothing undone. The Keeper of the Graal, as we have seen, must communicate his mystery before he departs hence. The mode of communication presupposes the arbitrary question which is a pretext for unveiling the mysteries, and the issue, which is clear from the beginning, is not clouded subsequently by extraneous matters. The king is healed—that is to say, he is relieved of the long burden of the centuries, and he is enabled to pass in peace. In the *Great Prose Quest* it is the hands of Galahad which are the hands of healing. The Hallow of the ensanguined lance inflicted the wound from which the unknown king Pellehan suffered through the whole period during which the Quest was prepared and achieved. The restoration was accomplished by Galahad with the blood from the same weapon ; therewith he anointed the king. It is after this or another manner that the remedial elements are sometimes in the House of the Graal, but they must be administered by one who comes from external places. It may be admitted that, at least on the surface, both wounding and healing in the Galahad Quest are a burden to the logical understanding. For what it is worth—which is little—in other respects, there is on this point a certain consistence in the *Conte del Graal*. At the beginning it carries the implicit of a vengeance legend, and though something is forgotten in the antecedence by Gautier and something else by Manessier, as if they had not read fully their precursors, that is explicated in fine which was implied at first. The *Longer Prose Perceval* has a root-difficulty, because there is no attempt to explain either why the question was necessary, when all was well with the king, or why—whether necessary or not—the failure of Perceval should have caused the Keeper of the Holy Graal to fall into such languishment that ultimately he died unhealed. For these are the distinctions, among many, between the *High History* and all other Perceval Quests—that it begins at the middle point of the story and that the Keeper perishes. Among the correspondences in the reverse order of these differences is the Quest of Gawain, according to *Diu Crône* by Heinrich, where the king indeed dies coincidently with his release, but this is his desired liberation from the condition of death in life. Speaking generally, the death of the wounded keeper is designed thoughout to make room for his successor. In the *Didot Perceval* he is released according to his yearning, and that almost at once; in the *Conte del Graal* Perceval, far from the Castle, awaits the keeper's demise, which occurs in the natural course. In the *Parsifal* of Wolfram there is a kind of abdication by Amfortas in favour of the Questing Knight, but the two abide together, and, as in the *Didot Perceval*, there is, in fact, a trinity of keepers. In the *Quest of Galahad*, that glorious and saintly knight can be called a keeper scarcely; if I may be pardoned the expression, he and his companions act as the transport agents of the Sacred Vessel, so far as the term is concerned, though we may still regard Galahad as the keeper in heaven. We are not concerned with the healing of King Pellehan, because he is not the keeper of the Graal, as the text stands, though we feel that some editor has blundered. I will leave him therefore with the last word which he might have addressed to Galahad : *Domine, non sum dignus ut intres sub tectum meum, sed tantum dic verbo et sanabitur corpus meum.* I will leave also at this point the mystery of the healing of the king. For us and for our salvation, the quests of the Graal are the exteriorised zeal of the hearts which desire the bread of heaven and a visible sign that it is more than the daily bread. Such a romance of sanctity they appear in the story of Galahad, whose kingdom is not of this world ; he is crowned indeed at Sarras, but it is contrary to the will of him who sought only to be dissolved and to be with Christ. The first term of the other quests sometimes carried with it a species of kingship, and, as to these, it was on the king's healing that it was said of his successor : Long live the King !

XII

THE REMOVAL OF THE HALLOWS

We have now seen that the Rich Fisherman, King and Warden of the Graal, was healed as the consequence of the Quest, or that, this failing, a provision was made for his successor after some other manner. Now, this is the penultimate stage of the mystery regarded as a whole, and the one question which still remains to be answered is—what became of the Graal? Subject to characteristic variations which are particular to each text, it will be found—as I have said—that the several romances follow or forecast one general process, suggesting a prevailing secret intention, and it is for this intention that my study will have to account. At the moment the external answer to the problem above propounded, resting on the evidence of the documents, is an example of variation—which tends, however, to one term ; this term is that either the Holy Graal and the other Hallows of the Passion were removed altogether or they were taken into deeper concealment. The specific testimonies are as follows. After the death of King Fisher, Perceval inherits his kingdom—in the *Conte del Graal*—and he reigns for seven years. He appoints his successor, who does not become the Warden of the Hallows, and he passes himself into the seclusion of a hermitage, where he remains for ten years, having been ordained a priest. The Graal follows him, and he is at length assumed into the joy of Paradise, since which time the Sacred Vessel and the other precious objects have never been beheld so openly. As a rider to this, it is added that no doubt they were taken to heaven, which is an argument from the unworthiness of the world. In the *Didot Perceval* the Knight of the Quest and a certain hermit, who is a character of importance in the Lesser Chronicles, become the guardians of the Graal, and the prophet Merlin also abides with them. Merlin, in fine, goes away, seeking a deeper seclusion, and neither he nor the Graal are heard of subsequently. The inference is that the Graal remains in the asylum of the Holy House, under the charge of its wardens. The *Longer Prose Perceval*, after a faithful picture of the Questing Knight in loneliness and rapture, surviving all his kindred, says that a secret voice commanded him to divide the Hallows among a certain company of hermits, after which a mystic ship anchors by the Castle, and Perceval, taking his leave of all those who still remained about him, entered that vessel and was carried far over the sea, "nor never thereafter did no earthly man know what became of him, nor doeth the history speak of him more." In the *Great Prose Quest* the most holy companions—Galahad, Perceval and Bors—are conveyed in the ship mystic of Solomon to a place in the East, named Sarras; the Hallows with which they are charged are the Sacred Vessel and the Lance, together with the Sword of David, wherewith Galahad is girded. For a certain allotted period of days that are sad, consecrated and strange, the companions watch over the Hallows in the city of Sarras;

and then the call comes to Galahad. "There with he kneled doune to fore the table, and made his prayers, and thenne sodenly his soule departed to Jhesu Crist and a grete multitude of angels bare his soule up to Heuer., that the two felawes myghte wel behold hit. Also the two felawes sawe come from heven an hand, but they sawe not the body. And thenne hit cam ryght to the vessel, and took it and the spere and soo bare hit up to heuen. Sythen was ther neuer man soo hardy to saye that he had sene the Sancgreal." In the German cycle, the *Parsifal* of Wolfram leaves the Graal where it was always since its first manifestation, but the *Titurel* of Albrecht von Scharfenberg—a text which is so late that it is excluded generally from the canon of the literature—narrates the rise and growth of an evil time, wherein, for its better protection, Parsifal and the chivalry of the Graal, bearing the Blessed Palladium, go forth from Mont Salvatch into the far East, where is the kingdom of Prester John, and there it may remain to this day—most surely in another kingdom which is not of this world. After these high memorials it is almost unnecessary to speak of the Quest in Heinrich, at the term of which the Graal and the ghostly company dissolve before the eyes of the Questing Knight, and thenceforth the tongue of man cannot show forth the mysteries.

Seeing now that the great sacraments do not pass away, it must follow that in the removal of the Holy Graal, as it is narrated in the texts, we are in the presence of another mystery of intention which appears the most obscure of all. The cloud that dwelt on the sanctuary, the inhibition which was on the world without, the hurt almost past healing which overtook the hereditary keeper, are ample evidence in themselves that evil had entered into the holy place, despite all the warrants which it held and all the Graces and Hallows which dwelt therein. With one curious exception, the Keeper was, in fine, healed; the enchantment was also removed; and the achievement of the last Warden, at least in some instances, must have been designed, after a certain manner and within a certain measure, to substitute a greater glory for the cloud on the secret sanctuary. All this notwithstanding, the end of the great quests, the term of the whole mystery, was simply the removal thereof. It occurs in each romance under different circumstances, and it was not, as we shall learn more fully, always of an absolute kind. In the *Conte del Graal* it is said—and we have seen previously—that it was taken away, possibly to heaven ; in the *Didot Perceval* it was seen no more ; in the *Longer Prose Perceval* it was distributed, so far as we can tell, with the other Hallows, to certain hermits, and it ceased simply to manifest ; in Wolfram the whole question is left open in perpetuity, for at the close of the poem the keeper remains alive ; in the *Titurel* of Albrecht von Scharfenberg the Vessel was carried eastward into the dubious realm of Prester John, and there apparently it remains ; in the Quest of Galahad it is assumed by Heaven itself, and the last keeper followed ; but, in spite of this, the lost recension, as represented, faithfully or otherwise, by the Welsh Quest, says that though it was not seen so openly, it was seen once by Sir Gawain, the least prepared and least warranted of all the Graal seekers, whose quest, moreover, was for the most part rather accidental than intended.

Speaking now from the mystic standpoint, the removal of the Holy Graal has in a certain sense the characteristics of an obscure vengeance. The destruction of the external order would appear to have been decreed. The Graal is carried away and its custodians are translated. The removal certifies the withdrawal of an object which we know, mystically speaking, is never taken away, though it is always hidden from the unworthy. In respect of its imputed removal, it is taken thither where it belongs ; it is the same story as that of the Lost Word in Masonry. It is that which in departing hence draws after it all that belongs thereto. In other words, it goes before the cohort of election as the Pillars of Fire and Cloud before Israel in the Wilderness. The root and essence of the matter can be put shortly in these words: The Graal was not taken away, but it went to its own place, which is that of every man.

The Galahad Quest closes the canon of the literature. Other romances have said that the Sacred Vessel was not seen so openly, or that it was heard of no more, or that it had passed into concealment, and so forth ; but this crowning legend carries it into complete transcendence, amidst appropriate ceremonial, though otherwise it leaves the Arthurian sacrament sufficiently unfinished. That is to say, it is still to be communicated for the last time to the whole world on the return of Arthur. The Graal is in hiding, like Arthur ; but the Graal is, like Arthur, to return. Meanwhile, the chivalry of the world is broken, and the kingdom is destroyed. The master of all chivalry has received in his turn a dolorous stroke and is removed through a mist of enchantment, under dubious wardens, to the land of the setting sun, even into an exile of the ages. But he also is to be, in fine, healed and to return, though at what time we know not, for centuries pass as days, within the certain knowledge of Ogier the Dane. So much as this may perhaps be hazarded on the point of time, namely, that the King's rendering shall be when the King's dark barge, sailing westward, like the lighter craft of Hiawatha, shall meet with the Graal, which set forth eastward, since the Graal must heal the King, and these shall meet truly when justice and mercy kiss. The Graal is not therefore lost, but gone before.

Of such are the mysteries of the Graal, considered in their manifestation and considered also in their removal. I have passed through many houses of initiation in literature, but I know of nothing in suggestion and allusion to compare with the House of the Graal.

BOOK III

THE EARLY EPOCHS OF THE QUEST

THE ARGUMENT

169

The Hidden Church of the Holy Graal

—(*C*) *The continuation of Gautier—The development of Perceval's story—The point to which it is taken—The historical texts of the Graal which intervened between Chrétien and Gautier—The unfinished Quest in Gautier—(D) The conclusion according to Manessier—Intervention of the Vengeance Legend—Elements of Graal history in this conclusion, and inferences therefrom—The ordination of Perceval as a specific departure from tradition—The assumption of the Hallows—(E) The alternative conclusion of Gerbert—The dual failure of Perceval—His penitence and expiation—The conventional intention of his marriage—His later and higher intention—An adornment of a spiritual marriage—The Knight of the Swan—An analogy with Alain le Gros—The process of departure from Folk-lore in the Conte del Graal—Absence of the Vengeance Legend in Gerbert—Further consideration of the Prologue to the whole story—(F) In which Sir Gawain is considered briefly as a Companion of the Holy Quest—Modern speculations and inferences as to the primary claim of this hero—The light upon these which can be gathered from the poem of Heinrich—The judgment of the prose Lancelot and the Quest of Galahad—Sir Gawain in the story of Chrétien—The burden of this Quest in Gautier—His recognition that the courtly Knight was predestined at least to some measure of success—How the false experiment is not repeated by Manessier or Gerbert—An Advance Note on Gawain in the Parsifal of Wolfram—The Knight of Courtesy in the Longer Prose Perceval.*

BOOK III

I

THE ANTECEDENTS OF THE LEGEND IN FOLK-LORE

THE beginnings of literature are like the beginnings of life—questions of antecedents which are past finding out, and perhaps they do not signify vitally on either side, because the keys of all mysteries are to be sought in the comprehension of their term rather than in their initial stages. Modern scholarship lays great and almost exclusive stress on the old Celtic antecedents of the Graal literature, and on certain Welsh and other proto-types of the Perceval Quest in which the Sacred Vessel does not appear at all. As regards these affiliations, whether Welsh, English or Irish, I do not think that sufficient allowance has been made for the following facts: (*a*) That every archaic fiction and every legend depends, as already suggested, from prior legend and fiction; (*b*) that the antecedents are both explicit and implicit, intentional or unconscious, just as in these days we have wilful and undesigned imitation; (*c*) that the persistence of legends is by the way of their transfigura-tion. We have done nothing to explain the ascension of the Graal to heaven and the assumption of Galahad when we have ascertained that some centuries before there were myths about the Cauldron of Ceridwen or that of the Dagda, any more than we have accounted for Christianity if we have ascertained, and this even indubitably, that some ecclesiastical ceremonial is an adaptation of pre-Christian rites. Here, as in so many other instances, the essence of everything resides in the intention. If I possess the true apostolical succession, then, *ex hypothesi* at least, I do not the less consecrate the Eucharist if I use the Latin rite, which expresses the words of institution in the past tense; or some archaic oriental rite, by which they are expressed in the future, and to which there is added at some point the *Epiclesis* clause, being the invocation of the Holy Spirit.

There is, in any case, no question as to the Graal antecedents in folk-lore, and I should be the last to minimise their importance after their own kind, just as I should not abandon the official Church because I had been received into the greater Church which is within. I believe personally that the importance has been magnified unduly because it has been taken by scholarship for the all in all of its research. But there is plenty of room for every one of the interests, and as that which I represent does not interfere with anything which has become so far vested, I ask for tolerance regarding it. My position is that the old myths were taken over for the purposes of Christian symbolism, under the influence of a particular but not an expressed motive, and it was subsequently to this appropriation that they assumed importance. It is, therefore, as I have said, simply to clear the issues that I place those of my readers who may feel concerned with the subject in possession of the bare elements which were carried from pre-Christian times into the Graal mythos, as follows:—

1. We hear of an Irish legend concerning the Cauldron of the Dagda, from which no company ever went away unsatisfied. It was one of the four talismans which a certain godlike race brought with them when they first came into Ireland. As the particular talisman in question, though magical, was not spiritual, it is useless to our purpose; but it connects with the palmary

Hallow of the Graal mystery, because that also is reputed to have been food-giving, though this property was the least of its great virtues, just as the stone of transmutation by alchemy was classed among the least possessions of the Rosicrucian Fraternity.

2. There is the Cauldron of Bendigeid Vran, the son of Llyr, in one of the old Welsh *Mabinogion*, the property of which, says one story, is that if a man be slain to-day and cast therein, to-morrow he will be as well as he ever was at the best, except that he will not regain his speech. He remains, therefore, in the condition of Perceval when that hero of the Graal stood in the presence of the mystery with a spell of silence upon him. It follows that the Druidic Mysteries, as we find them in Welsh legend, are like other initiations : the candidate is passed through the experience of a mystical death and is brought back, as, for example, by the Cauldron of Ceridwen, to a new term of existence ; but although in this sense the dead are raised, they are not, or at least in this case, restored with the gift of tongues—life, but no word of life. In other language, the silence of the great pledges is henceforth imposed upon them. The dead rise up, but they do not begin to speak. Except in so far as the Cup of the Graal legend concerns a mystery of speech and its suppression, it is difficult to trace its correspondence with this cauldron, which I should mention, however, came into Wales from Ireland. If these things can be considered as so much raw material out of which the Graal legend in fine issued, the fact extends rather than reduces the transformation which so operated that the Holy Vessel of Christian symbolism was brought forth from a Druidic cauldron, which is sometimes that of Ceridwen and sometimes of Bendigeid, being at once the fountain of Bardic inspiration and the provider of a feast of good things. In this connection we may remember further that the chief mystic hero of Wales was not so much King Arthur as Cadwaladr Fendigeid. Paulin Paris was the first who attempted to identify this

chieftain with Galahad, but one essential distinction is that in the Welsh myth Cadwaladr is destined to return, whereas in the romance Galahad comes no more.

It so happens that institutions of analogy are made occasionally by scholarship on warrants which they would be the first to repudiate if the object, let us say, were to establish some point advanced by a mystic. I do not reject them exactly, and I do not intend to use similar comparisons on evidence which appears so slight; but I must place on record that the derivations here mentioned, if true, are unimportant, even as it is also unimportant that Adam, who received the breath of life from the Divine Spirit, had elements of red earth which entered into his material composition. The lights which shine upon the altar are not less sacramental lights because they are also earthly wax; and though the externals are bread and wine, the Eucharist is still the Eucharist.

In addition to analogies like those which I have just cited, there are two versions of the quest or mission of Perceval into which the mystery of the Graal does not enter as a part. In their extant forms they are much later than any of the Graal literature in Northern French. One is the story of Peredur, the son of Evrawc, in the Welsh *Mabinogion*, and the other is the English metrical romance of *Syr Percyvelle*. Scholars have compared both to the *Lay of the Great Fool*, and I think that the analogy obtains not only in the Welsh and English fables, but even in such masterpieces of nature-born poetry as the work of Chrétien de Troyes. On the other hand, the English poem is a thing of no importance except in respect of its connections, its perfect form as a narrative, and its high literary value. These claims notwithstanding, it will be sufficient to say that even scholarship values it chiefly for its doubtful traces of some early prototype which is lost.

The scholarship of Dr. Evans is thought to account for certain opinions which he holds regarding the high importance of the *Longer Prose Perceval*, but he is correct at least in his instinct by the consequence of its comparison with other quests outside the *Parsifal* of Wolfram and the *Quest of Galahad*. The Welsh *Mabinogi* is like the wild world before the institution of the sacraments, and from any literary standpoint we shall see that it is confused and disconcerting ; the poem of Chrétien is like the natural world with its interdict just beginning to be removed ; it is also like the blind man in part restored to sight, seeing all things inverted and devoid of their normal proportions. The *Longer Prose Perceval* occupies a middle position between the Great Quest and Wolfram ; the enchantment of Britain—as if Logres were this visible Nature—has dissolved partly ; Grace is moving through Nature ; the Great Mystery is being declared and testified to everywhere. In the *Parsifal* the things which are without have suffered a certain renewal, and yet the German epic is not the nearest correspondence and equivalent of the Galahad Quest.

It follows from these considerations, so far as they have now proceeded, that the folk-lore antecedents of the Graal are Celtic ; but I should mention that it has not been determined finally by scholarship whether we should look to Wales through Norman-French poets or to Armorica through poets of Northern France for the primordial matter of romance in respect of the literature. Such a question, except as a preliminary gleaning leading up to another concern, is a little outside our horizon, but the concensus of opinion in England and France favours the first alternative. To direct our attention thither is by no means to set for our consideration a clear vista or to open an easy pathway. It happens, unfortunately, that as regards Wales there is as yet no certain canon of criticism to distinguish the genuine memorials of archaic literature from the vast mass of false seeming which wears only the vestures and mask of antiquity. It is now many years since M. Villemarqué, the Breton, illustrated what it was possible to do in the production and extension of Armorican remains, and in the Principality there have been more than one Ville-marqué—*fabulatores famosi*—whose results obtained, if they have not been calculated to deceive even the elect, have at least made the specialist wary, sometimes about rejecting, but always of accepting anything in the definite and absolute degree. Having regard to my own limitations as one who has observed the strife scarcely, much less shared therein, I seek only to note a single question of parallel. The antecedents of folk-lore passed into the literature of the Graal undergoing great transmutations, and so also did certain elements of old Druidism merge into Christianity; Rite and Myth and Doctrine were tinged by Tradition and Doctrine and Rite; for things which co-exist tend to dovetail, at least by their outer edges; and there are traces, I think, of a time when the priest who said mass at the altar was not only a Druid at heart, but in his heart saw no reason also for the Druid to be priest any less. Long after the conversion of the Celt, enigmatical fables and mystical Rites lingered in Gaul and Britain, and if one could say that the Cauldron of Ceridwen was a vessel of pagan doctrine, then in an equal symbolical sense it became a vessel of hotch-potch under the strange ægis of the Celtic Church. There were masters of mysteries and secret science, whose knowledge, it is claimed, was perpetuated under the shadow of that Church and even within the pale thereof. The Bardic Sanctuary, by the evidence of some who claimed to speak in its name, opposed no precious concealed mysteries, and perhaps on its own part the Church received into its alembic much that was not of its matter expecting to convert it therein and turn it out in a new form. In the fourth century there were professors at Bordeaux who had once at least been Druids, and for the doctrines of their later reception the heart of their old experience may have been also an alembic. St. Beuno in his last moments is recorded to have exclaimed: "I see the Trinity and Peter and Paul, and the Druids and the Saints!"—a choir invisible, the recognition of which would, if known, have imperilled his canonisation, supposing that its process had been planned in Rome. At a much later period, even in the twelfth century, we have still the indication of perpetuated mysteries, and there is no doubt that the belief in these was promoted generally by the bards. The twelfth century saw also the beginning of a great revival of literature in Wales. There are certain Iolo manuscripts which are late and of doubtful authenticity, but accepting their evidence under all necessary reserves, they refer the revival in question to Rhys ap Twdur, who assumed the sovereignty of South Wales, bringing with him " the system of the Round Table, as it is with regard to minstrels and bards." And when the time came for the last struggle between the Celtic and Latin Rites for the independence of the British Church, I can well believe that all which remained, under all transformations, of that old mixed wisdom of the West was also fighting for its life. When pseudo-Taliesin prophesied the return of Cadwaladr, who had passed into the unmanifest, like Arthur, and, like Arthur, was destined to return, I believe also that this allegory of rebirth or resurrection, if it referred on one side to the aspirations of the Celtic Church, did not less embody on another the desired notion of a second spring for the mysteries which once dwelt in Wales, which even after many centuries were interned rather than dead.

We can imagine—though perhaps at a far distance—what kinds of medley resulted from such interpenetration of mysteries as I have here indicated: the sacrifice of human victims in the ceremonial rites, on the one side; the eternal sacrifice of the Victim who was divine and human, on the other; the renovation of the candidate as the term of symbolical ritual, and the Resurrection of Christ as the first-fruits of the redeemed in the signal degree. With these as the analogies of opposites, there were meeting-points and enough in the Lesser Mysteries, while encircling all as an atmosphere there were, on the one hand, the presages, the signs, the omens, the vaticinations, the inspirations, dark and strange, of seers and bards; but, on the other, there were the great consecrations, the holy objects, the sacred traditions, the inspired writings and all the annals of sanctity. In fine, against the solemn pageants of pagan ceremonial performances there was the Great Mystery of the faith of Christ, the white sacrifice and the clean oblation of the Eucharist. I confess that if there were otherwise any evidence, I can imagine that secret words, exceeding *ex hypothesi* all words of institution in the Ordinary of the official Mass-Book, and strange claims of a priesthood which had never been seen at Rome, might well issue from so enigmatic and dubious a sanctuary.

From all this matter of fact, matter of speculation and high matter of dream, we can infer that wherever the cradle may be of the true legend of the Graal—Gaul, Armorica, or Wales, but the last as a probability apart—there was at work, less or more everywhere in the Celtic world, what I have called the alembic of transmutation. I care not what went therein—Cauldron of Ceridwen, Cauldron of the Dagda, head of Bran and poisoned spear which smote him, *Lay of the Great Fool*, Expulsion and Return Formula, Visitations of the Underworld, and so forward for ever and ever—but that which came out was the Mystery of Faith manifested after a new manner, and the search for that sanctuary wherein, among all waste places of the world, the evidence of things unseen became palpable to the exalted senses of the great Quest. Little and less than little it matters how that began which ends at this high point, and for us, therefore, who "needs must love the highest when we see it," we can only bless the beginning which brought the term we find; but its work is done, and it is not a concern of ours.

In our childhood we passed through the realm of fables from Bidpai to Lafontaine, but these were not everlasting dwellings. In our youth there may still have been some of us who looked to see great lights in *L'Origine de tous les Cultes* and in *The Ruins of Empires*, but again there was no abiding place. At this day it seems weariness, as it is indeed idleness, to go back to the solar mythologies, or otherwise than with great caution to folk-lore, when in far different flights we have touched the hem of His garment. I do not propose to include the study of folk-lore in the same category as the imaginings of Dupuis, Volney and Godfrey Higgins; but unless we can pre-suppose a certain enlightenment, it proves a morass sometimes rather than a pathway. However this may be regarded, in establishing a new scheme of interpre-tation, it is perhaps necessary rather than desirable that a beginning should be made by doing justice to old schemes, the office of which is at once recognised and reduced by the entrance of an overlord into his proper patrimony. I wish, therefore, to say that the appeal of scholarship to the derivation of the legends from folk-lore and the anxious collection of fresh data from this source have acted in the past upon several groups of students like the head of Braid's lancet-case on his hypnotic subjects. They are pretexts which have entranced them. There was never an occasion in which folk-lore was more important at the beginning and mattered in finality so little; it is a land of en-chantment, withal somewhat dreary, and through it the unspelling quest passes laboriously to its term.

An old metaphorical maxim of one of the secret sciences once said: "The stone becomes a plant, the plant an animal, and the animal a man"; but it did not counsel its students to consult the stone that it might better understand a man, though the stone re-mains a proper subject of investigation within its own limit. I leave it to readers who are after my own heart and within the classes of my proper school to apply this little parable to the question which is here at issue in respect of the Graal in folk-lore. It remains to be said that one field of Celtic research has been so far neglected by scholarship, and it is that precisely which throws light on the Christian aspects of the Graal legend apart from the aspects of old non-Christian myth. If there are analogies in the root-matter between the Hallows of Cup and Lance and folk-lore talismans, there are others which are far more intimate between the lesser matters of the literature and Celtic Christian hagiology. But this is a point which I note only, because it belongs to the close rather than the beginning of our research. It seems a commonplace to add at the moment that particular Christian tradition has for its environment the general traditions of Christianity, and, for explanatory purposes, that may be best which lies the nearest to hand, but at least it enters reasonably into the full consideration of the whole subject.

Apart from the fixed purpose in the direction which I have specified—that purpose which having exhausted, and this too easily, the available fields of evidence, begins to imagine new—apart from the thousand and one things which, by the hypothesis, would be referable to folk-lore if the wreckage of that world had not been disintegrated so thoroughly by the mills of the centuries, the antecedents of the Graal legend in folk-lore have been a wide field for patient research, nor is that field exhausted ; it has also offered an opportunity for great speculations which go to show that the worlds of enchantment are not worlds which have passed like the Edomite kings; but as I know that there was a king afterwards in Israel, I have concluded at this point to abandon those quests which for myself and those whom I represent are without term or effect, and to hold only to the matter in hand, which is the development of a sacramental and mystical cosmos in literature out of the strange elements which strove one with another, as in the time of chaos so also in pre-Christian Celtic folk-lore.

II

THE WELSH PERCEVAL

This is one of the two texts which have been held to offer independent traces of a pre-Christian and pre-Graal period of the Quest, but in their present state they are among the latest documents of the literature. It is perhaps more difficult to speak of the *Mabinogi* concerning Peredur, the Son of Evrawc, than of anything in the Graal literature; its elements are simple, its dimensions small, but its difficulties seem almost insuperable. The *Red Book of Hergest*, of which it forms one of the stories, is found in a Welsh manuscript which belongs probably to the end of the thirteenth century, but the contents of the collection are held to have existed in a much earlier form, and this is now unknown. The voice of criticism concerning the *Peredur* has become less assured of late years, but in matter and manner the story exhibits some elements which, even to the unversed mind, might suggest its correspondence in essentials with the claim which is made concerning it— or that it is among the oldest of the quests. On the other hand, there is little to support the unimaginative and frigid criticism which, because the plot turns on a conventional and not very purposeful vendetta, terms the narrative logical and straightforward. I have intimated already that it is really confused and disconcerting. It is, indeed, the idlest of all stories, and it leaves several of its episodes unfinished. We can accept, however, the alternative construction which criticism has placed upon the document; it may be either an intermediate between folk-lore and Graal literature, or otherwise a chaotic reflection from French sources. Probably it is a combination of both. The question is very interesting from some points of view, but hereto it matters little. The *Mabinogi* contains in any case the root-matter of the Perceval legend, and it includes, therefore, some part of those elements which were taken over by the Graal literature and were perpetuated through all the Graal-Perceval quests, though some part was abandoned when that quest was carried into transcension. For example, the personal history of the hero has certain uniform elements which persist throughout; the *Peredur* is, moreover, a pure vengeance legend, which characteristic prevails in the *Conte del Graal*, but has been eliminated from the *Longer Prose Perceval*. I should add that the *Didot Perceval* stands apart from the other texts not only by the absence of any vengeance motive, but by the fact that its early history of the hero must be held to differ in totality.

Whether regarded as a sacrament or a talisman, it is understood that there is nothing in the Welsh Perceval which answers to the Holy Graal, but it enters into the category of the literature for three palmary reasons : (1) Because it embodies the idea of a quest; (2) because this quest is connected with asking a conventional question concerning certain talismans; (3) because these talismans are in the house of a king or lord who is maimed and whose healing would have resulted from the question. Outside these specific correspondences, it is obvious that Peredur of Wales is the Perceval le Gallois of the *Conte del Graal* and the other Graal romances, while, all variations notwithstanding, the history of the one, in a broad sense, is also the history of the other. Some important details on these several points may be scheduled as follows: (1) The motive of the Quest does not enter into the story until nearly its very end; (2) the question is never asked; (3) there is no record that the king is ever healed; (4) the one accredited talisman of the whole story does not figure as that weapon which caused the maiming of the story.

It should be noted, however, with due consideration for what has been said to the contrary by criticism, that shadows of the characteristic Graal Hallows are to be found in the story, but they serve no real purpose therein. (*a*) THE CUP: there are, in fact, two cups, both filled with wine and presented with their contents to Perceval, on condition that he fights with their bearers. (*b*) THE BOWL, also filled with wine, and this passes on similar conditions. Perceval slays the bearers, and we shall see that he is afterwards entertained by an Empress for fourteen years. This incident has no analogy with anything in the other documents. (*c*) THE STONE, which is guarded by a serpent and is carried on the tail of the reptile. The virtue of this stone is that whosoever possesses it and holds it in one hand may have in the other as much gold as he desires. The analogy is therefore rather with the purse of Fortunatus than with a Feast of Good Things, but incidentally it recalls the latter. (*d*) THE SPEAR: this is of mighty size, with three streams of blood flowing from its point to the ground. It is the only so-called talisman of the story, and its purpose is to occasion the question which, if answered, will lead to the king's healing. Why it is a spear and why it distils blood the story does not explain. It has either been transferred from some other legend, as, for example, a genuine Graal romance, and placed without much reason in its present setting, or there is no better instance of such an alleged transfer in the whole cycle. The spear is seen once only, and on that occasion is accompanied by a large salver in which is a man's head surrounded with a profusion of blood.

The question which Perceval should have asked was the meaning and the cause of these wonders. He is cursed the next morning by his foster-sister, but it is not because he forbears at the instance of his maternal uncle. It is only after long years that his silence is denounced by a boy disguised as a laidly woman, but at the end of the whole business the question is never asked. Apparently it is too late, and Perceval had only a single chance, as he had in the poem of Heinrich and, after another sense, in the *Longer Prose Perceval*. The penalty of his failure is that "the lame king will have to endure battles and conflicts, and his knights will perish, and wives will be widows, and maidens will be left portionless." It does not appear that any of these disasters come to pass, but certain sorceresses of Gloucester, who caused the king's lameness among other misdeeds, are destroyed, which does not heal the king, so that the vendetta is a vain affair.

The father of Peredur was Evrac, who owned the earldom of the North and had seven sons, with six of whom he was slain, for they began in the folly of tournaments and so ended. Peredur, the surviving and youngest son, was taken by his mother into the wilderness, where he could see neither horses nor arms, lest he also should become a great warrior before the face of the Lord, and die in battle, with all that violence which signified the perfection of valour in those days of harsh adventure. His companions were the women of his mother, with some boys and spiritless men. In spite of such precautions he was destined, however, to depart from the house of his childhood in the wild and solitary ways, where the life which he led was like that of a savage hermit. He was the cutting of a fruit-tree and was sadly in need of grafting: grafted he was in the end on the great tree of Knighthood, yet he behaved throughout with the thoughtlessness of the impassioned man. It is only in the Graal romances that he puts forth many blossoms, and sometimes splendidly, but even then he does not bear the good fruit after its own kind in anything but the latest texts.

One day Peredur saw three knights, but his mother said that they were angels. He decided to become an angel, but the questions which he put to them subsequently having obtained a more reliable account, he resolved further to follow their vocation. Finding that she could not dissuade him, his mother gave him some notable instructions, as, for example, that he should pay court to a fair woman, whether she would or no, and that if he obtained anything precious he should bestow it, and so earn fame for his largesse. In fine, she told him to repair to the court of King Arthur. He mounted a sorry hackney and began a long journey. Arriving at a rich tent, he mistook it for a church and repeated his *Pater noster*, for he had little knowledge of religion; but the tent contained a beautiful lady, who gave him refreshment and allowed him to take a ring from her hand. Now, the lord of the glade became angry because of Peredur, and said that the lady, who was his wife, should not rest two nights in the same house till he had visited vengeance upon him.

As the youth drew towards the court of King Arthur, a Red Knight entered the palace, and seeing how the Queen was served with wine by a page from a golden goblet, he dashed the liquor in her face and smote her on the face also; but, despite his challenge, such was the unknightly condition of the Round Table that all present feared to avenge the insult, believing that the aggressor had magical protection; and so he retired with the vessel. Peredur then rode in, and asked for the honour of knighthood; but because of his outlandish appearance, he was treated with indignity by Kay and others of the household. A male and female dwarf, who had dwelt in the palace for a twelvemonth, uttering no word, found their tongues suddenly to praise him as the flower of chivalry, for which they were beaten by Kay. When Peredur demanded the accolade, he was told jeeringly to follow the Red Knight, recover the goblet, and possess himself of his horse and armour. He found no difficulty in obeying, and by slaying the Knight he accomplished his first mission of vengeance, which contains a more important implicit than the vindication of Arthur's Queen; for, unknown to himself, the Red Knight was he who had slain his father. The removal of the armour he could not accomplish till Sir Owain of the Round Table came to his help, after which he assumed it and mounted the dead man's horse. He restored the goblet to Owain; but to return and receive knighthood at the King's hands he refused until he had punished Kay for the insult which he had offered to the dwarfs. In this manner he began his second mission of vengeance, the implicit whereof involved his own vindication, because he, too, had been treated injuriously. After various encounters, the result of which is that many are sent to place themselves at King Arthur's mercy, on account of the dwarfs, he met with an ancient man, richly vested, whose attendants were fishing on a lake, and who was therefore the substituted Rich Fisher of the Graal stories.

It does not seem to follow that the servants caught anything, but if they did it was not to our purpose. The ancient man was lame, and he is therefore an alternative of the maimed king. He retired into a castle at hand, whither Peredur followed, and being there welcomed he learned that the host was his own uncle. By him he was taught chivalry, was cautioned, for no apparent reason, against asking questions, and was assured that any reproach involved by his silence should not fall on the boy but on himself only. It was as if this uncle said : "Do not explore the concealed mysteries : I will account." He accounts so badly, however, that the disgrace is ultimately on Peredur.

The next day the youth reached another castle, where he found a second uncle, at whose bidding he smote a great staple three times with a sword, and both things were shattered. The first and second time he rejoined the pieces of the sword, and the staple was also made good, as if automatically. The third time neither would unite, and we thus have an alternative of the Broken Sword in the Graal legends ; but nothing follows in the Welsh story, nor is the weapon heard of afterwards. What next occurred at the castle was a Rite as of a Lodge of Mourning. Two youths entered the hall bearing the mighty spear, from which poured torrents of blood, and at the sight of this all the company fell into grievous lamentation. Two maidens followed carrying a large salver, whereon was the man's head; and this, which was swimming in blood, as we have heard, caused another great outcry. Peredur, however, had been well counselled, and he asked nothing concerning these marvels, which fact constitutes the great mystery of the voided question and the prolonged sorrow of the lord. Now, either the two uncles are distinct persons inhabiting two castles, in which case (*a*) the story afterwards identifies them, although vaguely, and (*b*) the relations are working one against the other, unless there was some cryptic understanding between them; or they are one person strangely confused, while the castles are one castle, in which case the lame uncle himself issues that decree of silence which will delay his healing indefinitely and testifies to his separate existence as the brother first seen by his guest. Whatever alternative is chosen, the story rests distracting.

On the morning which followed these occurrences Peredur rode away from the castle, and while still in its vicinity he came upon a beautiful maiden, who was watching by the side of her dead husband. She told the youth that she was his foster-sister, that he was responsible for his mother's death because of his desertion, and that he had therefore become accursed.

We shall see in the sequel that he was under interdict after two manners, but in neither case does it appear to carry a consequence. After this meeting, in which he does everything to assist the distressed lady, and to recognise a relationship for which there is nothing to account in the story, he continued his journey and reached a castle, wherein was another maiden, also in stress and besieged by an earl whom she would not consent to wed. The unwelcome suitor was vanquished by Peredur, who sent him to the court of King Arthur, restored all her possessions to the despoiled lady, and after the space of three weeks again rode away. It should be noted that this maiden is the Blanchefleur of the Perceval-Graal romances, the bride-elect of the hero in some parts of the *Conte del Graal*, his wife in the conclusion of Gerbert, and so also in the *Parsifal* of Wolfram.

The distress of damsels is a lesser keynote of the story, and Peredur met now for a second time the lady of the tent and pavilion, only to find her in sorry straits through her lord's treatment, owing to the intrusion of the youth in the early part of the story. He overcame the knight in due course, enforced the usual pilgrimage, and pledged him to deal loyally with the lady in future, she having been at fault in nothing. In the adventure which next followed, he found that a whole country had been wasted by nine sorceresses of Gloucester, and they were now attacking the sole remaining castle. Over one of them Peredur prevailed, and she—though aware from of old of all that they must suffer at his hands—invited him to their palace. During three weeks he led a hidden life among them for the ostensible purpose of learning chivalry, which he knew already by its practice and otherwise by the instruction of his uncle; it is thus certain that they could teach him little thereof, and of sanctity nothing. The episode remains so unreasonable that almost surely it must have followed some prototype embodying another motive. By this time Peredur had sent so many knights as hostages to Arthur's court, in part to justify the dwarfs, that the king determined to seek for him. The search began accordingly, and after he had taken leave of his imputed instructors, the youth was found by the companions of the Round Table at the moment when he was wrapped in a love-trance, thinking of the lady of his heart. This incident, so trivial in itself, is included here because all the romances repeat it in one or another form. Kay, among others, disturbed Peredur rudely, and was chastised with violence. In this manner was accomplished the second mission of vengeance, or rather its implied part. Gwalchmai, who is Gawain, approached Peredur gently and courteously, and so brought him to the king. All went to Caerleon, and there Peredur, who, by inference from his trance and a certain period of tarrying, may be supposed to have loved previously the lady of the castle, became deeply enamoured of another maiden ; but seeing that she failed to respond, he vowed himself to silence in all Christendom till she should love him above every man. He left King Arthur's court and passed through various adventures, from which little follows in respect of the other romances. The time came when he yearned to revisit Caerleon and again have the maiden's society, besides that of the knighthood. At the court on account of his silence he suffered further indignity, still on the part of Kay ; but after many signal examples of chivalry, the lady of his affections, although she did not recognise him, confessed that if only he could speak, she should love him best of all men, as she did indeed already, his dumbness notwithstanding. So was his vow fulfilled ; and as he had sent many living gifts to the male and female dwarfs, after a votive manner, it is to be inferred that his second vengeance was further and fully accomplished by the disgrace which his deeds reflected upon the unworthy Kay.

At a later period, he being again on his travels, Peredur arrived at a castle, where the lord was a black man who had lost one of his eyes, and it was his custom to destroy every visitor who went to the place unasked. One of the lord's daughters interceded vainly, for he who at the time of need neglected to question his own uncle now demanded an explanation of the circumstances under which his present host had been deprived of his eye. For this he was informed that he should not escape with his life. However, in due course, he conquered the Black Master of the House and slew him, after learning his secret. That secret caused him to visit another castle, the knights in which rode out daily to do battle with an obscure monster, which is termed an Addanc in the story ; their bodies were brought back by the horses, and they themselves were raised up again nightly by the women of the household. Peredur, as will be expected, went forth to destroy the monster and, in return for the pledge of his future love, he was presented by a strange woman with a stone which ensured his success. As regards the covenant between them, he was told when he next sought her to seek in the East—that is to say, in India. Omitting an intermediate episode on which nothing depends, he came to the Mound of Mourning, where three hundred nobles guarded a serpent until the time should come for it to die. The explanation is that the tail of the serpent contained that mysterious stone to which I have referred already—the stone of wealth inexhaustible —and the intent of the whole company was to compete for this jewel. Peredur destroyed the serpent, which they did not dare to attempt, and, having compensated the other seekers, he bestowed the prize on a knight who had been in his service, thus fulfilling one behest of his mother. He next reached a galaxy of tents, gathered about the pavilion of the Empress Cristinobyl, who was resolved to wed the most valiant man in the world, and him only. This was the unknown enchantress by whose aid he was enabled to conquer the Addanc. The place was filled with competitors for her hand, but Peredur overcame them all, and was entertained by the Empress for four-teen years, as the story is said to relate; it is the only appeal to some antecedent source which occurs in the whole text. In this way the hero's variable affections find their rest for a period—by inference, in such a fairy-land as was visited by Ogier the Dane.

Peredur came back at length to the Court of King Arthur, without having attracted apparently any sur-prise at his absence; and, almost immediately after, the palace was visited by a laidly damosel, through whom it transpired what misery followed the failure to ask the question at the Castle of the Lame King. It is to be noted that so only, almost at the end of the story, does the hero learn anything concerning his omission and the fatality which it involved. He was reproached, as we have seen, bitterly by his foster-sister, but not about this matter; and the inference is that so far he had only reason for satisfaction in having followed the counsel of his first uncle—until the time came when he forgot the injunction at the castle of the one-eyed lord. Being now undeceived, he vowed to rest never until he knew the story of the Lance. He departed accordingly, while, at the suggestion of the same visitant, Gawain went in quest of a castle on a high mountain, wherein it is said that there was a certain maid in prison, and the fame of the world was promised to him who released her. This is the only instance, and a shadow at that, in which any quest is allotted to the hero of all gallantry in this story, though his adventures occupy so large a space in other romances of Perceval. We hear nothing, however, as to the term reached by Gawain. Peredur, after long wanderings in search of the laidly maiden, whom he seems to have regarded as a guide, was accosted by a hermit, who upbraided him for bearing arms on so holy a day as Good Friday. Recalled to that sense of religion which he had forgotten apparently, he responded in a becoming manner and received some directions which brought him ultimately to the Castle of Wonders. The first marvel which he saw therein was a chess-board, whereon automatic pieces were playing the game by themselves. The side which he favoured was defeated, and in his anger he cast both board and men into a lake. The laidly maiden appeared thereupon and reproached him. He was set certain tasks, under the pretext of recovering the playthings; they included that adventure of stag and hound with which we shall be concerned later; but the term of all was to bring him for a second time to the castle of his maimed uncle and to the end of his quest. Thither Gawain had preceded him, and in this manner, as in several of the Graal romances, the knight of earthly courtesy is somehow connected with the quest—whether he has undertaken it himself, or by accident, as in this instance.

Peredur found no Lance and he asked no questions, but he was told by a yellow-haired youth, who begged the boon of his friendship since they two were cousins, that it was he who in the far past carried the ensanguined talisman, that he bore also the salver, and at the end of long years of adventure, long years of faerie life, that he appeared as the laidly maiden. As the question had passed into desuetude and, all his vow notwithstanding, as he learned nothing concerning the Lance, it is possible, as I have suggested, that the opportunity of asking and of receiving knowledge was not granted a second time to the seeker. With these things also the head in the dish of blood passed into the limbus of desuetude, like the foster-sister of Peredur and his dubious alternative uncle; no one thought further about them, though the seeker did learn that the head was that of another cousin, who was killed by the sorceresses of Gloucester. It was they also who lamed his uncle, and for this he was to wreak vengeance upon them. Here, therefore, was the third and final vendetta which Peredur accomplished, with the assistance, curiously enough, of Arthur and all his household, by the destruction of the nine priestesses of evil magic. Whether this healed his uncle or relieved the land and the people is not told in the story, nor do we learn anything further concerning the hero, or what, in fine, became of him. Perhaps in the castle of his uncle he completed a third period of hidden life.

I have not entered into the Quest of the Holy Graal for the unsatisfying purpose of reproducing the romances in synopsis, and those more especially which are outside the high issues of my real concern. But in respect of the claims which have been and are still advanced concerning it, as the last reflection of some primordial type of quest, the Welsh Perceval seems to call for presentation adequately, that my readers may understand, firstly, the scope of the points of contact, and, secondly, may thus appreciate the better those greater points of divergence between this text and the true traditional tales of the Holy Vessel. The same motive will occasion the same treatment of the next and more excellent version, which is now posed for our consideration.

III

THE ENGLISH METRICAL ROMANCE OF SYR PERCYVELLE

Among the extrinsic evidences that the Welsh non-Graal quest of Peredur contains the fibrous roots of a legend which was earlier than the Graal period of literature, there is the analogical story of *Syr Percyvelle*, which belongs in its present form to the fifteenth century, being therefore far later than the *Mabinogion*, though there is an Italian story which is even later still. Among the intrinsic evidences are the wild elements which characterise the *Mabinogion* generally of the *Red Book of Hergest*, suggesting an archaic state. I do not know that the last word has been said upon either testimony, but I do know that the *Peredur* is not a Graal story, and if its roots could be traced to Atlantis it would still be nothing to our purpose. When the bells began to ring at the outset. of our great speculation, we said in our hearts: *Sanctus, Sanctus, Sanctus.* We look, therefore, for the elevation of the Graal on our high altar of research, and our password is, *Sanctum Graal.*

There is very little question that this poem is in the position described by scholarship—that is to say, it is a fifteenth-century presentation of a legend which may be far older than any of the Graal quests in which Perceval is the hero. Its elements are simple and primitive. They are much simpler and perhaps far more primitive than are those of the *Welsh Peredur*, while they are less disconcerting and aimless. The poem is in perfect harmony with itself; it has a conclusion proper to its beginning and intervening incidents which so work that the term indicated at the start is brought logically about.

It is the antithesis of any of the Graal romances—there is scarcely any quest at all; secondly, there is no question; there are no hallows of any kind, either Lance or Sword or Cup; finally, there is no enchantment of Britain. It is a savage story—naked and not ashamed; it calls on the kingdom of blood to be manifested about the hero, and he ensures its coming.

The mere skeleton of the poem will exhibit its points of contact with the Welsh Perceval and those of its divergence therefrom. The father of Perceval, who had also the same name, was for his valiant deeds married to the sister of King Arthur. She bore him only the one son, for a great tourney was held to celebrate the birth, and thereat the father was slain by a knight in red armour. As in the previous story, his widow fled into the wilderness, taking the child with her, so that he should know nothing of deeds of arms. He was brought up in the wild wood, with the wild beasts for his companions. However, as the boy grew up the mother gave him a small Scotch spear, and with this he became so dexterous that nothing could escape him. He was clothed in skins, and for a long time seems to have been reared as a heathen; but it came about at length that the lady taught him some prayers to the Son of God, and shortly after he met with three knights of King Arthur's court, one of them being Gawain and another Kay. He inquired which of them was the great God about whom his mother had taught him, and threatened to slay them if they refused to answer. He was told who they were, and then asked whether King Arthur would knight him also. He obtained a sorry horse, took leave of his mother, and rode to court clothed in his skins of beasts, and nourishing a firm resolution to slay the king if he would not grant his request. At parting the mother gave him a ring to be kept as a token, and she promised that she would await his return. On his road he reached a pavilion wherein was a lady asleep. He kissed her and exchanged a certain ring which she wore for the one that had been given to himself. He arrived at the court of all chivalry, and King Arthur recognised the boy's likeness to that older Perceval who had received his own sister as wife. The king, however, and apparently the whole chivalry had been reduced to recurring distress through fear of the Red Knight, who came regularly to rob the king of the cup out of which he was drinking. Perceval's arrival was coincident with another visitation of this kind, being the fifth during as many years. The Cup was of red gold, and it was seized while the king was in the act of putting it to his lips. Perceval, who was a witness, offered to bring back the vessel if the king would knight him, and the king promised to do so on his return. He went to fetch armour for the child, but Perceval in the meantime departed. The Red Knight did not wish to do battle with so sorry an opponent, but in the end there was a momentary combat, Perceval slaying the champion by throwing his dart, which passed through one of his eyes. For what it is worth, we have here an instance of that vengeance legend of which folk-lore traces examples in the Graal literature. It is true that Perceval slays the Red Knight, but, as in the *Welsh Peredur*, he does so without knowing that his victim was responsible for his father's death ; his sole and simple object is to wipe out the affront offered to the king. After the encounter Perceval, with the assistance of Gawain, who had followed and come upon the scene, stripped the body of the armour, and the youth was clothed therein. He did not return to claim the promised reward of knighthood, and Gawain was the bearer of the Cup to the king. His next office was to destroy a witch who was the mother of the Red Knight, and on account of his armour he was taken then and subsequently for that personage himself. He arrived at a castle, to which there came presently from the Maiden Land a messenger who was on his way to King Arthur entreating assistance for his mistress, the Lady Lufamour. She was being oppressed by a sultan who desired her for his wife, and because of her refusal he had slain her father and brother and had wasted her lands, so that she had only one castle left in which to take refuge. To this castle Perceval asked the way of the messenger, with the intention of destroying the Saracen, but the messenger preferred to continue his own road and get help from the king. Perceval, on his part, determined to discover it for himself, and the three sons of his host insisted on accompanying him, which they did for a certain distance, after which he contrived to shake them off. Meanwhile the messenger reached the court and had a very indifferent answer from the king, who, together with his knights, appears in rather a pitiful light throughout all the early portion of the story. The king, in fact, tells him that there is no lord in his land who is worthy to be called a knight. However, on hearing of the description of the chivalrous youth who was seen by the messenger from the castle on his road to court, the king concluded that this was Perceval, and called for horses, arms and companions of his table to follow in quest of the hero, fearing that he might be slain before they could reach him. By this time Perceval had arrived at the Maiden Land, and found a host of tents marshalled about a city. He set to and slew many, his ingenuous warcry being apparently that he had come to destroy a soldan. He slept in the open field, with his dead round him. The Lady Lufamour came to survey the slaughter from the height of her walls, and descried the knight whom she supposed to have effected it. She sent her chamberlain to bring him into the city; therein she made him good cheer, and fell in love at first sight. He returned to do battle in her cause, she promising herself and the kingdom if he destroyed the soldan. He behaved in a manner which recalls the worst combats in the Spanish romances of chivalry, wherein one knight scatters a thousand paynims. Meanwhile, King Arthur and his companions arrived, but were mistaken by Perceval for enemies, and he fought with Gawain. However, ultimately they recognised each other and embraced. All proceeded to the castle, and Arthur recounted to the lady the early history of Perceval. The next morning he was knighted by the king, and again went forth against the soldan, whom he slew finally. He was made king of the country, and wedded Lufamour. He was still in the first year of his marriage when he remembered his mother, and rode away to find her. This is the quest of the story, and on the way he had to champion the lady of the pavilion, who had fallen into the hands of her husband for the business of the ring. He reconciled them *vi et armis*, and learned that the ring which he had borrowed had such virtues that the wearer could be neither slain nor wounded. He proposed to exchange again, but the husband had given that which was Perceval's to the lord of the land, a giant of whom none would dare to ask it : he was, indeed, the brother of the soldan, but there is no need to say that Perceval in due course not only defeated but dismembered him. He recovered his ring at the giant's castle, and learned from the seneschal that his master had offered it to a lady whom he besought in marriage ; that she recognised it as her son's ring, and, supposing that he had been slain by the giant, she fled distracted into the forest hard by. Perceval was now close on the track of his quest-object ; he assumed a garment of skins, that she might know him the more easily ; and it was not long before the mother and son met and were henceforth reunited. They repaired to the giant's castle, till the lady was restored to health and sanity. In fine, he carried her home, where she was welcomed by his queen and the great lords. This was the good end of Perceval's mother, and in this way the story describes its perfect circle. The end of Perceval himself was in the Holy Land.

IV

THE CONTE DEL GRAAL

§ *A.*—PRELIMINARY TO THE WHOLE SUBJECT

The elements of Robert de Borron's poem are those of the apocryphal gospel rather than of the romance, as we now understand that term. I do not wish to be construed too expressly, as I am simply creating a comparison or instituting a tolerable approximation. In the *Conte del Graal* of Chrétien de Troyes and the group of poets who continued what his zeal had begun, we enter into a different atmosphere from that of the two texts with which we have been concerned previously, and yet it has analogies therewith. As a whole, it is the sharpest possible contradistinction to the hypothetical non-Graal quest; but in its first part, being that which was furnished by Chrétien, it represents more especially the transition from the folk-tale to the true Graal romance, and it offers in itself a certain typical specimen of the developing process. There is therefore little which distinguishes especially and signally this branch from the old tale of Peredur, as we can conceive it in its original form; there is a great deal by which several parts of Manessier's conclusion are distinguished from both, and still more the alternative rendering of Gerbert. Between all of them and the *Quest of Galahad* it is understood, this notwithstanding, that the deep abyss intervenes. The elements of Chrétien's poem are perhaps the most natural born that it has entered into the heart to conceive. The narrative is beautiful, or perhaps I should say that it is charming, after the manner of Nature; it is like a morning in spring. It has something more than the touch of Nature which takes us at once into its kinship; it seems actually Nature speaking; and so much of the Graal Mystery as can be said to enter within its dimensions is that Mystery expressed in the terms of the outside world, though still bearing a suggestion of translation direct from a strange and almost unknown tongue. The poem, taken as a whole, has few symbolic elements, and they are so entirely of the natural sacraments that it is difficult to recognise one touch of grace therein. Again, I except from this description what is termed the interpolation of Gerbert, which in comparison with the rest is like a Masonic tracing-board lecture compared with an essay of Goldsmith. This analogy is instituted expressly to show that in the widest construction Gerbert is also far from the goal.

Well, the *Conte* is a product of successive generations, but this granted it is the work of a single epoch. If it be approached simply from the poetic standpoint, there is no doubt much to repay the reader, if he be not deterred by the difficulties of extremely archaic French verse. But of the *odor suavitatis* of the sanctuary, of that which criticism has agreed to describe as the ascetic and mystic element, of that element which I and those whom I represent desire and look for, there is so little that it can barely be said to exist. Many who know and appreciate the sacramental mystery which attaches in certain parts to the Graal Quest in Malory and to the *Longer Prose Perceval*, which has been termed *The High History of the Holy Graal*, by Dr. Evans, its translator, will appreciate exactly this contrast, and will understand that in Chrétien de Troyes there is little of the secret once delivered to the saints of any sanctuary, though he made use of materials which may have carried this suggestion with them. He is described by his one editor as the poet of love, and as the poet who created the poetry of sentiment. He is fresh, natural, singularly direct, and he carried his intention very plainly on the surface in respect of his presentation of the story, so far as he is known to have taken it. To put it briefly, anything that is recondite in its significance is that which is typical of the entire cycle, while that which is obvious is of the poet.

The *Conte del Graal* was begun, approximately speaking, about the third quarter of the twelfth century, and this metrical romance is the longest of the whole cycle, unless we elect to include the compilation which passes under the name of the Dutch *Lancelot*. It is the work of several hands, first among whom, both as to time and merit, is Chrétien de Troyes. He derived his materials from a source which is no longer extant, and is responsible for something less than one-eighth of the entire medley, unless, indeed, his editor, M. C. Potvin, is correct in his opinion that certain preliminary and certain subsequent matter, now regarded as later, should be included in his work. But this, I believe, is rejected with no uncertain voice by all later criticism.

Speaking generally of those quests of the Holy Graal into which we are here entering by a kind of anticipation, in order to dispose of one which offers too little to our purpose, it is not very difficult to follow the mind of romance in its choice one after another of several heroes, though these are exclusive of each other. In a subject of this kind, I care little for antecedents in folk-lore as such, and many speculative constructions of scholarship may also be set aside reverently. It does not appear, for example, by the texts themselves that Sir Gawain was at any time the typical hero of the quest, not even in the mind of Chrétien, though I have said that he was after the manner born of Nature in his general treatment of the theme. There are two heroes only, whether typical or otherwise, and these are Perceval and Galahad, but among these Perceval is neither the ideal questing Knight nor one who can be called possible until he has undergone the transmuting process of the later texts. Perhaps at the highest he represents the spirit of romance when it was tinctured only in part by sacramental mystery; Galahad represents that spirit when it has undergone the complete change. From this point of view, we may say that there are three epochs of the Quest in Northern France :—

The Early Epochs of the Quest

(*a*) The epoch of Chrétien, all continuations included, and of the *Didot Perceval* considered as a derivative of Robert de Borron, one of growth and development after its own manner.

(*b*) The epoch of the *Longer Prose Perceval*, deriving from the putative Walter Map and the later Merlin romances.

(*c*) The epoch of the *Great Prose Lancelot* and the *Quest of Galahad.*

It is understood that I am using the term epoch to characterise a condition of mind rather than one of time, and, secondly, that the German cycle of the Holy Graal remains over for consideration. It should be observed in the first epoch that Chrétien and Gautier are the only French writers who tolerate the notion of an alternative Graal hero in the person of Gawain. In the second epoch there is Perceval shining in the kind of light which is native only to Galahad, for the visit which is paid by Gawain to the Graal Castle is not a part of the Quest but a pure matter of chance, and he is reflected in a high mirror of idealism. In the third epoch we have the Quest in its final exaltation, and there are many heroes, each of whom is dealt with according to his merits, with Galahad as the Morning Star among all the lesser lights. Gawain " died as he had lived, in arms " and spiritual inhibition. It is in the *Conte del Graal*, the *Longer Prose Perceval* and in more than one dubious text of the German cycle that he is represented as an intentional Graal quester. It is true that he proposes the experiment in the prose *Galahad*, but he takes none of the instituted precautions, and he abandons it easily and early. Those who imputed a certain righteousness to Nature allowed him some qualified success within the measure of their capacity, but it came about that the mystic mood intervened and, having found that Nature was of no effect, the Quest was transferred thenceforward into the world of mystery.

§ *B.*—The Poem of Chrétien de Troyes

By our previous considerations we have ascertained that after certain preliminary matters which are curious, but late in comparison and dubious, the *Conte del Graal* was opened in ample form by a master-singer of his period —that is to say, by Chrétien de Troyes. Now, if it be agreed that the *Peredur* and *Syr Percyvelle* are reflections of a lost primordial quest, it is desirable to note that they offer nothing concerning the feast of good things and the Bowl of Plenty. How, therefore, from the standpoint of scholarship, did this element, confessedly foreign thereto, in the beginning of things, come to be imported therein? There is no trace of it, as we have seen, in the long section of that great poem which is now set for our consideration, though it is supposed to have heralded and inaugurated everything which belongs to the seeking part of the Graal literature. It was not evidently from this source in folk-lore that Chrétien derived his knowledge of that mysterious object which he calls a Graal and from which was diffused so great a light, though nowhere in his long contribution does he term it the Holy Graal. It was carried by the maid who had charge of it in her two hands, from which it may follow either that it was a heavy object, as might be a large dish, or something exceedingly sacred—to be exalted with reverence—as it might be, an Eucharistic Chalice or a most holy Reliquary. That it was not certainly the first of these objects is made evident by the fact that a Dish was carried separately in the pageant at the Graal Castle. We know further from the brief description that it was a jewelled vessel :—

> " Pières pressieuses avoit
>   El graal, de maintes manières,
>   Des plus rices et des plus cières
>   Qui el mont u en tière soient ;
>   Tote autre pières pasoient
>   Celes dou grèal, sans dotance."

That it connects with the second or the third in my enumeration of possible objects is shown at a much later stage
to Perceval in the narrative of his uncle the hermit, who
tells how some hidden King of the Graal is sustained and
comforted by a Sacred Host therein. Whencesoever the
German poet Heinrich drew his materials, it is obvious
that he and Chrétien speak of the same vessel and, as I
have shown otherwise, rather of a *ciborium* than a Reliquary. The essence of a Reliquary is that it should
contain an invariable sacred deposit, as, for example, the
Precious Blood of our Saviour or the liquefying blood of
St. Januarius. We are therefore at once in the region of
great sacramental wonders. The legends of sanctity had
already in far other texts borne witness to those cases in
which the supersensual Bread of Life had served for the
saints as their only daily nourishment. This is therefore
the manner in which Chrétien de Troyes understood—
had he indeed heard of them—the feeding properties of
the Graal. It follows—and we shall see duly—that
three poets—Wolfram, Heinrich and Chrétien—who are
at the poles sometimes in variance over matters of symbolism, do yet, in the most important of all their concerns, tell the same story. And we who know better
than they could have ever known all that is involved in
the root-matter of their testimony, can say in our hearts,
even when we hear these dim echoes which are far from
the term of the Quest :—

> " Tu qui cuncta scis et vales,
>   Qui nos pascis hic mortales,
>   Tuos ibi commensales,
>   Cohæredes et sodales
>   Fac sanctorum civium."

We have no doubt as to the service or the table, and can
bear witness on our own part that " many men, both of
high and low condition in these last years past," have to
our knowledge seen the mystery of all sacredness and
sweetness unveiled before their spiritual eyes. It follows
that if there were many antecedents, the Graal is still one,

and that even at the epoch of Chrétien the true nature of the Sacred Vessel was known, and that clearly. Of himself the poet knew nothing, but in some book which he followed there must have been strange materials. One of the keynotes may be—among many others—that Hugh, Bishop of Lincoln, investigated about 1140 a case of miraculous sustenance by the Eucharist.

As regards the source of his story the poet himself gives us an exceedingly simple explanation. He says that he wrote by command of a certain Count—that is to say, Count Philip of Flanders. The order was:—

> " À rimoir le mellor conte
>   Qui soit contés en court roial."

The materials were written materials, namely, *li contes del Gréal*, as to which *li Quens li bailla le livre*. Such was the source of the earliest Quest-matter; and the earliest extant History-matter depends also from a great book, wherein great clerks wrote " the great secrets which are called the Graal " :—

> " Ge n'ose conter ne retreire,
>   Ne ge ne le pourroie feire,
>   Neis, se je feire le voloie,
>   Se je le grant livre n'avoie
>   Où les estoires sunt escrites,
>   Par les granz clers feites et dites :
>   La sunt li grant secré escrit
>   Qu'en nvmme le Graal et dit."

Whereas therefore his patron communicated to Chrétien, it was Robert de Borron who communicated to Walter Montbéliard, in whose service he was. We see in this manner that the first poet of the *Conte del Graal* depended on antecedent authority which was not of the oral kind; by one stage the question of source raised here has been moved back, and there must be left for the present.

We saw in the Welsh Perceval that there was a sword which broke and was rejoined, but in the stress of the last trial it was shattered beyond recovery. The episode in Chrétien which corresponds hereto is represented sufficiently for my purpose by the details already given when considering the Hallows of the Legend. I may add only that while certain codices make no attempt to account for the return of the Broken Sword to the Graal Castle, there are others which illustrate the foreknowledge of the king by his despatch of a messenger to follow Perceval in his travels till the mischance of the promised peril overtakes him. In yet others the fragments of the mystic weapon seem to have been spirited away. It will be seen that in the Welsh Perceval there is nothing to connect the maiming of the Lord of the Castle with the gigantic Lance which is carried about therein. The connection remains naturally a reasonable inference, but we cannot tell. The Sword certainly serves no purpose but that of a trial of strength. In Chrétien it appears, on the other hand, almost as a part of the plot, and the scheme is carried out by the sequels in accordance with so much as may be called manifest in the intention of the first poet.

Turning from the Hallows of the story, it so happens that it is after the manner of Chrétien to furnish his most important elucidations with the least suggestion of intention. I have spoken of the mystery of that Chamber wherein the Graal enters or re-enters after its manifestation in the pageant, or into which alternatively the dove flies in one Quest of the Greater Chronicles, before the Sacred Vessel is displayed. It is Chrétien only who discloses the secret of the hidden place, or at least manifests up to what point he understands it himself, when he says of the king, whom I interpret as sometime king of the Graal :—

> " . xx . ans i a estet ensi.
> Que fors de la cambre n'issi
> Û le Gréal véis entrer."

It was the bedchamber of that Warden of the Hallows who was far more concealed than he who is called or miscalled the Rich Fisher in the same text. The further question which arises for our consideration concerns, therefore, this nameless being who is the father of the king in evidence. The allusions to him are so brief and so vague that those who continued the story thought it best to ignore them, though I hold it as certain that Gautier had the elements of an explanation in his hands. Without forestalling what there is to say on this point in the next sub-section, I will refer back to an earlier part of our inquiry, when it was noted that the quest in Chrétien presupposes an early history and—notwithstanding certain confusions, as, for example, regarding the origin of the title King Fisherman—that this history may have corresponded, in respect of its essence, to the first draft of the metrical romance by Robert de Borron, or alternatively to the source from which the latter drew, and in which it may be hazarded that there seem to have been several histories. It is too early to speculate whether the texts which had come into the possession of the pious minstrel included the single story which the Count of Flanders placed in the hands of Chrétien, but there must have been a general prototype. Apart from the *Longer Prose Perceval*, which is extra-lineal in most details of its tradition, there are three persons connected immediately with the Graal in the various quests. In the *Parsifal of Wolfram* there are (*a*) Titurel—precisely in the position of the mysterious king in Chrétien, and like him abdicated; (*b*) the reigning king Amfortas, who is fed by the Graal; and (*c*) Parsifal, the king who is to come. In the quest of Galahad there are (*a*) the maimed king, Pellehan; (*b*) the reigning king, Pelles; and (*c*) Galahad, the king who is to come. In the *Didot Perceval* there are (*a*) Brons, who is sick of the centuries, but still the Graal king; (*b*) his son Alain, but in this case he dies, without it being possible for us to assign his special place in the mystery; and (*c*) Perceval, as a coming king who is in the warfare of his training. Now, this notion of a triple guardianship was first put forward in the romance of De Borron, and is evidently one of the root-ideas of the historical branches; and if in a certain sense it is broken in the *Book of the Holy Graal* to establish some phantom of a chronological succession, the Quest which follows therefrom recurs, as we see, thereto. I should add that the Royal Family of the Holy Graal—in the story of Chrétien and its sequels—has no names in the canonical texts till Perceval comes into his own, but there is a variant or interpolation in a Berne manuscript which follows the keepership in De Borron.

Separating from the poem of Chrétien not merely the prologue, which is by another hand, but an introductory part which is also of uncertain authorship, while it has elements in rather close correspondence with the Welsh *Mabinogi* of Peredur, and adhering to the more authentic poem itself, there is a diversity of the circumstances under which Perceval was born whereby it is set apart from the Welsh story and from the English poem. In the introduction there are variants from these, but they are matters of detail. According to Chrétien, it is the maiming of Perceval's father which takes the family into the woods. Perceval is the youngest of three sons, and the time comes for the others to be sent into the world. They are commissioned to the courts of two kings, where they are both knighted on the same day, and, though widely separated, both are also slain. It is this misfortune which causes the death of the father and the desire on the mother's part to isolate her remaining boy from all knowledge of chivalry. While the result is a certain inexperience, he does not seem so savage or untrained as in the texts which we have considered previously, and the surroundings of his father's house are those of a knight who has retired to a country estate on account of his health. Seeing that there is nothing so little to my purpose as to be at any unnecessary pains regarding the conventional story part of successive texts, I shall deal very shortly with points of minor variation in the life and adventures of the hero, and as regards the major episodes, they may be thus recited in summary:—The adventure of the Pavilion; the initial visit to the Court of King Arthur; the struggle with the Red Knight; the sojourn with an instructor in chivalry; the liberation of that Lady of the Castle who is here named Blanchefleur; the first visit to the House of the Graal; the meeting with Perceval's kins-woman afterwards; the exoneration of the Lady of the Pavilion; the search of the King and his knights after the hero whom they had once rejected almost; the love-trance; the denunciation of Perceval by the laidly damosel; his godless wanderings; the episode of Good Friday; the renewal of grace which he receives at the hands of a hermit, who—in this case—is his uncle: all these follow in due order, and though it is not throughout the exact order which we find in the Welsh *Mabinogi*, that text remains the artificial prototype representing the early narrative portion, and to this Chrétien has added the Holy Graal as his ostensible motive in chief. The first sojourn of Perceval at the Graal Castle takes place in the absence of any design on the part of the hero; he is not, in other words, on the Quest of the Sacred Vessel and he knew nothing about it. When he has liberated Blanchefleur from her thraldom in the castle of Beau-repaire, his avowed quest is that which will bring him to his mother, but when he has found her he will return to the maiden, will marry her and share her rule. The other maiden who reproaches him for his failure immediately after his departure from the Graal Castle is his cousin-german instead of his foster-sister, and in addition to his responsibility in respect of his mother's death, she denounces him for not asking the redeeming questions concerning the Vessel and the Lance. In this manner the subsequent reproaches of the laidly damosel at the Court of King Arthur—which is in camp on the quest of Perceval, and not at Caerleon—concern a twice-told tale. The adventures of Perceval are carried by Chrétien as far as his visit to that uncle who has em-braced the life of a hermit.

§ C.—The Extension of Gautier

It is certain that the poet who took up the thread of the story which was left by Chrétien had antecedent texts to go upon outside the work of his predecessor, and that one at least of these is not to be identified with purely folk-lore materials. It is considered that the metrical romance of De Borron was not one of his documents, and on the hypothesis—or perhaps I should say on the theory—of a primordial non-Graal Quest—as reflected into the Welsh *Mabinogi* and the English *Syr Percyvelle* —it would follow that he had seen this. Now, there are traces in the *Mabinogi* of an intention which might have led up to the marriage of Perceval and Blanchefleur, if his enchantment by the empress had not extended over a period which put such a possibility out of the question. In the English metrical story the marriage is a natural conclusion, and we have seen that it takes place accordingly. In Chrétien there are the same traces, and they reappear more strongly in Gautier, but the term of his intention is unmanifest because he failed to conclude. The common consent of scholarship would hold probably that the prototype of both poets celebrated a bridal at its end. It contained also the widely diffused story of the maiden and the hound, or *brachet*, which I have held over from the Welsh story to speak of in this place. Finally, in some form it had the curious episode of the chess-board. But, fully developed as they are in the long extension of Gautier, these things are of his accidents only, while of the essence is his zeal of the Graal Quest, which overrules all things else in his ingarnering of diverse memorials. Of that quest he has practically two heroes, and though a superior success attends the search of Perceval the adventures of his alternate Gawain are recounted at still greater length. This latter part, taken over from the first poet of the *Conte*, at once so extended and so important in its Graal elements, is postponed for consideration separately, registering here the bare fact only that in the section of Gautier and in the *additamenta* thereto belonging, Gawain appears most expressly as one of the heroes connected with the vision of the Holy Vessel. Of their comparative merits there need be no question, as the grace of sanctity had not entered into the heart of the poet who began or of him who extended the Graal story. The Sacred Vessel was *glorieus* and the Sacred Vessel was *sains*, but the election thereto was that of the best Knight in the world, or his nearest co-heritor in chivalry, and not of him who was resplendent in the arms of spiritual achievement. Gawain was therefore, in this sense, scarcely less eligible than Perceval, and the ground of his comparative failure was either an implied incapacity from the fact that he was not of the Keepership lineage or that for some reason it had been decided to regard Perceval as the more elect hero among two exotic flowers of Knighthood.

Of Perceval himself, however, who for the purpose of introducing Gawain had been left far behind in the narrative of Chrétien, we hear no single word till nearly half the work has been accomplished by Gautier. His story is then resumed at the point when the hero has departed from the hermitage of that uncle who has brought him into a tolerable state of repentance, purging him by the offices of the Church, and has communicated, as if it were in secret Mass or sacred Eucharist, the first mysteries of the Graal. Perceval had been denounced previously for the omission which he had almost covenanted to make, and no hope had been extended that he should yet act as repairer in fine, so that from initial point to term, as he could then perceive it, some blind and implacable fatality appeared to have been at work alone. Now, on the other hand, and if not all too plainly, it looked as if there followed by inference that a high hope of achievement was held out to him by his uncle's words; he resolved therefore that he would not return to King

Arthur's court till he had revisited the Fisher King's Castle and inquired concerning the Graal. But all without that secret fastness was not only beset by perils and hard encounters, but it turned in a glass of strange vision and great deception. Once more, I am not concerned in summarising the story to take in all its details, because, as usual, several of its episodes are idle and extrinsic in respect of our proper purpose. The Castle of all Desire moved near or far upon the confused horizon of adventure, and at a certain point Perceval reached a river, beyond which he was assured that the bourne rose up grandly, in a rich and peopled land; but he could find no means of crossing. The day passed from noon to vespers, and still on the further side he came to a vacant palace, beautiful exceedingly in situation, *moult bien séant*, but now standing drearily in ruins. There he found a maiden who was prepared to show him a place of crossing and mounted her mule for the purpose, but her intention was only to drown him. Unless we can connect this incident with something which will follow presently, I find nothing therein except an unmeaning hindrance, and the same may be said of an episode which occurs hereabouts in certain manuscripts, being the meeting between Perceval and a huntsman who reproached him for the fatality of the unasked question at the Graal Castle. It shows only that the rumour of the ill-starred visit had gone about the district, which was acquainted otherwise, and too well, with the sorrows of the Holy House and their effects beyond the precincts. As regards the maiden and the mule, I would note further that in the *Conte del Graal* there is a curse on Logres which occupies a middle term between times of adventure and times of enchantment, and one inference may be that Perceval had fallen into the hands of a water-fairy, belonging to the kelpie type, as the malice of an earthly maiden could be assumed scarcely in connection with such a meeting between complete strangers; or—that which is still more probable—the brief occurrence may be due only to the sporadic invention of the writer. In any case, the Knight, having been better counselled, learned of a ford, and so entered presumably on the direct road which led, by the hypothesis, to the desired House of Great Hallows. Yet he was still far from his term, and many adventures in the vicinity intervened without him reaching the goal. First among these was a visit to another deserted castle—such desolation being perhaps a part of the curse—and therein he found the chess-board of which we have heard something in the metamorphoses and adventures of the Welsh *Peredur.* Here it was no hideous damosel who came in to upbraid him, but a maid of great beauty, who rose from the midst of the lake into which Perceval had proposed to cast the board and pieces. The fact that she held his hands substituted another quest for that of their recovery in the alternative story. A white stag ranged in the park of the castle, and if the knight would receive those favours which her beauty led him to demand he must bring her the head of this animal, to facilitate which she lent him a hound with express injunctions to return it. I do not propose to follow the adventures which arise out of this undertaking. The favours involved by the covenant had unhappily been granted to Perceval in the case of Blanchefleur, though not perhaps when her distress, at their first meeting, had brought her to his bedside, and into his arms afterwards, through the whole night. Her true love was to follow her liberation by him from the violence of an undesired suitor. But it was granted indubitably in the plenary sense when he reached her castle unexpectedly for the second time. Still it was under circumstances which do not occur commonly in romances of chivalry unless the consummation of marriage is intended at the close of all. That she was a bride elect is clear beyond all in the poem, and in yielding, it was to her husband that she yielded only, which makes one later episode in Perceval's story the more iniquitous for this reason. That Perceval was self-devoted to

Blanchefleur follows from the episode of the love-trance, but his inclinations are variable in the *Conte*, as they are in the Welsh story; for the love of the Lady of the Chess-board he goes through long-enduring quests which so end that at length he attains his desires. In all this there are only two points that concern us—firstly, that the attainment involves the desertion of Blanchefleur under circumstances that for the knight are disgraceful; and, secondly, that the prolongation of the adventures which follow the slaying of the stag are due to the daughter of the Fisher King, or at least in part, and are designed to punish Perceval for not having asked the question.

I have said that the locality of the Graal Castle is as if it were a place in flux; there is nothing in the opening of the story to lend colour to the supposition that the Sacred Vessel and the Mystery and the House of these were close to the manorial residence and rural retreat wherein Perceval passed his childhood; hence it is doubtless by reason that the Castle was here to-day and gone to-morrow that they are brought suddenly into comparative proximity. Perceval was still in the course of his stag adventures and still seeking the prize which was to follow their completion; still also he was hearing casually concerning the Graal, or at least was in occasional speculation regarding its whereabouts; when he found himself, without expectation and without intention, at the door of his old home, for the first time only in ten years. There he entered, there he tarried but too briefly, and there he met with his sister—of whom Chrétien knows nothing, even as Gautier elects to ignore entirely the cousin-german of the earlier poet. He seems, however, to have been following some earlier stage of the legend, to which the *Longer Prose Perceval* and the Great Quest also conform, and in that last and glorious text the personality of the sister is exalted to a high grade of sanctity, of which we find nothing but the first traces—for the first traces are present—in the account of Gautier.

Herein she is a spirit of recollection and a meditative recluse—

> " Une moult très cointe pucièle,
> Blanc com flours en may novele."

But she is clothed richly withal and encompassed by a fair retinue, so living sad and unfriended in the woodland, lamenting the loss of her brother, of whose fate she had heard nothing. When Perceval declared himself there was great joy between them, and of her he learned the particulars of their mother's death, through the love and the loss of him. Together they visited a hermit uncle who is not to be identified with the former, being on the father's side ; to him Perceval made his confession—though of all prayers he knew only the *Pater noster*—heard at his celebration a Mass of the Holy Ghost, knelt at the tomb of their mother, and of his uncle prayed piteously that he might learn concerning the Graal and the other Hallows. But his uncle would tell him nothing at that time, though he gave him high instruction regarding holy mysteries of religion. That the heart of Perceval was not reached, his reverence notwithstanding, was too soon made evident by the fact that he bequeathed his sister to renewed isolation, with a mere promise to return which is never fulfilled, and soon or some time afterwards he was in a position—as we shall see—to claim and receive his dues from the Lady of the Chess-board.

Neither sin of concupiscence nor sin of desertion have disqualified him for the Quest of the Graal in the opinion of Gautier, and he was still less or more on that Quest when he came to a Castle of Maidens, who were reputed to have raised the beautiful edifice with their own hands—

> "Ains le fisent . IIII . pucièles,
> Moult avenans et moult très bièles."

Of these things he heard the story, though he was weary and looked rather for rest. So was he delivered to his slumber, but the place was all work of faerie, and he reposed in enchantment that night. Faerie houses are, however, like faerie gold—dead leaves and dry in the morning, or mere shadow and rainbow semblance which dissolve in the eastern light. So Perceval woke in a meadow with an oak murmuring above him. From all this there follows nothing, but it is designed that the next adventure should take him a further step in the direction of his term. It seems that in the neighbourhood of the Graal Castle there was always a river to cross, and as on the first occasion he met with a lady and a mule from whom followed his destruction almost, so now there was another maiden with a similar beast in her charge, thus creating a kind of equilibrium between false and true assistance. The story is very long, and much of it is outside the object, but it may be reduced under three heads : (1) Perceval was riding with the lady, whom he lost at night in the forest. Alone and so lost, he beheld a great light —very clear and very resplendent—but it was followed by tempest. (2) In the morning he recovered the damosel, who said that it was the light of the Graal, which the Rich King Fisher was accustomed to carry in the forest, so that no infernal temptation should have power over him. In the *Conte* therefore, as in the *Quest of Galahad*, the Graal goes about, but it is not for the same reason. (3) The maiden described the Vessel as that which contained the glorious blood of the King of Kings which was received therein as He hung upon the cross. This is rather the account of the *Vulgate Merlin* than of Robert de Borron, but the distinction is one of detail, and it follows that the Early History which was known to Gautier was that of a relic of the Passion. (4) More than this the lady would not reveal, because it was a thing too secret for dame or damosel to recount; it was also a tale of terror, though a man of holy life might express the marvels. (5) That which she could do she would do, however—namely, lend him her white mule—the beast which another romance declares to be on God's

side—and she would lend him also her ring, by which
the mule was governed. Thus assisted, he would be able
to cross a certain bridge of glass, from which he might
travel direct to the King's Castle. Thereafter the mule
would return of itself. He was not all the same destined
to continue the journey far beyond the waterside. He
was riding the mule, and leading his horse by the bridle,
when he encountered a knight who gave him news of a
tourney about to be held by King Arthur, and—ignoring
his original resolve—he turned aside from the straight
path to attend it. The digression delayed his achievement, but it left him the best knight of the world, and
this was a condition of the achievement. It did not,
however, meet the views of the damosel who was owner
of the mule and the ring, for she reappeared and demanded their return, on ascertaining that his Quest was
not achieved. They were both delivered, and thereafter
—without salutation or farewell—he was left to shift as
he might on the way, now all unknown, to the Holy
House. It was at this time, as if once more without
God in the world, that his road took him to the Castle
of the Chess-board, for during all these scenes and times
he had carried the stag's head and the dog of the damosel.
The term of this foolish business should have increased
the difficulties of his Quest, but—on the contrary—the
lady was to a certain extent his conductress in place of
the maiden of the mule, for she it was who took him
again to the waterside and to a great boat there at hand
which carried him—horse and all—to the opposite shore,
beyond which stretched that broad way which led to the
Court of King Fisher.

The subsequent occurrences are all intended to connect
intimately with his arrival thereat and with the Rite of
Questioning which is his prime object, but we shall see
in their later understanding that they are fantastic rather
than important, which also appears on their surface.
He found a child of apparently five years old, clothed
in rich vestments and seated on a branch of a tree

higher than any lance could reach. Of him Perceval, now full of his mission, inquired concerning the Fisher King but was told only that if he would learn news which might prove good and pleasant he must go to the Mount Dolorous, after which the speaker put a period to further questioning by ascending higher in the tree and thence vanishing. Perceval reached the mountain and met with a maid coming down on a palfrey who counselled him against the adventure, but he began the ascent and at the summit found fifteen crosses, of which five were white, five red and five blue. These encircled a pillar, to which he must fasten his steed. To fail was to lose reason. The achievement seems childish, but it was a proof of valour devised of old by Merlin in order that the flower of chivalry should alone serve King Arthur, and the maid who told this story was Merlin's daughter, of whom we find nothing otherwise in the canonical romances of the Graal. Seeing that very few knights of the Round Table ever heard of Mount Dolorous and much less of the testing, the account seems an idle invention, but it is regarded as important for early Arthurian history. Perceval being still on his journey, at the conclusion of this adventure, came next to a great tree which was illuminated by innumerable candles, like a high altar at the exposition of the Most Holy Sacrament. It was the spectacle of a moment only, for the lights vanished on his approach, and he found himself at a wonderful chapel, where a dead knight lay in repose on the altar and a black hand, appearing behind the altar, extinguished one great light thereon. The significance of these things appears in the sequel and does not signify especially. In fine, Perceval arrived at the Graal Castle, wherein he found the King and told him of his latest adventures, namely, those on his way to the Castle. The Hallows appeared, and for the first time in the poem the expression *Saint Greal* is used in connection with the actual vision of the object. When the procession had passed and repassed, Perceval asked, as we know, the required questions, whereat the King told him that these were great matters, and in the first place he recounted the meaning of the child seated on the branch of that tree which the knight passed on his way thither. Perceval did not learn what he wanted, because of his sins, and the episode as a whole indicated that the thought of man should be raised towards his Creator—an allegorical trifle which is after the manner of Masonic teaching, as this appears on the surface, or much ado about little. Before he could hear further Perceval was invited to piece the broken sword together, which he did, apparently by the power of his magnetism as the best knight in the world. He left only a slight crevice at the point of junction, which I should account for as signifying that other point in time at which the sin of sense entered into his life—but this is without prejudice to the explanation provided in one of the sequels which stand over for consideration. The partial success led the Keeper of the Hallows to hail Perceval as one of the lords of the House, though he was told at the same time that the Quest was yet unfinished. As Gautier dwells more especially on the resoldering of the Broken Sword, it may be inferred that what still remained was the perfect completion of this work. The next teller of the story will be found, however, to import another element, which so far may have been an implicit of the poem but has not been explicated. For the rest, Gautier explains nothing concerning that withdrawn and abdicated king, of whom we hear something in Chrétien, nor does he make more than the one reference, which I have cited, to the daughter of the Rich Fisher, except that to all appearance she continued her office as Bearer of the Holy Graal.

The Early Epochs of the Quest

§ D.—The Conclusion of Manessier

There is a disposition to think that the extension of
Gautier broke off in the middle of a sentence, which was
brought by the poet who followed him to its due point,
and the narrative continues thereafter, in his hands remaining to the very end. This poet was Manessier.
We have, however, to remember that at or about the
alleged break there intervened another singer, who intended, almost certainly, to furnish an alternative or independent conclusion, the term of which may have been
by possibility at the penultimate completed sentence of
Gautier's version, wherein the Fisher King calls Perceval
to enter within the fold of the house—

> " Sires soiés de ma maison,
> Je vos mec tout en abandon
> Quan que jou ai, sans nul dangier;
> À tous jours vos arai plus cier
> Que nul homme qui jà mais soit."

It would be in this case much the same ending as that
of the Berne Perceval. Alternatively, there may have
been some further extension which is not now extant, or
Gerbert, on his own part, may have failed to complete
as he proposed. I speak with considerable diffidence,
because the only editor of the text has given such a
vague account of that which preceded the interpolation
and followed it that it is impossible to decide whether
he has mistaken the line of Gautier, which is said to be
the point of intervention, or whether the experiment of
the Broken Sword is repeated a second time—with
glaring inconsequence—and proves a failure, soon after
it was resoldered in Gautier's text. Again, the welcome
among his household by the Fisher King is repeated at
the end in the one manuscript which gives—according
to the editor—the narrative of Gerbert *in extenso*. There
is, of course, another alternative which would exonerate

M. Potvin—the editor in question—and this is that the scribe of the codex brought in the Gerbert version at an arbitrary point without reference to that which went before and came after in the text of Gautier. The two poets are in any case of one mind as to the unfinished state of the Quest, and so also is Manessier, but the latter is of opinion evidently that Perceval has accomplished enough to have, on taking up the thread of the narrative, as much information concerning the Graal and Lance as he intends to provide under any circumstances whatever, together with so exhaustive a history of the Broken Sword that the hero shall be equipped fully for the undertaking which remains to be accomplished. I have said that Gautier is concerned more especially with the resoldering of this weapon, and it is out of the same talisman that Manessier obtains his keynote, or that which concerns himself in the palmary sense—namely, the vengeance-legend. It was the sword which inflicted the dolorous stroke and by fraud encompassed the destruction of the king's brother. It was the sword which wounded the king himself by a chance in which lurked a fatality, and his healing depended, as we know, on the visitation of tardy wrath and delayed justice upon him who used and misused the weapon. With the explanation of the Graal and the Lance we are already acquainted, but the inter-relation between the two Hallows is much closer in Manessier than it is in some other versions; as the Sacred Spear penetrated the side of Christ, the Graal was raised up to receive it, and the historic account which follows shows that the poet was acquainted with some early rendering of the *Book of the Holy Graal* which differed materially from the now extant form, as it knew nothing of the Second Joseph—the son of Joseph of Arimathæa, to whom such prominence is given in the later text. It was the elder or, for the early version, the only Joseph of the Graal, who brought the Hallows into Britain, who erected the Manor or Castle in which the King was now speaking to Perceval, and the speaker was of his own lineage. If there were any comparative connection in the romances, it would follow that the Castle was Corbenic and that the king was Pelles; but as the latter is not certainly this personage, so in the former case there is tolerable reason to suppose that the nameless House does not correspond to the mighty pile built of old by a converted pagan ruler, for which he was visited so heavily. After allowance has been made for several obvious disparities, it remains of no little importance that the early history of the Graal, so far as it is given in the *Conte*, is not that of Robert de Borron but of the putative Walter Map, and that in the sequence of texts as we have them the source of this Early History leads up to the Quest of Galahad and not to that of Perceval. Apart from the German cycle, for which there appear to be two sources —the one being in Northern French and the other in something so far untranslatable—the root-matter of Graal history was a text which corresponded of all things most closely with the metrical romance of De Borron. It was sometimes reflected through that medium and at others through the early form of the *Book of the Holy Graal*—and this history was one of Christian symbolism and religious legend, not one of folk-lore—by the elements of which it was contaminated in the course of development in romance.

Perceval, on the great night of his visit to the Graal Castle, heard other wonders than those of the Relics of the Passion and the Sword of wrath and vengeance. He heard that the maiden who carried the Graal was of royal lineage and so also was she who bore the salver, but the former was the King's daughter. He heard that the illuminated tree which he passed in his journey was the Tree of Enchantment, where the fairies assemble; for the powers of the height and the powers of the deep and the powers of the intermediate world encompassed the Graal Castle, that the times of enchantment, times of adventure, times of wonder might be illustrated by abundant pageants. He heard, in fine, of the Chapel and the

Black Hand, to which I have alluded as a tale of little meaning, wherein the Graal has no part, and there is no need to repeat the explanation here.

After all these narratives, Perceval covenanted to visit the death of the King's brother on the person who accomplished it. On the morning following he took his leave, commending his host to God and refusing all invitations to tarry. Perhaps Manessier did not know what to do in order to retard, for the purpose of story-telling, the accomplishment of his Vengeance Quest. Alternatively, perhaps he regarded it as a point of honour to follow his precursors by giving an inordinate space to the adventures of Gawain, with whom he couples those of Saigremor, another knight of fame in Arthurian romance. In any case, there are various digressions at this point which account for one half of the poem. When the story returns ultimately to Perceval he was again in the Chapel which he had visited previously—that of the Black Hand, the extinguished candle and the corpse on the altar. He did battle with and expelled a demon, purified the place and slept therein. The next day he assisted three hermits to bury the body of the person whom the Black Hand had slain. All this notwithstanding—indeed, perhaps because of it—for a considerable part of his mission the powers of the deep attacked him. On one occasion the Accuser, in the form of a horse, endeavoured to carry him to hell, but he was saved by the sign of the Cross. Later on he arrived at that river which he had crossed originally, and there the demon sought once more to deceive him, assuming the guise of Blanchefleur coming to him in a wherry. But at the right moment another vessel appeared, with sails of samite, bearing a holy man, and Perceval took refuge therein.

It is evident that the story has reached that point when its proper term is on the threshold rather than in sight merely, and the various delays which intervene can be dealt with in a few words, if we omit miscellaneous adventures which serve no important object, as they are nothing to do with the Graal. The most purposeful of all was the arrival of a messenger from Blanchefleur, who was again in peril, and so he paid his third visit to Beaurepaire, which he delivered duly and again departed from the lady, but this time in all chastity and reserve. She who had declared to him her love, now in the far past, she who expected to wed him, was destined to see him no more. The next most important episode was a stormy encounter with Hector of the Round Table, as a result of which both were destroyed nearly; but in the dark of the midnight there shone a great light about them, which was the Graal carried by an angel, and thereby they were again made whole. It follows, once more, that here, as in the Quest of Galahad, the Graal was going about, at least on occasion, and we have had an instance previously in connection with the wanderings of the Fisher King. Like all hallows the efficacy of which is transcendent and even of the absolute degree, there was no active ministry on the part thereof and nothing was done by the angel. He moved simply about them, holding the Precious Vessel, and their wounds, with the pains, left them. Doubtless after such manner was the company of the Blessed Joseph sustained and fed in the wilderness.

After this miraculous healing, Perceval, departing from Hector, as those who after great experiences have quenched all hatred in their heart, continued his way, as we may suppose, concerned now only with the accomplishment of his mission; and so in the fulness of time he reached that castle wherein there dwelt the knight who slew the brother of the Fisher King. Sorrow and outrage had the evil master of chivalry brought to his intended victim, and more even than that to the keeper of the Sacred Vessel. Why it had entailed such consequences nobody knows—perhaps also no one would care to speculate. The Graal had healed Perceval, and it had healed Hector, even in the absence of any desert on his own part, for he was the unworthy kinsman of Lancelot; but its own custodian it could not cure of the wound which a mere accident had inflicted. After a long encounter, Perceval despatched the worker of this mischief and started on his return journey to the Graal Castle, carrying the head of the destroyer with him. His mission once accomplished, all the hard and doubtful roads ran behind the hoofs of Perceval's horse; all the hindrances were taken out of the way. Of that way he knew nothing probably, and there was no need that he should. To the right he went and the left, with a certain sense of questing; the moons of the magical summer waxed and waned above him; and all suddenly the Castle rose up before him. A herald on the walls without beheld his approach and hurried to the Master of the House, not so much with the news of his coming as of that which he bore slung from the front of his saddle; whereupon the Fisher King rose up healed—with a great cry. Perceval presented his terrible gift, and it was fixed on the summit of the tower belonging to that Castle which so far was a place of vengeance rather than of mercy. Thus finished the last and crowning adventure. Whether it was the implicit of Chrétien that the question properly put would have restored all things within and without the Castle we cannot say; perhaps it would only have led to the vengeance quest, but again we cannot say. There is nothing in Chrétien to make us infer that quest and in the *Didot Perceval*—the prose romance which corresponds in the French cycle most nearly to the first portion of the *Conte del Graal*—the whole mission is one of asking and receiving a true answer. The relationship between the King and the knight was now for the first time declared by one to another; the King appointed his lands to the hero, promising to make him King in succession at Pentecost—as one who devises to an heir, or perhaps as if he also were a priest having power to consecrate. To this, however, Perceval would not accede so long as his uncle was alive, and he was also under covenant to visit the court of King Arthur, which he departed to fulfil accordingly. He was still there when a maiden arrived with the news that the Fisher King was dead, and that there was a vacancy of the royal office in the House of the Graal.

King Arthur accompanied Perceval to the Castle with all the chivalry of the Round Table—remaining a full month and being served daily by the Sacred Vessel. It does not appear who consecrated Perceval, whether this was effected, in the ordinary way, by a prelate of the church, or whether the office itself carried with it its own anointing. The text says only that he was crowned at the Feast of All Saints. After seven long years of reign in peace he bequeathed the lands in turn, and the official part of his royalty, to the King of Maronne, who had married the daughter of King Fisher; but the Hallows he did not bequeath. He retired into a hermitage, whither the Graal followed him. By a departure from tradition, he was consecrated acolyte, sub-deacon, deacon, and, in five years, he was ordained priest and sang Mass. Thereafter so did he serve God and so love Him that he was called at length from this world into the joy of Paradise. During the last period of his earthly life one codex says that he was fed only by the Holy Graal—that is to say, by the Eucharist.

§ *E.*—THE ALTERNATIVE SEQUEL OF GERBERT

It will be seen that in his wonderful kingdom Perceval had entirely neglected Blanchefleur, who is no longer even mentioned: he went into his own, and his own seem to have received him with no interrogation of the past. Had his sins been scarlet, the fulfilment of the vengeance mission and the consequent healing of the King would have made them white as snow, so far as we can follow Manessier; and yet in some obscure manner the poet knew that the things which he dealt in were sealed with holiness and that the office of the Warden, if it did not begin with priesthood, and all its sanctity, must end therein. The sense of poetical justice might have suggested another conclusion, and so did, but this was not to the mind of Manessier. There is, as we are aware, a long and long sequel by another writer which interpenetrates the last lines of Gautier, and it is a romance truly which is full of entrancements and hints of spiritual meaning. It has been summarised very fully indeed by the one editor of the *Conte del Graal*, but it has never been printed in full, as it demands and deserves. I do not know what Gerbert thought of the chessboard episode and that which followed thereafter as the term of the whole adventure. He seems to have isolated it from his mind and thus contrived to ignore it. Certainly a subsequent action, or a denial, as I should say rather, which he attributes to his hero, seems to assume tacitly the previous continence of his life. Putting aside this question of an implicit, there are three express pre-occupations to which the poem confesses: (*a*) that the desertion of Perceval's mother was an offence which called for expiation; (*b*) that the neglect of his sister must be overglossed by proper care in the future ; and (*c*) that the rest of his life must atone for all his pre-vious deficiences in respect of Blanchefleur, who—as I do not doubt that he determined in his secret mind—must be united through him with the Graal. Of such was his programme, and after what manner he fulfilled it can be told shortly. Perceval had reason to say in his heart: *mea culpa, mea culpa, mea maxima culpa*—for three offences and of these one was the greatest. I have indicated that in the midst of the editor's con-fusion, or at least as the allocation is found in the printed text, it is difficult to understand whether it is assumed by Gerbert that the Broken Sword had been resoldered partially before he begins his narrative, but even in this case it was clear to Gautier that the task of his hero was unfinished. That which he intended to do with him subsequently, there is, of course, no means of knowing; what he ought to have done, Gerbert has designed to illustrate. Perceval was to be treated, in the first instance, precisely as we shall find that Gautier presents the treatment of Gawain over his particular failure—he was not to know the truth concerning the Graal—the mystery, that is to say, of all secrecy. A state more approaching perfection was to deserve so high a prize. The King, who pronounced the judgment, consoled him, and him counselled, after which the knight was left to his repose in the holy and glorious Castle. The night of sleep was a night also which was intended to recall him to the sense of his first duty. The clear strokes of a clock, proclaiming the hour of midnight, awoke him; he saw a great light and he heard sweet singing, after which came the voice of one who was unseen, warning him concerning his sister, who was encompassed by great danger in the manorial house of their mother. He passed again into deep wells of slumber, and again —but now in the morning—he awoke, as others had awakened previously, to find himself lying on greensward, since the Castle had passed for the time being beyond the witness of the senses. He mounted his horse, which stood caparisoned and ready; he went forward, and soon—as it might seem, suddenly—a wonder of great wonders awaited him. It took the form of crystal walls, within which he heard all manner of instruments making a joyful music. The door in the hither wall being fastened, he smote it three times with increasing vehemence, using his sword for the purpose. It should be noted that this weapon neither was nor could have been the Graal Hallow, but on the third occasion it broke with a great clatter. Thereupon the door moved back, and one who was in white shining appeared and challenged. For Perceval it was a rebuff in more senses than he could understand at the moment, and though he entreated earnestly, not only was he denied entrance, but he was told by one who knew all his failure and success at the Graal Castle, that this his business with the sword must cost him another seven years of quest and exile. Apparently for the King's sake and the relief of him, he had striven in the first place, though the measure of his intention was small; now it was his own purification that was the chief work in hand. So he knocked and he did not enter, even as in the youth and inexperience of his brave spirit he saw the Pageant and the Hallows, but asked nothing concerning them. On both occasions, it was accounted to him as if he had sinned with knowledge. The truth is that the counsels of prudence do not obtain in the presence of the Mysteries, nor do the high conventions of good conduct, at least utterly. This was in the earlier case, and in the present one, while it is true that the Kingdom of Heaven is taken by violence, no one can enter unwarranted into the secret sanctuaries that have been instituted on earth to guard the memorials of the Kingdom which as yet is not upon earth, though with harp and viol and lute, and with all manner of music and psaltery, we pray that it may come quickly.

What, it will be asked, was this enclosure—within walls as the luminous shadow of the Jerusalem which is above? What manner of castle was this which resounded with the hallowings and enchantments of melody? Was it not, indeed, the Graal Castle, to which he had returned unwittingly by a devious way? According to the answer which the text furnishes, it was the Earthly Paradise, but another text tells us that among the added names of the Graal Shrine there was to be included the Castle of Eden, that it was the Castle of Joy also—as of music for ever sounding—and that behind it there was the Earthly Paradise, one of the rivers of which encircled the sacred enclosure. Therefore I leave those who will to draw the conclusion which pleases them, knowing, as at least I do, that places of this unquestionable order may be now on the crown of a causeway which the sea lashes, and again

" ·I· clos de mur fait à crestiax."

Perceval retired discounselled, but had he been advanced further in the knowledge of secret things, he would have recognised perhaps that there was encouragement and high hope which he could put to his heart because he had not been met by swords of fire, keeping the way of the Tree of Life, but by one in his own likeness, exalted gloriously, who had said to him : Not yet ! Moreover, at the end of the terse interlocutory discourse, he was given what is termed in the poem a Brief, Charter or Warranty, which—so long as he bore it—would ensure that through all his subsequent exile he should suffer no grievous harm, for thereby was he rendered invincible. We see in this manner that all kinds of miracle in medicine and every form of palladium were available there and here for knights of quest and pilgrimage ; that they seemed to be reflections or radiations from the central star of the Holy Graal; and hence that when he who was served thereby and maintained thereof could find not even a palliative in its vision and mystery, the explanation can only be that his sickness was not of this world.

Thus equipped, Perceval resumed his pilgrimage, much as the novice in some temple of the Instituted Mysteries circumambulates the Hall of Reception under the guidance of its Wardens, having only a vague notion of what is the intention and the term, but still progressing thereto. Again the road was strewn with wonders before him, but to his exaltation on this occasion. The world itself had assumed an aspect of May-time on a morning of Fairyland, and hold and keep and city poured out their garlanded trains, as with bells and banners and thuribles, to honour and acclaim him. Of the reason no one knew less than Perceval, or divined as little, but he had asked the question at the Castle, and although it had not been answered, although he had learned nothing of Graal and

Lance, and was therefore less instructed than Gawain, the interdict had been lifted from Nature, the winter was over and done, and all the cushats and turtles in all green places of the land—and all the ballad voices—broke into joy and melody, as if the Rite of Marriage had been celebrated between Heaven and Earth. He was clothed at castles in rich vestments, and from high-born maiden to simple peasant all hearts were his and all welcome.

It must be said at this point that we know little, and so little, of Gerbert that it may be reasonably a matter for speculation whether the place at which his sequel is introduced by the scribes of certain codices corresponds or not to his intention. There are some respects in which it could be allocated better if it were possible to suppose that it was part only of a Graal poem which was meant to follow immediately from the section of Chrétien; a very pertinent case in favour of this view is the palmary fact that Gerbert seems to assume almost certainly the virginity of Perceval up to, and, as we shall see, after his marriage night, which supposition is doubly impossible in view of the Gautier section. It must further be noted that in one remarkable reference to *Crestiens de Troie*, he speaks of himself as the poet who resumed the task, following the true history :—

" Si com li livres li aprent,
Où la matière en est escripte."

I feel that in making this suggestion I am exceeding my proper province, which is not that of textual criticism, and I recognise that it has its difficulties, assuming, as it does, that the Gerbert sequel must have existed in a much more extended form, because at the opening Perceval is at the Graal Castle for a second time, which is either pursuant to the account of Gautier or to some unknown portion of his own narrative. If, however, he followed Gautier, then he chose to forget or ignore him at several crucial moments. Sometimes he seems to forget Chrétien himself, for except on this hypothesis it is difficult to understand his introduction of another Broken Sword, being that which was shattered on the door of the Earthly Paradise. Now we have, in all respects, to remember that the putative Hallow which causes this confusion is in the position that we should expect it to occupy, seeing that it has no true place in the Legend of the Holy Graal. Not only does its history differ in every quest, but within the limits of the *Conte del Graal* it is contradictory under circumstances which exclude one another. At the poem's very inception the weapon is adjudged to Perceval and he carries it away. In certain codices the only further reference made to the Hallow by Chrétien is found in the warning which the questing knight receives from his cousin-german immediately after his departure from the Castle; in others we hear how the Sword splinters in the hands of Perceval, and thereafter how it is restored to the Castle. It is there, in any case, not only on the hero's revisit but long previously—in connection with the arrival of Gawain. Manessier tells a story concerning it from which it follows that in breaking it occasioned the wounding of the King at a period which was antecedent to all the quests. Therefore it could not have been at any time offered to Perceval, but must have remained in the Castle, with its resoldering always as the test of success in the case of each questing knight. Now, either Chrétien had conceived a different history of the Hallow or he told the wrong story, for the cousin-german of Perceval testifies in his poem that the Rich King Fisher was wounded in the thigh with a spear. When Gerbert intervened he left Chrétien's intention dubious, and substituted another sword, which was not a Hallow, though, like that of his predecessor, it was one that had been forged specially—would break in one peril only and must be re-soldered where it was made. After the triumph of his welcome, as related already, Perceval came to a castle in which the smithy was set up under the guard of serpents, for there were reasons why the craftsman who forged the weapon did not wish it to be mended, and the duty of the serpents was to destroy any one who brought the pieces to the smithy. These reasons are not explained by Gerbert, but—as we have seen—in certain codices of Chrétien the life of the smith is somehow dependent on the sword, and its reforging foreshadows his death approaching. If we can suppose that Gerbert's continuation began at a much earlier point than is now established, some explanation might be possible, though his own evidence seems to be against this view. Perceval conquered the serpents, and the weapon was therefore reforged. It does not appear to serve him in any special event subsequently, and as thus nothing follows from the episode we must conclude that its introduction is idle, that in this respect Gerbert did not know what to do with the materials which had come into his hands; and this is perhaps the conclusion that we should desire in respect of the Sword.

The next episode in Gerbert is a kind of addendum to that of Mount Dolorous in Manessier, and to this again no consequence attaches, except that it is an accident by which the hero is brought to Caerleon and to the court of King Arthur, when the poet gives us a new and revolutionary explanation concerning the Siege Perilous of Arthurian romance. The Siege is a decorative chair of jewelled gold sent from Fairyland—possibly that of Avalon—for occupation by the best knight in the world, and by him only with safety. For others who sit therein, the earth opens and swallows them. This chair is taken by Perceval, as at a great Rite of Exaltation, and the earth does open; but the Siege remains suspended in middle air, and the result of this achievement is that the previous ill-starred heroes, who have been engulphed but not destroyed, are restored to light and air. Perceval's next adventure is intended to illustrate his continence when tempted by a demon in the guise of a very fair woman. He emerged unsullied, and reached the abode of his sister, to her unspeakable joy and comfort. They visited the tomb of their mother, and then set forth together. Some time after they arrived at the Castle of Maidens, where Perceval in fine left her in hands of safety. Here there was another office of healing, which is of medicine rather than of anodyne; but though all the ways of wonder lead to and from the Castle of the Holy Graal, the King of that Castle knew too well the fatality by which he was encompassed to seek, for he would have sought vainly, his relief thereat. Within the merciful precincts of her new asylum Perceval's sister was enrolled henceforth as a ministering spirit, and thereat the questing knight learned something more concerning the antecedents of his Quest and also of his own family. The Castle of Maidens received wanderers, but sheltered in its ordinary course women only, and a reverend dame—under whose rule the whole company abode—declared herself a kinswoman of Perceval, being his mother's cousin. The name of his mother was Philoso-fine, and they two had entered Logres together, carrying the Sacred Hallow; but this event of the past was evidently a part of the historical mystery, and was not to be declared even to the knight of Quest until he had proved himself. He knew now that even from his very beginning he was a scion of the Sacred House, and he might have rested content in his heart that the house would at length receive him. He knew also that it was the sinful state of the land which had caused the Holy Graal to be placed in a concealed sanctuary under the ward of the good King Fisher.

Meanwhile the closing had been taken in the degree of his duty towards his sister, and, in the next place he was called to a subsidiary work in the region of filial duty. With whatever offence he could be charged in respect of his mother, she was past the reach of his atonement; but his father in chivalry, now in the distress of sorcery—as at the hands of the sorceresses of Gloucester in the Welsh romance—demanded his vengeance. This incident is one of many which would make the investigation of Gerbert's materials a quest of high enchantment if only the road were open. Of the duty which was thus imposed and accepted in all the honour of his knighthood, Perceval acquitted himself with credit, his brief from the Earthly Paradise coming to his aid, and the providence attached thereto; though—differing from the putative archaic romance—the event did not lead to the utter destruction of the people of the witch-craft, but of their military hirelings only. The episode, however, has a second object, more important to Perceval than itself, which is to aid in recalling a relationship between Blanchefleur and his father in Chivalry —as the same is recorded by Chrétien—and so forward to the root-matter of the poem, which is the marriage of Perceval. As regards this marriage there are two noticeable points, outside the fact that the union itself was the head and crown of exile ordeal. There is (*a*) the ideal set before the poet, which was to preserve the virginity of Perceval till he had accomplished the Quest of the Graal; and (*b*) the promise that at some time subsequently—when that was removed which hindered the consummation of the marriage in chastity— there should arise, as issue from those high nuptials, the mystic genealogy of the Swan Knight, whereby the Holy Sepulchre would be delivered. It is for this reason that—by a convenant which was made between them—Blanchefleur remained a maid on the night of her bridal. Of such was the marriage of Perceval, and thereafter he who was lord henceforth of all her lands, holding the sworn fealty of many princes and barons, went forth again into the world to prosecute the Great Quest. Of the virgin bride we hear nothing further, but there can be no doubt that if he had finished with her, as he seems to have planned, Gerbert would have recounted, and did perhaps, the re-union of Blanchefleur and Perceval.

I do not conceive that there is any object in prolonging this summary of a narrative which is protracted in various ways, but has reached its proper term. Some of its later, and, as one would say, redundant episodes occur or recur in the *Longer Prose Perceval*, but we have no criterion of judgment by which to decide whether one drew from another or both from that common source to which they appeal both. At the end of his probation Perceval is again at the Graal Castle, ostensibly for the third time, and the last lines of Gerbert repeat, as they stand in my text, those which are last of Gautier. I have stated my opinion already, under the necessary reserves, that Gerbert carried his sequel further and produced a conclusion which did not impose upon Perceval— under the genius of Manessier—two other pilgrimages outwards, but, as in the *Parsifal* of Wolfram, reconciled his own institution in the Graal Castle with the healing and concurrent prolongation of the old king's life. As regards the sources of the *Conte del Graal* in what is termed early historical matter, it is only at a late period that we reach accounts which are not interpolated obviously, and then they connect with the *Book of the Holy Graal* and not with the simpler history of De Borron. This is true of Manessier and true in part of Gerbert, but on the understanding that the story of Perceval's mother—in the latter case—does not represent any other extant narrative, more especially in respect of the circumstances under which the Fisher King became the guardian of the Graal. On the other hand, Gautier gives a few indications which are of the matter of the putative Walter Map.

§ *F.*—In which Sir Gawain is considered briefly
as a Companion of the Holy Quest

There are three that give testimony on earth concerning the Mystery of the Graal—Perceval, Bors and Galahad —and the greatest of these is Galahad. This notwithstanding, as there are persons who, through a certain mental deviation, turn aside from the highways of Christendom and look for better paths, out of the beaten track, in the issues of obscure heresy, so it has happened that scholarship, without setting aside the great heroes of research, has discovered some vague predilection for the adventurous and courtly Sir Gawain. They have been led even to think that he was the first popular hero of the Great Quest. If the evidence can be held as sufficient—and it is tolerable in certain directions—I suppose that I should waste my time by saying that it does not signify, any more than the preference of Jewry for Barabbas rather than Christ could accredit the Jewish robber with a valid or possible title. In order to strengthen the view, scholarship has supposed certain speculative versions, now more lost than regrettable, which present Gawain more fully as the quest-hero than any document which is extant. In such event these versions were like the poem of Chrétien de Troyes, as it was judged by Wolfram—that is to say, they told the wrong story. At the same time there are several accessory considerations which call for mention. Gawain was exactly the kind of character who would be disposed to initiate and undertake all kinds of quests, high and low. That he was a popular Graal hero might mean that some of his chroniclers did not see exactly why his methods and mode of life should create a barrier. It must be admitted also that for many purposes of the Greater Mysteries it is possible that the merely continent man requires a more express preparation than one of the opposite tendency in certain cases. I think further that the old romancists had in their minds a distinction between the continuity of the sin in Lancelot and the sporadic misdemeanours of Gawain, as also between the essential gravity of the particular offence in the two contrasted instances. There is the fullest evidence of this in respect of Guinevere, when considered side by side with other heroines of the cycles. Moreover, the romances reflected the unquestioned concensus of opinion at the period regarding the barren woman, and it seems clear that the unfailing fidelity with which plenary favours were granted by maidens in the matter of a covenant fulfilled, and the frankness which permitted such favours to rank as the term of reward, had its root in the sentiment that, except in houses of religion, the womb which bore no fruit was under a greater interdict than that which conceived without consecration by the sacred offices of the Church. This must be remembered when the literature suggests, as it will, that the chivalry of King Arthur's court translated in an inverted manner the institutes of heaven; that it was not very particular about marrying and giving in marriage; and that it seemed to have assumed to itself an indulgence, both general and particular, to follow the untinctured office of Nature without much consciousness of a stigma attaching thereto. Finally, it is. just to add that the later romances manifest a set purpose to depict Gawain in blacker colours exceedingly than the earlier texts warrant.

For the rest, and from the mystic standpoint, it seems pertinent to say that while there is no period at which it was customary on the part of the Church to impose celibacy as an ideal on those who lived in the world, and while from most of the higher standpoints the grace of chastity is less in its simple possession than in its impassioned recovery, we have to remember that the great masters do not marry because of the Divine Union. The connection in Chrétien between Gawain and the Graal Quest arises out of a challenge which he had accepted to clear himself of a charge of murder, as to which it was a matter of agreement that if he could find and bring back the Lance which bleeds he should be excused from returning to withstand the ordeal by battle. Out of this condition certain codices present the visit of Gawain to the Graal Castle very early in the version of Gautier. He beheld, firstly, a bier and, secondly, all the Hallows, asked the required question, and was told by the Royal Warden that if he could resolder the Broken Sword he should know (*a*) why the beautiful maiden who carried the Sacred Vessel was dissolved in tears; (*b*) why a bier formed part of the pageant; and (*c*) whose body was laid thereon. These points are peculiar to Gautier and his connections. The experiment with the Sword proved, however, a failure; Gawain learned nothing; he fell asleep after hearing the discourse of the King, who explained what was wanting in him; and on awaking next morning he discovered himself in the open country, with his horse and his arms close by him. It is obvious that he had found the Lance, but he had not carried it away, and for this reason he set out to take up the challenge. King Arthur, however, intervened, and the matter was settled in peace.

The codices which embody this account give much more extended particulars of another visit which was paid by Gawain to the Castle; but it is obvious that they are exclusive mutually, and the alternative texts which omit the first visit, and determine in a different sense the question of the accusation and the ordeal, are for the quest of Gawain the logical and preferable texts. Second or first, on this occasion, nothing was further from the mind of the character in chief than to go on the Quest of the Graal, nor was he concerned with the covenant of any challenge. He assumed the responsibility of a knight who was slain by a hand invisible when riding under his safe conduct. The identity of this knight is never disclosed, but Gawain wore his armour and was carried by his steed, who had mysterious foreknowledge of the way, to a destination of which he himself could dream nothing. He arrived at his term in due course, but what took place was the reception of a masquerading neophyte, who was unintroduced, unwarranted and unqualified. In place of being he that was to come, they had still to look for another; but his harness for a moment deceived the company about him.

The Early Epochs of the Quest

Chrétien knew nothing of a bier and a dead body, in that place where the sign of arch-natural life abode in perpetuity; those who took up the story in the footsteps of Gautier knew nothing also, and agreed to ignore his intimations of unexplained disaster. But Gautier or another, the bier was again seen at this visit of him who was unexpected, and a procession of canons and clerks recited thereover the Holy Office for the Dead, with a great ceremony of solemn voices intoning. The King also visited the bier and lamented over it. The pageant of the Graal was manifested, after the manner which I have described elsewhere, and Gawain saw it openly. At the conventional feast it was the Sacred Vessel which served so far as the food was concerned, but the sacramental communication was in one kind only, since the wine, as we have seen, was brought round by the butlers. Gawain, as in the previous case, asked all the necessary and saving questions, and was invited to solder the Sword, but he failed, as before, in this ordeal and learned only concerning its history. A stroke which was dealt therewith destroyed the realm of Logres and all the surrounding country. In the midst of this narrative Gawain fell asleep at the table, and was left to repose. When he awoke there was neither hall nor castle, neither King nor chivalry about him, but a fairly garnished land lying on the brink of the sea and restored by so much of the belated question as he had asked the King. The common folk blessed him, and the common folk accused him, because he had not finished his work or insured their full felicity.

Of such is the Quest of Gawain as it appears in the *Conte del Graal*, even as the pillars of a temple which was never finished. It intervenes between the first and second visit of Perceval to the High House of the Hallows, but on Perceval's own Quest it has no effect whatever, and the narrative of the one ignores that of the other. It is said in some old fable—which is not, I think, of the Graal,—that Arthur and Gawain at last re-

239

posed in Fairyland. There are two classes of Knighthood —that which goes in and returns, and thereof is Ogier ; that which enters but does not come back evermore, and thereof is Launfal. Now, Arthur returns in the fulness of the times that are to come, and, however these dreams may be, it is certain that the Peace of the King is not the peace of Gawain. In conclusion as to the *Conte del Graal*, after every allowance has been made for one statement in Chrétien, from which it follows that the father of the Fisher King was, as we have seen, sustained by a Sacred Host taken from the Holy Graal, the keynote of the whole cycle is that it has no sacramental connections such as we find elsewhere in the literature. On this account, if indeed on no other, the *Conte del Graal* has nothing to tell us which signifies in respect of our true affair, except by way of its echoes and reflections from sources which do concern us nearly, and are better and fuller witnesses. It has every title to possess in perpetuity the kind of Perceval which it has helped materially to create —in whom the Parsifal of Wolfram has little and the transfigured Knight of the *High History* has next to nothing at all.

BOOK IV

*THE LESSER CHRONICLES OF THE
HOLY GRAAL*

Q

THE ARGUMENT

BOOK IV

THE LESSER CHRONICLES OF THE HOLY GRAAL

I

THE METRICAL ROMANCE OF JOSEPH OF ARIMATHÆA

ROBERT DE BORRON was imbued, and even deeply, with the religious spirit of his period. I think also that in him there was a spiritual tincture which must have been a little rare at that epoch among courtly minstrels. He had seen, according to his story, some part at least of the Great Book of the Legend, and perhaps it had changed his life. After the manner of his time, he was attached to a patron, and he wrote his poem for the *preux* and noble chevalier Walter Montbeliard—a crusader when the Temple was at its glory. The poem opens with an account of the circumstances which led ultimately to the incarnation of Christ and is based on the fact that prior to this event, and prior indeed to the descent of Christ into Hades, good and bad were alike in Hell and less or more in the power of the evil hierarchy. The root-matter of the story can be expressed in a few words, and may be so offered to simplify the issues which are important to our purpose and must be dealt with therefore more fully. The vessel in which Christ prepared His sacrament, according to those words of the text with which we are already acquainted, was taken from the house of Simon by a Jew and delivered into the hands of Pontius Pilate.

Joseph of Arimathæa, with the assistance of Nicodemus and by permission of Pontius Pilate, took down the body of Jesus after the Crucifixion. The permission was a reward asked by Joseph in return for years of military service, and Pilate gave him in addition the vessel which the Jew had brought him. In that vessel Joseph received the Blood, which was still flowing from the wounds of Christ when the body was being prepared for burial. He laid the body in a sepulchre prepared for himself, and he concealed the vessel in his house. After the Resurrection the Jews sought Nicodemus, who eluded them by flight, and Joseph, whom they seized and imprisoned in a dark tower ; the only issue therefrom was at the summit, and this was sealed effectually by a heavy stone. Christ came to Joseph in the tower, brought him the Sacred Vessel and communicated to him certain secret words which were the grace and power thereof. Joseph remained for forty years in his prison and was sustained by the Blessed Vessel, as if in a condition of ecstasy and apart from any normal consciousness concerning the flight of time. Towards the end of that period, Vespasian, the son of Titus, being afflicted with leprosy—and a pilgrim who reached Rome having recounted the wonderful miracles of Jesus of which he had heard in Palestine—a commission was sent to Jerusalem to bring back some relic of the Master, if the report of His death were true. The commission in due time returned with St. Veronica, who carried the *Volto Santo*, or Sacred Face-cloth, and this effected the desired cure immediately. Titus and Vespasian proceeded with an army to Palestine to avenge the death of Jesus. It was in this manner that Vespasian found Joseph still alive in the tower ; the stone was removed from his sepulchre, and he who had been entombed, like Christ, like Christ also arose ; after this rescue was effected, the Emperor's son was converted by Joseph.

The vengeance on the Jews being in fine accomplished, Joseph collected his relatives and many companions who had embraced Christianity at his instance, and by the will of God the party started westward, carrying the Holy Graal. For a considerable period they took possession of a certain district and placed it under cultivation. At length a part of the company fell away from grace, with the result that a scarcity followed in the land, and the vessel was used to separate the good from the evil within the ranks of the people. For this purpose a table was dight after the manner of that which served for the Lord's Supper, and the vessel was set thereon. Before it there was placed a single fish, which the Divine voice of the Graal had directed Brons, who was the brother-in-law of Joseph, to catch in a neighbouring water. Between Joseph and Brons there was left a vacant seat corresponding to that which had been made void by the defection of Judas Iscariot. Under circumstances which remain vague in the story, a certain part of the company, being those who had kept in a state of grace, sat down at the table, and the rest who gathered about were of those who had lapsed into sin. The good people experienced all spiritual delight and inward refreshment, but the evil were not filled, and they beheld nothing. When a question, put to them by one who was named Petrus, had elicited this fact, they were denounced as those who were guilty, and they departed in shame. It is indeed quite clear that they seem to have separated from the company once and for all. The exception was a certain Moses, who manifested great sorrow, though he was really an unbeliever at heart. His prayers in fine obtained him permission to take a place at the table, but the void seat was the one which alone was available, and when he sat down thereon, the Siege and its occupants were both swallowed by an abyss which opened beneath them. Meanwhile the office of the table had become a daily, as it were, a divine service, and so continued till the company was divided further to continue the journey westward in successive parties. Alain, the son of Brons, and his eleven brothers under his guidance were the first to start, he carrying a certain proportion of what must be termed the revealed knowledge of the

Holy Graal, but it did not include apparently the Secret Words. The communication which had been made to Alain was because when the time came for Brons and his wife to seek for their twelve boys some kind of settlement in life, the eleven had elected to marry and were therefore provided with wives, but he who was the youngest of all chose a life of celibacy; he was therefore put over his brethren, and was taken by Joseph into his heart after a special manner. This party was followed by that of Petrus, whose connection with the family of Joseph, if any, is not stated; but he was favoured in another manner which would seem to be more distinctive, since he carried a brief or warrant sent down from heaven itself, but of its contents or their purport there is no account given. His destination was the *Vaux d'Avaron*. The last to depart was Brons, apparently with the remnant of the people, and to him Joseph, by the divine ordination, delivered the Sacred Vessel and communicated the Secret Words. Joseph of Arimathæa seems to have remained behind—though the text is corrupt at this point—his mission being accomplished, and it would follow in this case that shortly after he was taken into *la joie perdurable* of the Paradise which is above.

The theology is in part of the popular legendary character and may seem a little fantastic even within these limits. For the early church and the writers thereto belonging in places remote from the centre, the world of Christian doctrine was a world not realised, and Rome might well have been astonished at certain things which were said and sometimes taught with all innocence of intention on the verges of the horizon westward. It would be easy to furnish examples of elements in De Borron which are not less than heretical from the doctrinal standpoint, but there are indications also of curious learning and traces of strange sympathies. Among the latter may be mentioned a certain tenderness towards Pontius Pilate, the difficulty of whose position as the Procurator of Judæa, when acting almost under the compulsion of a Jewish faction, was from any point of view undeniable. The important point, however, is that the sympathy reflects at a far distance the apocryphal legends which represent Pilate as one who was converted ultimately, who became a bishop of the Church and sealed his testimony with martyrdom. More noticeable than this, perhaps, for the ordinary reader is the writer's seeming ignorance concerning the Jewish doctrine of rest in the bosom of Abraham for those at least of the faithful departed who died in the peace of Israel.

In the kind of research with which we are concerned here, we must be careful not to mistake the unintended blunder for the express statement. As a rule, it is easy to distinguish the simple errors, but occasionally a specific point may puzzle the most careful reader. While De Borron seems wholly unconscious of opposition to the claims of Rome, there is, of course, very full indication of a secret which inheres in the Graal and some ground for thinking that the rumour of this secret had gone forth abroad in the world prior to his poem. It is, however, a verbal formula, not apparently a doctrine. "Those who can learn and retain these words," says Christ to Joseph, "shall be virtuous among people and pleasant unto God; they shall not be forejudged in court, nor conquered in battle, so only that their cause is just." There is, however, a particular point which is a little opposed to my general view herein. Speaking of the common hell into which all souls went prior to the coming of Christ, De Borron says: "It was necessary that the ransom of our first fathers should be provided by the Three Divine Persons who are one only and the same substance." Now, the identity of the Three Persons in Christ is unquestionably a heresy, but, as it so happens, this is the express teaching of Swedenborg, for whom Christ was the manifested Trinity. It is curious to recall the analogy, but such a notion could at no time have formed part of any secret doctrine, supposing that this were otherwise to be found or expected in De Borron.

So also we must not interpret as a trace of any secret doctrine the implicit of his comparison between the conception of Eve and the most Holy Virgin. He says in effect that Eve conceived in suffering, that the posterity of our first parents were, like them, doomed to die, and that the possession of their souls was claimed by the demon as his right. To purchase them from hell our Saviour was conceived in the womb of the Virgin Mary, and in this manner the sin of generation according to the common course of Nature was annulled by a virginal conception. But in the analogy there is no ulterior motive, no *arrière pensée*.

The apostolic priority of Peter seems to underlie the following statement, which is put into the mouth of our Saviour: "I leave this example to Peter and to the ministers of the Church." Comparatively early criticism looked upon this as equivalent to an acknowledgment of St. Peter as the official chief of the Catholic Holy Assembly, and remarked that no such admission is found in the *Book of the Holy Graal*, which, it should be said, is however untrue. If we pass now to the consideration of the Sacred Vessel and to the question what De Borron designed to signify thereby, we may note in the first place that, by the hypothesis of the poem, it is not visible to evil-livers, though it is evident that they encircled the table at which they could not sit on the occasion when it was first manifested to the elect. The correspondence of this will be found much later on in the *Parsifal* of Wolfram, wherein the object which corresponds to the Graal was invisible to a pagan, though he was a man of noble life and a kinsman of the Secret House. De Borron speaks (*a*) of a vessel, not otherwise named, in which Jesus washed the feet of His disciples; (*b*) of that passing fair vessel, already described, in which Christ made His sacrament, but the institution of the Eucharist is not mentioned more specifically; (*c*) of the use by Pilate either of this vessel or another—for the text seems doubtful—when he washed his hands to signify that he was not responsible for the judgment which he had pronounced unwillingly. As regards (*b*) I have explained in the summary that a Jew carried it from the house of Simon, when Jesus had been led forth therefrom, and brought it to Pilate. At a later stage Pilate took the vessel, and remembering thereof that it was beautiful, he gave it to Joseph, saying : "Much hast thou loved this man." Joseph answered : "Thou hast said truly." But the gift was less an instance of generosity than of the procurator's desire to retain nothing which had belonged to Jesus, whereby it was possible that he might be accused. Either the present state of the text or the poet's method of expression leaves things so much in confusion that a further question has arisen whether the *piscina* used for the washing of the feet was identical with that vessel which became ultimately the Graal. It has been suggested that for the last word in the line

"Où Criz feisoit son sacrement,"

what was written and intended originally was the word *lavement*, but this is extremely unlikely in view of the general content and is not countenanced certainly by the *Lesser Holy Graal*. It has been suggested further that (1) St. John does not mention the Institution of the Eucharist and is the only Evangelist who does describe the washing of the Apostle's feet ; (2) Robert de Borron knew only the Fourth Gospel, possibly through that of Nicodemus in the Christian Apocrypha. But all these questions are settled by the text itself in the discourse of Christ to Joseph at the beginning of his imprisonment in the tower. It is there said (1) that at the Last Supper on the Thursday Christ blessed the bread and the wine and told His disciples that they partook in those elements of His flesh and blood ; (2) that the table of that Supper should be represented in many countries ; (3) that the sacrament should never be consecrated without commemoration of Joseph, who had taken down the Divine Body from the

Cross and laid it in the Sepulchre; (4) that this tomb should be signified by the Altar; (5) that the winding-sheet in which the Body was wrapped should be called the corporal; (6) that the Holy Vessel in which Joseph received the Blood should be called the chalice; (7) that the stone with which the sepulchre was sealed should be signified by the paten. Nothing can be more express, both as to the Mass and the Eucharist. Unfortunately, nothing can be clearer also in the mind of the poet than the content of the Palladium of his legend—being the blood of Three Persons in one God. And this, I think, is all that need be said in this place concerning the Cup of the Holy Graal in Robert de Borron.

That Christ had in nowise forgotten one who had at need befriended Him was shown by Him bringing it into the prison, holding it in the hands of Him, while the whole tower was illuminated by its great light, for it was all full of the Holy Spirit.

The Divine Discourse which occurs in this tower between the visionary Christ and Joseph is remarkable from several points of view, and especially by the categorical assurance that the Risen Saviour brought none of His disciples to the conference, because none were acquainted with the great love which subsisted between Himself and His auditor. It seems, however, to have been a prototype of that love which is the immanence of Christ in the believing soul, and the palladium in Joseph's case was the symbol of the Redeemer's death, as it is the Eucharist in the external church. The specific and material explanation is that Joseph took down the body of Jesus from the Cross, and for this reason he was to be a partaker in all glory. Of the colloquy there were, in any case, no witnesses, and the Gospel narratives could offer no contradiction. I suppose that I should add an implicit which seems almost evidently to have been in the poet's mind—that Joseph had made the Resurrection more, humanly speaking, possible by preserving the body as nearly intact as the circumstances of the Crucifixion would permit. The difficulty which seems to have been present to the sub-surface mind of De Borron was perhaps not unknown to one Gospel narrative, which is careful to indicate that the bones of Christ were not broken on the Cross.

The especial direction to Joseph was that he should guard well the Sacred Vessel, committing it only to those persons who were designed thereto, and by these it should be taken as given in the Name of the Father, and of the Son, and of the Holy Spirit. The possessors were to be three and no more, because of the Trinity; they were: (*a*) Joseph; (*b*) Brons; and (*c*) the grandson of Brons, who was to be born in the fulness of time. It must be said that this enumeration appears to omit one person who, according to the text itself, was intended for some high office. When Joseph prayed before the Cup for guidance over the future of his company, recalling an ordinance which had told him that at what time soever he desired secret knowledge, he should come into the presence of the Reliquary wherein was the glorious blood, he was answered by the Voice of the Graal that the celibate son of Brons was to be shown the Sacred Vessel so that he could see the content thereof. Now this son was Alain, and it might be supposed that the venerable charge would pass to him from his father, more especially as, in spite of his choice, he was to beget the keeper in fine, and was not dedicated therefore to permanent celibacy, but held rather in maidenhood for a marriage which was predestined already. The instruction to Petrus announced that he was to await the arrival of Alain's son, who would reveal to him the virtues of the Holy Vessel—being something omitted apparently in his undeclared brief or charter—and would make known to him what had become of Moses.

As to this ill-starred personage, who had suffered so strangely for parading a spurious election with intent to deceive those who were chosen in truth and faith, it is decreed that he shall be heard of no more in song or fable till the knight comes who will fill the void seat. In this dubious manner it seems to be indicated that the wrath of the Graal would not be visited to everlasting.

After the departure of the several bands of pilgrims, the poem comes to its conclusion for want of written materials. The author had carried it so far on the evidence of the sacred book to which I have cited already the chief reference. He leaves it in the expectation that he will recount later on as follows :—

(*a*) What became of Alain, whither he went, whom he married, and what heir was born to him.

(*b*) Whither Petrus proceeded.

(*c*) The fate of Moses, so long lost.

(*d*) The destination of Brons, who, outside all inferences of the logical understanding, had received the title of the Rich Fisher, on account of that single occasion when he angled in a certain water and caught one fish.

Meanwhile, De Borron had apparently the records of the Fifth Branch, and to that he passed on, so producing a metrical romance concerning the prophet Merlin. Let us therefore on our part conclude also as follows : (1) The formulary which incorporated the Great Secret of the Graal was, without evasion apparently, recorded in the prototypical chronicle by which the poet was guided. (2) The Secret was itself denominated the Graal, as if by a general title, the name not being applied exclusively to the Sacred Vessel. (3) The last directions to Joseph regarding Brons, the second keeper, are these : Tell him how God did communicate unto thee the Holy Words, which are sweet and precious and gracious and piteous, which are properly called and named the Secret of the Graal.

Hereto, therefore, as the *obiter dicta* at this still preliminary stage, the English *Syr Percyvelle* may be the nearest reflection of the quest-element in folk-lore, but the *Metrical Romance of Joseph* is the nearest and earliest reflection of all that which could have been imputed as historical in any lost book. It is unalloyed by folk-lore admixtures, for no two things can be well less alike than the pre-Graal Feeding-dish and the Hallow of De Borron's Christian legend. The distance between the old myths and this devotional poem is too great for us to say that the latter is the archetypal state of this mythos after assumption by Christianity. There is no kinship. It is that from which the Lesser Chronicles and the Greater Chronicles draw at their respective distances, though from otherwhere they gathered many elements. Here at least there are no adventitious Hallows; it is the Graal as the one thing only. And the Holy Graal is a symbol of the Angel of Great Counsel made visible.

II

THE LESSER HOLY GRAAL

The first and only editor of this text put it forward as the original prose romance from which the poem was produced subsequently by some unknown hand, not so much writing ostensibly under the name of Robert de Borron as reflecting in rhymes and measures the actual words of the original. This view did not obtain at its period any special acceptance and has been long abandoned. The codex as it stands is an accurate rendering of the poem, *plus* certain variations and expansions, of which some are important to our purpose and must be recited briefly. But any literary or other distinction between the metrical story and its disposition in another vesture leaves the narrative untouched, both versions working from the same beginning to the same term, so that any general description of the *Lesser Holy Graal* would be superfluous in this place.

The circumstances under which certain secret words were communicated originally, their transit westward, and the scheme designed for their perpetuation, constitute the mystery-in-chief of the metrical romance, and we have brought away from it an irresistible inference that these words were a formula of Eucharistic consecration. The negative proof is that they were not used by Joseph when he had occasion to appeal for guidance to the Divine Voice which spoke from within or about the Sacred Vessel, or when he separated the grain from the tares in his band of pilgrims. The proof which assumes some aspect of a positive kind is that wonderful analogy which the text indicates between the Sacrament of the Altar and the Vessel, with its antecedents and environments. But the Eucharistic character of the Secret Words is made much more explicit in the *Lesser Holy Graal,* for it is said, speaking of the Discourse in the tower : " Thereupon did Christ Jesus teach him those words which cannot be spoken or written, should any one wish to do so, except he have read the great book wherein they are recorded, and this is the secret which is uttered at the great sacrament performed over the Graal, that is to say, over the chalice, and I—Robert de Borron—do, for God's love, pray all those who shall hear this present book in the reading thereof that they ask no further herein concerning the said matter, for he who should try to say more might well lie concerning it, since more he could in nowise tell, and such falsehood would profit him nothing." That the Secret Words were therefore committed to writing follows from both versions, and the suggestion of the *Lesser Holy Graal* is that the Great Book was written by Joseph himself. The additional light which is gained concerning the Holy Vessel is (1) that it was the blessed and very object wherein Christ sacrificed ; but this is less express than the words *feisoit son sacrement,* which I have quoted more than once from the poem ; (2) on the other hand, the prose version makes it plainer than the poem that the Vessel brought by the Jew was given to Pilate after the death of Christ, or coincidently therewith, for which reason it could not have been used by the procurator to wash his hands before he pronounced sentence; (3) the Vessel is described by Christ as *la sénéfiance de ma mort*.

Among points left dubious in the poem we have seen that there is the question whether Joseph of Arimathæa remained where he was, not proceeding further westward than the point of separation determined for the whole company. It would follow in this case either that one legend concerning the evangelisation of Britain was unknown to Robert de Borron or that it was by him ignored. Now that which is left doubtful in the poem is carried into triple confusion by the prose version. One of its codices says that Joseph went into that country wherein he was born ; another says that he departed and came to his term in the land whither he was sent by Jesus Christ, yet it seems to follow from this second text that the whole company was already in *la bloie Bretagne* and that Joseph had converted it newly to the belief in Jesus Christ.

It will serve no purpose of mine to enlarge upon minor debatable points which occur in the prose version, as, for example, on the doubt which it creates whether (*a*) the third keeper of the Graal will be the son of Brons, by which we should understand Alain ; (*b*) whether he shall be the son of his son, as in the metrical romance ; and (*c*) whether the triple guardianship, corresponding to the Holy Trinity, should be enumerated after Joseph has surrendered the symbol of his mission, which is the reading of one codex and follows also from the metrical romance. It is sufficient to state in conclusion that as regards the second table, and the reason why it was established, the texts in verse and prose are both in agreement that whatever the needs of the company there was (*a*) no miracle in the multiplication of food ; (*b*) only a spiritual refection ; (*c*) the essence of which was to fill the participants with grace ; (*d*) one proof being that the fish of Brons becomes wholly symbolical and figures continually at the service.

III

THE EARLY HISTORY OF MERLIN

The Mystery of the Holy Graal was a mystery of grace behind Arthurian literature till the time came for it to be manifested at the period of the Quests, and among the texts in which it is exhibited as if working from afar and vaguely there is that which I have termed for convenience the *Early History of Merlin*, being the transcript in prose of another metrical romance by which Robert de Borron proceeded, for want of intermediate materials, from the history of Joseph to the period which just antedated the birth and life of King Arthur. The tradition of the one romance is carried over by the other, and as such it is at once interesting extremely and important for our purpose. With the story itself we are concerned only in the least possible degree. It narrates, in the first place, a conference of demons that seems to have been summoned immediately after the Descent of Christ into hell to consider the best means of reducing to a minimum the opportunity of human redemption which had been inaugurated by the sudden translation of all the just of old from the supposed power of Infernus into the joy of Paradise. The conclusion attained was that if only some emissary of theirs could be born on earth, having for his father one of the evil *personæ* and for l is mother a woman in the flesh, they would recover some part at least of the patrimony which they claimed in souls. There was one in the council, belonging to that averse hierarchy which is termed the Powers of the Air, who had the gift under certain conditions to make earthly women conceive, and he went forth upon this mission. What he did, however, was to surprise a pure maiden, apart from all knowledge of hers, at an unwary moment. After this manner was Merlin born into the world, in the accomplishment of which plot we are translated, with no suggestion or manifest sense of the intervening centuries, from the days which preceded the Ascension to the reign of Vortigern in Britain. The device of perdition had gone, as usual, astray, and that utterly ; for the mother was saved spiritually by her innocence and, on the discovery of her predicament, by recourse immediately to the offices of holy religion. She was accused indeed before the judges of the country, but the child himself saved her, for, being a babe, he yet spoke—now with the cunning which might be ascribed to his father in Sheol, and now with the subtlety and foresight which suggested the intervention of another and higher power, as if this had taken him for its own purpose into its safe custody.

Throughout the story Merlin, in virtue of his dual origin, is in part true steel and in part clay. Robert de Borron borrowed from antecedent materials which we can trace in their larger proportion, but the high spirit of his religious disposition worked upon that which he assumed, and wrought a great change therein. His Merlin has come really as if in the power of a mission which had been imprinted with a Divine seal, and though he is at best an admixture, and though the character of some of his actions is stained enough, he who has created him in literature more even than he has derived, does not weary of saying that God, who spared Merlin's mother in the body of her was able to save him in the soul, or at least contribute thereto, because of her perfect reconciliation with Holy Church. She had indeed sinned not at all, but had once, under great stress, forgotten to pray, and the visitation which came upon her was the hand of a providence rather than a hand which chastised. According to one text, with which we shall deal later, she became at length a nun, and so passed in sanctity. To pass thus also was evidently De Borron's intention as to the son's destiny, and at the end of the Lesser Chronicles we shall see how it was fulfilled. Meanwhile, the expressed mission of Merlin was after an unwonted manner to teach the love of Jesus Christ and the life everlasting. The note of this intention occurs early in the story, when it is said that God took the fiend-born child to His own use, though the mystery is the manner of that use ; his double nature was such and so granted that he might yield to God His part and to the fiend also his own. There are other stories which tell how Merlin dwelt amidst illusion, and how at the end he passed therein, but these are not of Robert de Borron.

The exigencies of intention rather than of the story itself take Merlin to Britain at a period which, according to his years, would be early out of reason for his work, but he who was never a child was more already than a man. There is no need to recite under what circumstances, initial and successive, he became the high councillor and worker of many miracles to four kings, each after the other : Vortigern, Pendragon, Uther Pendragon and Arthur. What remains to be said of his history will best fall under the considerations which now follow.

It is perhaps the Merlin cycle which offers the most curious among what I have termed the Lesser Implicits of the Graal literature. I must put them at a certain length because of their apparent importance, and will say in the first place that on Robert de Borron's part, as on that of certain other and unknown writers, there were two tangible purposes in full view : (1) To connect Merlin with all that Graal Mystery which was antecedent to the ascribed times of the prophet ; (2) to identify his function with the termination of the Graal marvels under the pretext of times of enchantment or times adventurous. We are drawn through far tracts of speculation in seeking to understand what sub-surface disposition of mind could have actuated these purposes, but at the moment we are concerned in ascertaining how they are carried out in the story.

There was a hermit named Blaise, to whom the mother of Merlin had recourse in her unexpected difficulties, who had been also her spiritual adviser previously. The text says that this hermit was an exceeding good clerk and subtle, for which reason Merlin prayed that he would become his recorder-in-chief, not only of all his deeds, but of things heard and seen which he might well think that no creature could express. A consent was obtained only after the holy man had conjured the querent in the Name of the Divine Trinity that he should deceive him in nowise; but Merlin answered that the records would rather keep him from sin than dispose thereto. It is in this way that Blaise is one of its characters even from the beginning of the romance, but his chronicle itself began long prior to the birth of Merlin, for at the instance of him who was to prove himself a prophet in Britain, he wrote first of the great love between Christ and Joseph of Arimathæa, of the lineage of Joseph, the names of those who were to be the guardians of the Graal, of Alain and his companions and whither they journeyed, of the departure of Peter westward, of the transmission of the Holy Vessel from Joseph to Brons, and of the death of Joseph. The history of these things was to be joined with that of Merlin, and the two recitals were to form a single book, complete in respect of everything, save only the Secret Words revealed to Joseph by Christ, whereof Merlin could say nothing—the reason of which is to be inferred from the Quest-matter of the Lesser Chronicles, namely, that he had not received them.

In accordance with the general trend of the earlier history and of the personages concerned therein, Merlin announced his intention to go west—that is, apparently out of Brittany into the land of Vortigern, or Greater Britain, and Blaise was also to follow, betaking himself to Northumbria, where it is said that the guardians of the Graal were then dwelling, though they are not specified by name. The first recompense of Blaise in this life was to be united with these Wardens, but thereafter it was to be *joie perdurable*. The Graal is the talisman of the whole story, and hereof is the repose of the Graal—that they who have achieved the search shall have rest in the term thereof. And the book made by Blaise was to be called while the world endured the *Book of the Seynt Graal*. In this manner did Merlin, though he was not in any sense a custodian of the Hallows, make a certain claim upon them in the dispensation of their graces and rewards. It was not, in the symbolical sense, of an idle nature, not the artifice of an impostor; rather it was of set purpose and as if the external sign of some secret warrant, in virtue of which the highest branch of the Graal history is connected indissolubly with Merlin. He laid the scheme, and the Hallows conformed thereto, the end being the termination of those dubious times, the dereliction of which we have heard of so often and can as yet understand so little.

Of such is the Graal in the *Early History of Merlin*. But this is also the first romance which, in the chronological succession of texts, apart from priority in time of literary production, introduces the Third Table and the mystery of the Siege Perilous. It may be held to constitute another side of its particular claim concerning the British prophet. Those who have followed so far the history of the Second Table will perhaps have recalled already that a vacant seat was left of old at the Passover for the unexpected guest, and it is still left by the Jews. There is also that custom, beautiful and piteous, of leaving a vacant seat for the Angel of Peace. I do not know what memories of this kind were present to the mind of De Borron when he borrowed from those who had preceded him the idea of the Round Table and attributed its foundation to Uther Pendragon, not to King Arthur, Merlin, however, being in either case the instigator of its institution. With his reflex of the spirit of sanctity, as conceived by the British prophet, the knightly table was something more than a substitute, and assuredly, in some later aspects, it reflected on earth that which belongs to heaven.

In the course of his proposal, Merlin told Uther

Pendragon the story of Joseph of Arimathæa, and how in the desert places, the sowing of which had become void through the sin of some who went forth, the Second Table had been instituted to separate the good from the evil. The Third was to be established by Uther in the Name of the Trinity, and it was to be set up at Cardoil in Wales for a certain Feast of Pentecost—that is to say, of the Holy Spirit. As there was a place that was void at the Table of Joseph so there was to be one now, which should not be filled in the days of Uther Pendragon, but of the king who was to come after him. The knight who would then fill it was not as yet born, which is colourable enough as a pretence in respect of the Perceval who was to follow as questing knight according to the Lesser Chronicles. But the codices have been edited in variant interests and the English rendering, represented by an unique text and drawing from what source I know not, adds words as follows which could apply only to Galahad: "Ne he that shall hym engendere shall not know that he shall hym engendere." On the other hand, the *Huth Merlin* says that he will be engendered by him who ought so to engender him, but as yet he has not taken a wife, nor does he know that he ought to engender him—a passage which, after much circumlocution, comes to nothing. The text suggests otherwise that before the predestined hero takes the void seat he must accomplish the adventures of the Graal, which is contrary to all the texts, historical and otherwise. The *Vulgate Merlin* says in effect that he who fills the one will fulfil the other. And the English version: "And he that shall a-complysshe that sete must also complysshe the voyde place at the table that Joseph made." This seems to create on the surface an almost insoluble difficulty, but the meaning is probably that in the secret and holy place where the Graal abides, the service of the Second Table is held still, as it was in the days of Joseph, that he who enters into the House shall take the seat reserved for him, and that the Table shall be in fine complete.

Of such was the second mission of the prophet Merlin; but the third was the conception of Arthur and the conduct of all those events which should lead to his high coronation as King of Britain. I need not reproduce in this place the familiar story of Ygerne, the faithful wife of the Duke of Tintagel, and of the sorcery by which she received Uther Pendragon in the likeness of her husband and so brought forth the great king who was to come. The circumstances of the imbedded sword which led to his ultimate recognition, though he had been reared as the reputed son of a simple knight, are or ought to be familiar. It was to achieve his prophetic purpose that Merlin assisted Uther over those things which led up to the conception of Arthur, since the latter was to consummate the great intent of the Round Table which was begun by his father. The conception was one of a triad —of Merlin, of Arthur, of Galahad—which all took place under false pretences. Merlin was conscious that he had sinned in respect of this business, and apparently he sought to make amends by assisting the subsequent marriage between Uther and Ygerne and by his arrangements in respect of the charge of Arthur in childhood.

It should be noted in fine (*a*) that no Keeper of the Graal is mentioned in the *Early History of Merlin*, though the locality of its abode is indicated; (*b*) that there is only a covert reference to Moses; (*c*) that certain sources are obvious for certain texts, but there are important respects in which all the early romances seem echoes from far away of a book that had never been seen by their writers, though it had been heard of by a general report; and (*d*) that this statement is intended to override all their reference, actual or imaginary, to mysterious sources of information which are not—if they were ever—extant.

IV

THE DIDOT PERCEVAL

Without instituting in the present stage of the question more than a parallel, the Quest of the Graal is the adventurous mission of those who go forth out of earthly houses, who depart from tables of wonder, from the enchantments and illusions of magicians after the manner of Merlin—when Merlin was not at his highest—and issue into strange lands, some unprepared enough, but some under spiritual guidance, observing the ordinances of instructors and looking for a mystical place. Few are destined for the perfect fulfilment of their object, but that which opens for these is the path of heaven. Though time and place are imputed, and this of necessity, it can be said scarcely that such limits are native to this manner of research. There is, according to the Hebrews, a palace at the centre which sustains all things, and in the terms of another symbolism it is the sanctuary of that which in later times was called the Holy Graal. The first consideration which must be kept present to the mind, as if here were also an implicit, in dealing with our whole subject, is that nothing on its surface differs in doctrine or in specific institutes from the beaten tracks of the faith delivered to the saints, and yet all undergoes a great transfiguration. There are many quests in folk-lore which, in their bare outlines, are analogous to this quest, with due allowance for the distinction of motive and all that belongs to the class of voided marvels. There is also the great debate concerning initiation and its purport, which seems to hold a middle place between that which is below—and is nothing—and that which is above—and is all, tending to the same term as the higher, and exhibiting after what manner that which is mortal puts on immortality in virtue of high election. It is well to recall these things, because the text with which we are dealing, though it has its claims and intentions, is far from this term.

From the Merlin there follows directly the *Didot Perceval* as the Merlin Quest *par excellence*, but it gleams dimly through a vague species of cloud; and as there is much which preceded the romance of the prophet, and remains among the implicits of the literature, so there is much which might be supposed to come after the Quest, as, for example, the rewards which are somewhere held in reserve for those who practise holiness.

There is no doubt that up to a certain point the *Didot Perceval* connects logically with the two poems which, by the particular hypothesis, were designed to lead up thereto. Its ascription to Robert de Borron, by the secondary and reflective way of a prose version, has been rejected by certain students in the past, but the state of the case is doubtful and opinions vary. It is almost impossible to read the opening portion without feeling that here is the genuine third part of the trilogy; while the fact, so frequently exemplified, that Perceval remains throughout a *virgo intacta*, is in perfect harmony with the mind of the metrical romance. The *Early History* or first part of the *Vulgate Merlin* follows directly from the poem of Joseph of Arimathæa, and so far as we can ascertain it closed for Robert de Borron at that stage, when it could, without any violation, be merged in the Perceval legend, by which the tradition is continued without a break of any kind. One other favourable point, and assuredly these points are many, is that—unlike the *Book of the Holy Graal*, which makes an effort in this direction but fails manifestly—it does not seek to fill the gap left by De Borron's missing branches; it does not mention Petrus, his Brief notwithstanding; as to Brons, it says only that he is old and full of infirmity; as to Alain, he is dying. All this tends to show that the intermediate promised branches were non-existent rather than lost, and I say this remembering that one of the unprinted Merlin codices speaks of a text which contains the marriage of Alain.

To conclude as to this question, the early history of the prophet specifies at the term thereof that Arthur, after his coronation, held the kingdom of Logres long in peace, while it leaves Merlin as his councillor. The Perceval opens with an account of the prophet's instruction to the King concerning the Round Table and the Graal mysteries which went before its institution; it is only at the term of the Quest that Merlin passes into voluntary and, as one would think, ascetic retirement, free from personal enchantment and having delivered Britain from spell. The later Merlin texts, on the contrary, intern the prophet, and then, and not after, lead up to the Galahad Quest. It is difficult therefore to say that the *Didot Perceval* does not reflect, from at hand or afar, the lost romance which completed the trilogy of De Borron.

Perceval was the son of Alain le Gros, the grandson of Brons, and the third of that earthly trinity which was destined to possess the Graal. While Arthur was holding high festival at London and was listening to the counsel of Merlin, the voice of the Holy Spirit spoke to Perceval's father—he being near his end—and informed him that Brons, the Rich Fisherman and the Warden of the Graal, was in the isles of Ireland, and that the Holy Vessel was with him. He was old, as I have said already, but he could not seek refuge in death till he was found by the son of Alain, had communicated to this son the grace of that vessel, and had taught him the secret words which he learned himself from Joseph. To express it more nearly in language of romance, the Quest, which is the intention of the story, must be fulfilled in all perfection. Thereafter his infirmity would be healed, apparently by the medicine of eternity, or, as the text says, by his entrance into the great joy of that Father in Heaven whom he had served always in time. The youth, Perceval, was therefore directed to repair to the court of King Arthur, and it was promised him that in this place he should hear such tidings that he would be brought in due season to the house of the Rich Fisher. When Alain had received this direction, he bowed his head and entered himself, as one who arrives beforehand, into the Company of Christ.

Perceval, in his outward seeming, has little title to participate in the mysteries, except the title of his geniture. He is brave, savage and imperious; he is also chivalrous, but he is without the spiritual chivalry which we find in the great Quest. He was then living with his mother, who, as we can infer subsequently, sought to dissuade him from the journey; but obeying the Divine Voice, which had come also to him, he set out for the court of King Arthur; there he abode for a season; there he received the grade of chivalry. At the court he saw Aleine, the niece of Gawain, the niece also of the King, and the text says that she loved Perceval with all love that was possible, because in addition to his bravery he was also beautiful. It came about that she sent him red armour to wear on her behalf at a tournament; in this manner he was accounted her knight, and she shared in the glory of his achievements. But hereafter nothing follows concerning her. Perceval was proclaimed the best knight of the world after overcoming Lancelot and others of the high company at the joust, it being then the Feast of Pentecost. There was high feasting in the hall after the tournament, and Perceval, who was to some extent exalted, desired to occupy the seat left vacant at the Round Table for the predestined third custodian of the Holy Graal. King Arthur endeavoured to dissuade him, remembering the fate of Moses, but the prayers of Gawain and Lancelot prevailed with the monarch. A tremendous confusion ensued notwithstanding, over which rose the voice of an invisible speaker, bearing once more the same witness which the Voice of the Spirit had borne recently to Alain, but revealing further that the healing of the Rich Fisher depended on a visit to his castle which must be paid by the best knight of the world, who must ask further concerning the secret service of the Graal. By the instructions which would follow, a period should be put to the enchantments of Britain. The voice also spoke of the dolorous death of Moses, who, according to the text otherwise, was to remain in the abyss until the days of Anti-Christ. The Quest was undertaken by Perceval, and there were others, Gawain included, who also ventured forth therein, but it is stated that of how they fared the book, which is the proto-type, says nothing. Our text, however, shows on its own part that one of the knights was slain. King Arthur deplored the Quest, as he does in the romance of Galahad.

The course of Perceval's adventures covers many of those incidents with which we are acquainted already in the *Welsh Peredur* and the *Conte del Graal.* There is, for example, the visit to that strange castle wherein he plays chess with an invisible opponent, and is mated. From this follows some part of the episodes which concern the quest of the Stag's Head in company with a hound belonging to a maiden of the Castle. For our purpose it is more pertinent to mention that Perceval visited his sister, from whom he learned the story of their father, his own early history, and the prophecy concerning the Graal. He heard further that his mother was dead at grief for his departure, and though, under the direc-tion received, he cannot be said to have deserted her, it is accounted to him somehow as a sin after the con-fused manner of materials drawn from many sources. He visited also his uncle, the hermit, who is the brother of Alain, and is seemingly one of the twelve brethren who were children of Brons. It is obvious therefore that the note of time is again wanting entirely, as for any purpose of the story this perpetuation of ordinary life through the centuries has no meaning. Perceval confessed to his uncle and heard from him that at the table instituted by Joseph —he also assisting—the Voice of the Spirit commended them to journey far into the countries of the West, and ordained in particular that the Rich Fisher should go forth into those parts where the sun set. In fine, the hermit told him how the son of Alain le Gros would perform such feats of chivalry that he should be called the best knight of the world. It is obvious that this information does not correspond very closely with any extant text of Graal history. The uncle continued to speak of that peculiar and holy service to which the youth had been called, and counselled him to be pure in his life; but he did not, as in other quests, advise him to beware of idle speaking or of the curiosity which leads to questioning. After these things Perceval continued the Quest, and among other adventures he met with a knight who, owing to this encounter, had missed by seven days the crown of the world's knighthood, but who ultimately vanished from sight. He saw further the wonder of two children disporting themselves in a tree; they spoke to him of the Terrestrial Paradise and of the Holy Spirit; they also directed him on his Quest, so that he fared better according to this story than he did in the corresponding episode of the *Conte del Graal.* Perceval reached in fine the Castle of his grandfather, the Rich Fisher, where he was received after the mode of chivalry, and the Warden of the Graal was borne into his presence in the arms of sergeants. They sat down to table and the procession of the Hallows entered in the accustomed manner. Perceval was said, however, to remember one counsel of caution which he had received from his uncle in the matter of questioning, from which it is certain that the text follows some prototype which it does not reproduce faithfully. He was also outwearied by vigils on two previous nights, and his host, when he noticed this, directed the table to be removed and a bed to be prepared for the knight, who retired thinking deeply of the Lance and the Graal, promising himself that he would inquire of the pages tomorrow. The voice of the invisible speaker which had directed him and the others with such utter plainness at the court of King Arthur had lapsed apparently from his mind, and from that fatal inattention he passed into the forgetfulness of sleep. On the morrow he went down into the courtyard, to find his horse and arms awaiting him, but there was no one else to be seen. He was cursed by a maiden in a forest adjoining the Castle, and was told that, so only that he had asked the question, the prophecy of our Saviour to Joseph would have been accomplished; but of this prophecy we find no particulars in the antecedent texts. The Fisher King would have been restored to health, and there would have ceased those enchantments of Britain the nature and cause of which still fail to appear. Perceval sought in vain to rediscover the Castle, for over the whole land he could find its trace no longer. As in previous texts, he returned to the maiden of the chess-board, with the dog to her belonging and a stag's head. She desired him to remain in her company, but he left, with a promise to return, saying that otherwise he would be false to the vow which he had made. I infer that in this manner he preserved his desired purity, but he fell into other evils during a pilgrimage of seven years which followed thereafter. Through distress at being unable to find the Fisher King, he lost all memory of God until he met with the pilgrim company on Good Friday, who asked, as in previous texts, why he rode armed for purposes of destruction on such a sacred day. His better nature then returned to him, and before long he was knocking once more at the door of his uncle the hermit, to whom he confessed all. It was his intention to revisit his sister, but he was told that she was dead these two years past. After certain further episodes he met with Merlin, who reproached him for neglecting the Quest, much as he was reproached by a certain hutsman in one of the *additamenta* to the poem of Gautier. Perceval heard also that the health of the Rich Fisher was still such that he remained at the point of death, though he could not pass away. But his prayers were going up for his grandson, and by the will of God he was to be the guardian of the Precious Blood. The authority throughout is the record of Blaise, to whom Merlin returned after this conversation and recounted that which had passed, as he does so continually in the course of his own romance.

Perceval at last reached the Castle of the Rich Fisher for the second time; again he beheld the Graal, and on this occasion asked concerning its service, at which the King was cured, and in a moment, in the twinkling of an eye, all was changed about him. The relationship between them was declared, and Perceval being instructed in the history of the Hallows was led into the presence of the Holy Vessel, where the Voice of High Counsel told Brons to communicate the Secret Words. In the fulfilment of this command the ancient Warden might have been still speaking when the soul passed from his body, and Perceval saw how the angels bore it to the kingdom of Heaven, unto the Father whom he had served so long. Perceval remained in the Castle, practising wisdom, and there was an end to the enchantments of Britain. It was as if an interdict had been imposed and a legate had removed the interdict.

While things were so ordered in the secret sanctuary, there were events in the outer world which led up to the passing of Arthur, who was carried into Avalon to be healed of his grievous wounds by his sister Morgan le Fay. Merlin was still in evidence, passing to and fro between the king's court and the sanctuary of the Holy Vessel, where then, as subsequently, Perceval seems to have divided his office of Warden with the scribe of the records thereof. After the death of Arthur, Merlin appeared for the last time, recounting the woes which had befallen, whereat the place of the Hallows became a house of mourning and a chapel for the office of the dead. The prophet took leave of the Wardens, because it was God's will no longer that he should go to and fro in the world, and he would therefore betake himself, as if for a last refuge, to a hermitage in the forest which encompassed the castle. It follows that the term of Merlin is revolutionised in this romance; he does not pass in enchantment, inhibition and the folly of morganatic ties, but seeking the peace of God, and choosing the life of contemplation. Thereafter he was seen no longer, and there was no further story concerning the Holy Graal.

The *Didot Perceval* and the *Parsifal* of Wolfram are the only texts which leave the last Warden alive and dwelling in the sanctuary. It should be noted further that the Quest in this instance does not involve the destruction of Logres or a fatality to the Round Table, though this fatality occurs. The point is important, because it is another note of the correspondences between the *Didot Perceval* and the *Early Merlin*. The secret conspiracy, planned, as one might say, in the sanctuary, against the great chivalry was undreamed of by Robert de Borron and is peculiar to the Greater Chronicles. The unanimity of the Lesser Chronicles resides, among other things, in the fact that they are all texts of the Secret Sanctuary, and they emanate by the hypothesis therefrom. They suggest no public office; there is no travelling of the Graal. Britain suffers during the Quest period from an enchantment, but it is not described, and it is to be doubted whether Britain knew of it. It is the most occult of all processes and the most withdrawn of all localised mysteries. Brons and Alain have done nothing in the land; they are aliens of sanctity, with the burden of the years of the *Juif errant* upon them; and they abide in seclusion.

The *Didot Perceval* is scarcely at peace with itself over some of its elements, nor is it at peace with those texts antecedent from which it follows that the third keeper will (*a*) meet with Petrus, who carries the Sacred Brief, and with him compare their knowledge in common of the Graal Mystery; (*b*) find Moses, and this under circumstances which suggest some palliation at least of that which he has suffered through the ages. I do not think that these points make void its place in the trilogy, because there are several respects in which all the Graal books, like other romances of chivalry, are conventions of the cohorts of sleep, and there is sometimes a distracting spirit moving through the great dream.

BOOK V

THE GREATER CHRONICLES OF THE
HOLY GRAAL

THE ARGUMENT

I. THE BOOK OF THE HOLY GRAAL AND, IN THE FIRST PLACE, THE PROLOGUE THERETO BELONGING.—*The claims and defects of the Text regarded generally—The secret of this cycle—Its imputed authorship—Its hypothetical divisions—The Hermit of the Legend—What he read and saw at a Mass of the Presanctified—Disappearance of the Secret Book—The Quest of its recovery—The time for the transcript thereof.* II. A NEW CONSIDERATION CONCERNING THE BRANCHES OF THE CHRONICLE AND CONCERNING ITS MAJOR BRANCHES.—*Divergence of the extant manuscripts—The incorporation of De Borron elements—The point at which their tradition is broken, and this completely—The arrival at Sarras—Events which lead up to the conversion of this city—The Spiritual Palace—The ordination of Joseph II.—His later life—Of Evalach, the King of Sarras, who was afterwards Mordrains—Of Queen Sarracinte—Of Seraphe, who was also Nasciens—Of Celidoine, the son of Nasciens—The Ship of Solomon—The Building of Corbenic.* III. THE MINOR BRANCHES OF THE CHRONICLE.—*The Later History of Joseph of Arimathæa—The Life of Petrus in Britain—Of Brons and Alain—Variations in the History of Moses—Of Simeon and his Brethren—Concerning the first Galahad—The Genealogies—Conclusion as to the Book of the Holy Graal.* IV. SOME LATER MERLIN LEGENDS.—*And firstly as to the scope of these Texts—(A) The Vulgate Merlin—Its Antecedents in*

277

The Hidden Church of the Holy Graal

History — Merlin as the chief promulgator of the Graal
Mystery—The House of the Holy Vessel—Of the second
Nasciens and his history—King Pelles of Lytenoys—The
Maimed King—The Daughter of the House—A son of King
Pelles—Tidings of the Graal in Britain—(B) The Huth
Merlin—Its false ascription—Its consideration as a stately
romance—The intention of the story—Of secret records—
The branches of the story—The Internment of Merlin—
Concerning the father of Perceval—The Institution of the
Round Table—The Vacant Seat—The Hidden Life of the
Holy House—The Dolorous Stroke—The Secret Powers of
Avalon. V. THE GREAT PROSE LANCELOT.—The ante-
cedents of the story—An undeclared Mystery of the Graal
—Of Perceval in the Great Quest—Particular Graal tra-
ditions — Missing elements of Quest—The Genealogy of
Lancelot—His life in Faerie—Of Moses and Simeon—Of
Gawain at Castle Corbenic—Of Lancelot and the Lady of the
Bath—Helayne, the Maiden of the Graal—The conception
of Galahad. VI. A PREFACE OR INTRODUCTORY PORTION
APPERTAINING TO ALL THE QUESTS.—Claims of the questing
Knights—And further concerning Gawain—A pentagram of
chivalry—The Mystery of Divine Providence manifested in
flesh. VII. THE LONGER PROSE PERCEVAL.—Its imputed
antecedents—The initial point which constitutes a departure
from tradition—After what manner the departure is per-
petuated throughout — Of pageants abroad in the land—
The Earthly Paradise—The state of King Arthur—Of
Gawain's visit to the Graal — And that of Lancelot—
The death of Guinevere—Visions of the King—The King
of Castle Mortal—The death of King Fisherman—The
capture of the Graal Castle—The removal of the Hallows—
The siege and victory by Perceval—The reign of the last
Keeper—The distribution of the Hallows—The departure

of Perceval. VIII. THE QUEST OF THE HIGH PRINCE.—
*Of the generation of Galahad—Of some things which
followed thereafter—The circumstances of his first mani-
festation—Its mystic environment—Of the Eucharist in the
Quest—Of arch-natural feasting—The Quest in brief outline
—The liberation of Simeon—The release of King Mordrains
—The voyage in the Ship of Solomon—The term of Quest at
Corbenic—The Mystery unveiled—The Ascent of Galahad
—The doom of earthly Knighthood.* IX. THE WELSH QUEST.
*—The position of this version—Its variations in summary—
Wanderings of the Graal—The Dolorous Stroke—Specifics
of the last scene—Additamenta to the Greater Chronicles.*

BOOK V

THE GREATER CHRONICLES OF THE HOLY GRAAL

I

THE BOOK OF THE HOLY GRAAL AND, IN THE FIRST PLACE, THE PROLOGUE THERETO BELONGING

THE *Book of the Holy Graal* is the most conscious, most cumbersome, most artificial romance in the literature. It is that also which is beyond all prodigal of wonders, and its wonders are the least convincing. In so far as concerns the history of the Sacred Vessel, it must be said that it materialises the symbol and it also distracts the legend. Robert de Borron finished his metrical romance by confessing that for want of materials he must, for the time being, hold over those branches of his chronicle which were intended to deal with the further adventures of Brons, Alain, Petrus and the connected characters of the story. In the meantime he proceeded to the life of Merlin, bridging the gulf of centuries by a promise to retrace the path when he had obtained the necessary data, though it is possible enough that the intervening distances of time may have spelt little to his mind. All that could be construed as wanting is supplied by the *Book of the Holy Graal*, leaving nothing undone, but working through I know not what mazes of great enchantment. I have said that the artifice of the design—which obtains also for its expression—stands forth in full manifestation, even upon its surface. A hand more sparing might have worked greater marvels and left some sense of realism, at least in the order of faerie. And yet the prolix history has a certain touch of enchantment, all paths of disillusion notwithstanding.

From whatever point of view it is approached, the entire text will prove to be sown with difficulties—curious things in truth of the worlds within and without, but even as difficulties these have also their secret charm. It has vast sections of unnecessary matter which suggest an imperfect art of mere story-telling, and it also deals with materials which do not belong, more especially at its own period, to the horizon confessed by that art. Moreover, nothing is really finished, for, as one of its sub-titles indicates, it is the first branch of the romances of the Round Table, or it is rather the prolegomenon to these. A cycle of the literature of chivalry is supposed to follow thereafter, which may mean that the writer had a mind to go further, or, alternatively, that his intention was to present the collated antecedents leading up to other documents which in one or another form were there already in being. Accepting either alternative, this prolix introduction in general, which presupposes and from which *ex hypothesi* there follows so great a cloud of romance, offers herein a first point of distinction from the trilogy ascribed to Robert de Borron. The latter lies, comparatively speaking, within such a narrow compass and yet has a claim to completeness within its own lines and measures. There are other distinctions, however, which are not less marked in their character and are very much more important. The account which I propose of the document will differ from ordinary critical and textual apprehension by way of direct summary, since it is actuated by exclusive objects which connect with the design of my study.

As the Lesser Chronicles of the Holy Graal are concerned with the reservation of a great secret or sacramental formula, so there is also a secret in the *Book of the Holy Graal,* and herein is the second distinction which we are called to make between them. That particular form of the Eucharistic mystery which we find in Robert de Borron and his line of anonymous successors is made void by the later romance; as if it had planned to show that there were no secret words of consecration, the actual mass-words are given in full, and although they are those of a liturgy which differs from the formula of the Latin rite and betrays oriental influences, the variations are local and accidental, and, except for liturgical history, they wear no aspect of importance. At the same time, when the Hermit of the *Book of the Holy Graal* is first received into that state of vision from which the transcript of the text follows, what he is promised by Christ is the revelation of the greatest secret of the world. But this is the book itself, which is invariably spoken of as very small—so small indeed that it can lie in the hollow of his hand. This notwithstanding, it is the greatest marvel that man can ever receive. In its original form it was written by Christ Himself, who committed to writing only: (*a*) the *Book of the Holy Graal;* (*b*) the Lord's Prayer; (*c*) the words written in the sand, according to the New Testament. To pronounce aloud the words contained in the book would convulse the elemental world, and it must therefore be read with the heart.

Not exactly on this consideration but not for less cogent reasons, the first thing which is apparent concerning it is that although the Hermit is covenanted to transcribe it and to occupy in this task the period which intervenes between the fifteenth day after Easter and the day of the Ascension; although further he states expressly that what he wrote down is that which follows his prologue; the secret book committed to his charge is not that which he transmits as a memorial for those who come after him. I suppose that in registering this with a certain touch of fantastic gravity, my motive can be scarcely misconstrued; we are dealing with a parable or pretence, and the point is that it is not especially consistent within its own lines. After making every allowance for the variations of late editing, both intentional and otherwise, it remains that the text of the story voids the claim of the prologue, and this to such an extent that a substitute only is offered for that which was brought from heaven for the assumed illumination of Logres.

The Book of the Transcript is by the hypothesis of the prologue divided into four branches, of which the first concerns the lineage of the Hermit himself; and on the assumption that the *Huth Merlin* is correct in identifying the latter with that second Nascien, who, in the days of the enchanter and those of Uther Pendragon, was at first of the order of chivalry and afterwards a holy recluse, it will follow that the entire romance corresponds to this designation rather than an individual part. The second branch is that of the Holy Graal, which is the title of the collection itself: *Li Livres du Saint Graal*, and it cannot be allocated to a section. The third branch is called the beginning of the Terrors, and the fourth is that of the Marvels, which in like manner will not assist towards any logical classification, as we are concerned with something which answers in all its modes to the title of a wonder-book.

The most express, most ordered, most reasoned part of the entire history is assuredly what is termed the prologue; it is there that the Hermit accounts for the manner in which he came for a period into the possession of the original text. It reads in certain passages like a story of initiation. The *parti pris* is quick to self-deception, and one sees too easily that for which one is looking; but here are words which are exceedingly like the sign of recognition in a secret society: "The first Knight," says the Hermit, who has found refuge in a house of chivalry, "recognised me, as he believed, by a sign which I bore about me; he had seen me in a place which he named." But the Hermit evaded disclosures, for he was bent on concealing his mission, even as through the whole of his narrative he veils also his personality, though perhaps for the express object that it should transpire in the subsequent texts.

The circumstances under which he came to begin his story took place in Britain, 717 years after the Passion of Christ. It is to be inferred that prior to his mission he knew nothing concerning the Mystery of the Holy Graal, though he did know of his lineage, which may be intended according to the flesh or according to the mystical spirit, if its reference is to the grades of his initiation. On Maunday Thursday, after the office of *Tenebræ*, the Grand Master awoke him from sleep and gave him a book to ease his doubts on the subject of the Trinity. His immediate experience thereafter was the possession of a further gift, which was that of an infinity of tongues. He began reading the book and continued till Good Friday, when he celebrated a Mass of the Presanctified; between the breaking of the Host over the Chalice and his reception of the elements he was transported to the Third Heaven, and there was enabled to understand the Trinitarian Dogma by the dilucid contemplation of the Blessed and Glorious Trinity, with its distinction of Persons combined in the mystery of their Unity. In other words, this was the ecstasy of the Eucharist consequent upon his initiation into the sacramental power and grace enshrined in the *Book of the Holy Graal.* After Mass he placed the book in the Eucharistic dovecote, or tabernacle, with the intention not to reopen it till Easter Sunday, when he found that it had been abstracted strangely, and he undertook a wonderful pilgrimage in search of it. The explanation of this disappearance is perhaps that the Mystery of the Graal is of that which was buried with Christ and with Him rises, and the subsequent communication of the priest signifies that Christ is placed spiritually in many sepulchres.

That he might be directed rightly on his journey, the Hermit was led by an animal which combined the characteristics of the lamb, the dog, the fox and the lion; it was in fact that questing beast which reappears in later romance, and, according to its mystical sense, is explained by the *Longer Prose Perceval.* Ultimately he recovered the book; and this restoration was followed by a vision of our Saviour, who ordained its transcription, and on Ascension Day the original was reassumed into heaven. It will be seen that no pains are spared to exalt the work which follows this introduction; it is of mysterious and divine origin; a parchment copy is produced for earthly purposes by the highest of all ordinations; and as regards its source and nature it takes precedence of everything, even the canonical gospels.

The Doctrine of the Trinity was the great crux and mystery which seems to have exercised the minds of those who had entered the Path of Sanctity at the period immediately preceding the literature of the Holy Graal. It was the triumph of Faith to accept it, and he for whom it presented no difficulties had attained a very high grade of illumination. The hermit of the prologue to the *Book of the Holy Graal* is moved profoundly by the question, and its solution is the great incentive which is offered him when he sets out on his pilgrimage to recover the vanished book, which, in spite of the content exhibited by its assumed transcript, is intended of itself—as we have seen—to allay his doubts on the subject. We should remember that in the year 1150 the Church had established the Festival of the Most Holy Trinity, and it was a quarter of a century later that the transformed Graal legends began to manifest on the horizon of romantic literature.

II

*A NEW CONSIDERATION CONCERNING THE
BRANCHES OF THE CHRONICLE*

Not the least difficulty in the *Book of the Holy Graal*,
regarded as a work of " truth in the art " of its particular
mystery, is the divergence exhibited by the extant manuscripts. These differences meet us, perhaps chiefly,
at the inception of the story, though they are with us
even at the end. In respect of the latter there are texts
which incorporate a distinct romance which is impertinent
to the design of the story. In respect of the former, it
should be understood that it is of the essence of the
whole design to make a beginning from the same point
of departure at which Robert de Borron started his
metrical romance, and all recensions present therefore
some kind of prose version reflecting his narrative. One
of them—and it is the most available of the printed texts
—has only moderately grave variations from the *Lesser
Holy Graal* up to that epoch of the story when the company of Joseph of Arimathæa set out on their journey
westward ; but another presents a brief summary which
scarcely stands for the original. It is not part of my
province to express opinions belonging to the domain of
textual criticism, but I think that the design of the *Book
of the Holy Graal* is represented better and more typically
by a manuscript like that which was made use of by Dr.
Furnivall for the *Early English Text Society*, and this is
the summarised form, than it is by a manuscript like
that which Hucher selected for the first printed edition,
and this is the extended version.

The incorporation of De Borron elements serves one
purpose which is material from my own point of view, as
it sets in relief the distinction *ab origine symboli* between
the actuating motives of the two cycles of literature. It
will be remembered that in the metrical romance and its

later reflections the narrative is broken rudely at that moment when the horizon has begun to expand by an inspired resolution of the company to part into several groups and proceed westward separately. Three subsequent divisions were involved hereby, and these Robert de Borron promised to expound in their proper order when he received true reports concerning them. The author of the *Book of the Holy Graal* undertook to supply these missing branches, but as the results differ, and in no light manner, from the manifest intent of De Borron, it may be deduced that they are not the real history, as this might have been set forth by the pious minstrel. On his part there was probably no design to bring Joseph of Arimathæa either to the *Vaux d'Avaron* or another part of Britain. The doubtful meaning of some of his lines must be taken in connection with the general scheme of his narrative. That scheme was to establish the mystery of sanctity in great seclusion under the government of a single keeper, with a life protracted through the centuries, until the time of its possible manifestation came. The *Lesser Holy Graal* is a reasonably faithful version of his nearly complete poem, though it is doubtful regarding Joseph's final destination. The *Early History of Merlin* is also faithful to what remains of De Borron's second metrical romance. Of the *Didot Perceval* we cannot speak so certainly, but in several points about which we have materials for judgment—and more especially regarding Moses—it does not correspond properly. It is even possible that the *Didot Perceval* is a speculative completion of the trilogy, characterised by remarkable insight, and yet without any accurate notion of De Borron's design, this being manifested imperfectly by his extant literary remains.

It will be understood, therefore, that the *Book of the Holy Graal*, or the great romance which follows the parable of the prologue, begins, in the codex here followed, with a short account of the chief incidents in the life of our Saviour and the condition of Palestine at the period.

It repeats the familiar story of the *Lesser Holy Graal*, but sometimes, as we have seen, only by way of summary, and always with many variations. The fact that Joseph is married and has a son in his infancy at the time of the Passion of Christ may be taken as the first important point of difference; he is named after his father, and to distinguish between them the orthography adopted by the romance to designate the son is Josephes, for which in the present account I shall substitute Joseph II. The next point of difference, with which we are also acquainted already, concerns the identification of the Holy Graal with the dish of the Paschal Supper—*en quoi li fiex dieu avoit mangie*—instead of with the Eucharistic vessel of sacrifice; but it should be said that there is another text which follows the description in the *Lesser Holy Graal*. The circumstances under which the Great Hallow was discovered, after the apprehension of Christ, also vary, and in place of its abstraction by a Jew, who carries the Hallow to Pilate, it is found by Joseph himself in the house where the Pasch was eaten, and is removed by him to be kept for a memorial of the Master. As in the other romances, it is used to collect the blood, which, however, is done no longer on Calvary, but in the sepulchre itself. The general lines established by Robert de Borron are followed as regards the imprisonment of Joseph, the circumstances under which he was released by Vespasian after a term of forty-two years, and the vengeance wreaked upon the Jews. All lapse of years notwithstanding, Joseph is reunited to his wife and son, is baptized, with a great number of his relatives, and he is directed by Christ to go with those who will follow him into distant countries, carrying neither gold, silver, nor any material possession except the Holy Graal. It is after this point that the prototype of Robert de Borron is abandoned once and for all. The first destination— reached by way of Bethany and the Wood of Ambush— is the city of Sarras, situated in a country of the same name on the confines of Egypt. From this land it is stated that the Saracens originated; the people are described as worshippers of the sun, moon and planets. It is also this place which is termed in later romances the spiritual city, though it is not on account of the faith found in its citizens—who appear to have been a perverse nation at the beginning and end—but because, according to the story, it contained the *palais esperiteus*, which name was given it by the prophet Daniel, who emblazoned it on the door thereof. The story is apocryphal, but the design is to show that even the seers of Israel were aware of the coming of the Graal, for it was in this palace that the Eucharist was first consecrated. It was the witness on the dry land, as the ship of Solomon was the witness on the open sea.

At Sarras Joseph found Evalach, its aged king, in great trouble through an invasion of his country by the Egyptians under Ptolemy. Joseph commended his conversion as a certain guarantee of his victory, but the king, though not disinclined, was not baptized actually until his enemies were dispersed with final slaughter. The power operating in his favour rested chiefly in a cross painted on his shield by Joseph. The story of the war and its wonders occupies a substantial part of the narrative, and before Joseph departed on his further journey westward the whole population of the country appears to have embraced Christianity. Several churches were built in the city or its vicinity, bishops and priests were ordained, and masses were celebrated therein.

England is the Promised Land which the special providence of the story has allocated to the spiritual and material lineage of Joseph of Arimathæa; and after the departure from Sarras the sole concern of all the involved adventures is, separately or collectively, to bring the various characters to this country and to reunite them therein, the evangelisation of the existing inhabitants being the palmary term of all. Speaking of the rank and file, apart from several of the more important personages, the good Christians are transported hither miraculously on a garment belonging to the second Joseph, but those who are imperfect come by ship. Some of the great heroes arrive independently under circumstances which I shall describe in the considerations to each allotted. Joseph of Arimathæa reaches the general bourne, and though the superior importance of his son causes him to be almost effaced, we hear of him from time to time during long years of continued existence. At length he left this world to be united with Christ, to whom all his love was dedicated. He was buried at the Abbey of the Cross in Scotland, for which one codex substitutes Glastonbury.

There is a general sense in which the *Book of the Holy Graal*—like the metrical romance of De Borron—is the Book of the Divine Voice which speaks from the Sacred Vessel, though this is not used to pronounce oracles or to separate the good from the evil as it does in the earlier text. The difficulties which are raised by the story regarding that Mystery of Faith which it exists to show forth are so grave and so numerous that I must be satisfied with the registration of the fact and its illustration by one instance. The whole notion of the Eucharist is changed by the supposition that, on occasion, it is administered to angels, for by no hypothesis can Christ be regarded as their Saviour.

Seeing that there is no clear division of episodes in the story, so that one section can be separated definitely from another, I shall attempt only a general grouping. The master-branch of the whole prodigal romance is that which embraces the mission of Joseph II.—this is of the essence, and all else is, in comparison, of the accidental order. About this central figure the wonder of the Graal converges and the confused cloud of marvellous incidents; from the first even to the last, he is thus steeped in a light of mystery that "never was on land or sea." Prior to the arrival at Sarras a command was received from the Son of God to build an ark, similar to that of the Old Covenant, for the reception of the Holy

Graal. Public devotions were to take place before it, but only Joseph and his son had a right to open the Shrine, to look into the Reliquary and to take it in their hands. Two chosen men were deputed to carry the Ark on their shoulders when the company was on the march. The intention was evidently to invest the new symbol with the same authority as that palladium which once belonged to Israel. To provide sustenance for the band during the journey, each disciple—after the daily service of prayer—found in his lodging the food which he desired in abundance, but it is not said that it was provided by the Holy Graal.

While the conversion of the King and the issue of the war were still pending at Sarras, things of far other importance were taking place in respect of the Sacramental Mystery under the charge of Joseph and his son. The pilgrims on their advent had been lodged in that building which was named the Spiritual Palace. The inhabitants of Sarras did not know why it had received this designation, but the arrival of the Christian cohort was to reveal the prophetic mystery—firstly, by the presence of the Ark and the Graal therein, and, secondly, by the sacred wonders which accompanied the ordination of Joseph II., with Christ manifested visibly as the Celebrant-in-chief. In that Palace, on the day following their arrival, the Holy Spirit advised Joseph the father that his son had been chosen to guard the Graal, as the Aaron of the new Rite, that he was to be ordained by the highest consecration, and was to transmit the priesthood to those whom he deemed worthy thereof. Joseph II. received also the power to hand on the Sacred Vessel to whomsoever he would, and it is to be inferred that he committed everything in the plenary sense—as if Christ said to His successor: "My peace I leave with you; My peace I give unto you."

When the company were worshipping before the Ark in the Spiritual Palace, the Holy Spirit descended in still fire, as at another Pentecost, and entered into the mouth of each one of them, like the Eucharist of some final dispensation which has not been declared on earth. It communicated, however, the gift of silence instead of the gift of tongues. A Voice also spoke and though apparently it was that of the Spirit, it was also the voice of Christ. The discourse was memorable enough, but I can speak only of its end, when the younger Joseph was directed to approach and receive the most great honours which could be conferred on earthly creature. He opened the door of the Ark and beheld a man clothed in a terrible vestment of scarlet flame. There were also five angels apparelled after the same manner, each having six wings of fire, like the vision of Ezekiel. In their right hands they held various symbols of the Passion—about which we have heard already—and each in his left carried an ensanguined sword. The human figure was that of Christ, with the five wounds upon Him. It is said by the text that the Ark had been magnified strangely, so that it would hold the Divine Personalities of the vision : but I conclude rather that when the door was opened, those who were empowered to behold looked as into a seeringglass, which contains at need the earths of the universe and the earths of the starry heavens, with all that dwell thereon. The state of the second Joseph is shown by the words addressed to his father, praying that he should touch him in nowise, lest the speaker be drawn from the joy of his entrancement. That which he next beheld was the crucifixion itself, presented in ritual form, with the angels for the actors therein. It seemed even as in one of the Greater Mysteries which I have seen with my own eyes, when the Adept Master is set on a cross of dedication and the officers of the high ceremonial are those who combine to immolate him. But the design in the case under notice was rather to certify concerning the Vessel of the Graal, for the side of Christ was pierced and the *sang réal* poured therein. The scene closed and a new scene was opened, this time more especially before the eyes of Joseph the father. What he beheld was an altar within the Ark draped in white over red, bearing the Sacred Dish, the nails of transfixion and the ensanguined head of the Lance. These objects were arranged on the epistle and gospel sides, but in the centre—or place of consecration—covered with a white corporal—there was a rich golden vessel with a covercle, also of gold, and it is recorded that all precautions were taken that the contents should remain hidden. A procession of angels entered with lights, aspergillus, thurible, incense-boat, and then—out of all knowledge—one carrying a head, as I suppose, on a salver, and another with a drawn sword. This pageant went about the house, as if for a Rite of Consecration, the Graal being also carried, and Christ entered, even as the Priest of the Rite, clad in sacramental robes for the celebration of Mass. The circumambulation being finished for the cleansing of the whole place—which, in spite of its name, had been the abode of evil and the spirit thereof—Christ told Joseph II. that he was to receive the Eucharist, and, as if constituted a secret pope, he was made and ordained sovereign bishop reigning over the world of Christendom. He was clothed with rich episcopal vestments and set in an episcopal chair, which the text says was still preserved at Sarras, where it proved to be another Siege Perilous and whosoever sat therein was maimed or destroyed utterly. Joseph was anointed by Christ, and with the oil which was used for this purpose the Kings of England were consecrated in later years up to the time of Uther Pendragon; but it was missing at his coronation. The ring of investiture, given to the prelate thus hallowed strangely, could be counterfeited by no human skill, nor could words express the virtues contained in its jewel.

When the ceremony was at length over and the divine discourse had explained one by one the spiritual significance of each part of his clothing, Joseph II. was instructed by Christ to consecrate the sacred elements, and it thus came about that the people of the new exodus communicated for the first time: but the Host which was elevated by Joseph was the body of a child and that which was received by the faithful, in the mouth of each one among them, was living and undivided flesh. The administration to the cohort of worshippers was, however, performed by angels, one of whom took the paten together with the chalice and placed both of them in the Holy Vessel of the Graal. Whether the Precious Blood adhered to the Eucharistic Vessel and the content of the Reliquary thus suffered diminution we do not know, nor the purpose otherwise of the ceremony, which, fortunately for the spiritual side of *la haute convenance*, is not repeated either in the romance itself or anywhere in the literature.

Thus was the second Joseph consecrated in the super-apostolical degree, and thus did he see—at least in the sense of the story—all Christ's mysteries openly. The issues which are raised by the narrative are much more complicated than will be gathered from the preceding summary. Scholarship has paid little heed to the importance of the sacramental question and all connected therewith, but it has not overlooked the pontifical supremacy which is ascribed to the reputed founder of Christianity in Britain. While the ecclesiastical consequence to these islands is perhaps the only thing which can be said to stand forth clearly, it must be added that if the intention was to make void one claim of the Papacy, there was never a design so clouded and veiled so sedulously. The brief for any secret pontificate is proclaimed much less openly than the general brief for the official Church, with all its ways and laws, as we are acquainted with its body—politic and spiritual—at the period. Still it is said expressly, in words ascribed to the Master: (*a*) that Joseph has been chosen as the first pastor of a new flock; (*b*) that his eminence is comparable explicitly in the New Law with that of Moses, the Leader of Israel, in the Law which had been now superseded; (*c*) that wherever he went, converting people and places, he was there to consecrate bishops and ordain priests, who would have power to bind and loose, even as the apostles; and that, in fine (*d*), to the younger Joseph was committed the government of souls, but to the elder that of bodies—the spiritual and temporal powers. It does not appear especially that the latter ever exercised his prerogative; but it may be recalled that whereas the first issue of the temporal power was after the spiritual kind, the second was after the material—on the one hand, Joseph II., who never married, whose office was devised by election; on the other, Galahad le Fort, who became an earthly King, who was anointed with the mystic oils by his brother Joseph, and who reigned gloriously. We may speculate, but it will be all in vain, as to what was in the mind of the author when he substituted a son for the father, and, as if further to confuse the issues, gave both of them the same name. Whatever the explanation may be, from that moment when the younger man assumed the reins of government in the spiritual degree, the older ceased to retain even the shadow of power. As regards Galahad le Fort, his birth took place in Britain, and it was foretold to his brother in a vision that he would be the ancestor of a holy lineage of many men of religion, who should maintain the name of our Saviour in all honour and all power throughout these islands.

His great election and his association in the highest notwithstanding, the second Joseph was not intended to escape without the purgation of suffering. When he and his company were at Orcauz, in the district of Sarras, he was punished for attempting to bind a devil who was hovering over the dead bodies of certain Saracens; for this indiscretion, a great vindicating angel, with a marvellous countenance, drove a spear into his thighs and left the weapon therein. Subsequently, he was healed by another angel, who drew out the head of the spear. That which Joseph II. should have contrived was apparently the conversion of the heathen, and in this having failed he was not to intervene between the destroyer and the victims. I mention these matters, firstly, because the office of wounding in the thighs recurs so continually in the romances, and, secondly, to note that for some obscure reason the injury in question never befalls the questing knights. The Lance used on this occasion is also important because of its after-history, for it was destined to prove the beginning of those great marvels which would occur in the land of Britain. At that time it is said that the Lance will drop blood and will strike—also in both thighs—another personage of the mystery, a knight full of charity and chastity, who will suffer for as many years as Joseph had carried the weapon in his own wound for days. These, on the computation of the victim, proved to be twenty-two. The reference is here to King Pellehan, whose wounding is narrated, as we know, in the *Huth Merlin*, and who is healed in the *Quest of Galahad*; the wounding in question is the Dolorous Stroke inflicted by the poor knight Balyn; and it follows that the *Book of the Holy Graal* gives an origin of the Lance-Hallow which either differs from that of all other texts or it has omitted to mention that the angel of the judgment used the Spear of the Passion.

When the company of pilgrims at length reached the sea-shore, from which they must cross over to Britain, those who bore the Ark of the Graal on their shoulders walked over the intervening waters as if upon the dry land; of the others, those who were in a state of grace crossed on the shirt of the second Joseph, as if on a raft; but the evil livers were left to fare as they could till ships could be found to carry them. I am not concerned with the events which followed the arrival of all and sundry in the promised land of their inheritance, but as regards Joseph II., his evangelical journeys through England, Scotland, Wales, Ireland and, as it is said, other strange countries, continue through the rest of the narrative, till at last he visits King Evalach in an abbey which had been founded by the latter and informs him of his own immediate death on the following day. This occurs accordingly at the hour of prime next morning, and he was buried in the abbey. So was Joseph II. gathered into the Kingdom of the Father, and I pass now to the history of one who was designed as a witness through the centuries to that mystery which was from the beginning of the Christian times, who, in fine, could enter into his rest only through the arms of Galahad.

King Evalach received the name of Mordrains in baptism, and he remained in his kingdom after Joseph and his company continued their journey westward. The design of the story, as we have seen, is, however, to bring all its characters into *la bloie Bretagne*, and with this object it puts the most complicated machinery in motion for some of the palmary heroes. I must speak only concerning the term in its attainment, omitting in the present case the visions and the bodily transportations which befell Mordrains for his further instruction and purgation. He left Sarras ultimately and for ever, taking his wife with him and three hundred barons, and proceeding to the rescue of Joseph, whom a revelation had told him was imprisoned by the King of North Wales. His own realm was committed to the charge of the good knight Aganore, who was to be King in his place and so to remain if he did not return himself. He carried with him the white shield by the help of which he overcame the powers of Egypt, so that this also passed into the West and was kept in perpetuity as one of the Lesser Hallows. The journey took place by ship in the ordinary way; Joseph and his people were rescued in due course, and of all their enemies not one was left alive. For this providence public thanksgivings took place in the presence of the Graal, the Ark of the New Covenant being set open for the purpose. Evalach, who had experienced already the delicious effects which followed an exposition of the Sacred Vessel, desired to see with his own eyes the interior of that Sanctuary from which the grace appeared to emanate. Though incapacitated by wounds received in the recent combats, he went to the door of the Ark and looked in. He saw the Holy Dish and the Chalice used for Eucharistic purposes. He saw also Bishop Joseph clothed in the beautiful vestments in which he had been consecrated by Christ. The romance says that no mind could conceive and much less the tongue express all that which was discovered to him. So far he had been kneeling with head and shoulders bent forward, but he now arose and pressed nearer. In vain a voice issued from a burning cloud and warned him to desist; he advanced his head further, when paralysis and blindness overtook him. Of all his members he preserved only the use of his tongue, and the first words which he pronounced were those of adoration, even for the misfortune which had befallen him and which he also recognised that he deserved for surprising Divine Secrets. Even at the price of his health, and of age-long suffering thereafter, he would not have renounced the knowledge which he had attained in the Ark. One of the spectators asked what he had seen, and he answered: " The end of the world, the Marvel of all marvels, the Wisdom which is above wisdom, the King of every king." The last wish recorded on the part of Evalach, who henceforth was to be termed Mehaigné—that is to say, the Maimed King—was that he should be carried to a hermitage far from other habitation, as the world and he had no further need for one another. The second Joseph approved, because the day of Evalach's death would not be witnessed even by his children's children. He was carried on a litter to the hermitage and placed before the altar, where he would be in the presence of the Body of the Lord whenever Mass was celebrated thereat. Upon the site of the hermitage a fair abbey was built subsequently, and there Mehaigné remained till the coming of the younger Galahad—or, as the chronology of the story states, for 200 years. On the day which preceded the death of Joseph II. that First Bishop of Christendom anointed the King's White Shield with his own blood, thus making a second cross upon it. It was reserved for the Knight Galahad, and should any one attempt to use it in the meantime he would repent it quickly. Mehaigné regained his sight so that he could behold this shield and the ceremony of the Unspotted Sacrifice.

With the story of Evalach there is connected that of his wife, Queen Sarracinte. While her husband was in warfare with the hosts descended from Egypt, she sent for Joseph to ask news concerning him, praying the apostle to intercede with God and to turn him to her own belief. Her mother had been converted through the offices of a certain hermit, and this, assisted by a vision, led to her own christening. Thereafter she was permitted to see a white box which was kept by the elder lady among treasures of jewels, and on being opened it proved to contain our Saviour under the element of bread. The mother received the Host, for it proved that she was departing this life, and she charged her daughter to keep the box secretly, and so have Christ every day in her company, as by a high dispensation had been permitted in her own case. When she was dead Queen Sarracinte went to the hermit, obtained Christ from him, as a sacred treasure, received the Host in the secret tabernacle and performed her devotions in Its presence. Outside this amazing reservation, the point of importance is that although Joseph II. was, by the hypothesis of the story, the first priest to consecrate the elements of the Eucharist, this was being done already—apparently long before—by a hermit in Sarras, who must have derived from the ordinary apostles. There is a suggestion of strange implicits in the names of the next character which I have placed on my list for inclusion in these major branches. He was Seraphe in his days as a paynim, carrying an axe keen as a serpent of fire and evoking in his need out of the invisible the vision of a white Knight mounted on a white horse, from which he dealt archnatural destruction. In baptism, with the others who elected to be redeemed out of Sarras, he assumed the name of Nasciens, as if in a new generation he had been received into the *militia crucifera evangelica*, with a mission to enter the West and preach the Gospel with his sword. Seraphe was the son-in-law of Evalach the king—a large man, strong-boned and broad-shouldered. Great and many were the miracles which brought him by slow stages to the Isles of Britain, but I will speak only of his sojourn on the Turning Island, from which he was rescued by that Mystic Ship of Solomon which fills so important an office in the *Quest of Galahad*.

Nasciens watched the vessel coming to him fast over the sea; it was richer than any other in the world, but no one was visible therein. He prepared to go on board, when he saw golden letters in the Chaldaic tongue giving warning that those who entered must be full of faith and clean in every respect. He was deterred at first, but after fervent prayer he entered, believing that it had been sent by God. He found therein a mysterious couch, having at its head a crown of gold and at the foot a marvellous sword, which was drawn ten inches out of the scabbard. Connected with the bed there were three spindles of strange colourings, though not as the result of artificial tincture; one was red, another white, and the third green. The story of the Ship is recounted at great length, and to express it as shortly as possible, the royal prophet of Israel had learned by a message from heaven that the last knight of his lineage would exceed all other chivalry as the sun outshines the moon. By the sage counsel of his wife, he built this ship to last for 4000 years, with the double object of making known to Galahad not only the royalty of his descent, but the fact that the wise king was aware of his birth in due time. The building was accomplished in six months, and then the Queen told him to provide King David's sword as an arm of might for his descendant. It was adorned with a new handle, pommel and sheath—all of great virtues—and a writing about it said that no man should draw it with impunity, save one who passed all others in prowess and perfection of virtue.

Solomon would have also provided rich hangings, but was deterred by his wife, who testified that they must be foul and of her own making, till another woman should, in the coming time, provide draperies that were glorious. The high office was reserved therefore for the most fair, faithful and unearthly sister of Perceval. In this connection, I may say that one of the side-problems of the whole narrative is that in spite of the wonderful counsel which Solomon receives from his wife, and in spite of the sacred, exalted meaning attached to the ship which was built by her directions, she is described as a woman who had deceived him and had embittered him regarding her sex.

The wooden bed seen by Nasciens was also placed in the Ship, and the sword was laid thereon as well as the crown, which was also that of David. By the same unaccountable directions the three spindles were of wood derived from the Tree of Knowledge in the manner here following. Adam and Eve ate the forbidden fruit; the apple which she gathered brought with it a branch; the fruit was separated by Adam and the branch remained with Eve, who preserved it in their exile as a memorial of her misfortune. It was planted by her and became a great tree, which—both within and without—was white as snow. One day, when they were seated beneath it lamenting their unfortunate condition, Eve called it the Tree of Death, but a voice bade them comfort one another, for life was much nearer than death—whereupon they termed it by substitution the Tree of Life. They planted cuttings thereof, which grew and flourished; these were white like the parent tree, but after the conception of Abel they all turned green, bearing flowers and fruit. It was under the first tree that Abel was murdered—when it changed from greer to red and no longer bore flowers or fruit; in later times it was called the Tree of Counsel and of Comfort.

When the Ship was fully garnished, Solomon placed a letter beneath the crown, giving warning to his de-

scendant against the wiles of women and asking to
be held in his remembrance; he recounted also the
building. The Ship was launched; the king saw in a
vision how a great company of angels descended and
entered therein, as it sailed far out of sight.

Nasciens learned further that the Ship typified the
Holy Church of Christ, and as the latter has only
faith and truth therein, so in its symbol no faithless
men could have part; confession and repentance were
necessary qualifications to enter Church or Ship. The
inscriptions in the Vessel were Holy Scripture; in a
word, as the text suggested, it was a symbol rather than
a ship. The sea over which it sailed signified the world;
the bed was the Holy Altar, on which the Divine Son
is consecrated and offered daily; in another sense, it
was also the Cross of Christ. The white spindle meant
Christ's virginity, the red one His humility and love,
while the green one signified His patience.

So far as regards the Ship of Solomon, and in respect
of Nasciens himself, before closing his story, I must speak
of two visitations which befell him. Soon after his
conversion he was filled with the same desire to know
the Mysteries of the Graal for which Mordrains paid
afterwards so heavily and yet was so well recompensed;
he raised up the paten which covered the Sacred Vessel
and by his own account he beheld the foundations of
knowledge and religion, the beginning of all bounty
and all gentility. We may remember here the old
poet who said that Christ was "The first true gentle-
man that ever breathed"; and doubtless the sacramental
mystery is also a mystery of courtesy. Nasciens was
blinded for his presumption and remained in this affliction till the healing of Joseph II. from the wounding of
the angel. His second visitation occurred on board the
Ship of Solomon, wherein he had been united with his
son and subsequently with King Mordrains. To the latter
he showed the Sword of David, but when the King took
it in his hands the weapon broke in two pieces and re-

joined as suddenly. At this moment they were warned
to leave the Ship, and in the act of obeying Nasciens was
wounded grievously between the shoulders by the Sword.
He regarded this as a chastisement in loving-kindness
for his sins, but the episode is made more intelligible by
another codex, which shows how he was tempted to draw
the Sword from its sheath and use it as his defence against
a giant when no other weapon was available. It broke in
the mere brandishing and so remained, but it was rejoined,
unaccountably enough, by the handling of Mordrains.
Towards the close of the story, a certain King Varlans
too finds the Sword of David in the Ship of Solomon and
uses it to slay Lambor, who was one of the twelve sons
of Brons and at that time Keeper of the Graal. There
followed great sorrow and suffering in the lands of both
rulers ; both were ruined by the stroke ; and Varlans, on
restoring the weapon to the Ship and therein sheathing it,
fell down dead. It will be seen that a kind of enchantment thus befalls these parts of Britain, though the *Book
of the Holy Graal* is rather the cycle of adventures than
that of enchantments. The Sword was to remain sheathed
until drawn by a maiden—that is to say, by the sister of
Perceval.

There is another story of a sword which belongs
properly to a different branch of the romance, but it
may be mentioned in this place. Joseph of Arimathæa
is wounded, as usual, in the thigh by a false steward,
leaving half of the sword in the wound. With the upper
half Joseph heals a Saracen Knight, whom he has converted
newly, and then uses it to withdraw the point from his
own flesh ; it comes out unstained by blood, and Joseph
foretells that the two parts shall not be joined together
till he arrives who shall end the adventures of the Graal.
This is the Hallow which is resoldered by Galahad at
Corbenic when the Holy Quest has ended.

So far as Nasciens is concerned the remainder of the
story deals more especially with his deeds of valour in
connection with the conversion of Britain, which he

reached at length by ship and was instrumental in bringing over those who had been left on the further shore by reason of their departure from grace. His death took place prior to that of the second Joseph, and he was buried in the abbey of white monks where Mordrains awaited his end.

Celidoine, the son of Nasciens, is in one sense a lesser character, but in the symbolism of the story he seems to stand for something that is important. He is said to have been born under the happiest of starry influences and was himself a reader of the stars, from which he drew presages and on one occasion ensured a Christian victory in consequence. The meaning of his name itself is explained to be the Gift of Heaven. One day Mordrains had a vision concerning him, and therein he was represented by a lake, into which Christ came and washed His hands and feet. This signified that God visited Celidoine daily because of his good thoughts and actions. Nine streams issued from the lake, typifying the boy's descendants. Into eight of them Christ also passed and made a similar lustration. Now the ninth was troubled at the beginning—foul even and turbulent—but in the middle it was translucent as a jewel and at the mouth more sweet and pleasant than thought can picture. Before entering this stream Christ laid aside all His vestments and was immersed wholly—that is to say, in the good works of Galahad. The troubled source signified the stain on that knight by reason of his conception, and the removal of the vestments meant that Christ would discover to the *haut prince* all his mysteries, permitting him in fine to penetrate the entire secrets of the Graal.

The external life of Celidoine, who reached Britain by himself in a boat, does not concern us except in broadest outline. As his father wrought with the sword of earthly knighthood in the cause of Christ, so did the son fight with the sword of the spirit—that is to say, with the tongue of eloquence, and paynim clerks and sages could not withstand him. Among many others he

U

converted the Persian King Label and was married to his daughter. As he was a prodigy from the beginning and was knighted in his eighth year, he is comparable to a sanctified Merlin.

One section of the romance which certainly calls to be included among the major branches, and may even be considered by some as important of all, has been reserved here till the last, and this is the permanent House of the Holy Graal. During the keepership of Joseph II. the Vessel, and the Ark which contained it, shared in the travels of the apostolate, but it found a place of rest during the reign of his successor—who was Alain, as we shall learn later. With a hundred companions he had proceeded to the realm of Forayne, where the King was a knight of worth, but a paynim and also a leper. He inquired whence his visitors came, and was told from Jerusalem; he asked further whether his disease could be cured, and was assured that it was more than possible if he forsook the evil law and became a Christian. To this the King consented, and after his conversion and baptism he was healed by the sight of the Graal, this being the only occasion on which the Vessel was shown to a stranger. It is important also to note that though Alain was the Keeper of the Hallows, he was not an ordained priest and he employed one for the purpose of baptizing. It follows, therefore, that the episcopal functions of Joseph II. did not devolve on his successor, and it is certain also that there was no sacerdotal character attributed to the still later wardens—or, among others, to King Pelles, who was the Keeper in the days of Galahad. The new convert was christened Alphasan, and he proposed to build a castle for the reception of the Graal, to marry his daughter to Joshua, the brother of Alain, and to make him the heir of his kingdom, if the Graal remained therein. Hereto Alain consented; the castle was built; and at its completion they found an instruction emblazoned in red letters on one of the gates, saying that it should be called Corbenic, the meaning of which, as we know, is the Treasury of the Holy Vessel. This is on the authority of the text and it is not an unreasonable persuasion to believe that the author knew what he intended to convey by the word which he seems to have compounded ; but as it has not given universal satisfaction we have variants, of which some are as follows : Carbonek = Caer Banawc—the Castle of the Corners, or the Square Castle, but this has nothing to commend it ; Corbenic = *De Corpore Benedicto*, which is high phantasy, but is charming in that sense ; Cor-arbenig = the Sovereign Chair, which is perfect past all desiring if the House of the Graal was the seat of a secret doctrine.

The Holy Vessel was placed in a fair chamber, as if on an Altar of Repose, and on the next Sunday Joshua was married to the King's daughter. His coronation also took place, and in the feast which followed the company was replenished by the grace of the Graal with all manner of delicacies. That same night the King made the fatal mistake of sleeping in the palace which he had built, and he awakened to witness a Mass of the Graal, celebrated in his room apparently. It was, I suppose, at the term of the service that the Vessel is said to have been removed suddenly, and there appeared one wearing the likeness of humanity but composed as if it were of flame. He upbraided the King for reposing in a House so holy as that where the Vessel was worshipped, and as a warning to all who should come after he smote him through both thighs with a sword. The sword was withdrawn, the figure vanished, and Alphasan died ten days afterwards. It was in this way, and at first by the voice of the victim, that Corbenic came to be called the Palace of Adventure ; many knights attempted to sleep therein subsequently, but they were always found dead in the morning, one strong hero of Arthur's chivalry excepted, and he suffered for it otherwise.

III

THE MINOR BRANCHES OF THE BOOK OF THE HOLY GRAAL

The things which remain over from the last section for consideration at the term of this inquest are chiefly derivatives from the metrical romance of De Borron, including those further adventures and histories which he promised to provide if he could. It was not sufficient for the putative Walter Map that England was the spiritual patrimony guaranteed to the eldest son of the new Church of Christ and the first Bishop of Christendom, but that he might exalt it further he transferred thereto several palmary episodes which in the work of his precursor had been allocated to the regions on the hither side of Syria, or wherever he brought the company of Joseph to its first prolonged halt. The most important of these postponements is the doom which befell Moses; it is also told differently, and is connected with a collateral story concerning one who was fated to suffer a similar punishment, of which the Lesser Chronicles know nothing. This personage is Simeon, who is sometimes said to be the father of Moses, and he is first referred to when the company are crossing the channel on their way to Britain. Simeon and his son sink then into the water because they have broken their vows of purity, and they have to be saved by the others. Long after the arrival of the whole fellowship at the term of their voyaging we hear first of the Graal table, at which Joseph II. and Brons sit together with a wide space between them; but the explanation of the empty seat differs from that of De Borron, signifying the place occupied by Christ at the Last Supper. It can be so occupied only by one of greater sanctity than are those at the Second Table. It follows that for the purposes of this romance the consecration of Galahad was greater than that of the first Bishop of

Christendom, who held the warrant of his ordination from Christ Himself. When the information was made public, Simeon and Moses speculated as to its truth and reason. Being sinners, they regarded it as false, and Moses undertook to occupy the seat if permission could be obtained from Joseph II. The latter was told by those who were parties to the conspiracy that a man counted among the sinners was worthy to take his seat at the Graal. Joseph was much astonished, knowing under what circumstances he had crossed over to Britain, but his informants persisted, and though he could not believe in the goodness of Moses, he gave him leave to try. This was without reference to the voice of the Graal, which was consulted on the occasion according to Robert de Borron, and it illustrates my previous statement that in the later romance the Sacred Vessel does not pronounce oracles or act as a touchstone. Joseph, however, warned Moses himself, when the time came for the trial, not to make the attempt, unless he knew that he was worthy, as he would repent thereof, seeing that it was the place of the Son of God. Moses was struck with terror but still persisted, and, before he had sat long, seven burning hands came from Heaven, set him on fire like a dry bush, and carried him off through the air. Shame fell upon his sinful companions, who inquired whether he was lost or saved; they were told that they should see him again, and that then they would know his fate.

At a later period, when the company were approaching the forest of Darnantes, they were directed that they must enter therein, and were told that they should see Moses. In a valley they came presently upon a great house and, passing through open gates, they entered a great hall, wherein burned a great fire. Out of the fire came a voice, which begged Joseph to pray for the speaker, that his sufferings might be alleviated by the mercy of God. This was the voice of Moses. Joseph II., who was present, demanded whether he was saved or lost, and the answer was that still he had hope of grace. He had been transported by devils, who meant certainly to plunge him in hell; but a hermit compelled them to release him, as in spite of his sin he had not deserved endless torment. The fire was destined to encompass him till he was delivered by that good knight who would end the adventures of the Graal. Alain, who was also present, asked more specifically who he was, and was told that it was his cousin Moses. Simeon also spoke to him, when he was advised, and Canaan—another of the evil fellowship—that they should seek to be better than they were, and to be cleansed from sin by the Bishop. Joseph II. and Alain prayed for Moses, that his suffering might be lessened. A beneficent rain then came down into the fire, softening its fervour by extinguishing half thereof, so that the poor sufferer was eased greatly. Simeon inquired how long such flames might endure, and was told by Moses that it would not be so long as he deserved, because he would be released by Galahad, who would not alone end the adventures of the Graal but all those of Britain.

In spite of the warning which came to them from a source that illustrated so bitterly the neglect of warnings, Simeon and Canaan not only remained without grace but made haste to complete with that which remained for them to do in the order of heinous offence. Joseph of Arimathæa and some part of the Christian cohort had now entered Scotland, where we have seen long ago that they were sustained by the Holy Graal. In this benefit of refection Simeon and Canaan were precluded by their condition from sharing, with the result that they had nothing to eat for two days and nights. Simeon claimed that he had done more for God than either Joseph or Petrus, and that he was suffering for their sins; on the other hand, Canaan declared that he was punished for the deficiencies of his own immediate kindred. Simeon covenanted to take vengeance on Petrus and Canaan on his brethren. The issue was that, grievously and almost incurably,

Petrus was wounded in the neck with a poisoned knife, and
the twelve brothers of Canaan were despatched with a
sword. The visitation of these crimes is varied strangely
in respect of severity, and it illustrates, I think, some
vague and undeclared sanctity in the mission of Petrus.
If so, it is a reflection from Robert de Borron, though in
the later story there is no brief from Heaven, or other warrant, as the evident seal of mission. In any case, he who only
wounded Petrus was transported, like Moses, by spirits of
fire, while he who was a twelve-fold fratricide was, by the
comparative mercy of earthly judgment, only buried
alive, with time to repent before death overtook him
almost in the ordinary course. Long and long afterwards,
when Galahad le Fort, who had become King of Wales, was
riding through that country, he saw a great fire burning
in a dry ditch. A voice came therefrom which proved
to be that of Simeon, who was expiating in this manner
his outrage on Petrus. At the same time—and again
like Moses—he was not beyond redemption, and he entreated his auditor to found a place of religion, wherein
monks could pray for his soul. Galahad le Fort
promised to erect an abbey and to be buried himself
therein. Simeon said further that his torment would
cease when a pure and worthy knight should come and
extinguish the flames. This would be he by whom the
adventures of the Holy Graal should be brought at last
to their term.

It is towards the close of the story that Petrus is first
mentioned in the *Book of the Holy Graal*, and the reference
is at that point which corresponds rather thinly to the
institution of the Second Table. It is he who inquires
why there is a vacant seat left thereat, and who is told that
it is the place of Christ. After the assault of Simeon, the
wound of Petrus was examined and a healing by herbs
was attempted, but this did more harm than good. He
was at length left in the charge of a single priest, while
the company proceeded on their way; but, seeing that
he expected to die, he asked to be carried to the seashore

and to be placed in a ship which was found lying thereby, with its sails set. The priest was not allowed to go further, and the vessel put out presently with its solitary occupant. He was taken to the Isle of Orkney, where ruled the pagan King Orcaut, whose daughter witnessed his arrival. She went on board the ship and so contrived that Petrus was healed in the end by a Christian prisoner who was in the hands of her father. As the issue of the whole adventure the heathen King was converted ; Petrus married the daughter ; he lived a long and worthy life as the successor of Orcaut ; and he had a valiant knight for his own heir. He died in fulness of years and was buried at Orkney, in the church dedicated to St. Philip.

It will be seen that if the author of the *Book of the Holy Graal* designed in this account to supply the missing branch of Robert de Borron concerning Petrus, he again —and quite manifestly—told the wrong story, for setting aside all question of the written warrant, the true destination of Petrus was not Orkney but Avalon, and there is no correspondence otherwise.

In nearly all those incidents which, from other points of view, are similar to some of Robert de Borron, the part assigned by the poem to Joseph of Arimathæa is transferred to the son in that prose romance which is its wresting rather than its extension. A notable instance is the demand for advice by Brons concerning his twelve boys. It is late in the story and long after the arrival of the pilgrims in Britain that the question arises which appears pregnant with consequence in the metrical romance. Brons has been himself so insignificant throughout that his name appears scarcely, though he is entitled to sit with Joseph II., each on one side of the vacant seat at the Second Table. As in the earlier text, eleven of the sons expressed a desire to marry, while the twelfth elected to lead a life of virginity. Joseph II. manifested great joy at the choice thus made and foreshadowed the reward which was to follow. It is indicated further by the fact that the son, and not Brons, was directed to fish in the lake and obtain that slender catch which gave him thenceforward the title of the Rich Fisher. In this case, however, it was used by a miracle to feed those whose desert did not allow them to share in the graces and favours of the Holy Table. When Joseph II. was dying there stood Alain by his bedside, and, being asked why he was weeping, he answered that it was because he was to be left like a sheep that has lost its shepherd. He was then told that he should be the shepherd after Joseph, having the lordship of the Sacred Vessel, with power to deliver subsequently to another inheritor full of grace and goodness, on condition only that the Hallow remained in the land.

We come in this manner to speak of the successions and genealogies, and in the first place concerning the Keepers of the Graal. Alain, by a curious disposition, died on the same day as Alphasan, the builder of Corbenic, and they were both buried in the church of that city dedicated to Our Lady. The text at this point is a little vague in expression and has been interpreted wrongly, but the succeeding warden was evidently Joshua—that brother of Alain who was most loved by him. He was succeeded in due course by his son Eminadap, who married the daughter of a King of Great Britain and had Carceloys as issue. He in turn begot Manuiel, and from him sprang Lambor, whose death and that which followed I have mentioned previously. This was the first Maimed King of the Graal, and on him followed immediately one who was the Maimed King *par excellence* of suffering and miracle of final healing—that is to say, Pellehan. But the *Book of the Holy Graal* says that his wounding was in the battle of Rome, and it knows nothing therefore of the Dolorous Stroke inflicted by Balyn. Seeing, however, that both texts testify that Galahad will heal, and he only, I think it must be inferred that the two accounts refer to the same person, who must be distinguished from King Pelles, though there is an inclination in some criticism to conclude otherwise, and I have shared it tentatively. The genealogy is quite clear that King Pelles was son of

Pellehan, and there is not any real difficulty about the son succeeding in the life of the father, as this occurs in the case of Joseph II. and is the rule rather than the exception in the counter-succession of the Perceval Quests. It follows from the *Book of the Holy Graal* that four of the Kings whom I have enumerated were termed Rich Fishers in succession and that all of them reigned in *Terre Forayne*, which the *Vulgate Merlin* terms—or for which it substitutes—Lytenoys.

The other genealogies are useful only in so far as they show the descent of the persons-in-chief who appear in the Greater Chronicles. The most important is that of Nasciens, which leads up through many names—but they are names only—to King Ban of Benoic, the father of Lancelot, and hence to Lancelot himself, as well as Galahad. The *haut prince* was therefore descended on the male side from the royal line of Sarras, over which he reigned himself after the Quest was finished; on the female side he was descended from Joseph of Arimathæa, through Galahad le Fort, as the *Romance of Lancelot* shows. Sir Gawain is also represented as coming from this root, which was that of King David, but his descent was through Petrus, the genealogy of whom is clouded rather deeply in the text, as it is indeed in the romance of De Borron.

At the conclusion of the *Book of the Holy Graal* the story professes to turn to the life of Merlin. Two of its codices contain a long interspersed digression concerning the two countries belonging to Mordrains and Nasciens after they had departed therefrom. Their power and influence were much increased under Grimaud, the son of Mordrains. When Sarras was destroyed, with the exception of the Spiritual Palace, it was rebuilt more splendidly than ever. These things do not concern us, for in dealing with the great prolix romance I think that my summary has been confined, in accordance with my design, to those matters which belong to the Mystery of the Graal as it is manifested in the Greater Chronicles, and where it has been possible to the Eucharistic side of that Mystery as the most holy motive of all my long research. On this subject there is one thing further to say. The doctrine of transubstantiation, as it is presented in the *Book of the Holy Graal*, and its continual transition into the notion of physical sustenance, are things which scandalise rather than discounsel the soul; but as we saw in the poem of De Borron that Eucharist and Reliquary were alike understood spiritually, so here it will be found in the last sifting that the spiritual side also emerges and becomes at times prominent. When Joseph II., in obedience to the heavenly voice, departed from Sarras and its King, that he might preach the new faith to the Gentiles, it came about in the course of the journey that provisions were wanting. In this extremity he knelt before the Ark, wherein was the Holy Vessel, and implored the help of God. Following the directions which he received, cloths were laid on the greensward, and the people took their places. The elder Joseph, pursuing his care of the physical bodies, ordained that his son should take the Graal in his hands and follow him round the cloths while he circumambulated three times, when—this being accomplished—all who were pure of heart would be filled with the rare sweetness of the world. This office took place at the hour of prime; the father and son sat down with a vacant place between them—as if something were lacking which at a fitting time subsequently would make perfect all holy ministry; the Vessel was covered with paten and corporal; and the result was that those who were privileged to take part were filled with Divine Grace, "so that they could neither conceive nor desire anything beyond it." That was a refection in which material nourishment shared not at all, and though the episode does not occur in all the codices, there is something that corresponds to its equivalent. An instance in point is found in Mordrains, the King, who, after he has attained all earthly knowledge, and has received as the price of attainment the orbicular wound of Plato, is maintained through the centuries by the

Eucharist, as Amfortas in the German cycle and the *alter ego* of both in the *Conte del Graal*. There are otherwise indications, and they obtain through the Greater Chronicles, that the proximity of the Holy Graal transformed the earthly festival into an experience in *extasis* and the good things here below become the *bona Domini in terra viventium*.

IV

SOME LATER MERLIN LEGENDS

§ *A.*—THE VULGATE MERLIN

There are many questions, and some of them may be insoluble, which are concerned with or arise out of the legend of Merlin, but there is perhaps one only which enters at all deeply into the collateral legend of the Graal ; it is why the British prophet, partly magician and enchanter, but in part also God's messenger, with his consequent strange mixture of motives, should have been selected in the mind of romance, or in any more withdrawn mind, as the promulgator of the Graal Mystery in Great Britain—perhaps more correctly—as the semi-supernatural power which was at work in connection therewith ; why also it was he who brought about the institution of the Third Symbolical Table, and set up that Siege Perilous which was, in the first place, to terminate the enchantments of Britain, and, in the second, by the alternative intervention of the adventurous times, to make void—but this is long after he has himself passed away—the high mystery of chivalry so far as the Round Table was concerned. The *Didot Perceval* intervened in respect of the latter vocation, with results which we have seen already, but in this respect it is scarcely the voice of the literature.

There are those who maintain that the late prophecies

of the fourteenth and fifteenth centuries attributed to Merlin were produced with a political object; but the object of the Graal was, speaking broadly, mystical, and as regards the literature which embodies it, this is either the reflection at a distance of secret sanctuary doctrine, or it stands in some dubious manner for the aspirations of the Celtic Church, and admits therefore a political object to the extent that such aspirations responded to particular ambitions which we know to have been cherished by English kings at or about the period during which the literature was developed. There are those who look to Armorica for the original book of the legend, and say that this was latinised by Geoffrey of Monmouth; but the question as to the origin of the romance elements is too complicated for so simple a settlement, and if it had ever a single source in writing, it was at a period when it was apart from romance, and personally I do not question that it was in the Latin tongue. There are those who consider that Scotland was the home of the Arthurian myth, but the land of second sight is not really that of the Mysteries, and though the old Cumbrian kingdom may have contributed to the story of Merlin, the latter must have been enriched from other sources. It was transported, we have been told, into Brittany, and there it may have undergone an express transformation; but, in common with so much of the Arthurian cycle, it was codified, extended and enriched by the process of late editing in some particular, though unexplained, interest, the method adopted by which was the collection of all the great texts of Arthurian literature about the Holy Graal. The hypothetical book of that legend was the central sacred point, and all the extant texts stand about it like subsidiary Hallows.

The break between the *Early History of Merlin*, which ends by saying that King Arthur held his land and kingdom long in peace, and the *Vulgate Merlin*, which begins by reciting how the nobles who had acknowledged him unwillingly went against him into prolonged rebellion, is sufficient in itself to open a new branch of the literature. My classification, however, does not make it impossible that the later text should reflect something from the Lesser Chronicles, two of the texts in which are by necessity the root-matter of all the Greater Chronicles; but its more important derivations are from the *Book of the Holy Graal* and the appurtenances thereof, including the prose *Lancelot*. We are only concerned with the text in respect of its Graal references, and of its content otherwise it will be sufficient, therefore, to say that it embodies an exhaustive account of King Arthur's wars with the Saxons, a certain group of adventures of the less indubitably romantic kind, and thereafter the various circumstances which led up to the internment of Merlin. In this manner it is the close of the prophet's chronicle, though it is still only the early history of Arthur.

Here, as elsewhere, the re-editing of romances in the Graal interest is to be distinguished from the innumerable alterations made otherwise by intelligent and other transcribers, but to which no ulterior motive need be attributed. Perhaps the most signal instance of all the major editing is the production of two, if not three, sequels, executed independently, to the Merlin of Robert de Borron, both of which were less or more exclusively made in the interest which I have mentioned, while both are also ascribed falsely to Robert de Borron. We could better understand the *Vulgate Merlin* and the *Huth Merlin* could one of them be accepted as carrying further forward the De Borron tradition, and thus leading up to a Perceval Quest, whether that of the Didot manuscript or another; but the derivatives of both texts make insuperable difficulties in respect of this course. At the same time the process of codification is nowhere complete in the literature. We must assume, for example, on the basis of textual criticism, that the prose *Lancelot* had in some form already enriched the cycle when the *Vulgate Merlin* came into existence, but in several particulars the Merlin allusions

318

in the *Lancelot* do not correspond with anything in those later Merlin stories with which we are here concerned. These, on the other hand, when they reflect elements which are particular to the *Lancelot*, may be reproducing in summary merely, or they may offer new materials by way of variation over details.

The *Vulgate Merlin* says that God has given to the prophet that skill and discretion which he possesses so to assist him that he shall in fine accomplish the adventures of the Holy Graal, which adventures are predestined to take place in the time of King Arthur, and Blaise, the hermit and scribe, shall live to behold the end. This is true in respect of the *Didot Perceval,* but not of the other quests, in which this personage is forgotten, or is lost, at least, among many recording clerks. But as it follows from the reference, by implication, that Merlin will not himself survive, the Vulgate text cannot be said to lead up to that document. In the interminable account of the wars with the King Rion, there is some stress laid on the achievements of Nasciens, who is the second of that name, and was a young knight at the time in question. He was a cousin of Perceval le Gallois, and was of near kinship to Joseph of Arimathæa, as also a cousin of Celidoine. Here the derivation is from the *Book of the Holy Graal*, but the genealogy is a little distracted. Subsequently Nasciens had Galahad in his keeping, which statement is reflected into the Welsh Quest. When he left chivalry, Nasciens became a hermit and was taken by the Holy Ghost into the Third Heaven, where he beheld unveiled the Divine Persons of the Trinity. He had subsequently the story in his charge, and by the ordinance of the Great Master he announced that which he had read therein—that is to say, in the Record of Blaise. It follows that the secret chronicle which, according to the *Book of the Holy Graal*, had been written by Christ Himself, was in reality the work of the hermit performed under the dictation of Merlin, and that the anonymous author of the *Book of the Holy*

Graal is here identified by the device of another author, who is himself also anonymous.

There is one reference to Helayn, the daughter of King Pelles, of the Castle Corbenic, the niece of King Fisher and of Alain who was wounded through both thighs by the avenging spear. She was the fairest lady in the land, and had the Blessed Vessel in her keeping till the time of Galahad's conception. After what manner Helayn was dispossessed of her high office the text covenants to declare at a later time, but seeing that it fails herein, it is reserved on my own part for the branch which belongs to Galahad. We learn also concerning a son of King Pelles, who—as in the romance of Lancelot—is named Eleazar. At the age of fifteen years he told his father that he would never be made a knight till the best knight of the world should give him his arms and the accolade after three years of service. In return for the dignity of chivalry, he believes that he shall take the knight to the country of King Pelles and the place of the Graal. At this time the king's daughter, though the bearer of the Sacred Vessel, is only seven years old. Seeing that Galahad during his brief career of knighthood does not confer the high degree on any squire of his service, save only Melyas de Lyle, the son of the King of Denmark, and much less on one who would be his uncle according to the flesh, whom also he was destined to meet in the Graal Castle at the term of all, we have here the source of a legend which differs in certain respects from any extant chronicle of the perfect knight. But it should be understood that, in the end, Eleazar serves Gawain and receives the accolade from him.

I do not know what construction is to be placed upon the position of King Pelles; to all intents and purposes he is the Warden-in-chief of the Graal in the *Quest of Galahad*, but neither there nor in the *Vulgate Merlin* is he called the Rich Fisher, which is the characteristic title of the Warden. The romance with which we are here and now concerned tells us, this notwithstanding, that he is spoken of as the Rich King, which seems by way of alternative; he is also a full noble king and a true one. But there is under his charge King Pellenore of the Welsh Lands, that is to say, Pellehan, who is sick and will never be healed till he is manifested who shall bring to an end the adventures of the Holy Graal. This comes to pass at the close of the times of Galahad. But there is another brother, who is Alain of the Forayn Lands; he is in sickness also, and will never be cured till the best knight of all Britain shall ask him why he is stricken by that malady and what it is that will help him. It follows that there is here the analogy of Perceval's question, but it is never asked in the sequel, nor do we hear further of Alain.

In the *Vulgate Merlin* the place of the Graal is Corbenic; it is situated in the realm of Lytenoys, which might signify Lyonesse; and just as we know that the Castle is one of perilous and even fatal adventure, so the kingdom to which it belongs is in nowise a region of peace, and I have said already that its ruler is a king in warfare. The great romance contains few other references to the Sacred Vessel and the history or the quest thereof. The tidings of the Graal in Britain are still tidings only; the Quest is still not a search after the place of the Hallows, but of knights who are proper to undertake it. On matters of so-called early history we hear that Joseph of Arimathæa received the blood from the side of Christ into the Sacred Vessel when the body was still hanging on the Cross—representing a tradition that differs from the Lesser Chronicles, though it is reflected from one of the visions in the *Book of the Holy Graal*. We hear further that the Graal came from heaven above into the city of Sarras, which may be a description by inadvertence, or it may represent a reflection from some source which corresponds to the antecedents of Wolfram. The spear which opened the side of Christ was brought to Logres, presumably—for it is not stated—by him who was the first to consecrate and offer the Eucharist, that is to say, by the second Joseph.

So far in fine as the *Vulgate Merlin* can be said to end at all—seeing that it stops or breaks off without redeeming its pledges—the close is taken soon after the enchantment of Merlin by arts of his own instruction given to the Lady of the Lake; the record of Blaise ceases for want of materials; but in the meantime the clerks of the court of King Arthur have taken up the story in a sense, though their task is confined to the registration of the prowess exhibited by those who are admitted newly to the fellowship of the Round Table, and are therefore at once postulants of earthly chivalry spiritualised and possible seekers for the Graal.

§ *B.*—THE HUTH MERLIN

I speak under correction in respect of all matters which are not in the kinship of near consanguinity with my proper subject, but there is one thing, I think, which may occur to many who make acquaintance with the Merlin sub-cycle in the original texts, and this is, that despite all the archaism of its language and the consequent difficulties which it must cost to the English reader, the method and the atmosphere of the whole seem modern in comparison with the books of the Lesser Chronicles. The devices and conventions suggest a later period, all which may perhaps seem to follow from its express attempt to codify a number of traditions and weld them into a harmonious whole. The Huth manuscript is for our purpose one of considerable and occasionally of great importance. Criticism speaks of it in much the same strain as it has spoken once or twice of the *Longer Prose Perceval,* which is equivalent to saying that it misses some vital points in a judicial appreciation of its merits on grounds that are within measure of the literary order or in respect of the claims put forward concerning its authorship. As regards the second point, there are two false

Roberts de Borron, being him of the *Vulgate* and him of the *Huth Merlin*, but the claim of the latter is interesting from my standpoint perhaps for the very reason which makes it suspected by the official critic. The inexpress collaboration which it indicates between its unknown author and another who is also unknown, though not indeed unnamed—that is, Hélie de Borron—is exactly after the manner of codifications of this kind at that period, thus providing us with a putative concordat on the external side of the literature as an equipoise to the mystical concordat between Merlin and Blaise. In this manner it suggests more than it expresses, but in virtue of their supposed understanding the Graal Mystery was more especially in the charge of that other artist Elias of whom the later Paracelsus had not dreamed. The date to which the work is assigned somewhat speculatively is between 1225 and 1230, and it is divisible for our purpose into four sections: (1) the prose version of De Borron's *Joseph of Arimathæa*; (2) the constituents of what is held to be the prose version of De Borron's metrical romance of Merlin; (3) that later history of Merlin which is exclusive to this manuscript; (4) a Quest of the Holy Graal, but this has not come down to us— at least in the French language. We know that it was a Quest of Galahad, and we are enabled to follow some of its variations from the extant Galahad romance by the allusions in the *Huth Merlin*, and not by these only, for it is supposed that the *Vulgate Merlin* also borrowed therefrom, that it was consequently an anterior document, so that the two later competitive Merlin codices had texts which were identical at the beginning and a text which was the same at the end. As regards the intermediate portions which differ so completely, their distinction is without prejudice to the fact that the prime inspiration of both is the *Book of the Holy Graal*, and that both in a subsidiary sense are indebted to the *Lancelot*.

The express purpose which has been noticed in the *Vulgate Merlin* is present in the alternative text, and is indeed marked more strongly. It may be accepted that the first part, as we have agreed to call it, offers no deviation of importance from other texts of the *Lesser Holy Graal*, and that it therefore reflects almost literally the metrical romance of De Borron. It has not, however, been printed. In the second part there are also no really important deviations, but when Blaise is engaged by the prophet to write the history of Joseph, and therewith to incorporate his own proposed records, it appears that the custodians of the Graal had their independent memorials, to which access was apparently possible, and these also were to be embodied by the scribe. In other words, he kept the minutes of the Mystery, and the claim is that there was therefore a great Graal book in the form of a general prototype. As regards the third part, with which we are concerned henceforward in the present section, it may be said generally that, in place of the unending, sanguinary battles with so-called Saxon Saracens, we are brought into the world of romance, high enchantments and pageants marshalled gorgeously; after what manner this distinction appealed to those who came after is evident from the use which was made of the text by Malory.

We are concerned as before only with the intimate things of the Sacred Vessel and the appurtenances thereof, but as to the latter the undivided text might be embodied almost in any complete schedule. Merlin moves through the story as the ambassador rather than the messenger of those who are the custodians of the Graal, but the advertisements concerning it are still as of a Parnassus which is remote. About the time of a certain tourney held in Logres, a great rumour passed over the land regarding the Sacred Vessel and its location in Britain. Where it abode was unknown—for if Merlin spoke in season, he told little—but the grace of its discovery and the limit of the adventurous times were reserved for the best knight of the world. The Companions of the Round Table set themselves—as they do also in the *Vulgate*—to follow the Quest, and—as again they do therein—to report concerning any Good Knight unknown heretofore among them. If such were found, he was straightway led to the Court, his chivalry was proved—as if a stranger knocked for admission at a lodge of the craft degrees—and on withstanding the tests, he was received into the great company. Each Knight who returned from the Quest recited his adventures, and these were reduced into writing by four clerks retained in the service of the Queen. In this manner they were transmitted to later times. It was an age of secret chronicles, of their sealing and the breaking of the seals. On the pre-viewed approach of his doom, and before finally parting from Blaise, Merlin indited that prophecy concerning the times of the Quest, to which I have referred previously. It opened as follows: " This is the beginning of the adventures in the land of Britain, whereby the mighty Lion shall be overthrown: these adventures shall be taken to their term by a King's son, who shall be chaste, and the best Knight of the world." After this manner did he who instigated the Quest seem thereby to encompass rather than foresee the destruction of the Round Table, its king also and its chivalry. It is said further—and still on the ground that he had not much longer to remain in the world—that Merlin engaged King Arthur to record all the occurrences which took place at the royal Court, and that fifty clerks were set aside for this office. Finally, as regards such memorials, another book was written by the own hand of the prophet, giving before the event an account of the death of Arthur and of Gawain. It was in the keeping of Morgan le Fay, but with its contents she was not acquainted, and it was presumably therefore a cipher manuscript.

The Hidden Life of the Holy House is a prolonged mystery of the ages through all the literature, and if one corner of the veil is lifted for a few moments by the *Vulgate Merlin* in its unconcerted allusions to King Pelles, the Huth manuscript does not compete with even this vague quality of candour, nor is there any certain ray of light cast upon the Graal itself. It is only the two great texts of transubstantiation in the days of quest which claim to have drawn aside the curtains of the Temple and to have manifested the secret things, though they continue to say that these should be kept covertly, and thus even in the unveiling they suggest that there is a deeper hiding. In the *Book of the Holy Graal* Corbenic is not more accessible because it is portrayed so openly, and it is not perhaps more withdrawn because it is in nowise named by the *Huth Merlin*. This text has allusive and hinting methods which are particular to itself, and there is one among them which seems to suggest a wilderness of strange meaning behind its simple words. When Bademagus, like other of the knights to whom no attainment was destined, was concerned for a period in the Quest, he found a branch of an holy herb, which was a sign of the *San Greal*, and no knight came upon such token unless his life was good.

The tradition of the Third Table is carried over from the *Early History of Merlin*, in which Robert de Borron is credited with inventing, rather idly, its institution by Uther; but all discrepancy notwithstanding, the Huth text, following the prose *Lancelot*, refers it to King Leodegan of Carmelide, the father of Guinevere, in which case it would seem to be independent of the prophet and of all logical Graal connections. The apparent discrepancy is explained, however, by the *Vulgate Merlin*, which says that the Knights of the Round Table, being weary of the evil estate into which all the country had fallen, retired to the realm of King Leodegan. It does not say what appears to follow from the text of the *Huth Merlin*, namely, that the material table itself is in the palace of the King of Carmelide. The story of the Siege Perilous is given much after the usual manner, and stress is laid upon the fact that each Knight on rising from the table finds his name inscribed miraculously upon the seat to him belonging—an incident which, according to the mind of the romance, exhibits the high pleasure taken by God in the institution of the Round Table.

Among the signs and tokens which go before, or are conterminous with the Quest, there is the appearance of a strange, nondescript animal, which is a combination of many creatures, and because within her there is the noise of hounds baying, she is called the Questing Beast. In the *Huth Merlin* she appears, as if it were out of due season, during the reign of Uther, who is told by his great counsellor that she concerns one of the adventures of the Graal, which will be explained to him by Perceval le Gallois, who will be the son of the knight that at that time is chasing the beast in question. As Perceval is therefore unborn, and as Uther dies on his day, the prophecy does not come to pass, but it serves to introduce Pellinore, who is now represented as a king and again as a knight, and he it is who follows the Questing Beast. After his death, we know from Malory that she was long followed by Palamedes, in both cases, to no purpose apparently, for nothing comes therefrom. It is only in the *Longer Prose Perceval* that the mystical interpretation of the interminable pursuit is given to Perceval himself. At this time I have said that Pellinore had not begotten Perceval, and though on his first introduction in the days of Arthur, his jousting seems to have constituted a kind of guerilla warfare against the chivalry of the Court, he is married ultimately to one of the King's sisters, and when the Round Table is sent by Leodegan of Carmelide as his daughter's dowry, he is chosen by Merlin to fill one of two vacant seats which were left thereat by the prophet's ordinance. Moreover, when other seats fall vacant, owing to death, he assists the king to fill them, and he serves him also in warfare. Pellinore was in fine slain by Gawain, whose father had fallen at his hands. It will be seen that the genealogy of Perceval, according to this romance, makes void that of the Lesser Chronicles, as it does also the corresponding account in the *Longer Prose Perceval*.

These things connect with the Holy Graal, though it

is in the subsidiary sense only, but the root and centre of the story is the great device by which the *Huth Merlin* brings war upon the House of the Hallows, devastation on the surrounding country, and a living death upon one of the Hereditary Wardens by means of the Dolorous Stroke. Of this fatality I have given some account already in a previous section, and I must speak of it here without covering precisely the same ground. The romance shows that the Secret Powers of Avalon were hostile in respect of King Arthur even from the beginning. From those realms of dream and faerie the Lady Lilith or Lylle brought a mysterious sword to the royal court, then being held at London. The weapon was her great encumbrance, but she was condemned to carry it till some knight should succeed in unsheathing it. Arthur and all his companions made the attempt in vain, but the poor Knight Balyn, who had just been released from prison, fulfilled the task easily. He refused to restore the sword to the damosel, and though he was told that it would cause his own destruction, he agreed to take the risk. Thereupon a Lady of the Lake entered and demanded either the head of the knight who had won the sword or that of the maiden who brought it. Balyn, however, cut off her own head, saying that he had been in quest of her these three years past, she having slain his mother by her arts of enchantment. In this manner he saved the other damosel, though Merlin showed that she was of evil ways and life, never appearing for good, but for great harm only. So begins the story of Balyn and Balan, as a tale of dole from the first, and such it remains to the end. But the Dolorous Stroke itself came about through a knight who had the power to ride invisible, and thus had others at his mercy. Balyn was in chase of this knight, to put an end to his evil deeds, and after the episode of the sword he overtook him in the castle of his brother, who is the King Pellehan. There he destroyed him in open court at a festival, and he was pursued by the king from room to room of the building to avenge what appeared to be an act of wanton murder. They met in a richly dight bedchamber, where there was a table of gold on four pillars of silver, and on the table a marvellous spear strangely wrought. Therewith Balyn smote his pursuer, who fell down in a swoon. The castle roof and walls broke and caved in. Merlin appeared and prophesied that the King Pellehan would remain sorely wounded for many years—that is to say, until Galahad healed him in the Quest of the Holy Graal. Merlin said also that there was preserved in the castle a part of the Precious Blood of our Lord Jesus Christ, which Joseph of Arimathæa had brought into this land, while the spear was that of Longinus, and the king himself was nearly of Joseph's kindred. Balyn rode subsequently through fair lands and cities, of which many inhabitants were slain on all sides, while those who remained cried out piteously against him. Such was the visitation of the Graal—a strange and unheard of enchantment. The story continues, multiplying dole and doom, with greater doom foretold, till the two brethren, Balyn and Balan, destroy one another unwittingly—truly adventurous times, from which all might pray to be delivered.

The opening incidents of this story are found in the *Chevalier aux deux épées*, and, so far as these are concerned, it may have drawn from some unknown source which is common to both. On the other hand, the passing of Merlin through the arts of Vivien or Nivienne, that Lady of the Lake who was the foster-mother of Lancelot, owes something to the great romance which is concerned with his story. When of his entombment the story ceases to speak, it promises henceforth to be concerned with the Graal only, but in the imperfect state that we possess the text it ceases to speak at all. As a final word on my own part, the fact may be cited that the Knight Pelleas is said to be one of great worship, and one also of those four who achieved the Holy Graal. It follows herefrom that the missing Quest of the *Huth Merlin* had grave variations from that with which we are acquainted, because it is not to be assumed that he was one of the nine knights, mostly unknown, who presented themselves, demanding and receiving admission, in the Graal Castle at the term of the Holy Quest.

V

THE GREAT PROSE LANCELOT

By many ways do all the antecedent texts of the Greater Chronicles lead up, in the hands of their editors, to the romance of Lancelot. Therefrom, or therein, all reflect, according to their respective measures, and itself is the great text which goes before the romance of Galahad, as a royal prince may herald the king of all. The prototype of the story in respect of early Graal history is the *Book of the Holy Graal*, but some of its references have no authority in that document. In comparison with its vast extent, the allusions to the Sacred Vessel are rare and brief. I will take all the necessary points in their order, beginning with two pregnant statements, the first of which is conclusive as to the historical source, for it is said that the Holy Graal was that Dish in which Christ ate the Paschal Lamb with His disciples. But the story is late chronologically in the sequence; it reflected much; its ambition was to include all Arthurian chivalry in its province; and none knew better than the successive authors, who are thought to have welded it into one whole, that the true service of the Sacred Vessel took place at no festival of earthly meats, but at an arch-natural mass. It is haunted therefore with the same idea as we shall find in the *Longer Prose Perceval*—that what besides it was, the Graal was also a chalice, and it is so described accordingly in one of the later branches. In evidence of this it may be noted that it is apparently the dove's censer in the story of Lancelot which brings the good meat and drink. The second statement occurs in a printed codex, and scholarship, which misses so little within its own province, has somehow over-looked this: the book says, however, that the natural Graal is to be distinguished from that which is super-natural, and this I take to mean that on the one side there is the festival of the Feeding Dish and on the other the Feast mystical of Transubstantiation, at the revelation of the whole mystery in the *Quest of Galahad*, foreshadowed, as a thing done out of due season, at the ordination of Joseph II. in the old time of Sarras.

It will not be found, otherwise than as I have here specified, that the Graal elements differ so much from the earlier versions as the actuating sentiments regarding the heroes of the Quest and the qualifications thereto belonging. A certain new spirit has entered—perhaps even a higher quality of the secret life of the Church—and it has moderated, among other things, the final aim regarding the Stewards of the Graal and the persons with and for whom it is represented as sojourning on earth. Speaking of the romance as a whole, it may be said that it is a Wonder-Book rather than a Book of Initiation, though at certain points it embodies very high mysteries. According to its own description, it is a branch of the great book of the Holy Graal, but the implied reason is that Lancelot was the father of Galahad. Make as it may for confusion, it is just to add here that, in this connection, one of the unprinted manuscripts speaks of Perceval as the leader and term of all stories told about other knights; it was he who achieved the Great Quest, but his story also is a branch of the high story concerning the Graal, which is the head and crown of all stories. This would seem to indicate that Galahad was not the final hero of the Quest, so far as this codex is concerned, but it may also and more probably mean that he had his own great place at the last consummation, or that he was an intermediate seeker, as were Lancelot also and Gawain.

We have seen in the *Huth Merlin*, firstly, that it has allusions to various occurrences in the *Quest of Galahad* which are not found in the extant romance, and, secondly, that much of its material is derived from the *Great Prose Lancelot;* so also in this text there are references to the succeeding branch of the Quest which we have now no means of checking, but they are not identical throughout with those in the *Huth Merlin.* It is said (*a*) that the story will recur in this part to the Knight Meliadus, but we hear nothing concerning him; (*b*) that it will speak of Helain the White, who became Emperor of Constantinople, but this it does not do; (*c*) that many marvels concerning the Tower of Merlin will be recounted therein, but we hear nothing; (*d*) that Orpheus, a certain enchanter, is doomed to remain in the Castle of the Holy Graal, with two snakes about his neck, until the Quest has been achieved, but he is forgotten entirely therein. These items may be contrasted with those which have been specified in respect of the *Vulgate* and the *Huth Merlin;* if there are others, as a more exhaustive analysis would find, and this assuredly, I believe that my purpose has been served within the measure of reason, and I will turn therefore to some further Graal references found in the *Lancelot,* and of which we hear otherwise.

There are several intimations concerning the close of the adventurous times in Great Britain, and the occupation of the Siege Perilous at the Round Table; the commencement of these times was on the occasion of the war declared by Uther Pendragon against King Urien. There is also a certain knight, named Elias, who carried two swords, after the manner of Balyn; one of them was enclosed in a priceless scabbard, and is said to be that in the old days which pierced the loins of Joseph of Arimathæa and was broken therein, as narrated in the *Book of the Holy Graal.* It was destined not to be re-soldered except by the Lord of Chivalry, who was to put an end to the adventurous times, with all the wonders and mysteries of the Holy Vessel.

A few other points will be best taken with the personal history of Lancelot, though it is not within my province to provide a formal analysis of the romance itself. Lancelot was the son of King Ban of Benoic, and his mother Helen was of the race of Joseph of Arimathæa, through whom she was of the line of King David. It is therefore said that, through his mother, Lancelot had the same blood in his veins as the King of Heaven Himself had deigned to take.

His baptismal name was Galahad, and, according to the *Huth Merlin*, Lancelot was that which he received in confirmation, though I find no record concerning this sacrament in his own romance. He was carried away in his infancy by one of the Ladies of the Lake ; she is really that Vivien who deceived Merlin, and who, under a cloud of poetic modernism, is familiar to the readers of Tennyson. The part which she plays through all the tale of chivalry is out of true kinship with what we have been disposed to conceive as she is pictured in the laureate's glass of vision. By the knowledge which she derived from Merlin she entered that unincorporated hierarchy of fairyland of which we hear in the books of chivalry ; she became a fay-lady, which signifies not an extra-human being of some minor or elemental order, but a woman proficient in magic. It should be noted here that whereas, in the ordinary acceptation, a fairy may correspond either to male or female, the term is never used in the Arthurian books except with reference to a woman. For example, the Fountain of Fairies, which is mentioned once in the *Lancelot*, received that name because beautiful unknown ladies had been seen thereat. The Lake into which the child was carried was therefore a Lake of Magic, concealing from public view the palace or manor in which his guardian dwelt, and the great park-land about it. The account of the region within this water of enchantment recalls one of the romantic episodes in the *Le Roman de Jaufre*, and, speaking generally, there are distinct analogies between this comparatively unknown Provençal poem and other tales of the Round Table.

Lancelot remained in the charge of the Lady of the

333

Lake until he was eighteen. About this period she told him the story of his ancestor Joseph, and also of Joseph's son, the first Galahad, who became the King of that country which was afterwards called Wales. She referred to King Pelles of Lytenoys and his brother, a second and later Alain le Gros, who had never ceased to maintain themselves in high honour and glory before the world and in the sight of God. As regards his own future course, she told him that he was called to carry to their term many wonderful adventures, while those which he did not achieve would remain over for a knight who was yet unborn, that is to say, for the last and true Galahad. But of the Graal she did not tell him, though at a later time he heard of the tomb of Lucan, connected with a house of religion, wherein was buried the godson of Joseph of Arimathæa, who was once charged with the guardianship of the Sacred Vessel. The *Huth Merlin* says, however, that it was a granddaughter of the First Keeper, which seems to accord better with the general tradition.

Before parting with Lancelot, the Lady of the Lake gave him a wand or ring—for the codices differ—which had the power of dissolving enchantments, presumably other than her own, and it served him in good stead at many junctures. Thus equipped, he went forth into the world, followed by her secret providence, and repaired to the Court of King Arthur, where, in due time, he was entered as a Companion of the Round Table, a reception which was characterised by considerable ceremonial grandeur. So passed he into the world of chivalry, but through the glory of his after-life, and through the scandal of his unhappy, over-measured, too faithful love, we have no call to follow him. Before we come—in another section—to the great event of his history, outside these particular vocations, there are only three further points to be noted. On one occasion he has a vision of his ancestors, namely, Nascien, Celidoine, the second Nascien, Alain le Gros and Jonas, who begot the

first Lancelot, who was himself father to King Ban of
Benoic; but it will be observed that this is on the male
side, and is therefore without prejudice to his derivation
on the mother's side from the *radix Jesse*. On another
occasion Lancelot visited the tomb of the first Galahad,
King of Wales. He saw also the burning sepulchre of
Simeon, and spoke with that victim of the centuries,
who told him that the knight who should deliver him
would be of his own kindred, and as nearly as possible
the very flesh of Lancelot. It is said in explanation
that Simeon was the father of Moses and the nephew of
Joseph, all which is in opposition to Robert de Borron,
though it reproduces literally the *Book of the Holy Graal*.
Moses was tormented in a similar tomb, but owing to
the prayers of Lancelot both experienced a certain miti-
gation, and their delivery in thirty years was insured
further. Lancelot removed the body of the first Galahad,
which was transported to Wales and reinterred with great
honour. The third point concerns the visit of Gawain
and Hector to a graveyard which they are counselled not
to enter unless one of them is the recreant knight whose
evil living has caused him to forfeit the honour of achiev-
ing the adventures of the Graal. The reference is to
Lancelot, and the graveyard is said to contain Simeon,
Canaan and the twelve brothers whom they immolated.
But this does not seem to correspond with the previous
account of Simeon's tomb. It is conclusive, however, as
to the disqualification of Lancelot for the Great Quest.
Had he never loved the Queen, he would not have begotten Galahad, for whom no office would have remained,
seeing that he himself was the exotic flower of chivalry,
palm of faith and cedar of purity. But, as things were,
the great light of Lancelot was clouded deeply, nor ever
shone freely until that term of all when he was received
into the priestly sanctuary of the official church and was
clothed at last in incense. It is certain that, speaking
generally of the Greater Chronicles, there was no true
light of Gawain, though some of the romances issued

from the ministry of Nature have pictured him in glowing colours. Subject to one great and cryptic exception, the day of Chrétien and Gautier had given way to the day of the prose *Lancelot,* and Gawain had been stripped of nearly all his graces, a process first begun in the *Romance of Tristram.* Perhaps it may be said that although he saw something according to the *Conte del Graal,* therein is an episode of personation, on which I have dwelt shortly, though it was not consciously to the hero himself. In Heinrich's poem he enters only into a world of ghosts. In the prose *Lancelot* he is characterised by a constitutional incapacity, to which the Galahad Quest adds impenitence in evil-doing. The picture of Sir Bors is one of great beauty, but it does not carry with it any particular significance, except that of a witness on his way back into the world. Among the Graal heroes we are therefore reduced, as we have seen and shall otherwise see further, to Perceval and Galahad. Of these two there is little doubt that Perceval was the first in time, or that in a certain sense Galahad was an afterthought. I use the expression so that I may introduce the more probable theory that this elect knight represents a later but exceedingly express intention, as if it were the design of the legend to say that a day would come when that Arthurian sacrament of which I have spoken previously, would not only be communicated at last to the world without, but that the official church would receive also, on its knees, acknowledging that there are great consecrations. If, without seeming too fantastic, I may refer to an old symbol which has no special connection with the present order of ideas, Galahad is like the horn of the quintessence in the microcosmic and alchemical star, and the four other horns are the four aspects of the symbolical legend of Perceval, being (*a*) the *Didot Perceval ;* (*b*) the *Conte del Graal ;* (*c*) the *Longer Prose Perceval ;* and (*d*) the *Parsifal* of Wolfram. It does no real outrage to the order of time if I say that these aspects represent, symbolically speaking, the growth of the tradition. The *Didot Perceval* may be doubtless later than Chrétien, and from him may have borrowed something, but the two texts are near enough in time to make the question of priority, at least to an extent, unimportant. Let me endeavour to compare for a moment the intention of this strange pentagram in literature. Collectively or individually its documents are best taken in connection one with another, and in conjunction also with those which lead up to them. It is only the *Longer Prose Perceval* which stands to some extent alone in the Northern French cycle, though it has certain connections with the *Book of the Holy Graal.* In the German cycle the *Parsifal* is by no means without antecedents, for we can trace the hand of Guiot up to a certain point, and we can trace also the analogies with Chrétien, though Wolfram scouted his version. Finally, we have the Galahad legend, as if the closing were taken in a superlative grade of romance.

As in the *Conte del Graal,* so in the romance of Lancelot, there is one visit paid by Gawain to the Graal Castle, and it begins abruptly with an adventure at a pavilion by a certain fountain. Gawain, who is the actor-in-chief, reached a castle subsequently in some annex or quarter of which he found a maiden in the durance of a scalding bath, wherefrom no one could save her except the highest typical example of earthly knighthood. Gawain was not Lancelot—for whom the adventure was reserved—and he failed therefore, for which he was promised shame to ensue quickly. He was received with pomp in the castle, and came into the presence of the king, by whom he was welcomed after the true manner of chivalry. In a word, he was at Corbenic, the Graal Castle, and the herald of the secret ministry entered in the shape of a dove, bearing a censer in its beak. This vision was momentary only, and was not repeated, but it served as a sign for the company to take their seats at the tables, and this was followed by the entrance of a maiden— that daughter, fairest among women—who carried the chalice of the Graal, in her passage through the hall replenishing the dishes and filling the place with sweet odours. After what manner this multiplication of loaves and fishes takes place does not appear—a feature which characterises nearly all the coincident legends of this particular type. It is worth a passing note that it is perhaps the only instance in which the Graal bearer is unaccompanied entirely. So much was Gawain bespelled by the maiden's beauty that he had no eyes for anything else. She departed at length, and he, coming to himself, found that, for some fault which he could not identify, he only was left without refection of any kind—even as the evil livers in the company of Joseph. The meal proceeded in complete silence, and was disconsolate enough for the hero, who already began to feel the working of that shame which was promised him. At the end of the supper the whole company departed, still without any word, and a dwarf—who tried to chastise him, because of his presence in that part of the building—bade him at length go in search of some other chamber, where no one would see him. He remained, however, in the hall, and there had a certain partial vision of a Graal service. The presence of the Sacred Vessel healed him not only of a grievous wound which he had received from a spear a little earlier in the narrative, but also of various hurts in a long combat with an unknown knight in the hall. I omit any special account of this meeting, except that here again Gawain was attacked because he refused to depart. I omit also a clumsy parable concerning a dragon who gave birth to a vast progeny and afterwards strove with a leopard, only to be destroyed in the end by her own children, who likewise perished in the struggle. In a state of exhaustion Gawain at length fell asleep, and found on waking in the morning that he was being drawn through the public streets of the city in a vile cart. After being pelted with filth, he was released ultimately, and arrived at the hold of one whom men termed the Secret Hermit. From him he ascertained that he had been at the Graal Castle, which appears to be new tidings; of the Sacred Vessel and its mysteries he learned nothing, though it was foretold that he should know soon, but this does not seem to come to pass.

Of such is the message of the literature as it moved towards the greater heights of its root-conception. It should be added that whereas in the prose *Lancelot* Gawain is thus covered with disdain, the romance of Galahad paints him in darker colours. But between the one and the other I propose to introduce a different picture in the *Longer Prose Perceval*. Meanwhile, I do not know why there was such a revulsion of feeling in respect of one who in certain texts appears as the knight of earthly courtesy, and who assuredly in the *Conte del Graal* is not less entitled to consideration than Perceval himself.

After another manner is it dealt to another knight, who visited the castle also, but he was the diadem of chivalry which at that time had been exalted in the world of Logres. By this I mean that he was Lancelot, and he arrived not only as an expected guest, but as one whose advent had been decreed and led up to from the first times of the mystery. It was then that the great parable of the adventurous times passed into that other parable concerning the times of enchantment, because it was understood before everything, and was also accepted, that the faith of King Ban's son was with the heart of the Queen forever, and so utterly that, in the sub-surface mind of romance, it had even moved somewhere as if towards the sacramental order; or without being condoned therein it was believed to have carried within it an element of redemption. Dedicated and vowed as he was, no other willing union was possible; hence therefore the office of enchantment to bring about the conception of Galahad by the daughter of the House of the Graal, with Lancelot as the morganatic father, thus ensuring the genealogical legitimacy of the last recipient of the mysteries.

Of this conception I propose to speak in another

section, because the *Lancelot* dissolves into the *Quest*, of which the first condition is the birth of Galahad.

VI

A PREFACE OR INTRODUCTORY PORTION APPERTAINING TO ALL THE QUESTS

There is a certain sense in which we can say that the knight of old was consecrated like the priest of old, and we can picture the whole ceremony as if it were included in some unwritten part of the *Pontificale Romanum*. The institution of chivalry existed for a particular impression of ecclesiastical idealism on one domain of the life in the world. It was as if it were the outcome of some undeclared design to dedicate even warfare to the high ends of the Church, as if the implied covenant of battle were that a man should be so prepared through all his days that no sudden and violent death should find him unfitted for his transit. The causes of strife are many, and some of them are doubtful enough, but so clothed in the armour of salvation the natural-born hero experienced a kind of rebirth and came forth, so far as he himself was concerned, a soldier of the cross. One section at least in the romantic literature of chivalry was devoted to this ideal, and better than any formal catechism of doctrine and conduct did it uphold the authority of the Church and illustrate the principles of its practice. That section was the quest of the Holy Graal in its proper understanding, and on the authority of this fact I can say that this branch became a search after high sanctity expressed in the form of romance ; as such it does not differ from the quest-in-chief of holiness. It has been rendered after more than one manner out of the consecrated implicits imbedded in consciousness, as if this were the rare and secret book from which the texts, almost indifferently, claim to have derived their knowledge, and it happens—for our greater misdirection—that some of the modes of transcript are like *Frater Pereclinus de Faustis* in the old mystery of salvation—that is to say, they are far from the goal.

These statements—which are introduced like an interlude in a section apart and as if extrajudical—will sound strangely in the ears of those who have preceded me, and it must be understood that, of course, I am speaking of things as they are found at their highest in the great texts; but the evidence is there; it is there also in terms that it is impossible to elude and impossible also to discount. In respect of the *Conte del Graal*, we must surrender to Nature the things which are Nature's; but the *Longer Prose Perceval* says that of God moveth its High History, and I say likewise—but in a more exalted degree still—concerning the *Quest of Galahad*. Were it otherwise, the literature of the Graal would be like the records of any other princes of this world, and my predilections would have nothing therein. My true intent from the beginning of my life in letters has been for the delight of the soul in God, and I have not consented with my heart to the making of books for another and lesser end.

It was only by slow stages that the course of the literature rose up to that height at which it found rather than created the ideal of Galahad. We may take as our most obvious illustration of the developing process one crucial point which characterises the Perceval quests, and this is the loves of the hero. The earlier branches of the *Conte del Graal* show little conscience on the subject of restraint, the deportment of the hero being simply a question of opportunity. I know that we are dealing with a period when the natural passions were condoned rather easily, though the Church had intervened to consecrate the rite of marriage after an especial manner. Hence it was little stigma for a hero of chivalry to be born out of lawful wedlock, or to beget sons of desire who would shine in his light and their own subsequently. The ideal of virginity remained, all this notwithstanding, so that the makers of romance knew well enough where the instituted counsels of perfection lay. It is comparatively late in the cycles that ascetic purity became an indefectible title to success in the Quest of the Holy Graal, about which time Gawain and Lancelot were relegated to their proper places—ridicule and confusion, in the one case, and final, though not irreverent, disqualification in the other.

The *Didot Perceval* offers a frigid quality of abstinence, apart from either sympathy or enlightenment, and without one touch of grace to make it kindred with the ardours and solitudes of the Divine Life. The poem of Gerbert preserves the hero's virginity even on his marriage night, but the precaution—considering the texts which he had elected to follow—has the aspect of a leap in the dark. Wolfram insures the chastity of Perceval by introducing the marriage of his questing knight at an early stage. The *Longer Prose Perceval* is like heaven, knowing neither marriage nor giving in marriage, or at least nuptials are so utterly made in heaven that they are not reflected on earth. Blanchefleur has disappeared entirely, and it is never supposed that the Quest would be achieved in perfection by one who was not a virgin. If we turn now to the story of Galahad, we shall find that the Quest of the Holy Graal has become an unearthly experiment. There is illumination, there is sanctity, there is ecstasy, and the greatest of these is ecstasy, because it is the term of the others. All the high researches end in a rapture, and thereby is that change of location which does not mean passage through space. I believe that the author of the Great Quest knew what he was doing when—leaving nothing outside—he so transmuted all, and assuredly in the order of romance he spoke as no man had spoken before him.

Now, seeing that all subjects bring us back to the one subject; that in spite, for example, of any scandalous histories, every official congregation returns us to the one official Church; so, at whatever point we may begin,

I affirm that every quest takes us ultimately to that of Galahad. It would seem, therefore, that this is the crown of all. If Galahad had come in the good time instead of in the evil, the Graal would have been set up for adoration before the whole face of Logres. But the Quest says that the world was not worthy, though the *Parsifal* seems to say: "Behold, I am with you always."

Of Perceval and his great experiment there are several phases; but this is the lesser Quest. Of Galahad there is one phase only, led up to by many romances, but represented in fine by a single transcendent text. This text is the quintessence and transmutation of everything, allocating all seekers—Perceval, Bors, Lancelot, Gawain —to their proper spheres, over whom shines Galahad as an exalted horn in the great pentagram of chivalry. Of the Perceval Quest there are two great versions; one of them, as I have already noted, is an alternative conclusion to the cycle of the Greater Chronicles; and one—which is the German *Parsifal*—all antecedents notwithstanding, is something set apart by itself in a peculiar house of mystery. It is the story of the natural man taken gradually to the heights. There is also a third quest, that of the *Didot Perceval*, which, amidst many insufficiences, is important for several reasons after its own manner— that is to say, because of its genealogy. The fourth is the *Conte del Graal*, and this—apart from Gerbert—is of no importance symbolically, though it is a great and powerful talisman of archaic poetry. The truth is that for all the high things there are many substitutes, after the manner of colourable pretences, and many transcripts, as out of the language of the angels into that of man, after the same way that the great external churches have expressed the mysteries of doctrine in words of one syllable for children who are learning to read. But the absolute and direct message of the things most high, coming in the name of these, is alone commonly. In fine, it sometimes happens that as from any corner of the veil the prepared eyes can look through and perceive something of the immeasurable region which lies beyond the common faculties of sense, so there are mysteries of books which are in no way sufficient in themselves, but they contain the elements and portents concerning all those great things of which it is given the heart to conceive. Among these are the Graal books in the forms which present the legend at its highest.

VII

THE LONGER PROSE PERCEVAL

Amidst much that is dubious and belonging to the seeming of enchantment, one thing is certain—that the Perceval Quests leave behind them the Graal Castle and that nothing is taken absolutely away, for even the *Conte del Graal* presents the removal of the Hallows as a point of speculation rather than a thing of certitude. So much is true also of the only Perceval romance in the Northern French cycle which leans towards greatness. I have given it a name which is descriptive rather than its exact title, for, like the *Conte*, it is *Perceval le Gallois*, the *Perlesvaux* for modern scholarship, while for him who in recent years recreated rather than rendered it, the proper designation is *The High History of the Holy Graal*. By its own hypothesis, it is based upon and was drawn into romance out of a Latin book, said to have been written by Josephus, which scribe is meant possibly to be Joseph II. of the *Book of the Holy Graal*—that first priest who sacrificed the Body of our Lord. So, therefore, as the Lesser Chronicles derive from a Secret Book allocated to the first Joseph, does this reflection of the legends which are called greater draw from the records of his son. But the one is not rendered into the other, for the other derives from the one many points of reference which it does not set forth actually.

The *Longer Prose Perceval* is an echo of many texts, including the *Conte del Graal,* and of things unknown which suggest Guiot de Provence, or the group which is covered by his name. It would seem also that the author, though there was much that he remembered, had either forgotten not a few episodes of the antecedent legends, or alternatively he scouted some things and was bent on inventing more. We have seen that, according to Gautier, the failure of Perceval to ask the vital question involved the destruction of kingdoms, but the *Longer Prose Perceval* is the one story in the whole cycle which, firstly, accounts for the king's languishment, by this failure, as the sole actuating cause, and, secondly, represents King Fisherman as dying in the middle way of the narrative, unconsoled and unhealed, before the word of power is spoken. Further, it is the only story which describes the Secret Sanctuary as the Castle of Souls, or which specifies an evil brother of King Fisherman under the title of the King of Castle Mortal, though this character has analogies with the Klingsor of Wolfram.

There is little need to speak of the story itself, which is available to every one in the best of all possible versions, but it should be understood that its entire action is subsequent to the first visit paid by Perceval to the Graal Castle and the consequent suppression of the Word. In the course of the story such suppressions are several. For example, when the dismembered pageant of the Graal is going about in the land, a certain Damosel of the Car wanders from place to place, carrying her arm slung at her neck in a golden stole, and lying on a rich pillow. Sir Gawain, who meets and converses w h her, fails to inquire the reason, and is told that no greater care will be his at the court of the Rich King Fisherman. That reason is, however, explained to him subsequently, namely, that she was the bearer of the Sacred Vessel on the occasion of Perceval's visit, and nothing else will she carry till she returns to the Holy House. It will be seen that the romance has strange vicarious penances besides its strange quests. It does not appear why the Damosel of the Car is constrained to wander on account of Perceval's silence. But we are moving throughout the narrative in a high region of similitude, and although it is concerned so chiefly with the perpetuation of a mystery which is so divine, it creates no secret from the beginning as to the nature and origin of that mystery, nor does it fail to make plain the fact of the mystical significance which underlies many of its episodes and adventures. Sometimes its dealings in allegory are drawn from materials belonging to another side of the Graal legend, as in one reference to King Pelles, who for the great love of his Saviour had renounced his kingdom and entered into a hermitage. It is said that his son Joseus slew his own mother at a certain castle, which from that time forward continued burning, burning, and it is testified that from this hold and from one other there will be enkindled the strong flame which in fine shall consume the world.

Again, there are many intimations concerning the Earthly Paradise, which lay behind the Castle of the Graal, showing that this House was really a place of initiation—the gate of something that was beyond it. According to Josephus, the soul of any person who passed through the Castle went to Paradise, from which those who are qualified may infer what grades of initiation were conferred within its penetralia. The true spiritual place was therefore not at Sarras—which in this story has gone utterly out of being—but at the Graal Castle, though before the Earthly Paradise becomes the Home of Souls it must be assumed into the higher Garden of Eden. There is another facet of this jewel of meaning which says elsewhere that the Red Cross symbolises the redeeming blood, meaning that it is the tincture of the Divine Virtue by which the tree of the universal disaster becomes the Tree of Life. There are further allusions designed—as one would imagine—to exhibit the proximity of this world to the next, and it happens sometimes that one side of the world beyond thus realised is not of a desirable kind. Perceval visits a certain Castle of Copper, which is a

stronghold of evil faith and an abode of perverse spirits.
Beside it there rages a water called the River of Hell,
which plunges and ploughs into the sea with a fell hiss-
ing, so that it is a place of danger to those who sail by
the stars.

The story has many questers, and he who attains to
the Keepership is not he who can be said to enter the
Mysteries at a saving time. As King Arthur is accused
at the beginning of falling into a supine state, ceasing
from deeds of chivalry and scattering the flock of his
knighthood, so a certain poetical justice is done to him
by the assignment of an important place of vision in the
finding of the Graal. As regards the questers generally,
prior to the death of King Fisherman, the latter received
a visit from Gawain, who, in accordance with the prophecy
uttered by the Damosel of the Car, failed in his turn to
ask the vital question, though scarcely—as the romance
confesses—through his own fault, for at the sight of the
Graal and the Lance he fell into an ecstasy, and, for the
first and only time recorded of him in all the literature,
the thought of God overflowed his whole consciousness.
Lancelot also visited the Castle prior to the King's death,
but there was no manifestation of the Sacred Vessel on
this occasion, because of that which had been and was
between him and Arthur's royal consort, the reason
apparently being less on account of the past than of his
long impenitence in the heart. By the evidence of several
texts Gawain also had led an evil life, but at least for the
purposes of the Quest he had here put it from him in
confession. It is just to add that the exalted legend of
Galahad is not so severe upon Lancelot, permitting him
to see all save the inmost heart of the mystery. For such
a measure of success as inhered in his presence and vision
at the Graal Castle, Gawain was indebted to the prowess
by which, as a preliminary condition, he was enabled to
wrest from an unlawful custodian the Sword of St. John
the Baptist. Speaking generally, he was the favoured
recipient of many episodical mysteries in this romance, to

each one of which a suitable interpretation is allocated; in one case his adventures proved to be an excursion into the mystical domain of the Fall of Adam and that of the scheme of Redemption; in another he beheld three maidens grouped about a fountain who dissolved ultimately into a single maiden, as though they were another symbol of the Holy Trinity and the superincession of the three Divine Persons. If, this notwithstanding, he was allotted no better success than Perceval on his first visit, he learned much, and more indeed than he was qualified to understand fully.

The High Quest is dolorous enough in its consequences even to worthy heroes and others illustrious who undertake it without indubitable election. The realm of Arthur was left sufficiently discounselled when he set forth on that great errand; he suffered even the death of his Queen, in defiance of the whole tradition of the cycle. He is a pathetic and haunting figure moving through the pageant of that one romance which has enrolled him among the Knights of Quest, and though he saw the Graal in its processional travels when it was uplifted like a monstrance over the world of Logres, he did not reach the Castle till after the second entry of Perceval, as another king in warfare, had been ratified by the return of the Hallows. Then he was welcomed by Perceval and was led into the presence of the Graal, or at least into the chapel where it abode and was accustomed to appear at the serving of the Mass. It is at this point that the mystery of the subject deepens and that he is said to have beheld the five changes, corresponding to the five wounds which Christ received upon the Cross. But the vision had a more withdrawn meaning, which is held in utter reserve, because it is the secret of the sacrament. It was through his experiences in the Hidden House that Arthur, on his return to Cardoil, was enabled to furnish, as we are told, the true pattern for Eucharistic chalices, previously unknown in his kingdom, and, in like manner, of bells for church offices.

It is possible scarcely to say that the numerous allusions to the Sacred Vessel tend to the increase of our knowledge on the descriptive side of the object, but on that which may be called historical there is ample evidence that the story draws from some form of *The Book of the Holy Graal*, while its specific additions and extensions do not distract its harmony in respect of this source. It is clear from several statements that there is to be no rest in the land until the Graal has been achieved, but the tremor of adventure and enchantment which stirs Logres in its dream is not characterised clearly by either of those diagnoses which are found in the Greater or Lesser Chronicles. Prior to the first arrival of Perceval, and during his keepership subsequently, those maidens and holy hermits who, in one or another way, have been concerned with the Graal service have a devotional refuge therein which carries with it a species of youth renewal. Yet the vessel itself still lies under a certain cloud of mystery, and during the period of research there is no man, however well he may be acquainted himself therewith, who can instruct another in the quest or in the attainment of the Castle of Desire. The will of God alone can lead the seeker.

Though encompassed by sacramental protections, the Graal and its companion Hallows were not without danger from the assaults of workers of evil. We learn early in the story that King Fisherman is challenged by the King of Castle Mortal in respect of the Graal and Lance. The fact of this claim and the partial success which follows it constitutes a departure from the tradition of the whole French cycle, in so far as it is now extant; but we shall meet with its correspondences in the German cycle, and shall find that, as they do not derive from one another, they are branches with a common root which lies beneath the surface of the literature. The King of Castle Mortal is described as he who sold God for money; but although there is a full account of the evil ruler taking possession of the

Graal Castle, we know nothing of his antecedent life, except that he was a brother of him who was sealed with sanctity and the rightful custodian therefore of the sacred objects. It follows from this that he was reared, so to speak, in the sanctuary and must have either betrayed the sanctuary or have been cast out therefrom. The usurpation takes place after the death of King Fisherman, which seems to have created the opportunity; but when the enemy of the Laws of Light entered into the place of God, the Chapel of the Holy Graal was emptied of its Hallows, which were taken into deeper retreat. The sanctuary was not destined, however, to remain under the powers of the darkness, and as in the other romances Perceval returns in fine to ask the postponed question; as by so doing he restores health to the King and joy to the Hidden House; so here he visits the usurper with arms of the body, arms of the soul in purity, invincible arms of grace, and by his conquest of the Castle he reads himself into the Kingdom, while the self-destruction of the false King follows on that victory. The Hallows are then restored, though the witness does not say whether by hands of men, hands of angels, or borne by the wind of the Spirit. The sepulchre of King Fisherman was before the altar, and it was covered with the jewelled tabernacle, which seems to have been moved by a miracle.

Perceval abode in the Castle, except in so far as his toilsome life called him temporarily away, and there also were his mother—who did not die at the beginning of his adventures, as in several of the other texts—and his virgin sister, till they were called at length from earth. The call came also to Perceval, but not in the guise of death. He was instructed, as we have seen in another branch of our inquest, to divide the Hallows between certain hermits who possessed the " building word" for churches of all things holy and houses dedicated to sanctity. From this it follows that the Graal in this story may not in reality depart, but is removed and remains—as it would seem—in some undeclared sanctuary of Britain. Perceval was not instructed, and made no disposition in respect of his kingdom or the Castle, for there began the ringing of certain joyful bells, as if for a bridal. Into the harbour there entered a ship with white sails emblazoned with the Red Cross, and therein was a fair, priestly company, robed for the celebration of Mass. The anchor was cast, and the company went to pray in the Chapel of the Holy Graal, bearing with them glorious vessels of gold and silver, as if on the removal of those things which were without price in the order of the spirit there were left, as a sign of goodwill, the external offerings of precious metals of this world. Perceval took leave of his household and entered the ship, followed by those whose high presence made his departure a pageant. It is said, thereupon, that the Graal would appear no more in the Chapel or Castle, but that Perceval would know well the place where it would be.

There can be no question that in spite of several discrepancies this version of the Quest is the most significant of all its renderings into the fair language of romance, that being excepted only which is the exalted Quest of all. I record in conclusion as follows: (1) That there is no genealogy given of the Graal Keeper; (2) that among the discrepancies, or as something that is out of reason, there must be included the allocation of the King's illness to the paralysed inquisition of Perceval; (3) that so far as enchantments of Britain are mentioned in this text, the *Longer Prose Perceval* draws a certain reflection from the Lesser Chronicles; (4) that the final abrogation of the question through the King's death in misease, and the winning of the Graal by the chance of war, are things which place this branch of the Graal literature apart from all other branches; (5) accepting the judgment of scholarship that the *Mabinogi* of *Peredur* and the English *Syr Percyvelle* are the last reflections of some primeval non-

Christian quest, before all marriage with the Graal, it is desirable to note that the *Longer Prose Perceval* shares with them one characteristic in common, that in none of them is the question asked; and late though it be otherwise, as those texts are late, this also seems to embody a primitive element. I should mention further that the shield borne by Perceval is said to have been the shield of that Joseph who "took down the Saviour of the world from hanging on the rood," and that Joseph set in the boss thereof a relic of the Precious Blood and a piece of our Lord's garment. It seems obvious that this is a reflection from the *Book of the Holy Graal* concerning the shield of Evalach, but this was reserved for Galahad. And in fine, as regards the question, with all that followed in respect of the King's languishment, it should be noted —as a suggestion of deeper mystery behind one unaccountable mystery—that, on the evidence of King Fisher himself, he would have been whole of his limbs and his body, had he known that the visitor at the Graal Castle was Perceval, and his own nephew.

VIII

THE QUEST OF THE HIGH PRINCE

Having passed through many initiations, I can say with the sincerity which comes of full knowledge that the Graal legend, ritually and ceremonially presented, is the greatest of all which lies beyond the known borders of the instituted mysteries. But it is exalted in a place of understanding of which no one can speak in public, not only because of certain seals placed upon the sanctuary, but more especially, in the last resource, because there are no listeners. I know, however, and can say that the Cup appears; I know that it is the Graal cup; and the wonders of its manifestation in romance are not so far removed from the high things which it symbolises, whence it follows that the same story is told everywhere. It is in this way that on these subjects we may make up our minds to say new things, but we say only those which are old, because it would seem that there are no others. If Guiot de Provence ever affirmed that the Graal legend was first written in the starry heavens, he testified to that which is the shadow of the truth, or more properly its bright reflection.

Let us now set before our minds the image of the Graal Castle, having a local habitation and a name on the mountain-side of Corbenic. The inhabitant-in-chief of this sanctuary is the Keeper of the Hallows, holding by lineal descent from the first times of the mystery. This is the noble King Pelles, behind whom is that undeclared type of the consecrated royalty which was—the maimed King Pellehan, whose hurt has to be healed by Galahad. The maiden who carries the Sacred Vessel in the pageant of the ceremonial rite is the reigning king's daughter, the *virgo intacta* Helayne. To the Castle on a certain occasion there comes the Knight Lancelot, who is the son of King Ban of Benoic, while his mother Helen is issued from the race of Joseph of Arimathæa, and through him is of the line of King David. It is known by the Keeper Pelles that to bring to its final term the mystery of the Holy Graal, his daughter must bear a child to Lancelot, and this is accomplished under circumstances of enchantment which seem to have eliminated from the maiden all sense of earthly passion. It cannot be said that this was the state of Lancelot, who believed that his partner in the mystery of union was the consort of Arthur the King, and to this extent the sacramental imagery offers the signs of failure. In the case of Helayne the symbolism only deflects from perfection at a single point, which is that of a second meeting with Lancelot under almost similar circumstances. I must not specify them here, except in so far as to say that there was a certain incursion of common motive into that which belonged otherwise to the sacramental side of things, so far as she

353   z

was concerned. I can imagine nothing in the whole course of literature to compare with the renunciation of this maiden, on whom the pure light of the Graal had fallen for seasons and years, and who was called upon by the exigencies of the Quest to make that sacrifice which is indicated by the great romance. It is at this point that the Book of the Knight Lancelot sets aside finally all sense of triviality and is assumed into the Kingdom of the Mysteries.

The motherhood of King Pelles' daughter, because of her consanguinity with the mysteries, of which she is an assistant-guardian under the Hereditary Keeper, occurs as the result of an intercourse which has some aspects of a magical marriage, and, considering all its circumstances, it is difficult at this stage to speculate about all that which lies behind it. We may almost say that the Lesser Mysteries took flesh for a period under an ordained enchantment and were ill at ease in their envelope. Having regard to Galahad's election, the response which he made thereto, and the achievement which in fine crowned it, the manner of his birth is no longer even a stain; it is a triviality, the sufficing cause of which removes the suggestion of profanation in respect of the Holy Place which by that unusual conception drew to the term of its ministry. I can understand that the mind unversed in the harmony of the whole scheme may think that the generation of Galahad should have been left in a cloud of uncertainty and himself without declared father or mother, like the mystic King of Salem. We have, however, to remember that what we now term bastardy does not rank in the romances exactly as a stain upon origin; it is almost a conventional mode of begetting heroes-in-chief, and that which obtains for Galahad obtains for the ideal hero and king who was the son according to the flesh of Uther Pendragon. As no romances ascribe a higher importance to chastity, and even to virginity, than the Graal legends, so—antecedently at least—their writers had every reason to attach its proper degree of value to the pre-eminence and sanctity of the nuptial bond; but there was that in the antecedents of Lancelot which made him the only possible father for the most exotic flower of chivalry who was the predestined Graal winner, but at the same time nothing could insure that possibility, except in the absence of his marriage.

So, therefore, Galahad is begotten in the fulness of time, and over all connected therewith falls suddenly the veil of concealment. Though on one occasion he was seen as a babe by Sir Bors in the Holy Place, we do not know certainly where he was born or by whom nurtured; but if we are guided by the sequel, as it follows in the Great Quest, it was probably away from the Graal Castle and with mystic nurses. When we first meet him he is among the pageants and holy places of the mysteries of official religion. Subsequently he is led towards his term by one who seems a steward of other mysteries, and when the quest begins he passes at once into the world of parable and symbol, having firstly been consecrated as a knight by his own father, who does not apparently know him, who acts under the direction of the stewards, while Galahad dissembles any knowledge that he might be assumed to possess. He has come, so far as we can say, out of the hidden places of the King. He bears the outward signs of the Mysteries, and has an imputed prescience of events in a certain chain of cause and effect. He passes through adventures as a man passes through visions, and he has many combats, but they are chiefly of such an order that the alternative title of the Great Quest might well be the Spiritual Combat. In the quests which he undertakes, although there is nominally one castle in which the Graal has its normal abode, it is yet a moving wonder, and a studied comparison might show that it is more closely connected with the Eucharistic mystery than it is according to the other romances, the *Longer Prose Perceval* excepted. Still, an efficacious mass is being said everywhere in the world. The Graal is more especially the secret of high sanctity. Galahad himself is the mystery of spiritual chivalry exemplified in human form ; his history is one of initiation, and his term is to see God. As compared with the rest of the literature, we enter in his legend upon new ground, and are on the eminence of Mont Salvatch rather than among the normal offices of chivalry. It is more especially this legend which is regarded by scholarship as the last outcome of the ascetic element introduced into the Graal cycle; but it is not understood that throughout the period of the middle ages the mystic life manifested only under an ascetic aspect, or with an environment of that kind. The Galahad romance is not ascetic after the ordinary way, or as the term is commonly accepted; it has an interior quality which places it above that degree, and this quality is the open sense of the mystic life. But the gate of the mystic life is assuredly the ascetic gate, in the same manner that the normal life of religion has morality as the door thereof. Those who have talked of asceticism meant in reality to speak of the supernatural life, of which the Galahad romance is a kind of archetypal picture. Though Wolfram, on the authority of Guiot, may have told what he called the true story, that story was never recited till the creation of the Galahad legend. The atmosphere of the romance gives up Galahad as the natural air gives up the vision from beyond. It is the story of the arch-natural man who comes to those who will receive him. He issues from the place of the mystery as Lancelot came from fairyland, or at least a world of enchantment. The atmosphere is that of great mysteries, the odour that of the sanctuary withdrawn behind the Hallows of the outward Holy Places. Galahad's entire life is bound up so completely with the Quest to which he is dedicated that apart therefrom he can scarcely be said to live. The desire of a certain house not made with hands has so eaten him up that he has never entered the precincts of the halls of passion. He is indeed faithful and true, but earthly attraction is foreign to him, even in its exaltation. Even his meetings with his father are shadowy and not of this world—a characteristic which seems the more prominent when he is the better fulfilling what would be understood by his filial duty. It is not that he is explicitly outside the sphere of sense and its temptations, but that his actuating motives are of the transmuted kind. In proportion, his quest is of the unrealised order; it is the working of a mystery within the place of a mystery; and it is in comparison therewith that we may understand the deep foreboding which fell upon the heart of Arthur when the flower of his wonderful court went forth to seek the Graal. In this respect the old legend illustrates the fact that many are called but few are chosen; and even in the latter class it is only the rarest flower of the mystic chivalry which can be thought of as chosen among thousands. Of the Perceval Quest there are many versions, but of Galahad there is one story only. So are the peers of the Round Table a great company, but Galahad is one. So also, of the high kings and princes, there are some who come again, and of such is the royal Arthur; but there are some who return no more, and of these is Galahad. He has not been understood even by great poets, for there could be scarcely a worse interpretation of his position than a poem, like that of Tennyson, in which he celebrates his strength on the ground that his heart is pure. Let me add, in conclusion of this part, that at the time of his coming the Graal went about in the land, looking for those it belonged to, and that in this respect Galahad had the true secret of *Le Moyen de parvenir*. It has its secret place of abiding, its altar of repose, at Corbenic, the Graal Castle, but it appears at the King's court—and this is exclusive to the story. The voice of the Quest passed through all Britain, in part by common report—because all the Arthurian knighthood bound itself to assume the task—but in part also by the miracle of unknown voices and of holy fore-knowledge. The Graal itself is not the official sacrament, or it is that and something which exceeds it. If it were otherwise there would be no sense in the declaration made by a hermit that certain knights may seek but shall never find it. On the Eucharistic side, it is the vision of Christ Himself, and the mystery of Divine Providence is manifested strangely therein; it works through faith, represented as the way of vision and the gate of things unseen. In the poem of De Borron and other early versions, the Sacred Vessel is invisible—and that utterly—to persons of evil life; but, though still under its due veils, it is shown in the Quest more openly, and on one occasion even to all who are present—good knights and indifferent. The vision imposes silence, and this seems to have been always its office, but it is that kind of silence which comes about by the mode of ecstasy, and in the case of Lancelot it is described rather fully, as if there were a particular intention discernible in his advancement through those grades of his partial initiation, when he sees without participating. One form of this ecstasy seems to be connected with the working of the Holy Spirit. But there is no assurance to be inferred from favour to further favour, since, on another occasion, the Graal is invisible to Lancelot when it is seen at the same time and in the same place by a company of white knights.

Of such is the Vessel of the legend and as regards the search after it, the elect knight is told that God entered into this world to free men from the wearisome adventures which were on them and from the evil belief. A close parallel is instituted between the Knight and Christ, since Galahad came to terminate the adventurous and evil destinies in this island of Britain. For this reason he is likened to the Son of the High Father, who brought souls out of thrall, and even a demon confesses to him as the way of truth.

I conceive that there is little occasion to recite the story of the Quest which is available after so many manners of English vesture to young and old alike. At the Vigil of Pentecost, Lancelot was carried by a gentlewoman to a Holy House, where he was required to knight the son of his own body, but, as we have seen, without learning his name or recognising him after any manner. Galahad, who "was semely and demure as a dove, with all maner of good features," was acquainted, undoubtedly, with his geniture, but he made no claim on his father. After this mode, at the beginning of his progress, was he consecrated by the secular order and received into the degree of chivalry. He came forth from the sacred precincts, being a convent of white nuns, wherein it is said that he had been nourished, and was brought to the Court of King Arthur by "a good old man and an auncyent clothed al in whyte," who saluted the company at table with words of peace. Against this arrival the palace had been prepared strangely by the emblazonment of letters of gold on the Siege Perilous—testifying that the time had come when it should be at length occupied—and by the appearance of a great stone in the river outside, with a sword embedded therein, which none present could withdraw. The ancient man uplifted the draperies of the chair, and there was found a new emblazonment: "this is the sege of Galahalt the haute prynce." The youth is seated accordingly, as a prince who was not of this world, and it was seen that he was clothed in red arms, though without sword or shield. But he had begun to move amidst enchantments; the sword implanted in the stone was to him predestined, and by him it was withdrawn, after which he revealed by the word of his own mouth that it was that weapon wherewith the good Knight Balyn had slain Balan, his brother. At the festival which followed this episode the Graal, under its proper veils, appeared in the hall, illuminating all things by the grace of the Holy Ghost and imposing that sacred silence—already mentioned—in the presence of the Great Mysteries. As the light enlightened them spiritually, and to each uplifted the countenance of each in beauty, so the sacred vision fed them abundantly in their bodies; but because of those draperies whieh shrouded the vessel, the great chivalry vowed to go in quest thereof, that they might see it more openly. After this manner began the mystic inquisition which, by a messenger from Nascien the Hermit—who was the early Keeper of Galahad according to the *Vulgate Merlin* and the recipient of those revelations contained in the *Book of the Holy Graal*—was forbidden to natural women, like that of Masonry, though the ministers of the Graal were maidens, and if Masonry had retained its secrets in conscious memory they would be served by women who were virgins.

The first adventures of Galahad were those which befell him at an Abbey of white monks, when he who was as yet without shield received that which Joseph II. gave in the far past to Evalach that he might prevail against the King of Egypt—that also which Joseph crossed with his blood on his death-bed. It was a sign that the evil adventures would be ended by Galahad. Previously, it had been a shield perilous to all who used it, because it was predestined to one, but I do not find that it had a special office in the later part of the legend.

Of the Graal and the other Hallows, of their ministry and mystery, and of all things connected therewith, we have heard in their proper sections otherwise. After what manner Lancelot, Perceval and Bors passed through worlds of parable—as through places of purification—I do not speak here, and even in respect of the High Prince, I am concerned only in so far as his story completes the things which were left over from other branches of the Greater Chronicles ; the healing of Mordrains, the King—penitent of all the centuries; the release of Simeon ; and the manumission of the unfaithful Moses. But of this last I find nothing in the Quest. As regards Simeon, the abbey which was visited by Lancelot was reached by Galahad towards the close of his time of quest, and there he beheld a burning wood in a croft under the minster, but the " flammynge faylled, and the fyre staunched " as he drew thereto, and there paused for a space. The voice of Simeon from within greeted him in a good hour when he was to draw a soul out of earthly pain into the joy of Paradise. It said also that he who spoke was of his kindred, and that for three hundred and fifty-four years he had been thus purged of the sin which he had done against Joseph of Arimathæa. Galahad took the body in his arms, bore it into the minster, had service said over it, and interred it before the high altar. Of such was the rest of Simeon.

It was at another abbey that he came upon the age-long vigil of King Mordrains. Galahad had the hands of healing, and seeing that he was born in the sanctuary, it may be said that in this romance the healing comes from within. These were the words of the King: "Galahad the seruant of Jhesu Cryst whos comynge I haue abyden soo longe, now enbrace me & lete me reste on thy breste, so that I may reste bitwene thine armes, for thou art a clene vyrgyn aboue all Knyghtes as the floure of the lely, in whome vyrgynyte is sygne-fyed, & thou art the rose the whiche is the floure of all good vertues, & in coloure of fyre. For the fyre of the holy ghoost is taken so in thee that my flesshe which was of dede oldnesse, is become yong ageyne." When Galahad heard his words, he covered his whole body in a close embrace, in which position the King prays Christ to visit him, wherein and whereafter the soul departed from his body. So was the curious impertinent, who had been called but not chosen at that time, after his long penance, at length forgiven the offence, and was taken into the great peace, fortified with all Rites of the most secret and Holy Church of the Hidden Graal.

The Ship of Solomon had, prior to these episodes, conveyed the questing knights—Galahad, Perceval and Bors—from point to point of their progress; it had taken Lancelot a certain distance in his son's company, till they commended each other to God for the rest of their mortal life; it had borne the sister of Perceval, who of her own hair and of silk, combined with precious stones, had braided the true and proper girdle for the Sword of David, to replace the mean girdle attached to it by the wife of Solomon. But she had yielded her life before the healing and passing in God of Mordrains, and had been placed by her proper desire in another ship, with a covenant on her part that it should meet the questers at Sarras, when the Ship of Solomon brought them to that bourne of their voyaging. It remained only that those three should now gather at Corbenic for the healing of the maimed King Pellehan, about whose place and identity we have seen that the text offers some elements of minor confusion. This is he whom we must suppose to have received the Dolorous Stroke at the hands of Balyn.

As the path of quest drew towards its central point, the three, who had traversed various converging roads, met, as it is said, at travers, knowing that the adventures of Logres were at last achieved. They entered within the Castle, and King Pelles greeted them with great joy. In this as in some other romances grave importance is attached to resoldering the Broken Sword, and that which was brought by Eleazer, the King's son, was that with which Joseph II. was once stricken through the thighs. It was set perfectly by Galahad when the others had essayed in vain, and was then given to Bors, as a good knight and a worthy man. What followed thereon was the sustenance of the elect Graal knights after a spiritual manner, to the exclusion of the general assembly, who were dismissed from the presence. Those who remained were three and three, namely, Galahad, Perceval and Bors, for the first triad ; King Pelles, his son Eleazar, and a maiden who was the King's niece, for the second triad. To these were joined certain pilgrims who were knights also, namely, three of Gaul, three of Ireland, and three of Denmark. Finally, there was brought in the maimed King, and thereon a voice said that two of those who were present did not belong to the Quest,

at which words King Pelles—although he was the
Keeper—rose up with his son and departed. They were,
therefore, thirteen in all, and one of these was a woman,
who was present with them when Joseph of Arimathæa,
the first Bishop of Christendom, came down with angels
from heaven, and celebrated an arch-natural Mass in the
Holy Place. After the Kiss of Peace given to Galahad,
and communicated by him to his fellows, the celebrants
dissolved, but out of the Graal itself there came the
Saviour of all, with the signs of His passion upon Him,
and communicated to them all in the Eucharist. He also
vanished, and Galahad, who had received his instructions,
went up to the maimed King and anointed him with the
blood flowing from the Hallowed Spear. Thereupon,
he, being healed, rose up and gave thanks to God. It is
said that, in the sequel of time, he united himself to a
company of white monks.

"Sir," said Galahad to the Great Master at the close
of the Mysteries, "why shalle not these other felawes
goo with us?"—that is to say, unto Sarras, the reference
being to the nine mysterious knights. The answer
hereto was significant: "For this cause: for ryght as
I departed my postels, one here and another there soo I
will that ye departe, and two of yow shall dye in my
servyse, but one of you shal come ageyne and telle
tydynges." So, therefore, the company of the adepts
dissevered; but we have seen how Galahad, Perceval
and Bors were carried by the Ship of Solomon to Sarras,
"in the partyes of Babylone," called an island in the
Quest. There met them, in accordance with her covenant, that other vessel, which carried the body of
Perceval's most holy sister. We have seen also how
the soul of Galahad departed, and it rests only to say
that Perceval died in a hermitage, but Sir Bors returned
to Logres, bearing the messages of his brethren, but
especially of Galahad to his father: "And whanne he
had said these wordes Galahad went to Percyual and
kyssed hym & commaunded hym to God, and soo he

went to sire Bors, & kyssed hym, and commaunded hym to God, and sayde: Fayre lord, salewe me to my lord syr launcelot my fader. And as soone as ye see hym, byd hym remember of this unstable world."

The bodies of Perceval and Galahad were buried in the spiritualities of Sarras, which may have been in some sense a city of initiation, though until their coming it was ruled by evil rather than good. It was not the abiding place, but that of the final trial for the stewards of the Mystery, and at first they were imprisoned therein; but Galahad was afterwards made King. The Spear was taken into heaven, together with the Holy Vessel, but Bors returned—as it has been intimated—carrying the re-soldered Broken Sword, as if grace had been removed, but not that which now may have symbolised the coming destruction of the Round Table. Of the Sword of David we hear nothing further, nor do we know what became of the Ship of Solomon. As the symbol of Faith, it may have continued voyaging, but on other considerations it had done its work: there was no reason why it should remain when Galahad had gone.

But perhaps the saddest mystery of all is the end of King Pelles himself, and how it fared with him after the departure of the Graal. It will be seen that the Quest versions offer many alternatives, but there is one text only which says that the Hereditary Keeper was dispossessed utterly and left in an empty sanctuary.

We have now, and in fine, to account as we can for the great disaster of the whole experiment. The earthly knighthood undertakes, in despite of the high earthly king, a quest to which it is in a sense perhaps called but for which it is in no sense chosen. The result, as I have said, is that the chivalry of the world is broken and the kingdom is destroyed, while the object of all research is said to be taken away. It was not, therefore, the conceal-ment of the Sacred Vessel, but its manifestation rather, which brought ruin to the Round Table. It went about in the world of Logres, and the ruin followed, because the world was not worthy. In a certain manner it is the mystery of the Graal itself which gives forth Galahad as its own manifestation, in the order of the visible body, and sends him on designed offices of healing, with a warrant to close a specific cycle of times. When the Graal romances say that the Sacred Vessel was seen no more, or was carried up to heaven, they do not mean that it was taken away, in the sense that it had become unattainable, but that it was—as some of them say also—in concealment. It is certain that the great things are always in concealment, and are perhaps the more hidden in proportion to their more apparently open manifestation. In this respect, the distinction between the natural and supernatural Graal, which is made by the prose Lancelot, has a side of highest value. Let us reserve for a moment the consideration of the Hallows as mere relics, and in so far as the Cup is concerned, let us remember the two forms of sustenance which it offered — in correspondence closely enough with the ideas of Nature and Grace. It should be understood, however, that between the mysteries themselves there is a certain superincession, and so also there is in the romances what the light heart of criticism regards as *un peu confus*, namely, some disposition to talk of the one office in the terms of the other. At the same time certain romances give prominence to the greater and others to the lesser office.

IX

THE WELSH QUEST OF GALAHAD

It is considered that this translation, which is referable to the early part of the fifteenth century, was made from another codex than that which was used by Malory for the *Morte d'Arthur*, but it embodied material from the *Book of the Holy Graal*, which may mean that the anonymous author of the rendering was either the compiler of a harmony or the simple translator of a manuscript corresponding to the texts followed by Dr. Furnivall in his edition of the *Quest*. At the same time, outside all evidences of mistranslation, the Welsh version of the Quest itself differs unquestionably in several particulars from all codices which are known to scholarship, and it seems quite certain that the variations are not those of invention. On the one hand, there is a certain slight attenuation of the mystic atmosphere, though the general features remain; for example, that enhanced knowledge of one another which is attributed to the knights who saw the Holy Vessel, under the veils thereof, at the King's table, is unmentioned in the Welsh text. Alternatively, there are other respects in which there is an added disposition to lean on the spiritual side of things, and this is manifested plainly in a few crucial cases. The Table of the Lord's Supper is described as that which fed the body and the soul with heavenly food, while the Graal itself is said to provide a spiritual nourishment, which is sent by the Holy Ghost to him who seeks in grace to sit at the table thereof. The close connection between the Sacred Vessel and the office of the Divine Spirit—which is so evident in the metrical romance of De Borron—is also apparent, and one who is on the quest is told that by falling into sin he will fail to see that Spirit, even as Lancelot failed. Outside those wanderings of the Holy Graal which are recorded in the French texts, there are references to its manifestation at sundry places in Logres—or there more especially, but not there to the exclusion of all other countries. Finally as to this part, I recognise a note of undeclared mystery as regards the House of the Hallows. There was the permanent shrine of the Holy Vessel, but whether it was visible always to those who dwelt within or at certain times and seasons is not apparent, and remains indeed doubtful on the evidence of all the literature. It is therefore open to question whether it was the daily nourishment of the House, or whether its varied ministry was contingent on the arrival of a stranger who was prepared so far sufficiently that he was admitted within the gates. It was the latter probably, because Lancelot rested there for four days; but it was not until the fifth day, and then in the midst of the supper, that the Graal appeared and filled all with the meats most loved by them.

The Welsh Quest, like its prototype of Northern France, draws then from the *Book of the Holy Graal*, but not from one of those codices with which we have been made acquainted so far by the pains of scholarship. For example, the account of the Second Table is given with specific variations, though there is nothing to justify their enumeration in this place, except that the son of Joseph is said to have occupied the seat which corresponded to that of Christ, and no one ventured to take it after him. It was not so occupied in the parent historical text, and we know, of course, that the Siege Perilous in other presentations of the legend is that of Judas Iscariot.

What appears to be the Dolorous Stroke in the Welsh Quest is exceedingly involved, but the account is as follows: (*a*) King Lambor was father of the Lame King, and was at war with King Urlain, formerly a Saracen. (*b*) Lambor was forced to flight, and in doing so reached the seashore, where he found the Ship of Solomon. (*c*) He took up the Sword therein and smote Urlain, so that he and his horse were cut in two pieces. This occurred in England, and was the first blow that was ever given with the weapon. (*d*) The King who was slain is said to have been so holy that great vengeance was taken by God for that blow. (*e*) In neither kingdom for a long time was there found any fruit, everything being dried up, so that the land is called to this day the Decayed Kingdom. It will be seen that this is in direct contradiction to the particulars in the *Book of the Holy Graal* concerning the death of Lambor, the keeper at that time of the Sacred Vessel. It follows also that the story of Balyn and Balan was unknown to the Welsh translator.

The Lame King was the Uncle of Perceval, and so good was his manner of living that his like could not be found in the world. One day he was hunting, and came to the seashore, where he also found the ship. In spite of the warning written therein, he entered without fear, and drew the Sword partly from the scabbard. He was struck by a spear in the thigh, and was maimed from that time forward. In the French *Quest of Galahad* this episode is attributed to King Pelles.

As an illustration of general intention prevailing through the Welsh Quest, a hermit reminds Gawain that the dignity of knighthood was conferred upon him—among other things—for the defence of the Church, and as this specific statement is part only of the general atmosphere through which the romance moves, it is itself an eloquent comment on the alleged underlying hostility to official ecclesiasticism which is sometimes traced in the literature. The condition of Wales at the time of the Quest, as it is depicted in the Welsh text, is not an encouraging report regarding the last stronghold of the Celtic Church, but it is possible that the worst particulars are things which the translator has interpolated.

Whether in their agreement or variation, the details of the story do not call to be scheduled here, but there are a few points which may be noted with all brevity. Galahad is described as the foster-child of the abbey where Lancelot finds him, and he is commanded to watch his arms prior to receiving knighthood. He is introduced at the Court of King Arthur as the desired Knight descended from the line of the prophet David and Joseph of Arimathæa: on him rest all the adventures and wonders of Great Britain and all countries. He is called the son of the daughter of King Pelles, but the later story speaks invariably of the Graal Castle as that of King Pelour, whom I should identify as the maimed and abdicated Keeper who was healed by Galahad in the French version, of which, however, there is no mention in the Welsh Quest. The manifested festival of the

Graal in the hall of Arthur is heralded by an unknown messenger—a lady vested in white on a white palfrey, who gives warning concerning its advent, and this is found also in Malory's version, but he follows a defective text, for in him the prophecy is uttered after the event itself. So great are the delicacies at the table, by the provision of the Sacred Vessel, so much are they dwelt on in the Welsh version, that the resolution of the knights in respect of the coming Quest has the aspect of material appetite, and they resolve not to rest till they can eat at another table where they will be fed as rarely. According to Gawain, there is no such place on earth except the Court of King Peleur. When the Quest is thus undertaken Galahad says nothing. All this is an accident of aspect, for elsewhere it is stated (*a*) that no one shall see the Holy Graal except through the gate which is called Confession, and this is obviously the gate of the Eucharist; (*b*) that the final return of Bors was designed to exhibit the spirituality of that good which at the last end of things was lost by so many on account of their sins.

The time comes when Galahad swears upon the relics with the others to maintain the Quest, and, apart from this position—which has not been understood by scholarship—there are episodes and intimations which seem intended to show that the natural child of the sanctuary was not permitted to know all—though he had that which was implied in his heirship—until, in common with the others, he undertook the great enterprise. The Knights proceeded on their journey weeping and in great sorrow—that is to say, with failing hearts, foreboding the discounselling of so many and all the disaster coming after : *Euntes ibant et flebant.*

There is one reference to Eleazar, the son of King Pelles, and one to a Knight named Argus, who, by an unthinkable confusion, is said to be the son of Helayne, as if this daughter of the House had married or begotten subsequently. The hermit Nasciens, whose identity is so important for the *Book of the Holy Graal*, is described as the son-in-law of Evalach, instead of his brother by marriage, as he appears in the extant text. He is found on one occasion by Gawain in a very poor cell or hermitage, with a small chapel attached.

When the questing Knights arrive at the Graal Castle, it is not said that they see either Pelles or Peleur, nor are these or Eleazar present at the manifestation of the Holy Graal. The maiden who remains in the text of Malory is also bidden to depart, following in this respect the chief French manuscripts. He who comes down from Heaven as the first Bishop of Christendom is distinguished rightly from Joseph of Arimathæa, and is therefore the second Joseph. When he celebrates the secret mass of the Graal, he takes out a wafer from the Vessel, which shows that it was used as a ciborium. In the divine discourse thereafter, it is said by Christ that many a good man has come to the Castle through the grace of the Holy Ghost. As regards the nine mysterious Knights who are not to accompany the three on their journey to Sarras, the parting of those with these takes place amidst great brotherhood, and each of them says who he is, but the nine are not named in the text. Galahad asks them to salute Arthur if they go to his Court, and they reply that they shall do so gladly, but they do not say that they will go. Probably they went back by another way into their own countries.

Now, these are the chief points which I promised to set forth; and there is one thing more only—that the Spear was not taken to Sarras, nor was it removed to Heaven with the Sacred Vessel. In conclusion as to the *Quest of Galahad*, the presence of that maiden who was niece of King Pelles at the great vision of the Graal seems without authority in extant French texts; it is therefore peculiar to Malory and the version which he followed. If it were possible to trace the variations of the Quest through developments of the Tristram cycle, we should meet with very curious details, but they are not necessary to our subject.

BOOK VI

*THE GERMAN CYCLE OF THE
HOLY GRAAL*

THE ARGUMENT

BOOK VI

THE GERMAN CYCLE OF THE HOLY GRAAL

I

THE PARSIFAL OF WOLFRAM VON ESCHENBACH

THOSE who in recent times have discussed the poem of Wolfram with titles to consideration on account of their equipment have been impressed not alone by the signal distinctions between this German poem and the Perceval legends as we know them in Northern France, but by a superiority of spiritual purpose and a higher ethical value which are thought to characterise the knightly epic. For the moment, at least, it can be said on my own part that we are in the presence of a poet whose work is full of gorgeous pictures, all rude diction notwithstanding, and all contemporary reproaches made upon that score. To me—but as one who on such subjects speaks with a sense of remoteness—the traces of Oriental influence seem clear in the poem, partly in its decorative character and partly in its allusions to places —after every allowance has been made for geographical confusions. Such traces are allowed, and they are referred to the source of Wolfram, about which I must say something in this section to introduce the separate inquiry which will follow hereafter. But we are asked in our turn to recognise that the *Parsifal* is the most heterodox branch of the whole Graal cycle, though it

375

is said to be the work of an ecclesiastic. This idea is represented by authoritative statements on the part of scholars who have scarcely produced their evidence, and by sporadic discursive remarks on the part of some other writers who could have been better equipped. In this manner we have (*a*) the negative inference drawn from a simple fact—as, for example, that the *Parsifal* does not exhibit that hostility towards Mohammedan people and things which characterised Crusading times—but as much might be said about other texts of the Graal; (*b*) the positive opinion that the chivalry of the Graal Temple resembles an association formed without the pale of the Church rather than within—which on the authority of the poem itself seems untrue, and this simply. Those who expound these views look for an explanation to the influences exercised theoretically by Knights Templars and the sects of Southern France—which possibilities will be considered in their proper place in respect of all the literature. As a preliminary, by way of corrective, I desire to record here that if the *Parsifal* is heterodox, its elements of this order have been imbedded below the surface, and then deeply, but whether it implies in this manner any secret religious claims which are not of sect or heresy is another question. On the surface it would be easy to make a tabulation of many points which manifest an absolute correspondence with Church doctrine and ordinance; but it will be sufficient for the moment to say that Mass is celebrated and heard as it is in the other romances; that confession is not less necessary; and so far as there is allusion in particular to dogmatic teaching, that it is of the accepted kind, as of the conditions and day of salvation: Mary is the Queen of Heaven, and the Lord Jesus dies as man on the Cross; the Divinity of Three Persons is included in one God. Sometimes there is an allusion which looks dubious, but it is mere confusion, as when a hermit speaks of a soul being drawn out of hell, where the reference is of course to the purgatorial state.

The story of the Quest in Wolfram may be considered in the interests of clearness under two heads, the first of which is designed to develop the specific analogies with other romances of the Perceval cycle, while in the second there are exhibited the specific points of distinction. As regards the analogies, it is to be understood that I reserve the right to omit any or every episode which does not concern my purpose. It is to be understood further that all analogies are under their own reserve in respect of variation. Let it be recalled, in the first place, that the historical side of the Perceval legend in the *Conte del Graal* of Chrétien is in a certain state of confusion. That poet left so much to be desired on the score of clearness about the early life of his hero that another poet prepared some antecedent information, but he spoke according to tradition and forgot that the matter with which he intervened was not in complete accordance with Chrétien's own account, so far as he had one. All continuations of the *Conte* were either too late for Wolfram or were for some other reason unknown by him ; but it may be said that Gautier and Manessier produced their romantic narratives following several prototypes, not of necessity connected with their character-in-chief *ab origine symboli*. Gerbert, who was evidently under the obedience of a prototype which was peculiar to himself in the Northern French cycles, had perhaps some lost Perceval Quest, if not that actually which we connect with the name of Guiot. With the *Didot Perceval* Wolfram has only those points of concurrence which belong to the common primordial source, and with the *Longer Prose Perceval* his features of likeness are in so far as both texts stand together by themselves. Under these qualifications, the salient lines of correspondence by way of likeness with the French cycle may be collected as follows.

The genealogy in the *Parsifal* is simple ; it is the triad, which is permanent on earth as the Holy and Undivided Trinity is eternal in Heaven. But in most texts the Trinity of the Graal Keepership is by way of succession and therefore feeble; Wolfram, on the other hand, ends with a perfect symbol in the union of those who have reigned with him who shall reign henceforward, whereas all other quests of Perceval leave him alone in his kingdom at the end absolute of the great adventure. The German Kings of the Graal are Titurel, Frimutel and Amfortas. The first is the founder of the dynasty—in respect of the Graal Keepership—and he remains alive, like Brons in Robert de Borron, the maimed King Pellehan in the *Quest of Galahad*, and that nameless hidden sovereign who anteceded King Fisherman in the *Conte del Graal*. The second has died in war, which was not in the cause of the Graal, and it is partly for this reason that Perceval must intervene to renew the triad. The nearest analogy to this is in the *Didot Perceval*, which after the achievement of the Graal pictures the questing knight abiding in the place of the Hallows with Blaise and Merlin as two substituted keepers, though at the close it detaches the prophet and puts him into mystic retreat, as if at the term of the ages—when Avalon gives up its exiles—he might again manifest and testify. There is also another analogy, but this is of the implied kind, for in the *Parsifal* and the *Didot Perceval* he who has achieved the Quest remains, and the Sacred Vessel—in apparent perpetuity—that is to say, in the House of the Hidden Hallows. Both elect knights—shadows of a single personality—arrived, that they might stay in fine.

The father of Parsifal was a king's son—as he is occasionally in the other romances—and it is said in more than one place that he came of the fairy lineage. It was on the mother's side that the youth was by generation a son of the house, and therefore entitled, supposing that he was otherwise prepared, to return therein. She was Herzeleide, sister of the Graal King and Queen, in her own right, not only of Wales but Anjou. The father was named Gamuret, but in the course of knightly adventure he was slain shortly after his marriage and the birth of his only son in respect of this union. That he may be saved from the fatal knowledge which in those days was involved by the life of chivalry, there follows—with many variations—the concealment of Parsifal by his mother in the wild places and woodlands. It does not appear what she did to insure the rule of the kingdoms, but her result was that the two countries fell into other hands. She who had been born, as one may suppose, in that secondary light which is the shadow of the Holy Graal—since she does not seem to have been an inbred Daughter of the House—might have acted better and more wisely to have reared her son—in the spirit and intention at least—as a child of the Sacred Talisman instead of a wild boy of the woods. Far otherwise than she did the twice-born Hermit Nasciens, who had Galahad in his keeping; far otherwise did they of the White Abbey, among whom Galahad was found by Lancelot. But the fatality was working with greater power because she strove the more; Parsifal met all the same with the knights of King Arthur's Court, and rode forth as usual —not with her consent indeed, but with the dangerous folly of her cautions—in search of the Grade of Chivalry. Almost immediately after her parting with Parsifal, she died in the grief of his loss. He, as in other stories, reached the pavilion of the Sleeping Lady, and he took not her ring only but also a buckle. In this instance she seems to have been unwilling throughout, and the youth behaved brutally.

Before reaching the Court of King Arthur he met with his cousin Sigune, and it should be noted here that there is no sister in this version of the Quest. Of her he learned his proper name and so much of his genealogy as was requisite to assure him that he was the legitimate King of Wales, in the defence of which right there perished her own lover, whose body remained in her charge after the mad manner of the romances.

The Hidden Church of the Holy Graal

As geographical names signify little or nothing, the court of King Arthur was held at Nantes, and on his arrival thither the old episode of the dwarfs was exchanged for that of a maiden who could not laugh until she beheld the best knight in the world. She was struck and insulted by Kay for paying this honour to one of Parsifal's outlandish appearance, and a considerable part of the story is concerned incidentally with the youth's resolution to avenge her and a certain silent knight who, after the manner of the dwarfs, found speech to hail his advent and was also chastised. The Red Knight appeared as usual and Parsifal obtained his armour, the grievance being that the knight had taken a cup from the Round Table and spilt wine upon the robe of the Queen. But the secondary detail was a matter of accident and one regretted deeply, for in this story only the Red Knight is a hero after the true manner; he is also the youth's kinsman, and his death—which occurs as usual—is a stain on Parsifal rather than to the glory of his prowess.

So proceeds the story, and so far as it follows the long weariness of the worn way, even its decorations can lend it only a secondary interest. I think also, and it must be said, that even in his exaltation the hero kindles little sympathy, whereas Galahad enthrals for ever. The next incident in our scheme is Parsifal's instruction in chivalry, which took place at the castle of Gurnemanz, who was the brother of the Graal King, but this relation was not declared to his pupil. As in the *Peredur*, he is responsible for the fatality of the unasked question, and in both cases there is the same want of logic on the surface which probably covers a secret intention. The result otherwise of the instruction was that Parsifal ceased from his folly.

This experience completed, he asked his teacher at their parting to give him his daughter when he had done something to deserve her; but it appears to have been more in conformity with her father's implied wish than through a keen desire of his own, and we hear nothing further of either. His next task brought him to Belrepaire—in siege by sea and land and wasted by famine. There he succoured the Queen Kondwiramour, who corresponds to Blanchefleur, and there also he married her. We are now in that region which we know to have been travelled by Gerbert, and as for him the espousals left the lovers in virginity, so, according to Wolfram, the marriage was not consummated till the third night. But—whereas a high motive actuated the two parties in the French romance—in the German poem there was no mutual concordat but a kind of spurious chivalry on the hero's side which he overcame in the end. Parsifal, however, was still espoused only to the notion of adventure, on which he again set forth, this time to meet with the Fisher King and to learn that the Graal Castle was close at hand, like all things that are greatest. As regards his qualifications for the visit, it would seem that, even in the Holy Place, he thought chiefly of knightly combats and wondered how he should find them in such surroundings. The Fisher King was Amfortas, the Maimed King, and the procession was that which I have described previously and at needed length. The Castle was full of splendour and chivalry, but it was also full of sadness : the story is one of suffering and sorrow. The relation between host and guest was that of uncle and nephew, but as usual it did not transpire on this occasion. Parsifal also failed to ask the vital question, but it should be noted that, although grievous sin was attributed to him on this account, he had not been warned so distinctly—either here or in the *Conte del Graal*—that there would be a question to ask as he was in the *Didot Perceval*. He went forth unserved from the Castle, but there is no suggestion of any external enchantment, nor did he find that the whole country had been laid under a mysterious interdict which had rendered it utterly waste, or that the inhabitants were abandoned to various forms of distress. On account further of the normal offices of Nature, it is to be understood that he left the Castle as a knight who has finished his visit—that is to say, he rode away; it was not the Castle which left him by a sudden process of vanishing. In the world outside he was reproached by his kinswoman Sigune, who still had the body of her lover.

The familiar pursuant adventures must be mentioned briefly. The Lady of the Pavilion was fairly exonerated by Parsifal and sent with her vanquished lord to the woman who could not laugh at the court of King Arthur, where she proved to be the knight's sister, so that Kay was put to shame. Arthur rose up and set forth on the quest of Parsifal, who was found in the love-trance and brought to the royal tent. There he was made a Knight of the Round Table, and thither came the laidly Kundrie—that baleful messenger of the Graal, who was also God's minister—to curse and denounce him for his ill-fated course at the Castle. She told him much which belongs to the second branch of our subject, but also of his mother's death, by which news he was overwhelmed, and by the shame of the messenger's wrath tempestuous. He departed from that court as a man who had lost his faith, yet he went—*pro forma* at least—on the Quest of the Graal. After long wanderings he met again with his cousin Sigune, whose lover had found a sepulchre, near which she lived as an anchoress and received food from the Graal which was brought her by the sorceress Kundrie. At a later period, Parsifal, being still in his sins, and cherishing no thought of God, met with the pageant of pilgrims on Good Friday, but his better nature did not return to him so quickly as in the other stories. In due course he reached the hold of a hermit, who—here as there—was his uncle, to whom he confessed everything and from whom he learned—subject to certain variations —the story of the Graal in full.

When he is heard of next in the poem, the chance of war had brought Parsifal in collision with Gawain, and they failed to recognise each other until the latter suffered defeat. The victor was restored in this manner to the court of King Arthur, passing henceforth to and fro between that world and the more external world of adventure. To the court on a certain occasion, with no preface or warning, there again came Kundrie, sorceress and messenger, carrying the news of Parsifal's election to the Holy Kingdom of the Graal. Thereat he rose to his feet and recited the secret story of the great Palladium, as he had learned it from the lips of the hermit; he told how none could attain it unless he were called thereto; and in virtue of that calling, in his own case, he took leave of the chivalry for ever. He reached the Consecrated Castle, beheld the Hallows therein, and asked the necessary question, to the king's healing and the joy of those who were delivered from the thrall of his long suffering.

I have left out of this consideration all reference to Gawain, who occupies a third part of the whole story, and whose marriage is celebrated therein. He undertook the Quest of the Graal, and though much followed thereupon in the matter of high adventure he did not attain the term. To say this is to indicate in one word an important point of difference between this text and the stories which have been studied already. There are other variations, but I will mention one of them only, that I may have done with this extraneous matter; it concerns the character of Gawain, which is one of knightly heroism and all manner of courtesy and good conduct. Wolfram knew nothing apparently of that later fashion of calumny which was set by the *Romance of Lancelot*.

The reader is now in a position to understand how far this summary corresponds with the general outline of Chrétien and with the brief quest in the *Didot Perceval*. He will also trace the salient analogies with the *Welsh Peredur*, and, in a lesser degree, with the English *Syr Percyvelle*. In fine, he will see that so far as the schedule reaches, it has no correspondence in adventure with the *Longer Prose*

Perceval, which is the second part only of the knightly Quest. I have mentioned, however, that the last text has vague reminiscences of a source which may have been that of Wolfram, and the two romances converge in the path of their greatest divergence from other texts. We have now to consider the points of distinction in the *Parsifal*—which are a much more serious question—and I shall do so under three subdivisions, the first of which will deal with the romantic episodes, the second with the Graal itself, including its concomitants in symbolism, and the third with the source of Wolfram, thus leading up to the considerations of my next section.

A morganatic union was contracted by the father of Parsifal, prior to his marriage with Herzeleide, as one consequence of a journey eastward in search of adventure. He was the means of salvation to a heathen Queen Belakané, whose throne he shared for a period, and although no rite of wedlock is mentioned, she is described as his wife invariably. The inference is that this union was not one which the Church would recognise; but Gamuret is not exculpated, because it is quite clear that he had every opportunity to convert her and to lay the Christian religion like a yoke on the neck of her kingdom. He would be, therefore, responsible for not making the attempt, an episode which does not correspond to a very high sense of honour, while his subsequent marriage —which is not challenged by the poet—would be thought little less than disgraceful if the hypothesis of scholarship had not allocated the poem of Wolfram to so high an ethical level. The fruit of the first union was the pagan prince Feirfeis, who, being born in the East under such circumstances, is harlequined—that is to say, is represented as half black and half white, to indicate his dual origin. The death of Gamuret was the result of a second visit to the East. He heard that the King of Bagdad was beset by the princes of Babylon, and having served him in his youth he was impelled to go forth to his rescue. In one of the ensuing battles he took off his helmet and laid it down for a few moments on account of the heat. A pagan knight poured thereon the blood of a he-goat, and that which was previously like diamond in its hardness became soft as sponge. The result was that the King of Alexandria cut with his spear through the helmet and penetrated the brain.

I have mentioned here the first point of distinction between the more narrative part of the poem and the other quests of Perceval; the second concerns Kundrie, who acts as the messenger of the Graal. She is described as faithful and true, possessing all knowledge—according to the institutes of the period—and speaking all tongues. But she was repellent in appearance beyond the physical issues of Nature, as a combination indeed of gruesome symbolic animals. She was a sorceress also, as we have seen, though this is perhaps a technical description of the period, expressing only the sense of her extraordinary knowledge. She is not, however, to be identified with the evil side of the powers of Avalon, concerning which we hear so much in the *Lancelot* and later Merlin texts, nor is she exactly a fay woman—that is to say, the Daughter of a School of Magic—as conceived by the French romancers, since she does not practise magic or weave enchantments. Her impeachment of Parsifal at the Court of King Arthur turned wholly on his failure at the Graal, and was interspersed with prophecy which future events made void. I must say that her discourse reads only as the raving of one distracted, and that by which she was distracted was the sorrow in the House of the Graal. As Parsifal might have disarmed her by the simplest of all explanations—being that which he gave subsequently to the Round Table itself—and as thus he had at least his personal justification reposing in his own heart—it is curious, and particular to the story, that he should take her reproaches so deeply into his inward nature that he held himself shamed almost irretrievably, though the court did not so hold him. The effect was greater than this, for it hardened his heart against God and converted one who had never been ardent in faith, who had never so far experienced a touch of Divine Grace, into an utterer of open blasphemy. Other stories say that he had forgotten God, but in Wolfram he remembers and rebels.

The *Parsifal* does not give us an intelligible history of Kundrie; it does not explain why the messenger of the Graal was or had become unlovely; or why it connects, however remotely, that sacred object with one whom it terms a sorceress. We only see that she comes and goes as she pleases, or is thereby commissioned, in and about the Holy House : she carries the palliatives administered to the wounded King to a place where they become available for Gawain, and she brings the food of the Graal to Parsifal's cousin, Sigune.

The intervention of the magician Klingsor in the story leaves us also in doubt as to what he represents in the scheme. He came of the race of Virgil—whom mediæval tradition presents as a potent enchanter—and was originally a duke of noble life till he was ensnared by unholy passion, for which he was heavily visited, being deprived of the instruments of passion. Those who know anything of occult traditions will be aware that this affliction would have been an almost insuperable barrier to his success in magic, but Wolfram, who knew only by hearsay, and then at a very far distance, says that he was made a magician by his maiming, meaning that he visited the secret city of Persida, the birthplace of magic—on its averse side apparently—and received initiation in full, so that he could work all wonders. He erected *Chateau Merveil*, which is a sort of contradiction, in terms of diabolism, to the Castle of the Holy Graal, as his own life is an analogy by travesty of that of the King of the Graal, who had also sinned in his senses, at least by the desire of his heart. *Chateau Merveil*, however, seems to lack intention, for the magic which built it was not proof against the personal bravery of Gawain, who put an end to the enchantments and became the lord of the fortress. It should be added that Klingsor himself does not appear in the poem, so that he is a king in hiding.

I have little cause to delay over the history of Feirfeis, the brother of Parsifal, who came with a great host westward in search of chivalry and his father, only to learn that the latter was dead when he and Parsifal had nearly slain each other. Feirfeis married before leaving his native land, but as Wolfram von Eschenbach begins his knightly epic with one cruel adultery, so he ends it with another, eclipsing his previous record by uniting Feirfeis, within the sacred walls—after his baptism—to the pure and wonderful maiden who through all her virgin days had carried the Holy Graal. Now, I pray that God may preserve us from these high ethical values which we have known under rougher names. To make bad worse, when the wedded pair proceed on their journey eastward, the news of his first wife's death was brought to Feirfeis, which caused him to rejoice in the journey, though it seems an indecent satisfaction. I have read some weird criticisms which are designed to depreciate it, but—while God continues willing—I set my own heart on the *Quest of Galahad*. In fine, as regards this marriage the issue was a son, who received a name the equivalent of which was *Jean le prêtre*—that is to say, Prester John, the great, legendary, sacerdotal, Christian King of the furthest East, the rumour concerning whom went forth over Europe at the end of the twelfth century.

After the union of all the characters of the story—who are within the sphere of election—at the Castle of the Graal, which, as in Chrétien so here also, is never the *Holy Graal*, the poet passes to the history of Lohengrin —the son of Parsifal and Kondwiramour. He became the Knight of the Swan, whose legend was transferred by Wolfram from what is termed the Lorraine epic cycle. We shall hear further concerning him and the transmission of the Sacred Talisman to Prester John in the *Younger Titurel* of Albrecht von Scharfenberg. Kardeiss, the second of Parsifal's twin sons, was crowned in his infancy as King of those countries which were the more earthly heritage of his father.

A few matters of lesser importance may be grouped here together: (1) There is an account of the mother of King Arthur which is the reverse of the other legends; it is said that she fled with a clerk who was versed deeply in magic—one would have thought a reference to Merlin, who otherwise at least is unknown to Wolfram. Arthur is said to have pursued them for three years. (2) There is no Siege Perilous and no reference to Lancelot. (3) Parsifal is elected to his kingdom by the fiat of the Graal itself. (4) The mystic question in Wolfram seems to be the most natural and ineffective of the literature, its words being: What aileth thee here, mine uncle? (5) It is essential that this question should not be prompted, but Parsifal's uncle on the mother's side gives him the information in full and so makes void the condition; yet Parsifal asks in the end, and all is well with the King.

I pass now to the matter of the Graal itself, to the Hallows—imputed, or otherwise—connected therewith, and the subsidiary subjects, in so far as they have not been treated in the considerations of the second book. It will clear the important issues in respect of implicits if I say that in the German cycle there are no secret words, there is no strange sacerdotal succession, while the religious side of the mystery is distinct, and so utterly, from that of the French romances. The Graal is not a chalice—and much less a chalice containing the Blood of Christ: it is a stone, but this is not described specifically when it is first beheld by Parsifal. It is carried on a green cushion and is laid on a jacinth table over against the Warden. It is called the crown of all earthly riches, but that is in respect of its feeding properties, of which I shall speak presently. It is not termed a stone, which is the current account regarding it, till the Knight hears its history from the lips of his uncle Trevrezent. The names which are then applied to it are Pure and Precious,

Lapis exilis (literally, *Lapis exilix*, but this is a scribe's mistake and is nonsense), and it is also that stone which causes the phœnix to renew her youth. No man can die for eight days after he has seen it, and—although this virtue is forgotten in the case of Titurel, who is described as an ancient of days—those who can look on it daily remain in the appearance of youth for ever. It is subject, apparently, to a periodical diminution of virtue, and it is re-charged like a talisman every Good Friday by the descent of a dove from heaven carrying a Sacred Host : she deposits it thereon, and so returns whence she came. It follows that the mystery of the *Parsifal* is certainly an Eucharistic mystery, although at a far distance, seeing that it never communicates supersubstantial bread. What it does distribute actually we have learned elsewhere, for at the supper-table in the Castle it acts as an inexhaustible larder and superb hotch-pot, furnishing hot or cold, wild and tame, with the wine-cups of an eternal tavern. As a peace-offering to the rational understanding, there is a vague suggestion that the stewards of the Castle provide the salt, pepper and sauces. Wolfram von Eschenbach describes this abundance as (*a*) earthly delight in the plenary realisation thereof, and (*b*) joy which he is justified in comparing with the glories of heaven's gold bar. Long researches dispose the heart towards patience—perhaps because of their weariness ; let me be satisfied therefore with registering the bare fact that this story is supposed, by those who know, to be the high spiritual quest of all, on which authority I am casting about me for the arch-natural side of an alderman's dinner. The writing on the Graal Stone might well be : *esurientes implevit bonis.* I note also that in the pageant a stone is put upon a stone, but those who remember *super hanc petram ædificabo ecclesiam meam* may be asked to desist.

The sacred character of this wonderful object—which solves for those who are called the whole difficulty of getting a material living—is explained by the antecedent part of its history. It was brought to this earth by a company of angels, who gave it into the charge of certain baptized men, the first of whom was Titurel. In the Northern French cycle the origin of the Sacred Vessel is explained in a manner which, within its own limits, is quite intelligible; it may be almost said to begin in Nature, though it ends in the Great Mystery. To the Cup used by Christ at the Last Supper no unusual qualities attach; Robert de Borron says that it was *mout gent*, but it is only in the sense of an utensil at the period. This is probably the earliest description which we have, and it is left by most of the later texts in similar comparative simplicity. The arch-natural character resided solely in the content. To sum up, the chalice of the French cycle began on earth and was taken to heaven, but the history of the German Hallow is the converse of this; its origin is celestial, but in the end it is left on earth. Let it be remarked in conclusion that there is no reason assigned for the bringing of the Graal to earth, nor do we hear of its purpose or nature prior to this event.

The Lesser Hallows of the story have scarcely a title to the name, as they have no connection with the Passion of Christ or any other sacred history. The Graal King was wounded in ordinary warfare by a poisoned spear, and this was exhibited in the Castle, but not as a memorial or a symbol of vengeance to come, for the heathen who smote him died at his hands in the joust. We know already that the Lance has a prodigal faculty of bleeding, but it is to no purpose. The Sword seems to be merely an ordinary weapon of excellent quality and temper; it was used by the King before he fell into sickness; it is given to Parsifal as a mark of hospitality apparently; it will break in one peril, but somehow the poet forgets and the event does not come to pass. No Dish is specified as part of the official procession; and the two silver knives, though they have a certain history, for they were made by the smith Trebuchet, serve only some dubious purpose in connection with the King's sufferings.

As regards these, we know that the sin of Amfortas, for which he has been punished full long and in which he awaits the help of the mystic question, was a sin of earthly passion. The Graal is an oracle in Wolfram, as it is in Robert de Borron, but according to the latter it spoke, while here it writes only. In this manner it calls maidens and men from any place in the world to enter its service, but the maidens it calls openly and the men in secret. It also appoints the successor of the reigning King and the wife whom he must take unto himself. With his exception, the life of celibacy is imposed on all the chivalry of the Castle. With the women it seems to have been different, but those who married went out into the world. The sin of Amfortas, which led to his grievous wound, was—as I have just said—a sin of earthly passion, but not apparently of that kind which is consummated in shame. The Graal had not announced that this keeper should take a wife, and he had gone before its judgment by choosing a lady for his service, in whose honour he went beyond the precincts of his kingdom in search of knightly deeds. She was the Duchess Orgeluse, who became subsequently the wife of Gawain. In accepting the service of Amfortas, as later that of her future husband, she was pursuing only a mission of vengeance on one who had destroyed the prince to whom her love had been dedicated from the first days of desire. The King of the Graal was abroad on these ventures when he met in a joust with a heathen, who had come from the region about the Earthly Paradise with the ambition of winning the Graal. We have seen that the unqualified aspirant after the secret knowledge died in the tourney, but Amfortas went home carrying the poisoned spear-head in his flesh, and thereafter he abode as the King in suffering and even in punishment. It follows that the cause of battle was true and righteous, but the motive which created the place was, I suppose, the root of offence, and for that he was bruised grievously. All the resources of healing were sought in the world of

Nature and that of magical art: the Graal itself in vain; in vain the waters of Paradise; the blood of the Pelican, the heart of the Unicorn, that bough which the Sybil gave to Æneas as a palladium against Hades and its dangers, and the magic herb which springs from the blood of a dragon—but these too in vain. Finally, the appeal was referred to the Sacred Talisman by offices of prayer, and a writing which appeared thereon announced the condition of healing—to wit, the visit of a knight who should demand knowledge concerning the woe of the Castle. It is the only version in which this Mystic Question is shown to originate from the Graal itself. It is also the only version in which sin enters the Sanctuary, and it is therefore important to show that it is a sin of sense in the lowest degree; it is rather a transgression of obedience. There are stated periods in the story for the increase of the King's suffering, being the close of the wandering of Saturn, causing frost and snow in summer on the heights where the kingdom is situated. The cold is agony to the Keeper, and it is then that the poisoned spear is used to pierce him again; it re-opens the wound, but it keeps him alive, for it draws out the frost in crystals—which crystals are removed apparently from the weapon by the silver knives of Trebuchet.

The Castle in Wolfram is supposed to have been situated on the northern slope of the mountains of Gothic Spain, while on the southern side, or in Moorish Spain, was the Castle built by Klingsor—that is to say, *Chateau Merveil*, containing the *Lit Merveil* of the other romances. The name allocated to the first was that of the eminence itself—Mont Salvaage, Salväsch, or Salvatch. There is no account of the building or of the incorporation of the chivalry; but (*a*) the Graal Knights are chosen, as we have seen, by the Graal itself as opportunity offers or circumstances seem to require; (*b*) they may be elected in childhood; (*c*) they constitute an aggressive military order, going sometimes on long missions; (*d*) they cannot be regarded as a perfect nor

yet as an invincible chivalry, for one of them is overthrown by Parsifal in combat, when on his quest of the
Castle; and here, as in other respects (*e*) they recall and
are practically identified by Wolfram with the Knights
Templars, having also the same order name. Scholars
who have investigated this part of the subject trace a
distinct connection between the House of Anjou and the
Graal Brotherhood; it should be added that the lineage of Anjou is the subject of continual reference in
Wolfram's poem, and Parsifal is of that legitimacy.

At the beginning of his chronicle Wolfram testifies to
a single prototype from which alone he drew; he cites its
authority continually in the course of his poem; in one
place he gives a very full account of it; and he testifies concerning it at the end. He knew otherwise of
Chrétien's version, but he suggests that it was the wrong
story, with which the fountain-head might be reasonably
indignant. The authentic text was the work of Guiot
de Provence, and from that region it was brought into
the German fatherland. It was not invented by Guiot,
but was found by him under circumstances the account
of which is in one respect a little out of harmony with
itself. It lay rejected or forgotten in the city of Toledo,
and being in the Arabic tongue, the first task of Guiot
was to learn that language. This he accomplished by
the sacramental grace of baptism and the holy illumination of faith. Without these aids to interpretation the tale would have remained in concealment,
for, according to its own testimony, no pagan talents
could have expressed the great mystery which reposes
in the Graal. This is so far clear, but the difficulty is
that it was written in the first place by one who ranks
as a heathen for Wolfram—that is to say, one who on
the father's side was a worshipper of idols, though on the
mother's, apparently, of the royal line of Solomon. This
was in the days which preceded Christ, and the Jew was
the first in this world who ever spoke of the Graal.
That which enabled him to do so was his gift of reading

the stars, wherein he saw wondrous secrets, for the story
of the Graal was written in a celestial galaxy. On this
basis the scribe wrote more especially concerning the
descent of angels to earth carrying the sacred object and
concerning certain baptized men who were placed in
charge thereof. This being the record attributed to a
Jew before the first dispensation had suffered super-
session, no one will be surprised to learn that his name
was Flegetanis; but here ends the account concerning him.
Guiot may have been, reasonably or not, dissatisfied with
the transcript from the starry heavens, but he confesses
only to anxiety about the identity of those who had been
appointed the wardens, and after consulting old Latin
works, he went in quest of them through France, Britain
and Ireland, but did not attain what he wanted until he
arrived in Anjou, where he found the story of the
Keepers faithfully and truly registered—that is to say,
concerning Titurel, Frimutel and Amfortas. It is clear
therefore that the Jew of Toledo told the early history
of the Graal but gave no version of the Quest. I deduce
from these data two conclusions, one of which is speculative and personal to myself at the moment: (*a*) The
appeal of Guiot, like all the other romancers, is to
an antecedent authority and, like some of them, to a
primordial text; (*b*) the story of Flegetanis has suffered
what is termed contamination by the introduction of
extraneous matter, being all that which was not included
in the record of the starry heavens, for which reason I
set down as a tolerable presumption that neither Guiot
nor Wolfram told the true story, however ample the
evidence on which the version of Chrétien was condemned. I suppose that I shall be accused of fooling or
alternatively of preternatural gravity, but I mention these
matters because of what will be said hereafter concerning
a lost book of the Graal. Three points remain to be
mentioned here: (1) Guiot seems to have cautioned
those who reproduced his story to hide the chief matters
until the end thereof, and this is cited by Wolfram,

though it can be said scarcely that he carried out the injunction; (2) if Wolfram followed Guiot, and him only, it seems certain that Guiot himself recounted several adventures to which his translator alludes merely in passing; however, they do not concern us; (3) the authority of Guiot, though often held to be an invention of Wolfram to conceal his indebtedness to Chrétien, has of late years been demonstrated.

The consideration of the Graal as a stone belongs to a later book of my experiment, but that the coming event may cast its shadow on these particular pages, I will add here a few subjects of reflection; they will prepare the ground for those who have ears to hear me, even if they are as a rock of offence to some others who are impatient of ways in thought which they have not sought to enter. (*A*) For *Lapis exilis*—in any higher sense—I should read only *Lapis angularis*, but this is put forward rather by way of interpretation than of alternative or amendment. We have seen that the term *exilis* is the speculative construction of a nonsensical word, and as such it does not help towards understanding; if there were authority to support it, one would recall that passage in Wolfram's Quest which says that in the hands of her who was qualified by grace to carry it, the Graal was a light burden, but it was heavy beyond endurance for those who were unworthy. In this respect it was like the *Liber exilis*, which was held by the hermit of the *Book of the Holy Graal* in the hollow of his hand, but this unrolled in his rendering till it grew to be a goodly folio. (*B*) Whosoever says *Lapis angularis* in this connection should add *super hanc petram*. (*C*) It is true also that he who wrote *Lapis exilis*—if indeed he wrote it—implied as its complement: *nobis post hoc exilium ostende*. (*D*) This stone is the head of the corner and the key of the Royal Arch. (*E*) The Stone which tinges is also the Stone which burns; if not, the Phœnix would fail of rebirth. (*F*) There is another form of the Graal Mystery in which men ask for Bread and are given a Stone, but this is *Lapis exilii*—a healing nutriment, and it is designed to restore the Banished Prince on his return home. (*G*) It can be well understood that the stars over the Graal speak in a strange language. (*H*) I rule therefore that much remains to be said for the clear sight of that Son of Israel and Paganism who found the Graal-record in a galaxy of stars, and though the method by which that record is decoded will not be found in the course of a day's reading at any observatory, I am quite sure that the stars still tell the same story, that it is also the true story, which owes nothing to the Chronicles of Anjou. (*I*) When the Jew of Toledo read in the great sky, as in a glass of vision, it does not mean that he arranged the fixed lights into conventional forms, but that he divined as a devout astronomer. (*J*) The Mystery which the stars expressed is that by which, in the last consideration, all the material planets are themselves ruled.

Let those who will chide me on the ground that I "sit and play with similes," but this is the kind of symbolism which Guiot de Provence might have brought over from the place which he terms Toledo, and this the imputed Jew of that city might have read in the starry heavens. In the chronicles of Anjou, or their substitutes, Guiot might have found the remanents of the Bowl of Plenty and even some far-away fable concerning a certain Stone of which Templar initiation could speak to the higher members of that Order of Chivalry; but the two notions do not stand even in the remote relation which subsists between Aleph and Tau.

Lastly, and that I may act on myself as a moderator, if there or here I should seem to have suggested that an enthusiasm has exaggerated the *Parsifal*, I have spoken of things as they appear on the surface and as they have been understood thereon by those who have preceded me. We shall see in its place whether there is another sense, and the readers to whom I appeal may have marked enough in my bare summary of the text to conclude that there is. I place it at the moment only as a tolerable inference.

II

GLEANINGS CONCERNING THE LOST QUEST
OF GUIOT DE PROVENCE

Astronomers have recognised in the past the influence of certain planets prior to their discovery, and subsequently this has verified their prescience. In like manner, the influence of that French poem which is ascribed to the Provençal Guiot is discernible after several modes in the German cycle, and the fact is no less important, even if the providence of books should not in fine lead us to the discovery of the missing text. It is at present a lost planet which will not "swim into our ken." I think that there are difficulties in Wolfram's references to the poem which may be classed as almost insuperable by persons who are unacquainted with the literature of hidden traditions : to these they are the kind of difficulties which—as Newman once said in another connection—do not make one doubt. At the same time the legend of the lost story occupies a position in the cycles which, without being in any way abnormal, is in several respects remarkable. In the past, as I have said, there was one phase of criticism which regarded the whole *crux* as nothing more than the invention of Wolfram to conceal the real fact that he borrowed from Chrétien. Being the finding of certain German scholars concerning the work of their countryman, it was entitled to a tempered respect antecedently, but it was at no time tolerable in its pretension and has been since made void. Wolfram lays claim to nothing so little as origination, and I know not why his literary vanity should have been consoled better by a false than a true ascription in respect of his source, more especially as in either case he would be confessing to a French poet. The suggestion, in fine, would account only for a part of the field which he

397

covered, as we know that Chrétien fell far short of completing his task.

The bare facts of the existence of Guiot and his poem were determined, so far as I am aware, for the first time, and, as it is thought, indubitably, by the publication of the *Saone de Nausay* in 1902. It has attracted little attention, but the fact of its existence and the important evidence which it offers to our particular subject have been at least stated in England. It is an exceedingly curious text, and in respect of Graal matters it has weird and scoriated reflections of the Joseph legend. But one reference to his son as the first consecrated bishop indicates that cycle of French texts into which it would fall if there were occasion to class it. The Graal is represented in the light of a general healing vessel, which we know otherwise to be in a sporadic sense its office, though it could do nothing within the charmed circle of its own sanctuary for those who belonged thereto.

Much about the time that this poem was put at the disposition more especially of German scholarship, there was an attempt in the same country to show that the reputed Provençal Guiot was a priest of the Church in Britain, and that he died Bishop of Durham. I do not know how this opinion may have impressed those who are most qualified to judge, but at least in France and England it was passed over in complete silence.

The evidences and speculations with which we have been just dealing—while, on the one hand, they satisfy us regarding the existence of Guiot and the poem connected with his name, and, on the other, create some bare and tentative presumption regarding his identity—are of no material assistance in respect of the problems which are raised by his work as it is reflected in the Quest of Wolfram. If we accept the Durham hypothesis of Dr. Paul Hagan it follows not only that Guiot de Provence no doubt anteceded Chrétien de Troyes, but—so doing—that he was the first recorded writer who told the history of the Graal, regarded as a Christian Hallow, and the Quest thereof. If we set aside this hypothesis, I suppose that it is an open question as to the succession of the two poets in time, and whether one derived from another or both from a common source. There is a disposition —if speaking of it be worth while, when the subject is so precarious—to regard Guiot as first in the point of time. We know only that both poets appealed to a source, and that, on the surface at least, the appeals are exclusive mutually. To his authority Wolfram seems to refer as if he were an old writer, but in ascriptions of this kind the years tend to dissolve rather rapidly into generations. If, however, we assign the superior antiquity to Guiot, it may be thought not unreasonably that the alleged source of Chrétien—the *mellor conte qui soit contés en court roial*—was actually the Quest of the Provençal. Textual scholarship, however, which is much the best judge in these matters, is tempted, I believe, to conclude that it was not a quest at all. On the other hand, except for personal predispositions —to one of which I have confessed—there is little to warrant the supposition that it was a pious local legend, like that which was produced at Fécamp, because in Chrétien, as in Guiot, the Graal Hallows are not relics of the Passion. There is an inclination at the present day to account for Chrétien's vagueness regarding his central sacred or talismanic object by assuming that he had heard only vaguely concerning it on his own part; that he introduced it in an arbitrary manner; and that it was quite purposeless in his Quest. I do not think that this will bear examination, more especially in the light of Guiot, who, as we have seen, counselled those who followed him to hide the tale at the beginning till it was unfolded gradually in its narration. In accordance with this, Wolfram is not much more explanatory at the beginning than his antecedent in Northern France, though the latter falls short at the point where the German poet himself begins to develop—that is to say, in the interview between Perceval and his hermit uncle.

However this may be, it is most important to note (*a*) the absence of the Passion-relics in both poets, and (*b*) the absence of the feeding qualities of the Graal in Chrétien, thus, in my opinion, (*c*) disposing of any theory that he derived from Guiot, supposing that these elements were present in Guiot's text. On this last point, as the evidences which can be extracted from Wolfram leave much to be desired in respect of fulness, the question remains open. While he states in the first place that he knows of no other witness, the third book seems to speak in the plural of those who told the story before him and, at the same time, having regard to his judgment concerning Chrétien, he can scarcely have held that it was recited to any purpose by him. The Provençal, on the German's authority, gave it to the very end—which, I suppose, means to the winning of the Graal by Parsifal. Yet it is certain on the text only that he is responsible for (1) The Arabian source of the Graal story; (2) the names of its appointed Keepers; (3) the history of Gawain, or at least some part thereof; and (4) the kinship of Parsifal and Sigune. It is difficult in several respects to follow Guiot as he is represented by Wolfram solely, though *additamenta* gathered from later sources lie under the suspicion of false and invented ascriptions. The Graal itself is a case in point; there is a later report that it was originally a stone in the crown of Lucifer, which I do not find in the *Parsifal*. Assuming that this account was derived from Guiot, one is inclined to speculate whether the feeding properties of the talismanic object could have been a part of his scheme, as the two notions are quite foreign to each other, and yet the Dish of Plenty looms so largely in Wolfram that it is difficult to predicate its absence in his palmary source. At the same time, though Wolfram acknowledged, as I have said, no other exemplar, he did adopt extrinsic materials, as, for example, the legend of Lohengrin from the Lorraine epic cycle. To increase the confusion, the stone is identified in *Parsifal* with the fabulous or symbolic Phœnix, and thus recalls the Phenicite Stone of Dioscorides. In this connection, it has not been noticed that one of the myths incorporated by the *Book of the Holy Graal* concerns a bird similar to the Phœnix, but more extravagantly described. After laying her eggs this bird is said to make use of a stone called Piratite, found in the valley of Hebron, the property of which is to burn anything that rubs it, and it is supposed to consume the bird. It is not the *Lapis Judaicus* or *Thecolithos*, but apparently the Black Pyrites, which, according to Pliny, burns the hand when touched. The same fable says that the name given to the bird is Serpelion, but hereto I find no reference. Neither on this nor on another consideration can Wolfram's historical account of the Graal be held to explain its imputed sacred character, and it is not surprising that no spiritual exaltation seems to follow its presence. If the vague story does not imply the later legend of the Crown of Lucifer, there is no explanation of its origin or of its supposed custody by the fallen angels of the air, though part at least of this story is repudiated afterwards by the person who relates it to Parsifal. Why it was sent by God, what purpose was served by its presence on earth, in what sense the stone which consumes the Phœnix is identical with the talisman which supplies inexhaustible delicacies ready dressed and cooked at a banquet—these things remain a mystery, and if any explanation were possible on the assumption of a subsurface sense, the presentation would remain and is the worst form of the legend on the official and extant side.

Fortunately, its mere presentation disposes of the suggestion that Guiot was heretical in his tendencies. This has arisen in part out of the Templar element, which is so obvious in the *Parsifal*, and for the rest out of the Albigensian implications, which may be thought to underlie at the period any text connected, directly or otherwise, with the South of France. We have seen that the charge against Wolfram is without foundation, and utterly. There is no Mass of the Graal in the *Parsifal*, no priestly character in the Wardens, no kind of competition with Church claims, no interference with ecclesiastical matters. If it be said that the arch-consecrated Host brought down from Heaven to renew the virtues of the Graal constitutes a questionable element, that must depend upon the general context, and in the light of this it raises no difficulty. There is a significant absence of suggestion that souls are sustained through the Graal from a superior channel of grace than can be claimed by the official Church, for on the surface sense of the text it is the bodies of the confraternity which, owing to the Graal and its annual renewal, were fed by the Host, while the recipients, including the Keepers, were not preserved thereby in a catholic state of sanctity. This is folly and all confusion, but it is not heresy by intention ; it is a muddled thesis concerning a grotesque object, of all things least sacred in the world of imaginative writing ; it is worse than the Fécamp reliquary as compared with other legends of Joseph of Arimathæa ; in a word, it is on a due and just level with the moral elevation which is ascribed spuriously to the epic. The story of Perceval was never written at all till the task was undertaken by the unknown author of the *Longer Prose Perceval*, and so far as we can trace the hand of Guiot in Wolfram, those so-called Chronicles of Anjou must have taken him far from the term.

Varied and considerable learning is ascribed to Guiot de Provence, and, among many indirect evidences, this is suggested by the circumstances under which, in his own turn, he claims to have derived the fundamental part of his story. We know that his alleged source was written in the Arabic tongue ; that the recipient *in primis*, in far pre-Christian days, was a Jew who on one side of his parentage was also of pagan stock ; and that in fine the old and old chronicle was lying neglected and forgotten among the undemonstrable archives of Toledo. We have seen further that above this story on earth there was an eternal story in heaven, as the last possible antecedent of all records, and it was therein that the Jew read, while the beating of his own pulses alone throbbed in the silent spaces. But as it is desirable to give a certain local touch to these abstruse matters, I have mentioned that the Jew's name was Flegetanis, to increase the verisimilitude of which we may memorise the fact that he wrote in Arabic rather than in Hebrew. The baths of disillusion are colder than those of Apollo, and from all—if any there be—who can dream that these things were possible individually before, or collectively after, the manifested Light of the World, we may well cry with devotion our *Libera nos, Domine*. The fact which remains is that Flegetanis read in the starry heavens, and that in the *Book of the Holy Graal* a person of this name, or nearly, was the mother of Celidoine, who was born under such high stellar auspices and himself divined by the stars. In such strange ways does one of the latest histories seem to draw from another which is earliest by the high imputation of things; only these two texts contain the Celtic name in question, and these only produce from their hidden source in common the myth which exceeds explication concerning the Phœnix bird and the ardent stone. It is in connections of this kind that one occasionally obtains, out of all expectation, a certain extrinsic light. The suggestion that, at however far a distance, there may have been the hand of Jewry in the literature of the Holy Graal might well be a source of scandal. But the Provençal Guiot was, as we have seen, a man of curious learning, and by a somewhat precarious induction it is supposed that he was a student at Toledo in those days when the relations between Southern France and Northern Spain may be described as intimate. Whatever be the merits or otherwise of this supposition, it is certain that in one curious respect he gives evidence of an acquaintance with the secret ways of Israel. One of the interminable discourses comprised in the collection of the *Zohar* states that in the whole extent of the heavens, the circumference of which surrounds the world, there are figures and there are signs by means of which the deepest mysteries may be discovered. These figures are formed by galaxies and constellations of stars, which are for the sage a subject of contemplation and a source of mysterious delights. The simple indication in the great canon of the Kabalah is the root-matter of all Hebrew astrology, and the reader who is sufficiently curious may consult on the whole subject certain *Unheard-of Curiosities* collected by James Gaffarel, where he will find the celestial constellations expressed by Hebrew characters and the celestial Hebrew alphabet. It follows that all mysteries resident in the letters and their combinations would be indubitably in the starry heavens, and the mysterious inspiration which, according to Guiot's story, fell on the Jew of Toledo represents a mode of divination which in that place was well known and in practice at that period. It will, I hope, be understood that nothing follows from this fact except that by a curious instance I have illustrated the curious learning which must have been possessed indubitably by the Provençal poet.

The considerations of this section are far indeed from our term, but, as seen already, something remains to be said, when the pageant draws to its close, concerning the second sense of Guiot and his German reflection.

III

SIDELIGHTS FROM THE SPANISH AND PORTUGUESE QUESTS

The German cycle of the Holy Graal owes nothing to the romances of Merlin, and it embodies no attempt to incorporate Arthurian history, except in so far as this is in close consanguinity with its own purpose. A few fragments make it evident that archaic Provençal literature once included some translation of Merlin, but whether it exceeded the point reached by the poem of Robert de Borron or its prose rendering there is no evidence to show. Speaking antecedently, from the great body of romance which was produced in Spain, we might have expected many reflections therein, but we know only (*a*) of simple allusions scattered through the interminable books of chivalry, and (*b*) of three printed texts, two of which I have cited by a bare allusion already. *El baladro del sabio Merlin* is in substance a rendering of the Huth manuscript, and all that we have heard concerning it has been given us by Gaston Paris. The second text is *Merlin y demanda del Santo Grial*, so that the Quest—and it is the Great Quest—did enter the Peninsula. I do not know under whose eyes it has fallen in these places of the world, and it is only from sparse references in German authors that I have been able to certify even to this extent. There is, however, *La Demanda del santo Grial*, which appeared at Toledo in 1515, of which I shall speak in the Appendix.

Portugal had also its solitary version of the Galahad Quest, and probably it is much more important than that which we meet with in Spain, for it has been found to contain the missing final part of the *Huth Merlin*. Some years ago an attempt was made to re-edit it, not from the printed version, but from a Viennese manuscript. I cannot trace that the task was ever completed, and in so far as the text is available in this fragmentary manner, the variations from the normal versions of the Quest, though interesting to textual scholars, are not important to us. The Viennese manuscript seems to have included also some form of the *Morte d'Arthur*. It may be termed composite in character, as it introduces matter which seems extraneous to the Quest. It is also in another key; there is even a wooing of Galahad; Palamades reappears therein; so also does Tristram. As a note in fine on the whole subject, it should be said that, all communications notwithstanding between Southern France and Spain and all Spanish-Oriental allusions reflected into the

Parsifal of Wolfram from the Quest of Guiot, the rumour of the Graal which reached the Peninsula was of Galahad rather than another. The *Templeisin*, the Stone, the hierarchy of fallen angels, have no part therein. And so, as I have just hinted, there is a certain intellectual consolation in knowing that the *Quest of Galahad* did pass into the life of Spanish romantic chivalry. One would have thought that it must have had a great vogue where the sons and daughters of desire accepted so easily in their hearts some phase at least of desire in the life of devotion. This, of course, was not to be expected at the period of its production, but in that much later century when the literature of chivalry itself began to assume the official draperies of religion. The new aspect was unfortunately at once conventional and extravagant, and perhaps the Quest was too spiritual in the transcendental degree for it to be quite within the compass of the Iberian mind. The tendency which produced *The Book of Celestial Chivalry* in the middle of the sixteenth century originated much earlier, and that which made *Esplandian* or *Don Belianis of Greece* as if it were peers of Christ, when Christ became a knight-errant, had long before registered the vocation of Galahad as a thing unrealisable. Whether the Quest was known to Cervantes is interesting at once and insoluble, for it did not enter into the catalogue of Don Quixote's library, either for praise or blame. However this may be, those who are acquainted with the *Book of Celestial Chivalry* and kindred productions will be in a position to appreciate the kind of inhibition which seems to have befallen the flights of romance when they sought to body forth the aspirations and emotions towards things unseen. It is a condition which is the more curious when we remember the *Ascent of Mount Carmel*, the *Dark Night of the Soul* and all that which is told us of worlds too seldom realised by Peter de Avila and Molinos. In some of the books which are attributed, falsely enough, to Raymond Lully—but for which a Spanish source can perhaps be predicated reasonably—and in the theosophical quests and ventures through the tangled skein of the *Zohar*, there is more of the true spirit of romance than in all Spanish tales of chivalry, if we set aside those of *Amadis* and *Palmerin*. All that follows thereafter shows only that there were other and drearier enchantments than those of Logres.

The claims of this sub-section cannot be regarded as high in respect of sidelights, but seeing that my least concern of all is to establish an exhaustive scheme of texts, it follows that I must confess to some other motive for its inclusion, restricted as in space it is. My purpose is therefore to show that to none of the romance countries—France excepted—did the cycle of Perceval appeal, and, I believe, for another cause than the mere fact that the later *Merlin*, the *Lancelot*, the *Quest of Galahad* were in prose, while some of the *Perceval* stories were cast in verse, which may have offered a difficulty. Even if the fact were due to the accidents of that which was most available, I hold it a felicitous accident that only Seville produced a quest of Perceval.

IV

THE CROWN OF ALL ADVENTURES

The implicit, I must suppose, of each succeeding quest was that the earlier singer of *le meilleur conte qui soit conté en cour royale* had told the wrong story, and that some far higher flight of pure romance must justify the material which came into the hands of each. The most interesting contrasted instance is the *Longer Prose Perceval* put forward as an alternative to the *Quest of Galahad*, as if by one who cleaved to the old tradition concerning the hero of the achievement and yet had every intention of profiting by the high light of sanctity which overshone the symbol of Galahad. The least comprehensible contrasted instance is the competition instituted in the name of Gawain by Heinrich von dem Turlin in his poem of *Diu*

Crône. The ambition seems so impossible after the *Parsifal* of Wolfram, but that poem was not appreciated — on account of its setting chiefly—by the general profession of minstrelsy. The instance further was, in its way, a certain justification of Chrétien, who was followed in several respects and often appealed to by Heinrich. *Diu Crône* owes something also to the lost poem of Guiot, but whether by derivation through Wolfram or in a more direct manner is uncertain. That it justifies any claim to existence I do not think, but this notwithstanding it is a very curious romance, so much under the veils of enchantment that the whole action seems transferred into a land of faerie, while the gifts and dotations which are offered to the elect hero might have made any quest of the Graal almost a work of superfluity on his part. In place of the Castle of Maidens there is pictured a wandering island of the sea wherein dwell virgins only, and the queen of this wonderful people, exercising a royal privilege, offers the possession of herself in marriage and the rule of her kingdom to Gawain as her chosen knight; yet if this be incompatible with his purpose, she will tolerate their parting at need and will bestow upon him, as her token of goodwill, an elixir of unfading youth. The hero exercises his admitted power of choice in favour of the second alternative, and with good reason probably, since the island was doubtless one of those dreaming places where a thousand years are even as a single day, and after a moon of sorcery he might have issued bearing on his shoulders an age past all renewing, even by the Holy Graal.

The keynote of the story is in one sense the disqualification of Perceval, who—because he had failed once —had forfeited his vocation forever. The opportunity is transferred to Gawain, and Heinrich is indebted to Chrétien for the substance of those inventions by which he is covenanted to enter on the Quest of the Holy Graal. We, on the other hand, may be indebted to his own imagination for the aids that the powers of Fairyland combine to provide by means of telesmas and other wonder-working objects which safeguard the way of the Quest. Seeing that the failure of Perceval to ask the all-important question is held insufficient as a warning in the case of Gawain, when he seeks to follow in his footsteps, he is reinforced by a particular caution at the Castle of Wonders. What he receives is indeed a dual counsel: he is not only to ask and to learn, but, in order that he may behold the Graal, he is urged to abstain at the table from all refreshment in wine. The maiden who proffers this advice proves to be her who carries the Sacred Vessel in the pageant at the Castle thereof. The analogy by opposition hereto is Gautier's story of the trick played upon Perceval by the Daughter of the Fisher King when she carries off the stag's head and brachet to punish Perceval for not asking the question.

We have had full opportunity to appreciate Gawain's share in the great adventurous experiment within the horizon of Wolfram's poem; we have seen also in Chrétien how and why, as a part of his own vindication, he set forth to seek the Bleeding Lance, but the quest proved a failure. Except the promiscuous proposal and fleeting undertaking in the Galahad Quest, Gawain does not figure as a knight in search of the Graal in the French romances till we come to the period of the *Longer Prose Perceval*. Even in Gautier the fullest account of his visit to the Castle of Hallows is apart from all notion of intention, as he is simply a gallant of the period in attendance on Guinevere, who herself is awaiting the return of King Arthur after the reduction of Castle Orguellous. On the other hand, Heinrich's *Diu Crône* pictures him expressly, and as if in real earnest, seeking to achieve the Graal, enduring also many adventures because of it. After the poem of Wolfram, his success does not seem to improve upon his failure in the other stories; it is by way of superfluity, and it may be said almost that Heinrich takes him for another, as he was also hailed for a moment in Gautier's poem.

In the course of his progress Gawain arrived at a bountiful and smiling land, as if it were the precincts of an earthly paradise, and on the further borders thereof he beheld a vast fiery sword keeping the entrance to a fortress with walls translucent as glass. I do not know, because it is difficult always to adjudicate in his case, why he should have regarded this wonder in the light of an evil omen, but this is how it impressed him, and he missed perhaps one among the greatest adventures when he retired so incontinently—whether it was a way of entrance into the higher Eden or into the fascination of a false paradise. Great as are the accomplished enterprises of Graal literature, I think that greater still are some of those which therein are hinted only, remaining unachieved or unrecorded. It seems clear that this fortress, at no indefinite distance from the Graal Castle, is that which Perceval would have entered in Gerbert's poem, and his incontinent eagerness contrasts favourably with the terror and the flight of Gawain. The Knight continued to traverse a land flowing with milk and honey, and he rode for yet twelve days, when he came upon Lancelot and Calogreant—another companion of the Round Table—both in a manner on the Quest. So these three shadows of those who should finish the experiment in utter reality came at last to their bourne. It may have been a region of sorcery which encompassed that abode, which we know to have been the House of the Dead, but it was assuredly like the intermediate region between the life of this world and the life everlasting. There are few things in literature which savour so strangely of that visionary astral region, full of great simulations and full of false joy, which does not attempt to conceal the bitter heart of sorrow. The knightly company depicted on the meadow without the burg, performing evolutions in pastime, was like the "midnight host of spectres pale" which "beleaguered the walls of Prague." But the places of death are not places of silence; the burg itself had a noisy throng within it, and so had the castle or palace—that Ghost's

House and House of the Dead alive. The companions were brought under safe guidance into the hall in chief, which was like the Kabalistic sphere of Venus—a pomp of external splendour, heavy with the crushed-out fragrance of heaped roses — as some mansion in an eastern fairyland. In the Hall of Roses there was seated the host who was to receive them — another patient sufferer of the ages, diverted in his pitiful weariness by youths playing chess at his feet. That game is a feature which in one or another form is inevitable in all the stories till the highest of the high quests intervenes and makes void so many of the old elements. It is played elsewhere by pieces having self-moving powers, but here it is played by the dead amidst shadowy sport and raillery ; betwixt the one and the other there is perhaps suggested some vaguely mystic side of the old war in mimicry.

The questing knights had not been received to no purpose ; there was a work which they were required to perform, supposing that they were properly prepared ; for the unspelling quest is followed even to the grave. Lord or prince of the Castle, it is not said till the close whether the host is old or young ; he is not termed the Rich Fisher and his genealogy is unknown. So also are most antecedents of the Hallows. The guests were treated royally and were entertained at a banquet, but at that time the Master of the House neither ate nor drank. On his part, remembering the warning which he received, Gawain ate only, and this in spite of solicitations on his entertainer's side, the doom of whom seems to have been working strongly, seeing that it drew to its term, and he was compelled to entreat that which would operate against his salvation. Lancelot and the other companion quenched their thirst with wine, which overcame them immediately, as if it were nepenthe devised for that express purpose, and they fell asleep. The lord of the Castle fulfilled his office zealously, and again tempted Gawain ; but, finding no better success, he desisted, and thereafter began the high pageant, the foremost in

which were maidens, and she who was fairest among all
—the crowned priestess who carried the Most Holy
Reliquary—was recognised as her who had counselled
him previously in the Quest—counselled him above all,
as did other wandering messengers in the romances of
Perceval—not to forget the question did ever he come to
the place. If he could not be compelled therefore, he
could at least be prompted, and the convention recalls
that indicible word which *ex hypothesi* cannot be spoken
or written and yet is communicated to the initiate of
many mysteries, when he finds that he has been acquainted
always therewith.

Before the company—which was numerous within as
without—had taken their places at the table, a page
of the chambers brought in the Hallow of the Sword
and laid it at the feet of the Master. The inference is
that this was the fatal weapon which, in the midst of the
strife of kinsmen, had somehow brought woe on the
Castle, but the particulars are not given, and of itself the
weapon would be nothing to our purpose, except that it
is the antithesis of other swords in the legends. Not
only was it perfect then but would so remain for ever ;
it was adjudged to the successful quester and would
break in no peril—an office of relaxed observance which
shortened and simplified the Quest.

Now, the company in the Castle had feasted gallantly,
like the guests who sat with the Master ; though dead,
they yet spoke—and that, it would seem, volubly—
interchanging questions and answers, as if in mockery
of the real question ; but the strong wine of the banquet
had no effect on them, and the Lord of the plenty meanwhile, as I have said, had fasted. But the appearance
of the Graal procession was the signal that he was to
receive a certain shadow of nourishment—as if, after
some necromantic supper, a disqualified Eucharist were
communicated to one who had not partaken previously.
We know already that the Reliquary contained the semblance of a Host, as from the Lance there exuded blood—

neither more nor less, in this case, than those three mystic drops which ensanguine all the legends and connect them, as if undesignedly, with other and older mysteries. In the story of Wolfram the first nourishment drawn from the Graal at the banquet in the Castle Hall is described as bread, and Heinrich—following the prototype of Guiot or profiting by a caution in respect of the Feeding Dish—converts the sacred object into a simple ciborium. The Master of the Castle received therefore in bread and in the colouration of wine; but of the bread he took only a third part, as if it were the efficient oblation at the sacrifice of the Mass. There is no reason to think that these were consecrated elements, but there seems to have been a substituted Eucharist, in which the dead might be supposed to share, so that, prince or lord—or whatever it is right to term him—he was fed sacramentally and super-substantially in some sense, for this his only nourishment was administered once in a year. Therefore Gawain arrived at a happy season, to see and to speak; and on seeing these things, he overflowed in himself with the wonder and the mystery of it all, so that, acting on the spur of the moment, importunately he asked that which was vital to those who were suffering from death in life—the mystic question, the most conventional of all formulæ: What does it mean? There was no effect to begin with —no sudden change, I mean, as from life to death or from death to life; but if before there was the chaffer and traffic of light talk at a feasting, now it was the hubbub of a joy beyond suppression, as if the closing at last were taken in a great grade of long sorrow.

Gawain has asked indeed, but as regards the secrets of the Graal he is not told anything; it has come forth out of mystery and it passes away therein. It is said to be God's mystery—one of the Secrets of the King, and Heinrich has written about it—*abscondere bonum est*. Of the woe, the wasting and the endurance, when brother warred upon brother, he learned something, and we have heard enough; of Perceval's failure and the deepened misery therefrom he was told also, and the condition of release resident in the question. But the king himself was guiltless, and so also were the maidens; he, however, was dead with all the men of his household, but they were alive in the flesh and they would go forth in the morning. When that dawned presently, the released speaker vanished, the Graal also with him, and its mystery, never to be seen more.

The following points may be noticed in conclusion of this part: (*a*) There is no question anywhere of feeding properties in the Sacred Reliquary, except as regards the king—and him it feeds sacramentally; (*b*) the Spear does not distil blood until it is laid on a table, with the head apparently over the salver; (*c*) the recession of the Graal seems to have been adjudged because it has performed its work of feeding the dead Master, keeping him in the semblance of life, and once this office was perfected it went like a ghost. After what manner the variations which are introduced thus into the shifting pageant of the legend can be said to elucidate its object will not be determined easily. The doom that involves the dwellers in the Castle changes the symbolism but certainly does not exalt it. The romance, for the rest, is the work of one who has resolved to give the palm to Gawain at the express expense of Perceval, to the knight of this world in place of the knight celestial. It is the experiment of an inventor who has adapted some old materials to another purpose, at once indeterminate and undesirable.

The date ascribed to the poem is about 1220, and its ingarnering as a whole is regarded as a little chaotic. It reaches some 30,000 verses, and though we hear generally concerning King Arthur's Court and the Round Table, Gawain is the hero-in-chief. After his completion of the Graal Quest, various pageants of chivalry bring him back to his uncle and the fellowship, the story in this manner reaching its natural close.

V

THE TITUREL OF ALBRECHT VON SCHARFENBERG

The secret doctrine of Guiot de Provence and the high tradition of the starry heavens not only failed to convince the minstrel world in Germany concerning the indefectible titles of Parsifal, with its root-matter written in the starry heavens—of which our example is Heinrich—but it failed to hold even those who had no alternative and more elect hero to offer—of which the example, within certain limits, is Albrecht. It came about that at the end of that century which had seen the light of Wolfram there arose the succeeding light of him who was to follow, and, having regard to the welcome which he received, the German world was evidently looking for another. He came to announce—like the French romances before him —that the Graal was taken away. Albrecht von Scharfenberg was a Bavarian poet, who wrote about 1270. He undertook to carry the whole experiment to its term, which he did in a vast poem of 45,000 verses, written in the obscure style of his predecessor-in-chief, whence— and for other reasons—the distinct individualities were confused for a considerable period. He incorporated various materials, for there was firstly the intervention of an anonymous and unknown poet, who seems to have undertaken but not completed the task, and, secondly, there were certain so-called *Titurel* fragments which were the work of Wolfram himself. Of the first I can say nothing, except that he is believed to have projected a complete chronicle of the Graal and its keepers, drawing for this purpose on the source used by Wolfram. It is a matter of speculation at what point he broke off and for what reason, but his mantle fell upon Albrecht. Of the materials left by Wolfram we know all that is needful, and they are quite unconsonant with our purpose. They are two in number, and the opening lines of the first fragment explain why they have been termed a *Titurel* poem. They are really, by Wolfram's evidence, parts of the early history of Sigune and Schionatulander—respectively, the cousin of Parsifal and her lover, whose embalmed body she carries with her so long in the Parsifal poem. Contrary to the evidence of this, it appears from the fragments that the lover met his death in satisfying a whim of his mistress. Albrecht, or his precursor, incorporated these fragments, and in many ways otherwise the *Younger Titurel*, as it is called, while it covers the same ground, also supplants the earlier knightly epic and carries the history of the Graal—as I have indicated—to its final term. I have explained that the lateness of the poem has excluded it, in the mind of scholarship, from the canon of the Graal ; but it has some aspects of importance, and its consideration will help us better to understand the position and claim of the German cycle. To that cycle it makes a real contribution, and it differs in this respect from the metrical romance of *Lohengrin*, which is ascribed to the year 1300. This is an important document for the legend of the Swan Knight, but its allusions to the Holy Graal are mostly of the occasional kind. As such, however, they offer a complete revolution of the whole Arthurian cycle in respect of the close in disaster of all those gracious times of chivalry. The star of the king's destiny does not close in blood and warfare—

" In dark Dundagel by the northern sea "—

owing to that frightful fatality by which Arthur begat Mordred on the body of his own half-sister. Other stars intervened in their power to avert the doom and vengeance for that which was done in ignorance. In place of the dubious mercy of healing at the hands of Morgan le Fay in the mystic island of Avalon, the king—at the head of his whole chivalry—carries the Graal to India, and he and they are its guardians even to this day in the remote, undeclared places of the eastern world.

The *Titurel* differs also from that interned manuscript concerning Parsifal and the Round Table which is preserved among the treasures of the Vatican—being the sole copy that is known. It was written a little earlier than the year 1336, and it incorporates Manessier's conclusion of the *Conte del Graal* with materials derived from the *Parsifal* and *Titurel*. It is therefore a work of compilation, and does not as such concern us.

Now, one important point with regard to the poem of Albrecht is that he rejected the antecedent history of the Holy Graal bequeathed by his earlier German peer in poetry and reverted for his thesis concerning it to the more orthodox traditions of Northern France. In a word, the sacred object is no longer a stone, whether that in the crown of Lucifer or that which consumes the Phoenix and at the same time incubates the egg which the bird has laid. It is the Eucharistic vessel of Joseph, with whom its history begins, so that once again—and but once in the German cycle—we can kneel in spirit while Mass is being said in the Sanctuary, looking towards that time when we also, at the secret words of consecration, shall behold the five changes.

The *Titurel* claims to give the perfect and rectified history of the Vessel and its Wardens from the beginning to the end thereof. Considering that the first Graal King is the real centre of interest, an excessive space is devoted to Sigune and her lover—but this I refer to the anonymous poet who preceded. At the inception it gives the generations of the secret dynasty from the days of Vespasian, when Berillus the Cappadocian, who had great possessions and was moreover of the Christian faith, took service with the Roman general at the siege of Jerusalem and followed in his train subsequently when he was called to the throne of the empire. Berillus married Argensilla, the daughter of the emperor, and a considerable part of France was thereafter assigned to him in

fief. He had as issue Titurisone, who married Elizabel
of Aragon and of her—after long years and precious
offerings in pilgrimage at the Holy Sepulchre, because
of their childless condition—there was born Titurel, this
name being, as one writer has indicated, a contraction
of the parental names. It will be seen that the genealogy
takes back the so-called Angevin dynasty to a very early
period of the Christian centuries, as well as to those
districts which abut on the Holy Fields. The remaining
succession in the keepership follows the indications of
Wolfram, and the main outlines of the Quest are also
followed in substance, with no remarkable exception.
Wolfram knew nothing of that sister of Parsifal who
attained to such spiritual heights in the *Quest of Galahad*,
and Albrecht—who knew indeed, since he had fair opportunity to be acquainted with the whole cycle—does
not, if I remember, mention her; but, on the other hand,
he has not elected to ignore the marriage of Parsifal or
all reference to Kondwiramur. It follows that, in dedi-
cating that hero to the great exaltation, he considered
that his virgin celibacy was not a first qualification within
the domain of Nature. And these words may be called
an introduction to a short statement concerning the
ascetic aspects of *Die Jungere Titurel*. They are supposed to be somewhat pronounced, and to impress
upon the poem a peculiar ecclesiastical aspect, which
I interpret as meaning that it carries the seal of
sanctity rather than the seal of ethics and other preliminary exercises in the school without the gates. At
the same time, I see nothing in the poem to connect
it with the mystical degrees, and I see nothing to indicate
the conscious existence on the part of the author of any
subsurface sense. It lends itself to a construction of
this kind only in the way that all great books of romance
—and greater than is this book—speak otherwise than in
the external tongues to the higher part of our nature.
It is only by reflection from the sources in Northern
France that the *Titurel* reproduces—as we shall see that

it does—the recession of the Graal. Perhaps—but I do not know—Albrecht may have divined dimly that the heaven of Galahad's attainment and the land of Prester John are neither of them out of this world, and, so far as distance goes, not especially more remote than the corner of the nearest street. In such case, by saying that it went to India he would know that he was telling the same story as he who testified that the hand which had no body came right to the vessel and so took it and bore it up to heaven. Perhaps—in the alternative sense—the episode spelt nothing more for the poet than a good illustration of that which follows from the common unworthiness of the world. He describes the evil time which fell upon things outside the precincts of the Temple, and it was in pursuance of their own counsels of prudence, rather than by an instruction from within, that the Keepers of the Holy Vessel in fine convened the cohort of the Templar chivalry and that Parsifal, accompanied by them and carrying the Hallows of the House, went in quest of his brother Feirfeis, so reaching India.

The *Parsifal* of Wolfram indicates that Prester John was the issue of this brother; but the *Titurel* represents him as an independent ruler in the East, despite his attributed genealogy, and gives such an account of himself and his wonderful kingdom that the reigning keeper is minded, and indeed prompted by Feirfeis, to bequeath the Graal to his care. When, however, he came into his august presence, bearing the Holy Vessel, the Priest-King offered his realm and crown to him who was the Graal King. Parsifal, on his part, desired to enter his service, for report had well assured him that all material and spiritual riches abode with Prester John, even the Seven Gifts and the Twelve Fruits of the Divine Spirit of Counsel. But the decision was not between them, for there was an intervention on the part of the Graal, by which it was ordained that Parsifal should remain as he was, the Guardian of the Holy Vessel. He became therefore the heir of Prester John and assumed his name. At the prayers of the keeper, the Castle and the Sanctuary of Mont Salvatch were transported in a single night to India, like a mystic city of Irêm, so that the great Palladium had again its proper asylum. It was this, I conclude, that led to the whole chivalry remaining as they were in the East, whereas, if they had relinquished their trust, they would have returned whence they came. So does the House of the Doctrine follow the transit of Doctrine, as the house of man at his highest is wherever the highest is attained. It is for this reason that Wisdom has finished its temples, seeing that its proper habitations are waiting all over that world which once was built in Wisdom.

It is to Ethiopia or Turkey that other legends refer the retreat of Prester John, which really was "built in the unapparent." There is therefore no need to co-ordinate rival versions, nor would such a task be possible in the conflicting accounts of Albrecht and Wolfram. To vary the issues of confusion, I will mention only that, according to the *Dutch Lancelot*, the Priest-King appears to have been Perceval's son. It is thought that the reticence of Wolfram on the whole subject is explicable by the fact that there were few materials at his period, while in the fifty subsequent years the rumours of the eastern legend had extended and was available to Albrecht. But it should be mentioned that the first rumour is referable to 1156, and before the end of the twelfth century it had the support of Maimonides as well as of the wandering Israelite, Benjamin of Tudela. The seat of Peter had done more than confess to an attraction when an embassy was sent to Prester John bearing a written communication from Alexander III.; and before 1180, or at and about this time, the Emperor of Constantinople is supposed to have received the celebrated letter in which the mysterious potentate announced his own existence with consummate grandiloquence. It was a pretentious and impossible document in the worst style of false-seeming, but it created great interest and great wonder. It concerns us only because it may have provided certain materials both for

Wolfram and Albrecht. The palace of Prester John is like the Castle of Mont Salvatch drawn out into a greater wilderness of building, and the *Parsifal* allusions to the Earthly Paradise are recalled by the account of that spring which is three days' journey from the Garden of Eden. Whosoever can drink of its water will have, through all his later life, the aspect of thirty years— precisely that period which was maintained by the Templar chivalry owing to the presence of the Graal. The myth has been noticed exhaustively by several writers ; it never required exploding, but that work was done in the seventeenth century by Julius Bartolocci in his *Magna Bibliotheca Rabbinica.*

I have only to add concerning Albrecht and his *Titurel* (*a*) that in the earlier part of the fourteenth century it was not only allocated to Wolfram, as we have seen, but was held to be his master work ; (*b*) that all assertions notwithstanding, the hypothesis of Albrecht's acquaintance with the poem of Guiot is regarded as precarious ; (*c*) that the *Titurel* represents King Arthur and his knights as travellers in search of the Graal after it had been taken away : it was a vain journey, of which Parsifal had calculated the probabilities beforehand when he took leave of the Round Table ; but the adventure—as we have seen—is the root-matter of that other fable which was conceived subsequently by the author of the metrical *Lohengrin.*

VI

THE DUTCH LANCELOT

The quest undertaken in our work of high research is long enough, and it is also toilsome enough, to spare us from the consideration in full of any extraneous issues, though these are yet of our kinship ; but I am speaking of a great literature to those who are unversed therein, albeit they are not otherwise unacquainted with the mysterious ways in which God declares Himself. I am called upon therefore to say something of all the branches, but must touch lightly where we are not concerned deeply. The *Dutch Lancelot* is a compilation which is known only by a single text, and this is incomplete, unfortunately, the first part out of four original parts being now wanting. The authorship is unknown and so is the date of composition; but, by those who are competent to speak, the extant manuscript has been assigned to the early part of the fourteenth century. Were it otherwise, it might be said with greater certainty than is now possible that it had taken the chief field of Graal romance for its province. The missing first volume must have contained indubitably the earlier life of Lancelot, and it may have included by inference some part of the quest and initial failure of Perceval at the Graal Castle. The second book contains the adventures of Agravain, the brother of Gawain, a knight of pride and violence; but this is already late in the history of the hero-in-chief, and it is in the so-called Agravain section that Lancelot pays his first visit to Castle Corbenic and that the conception of Galahad is encompassed. The poem reverts thereafter to dealings with Perceval, and has traces of a tradition which is not extant in the romances of Northern France. There are variations, for example, in the development of the tasks proposed by the messenger of the Holy Graal to the knights of King Arthur's Court. Correspondences are traced: (*a*) with the variations in the Montpellier MS. of the *Conte del Graal;* (*b*) with the Vatican German Perceval; and (*c*) at a distance, with Wolfram's *Parsifal.* The *Quest of Galahad* occupies the third book, and the fourth brings all to its term in the *Morte d'Arthur.* The Dutch romance is a poem, and even in this, its present dismembered form, it is a work of vast extent. As in respect of my own province I have not assumed all languages, I know the original only by the collation of available channels of research. That which has impressed me concerning it is the important, though fluidic, analogy which it offers to the poem of Heinrich in its judgment on Perceval. Therein the Lord of the Hallows and those by whom he was engirded had great hopes of the latter, but because he had entered the Castle and did not ask the question he was discarded once and for all. Now, the *Dutch Lancelot*, at the conclusion of the second book, has a text of unknown origin which I have held over in my previous enumeration to speak of more adequately here. This is the episodic or biographical romance of Morien, the son of Agloval and the nephew of Perceval, a black knight, corresponding to Feirfeis, who is Perceval's half-brother in the romance of Wolfram. Morien is, however, a Christian when he arrives in the realms of the West, and he is in search of his father, to whom he is in fine united. It is in the course of his story, which is otherwise unimportant to our purpose, that we learn as follows concerning the Holy and Sacramental Mystery :—

(1) King Arthur—who here, as otherwhere, manifests his unfailing love and anxiety for Perceval—is represented lamenting his loss because he had gone in search of the Graal and the Sacred Lance, but there were no news concerning him. Now, the text states—and this is on the part of the King, by the way of foreknowledge or prophecy— that he will never find them—that is to say, upon earth. (2) The same conviction may have entered into the proper heart of the Son of the Widow Lady; but Sir Gareth, the brother of Gawain, is he who announces the reason, which is not on account of his failure but because Perceval sinned in leaving his mother to die of grief at his absence. On this account he might search till the Kingdom which is above descends on the Kingdom which is below but his pains would be his only meed. We see here that a responsibility which is of right made transient only becomes permanent and insuperable for a moment—but this is in appearance solely. (3) Perceval, on his part, has been convinced of his sin and has embraced the life of a hermit as the proper path of

atonement. (4) But Arthur and Gareth notwithstanding, the intention of the tale is to restore Perceval forgiven to the higher life of chivalry, and we have accordingly (5) the vision of Sir Agloval, the brother of Perceval, who speaks of a Golden Staircase seen therein, which, by interpretation, is more than the sunbeam whereon the Graal enters in the Great Quest, for it symbolises the Sacred Vessel as another ladder of Jacob leading to the Throne and the Kingdom, and this is also for Perceval as the days of the life of him. It followed that he should yet have his place in the Quest, and it was foretold that in such high service he should pass to his reward on high. That which is here foretold is of course fulfilled to the letter in the part which follows thereafter —that is to say, in the *Quest of Galahad*.

The *Dutch Lancelot* is in some respects that which I indicated at the beginning, an attempt to harmonise all the cycles by dealing (*a*) with the Quest of Perceval and its initial failure ; (*b*) with that of Gawain, corresponding to the Montpellier intercalation of the *Conte del Graal ;* and (*c*) finally with the union of Galahad, Perceval and Bors, according to the plenary inspiration of the Great Quest. I recur now to the point which I made at the close of the third section. The *Dutch Lancelot* offers the position of a text which had every opportunity to profit in universals and not in particulars only by the poem of Wolfram ; but, though it is under the obedience of the prototype created by the *Parsifal* and the *Conte del Graal* for the early history of Perceval, it redeems him only at the close, by a kind of *tour de force*, in its adaptation of the story of stories.

The conclusion of all this inquiry into the German cycle of the Holy Graal is that the hand of Guiot is traceable, at whatever distance, through all its length ; at times it is the ruling hand, at others it intervenes for a moment. He seems also reflected into the Greater Chronicles in Northern French ; for, setting aside those almost accidental connections which are found in the *Book of the Holy Graal*, there are the similitudes, which I have termed haunting, in the *Longer Prose Perceval*. The King of Castle Mortal is drawn in much darker colours than Klingsor, the magician of Wolfram, but they derive from the same root.

It is obvious that in such a summary account of the German cycle there are points, and they are indeed manifold, which have been omitted from the foregoing sections. Those who have preceded me in England with valuable and extended monographs on individual texts and with studies of particular groups will be the first to dispense generosity towards a work which embraces the whole literature in a single volume, more especially if they are able to realise that I am not addressing their audience, but rather a school set apart and among whom no knowledge of the subject can be presupposed safely. It is for this reason that I have had to recover the same ground on several occasions, increasing the difficulty of my task, as it was not less important to avoid verbal repetition in devotion to the high canons of literature than to spare my readers the weariness of continual reference to anterior sections or books. Before leaving the German cycle, I will embrace in a brief schedule certain accessory matters, belonging to its several parts, which—without being essential thereto—are of sufficient interest to demand inclusion.

The Parsifal of Wolfram.—It should be noted (1) that there is no passage of Hallows from East to West; there is no enchantment of Britain; and there are no times which are termed specially adventurous; (2) that Parsifal's uncle, Trevrezent, confessed to having tampered with the truth in respect of his Graal history, so as to dissuade the hero from the Quest, and that this is possibly the root-reason of the uncle's misdirections in all the romances.

The Lost Quest of Guiot.—(1) There was a great movement of literature from Southern to Northern France and through Northern France to England at the period of Henry II. He married Eleanor of Guienne, who is said to have brought Provençal poets in her train. If therefore we can suppose that Guiot de Provence and his poem antedated all other Graal literature, they may have become known in this manner, and it will then seem at first sight that we have accounted for the appearance subsequently of Graal literature in Northern French. But this is an explanation with the disadvantage of a fatal facility, because Guiot, as we can divine concerning him, is incapable of accounting for Graal romance outside the one text that we know him to have influenced in Germany. (2) It was on an illusory assumption of this kind that the Perceval legend was classed as Celtic by Schulze, but the Graal, on the other hand, as Provençal. The first statement is true obviously, but the Graal of Guiot is not the Graal of Northern France. The marriage of Schulze's two classes is said to have been contracted about 1150 ; but I do not believe that any sacramental mystery was incorporated by southern romance ; only the shadow of the Eucharist is found in Wolfram. (3) The test of such a possibility is the affirmed traditional hostility to the Church of Rome on the part of most troubadours. Northern French romance had no such implicit : it is a literature written round the great heart of Christian catholicity. (4) The analogy of troubadour poetry with Graal literature is slight after all. If we set aside the *Conte del Graal*, love, for example, is only an accident of the cycle, and it is totally absent from two of the highest texts. The mystic side of human love in poetry and its Provençal reflections are a light of Moslem ecstasy. (5) Scholarship holds that Wolfram and Chrétien drew from the same source, more especially as regards the adventures of Gawain. This raises a question respecting the identity, language and real locality of Guiot. It is acknowledged on all sides that if he had written in the *langue d'oc*, he would not have been understood by Wolfram. One speculation identifies him with the author of the *Bible Guiot*, but this person was of Provins in the Alsace-Lorraine district. The suggestion, I suppose, is that Provins was mistaken for Provence by Wolfram. Had Guiot promulgated in the South so wonderful a legend as that of the Graal, it is incredible that his name should never have transpired among his contemporaries; though his poem is now lost, his memory should at least have lingered.

The Spanish Cycle.—(1) We have seen that Spain has no indigenous literature of the Holy Graal; it has only accidental reflections by way of translation, and with all deference to the curious implicits connected with the Jew of Toledo, I think that this is final as to anything of prototypical matter of the Graal having come out of the Peninsula. (2) This notwithstanding, if ever the missing Guiot should be discovered in fine, it will be probably in a Spanish monastery. Whatever language he wrote in, the poet had evidently Provençal sympathies, interests and erudition, and we know that in 1820, on the evidence of Fr. Jayme de Villanueva, there were large collections of unedited Provençal poets in the archives of Spanish churches. This is readily explained (*a*) by the intimate union between the court of Provence and that of Barcelona; (*b*) by the union of the crown of Provence and the crown of Aragon in the person of Alphonso the Second, and it is Aragon that once at least was especially rich in such manuscripts; (*c*) by the popularity of Provençal poetry in Catalonia during the twelfth and thirteenth centuries. A poem breathing the Provençal atmosphere and inspired by the Provençal spirit, though not actually in the *langue d'oc*, may well have drifted into Spain from Provence without leaving traces behind it at either point.

BOOK VII

THE HOLY GRAAL IN THE LIGHT OF
THE CELTIC CHURCH

THE ARGUMENT

I. STATEMENT OF A POSSIBLE IMPLICIT ACCOUNTING FOR ALL CLAIMS.—*The Celtic Church as an environment of the Graal literature—Its traces of Eastern influence—Of the spirit of the East in the Graal Legend—Its implicits as reflections of the Celtic Church—The source of British Christianity independent of Rome—Reference to the Johannine Rite—Certain considerations which would determine the present inquiry.* II. THE FORMULÆ OF THE HYPOTHESIS SCHEDULED.—*Of Britain as a microcosm of the world— An analogy from the Apocalypse—Celtic religious sympathies— The hypothesis under review—Celtic origin of the Graal Legend—The Legend as an ecclesiastical growth—The Graal Church—St. David and his miraculous Altar—The Fish Symbol and the Rich Fisherman—The Secret Words as an evasive reference to the Epiclesis clause—Nature of this clause in Eucharistic consecration—Celtic Hereditary Keepers of Relics—General characteristics of the Celtic Relic —Of Mass Chalices—Of mystic and holy cups—Of the Columbarium and the Graal Dove—The disappearance of St. David's Altar—Withdrawal of the Celtic Rite—The Celtic Church and the Druids—Cadwaladr and Galahad— The return of the British King—Claims connected with Glastonbury—The substitution of Joseph of Arimathæa for St. David—Further concerning Fish symbolism—And concerning Mass chalices—Of Mystic Bells—A Church consecrated by Christ—Super-Apostolical succession—The House of*

431

Anjou—A mystery of the Celtic Mass—Summary of the whole matter—The Celtic Book of the Graal and the Secret Mass-Book. III. IN WHAT SENSE THE PLEA MUST BE HELD TO FAIL.—*Some preliminary admissions—The Secret Tradition of the Epoch—Further concerning Super-Apostolical Succession—History of the Church in Britain—Further concerning the Johannine Rite—Absence of Passion-Relics in the Welsh Church—The Epiclesis clause does not explain the Secret Words—Greek mode of consecration—Distinctions between Cadwaladr and Galahad—Fantasy of the* VIR AQUATICUS—*The Altar of St. David a false ground of comparison—Substitutes for the sacramental Cup—True position of the Glastonbury claim—No substitution of Joseph for St. David—The Second Joseph—Another light on King Arthur's chalice—And on the Mystery of the Celtic Mass—Further concerning a Secret Book of the Mass—The Pan-Britannic Church and the Graal literature—The Celtic Church and the literature.* IV. THE VICTORY OF THE LATIN RITE.—*Of Rome and the other Assemblies—Why Rome prevailed—The conclusion that we must go further.*

BOOK VII

THE HOLY GRAAL IN THE LIGHT OF THE CELTIC CHURCH

I

STATEMENT OF A POSSIBLE IMPLICIT ACCOUNTING FOR ALL CLAIMS

AMONG all external organisations there is one institution —and there is one only—which, on the principle that the best is the nearest, might be expected to offer some of those signs and warrants that we should expect in a society, a sodality, a body—let me say, at once, in a church—which could and did connect with the idea of the Holy Graal—as something nearest to its source, if not indeed that centre from which the entire mystery originated.

The early history of the Holy Graal, as distinguished from the several quests undertaken for the discovery of that sacred object, is one of Christianity colonising. We know in the French cycle, by the universal voice of the texts, that it was a mystery which was brought into Britain, and seeing that the legend, as a whole, is— apart or otherwise from anything involved by the implicits thereof—assuredly of Celtic origin, its religious elements, in the absence of any special and extrinsic claims, must be accounted for most readily by the characteristics of the Celtic Church.

It is much closer to our hands than anything which has been suggested alternatively, and it was unquestionably that environment in which some of the legends developed. Those who have previously recognised, in their imperfect and dubious way, that the great legends have a mystic aspect, and that hence they are probably referable to something in instituted mysticism, have put forward bare possibilities, and, independently of these, scholarship has itself gone much further afield. It has thought of the Far East as the home of the Holy Graal, and some who are mystics by more than a predisposition on the surface, know certainly—even if it is in a certain sense only—that there is a country deep in Asia. Now, albeit the limits of our evidence concerning the Celtic Church are circumscribed somewhat narrowly, there seems no doubt that this Church bore traces of Eastern influence—by which I mean something stronger and plainer than resides in the common fact that Christianity itself came to us from the oriental world. If, therefore, the Holy Graal has any marks and spirit of the East, it might be accounted for in this manner by way of the most colourable inference. If, however, we prefer to consider without any further preface what is the palmary claim of all, and if therefore we appeal to the veiled suggestion of pre-eminence in the Graal priesthood in respect of an extra-valid form of consecrating the Eucharistic elements and of a super-apostolical succession, it may be advanced that here is simply an exaggerated reflection of that which was actually claimed by the Celtic Church and more especially by that Church in Wales. The claim was that it had a title to existence independently of Rome, Christianity having been established in these islands for a long period prior to the arrival of St. Augustine, which arrival, from this point of view, was an incursion upon territory already conquered and held to a defined extent rather than a sacred endeavour to spread the gospel of Christ; thus it brought spiritual war rather than the light of truth. I have classed these two points together—that is to say, the alleged oriental origin and the original independence of Rome—not because I regard the second as important in comparison with the first, but because as a fact we know that the Celtic Church had a certain autonomous existence long before the legend of Joseph of Arimathæa was devised in the local interests of Glastonbury. It was not, therefore, at the beginning any question of Angevin ambition. Further, we can, I think, understand very well how this claim may have been exaggerated in legend, so as to cover—as I have said—the special implicits which I have traced in the Graal literature, and therefore to account for it within as the general characteristics of the Celtic Church may account for it reasonably without. I propose now to set forth some other specific analogies, from which we shall be enabled in fine to draw a general conclusion whether we can be satisfied with the evidence as it so stands, or whether we must go further. Let us remember, in the first place, that the earlier point, if it can be taken apart from the later, would mean probably an origin for the Holy Graal independent of Celtic environment, like that of some Eastern heretical sects which passed into southern France; otherwise a derivation through Spain; or, as an alternative to both, the transit, for example, of the Johannine tradition westward. But if we abandon the earlier and are compelled to have recourse, or this mainly, to the later point, then the legend of the Holy Graal—because it contains elements which are foreign to the mind of romance, though it is expressed in the romance form—must belong to that class of fable which has been invented in an external interest, and its position is not much better than one of forged decretals; it is, indeed, a decretal in literature, put forward in many forms and with many variants, and it would be useless to look therein for any secret intention beyond that of the particular pretension which it was designed to support. With the merits and defects of Celtic Christianity in Britain, we are sufficiently acquainted to deal rather summarily respecting the value of any mystical suggestions which are discernible in the cycles or remanents of literature which must be regarded as belonging thereto.

The suggested implicit with which I am dealing, if found to obtain, would signify therefore the closing of the whole inquiry.

II

THE FORMULÆ OF THE HYPOTHESIS SCHEDULED

There are traces in the Anglo-Norman romances of a certain fluidic sense in which Britain and its immediate connections, according to the subsurface mind of their writers, stood typically for the world. They were familiar enough with the names of other regions—with Syria, Egypt, Rome—above all, with the Holy Places in the Jerusalem which is below; but their world was the Celtic world, comprised, let us say, between Scotia and Ireland on the one side and central France on the other. This region came, I think, to signify symbolically, and so we hear that the failure to ask " one little question " involved the destruction of kingdoms, while the belated interrogation seems to have lifted the veil of enchantment from the world itself. The cloud upon the sanctuary was a cloud over that world; its lifting was a glory restored everywhere. But as the enchantment, except within very narrow limits, and then *ex hypothesi*, was only of the imputed order, so the combined restoration of Nature in common with Grace was but imputed also; the woe and inhibition were removed as secretly as they were imposed. So again, when the chivalry of the Round Table —in the Greater Chronicles—covenanted to go forth on the Quest of the Holy Graal, the universal and proclaimed object was to terminate the hard times of adventure, which had become intolerable: *pour deliveir nôtre pais des grans mervelles et des estrainges auentures qui tant y sont auenues, lonc tans a.* The whole position reminds one of that chapter in the Apocalypse which presents a

436

sheaf of instructions to the Seven Churches of Asia. No one knew better than the Jews not only concerning Rome, Greece and Alexandria, but of the world extended further; this notwithstanding, when the great book of the secret Christian mystery was first written, the world of Christendom was confined chiefly within narrow limits in Asia, and this was the world of the Apocalypse. It was actually all *Assiah* of Kabalism, though the few who have dared to institute a philological connection between the one name and the other have gone, as usual, astray. Recurring to the fact out of which this analogy arises, let me add, as a matter of justice to an hypothesis which I seek to present adequately, that within this Celtic world the first and most natural sympathies in the religious order would be indubitably with its own aspirations, and I set aside therefore for the time being all speculation as to anything rich and strange in Rite and Doctrine which may have been brought from the Eastern world by those—whoever they were—who first planted Christianity on the known confines of the Western world. The chief points of the hypothesis may be collected into a schedule as follows:—

1. It is certain that the Graal Legend is of Celtic origin and making, because of the Celtic attributions of the romances and their Celtic *mise-en-scène* and characters ; because of the Celtic names, disguised and otherwise, which are found in the romances, even in those which belong to the Teutonic cycle ; and because of the undoubted derivations into the Graal Legend from Welsh folklore. This is agreed on all hands, and will therefore call of necessity for no extension or comment in this place.

2. The romance of the Holy Graal, regarding the cycles synthetically, is a glorified ecclesiastical legend of Celtic origin ; there are other ecclesiastical legends, referable to the same source, which suggest the Graal atmosphere. The "Graal Church" was in its earlier stages the Celtic Church contrasted with the Saxo-Roman.

3. The nucleus is to be found in the story of St. David and his miraculous altar. The apostle of South

Wales, with some other saints, made a pilgrimage in the legend to Jerusalem, where the patriarch of the Holy City invested him as archbishop and gave him "a consecrated altar in which the body of our Lord once lay." It was transported to Wales, performed innumerable miracles, but after the death of St. David it was covered with skins and was never seen by any one. According to a variant of the legend, this altar—and possibly some other Hallows—was carried through the air to Britain, and hence was often described as *e coelo veniens*. Though apparently it was the rock-hewn sepulchre mentioned in the New Testament, no man could specify its shape, its colour, or of what material it was fashioned ; in addition to its other wonders, it gave oracles—that is to say, a voice spoke therein, as it did, according to the romances, in the Graal itself. St. David died about 601 A.D. ; he gave the Mass to Britain ; he was of the lineage of Our Lady ; and his birth having been foretold by the finding of a great fish, he was termed the Waterman—*vir aquaticus*—which recalls the Rich Fisherman of the later legends. It might be said that this title was applicable especially to him, as one who was rich in the conversion of souls to Christ and in the greater gifts of sanctity. His ancestors bore the name of *Avallach*, whence that of the king of Sarras seems to be derived certainly ; and he is said to have provided sacred vessels for the celebration of the Eucharist.

4. The secret words of the Robert de Borron cycle refer to the *Epiclesis* of the Celtic Rite. The form of Eucharistic consecration in the Latin Rite is actually the words of Institution—that is to say, the New Testament's account of the Last Supper. In the East, however, consecration is effected by addition of the *Epiclesis* clause—that is, by the invocation of the Holy Spirit. In its more usual form, it is a petition for the descent of the Comforter, firstly, upon the worshippers, and, secondly, upon the Altar gifts, that the elements may be converted into the Divine Body and Blood. The liturgy of St.

John Chrysostom may be consulted on this point; indeed, from one passage it would seem to follow that what was communicated was the Holy Ghost, an idea in which all that is usually attached to the Eucharistic office seems to dissolve in a higher light. The evidence is, however, confessedly somewhat indirect, as no Gallican or other connected liturgy gives the words of institution, but they are found in full in a North Italian, perhaps a Milanese, liturgy, and elsewhere, as we shall see shortly. It has been said that between 750 and 820 A.D. certain words in the Celtic Rite vanished from the consecration of the Eucharist, which would correspond, I suppose, *ex hypothesi*, to the intervention of the Roman Rite. The Celtic was abolished formally about 850, but is said to have survived to the period of the Graal literature. The Welsh would have learned from the Crusades that the *Liturgy of the Holy Spirit* was still used in the East.

5. The hereditary Graal Keepers, so strongly emphasised in the romances, are derived from the Hereditary Relic Keepers of the Celtic Church. Mr. J. Romilly Allen, in his *Monumental History of the Early British Church*, has said: "The vicissitudes through which the relics passed in the course of centuries were often of a most romantic description. The story was generally the same. The book, bell or crozier belonging to the founder of the Church was supposed to have acquired peculiar sanctity and even supernatural properties by association with him; and after his death it was often enclosed in a costly metal shrine of exquisite workmanship. Each relic had its hereditary custodian, who was responsible for its safe keeping and who in return received certain privileges, such as . . . the title to inherit certain land, of which the relic constituted the tenure." The preservation of relics-under hereditary guardianship seems to have been common among Celtic families—as, for example, the banner of St. Columba. So also the relics of certain saints belonging to the Scoto-Irish Church were placed in the care of families of hereditary keepers;

these were consecrated objects, not human remains, and they were regarded as of great virtue when borne in battle by a person who was free from any deadly sin. Sometimes a venerable cup was deposited in a special shrine ; sometimes the book of the gospels was enclosed in triple cases—as of wood, copper and silver. The custody of such an object became an office of dignity from generation to generation in a single family. The general characteristics of the Celtic relic may be enumerated as follows, but it is not intended to say that every sacred object possessed all the qualities : (*a*) It came from heaven, like the Graal ; (*b*) it was of mysterious and incomprehensible matter ; (*c*) it was oracular ; (*d*) like the Graal, it had the power of speech ; (*e*) it healed the sick, as the Graal did also occasionally, though this was not its specific office ; (*f*) like the Graal, it must not be seen by unqualified persons ; (*g*) it had the power of miraculous self-transportation, and the Holy Cup, in certain romances, was also a wandering vessel ; (*h*) it acted as a guide ; (*i*) it was a palladium ; (*k*) it executed judgment on the wicked and profane, which is the characteristic in chief of the Graal in the metrical romance of De Borron.

6. In the *Panegyric of St. Columba*, a document ascribed to the last years of the eleventh century, it is recorded among his other good works that—like his peer, St. David of Wales—he provided a Mass Chalice for every Church —presumably within his special sphere of influence or perhaps even in the islands generally. Readers of the prose *Perceval Le Gallois* will remember that chalices were so uncommon in Arthurian days that the King, during a certain quest, seems to have met with one, and that miraculously, for the first time in his life. The explanation is that wooden bowls may have been used previously for purposes of consecration. This was at the Mass of the Graal which Arthur was permitted to see in the course of his travelling. We should remember at this point that it is only at the close of the cycle

in Northern French—that is to say, in the romance which I have just mentioned, in that of Galahad and in the *Book of the Holy Graal*, that the Sacred Vessel—its other uses notwithstanding—is connected expressly and indubitably with the administration of the Eucharist, though it is not always the vessel of communion.

7. There are historical memorials of mystic and holy cups, possessing great virtues and preserved in old Welsh families. Among these is the Holy Cup of Tregaron, which was made of the wood of the True Cross and its healing virtues were manifested so recently as the year 1901. The curious thing in the romances is that the Holy Graal heals every one except the Keeper himself, who in the Perceval cycle can be cured only by a question, and in the Galahad legend—but here it is a former Keeper—by the magnetic touch of his last lineal descendant.

8. In England during the Middle Ages—but this is a side-issue which is mentioned only for its possible greater antiquity and origin in Celtic times—the Eucharist was reserved, as we have seen otherwise, in a *Columbarium*, or Dove-House, being a vessel shaped like a dove. This was the Tabernacle of its period, and it recalls (*a*) some archaic pictures of a Cup over which a dove broods; (*b*) the descent of a dove on the Graal stone in Wolfram's poem; (*c*) the passage of symbolic doves in connection with the Graal procession as told by several romances, but especially in the *Quest of Galahad*; and (*d*) the office of the Holy Spirit in the Graal legend. But it is also suggested—and this, I believe, is by Huysman—that the Tabernacle was frequently in the form of an ivory tower to symbolise Christ in the womb of the Virgin, who is herself called *Turris eburnea*.

9. The vanishing of the Graal refers (*a*) to the actual disappearance of St. David's altar after the death of its custodian; (*b*) to the disappearance of the Celtic Church before the Roman; and (*c*) to the subjugation of the British by the Saxons. The Welsh Church was pre-

eminently a monastic church, and, in spite of the existence of bishops, its government was in the hands of monks. The claim of the ancient British Church generally, including its legend that the first Church of Glastonbury was consecrated by our Lord Himself, may help us to explain the undertone of dissent from Rome which has been noted here and there in the subsurface of the Graal literature, but especially, as it has been thought, in the *Longer Prose Perceval*. To appreciate the position fully, we have to remember that the Latin rite gained ground and influence with the Norman Conquest, though independently of that rite there were monasteries in remote valleys where the old liturgy and the ancient form of consecration may have been still used and where also the ancient wisdom of the Druids was preserved, though—in spite of certain testimonies—it could have been scarcely considered consistent for a man to be a mystic Druid and also a Christian. The Druidic secret was symbolised by the term *Afalon*, which means the Apple Orchard. The last Welsh Archbishop of St. David's died in 1115, and was succeeded by a Norman, that is to say, by a Roman prelate.

10. Cadwaladr is Galahad. Galahad took away the Holy Graal, because, according to the *Welsh Quest*, the world was not worthy. His prototype, in despair of his country, removed certain relics, and, by the testimony of one tradition, he died in the Holy Land, as if he also had departed to Sarras, with the intention of proceeding further. Another story says that he projected the reconquest of Britain in a fleet furnished by his kinsman Alain of Brittany, where he was then in exile; but an angel warned him to desist. He was to seek the Pope and confess, and he would be canonised after his death —which, according to this legend, occurred at Rome. This chieftain, who loomed so largely in the Welsh imagination, who, like Bran of pre-Christian legend, was termed the Blessed, was regarded as of the royal line of David; he is thought to have been the custodian of holy

relics belonging to his family before him, and when he died, in reality, as it seems, of the Yellow Sickness, in 664, his return was confidently expected. So many legends grew up around him that he appears to have gathered up in himself all the aspirations of Celtdom. His return is associated with the second manifestation of his relics and with the final felicity of the Celts. Awaiting that event, the entire British Church, for some reason not otherwise explicable, began to droop and decay. But I may note here that a great Welsh revival was inaugurated in the year 1077 A.D. by the return of Rhys-ap-Tewdwr from Brittany. Bards and Druids were at white heat, and Rhys himself was a descendant traditionally of Cadwaladr the Blessed, who was to restore all things. He even claimed identity with that departed hero.

11. When the particular set of claims connected with Glastonbury began to be manufactured about 1150, to centralise a wide field of interests at a defined point, Joseph of Arimathæa was substituted for St. David. There was the supposed body of Joseph, there the phial which he brought containing the Precious Blood, there also the body of King Arthur, and by imputation the *Sapphirus*, the lost altar of the Welsh apostle, the last of these recalling rather plausibly, and accounting for, the *Lapsit exillis*, or *exilix*, of Wolfram. From this point of view it is worthy of close attention (*a*) for its sacramental connection; (*b*) for its association with the body of our Lord; and (*c*) for the mystery attaching to its form, with which we may compare the vagueness which characterises nearly all the descriptions of the Graal vessel.

12. The descent of the Graal *prima materia* from folk-lore no more explains the Christian legend of the Gràal than the words *vir* and *virtus* explain the particular significance attaching to the term *virtuoso*. The mythological Salmon of Wisdom as a prototype of the Fish in De Borron's poem is a case in point. The real approximate progenitor is the primitive Christian symbol, which was familiar to Celtic Christianity, and seeing that

the latter was much like the Church at large of several centuries earlier, so it may have preserved things which elsewhere had passed out of memory—the *Ichthus* symbol among them. This signified Christ, and especially the Eucharistic species. It also symbolised the *Disciplina Arcani* and was the most general of Christian emblems; it passed into a specific form of expression for the concealment of the more interior mysteries, and to partake of the Fish was an evasion for the reception of the sacrament.

13. His connection with the Quest of the Graal not only enabled King Arthur to furnish chalices for churches but bells also, which seem to have been unknown previously in Logres. In the Celtic veneration for relics they bear, however, a conspicuous part, the examples being far too numerous for recitation in this place. I can say only that their cultus, their care, the keeperships instituted in connection and the wonders ascribed to them are common to ancient Wales, Scotland and Ireland.

14. Reverting once more to St. David, it is reported traditionally that the first church which he built was situated at Glastonbury, and in connection with this ascription, it is said to have been consecrated by Christ Himself, so that in more senses than in one sense merely the place was a source and fountain of all religion in the Kingdom of Britain, as affirmed by William of Malmesbury. It was therefore among ecclesiastical structures what the second Joseph was among the bishops of Christendom. If ever there was an arch-natural Mass celebrated and a noumenal Eucharist administered at a specific place in Logres, assuredly with these warrants it would have been only at Glastonbury, the connection of which with St. David raises one further point. The Celtic Church held that the Roman Pontiff was the successor of St. Peter, but the patriarch of Jerusalem—who ordained the Apostle of Wales—was the successor of Christ. The subsurface intention which created this legend seems to have been nearly identical with that which put forward the super-apostolical succession of Joseph

II., and it follows that Celtic imagination at work in the field of hagiology furnished the makers of romance—and the author in particular of the *Book of the Holy Graal*—with an ample groundwork. The substitution of the man of Arimathæa for the original patron of Wales was the appropriation of an independent legend, which served the ecclesiastical side of Angevin ambition without affording a handle to the troublesome principality on the western side of the vast dominions of Anjou.

15. There are " distinct traces of something 'queer' in the Masses of the earliest Celtic Church—before the coming of St. David in Wales or of St. Columba in Scotland and Ireland." An allusion to the " queerness " in question may be found in the following passage of the *Lesser Holy Graal*, forming part of the discourse of Christ to Joseph of Arimathæa when He brought the Holy Graal to console the prisoner in his tower: " *Et ensinc con ge lou dis à la table, seront pluseurs tables establies à moi sacrefier, qui sénéfiera la croiz, et lov vaissel là où l'an sacrefiera et saintefiera, la pierre où tu méis mon cors, que li caalices sénéfiera où mes cors sera sacrez, en samblance d'une oïste, et la platainne qui sera dessus mises sénéfiera lou couvercle de coi tu me covris,*" &c. Alternatively, seeing that there is no mention of the Blood, it may be " a manifesto of the party who wished the chalice to be denied the laity," or, finally, the utterance of some obscure party or sect. " The latter view finds some support in the Hermit's story "—referring here to the Prologue of the *Book of the Holy Graal*—" of his meeting with a knight who had seen him in a place that he named."

16. And now as regards the summary of the whole matter, the position may be expressed as follows: (*a*) The Graal legend is demonstrably of Celtic stuff— in part of Celtic folk-lore which has turned good Christian, but more largely of ecclesiastical legend; (*b*) it derives from the story of St. David and his altar; (*c*) the original Graal book was probably a legend following a special and peculiar Liturgy; (*d*) the legend told of

the Christianising of Britain by St. David, the celebration
of the Christian Mysteries on the saints' miraculous
altar, which was actually the sepulchre of our Lord, of
the wonders wrought by this altar, of the coming of the
heathens, the ruin of Britain, the flight of its King—who
was St. David's last descendant—bearing with him the
altar relic to the East. There he died, thence he shall yet
return, again bearing the relic ; the Britons shall triumph,
the Saxons shall suffer expulsion, and the mystic words
shall be uttered once more over the Thaumaturgic Altar.
It is obvious that, according to this hypothesis, the book,
which was far older than any Graal literature, remained
in concealment in Wales and perhaps was unearthed at
the Norman Conquest of Glamorganshire, when it was
modified, varied, exalted, transformed and allegorised by
successive makers of romance, being adapted specifically
as an aid to the House of Anjou, in its struggle with the
Pope, by the author of the *Book of the Holy Graal*—
whether Walter Map or another. But Rome proved
more than one part too strong and by more than one
interest too many for the ambition of Henry II., while as
regards Wales, it had long and long already succumbed
to the Latin Rite.

III

IN WHAT SENSE THE PLEA MUST BE HELD TO FAIL

It is indubitable, and we have seen in the plenary sense,
that folk-lore provided its elements as the crude matter
of the scheme of the Holy Graal. It is true, and also
indubitable, that many accidentals of the Celtic Church
became accidentals of the literature ; they were worked
into the Graal cycle as well as the pre-Christian elements,
the process arising in the most natural of all possible
manners. It was not exactly that the most early romancers
took the matter which was nearest to their hands, but

rather that there was no other; the external aspect of religion was of necessity therefore a reflection of the Celtic Church. But as folk-lore does not explain the Christian Graal and the high experiments of sanctity therewith connected, so the contributory memorials on the Celtic ecclesiastical side do not explain it either. Behind all there lies the secret tradition of the epoch, and it is this precisely which makes the whole research so remote and intractable in respect of its final issues. I need hardly say that the secret tradition had no claim to put forward in respect of super-apostolical succession in the form belonging, as we find, to the Graal literature, though it had—*ex hypothesi*—its own Divine Warrants. This claim may represent therefore, by a hazardous ascription, the ecclesiastical political programme of the Anjou dynasty in England, and it would be in this way a separable element in the literature. There is no other sense than this in which a Britannic Church shows any true correspondence with Graal subsurface intention, because that intention had neither hostility to Rome nor a plea to put forward in respect of religious independence and the institution of an autonomous pan-Britannic Church. It follows that the secret tradition and the glimpse which we obtain thereof in the Graal books are either a mere dream, or the point of departure for this sub-section must be a total denial of all that has been put forward previously in regard to St. David's legend. As it is premature, however, to make it a point of departure, I must lead up to it from other considerations, and I will therefore say a few further words concerning the Church itself in Britain, not that they are essential to the subject but for the information of those of my readers who may have had no call to consider it.

Brief as it is, the following schedule will, I think, be sufficient for the purpose, and I note: (*a*) that Christianity existed in Britain during the Roman occupation, and that three British bishops were present at the council of Arles, about 350 A.D; (*b*) that the extent of its diffusion is doubtful, but it was probably the religion of Romans and Romanised Britons in and about the garrison towns; (*c*) that it became universal early in the fifth century, which was the beginning of the age of Saints; (*d*) that it is doubtful whether the Celtic Church at this period was a descendant of the Roman-British Church or a colonisation *de novo* from Gaul, but it may have combined both sources; (*e*) that an episcopal mission from Gaul into Britain is certain, and its object is supposed to have been the extinction of Pelagian heresy, or Pagan, as it has been suggested alternatively; (*f*) that the derivation *ab origine symboli* was possibly from Ephesus through the Johannine Rite into Southern Gaul, and thence into Britain; (*g*) that, also possibly, there were other Oriental influences, and particularly from Egypt, in the fifth century, the evidence being: (1) The derivation of Celtic ornament from Egyptian ornament; (2) the commemoration in ancient Irish books of "Holy Egyptian hermits" buried in Ireland; (3) the correspondences between the Celtic monastic system and that of Egypt; (4) the practice, attributed to St. Columba, of removing his sandals before entering the sanctuary, a practice known otherwise only in Egypt.

As regards the hypothesis put forward in the previous sub-section, it is observable that we have not been invited to consider in the Celtic Church any traces of a particular theological or doctrinal tradition—such as might, for example, be inferred from the Johannine Rite—or of an evasive or concealed claim; it is not suggested that in Wales, Scotia or Ireland there is any trace of an ecclesiastical legend concerning a relic which at any distance might be held to offer a real correspondence with that of the Holy Graal or its companion Hallows, because the essential condition of the analogy must be indubitably the existence of memorials of the Passion of our Lord. Of these it is certain that there were none, because otherwise it is certain that they would be adduced. We are asked, on the contrary, to assume that a variant liturgical reading, the legend of an historical apostle after passing under a specific transmutation, and the mythical restitution of a Welsh King are the first matter in combination of the complex cycles of literature which are comprised in the Graal legend. If this hypothesis can be taken with such high seriousness that we may suppose it put forward—shall I say?—as an equivalent by analogy for that which has offered St. Dominic and the enchanting fable of a question which should have been put to the Pope as a real explanation of the Perceval-Graal myth, it will be sufficient, I think, to deal with it on general lines rather than by an exhaustive process of criticism in detail. Let us put aside, in the first place, all that part which is purely in the region of supposition, and take the actual facts as things for valuation in the schedule. Question of *Epiclesis* or question—as we shall see presently —of a particular tense, it is obvious that the oriental terms of consecration, when those prevailed in the West, were the secret of no particular sanctuary as distinguished from all other holy places in Britanny, Britain and Wales. They were catholic to these countries and also to a great part of that which we understand by Scotia, Ireland and Gaul. They connect in themselves with no keepership and with no Hallows. We know that the Roman rite colonised all these countries, and that in the course of time it prevailed. But the period between the public use of the words now in question and their final abrogation was one of centuries, and although during a portion thereof — *ex hypothesi*—they may have been perpetuated in concealment, there is no doubt that they had fallen into complete desuetude long before the third quarter of the twelfth century. It is impossible to suppose that there was at that time any one concerned in their perpetuation sufficiently to put them forward as a great mystery of sanctity inherent in the heart of Christianity, and it is impossible, mystically speaking, that they should carry this significance. The secret words do not appear in the metrical romance of Joseph as in any sense the material of romance; they appear with all the marks of a particular claim advanced for a special reason and maintained through more than one generation by the successive production, firstly, of a prose version of the early metrical *Merlin*, and, secondly, by the similar derivation or independent invention of the *Didot Perceval*, which carried on the same tradition, though it seems left unfinished, perhaps from the standpoint of narrative and assuredly of the term of its intention. In the second place two concurrent claims appear, and the second—which is stronger than the first—abandons the claim in respect of secret words. It does this so explicitly that it makes public the words of consecration, by which we are enabled to see at once how little they could have ever signified, if indeed it were possible to suppose that these are the lost words of Graal literature. Moreover, by a particular fatality, they do not happen to contain the *Epiclesis* clause. In its place, as we know so well already, we have the claim to a super-apostolical succession—as I have said, a much stronger claim and one for which there is little precedent in the dubious history of the Celtic Church. It is out of this pretension that the Galahad Quest arises, though at a period when the claim itself appears to have lapsed. We are agreed that, so far as there is a true story at all, it is that of Galahad, and the question of secret words never entered into the heart thereof. It is, therefore, useless to put forward the assumed fact of their existence in the Celtic Rite of Institution as something which is explanatory of the literature. In this connection it is of importance to remember (*a*) that the only prose *Perceval* which is of any importance mystically is that which depends from the *Book of the Holy Graal*, not from Robert de Borron; and (*b*) that the only metrical romance of Perceval which mystically may be also important is that of Wolfram. The first has abandoned the words and the second nearly all Eucharistic connection. The first puts the Roman dogma of transubstantiation in its most materialised possible form. It will be seen, therefore, that the Celtic hypothesis fails along what must be regarded as the most important line. I submit, therefore, that the pretension to a super-apostolical warrant is either part of a fraudulent scheme of pre-eminence as an argument for autonomy on the part of the British Church, with the advisers of a King for its spokesmen, or it belongs to another order of concealed sentiment and event, the details and motives of which are wanting on the historical side of things. In the former case it is not of our concern, and it is explanatory only of one branch in a large literature ; in the latter, we must go much further, and, if we can supply the missing events and motives, from certain hidden sources, we shall be in possession, for the time being at least, of a provisional explanation concerning things which are most important in the literature, and—*donec de medio fiat*—it must be allowed to hold.

The distinctive note of the Latin Eucharistic Rite is that, like the gospels of St. Matthew and St. Mark, it gives the first words of institution thus : *Accipite et manducate ex hoc omnes. Hoc est enim corpus meum* ("Take and eat ye all of this. For this is My body"). Hereto certain oriental rites added other words which should read in Latin : *Quod pro multis confrangetur* ("Which shall be broken for many"). The *Book of the Holy Graal* gives : *Venés, si mangiés et chou est li miens cors qui pour vous et pour maintes autres gens sera livres à martire et à torment*—the substantial equivalent of *pro multis confrangetur*. Compare the gospel of St. Luke in the Latin Vulgate, which uses the present tense : *quod pro vobis datur*.

So far as regards the really trivial question of tense. The mode of consecration by *Epiclesis*, or the Invocation of the Holy Spirit, may be unknown to some of my readers, and I extract it therefore from the *Liturgy of St. John Chrysostom*.

THE PRIEST (saith).—Blessed art Thou, Christ our God, who didst fill the fishermen with all manner of wisdom, sending down upon them the

Holy Ghost, and by them hast brought the whole world into Thy net, O Lover of men : Glory be to Thee.

R. Both now and ever, &c.

THE PRIEST (saith).—When the Highest came down and confounded the tongues, He divided the nations; when He distributed the tongues of fire, He called all to unity ; and with one voice we praise the Holy Ghost.

The Deacon, pointing to the Holy Bread, saith in a low voice :

DEACON.—Sir, bless the Holy Bread.

The Priest standeth up, and thrice maketh the sign of the Cross on the Holy Gifts, saying :

PRIEST.—And make this bread the Precious Body of Thy Christ.

DEACON.—Amen. Sir, bless the Holy Cup.

PRIEST.—And that which is in this Cup the Precious Blood of Thy Christ

DEACON.—Amen. (*And pointing with his stole to both the Holy Things*) Sir, Bless.

PRIEST.—Changing them by Thy Holy Ghost.

DEACON.—Amen, Amen, Amen.

PRIEST.—(*after a pause*) So that they may be for purification of soul, forgiveness of sins, communion of the Holy Ghost, &c.

I believe that in the Mozarabic Rite, which is thought to be in near consanguinity with the Celtic, the *Epiclesis* formula is used on occasions only. It is missing altogether from the so-called *Liturgy of St. Dionysius*, which only survives in the Latin. I should add that the existence of the clause in the Celtic Rite—whatever the strength of the inferences—is a matter of speculation, for the simple reason that no such liturgy is extant.

The other analogies and possibilities are a little attractive on the surface, and are of the kind which are caught at rather readily ; but they seize upon a single point where they can be made to apply, and the other issues in a long sequence are ignored. The name Cadwaladr naturally suggests that of Galahad, and on the appeal to certain laws of permutation, it seems for a moment justified ; but it is not justified in the legends. The last King of the Britons had indeed the hallows of his family by the right of inheritance, but there was no antecedent keeper whom he was required to heal, and there was no quest to undertake in order that he might secure his own. But this healing and this quest inhere in the Graal legend, and are manifestly at the root of the design, so that there is no connection possible between the two cases. Moreover, Cadwaladr is destined by his legend to return, while it is of the essence of that of Galahad that he comes back no more. The same remarks will apply to all traceable instances of hereditary Keepership in Celtic families, whatever the object reserved. It is even more certain that any comparison of St. David the Waterman with the Rich Fisherman who is wounded is highest fantasy; neither physically nor symbolically did the Saint suffer any hurt, but, again, one of the foremost Graal intentions resides in the King's wounding. The symbolical term Fisherman signifies the guardian of the Holy Mysteries; it can have nothing to do with DEVERUR = Waterman. We do not know why a great fish is said to have heralded the birth of the Welsh Apostle. To help out the argument, we may affirm that he was a guardian of the Christian Mysteries in the land to which he was commissioned, but we do not in this manner account, either in the historical or symbolical sense, for the fishing of Brons or Alain in the lake, or for the title of Rich Fisherman applied to the Wardens of the Graal. It is true that they also were Guardians of Mysteries, but this is an instance of concurrence and not of derivation. The *Lesser Holy Graal* may create a comparison between the Sacred Vessel and the Sepulchre in which Christ was laid; but it does not for this reason institute any analogy between that vessel and St. David's altar, nor is the appeal to Wolfram useful except in the opposite sense, for the Graal stone of the Parsifal, whether or not it was once in the crown of Lucifer, can tolerate still less the institution of its likeness to "a sepulchre that was hewn in stone, wherein never man before was laid." The altar of St. David is an interesting fable of its type, as preposterous as that of Fécamp, and between the tomb of Christ, *ex hypothesi*, transported to Wales, and the sacramental *ciborium* likened to the Holy Sepulchre there is no analogy in any world of correspondences.

It remains therefore that in this literature we have shown how evil fell upon the House of the Doctrine; how it overtook also the Keeper of secret knowledge; after what manner he was at length healed; how the hidden treasures passed under the care of his saviour; and how at the term of all they were removed because of a fell and faithless time. That would be a very pleasant scheme of interpretation which could say that the House of Doctrine was the Celtic Church and that the wounded Keeper signified the Church in desolation, but it remains that we must go further in our search for a key to these mysteries.

If the legend of the Holy Graal were the last light of the Celtic Church before it expired in proscription, one would confess that it was glorious in its death. But the most that we can actually say is that it left elements which in fine served a better purpose. The *Longer Prose Perceval*, the poem of Wolfram, and the sacred and beautiful *Quest of Galahad*, these are three records which bear witness on earth of the secret things which are declared only in the heavens. There are three tabernacles wherein transfiguration takes place.

In the extrinsic Celtic remains, the only substitute which offers for the great legend of the Holy and Sacramental Cup is an obscure and nameless vessel which is subject in its latest history to the irreverence of a pedlar, and this it was deemed worth while to avenge. From such inefficiencies and trifles it is certain that we must have recourse, even if for a moment only, to the Glastonbury legend, which did invent high fictions to glorify the British Church. This resource must however in its turn fail us, because Glastonbury is (*a*) of very small moment throughout the Graal literature; (*b*) is never the place of the sacred vessel, for even its most mythical allocations

—as, for example, Corbenic—cannot be identified therewith; and (*c*) it knows nothing of the second Joseph. The *Book of the Holy Graal* does, in one of its codices, speak of Glastonbury as the burial-place of the elder Joseph, but it only says *Glas* in England, for which other texts substitute Scotland. I doubt very much whether the Glastonbury legend was intended for more than the praise of a particular monastery; it represents Joseph of Arimathæa as the chief among twelve apostles sent by St. Philip to Britain, and they carried a phial or phials containing the Precious Blood. The Graal notion may have gratified Henry II., who concerned himself with things Arthurian, but beyond this we have only romance of history. It is certain in any case that St. David was not transformed into Joseph of Arimathæa, so far as Glastonbury is concerned. He and his *apostoli coadjutores*, his staff and his relics, belong to another story brought over from the Continent when St. David had passed into desuetude. Even so, of the Joseph claim, as we have it in the Graal romances, there is little enough trace in the historical writers of the time. The abbey of Noirmoutier in France laid claim to the original possession of Joseph's body, but it disappeared, or was stolen—as some said— by the monks of Glastonbury. If it be affirmed that the second Joseph, who is a creation of the *Book of the Holy Graal*, signifies some move in the strange ecclesiastical game which was played by Henry II., the evidence is in the opposite direction, so far as it can be said to exist; it is obvious that any game would have worked better with the original apostolical Joseph than with his imaginary son.

It is time to close these reflections, and there are only two points which remain, as I have not covenanted to deal with the *minima* as a whole. If King Arthur was enabled to make chalices for ordinary sacramental uses in official churches from the prototype which he saw in his vision, being a chalice that was arch-natural wholly, this occurred after the same manner that the Pilgrim Masons who discovered the body of the Master Builder were enabled to bring away certain things in substitution for the secrets that were lost at his death, and there are thus other analogies than the natural and reasonable gifts of the Welsh Apostle, but there is no need to dwell upon them in this place.

The quotation which I have given from the *Lesser Holy Graal* raises an interesting point, and, without being versed in the ecclesiastical side of things, we can all of us believe that a church so strange as that which once ministered in Wales had also some curious things belonging to the liturgical world; but the extract in question must be read in connection with the original metrical romance, where the symbolism is expressed differently.

> " Aussi sera representée
> Cele taule en meinte contrée.
> Ce que tu de la crouiz m'ostas
> Et ou sepulchre me couchas,
> C'est l'auteus seur quoi me metrunt
> Cil qui me sacrifierunt.
> Li dras où fui envolepez,
> Sera corparaus apelez.
> Cist veissiaus où men sanc méis
> Quant de men cors le requeillis,
> Calices apelez sera.
> La platine ki sus girra
> Iert la pierre senefiée
> Qui fu deseur moi seelée,
> Quant ou sepulchre m'éus mis."

The Blood is therefore mentioned and the analogy is complete; it is also gracious and piteous, as the poem might say itself; and, in fine, it is a true, catholic and efficacious comparison, which exhibits for those who can read in the heart one other side of secret Eucharistic symbolism—even the deep mystery of that mystical death which is suffered by the Lord of Glory in the assumption of the veils of bread and wine, that He may arise into a new life in the soul of the reborn communicant.

The Light of the Celtic Church

I do not propose to speak of the original Graal book, because this is for another consideration, but if there was a secret liturgy or missal at the root of the legend, I know that it was not especially Celtic and still less Welsh especially. Behind the hypothesis of the *Epiclesis* clause there lies a deeper speculation, for there are traces of a very wonderful and super-efficacious Office of the Holy Spirit here and there in the Graal literature, and I believe that this is one of the keys as to its source in doctrine. We shall open hereafter another gate which may bring us back to the Johannine Rite.

I have indicated already that if we accept the hypothesis of a Pan-Britannic Church, it has no operation outside the Book of the Holy Graal. Of Chrétien's intention we can discern little, nor does it signify; it seems fairly clear that he had no religious, much less ecclesiastical, implicits. Gautier is in the same position; Manessier was merely a story-teller; Gerbert offers a few allusions, but we cannot tell where he began, and his end is a thing frustrated. There is nothing so remote from all ecclesiastical programme in the official order as the Lesser Chronicles, and the *Parsifal* of Wolfram—which renders to God all that can be offered in ethics—like another Cain, though not of necessity rejected, offering the fruits of the earth—and to the spiritual Cæsar seeming to deny nothing—if the *Parsifal* has an ulterior motive, it is not of the Celtic Church nor yet of the House of Anjou, about which methinks that it protests too much, either for the Provençal Guiot or the lord of Eschenbach. There remain therefore only the Greater Chronicles and outside the primary text in place, which happens to be last in time—here, for the hypothesis in question, a moment surrendered formally —I know that of God moveth the *High History* and the *Galahad* of the King of all.

I do not much care on what materials the makers of the Graal romances may be agreed to have worked, since it is clear that they imported therein a new spirit.

If any one should like still to say that Cadwaladr who went to Rome or Jerusalem is to be identified with Galahad who went to heaven, they can have it that way since they so please, understanding that, on my part, I may reserve my judgment. I know that the one has suffered a high change before he has passed into the other. I know that every literature has its antecedents in some other literature, and that every religion owes something to a religion that preceded it. Sometimes the consanguinity is close and sometimes it is very far away. Only those who affirm that the one accounts for the other, and this simply and only, seem to be a little unwise. Christianity arose within Jewry and doctrinally out of Jewry, but this fact only brings their generic difference into greater relief. So also the Graal literature rose up in the Celtic Church ; its analogies are many therein ; they are many also in folk-lore ; but there are also as many ways in which the one, as we know it, does not account for the other, as we have it actually.

The Celtic Church has, however, assisted us to see one thing more plainly, though we know it on other considerations, namely, that in fine there is but a single quest, which is that of Galahad. We must make every allowance for the honest findings of scholars, for whom the Holy Graal, as it was and it is, has never spoken, for whom it is only a feeding-dish under a light cloud of imagery, and by whom it is thought perhaps in their hearts that the intervention of Christianity in the wild old pagan myth is on the whole rather regrettable. They turn naturally to those quarters whence issue the voices of purely natural life, and therefore they prefer Gawain and Perceval in his cruder forms, because these speak their own language. It is to be trusted, and this devoutly, that they will find more and more evidences for the maintenance of their particular view. Unmanifested now but still discerned darkly, if the true proto-Perceval should be at length found, that which went before the *Peredur* and the English metrical romance, and if, as there is no doubt, it should be devoid of all elements belonging to Graal or quester, our case will be the better proved which is (1) the natural succession of the Galahad Quest after the Graal history in its longer recension; (2) the succession of Perceval in the sequence of Robert de Borron, but rather as the scion of a dubious legitimacy; (3) the introduction of the late prose *Perceval le Gallois* as a final act of transmutation in the Anglo-Norman cycle, which so far assists our case that it manifests the unfitness, realised at that period, of Perceval as he was known by the earlier texts; (4) the derivation of the Wolfram *Parsifal* in part from Celtic elements, in part from some which are, or may have been, Teutonic, but also with derivatives through Provence from Spain.

IV

THE VICTORY OF THE LATIN RITE

I have now put forward the hypothesis of the Celtic Church as it has never been expressed previously; I have diminished nothing, and any contrary inferences have been proposed so far temperately; but the issues are not entirely those of the Graal legend, and in view of all that comes after a few words in conclusion of this part may perhaps be said more expressly. It should be on record, for those who have ears, that the Welsh Church, with its phantom and figurehead bishops, its hereditary priesthood, its fighting and sanguinary prelates, and its profession of sanctity as others profess trades, seems a very good case for those who insist that the first Christianity of Britain was independent of St. Augustine, which it was, and very much indeed, but on the whole we may prefer Rome. When we have considered all the crazes and heresies, all the pure, primitive and unadulterated Christianities, being only human and therefore disposed to gratitude, it is difficult not to thank God for Popery. But it would also be difficult to be so thankful, that is to say, with the same measure of sincerity, if we were still in the school courses and belonged officially thereto. I mean to say, although under all reserves, that there is always some disposition to hold a fluidic brief for Rome in the presence of the other assemblies. William Howitt, the historian of priestcraft *à rebours*, once said : " Thanks be to God for the mountains ! " It is well to quote from our enemies, but not in the sense of our enemies, and hence I read by substitution the seven hills and the city built thereon. Let therefore those who will strive with those who can over the dismembered relics of apostolical Christianity ; but so far as we are concerned the dead can bury their dead. We have left the Celtic Church as we have left carved gods. A Pan-Britannic Church might have been the dream of one period, and were that so, seeing that it never came to fulfilment, we could understand why it is that in several respects the Graal literature has now the aspect of a legend of loss and now of a legend of to-morrow. The Anglican Church seems in this sense to recall for a moment that perverse generation which asked for a sign and was given the sign of Jonah. It has demanded apostolical evidences to enforce its own claim and it has been given the Celtic Church. Let us therefore surrender thereto the full fruition thereof. There may be insufficiencies and imperfect warrants in the great orthodox assemblies, but in the Celtic Church there is nothing which we can regret. Gildas and St. Bernard are eloquent witnesses concerning it. The Latin rite prevailed because it was bound to prevail, because the greater absorbs the lesser. On the other hand, and now only in respect of the legends, let us say lastly that the ascension of Galahad is, symbolically speaking, without prejudice to the second coming of Cadwaladr. It does not signify for our purpose whether Arthur ever lived, and if so whether he was merely a petty British prince. The Graal is still the Graal, and the mystery of the Round Table is still the sweet and secret spirit of universal knighthood.

It follows, in fine, that we must go further, and in the next section, as one who has been in exile among *disjecta membra*, like Marius among the ruins of Carthage, I shall re-enter into my own patrimony. To my old friend, Arthur Machen, himself of Caerleon-upon-Usk, I owe most of the materials which have been collated for the presentation of the hypothesis concerning the Graal and the Celtic Church. He collected them in my interest out of his good heart of brotherhood, and I trust that in the time to come he will extend them further in his own.

BOOK VIII

MYSTIC ASPECTS OF THE GRAAL LEGEND

THE ARGUMENT

I. The Introductory Words.—*The Quest of the Holy Graal considered as a religious experiment—Counsels of Perfection in the Quest—Of poverty, obedience and virginity—Of partial success in their absence—Peculiarities in the election of Galahad—The state of sanctity—The descent of Grace—Perpetuity of conditions for the experiment—Further as regards virginity in respect of the Quest—The mystical idea of union—The term of the Quest—Separation of transubstantiation marvels from the final vision of the Graal—The experience of Nasciens—Collateral experience of the Mystics—After what manner grace manifested through the Eucharist—Of a gate of knowledge in the Eucharist—Declaration of the Graal in its mystic aspects.* II. The Position of the Literature Defined. — *A distinction concerning the literature — Of allegory in the Great Quest—A particular form of development in the Graal Legend—The Graal and the Official Church—The case concerning that Church—The implicits of the literature as elements of the mystic aspects—The Recession of the Graal—How this symbol was perpetuated from the beginning—A light from the Quest of Guiot—Meaning of the Stone in the Crown of Lucifer—The Graal and Eucharistic Wisdom.* III. Concerning the Great Experiment.—*The wonder of all sacredness as the term of Quest—An analogy from Ruysbroeck—Term of the Experiment—External places of the Quest—Of helpers therein*

465   2 G

The Hidden Church of the Holy Graal

*—Of Secret Orders—Communication of Divine Substance
—The Channel of the Eucharist—Of Integration in Secret
Knowledge—The Office of the Quests—Of Popular De-
votions in the Church and of such Fatalities—Our Inherit-
ance from the Past—The open Secret of Tradition—
Of things that stand in the way in respect of Christian
Mysticism—Latin Christianity—The true way of Experience—An eirenicon in doctrine.* IV. THE MYSTERY OF
INITIATION.*—Of the Graal in its correspondence with instituted Mysteries—The mind of scholarship on this subject
—Analogies from the literary history of Kabalism and
Alchemy—The sacramental message of the Graal—Points
of comparison between Graal literature and other cycles of
books—A distinction on the question of Initiation—The
Hidden Knowledge—An illustration from Masonry—Of a
certain leaven working in the texts of the Graal—Testimony
to the existence of the Great Experiment—The failure of the
external world—A caution in respect of interpretation—
The indubitable subsurface sense of Graal books.* V. THE
MYSTERY OF FAITH.*—A first summary of the whole subject
—The Graal Mystery as a declared pageant of the Eucharist
—Its distinctions from the official Sacrament—A profound
symbolism—Of secret memorials—The Five Changes of the
Graal—Of what remains over from the findings of scholarship—The Church teaching on the Eucharist—Limitations
of Graal books—And of books of the Mystics.* VI. THE
LOST BOOK OF THE GRAAL.*—Suggestion concerning a concealed Liturgy or Mass-Book—Superfluity of this hypothesis
in respect of the present interpretation—General testimony
of the literature to a primordial text—The schedule thereof
—Whether the evidences are applicable to one book—The
results obtained therefrom—Conclusion that the literature
could not have arisen from a single prototype—Of admitted*

The Argument

and indisputable prototypes—*The alleged Latin source*—*Southey's opinion*—*Statement of the Comte de Tressan*—*Middle ground occupied by Paulin Paris*—*A lesson from the literature of Alchemy*—*Of all which remains after abandoning the hypothesis of a single prototype in the ordinary sense*—*Further concerning the implicits and strange rumours present in Graal literature*—*Proof that these were not inventions of romance*—*Hypothesis of a* Sanctum Graal *which contained these elements*—*The negative view of its content*—*The positive view*—*The book not seen by those who wrote the romances*—*The presumable custodians thereof*—*The rumours thereof*—*How their prevalence does not involve the existence of any book.* VII. THE DECLARED MYSTERY OF QUEST.—*Exotics of the whole subject*—*Of faith and experience*—*Errors of the Mystic Quest*—*The Open Door*—*The Gates and their Wardens*—*A condition of progress in the Quest*—*The declared and the hidden knowledge*—*Suddenness of the Graal Wonders*—Obiter Dicta—*The expression of the whole Quest after a new manner.*

BOOK VIII

MYSTIC ASPECTS OF THE GRAAL LEGEND

I

THE INTRODUCTORY WORDS

SEEING therefore that we have not found in the Celtic Church anything which suffices to explain the chief implicits of the literature and that the watchwords call us forward, there remains another method of research, and of this I will now proceed to make trial. I suppose that there is no need to exhibit in formal words after what manner the Quest of the Holy Graal became in the later texts a religious experiment, and thus justified the titles from which it began in that story of Robert de Borron which is the earliest extant history. Any one who has proceeded so far in the present inquisition as to have reached these lines—even if he is wholly unfamiliar with the old treasury of books—will be aware that the Quest was ruled throughout by the counsels of perfection. These ruled in fact so strongly as to have reached that stage when two of them were implied only—that is, they were taken for granted : (*a*) Voluntary poverty, for the knights possessed nothing, and whatever came into their hands was distributed there and then ; (*b*) entire obedience, in dedication to the proposed term, and all the ships of the world burnt with fire behind them ; when change came there followed complete *avortement*, as that of Gawain in the Great Quest ; (*c*) perpetual chastity, as the only counsel which stands declared—and in this connection it will be remembered that Bors returned to Logres. The zeal of these counsels does not appear—as I have said—to guarantee election utterly: it is rather the test of merit. And I have said also that there may be a certain success without their fulfilment in the absolute degree. In the *Longer Prose Perceval* Gawain received signal favours, yet it is admitted that he was wanting in purity, and hence he could make no response when the questionable mystery appeared once in his presence. The King also beheld the arch-natural Eucharist on the manifested side thereof: but Perceval alone possessed the plenary qualifications in this text. On the other hand, in the story of stories there was one who surpassed him, but not so utterly that they were otherwise than classed together as companions of the Quest. The distinction seems to have been that Galahad dissolved temptation, as one more than human. Perceval carried within him the latent desires of the body, and after beholding the Graal he required the purgation of a hermit's life before he entered into the true inheritance of those thrones which are above. By some of my fellowship in research it has been said most truly, though they do not understand Galahad, that the *haut prince* was just as fit for the Quest at its beginning as he was at its end. Now, that is exactly the sign of perfect vocation—of election as well as calling; the criterion of those who are meant for heaven is that they might ascend thither at any moment. Another test of Galahad was that he knew really from the beginning the whole mystery by the tradition thereof.

I am enumerating here the general implicits of the subject which should be latent in the minds of those whom I address; they do not constitute a question put forward for sifting with a view to a settlement, but of fitness and power to see—of the *verus certusque intuitus animi*, in some degree and proportion. This being passed by those who can suffer the ruling, it will be obvious that the religious experiment about which I begin to speak can depend only from two considerations: (1) the attainment of the sanctified state in the Questing Knights, and (2) the descent of a peculiar Grace upon them. I enumerate both points, though it is obvious that one of them has in another form but now passed through review, but in dealing with a very difficult subject it is necessary to look at it in more than a single light, and I wish to make it clear that the specifics of the sanctified state—by which I mean the counsels of perfection—are not things that are determined in the given case by a trend of thought and emotion at the given period, and are not therefore to be dismissed as a presentation of the ascetic life or as the definition of canons which have now passed into desuetude. The same experiment always demands the same conditions for its success, and to set aside these is really to renounce that, or in this instance it is to reject the experiment as one of the old ecstasies which never came to a term. On the contrary, the experiment of sanctity is always approximating to a term, and the measure of success is the measure of zeal in its pursuit. I propose therefore to look a little closer at one of the counsels of perfection. The essential point regarding the condition of *virgo intacta*—not in respect of the simple physical fact, which has no inherent sanctity, but in respect of its conscious acceptance at what cost soever—is that there neither was nor can be a more perfect symbol of the prepared matter of the work. It is the analogy in utter transcendence of that old adage: *Mens sana in corpore sano*, and its nearest expression is: *Anima immaculata in corpore dedicato, ex hoc nunc et usque*, &c. In other words, the banns of marriage in the higher degrees cannot be proclaimed till the contracting parties are warranted in their respective orders to have that proportion and likeness apart from which no union could be effected. The consummated grade of sanctity is an intimate state of union, and the nearest analogy thereto is found in human marriage; as the latter presupposes in the sacramental order an antecedent or nominal purity, and has for its object the consecration of intercourse which in its absence is of the animal kind, so the antecedent condition in sanctity—or the life of perfect dedication —is in correspondence with the state of *virgo intacta*. I need not say that because these things are analogical so the discourse concerning them partakes of the language of symbolism or that the state itself is a spiritual state. Entire obedience involves no earthly master; voluntary poverty is of all possibility in a palace, and the law would not deny it at the headquarters of an American Trust; as regards chastity, that is guaranteed to those who receive the sacrament of marriage worthily, and it is to be noted that this sacrament differs from baptism, which is administered once and for all, while marriage, in the effects thereof, is administered in continuity as an abiding presence and a grace abounding daily so long as its covenants are observed. On the other hand, the perpetuity of spiritual chastity in the life within does not mean of necessity that man or woman has never known flesh in the physical order. Galahad in the story had the outward signs as well as the inward grace. His Quest was an allegory throughout and sometimes the allegorical motive obtrudes into the expressed matter, which is an error of art.

The term which is proposed in the Quest, as the consideration thereof, will be best given in the words of the Quest itself. " Now at the yeres ende and the self daye after Galahad had borne the croune of gold, he arose up erly and his felawes, and came to the palais, and sawe to fore hem the holy vessel, and a man knelynge on his knees in lykenes of a Bisshop that had aboute hym a grete felaushyp of Angels as it had ben Jhesu Cryst hym self, & thenne he arose and beganne a masse of oure lady. And whan he cam to the sacrament of the masse, and had done, anone he called Galahad and sayd to hym

come forthe the servaunt of Jhesu Cryst and thou shalt
see that thou hast moche desyred to see, & thenne he
began to tremble ryght hard, when the dedely flesshe
beganne to beholde the spyrytuel thynges.   Thenne he
held vp his handes toward heuen, and sayd lord I thanke
the, for now I see that that hath ben my desyre many a
daye.   Now blessyd lord wold I not lenger lyue yf it
myghte please the lord, & there with the good man
tooke our lordes body betwixe hys handes, and profered
it to Galahad, and he receyued hit ryghte gladly and
mekely. . . . And there with he kneled doune to fore
the table, and made his prayers, and thenne sodenly his
soule departed to Jhesu Crist and a grete multitude of
Angels bare his soule vp to heuen," &c.   In this citation
the most important point for our purpose at the living
moment rests neither in that which it expresses nor in
that which it conceals : it is assumed and realised that
such a term is always hidden because it always exceeds
expression, and is the closer veiled wherein it is announced
the most.   But here was the consummation of all, and
here was that more open seeing than was granted at
Corbenic wherein all the outward offices of things arch-
natural were set aside utterly.   Herein therefore was no
vision of transubstantiation changes, and as evidence that
this was of concert and not of chance, I have the same
report to make concerning the *Longer Prose Perceval ;*
when the questing knight comes to his own therein no
signs and wonders are connected with the Holy Graal.
As regards the vision itself, we may remember the words
of Nasciens when he attempted to penetrate the secrets
within the new Ark of the Covenant.   "*Et Nasciens
dist que il l'en descouverroit tant comme nule mortieus
langue em porroit descouvrir, ne deveroit.   Je ai, dist-il,
véut la coumenchaille dou grant hardiment, l'ocoison des
grans savoirs, le fondement des grans religions, le des-
sevrement des grans félonnies, la démoustranche des grans
mierveilles, la mervelle de totes les altrez mervelles, la
fin des bontés et des gentillèces vraies.*"   This extract

from the *Book of the Holy Graal* is thus rendered in the halting measures of Lovelich :

> " ' I have sein,' quod the sire Nasciens,
> ' Of alle manere of wykkednesse the defens ;
> Of alle boldnesse I have sene the begynneng,
> Of all wittes the fowndyng.
> I have sein the begynneng of Religeown
> And of alle bowntes, bothe al & som,
> And the poyntes of alle gentrye,
> And a merveil of alle merveilles certeinlye.' "

Other masters have expressed the same wonder in other terms, which are the same—as, for example : *quædam prælibatio æternæ vitæ, gustus et suavitas spiritualis, mentis in Deum suspensa elevatio*, &c.

The qualifications of Galahad and Perceval in the Great Quest are not therefore things which are the fashion of a period, like some aspects of what is termed the ascetic mind, but they obtain from *Aleph* to *Tau*, through all grades of expression. Those who speak of the ethical superiority of the *Parsifal* are saying that which, in all moderation and tenderness, signifies that they are still learning the elements of true discipline.

I have now dealt with the indispensable warrants of the state, and the mode of the descent of Grace belongs to the same category ; it was a manifestation to the spiritual flowers of Christian knighthood through the Eucharist—the form of symbolism made use of for this purpose being that of transubstantiation. I have already set down what I believe to be the Divine Truth on this subject, but here again we must as our research proceeds approach it from various standpoints ; and, for the rest, it must be obvious that of all men I at least should have no call imposed on me to speak of the Holy Graal were it not for its connection with the Blessed Sacrament. It is the passage of the putative reliquary into the Chalice of the Eucharist, the progressive exaltation of its cultus and the consequent transfiguration of the Quest which have substituted insensibly a tale of eternity for a mediæval legend of the Precious Blood ; in place of the Abbey of Fécamp, we have Corbenic and Mont Salvatch shining in the high distance, and where once there abode only the suggestion of some relative and rather trivial devotion, we have the presence of that great sign behind which there lies the Beginning and the End of all things.

The romance-writers, seeking in their symbolism a reduction to the evidence of the senses, selected and exaggerated the least desirable side of Eucharistic dogma ; but we have no occasion to dispute with them on that score, seeing that — for the skilled craftsman — any material will serve in the purposes of the Great Work. The only point which stands out for our consideration is that—following the sense of all doctrine and the testimony of all experience—the gate by which faith presses into realisation is the gate of that Sacrament from which all others depend—of that Sacrament the institution of which was the last act of Christ and the term of His ministry ; thereafter He suffered only until He rose in glory. When therefore the makers of the Graal books designed to show after what manner, and under what circumstances, those who were still in flesh could behold the spiritual things and have opened for them that door of understanding which, according to the keepers of the Old Law, was not opened for Moses, they had no choice in the matter, and it is for this reason that they represent the Bread of Life and the Chalice of the Everlasting Testament as being lifted up in the secret places of Logres, even in the *palais esperiteux*.

Hereof are the mystic aspects of the Great Quest, and it seems to follow that the secret temple of the soul was entered by those who dwelt in the world of romance as by those in the world of learning. The adepts of both schools were saying the same thing at the same period, seeing that during the twelfth and thirteenth centuries, which moved and had their being under the wonderful ægis of the scholastic mind, there began to arise over the intellectual horizon of Europe the light of another experience than that of spiritual truth realised intellectually; this was the experience of the mystic life, which opened—shall we say?—with the name of Bonaventura and closed for the period in question with that of Ruysbroeck.

II

THE POSITION OF THE LITERATURE DEFINED

The books of the Holy Graal are either purely of literary, antiquarian and mythological interest, or they are more. If literary, antiquarian and mythological only, they can and should be left to the antiquaries, the critics and the folk-lore societies. But if more it is not improbable antecedently, having regard to the subject, that the excess belongs to the mystics, and to those generally who recognise that the legends of the soul are met with in many places, often unexpectedly enough, and wherever found that they have issues outside that which is understood commonly and critically by the origin of religious belief. The ascetic and mystic element—to repeat the conventional description — outside the considerations which I have put forward, is for those of all importance, and it is otherwise and invariably the only thing that is really vital in legends. The impression which is left upon the mind after the conclusions of the last sub-section is assuredly that the "divine event" is not especially, or not only, that "towards which creation moves," but a term, both here and now, towards which souls can approximate and wherein they can rest at the centre. Over the threshold of the Galahad Quest we pass as if out of worlds of enchantment, worlds of færie, worlds of the mighty Morgan le Fay, into realms of allegory and dual meaning, and then—transcending allegory—into a region more deeply unrealised; so also, after having reflected on the external side of the romances and the preliminary analogies of things that are inward, we pass, as we approach the end of our research, into a world of which nothing but the veils and their emblazonments have been so far declared. No other romances of chivalry exhibit the characteristics which we discern in the perfect and rectified books of the Holy Graal, but if we do not know categorically why romance came to be the vehicle for one expression of man's highest experience, we have reasons —and more than enough—to determine that it was not automatic, not arbitrary, and yet it was not fortuitous; it came about in the nature of things by the successive exaltation of a legend which had the capacity for exaltation into transcendence. The genesis of the story of Galahad is not like the institution of the ritual belonging to the third craft grade in Masonry, which seems without antecedents that are traceable in the elements—actual or symbolical—of the early building guilds. By successive steps the legend of the Graal was built till it reached that height when the hierarchies could begin to come down and the soul of Galahad could go up. It is important for my own purpose to establish this fact, because in that which remains to be said I must guard against the supposition that a conventional secret society or a sect took over the romances, edited them and interpenetrated the texts with mystic elements. That is the kind of hypothesis which occult interests might have manufactured sincerely enough in the old days, and it would have had a certain warrant because there is ample evidence that this is exactly the kind of work which in given cases was performed by the concealed orders. The Graal, as a literature, came into other hands, which worked after their own manner, and worked well.

There is another fact which is not less important because of certain tendencies recognisable in modern criticism. I will mention it only at the moment, that the reader may be put on his guard mentally; there is no single text in the literature which was or could have been put forward as a veiled *pronunciamento* against the reigning Church on the part of any historical sect, heresy, or rival orthodoxy. The pure Christianities and the incipient principles of reform took their quack processes into other quarters. The voices which spoke in the books of the Holy Graal as no voices had ever spoken in romance were not putting forward a mystery which was superior specifically to the mysteries preserved by the official Church. They trended in the same direction as the highest inquisitions move, and that invariably. The most intelligent of all the heresies is only the truth of the Church foreshadowed or travestied. The reforms of the Church are only its essential lights variously refracted. Even modern science, outside the true prerogatives of its election as our growing physical providence, is the notification of the things which do not ultimately matter in comparison with the science of the Church, which is that of the laws ruling in the search after the eternal reality. The Graal at its highest is the simulacrum or effigy of the Divine Mystery within the Church. If she, as an institution, has failed so far—and as to the failure within limits there is no question—to accomplish the transmutation of humanity, the explanation is not merely that she has been at work upon gross and refractory elements—though this is true assuredly—but that in the great mystery of her development she has still to enter into the fruition of her higher consciousness. Hereof are the wounds of the Church, and for this reason she has been in sorrow throughout the ages.

So far I have defined, but in one sense only, the position of the literature. It remains to be said that what I have termed from the beginning the major implicits, as they project vaguely and evasively upon the surface, are integral elements of the mystic aspects. But they must be taken here in connection with one feature of the quests which is in no sense implied, because this will concern us in a very important manner in the next book. I refer to the Recession of the Graal. I have no need to remind any one after so many enumerations that the final testimony of all the French Quests is that, in one or another way, the Graal was withdrawn. It is not always by a removal in space; it is not always by assumption to heaven. In the German cycle the Temple was inaccessible from the beginning and the Palladium never travelled, till—once and for all—it was carried in a great procession to the furthest East. Wolfram left it in primeval concealment; but this did not satisfy one of the later poets, who married—as we have seen—the Graal legend to that of Prester John. Now, it might be more easy to attain translation, like St. Paul, than to find that sanctuary in India where, by the assumption, it must be supposed to remain. But having regard to the hidden meaning which seems to lie behind Wolfram's source he was within the measures of his symbolism when he left the Graal at Mont Salvatch, not removing to the East that which in his case did not come therefrom. Albrecht, who tells of the transit, first took the precaution to change the hallowed object. I believe that the testimony to removal was inherent to the whole conception from the beginning, concurrently with the Secret Words, and that the latter were reflected at a later period into the peculiar claim concerning sacerdotal succession. They were all Eucharistic in their nature. The testimony itself is twofold, because, in addition to the withdrawal of the Living Sign, the texts tell us of the House that is emptied of its Hallows; these are in particular the *Longer Prose Perceval* and the *Quest of Galahad*. There is also Manessier's conclusion of the *Conte del Graal*, but no very important inference is to be drawn therefrom. One of our immediate concerns will be to find the analogies of this prevailing conception elsewhere in the world; the present study of Graal mystic aspects is simply preliminary thereto, and the eduction of the significance behind the major implicits. It is at this point curiously that one element of Graal history which has been somehow ascribed to Guiot comes to our assistance, providing an intermediary between the literature of mystical romance and—as we shall learn—the obvious text-books of the secret schools. It opens, I think, strange vistas of intellectual wonder and enchantment. We have heard already that the Stone which is identified with the Graal in Wolfram was at one time a stone in the crown of Lucifer, and seeing that, according to other legends, the thrones left vacant by the fallen angels are reserved for human souls, it becomes intelligible why the Graal was brought to earth and what is signified by the mystic jewel. The Stone in the crown of Lucifer symbolises the great estate from which the archangel fell. It was held by the fathers of the Church that, when still in the delights of Paradise, Lucifer was adorned by all manner of precious stones, understanding mystically of him what in the text of the prophet Ezekiel is said literally of the Prince of Tyre : *In deliciis paradisi Dei fuisti ; omnis lapis preciosus operimentum tuum : sardius, topazius, et jaspis, chrysolithus, et onyx, et beryllus, sapphirus, et carbunculus, et smaragdus*—nine kinds of stones, according to Gregory the Great, because of the nine choirs of angels. And Bartolocci, the Cistercian, following all authorities, understands these jewels to signify the knowledge and other ornaments of grace with which Lucifer was adorned in his original state as the *perfecta similitudo Dei*—in other words, the light and splendour of the hidden knowledge. It follows on this interpretation (1) That the Graal Stone in no sense belongs to folk-lore ; (2) that it offers in respect of its origin no connection with the idea of physical maintenance, except in the sense that the things which sustain the soul maintain also the body, because the *panis quotidianus* depends from the *panis supersubstantialis ;* (3) that the wisdom of the Graal is an Eucharistic wisdom, because the descent of an archnatural Host takes place annually to renew the virtues thereof ; (4) that the correspondence of this is, in other versions of the legend, the Host which is consecrated extra-validly by the Secret Words, and so also the correspondence of the Stone which comes from heaven is the Cup which goes thereto; but in fine (5) that the jewel in the crown of Lucifer is called also the Morning Star, and thus it is not less than certain that the Graal returns whence it came.

III

CONCERNING THE GREAT EXPERIMENT

If there be any who at this stage should say that the term of the Holy Graal is not the end of the mysteries—which is the Vision that is He—I would not ask him to define the distinction, but the term in either case, for that which must be said of the one is said also of the other, and if he understands the other it is certain that he understands the one. The Quest of the Holy Graal is for the wonder of all sacredness, there where no sinner can be. The provisional manifestation is in the *Longer Prose Perceval* and the full disclosure—not as to what it is but as to what it is about—is in the romance of Galahad. If, after the *haut prince* had given his final message, "Remember of this unstable world," he had been asked what he had seen which led him to exercise his high prerogative and call to be dissolved, he might have answered: *Visi sunt oculi mei salutare suum*, yet he would have said in his heart: "Eye hath not seen." But it has been divined and foretasted by those who have gone before the cohorts of election in the life that is within and have spoken with tongues of fire concerning that which they have seen in the vista. One approximation has told us that it is the eternal intercourse of the Father and the Son wherein we are enveloped lovingly by the Holy Spirit in that love which is eternal. And him who said this the wondering plaudits of an after-age termed the Admirable Ruysbroeck. He knew little Latin and less Greek, and, speaking from his own root, he had not read the authorities; but he had stood upon that shore where the waves of the divine sea baptize the pilgrim, or in that undeclared sphere which is *Kether*, the Crown of Kabalism, whence those who can look further discern that there is *Ain Soph Aour*, the Limitless Light. The equivalent hereof is in that which was said by Jesus Christ to the men of the Quest : " My Knyghtes and my seruantes & my true children whiche ben come oute of dedely lyf in to spyrytual lyf I wyl now no longer hyde me from yow, but ye shal see now a parte of my secretes & of my hydde thynges." And in the measure of that time they knew as they were known in full, that is, by participation in, and correspondence with the Divine Knowledge. Meat indeed : it is in that sense that Christ gave to Galahad " the hyghe mete " and " then he receyved his saueour." The monk who wrote this might have exhausted all the language of the schools, but he also knew little Latin and less Greek, if any, so he said only of the communicants : " They thoughte it soo swete that hit was merveillous to telle." And of Galahad he said later : " He receyued hit ryghte gladly and mekely." But yes, and that is fuller and stronger than all the eloquence of the Master of Sentences. It is the voice of Ruysbroeck—but further simplified—saying the same thing : " And he tastes and sees, out of all bounds, after God's own manner, the riches which are in God's own self, in the unity of the living deep, wherein He has fruition of Himself, according to the mode of His un-created essence."

This is the Great Term of the Great Experiment followed by the Mystic Schools, and here by its own words the Graal legend is expressed in the terms of this Experiment. It has been made, within their several measures, by all churches, sects and religions, for which reason I have said elsewhere that the skilled craftsman does not quarrel with his tools. All materials are possible ; the ascent to eternal life can be made by any ladder, assuming that it is fixed in the height ; there is no need to go in search of something that is new and strange. And those who can receive this assurance will, I think, understand why it is that the Church of a man's childhood—assuming that it is a Church and not a latitudinarian chapel of ease or a narrow and voided sect —may and perhaps should contain for him the materials of his work, and these he will be able to adapt as an efficient craftsman. There is neither compulsion nor restraint, but the changes in official religion, the too easy transition from one to another kind, taking the sanctuaries as one takes high grades in Masonry, are a note of weakness rather than a pledge of sincerity, or of the true motive which should impel the soul on its quest.

There are, of course, many helpers of that soul on that progress:

> " We, said the day and the night
>   And the law of gravitation;
> And we, said the dark and the light
>   And the stars in their gyration;
> But I, said Justice, moving
>   To the right hand of the Throne;
> And I, said Fate, approving;
>   I make thy cause mine own."

Among these there are certain of the secret orders— those, I mean, which contain the counterparts of the Catholic tradition—and it is necessary to mention them here because of what follows. They offer no royal road, seeing that such roads there are none; but they do in cases shorten some of the preliminaries, by developing the implicits of a man's own consciousness, which is the setting of the prepared postulant on the proper path. There are, of course, some who enter within them having no special call, and these see very little of that which lies behind their official workings, just as there are many who have been born within the Church, as the body of Christ, but have never entered into the life which is communicated from the soul of Christ. They remain the children of this world, participating—as we hope—according to their degree, in so much of grace and salvation as is possible at the particular time. There are others who, out of all time, have received a high election, and for them the subject is often—in its undivided entirety— found resident in that state of external religious life in which it has pleased God to call them.

The Secret Doctrine in the religions equally and the schools is that of the communication of Divine Substance. I speak of it as secret in both cases, though it is obvious that in the official church there is no instituted reservation or conscious concealment on any point of doctrine or practice; but the language of the heights is not the language of the plains, and that which is heard in the nooks, byways and corners, among brakes and thickets, is not the voice of the rushing waters and the open sea. That is true of it in the uttermost which was said long ago by Paracelsus: *Nihil tam occultum erit quod non revelabitur;* but as there are few with ears to hear, it remains a voice in the wilderness crying in the unknown tongue. We know only that, according to high theology, the Divine Substance is communicated in the Eucharist—normally in the symbolical manner, but, in cases, essentially and vitally according to the true testimonies. It is therefore as if the elements were at times consecrated normally and at times by other words, more secret and efficient archnaturally. Then the enchantments terminate which are the swoon of the sensitive life in respect of the individual, who enters into real knowledge—the soul's knowledge before that supervened which is termed mystically the fall into matter. The Great Experiment is therefore one of reintegration in the secret knowledge before the Fall, and when, or if, the Holy Graal is identified with the stone in the crown of Lucifer, that which is indicated thereby is (*a*) the perpetuation of this secret knowledge, and (*b*) that under all circumstances there is a way back whence we came. So close also those times of adventure which— among other things and manifold—are the life of external activity governed by the spirit of the world, and this is accomplished by taking the great secret into the heart of the heart, as if the Blessed Sacrament, truly and virtually, into the inmost being.

Of such is the office of the Quests, but it is understood that it is not of my concern to enumerate these particulars as present consciously in the minds of the old monastic *scriptores*, who wrote the greatest of the books; they spoke of the things which they knew; without reference or intention they said what others had said of the same mysteries, and the testimony continued through the centuries. The story of the assumption of Galahad draws into romance the hypothesis of the Catholic Church concerning the term of all sanctity manifested; in both it is attained through the Eucharist. I mean to say that this is, by the hypothesis, the normal channel of the Divine Favour, and the devotion which was shown by the saints to the Sacrament of the Altar was not like the particular, sentimental disposition in minds of piety to the Precious Blood or the Heart of Jesus. Concerning these exercises I have no call to pronounce, but among the misjudgments on spiritual life in the Roman communion has been the frittering of spiritual powers in the popular devotion. If the Great Mysteries of the Church are insufficient to command the dedication of the whole world, then the world is left best under interdict, just as no pictures at all are better than those which are bad in art, and no books than those which are poor and trivial.

There is one point more, because here we have been trending in directions which will call for more full consideration presently. I have mentioned Secret Orders, and I cannot recall too early that any Secret Tradition—either in the East or the West—has been always an open secret in respect of the root-principles concerning the Way, the Truth and the Life. We are only beginning, and that by very slow stages, to enter into our inheritance from the past; and still perhaps in respect of the larger part we are seeking far and wide for the mystic treasures of Basra. It is therefore desirable to remember that the great subjects of preoccupation are all at our very doors.

One reason, of which we shall hear again in another connection, is because among the wise of the ages, in whatsoever regions of the world, I do not think that there has been ever any difference of opinion about the true object of research; the modes and form of the Quest have varied, and that widely, but to a single point have all the ways converged. Therein is no change or shadow of vicissitude. We may hear of shorter roads, and we might say at first sight that such a suggestion must be true indubitably; but in one sense it is rather a convention of language and in another it is a commonplace which tends to confuse the issues. It is a convention of language, because the Great Quests are not pursued in time or place, and it would be just as true to say that in a journey from the circumference to the centre all roads are the same length, supposing that they are straight roads. It is a commonplace, because if any one should enter the byways, or return on his path and restart, it is obvious that he must look to be delayed. Furthermore, it may be true that all paths lead ultimately to the centre, and that if we descend into hell there may be still a way back to the light: yet in any house of right reason the issues are too clear to consider such extrinsic possibilities.

On this and on any consideration, we have to lay down one irrevocable law—that he who has resolved—setting all things else aside—to enter the path of the Quest must look for his progress in proportion as he pursues holiness for its own sake. He who in the Secret Orders dreams of the adeptship which they claim, *ex hypothesi*, to impart to those who can receive, and who does not say sanctity in his heart till his lips are cleansed, and then does not say it with his lips, is not so much far from the goal as without having conceived regarding it.

Now, it is precisely this word sanctity which takes us back, a little unintentionally, to the claim of the Church, and raises the question whether we are to interpret it according to the mind of the Church or another mind. My answer is that I doubt if the Great Experiment was ever pursued to its term in Christian times on the part of any person who had once been incorporated by the mystical body but subsequently had set himself aside therefrom. When the Quest of the Holy Graal was in fine achieved, there were some who, as we know, were translated, but others became monks and hermits; they were incorporated, that is to say, by the official annals of sanctity. I am dealing here with what I regard as a question of fact, not with antecedent grounds, and the fact is that the Church has the Eucharist. It may in certain respects have hampered Christian Mysticism by the restriction of its own consciousness so especially to the literal side; it may, on the historical side, have approached too often that picture of a certain King of Castle Mortal, who sold God for money; it may in this sense have told the wrong story, though the elements placed in its hands were the right and true elements. But not only is it certain that because of these elements we have to cleave as we can to the Church, but—speaking as a *doctor dubitantium*—I know that the Church Mystic on the highest throne of its consciousness does not differ in anything otherwise than *per accidentia*— or alternatively, the prudence of expression—from formal Catholic doctrine. It can say with its heart of knowledge what the ordinary churchman says with his lips of faith; the *Symbolum* remains; it has not taken on another meaning; it has only unfolded itself, like a flower, from within. The Christian Mystic can therefore recite his *Credo in unum Deum* by clause and by clause, including *in unam sanctam catholicam et apostolicam ecclesiam*, and there is neither heresy in the construction nor Jesuitry in the *arrière pensée*. Above all, the path of the mystic does not pass through the heresies. It has seemed worth while to make this plain, because the Holy Graal is the Catholic Quest drawn into romance.

IV

THE MYSTERY OF INITIATION

The Mystic Aspects of the Graal legend having been developed up to this stage, the question arises whether they have points of correspondence with any scheme of the Instituted Mysteries, whether any element which is present in the romances can be regarded as a faint and far off reflection of something which at that time was known and done in any secret schools. The possibility has presented itself already to the mind of scholarship, which, having performed admirable work in the study of the Graal texts, is still in search of a final explanation concerning them. The shadow of the old Order of the Temple has haunted them in dreams fitfully, and they have lingered almost longingly over vague imagined reflections of the Orgies of Adonis and Tammuz. As behind the Christian symbolism of the extant literature there spreads the whole world of pagan folk-lore, so—at least antecedently—there might be implied also some old scheme of the epopts. It seems permissible therefore to offer an alternative, under proper judgments of reserve, as something which—if otherwise considerable —may be held tentatively until later circumstances of research either lead it into demonstration or furnish a fitting substitute. The Graal legends are comparable to certain distinct literatures with which the theory here put forward will connect them by a twofold consanguinity of purpose. Scholarship had scarcely troubled itself with the great books of Kabalism till it was found or conceived that they could be made to enforce the official doctrines of Christianity. Many errors of enthusiasm followed, but the books of the mystery of Israel became in this manner the public heritage of philosophy, and we are now able to say after what manner it enters into the general scheme of mystic knowledge. The literature of alchemy, in like manner, so long as it was in the hands of certain amateurs of infant science and its counterfeits, remained particular to themselves, and outside a questionable research in physics it had no office or horizon until it was discovered or inferred that many curious texts of the subject had been written in a language of subterfuge, that in place of a metallurgical interest it was concerned in its way with the keeping of spiritual mysteries. There were again errors of enthusiasm, but a corner of the veil was lifted. Now, it is indubitably the message of the Graal that there is more in the Eucharist than is indicated by the sufficing graces imparted to the ordinary communicant, and if it is possible to show that behind this undeclared excess there lies that which has been at all times sought by the Wise, that *est in sacramento quicquid quærunt sapientes*, then the Graal literature will enter after a new manner into our heritage from the past, and another corner of the veil will be lifted on the path of knowledge. It will be seen that the literature—contrary to what it appears on the surface—is not without points of comparison in other Christian cycles—that it does not stand exactly alone, even if its consanguinities, though declared by official religion, are not entirely before the face of the world but within the sanctuaries of secret fraternities. To suggest this is not to say that these stories of old are a defined part or abstract of any mysteries of initiation; they are at most a byway winding through a secret woodland to a postern giving upon the chancel of some great and primeval abbey.

Those who have concerned themselves with the subject of hidden knowledge will know that the secret claims have been put forth under all manners of guises. This has arisen to some extent naturally enough in the course of the ages and under the special atmosphere of motives peculiar to different nations. It has also come about through the institution of multiples of convention on the part of some who have become in later times the custodians of the mysteries, such wardens having been actuated by a twofold purpose, firstly, to preserve their witness in the world, and, secondly, to see that the knowledge was, as far as might be, kept away from the world. This is equivalent to saying that the paramount law of silence has of necessity a permanent competitor in the law of the sign. We may take the readiest illustration in the rituals of Craft Masonry. They contain the whole marrow of *bourgeoisie*, but they contain also the shadow of the great mysteries revealed occasionally. The unknown person or assembly which conceived the closing of the Lodge according to one of the grades had a set of moral feelings in common with those of all the retired masters in the craft of joinery, and a language like a journeyman carpenter, but this notwithstanding the words of the adepts had passed over them and they spoke of the Hidden Token as no one had ever spoken before. That closing gives the true explanation of the secret which cannot be told and yet is imparted quite simply; of that mystery which has never been expressed and can yet be recited by the least literate occupant of the chair placed in Wisdom. Nor does it prove in communication to be anything that is strictly unfamiliar. And yet the explanation, so far from making the concealed part of the rite familiar and a thing of no moment, has built about the concealment a wall of preservation which has made its real significance more profound and in the minds of the adepts more important.

The Graal literature is open to a parallel criticism, and the result is also the same. Whatever disappointment may await, in fine, the pursuit of an inquiry like the present, partly on account of the uncouth presentation of important symbolism to the mind of the early romancist, partly by reason of the inherent defect of romance as a vehicle of symbolism, and more than either by the fatal hiatus brought about through the loss of the earliest documents, there is enough evidence to show that a very strange leaven was working in the mass of the texts. Let me add in respect of it, with all necessary reservations and in no illiberal spirit, that the quality of this leaven can be appreciated scarcely by those who are unacquainted (*a*) with the inward phases of the life of Christian sanctity during the Middle Ages, after which period the voices sound uncertain and the consciousness of experience more remote, and (*b*) with the interior working of those concealed orders of which the Masonic experiment is a part only, and elementary at that. The most important lights are therefore either in the very old books or in the catholic motive which characterises secret rituals that, whether old or not, have never entered into the knowledge of the outside world.

The testimony is of two kinds invariably—first of all, to the existence of the Great Experiment and the success with which, under given circumstances, it can be carried to its term, and, secondly, to a great failure in respect of the external world. The one is reflected by the achieved Quest of the Holy Graal, and the other by the removal of the Graal. In respect of the one it is as if a great mystery had been communicated at one time in the external places, but as if the communication had afterwards been suspended, the secret had as if died. In respect of the other, it is as if the House of Doctrine had been voided. Did these statements exhaust the content of the alternatives, the testimony might be that of a sect, but we shall see at the proper time after what manner they conform to external doctrine, even if the keepers of that doctrine should themselves be unable to see the law of the union.

The great literatures and the great individual books may be often at this day as so many counters or heaps of letters put into the hands of the mystic, and he interprets them after his own manner, imparting to them that light which, at least intellectually, abides in himself. I make this formal statement because I realise that it is perilous for my position and because it enables me to add that though literatures may be clay in our hands, we must not suppose that they who in the first place put a shape of their own kind on the material which they had ingarnered were invariably conscious that it would bear that other seal and impression which we set upon it in our own minds as the one thing that is desirable. It is too much to suppose that behind the external sense of texts there was always designed that inward and illusory significance which in some of them we seem to trace so indubitably. The Baron de la Motte Fouqué once wrote a beautiful and knightly romance in which a correspondent discovered a subtle and complete allegory, and the author, who planned, when he wrote it, no subsurface meaning, did not less sincerely confess to the additional sense, explaining in reply that high art in literature is true upon all the planes. There are certain romances which are found to connect in this manner with the mystery of our science—that is to say, in the non-intentional way, and we must only be thankful to discern that there is the deep below the deep, without pressing interpenetration into a formal scheme. It is well to notice this position and thus go before a criticism which presents itself rather than calls to be sought out. The books of the Holy Graal are not exactly of this kind. A text which says that certain secret words were once imparted under very wonderful and exceptional circumstances is certainly obtruding a meaning behind meaning; another which affirms that a certain mythical personage was ordained secretly, owing to a similar intervention, and was made thereby the first Bishop of Christendom, manifests an ulterior motive, or there are no such motives in the world. And further, when the two great Quests of the whole literature are written partly in the form of confessed allegory, it is not unreasonable to infer that they had some such motive throughout; while, in fine, as their express, undisguised intention is to show the existence of an arch-natural Mass, the graces and the mysteries of which can be experienced and seen by some who are of perfect life, then the interpretation which illustrates this intention by the mystic side of Eucharistic doctrine in the Church offers a true construction, and its valid criticism is *vere dignum et justum est, æquum et salutare.* I will pour three cups to the health and coronation of him who shall discover the speculative proto-Perceval of primeval folk-lore, yet on the present subject let him and all other brethren in the holy places of research keep silence, unless God graces them with agreement. The unknown writers of the *Longer Prose Perceval* and the *Quest of Galahad* spoke of the Great Experiment as those who knew something of their theme and bore true witness on the term of the research.

We know in our own hearts that eternity is the sole thing which signifies ultimately and great literature should confess to no narrower horizon. It happens that they begin sometimes by proposing a lesser theme, but they are afterwards exalted; and this was the case with the Graal books, which were given the early legends of Perceval according to the office of Nature, but afterwards the legend of Galahad according to the Law of Grace.

V

THE MYSTERY OF FAITH

We have now reached a certain definite stage in the high debate and can institute a preliminary summary of the whole subject. It is known that the mystery of faith in Christianity is above all things the Eucharist, in virtue of which the Divine Master is ever present in his Church and is always communicated to the soul; but having regard to the interdictions of our age-long exile we receive only a substituted participation in the life of the union. The Graal mystery is the declared pageant of the Eucharist, which, in virtue of certain powers set forth under the veil of consecrating words, is in some way, not indeed a higher mystery than that of the external church, but its demonstration in the transcendant mode. We have only to remember a few passages in the *Book of the Holy Graal*, in the *Longer Prose Perceval*, and in the *Quest of Galahad* to understand the imputed distinction as: (*a*) The communication in the Eucharist of the whole knowledge of the universe from Aleph to Tau; (*b*) the communication of the Living Christ in the dissolution of the veils of Bread and Wine; (*c*) the communication of the secret process by which the soul passes under divine guidance from the offices of this world to heaven, the keynote being that the soul is taken when it asks into the great transcendence. This is the implied question of the Galahad legend as distinguished from the Perceval question. There are those who are called but not chosen at all, like Gawain. There are those who get near to the great mystery but have not given up all things for it, and of these is Lancelot. There is the great cohort, like the apocalyptic multitude which no man can number—called, elected and redeemed in the lesser ways, by the offices of the external Church—and of these is the great chivalry of the Round Table. There are those who go up into the Mountain of the Lord and return again, like Bors; they have received the last degrees, but their office is in this world. In fine, there are those who follow at a long distance in the steep path, and of these is the transmuted Perceval of the Galahad legend. It is in this sense that, exalted above all and more than all things rarefied into a great and high quintessence, the history of the Holy Graal becomes the soul's history, moving through a profound symbolism of inward being, wherein we follow as we can, but the vistas are prolonged for ever, and it well seems that there is neither a beginning to the story nor a descried ending.

We find also the shadows and tokens of secret memorials which have not been declared in the external, and by the strange things which are hinted, we seem to see that the temple of the Graal on Mont Salvatch is not otherwise than as the three tabernacles which it was proposed to build on Mount Tabor. Among indications of this kind there are two only that I can mention. As in the prologue to the *Book of the Holy Graal*, we have heard that the anonymous but not unknown hermit met on a memorable occasion with one who recognised him by certain signs which he carried, giving thus the unmistakable token of some instituted mystery in which both shared : as in the *Longer Prose Perceval* we have seen that there is an account of five changes in the Graal which took place at the altar, being five transfigurations, the last of which assumed the seeming of a chalice, but at the same time, instead of a chalice, was some undeclared mystery : so the general as well as the particular elements of the legend in its highest form offer a mystery the nature of which is recognised by the mystic through certain signs which it carries on its person ; yet it is declared in part only and what remains, which is the greater part, is not more than suggested. It is that, I believe, which was seen by the maimed King when he looked into the Sacred Cup and beheld the secret of all things, the beginning even and the end. In this sense the five changes of the Graal are analogous to the five natures of man, as these in their turn correspond to the four aspects of the Cosmos and that which rules all things within and from without the Cosmos. I conclude therefore that the antecedents of the Cup Legend are (1) *Calix meus quam inebrians est ;* (2) the Cup which does not pass away ; (3) the *vas insigne electionis.* The antecedent of the Graal question is : Ask, and ye shall receive. The antecedent of the Enchantment of Britain is the swoon of the sensitive life, and that of the adventurous times is : I bring not peace, but a sword ; I come to cast fire upon the earth, and what will I but that it should be enkindled ? The closing of these times is taken when the Epopt turns at the altar, saying *Pax Dei tecum.* But this is the peace which passes understanding and it supervenes upon the *Mors osculi*—the mystic

Thomas Vaughan's " death of the kiss "—after which it is exclaimed truly : " Blessed are the dead which die in the Lord from henceforth and for ever." It follows therefore that the formula of the Supernatural Graal is : *Panem cœlestem accipiam ;* that of the Natural Graal, namely, the Feeding Dish, is : *Panem nostrum quotidianum da nobis hodie ;* and the middle term : " Man doth not live by bread alone." I should add : These three there are one ; but this is in virtue of great and high transmutations. So, after all the offices of scholarship—pursued with that patience which wears out worlds of obstacles—it proves that there is something left over, that this something bears upon its surface the aspects of mystic life, that hereof is our heritage, and that we can enter and take possession because other claimants there are none. The books of the Holy Graal do tell us of a sanctuary within the sanctuary of Christendom, wherein there are reserved great sacraments, high symbols, relics that are of all most holy, and would be so accounted in all the external ways ; but of these things we have heard otherwise in certain secret schools. It follows therefore that we as mystics can lift up our eyes because there is a Morning Light which we go to meet with exultation, *portantes manipulos nostros.* We shall find the paths more easy because of our precursors, who have cleared the tangled ways and have set up landmarks and beacons, by which perchance we shall be led more straightly into our own, though in their clearing and surveying they did not at all know that they were working for us.

It is recognised by the Catholic Church that the Eucharist is at this time the necessity of our spiritual life, awaiting that great day when our daily bread shall itself become the Eucharist, no longer that substitute provided in our material toil and under the offices of which we die. The body is communicated to the body that the Spirit may be imparted to the soul. *Spiritus ipse Christi animæ infunditur,* and this is the illustration of ecstasy. But in these days—as I have hinted—it works only through the efficacy of a symbol, and this is why we cannot say in our hearts: *A carne nostro caro Christi ineffabile modo sentitur*, meaning *Anima sponsæ ad plenissimam in Christum transformationem sublimatur.* Hence, whether it is St. John of the Cross speaking of the Ascent of Mount Carmel or Ruysbroeck of the Hidden Stone, the discourse is always addressed to Israel in the wilderness, not in the Land of Promise. Hence also our glass of vision remains clouded, like the sanctuary ; and even the books of the mystics subsist under the law of the interdict and are expressed in the language thereof. Those of the Holy Graal are written from very far away in the terms of transubstantiation, presented thaumaturgically under all the veils of grossness, instead of the terms of the *Epiclesis* in the language of those who have been ordained with the holy oils of the Comforter. In other books the metaphysics of the Lover and the Beloved have been rendered in the tongue of the flesh, forgetting that it bears the same relation to the illusory correspondence of human unions that the Bread of the Eucharist bears to material nutriment. The true analogy is in the contradistinction between the elements of bodies and minds. The high analogy in literature is the Supper at the Second Table in the poem of Robert de Borron. That was a spiritual repast, where there was neither eating nor drinking. For this reason the symbolic fish upon the table conveyed to the Warden the title of Rich Fisher, and it is in this sense—that is to say, for the same reason—that the saints become Fishers of Men. We shall re-express the experience of the mystic life in terms that will make all things new when we understand fully what is implied by the secret words: *Co-opertus et absconditus sponsus.*

VI

THE LOST BOOK OF THE GRAAL

We have seen, in considering the claim of the Celtic Church to recognition as a possible guiding and shaping spirit of the Graal literature, that one speculation regarding it was the existence in concealment of a particular book, a liturgy of some kind, preferably a Book of the Mass. I have no definite concern in the hypothesis, as it is in no sense necessary to the interpretation which I place upon the literature; but the existence of one or more primordial texts is declared so invariably in the romances that, on the surface at least, it seems simpler to presume its existence, and it becomes thus desirable to ascertain what evidence there is otherwise to be gleaned about it. As it has been left so far by scholarship, the question wears almost an inscrutable or at least an inextricable aspect, and its connection with the mystic aspects of the Holy Graal may be perhaps rather adventitious than accidental, but it is introduced here as a preliminary to those yet more abstruse researches which belong to the ninth book.

We must in the first place set aside from our minds the texts which depend from one another, whether the earlier examples are extant or not. The vanished *Quest* of Guiot—priceless as its discovery would be—is not the term of our research. We must detach further those obviously fabulous chronicles by the pretence of which it is supposed that the several quests and histories were perpetuated for the enlightenment of posterity. No one is wondering seriously whether the knightly adventures of the Round Table were reduced into great chronicles by the scribes of King Arthur's court, for which assurance we have the evidence of the *Huth Merlin*—among several deponents. There are other sources which may be equally putative, but it is these which raise the ques-

tion, and I proceed to their enumeration as follows:
(1) That which contained the greatest secret of the
world, a minute volume which would lie in the hollow
of a hermit's hand—in a word, the text presupposed by
the prologue to the *Book of the Holy Graal*; (2) that which
is ascribed to Master Blihis—the *fabulator famosus*—by
the *Elucidation* prefixed to the *Conte del Graal*; (3) that
which is called the Great Book by Robert de Borron,
containing the Great Secret to which the term Graal
is referred, a book of many histories, written by many
clerks, and by him communicated apparently to his
patron, Walter Montbéliard; (4) that which the Count
of Flanders gave to Chrétien de Troyes with instructions
to retell it, being the best story ever recited in royal
court; (5) that which the Hermit Blaise codified with
the help of the secret records kept by the Wardens of
the Graal; (6) that which the author of the *Longer
Prose Perceval* refers to the saintly man whom he calls
Josephus; (7) that which the Jew Flegitanis transcribed
from the time-immemorial chronicles of the starry
heavens.

The palmary problem for our solution is, whether in
the last understanding a mystery book or a Mass book,
these cryptic texts can be regarded as "seven and yet
one, like shadows in a dream"—or rather, as many inventions concerning one document. If we summarise
the results which were obtained from them, we can
express them by their chief examples thus: (1) From
the prototype of the *Book of the Holy Graal* came
the super-apostolical succession, the ordination of
Joseph II., the dogma of transubstantiation manifested
arch-naturally, and the building of Corbenic as a Castle
of Perils and Wonders girt about the Holy Graal; (2)
from the prototype of the *Elucidation* we have the indicible secret of the Graal, the seven discoveries of its
sanctuary, the account of the Rich Fisherman's skill in
necromancy and his protean transformations by magical
art; (3) from the prototype of Robert de Borron we

have the Secret Words, by him or subsequently referred to Eucharistic consecration; (4) from the prototype of Chrétien we have the history of Perceval le Gallois, so far as it was taken by him; (5) from the putative chronicle of Blaise and his scribes, antecedent and concurrent, we have all that which belongs to the history of Merlin, the foundation of the Round Table and the Siege Perilous; (6) from the prototype of the *Longer Prose Perceval* we have Perceval's later history, his great and final achievements—unlike all else in the literature, more sad, more beautiful, more strange than anything told concerning him; (7) from the prototype of Guiot, we have the Graal presented as a stone, and with an ascribed antecedent history which is the antithesis of all other histories. Had I set up these varying versions in the form of seven propositions on the gates of Salerno or Salamanca and offered to maintain their identity in a thesis against all comers, I suppose that I could make out a case with the help of scholastic casuistry and the rest of the dialectical subtleties; but in the absence of all motive, and detached as regards the result, I can only say in all reason that the quests and the histories as we have them never issued from a single quest or a single history. We may believe, if we please, that the book of the Count of Flanders was really the *Quest* of Guiot, reducing the sources to six, and a certain ingenuity —with courage towards precarious positions—may help us to further eliminations, but the root-difficulty will remain—that the Quests, as we have them, exclude one another and so also do some of the histories. It follows that there were many prototypes, or alternatively that there were many inventions in respect of the sources. In respect of the Perceval legends there was the non-Graal folk-lore myth, which accounts for their root-matter but not for their particular renderings and their individual Graal elements; the nearest approximation to these myths and their nearest issue in time may have been the *Quest* of Guiot. One general source of De Borron was transparently the *Evangelium Nicodemi*, complicated by later Joseph legends, including the tradition of Fécamp, but more than all by another source, of which he had heard at a distance and of which I shall speak at the close. The *Quest of Galahad* makes no claim to a prototype, but it reflects extant manuscripts of the Greater Chronicles; for the rest, its own story was all important; it cared nothing for antecedents, and it is only by sporadic precaution, outside its normal lines, that it registers at the close after what manner it pretended to be reduced into writing. The prototypes of this text are in the annals of sanctity, except in so far as it reflects—and it does so indubitably—some rumours which Robert de Borron had drawn into romance. As regards Galahad himself, his romance is a great invention derived from the prose *Lancelot*. The *Longer Prose Perceval* is an invention after another manner; there is nothing to warrant us in attaching any credit to the imputed source in Josephus, but the book drew from many places and transmuted that which it drew with a shaping spirit; it is an important text for those rumours to which I have referred darkly. It works, like the *Quest of Galahad*, in a high region of similitude, and its pretended source is connected intimately with the second Joseph of the Greater Chronicles.

We are now in a position to deal with a further ascription which is so general in the literature and was once rather widely accepted—namely, that of a Latin source. It will be noted that this is a simple debate of language and it leaves the unity or multiplicity of the prototypes an open question. It is worth mentioning, because it enters into the history of the criticism of Graal literature. There is no need to say that it is now passed over by scholarship, and the first person to reject it was Robert Southey in his preface to the edition of Sir Thomas Malory's *Morte d'Arthur* which passes under his name, though he had no hand in the editing of the text itself. "I do not believe," he says, "that any of these romances ever existed in Latin,—by whom, or for whom, could they have been written in that language?" For the romances as romances, for *Meliadus de Leonnois*, *Gyron le Courtois*, and so forth, the question has one answer only, the fact notwithstanding that the prologue to *Gyron* draws all the prose tales of the Round Table from what it terms the Latin *Book of the Holy Graal*. There is one answer also for any version of the Graal legend, as we now know it. Even for that period, the Comte de Tressan committed a serious absurdity when he affirmed that the whole literature of Arthurian chivalry, derived by the Bretons from the ancient and fabulous chronicles of Melkin and Tezelin, was written in Latin by Rusticien de Pise, who was simply a compiler and translator into the Italian tongue and was concerned, as such, chiefly with the Tristram cycle. At the same time it is possible to take too extreme a view. In his preface to another work, *Palmerin of England*, Southey remarks that "every reader of romance knows how commonly they were represented as translations from old manuscripts," and that such an ascription, "instead of proving that a given work was translated, affords some evidence that it is original." The inference is worded too strongly and is scarcely serious as it stands, but the fact itself is certain; and indeed the Graal romances belong to a class of literature which was prone to false explanations in respect both of authorship and language. Still, there is something to be said for the middle ground suggested, now long ago, on the authority of Paulin Paris, that while it is idle to talk of romances in the Latin language, there is nothing impossible in the suggestion that the sacramental legend of Joseph of Arimathæa and his Sacred Vessel may have existed in Latin. From his point of view it was a Gradual, and he even goes so far as to speculate (*a*) that it was preserved at Glastonbury; (*b*) that it was not used by the monks because it involved schism with Rome; and (*c*) that, like the Jew of Toledo's transcript, it was forgotten for three centuries—till it was recalled by the quarrel between Henry II. and the Pope. This is, of course, fantasy, but the bare supposition of such a Latin legend would account in a natural manner for an ascription that is singularly consistent, while it would not pretend to represent the lost imaginary prototypes of the whole complex literature.

In this connection we might do worse than take warning by one lesson from the literature of alchemy. The early writers on this subject were in the habit of citing authorities who, because they could not be identified, were often regarded as mythical; but all the same they existed in manuscript; they might have been found by those who had taken the trouble; and they are now familiar to students by the edition of Berthelot. In matters of this kind we do not know what a day may bring forth, and from all standpoints the existence of a pious legend—orthodox or heretical, Roman or Breton—concerning Joseph and his Hallow would be interesting, as it must also be valuable. Unfortunately, the Quest of the Holy Graal in respect of its missing literature is after the manner of a greater enterprise, for there are many who follow it and few that come to the term of a new discovery. There are authorities now in England to whom the possibility of such a text might not be unacceptable, though criticism dwells rightly upon the fact that there is no mention of the Holy Vessel in the earliest apocryphal records of the evangelisation of Britain by Joseph. We have heard already of one Latin memorial among the archives of Fécamp, but of its date we know nothing, and its conversion legend does not belong to this island.

Having thus determined, as I think, the question of a single prototype accounting for all the literature, we have to realise that everything remains in respect of the mystery of origin—now the wonder element of things unseen and heard of dimly only, sometimes expressed imperfectly in Nature poems, which have no concern therein; now what sounds like a claim on behalf of the Celtic Church; now sacramental legends incorporated by Latin Christianity into the great body of romances. But I speak here of things which are approximate and explicable in an atmosphere of legend married to a definite world of doctrine. There is nothing in these to explain (*a*) the report of a secret sanctuary in all the texts without any exception whatever, for even the foolish *Crown of all Adventures* allocates its house of ghosts to the loneliest of all roads; (*b*) the Secret Words of Consecration; (*c*) the arch-natural Mass celebrated in three of the texts; (*d*) the hidden priesthood; (*e*) the claim to a holy and hidden knowledge; (*f*) the removal of this knowledge from concealment to further concealment, because the world was not worthy. These are the rumours to which I have alluded previously, and I have attached to them this name, because there is nothing more obvious in the whole cycle of literature than the fact that those who wrote of them did not—for the most part—know what they said. Now, it is a canon of reasonable criticism that writers who make use of materials which they do not understand are not the inventors thereof. It had never entered into the heart of Robert de Borron that his Secret Words reduced the ordinary Eucharist to something approaching a semblance; to the putative Walter Map that his first Bishop of Christendom put the whole Christian apostolate into an inferior place; to any one of the romancers that his Secret Sanctuary was the claim of an orthodoxy in transcendence; to the authors in particular of the *Longer Prose Perceval* and the *Quest of Galahad* that their implied House of the Hallows came perilously near to the taking of the heart out of Christendom. So little did these things occur to them that their materials are mismanaged rather seriously in consequence. Had the first Bishop of Christendom ordained those whom he intended to succeed him, I should not bring this charge against the author of that text which presents the consecration of the second Joseph in all its sanctity and wonder. But, as a matter of fact, the custody of the Holy Graal passed into the hands of a layman, and we are offered the picture of a priest anointed by Christ who does not even baptize, a hermit on one occasion being obtained to administer this simplest of all the sacraments. And yet this first bishop of Christendom had ordained many and enthroned some at Sarras. There is a similar crux in the *Lesser Holy Graal* and its companion poem. One would have thought that the possession of the Secret Words would be reserved to those bearing the seal of the priesthood; but it is not suggested that Joseph of Arimathæa was either ordained by Christ or by any bishop of the Church; his successor, Brons, was simply a disciple saved out of rejected Jerusalem; and Perceval, the *tiers hons*, was a knight of King Arthur's court. Of two things, therefore, one: either the makers of romance who brought in these elements knew not what they said, and reflected at a far distance that which they had heard otherwise, or the claims are not that which they appear on the surface; beneath them there is a deeper concealment; there was something behind the Eucharistic aspect of the mysterious formula and something behind the ordination in transcendence; there was in fine a more secret service than that of the Mass. I accept the first alternative, but without prejudice to the second, which is true also, as we shall see later, still on the understanding that what subtended was not in the mind of romance.

If it is necessary or convenient to posit the existence of a single primordial book, then the *Sanctum Graal, Liber Gradalis,* or *Missa de Corpore Christi* contained these elements, and it contained nothing or little of the diverse matter in the literature. It was not a liturgy connected with the veneration of a relic or of certain relics; it did not recite the legend of Joseph or account in what manner soever for the conversion of Britain. It was a Rite of the Order of Melchisedech and it communicated the arch-natural sacrament *ex hypothesi*. The prologue to the *Book of the Holy Graal* has what one would be inclined to call a rumour of this Mass, after which there supervened an ecstasy as a foretaste of the Divine Rapture. The term thereof was the Vision which is He, and the motive of the dilucid experience is evaded—consciously or not, but, I say, in truth unconsciously—by the substitute of reflections upon difficulties concerning the Trinity. No Graal writer had ever seen this book, but the rumour of it was about in the world. It was held in reserve not in a monastery at Glastonbury, but by a secret school of Christians whose position in respect of current orthodoxy was that of the apex to the base of any perfect triangle—its completion and not its destruction. There was more of the rumour abroad than might have been expected antecedently, as if a Church of St. John the Divine were planted somewhere in the West, but not in the open day. There was more of the rumour, and some makers of texts had heard more than others. We know that in the prologue to the *Book of the Holy Graal* there is what might be taken as a reference to this company, the members of which were sealed, so that they could recognise one another by something which they bore upon their persons. When, in the *Quest of Galahad*, the nine strange knights came from the East and the West and the North and the South to sit down, or to kneel rather, at the Table of the Graal, they entered without challenge, they took their proper places and were saluted and welcomed, because they also bore the seal of the secret order. King Pelles went out because he was not on the Quest, because his part was done, because he had attained and seen, for which reason he departed as one who says: *Nunc dimittis Servum tuum, Domine, secundum verbum tuum in pace: quia viderunt oculi mei*—elsewhere or earlier—*salutare tuum*. The minstrels and romancers knew little enough of these mysteries, for the most part, and on the basis of the rumours of the book they superposed what they had heard otherwise—the legend of Joseph, the cultus of the Precious Blood, clouds of fables, multiples of relics, *hoc genus omne.* But it is to be noted in fine that the withdrawal into deeper concealment referred more especially to the company as a hidden school, which would be sought and not found, unless God led the quester. And perhaps those who came into contact by accident did not always ask the question : Who administers the Mysteries ? Yet, if they were elected they were brought in subsequently.

It will be observed that in this speculation the existence of the rumours which were incorporated does not in a strict sense involve the existence of any book to account for their comparative prevalence.

VII

THE DECLARED MYSTERY OF QUEST

There follow in this place certain exotics of the subject which are not put forward as an integral part thereof, but are offered to those only who are concerned in the rumour of the Graal literature—as expressed in this book—so far as it incorporates that literature in the annals of Christian sanctity. They will know that the sins and imperfections of this our human life are attenuated by the turning of our intellectual part towards the Blessed Zion, and that, next after leading the all-hallowed life, the making of holy books to formulate the aspirations of our best part in its best moments is counted in a man towards righteousness. It is well, indeed, for him whose life is dedicated to the Quest, but at least— in the stress and terror of these our wayward times—in the heart and the inmost heart let us keep its memory green.

1. Faith is the implicits of the mind passing into expression formally, and knowledge is the same implicits certified by experience. It is in this sense that

God recompenses those who seek Him out. The Mystery of the Holy Graal is the sun of a great implicit rising in the zones of consciousness.

2. If, therefore, from one point of view we are dealing with great speculations, from another we are truly concerned with great certainties; and Galahad did not question or falter.

3. There is nothing in the world which has less to do with a process or other conventions and artifices than the ascent of a soul to light. Thus, the Quest had no formulæ.

4. The mistake which man has made has been to go in search of his soul, which does not need finding but entering only, and that by a certain door which is always open within him. All the doors of Corbenic were open when Lancelot came thereto, even that sanctuary into which he could look from afar but wherein he could not enter. The chief door is inscribed: *Sapida notitia de Deo.*

5. It is understood, however, that before the door is reached there are gates which are well guarded. So on a night at midnight, when the moon shone clear, Lancelot paused at the postern, which opened toward the sea, and saw how two lions guarded the entrance.

6. It is true also that the gates are not opened easily by which the King of Glory comes in; yet we know that the King comes. The key of these gates is called *Voluntas inflammata.* This will works on the hither side, but there is another which works on the further, and this is named *Beneplacitum termino carens.* When the gates open by the concurrence of the two powers, the King of Salem comes forth carrying Bread and Wine. Of the communication which then follows it is said: *Gustari potest quod explicari nequit.* Galahad and his fellows did taste and saw that the Lord is sweet.

7. For the proselytes of the gate which is external and the postulants at the pronaos of the temple, the Crucifixion took place on Calvary. For the adepts and the

epopts, the question, if it can be said to arise, is not whether this is true on the plane of history, but in what manner it signifies, seeing that the great event of all human history began at the foundation of the world, as it still takes place daily in the soul of every man for whom the one thing needful is to know when Christ shall arise within him. It is then that those on the Quest can say with Sir Bors: "But God was ever my comfort."

8. All that we forget is immaterial if that which we remember is vital, as, for example, the Lord of Quest, who said: "Therefore I wote wel whan my body is dede, my sowle shalle be in grete joye to see the blessid Trynyte every day, and the mageste of oure lord Jhesu Cryst"—in other words, *Contemplatio perfectissima et altissima Dei.*

9. The first condition of interior progress is in detachment from the lesser responsibilities which—because they have not entered into the heart of hearts—are external to our proper interests and distract from those high and onerous burdens which we have to carry on our road upward, until such time as even the road itself—and the burdens thereto belonging—shall assume and transport us. From the greatest even to the least the missions of knight-errantry were followed in utter detachment, and those who went on the Quest carried no *impedimenta.* So also is the great silence ordained about those who would hear the *interior Dei locutio altissimi.*

10. The generation of God is outward and so into the estate of man; but the generation of man—which is called also rebirth—is inward, and so into the Divine Union. The great clerks wrote the adventures of the Graal in great books, but there was no rehearsal of the last branch, the first rubric of which would read: *De felicissima animæ cum Deo unione.*

11. Most conventions of man concern questions of procedure, and it is so with the things which are above, for we must either proceed or perish. Sir Gawain turned back, and hence he was smitten of the old wound

that Lancelot gave him; but no knight who achieved the Quest died in arms, unless in Holy War.

12. In the declared knowledge which behind it has the hidden knowledge, blood is the symbol of life, and this being so it can be understood after what manner the Precious Blood profiteth and the Reliquary thereof. The other name of this Reliquary is Holy Church. But such are the offices of its mercy that *in examine mortis* even Gawain received his Saviour.

13. The root from which springs the great tree of mysticism is the old theological doctrine that God is the centre of the heart. He is by alternative the soul's centre. This is the ground of the union: *per charitatem justi uniuntur cum Deo.* Gawain entreated Lancelot to "praye some prayer more or lesse for my soule;" King Arthur as he drifted in the dark barge said to Bedivere: "And yf thou here neuer more of me praye for my soule," but Perceval and Galahad knew that their reward was with them; they asked for no offerings and no one wearied Heaven.

14. In the soul's conversion there is no office of time, and this is why the greatest changes are always out of expectation. The Graal came like angels—unawares. The *castissimus et purissimus amplexus* and the *felix osculum* are given as in the dark and suddenly. There is further nothing in the wide world so swift and so silent as the *illapsus Christi in centrum animæ.* So also it is said of Galahad that "sodenely his soule departed."

15. The five changes of the Graal are analogous to the five natures of man, and these in their turn correspond to the four aspects of the cosmos and that which rules all things within and from above the cosmos.

16. The consideration of eternity arises from that of the Holy Graal, as from all literature at its highest, and if I have set it as the term of my own researches, in this respect, it is rather because it has imposed itself than because I have sought it out.

Mystic Aspects of the Graal Legend

Obiter Dicta.

And now as the sum total of these mystical aspects, the desire of the eyes in the seeking and finding of the Holy Graal may, I think, be re-expressed as follows :—

Temple or Palace or Castle—Mont Salvatch or Corbenic —wherever located and whether described as a wilderness of building, crowded burg or simple hermit's hold— there is one characteristic concerning the sanctuary which, amidst all its variations in the accidents, is essentially the same ; the Keeper of the great Hallows has fallen upon evil days ; the means of restoration and of healing are, as one would say, all around him, yet the help must come from without ; it is that of his predestined successor, whose office is to remove the vessel, so that it is henceforth never seen so openly. Taking the Quest of Galahad as that which has the highest significance spiritually, I think that we may speak of it thus :—We know that in the last analysis it is the inward man who is really the Wounded Keeper. The mysteries are his ; on him the woe has fallen ; it is he who expects healing and redemption. His body is the Graal Castle, which is also the castle of Souls, and behind it is the Earthly Paradise as a vague and latent memory. We may not be able to translate the matter of the romance entirely into mystical symbolism, since it is only a rumour at a distance of life in the spirit and its great secrets. But, I think, we can see that it all works together for the one end of all. He who enters into the consideration of this secret and immemorial house under fitting guidance shall know why it is that the Graal is served by a pure maiden, and why that maiden is ultimately dispossessed. Helayne is the soul, and the soul is in exile because all the high unions have been declared voided—the crown has been separated from the kingdom, and experience from the higher knowledge. So long as she remained a pure virgin, she was more than a thyrsus bearer in the mysteries, but the morganatic marriage of mortal life is part of her doom. This is still a high destiny, for the soul out of earthly experience brings forth spiritual desire, which is the quest of the return journey, and this is Galahad. It is therefore within the law and the order that she has to conceive and bring him forth. Galahad represents the highest spiritual aspirations and desires passing into full consciousness, and so into attainment. But he is not reared by his mother, because Eros, which is the higher knowledge, has dedicated the true desire to the proper ends thereof. It will be seen also what must be understood by Lancelot in secret communication with Helayne, though he has taken her throughout for another. The reason is that it is impossible to marry even in hell without marrying that seed which is of heaven. As she is the psychic woman, so is he the natural man, or rather the natural intelligence which is not without its consecrations, not without its term in the highest. Helayne believes that her desire is only for Lancelot, but this is because she takes him for Eros, and it is by such a misconception that the lesser Heaven stoops to the earth ; herein also there is a sacred dispensation, because so is the earth assumed. I have said that Lancelot is the natural man, but he is such merely at the highest ; he is born in great sorrow, and she who has conceived him saves her soul alive amidst the offices of external religion. He is carried into the lesser land of Faerie, as into a garden of childhood. When he draws towards manhood, he comes forth from the first places of enchantment and is clothed upon by the active duties of life as by the vestures of chivalry. He enters also into the unsanctified life of sense, into an union against the consecrated life and order. But his redeeming quality is that he is faithful and true, because of which, and because of his genealogy, he is chosen to beget Galahad, of whom he is otherwise unworthy, even as we all, in our daily life, fall short of the higher aspirations of the soul. As regards the Keeper, it is certain that he must die and be replaced by another Keeper before the true man can be raised, with the holy things to him belonging, which Hallows are indeed withdrawn, but it is with and in respect of him only, for the keepers are a great multitude, though it is certain that the Graal is one. The path of quest is the path of upward progress, and it is only at the great height that Galahad knows himself as really the Wounded Keeper and that thus, in the last resource, the physician heals himself. Now this is the mystery from everlasting, which is called in the high doctrine *Schema misericordiæ*. It is said : *Latet, æternumque latebit*, until it is revealed in us ; and as to this : *Te rogamus, audi nos.*

BOOK IX

SECRET TRADITION IN CHRISTIAN TIMES

THE ARGUMENT

I. PRELIMINARY TO THE WHOLE SUBJECT.—*The atmosphere of the Middle Ages—After what manner the subsurface meanings in Graal books suggest the possibility of other concealments in literature about the same period—Mediæval mystic thought—Independent schools—The purpose of the present consideration—The assumption of a Secret Tradition—A question which arises therefrom—Multiplicity of traditions—A distinction between occult and mystic schools.* II. SOME ALLEGED SECRET SCHOOLS OF THE MIDDLE AGES.—*Albigensian sects and the misconceptions concerning them—Foolish attempt to connect them with the literature of the Holy Graal—The test question of Eucharistic doctrine in heresies—The Eucharist among the Manichæans—Albigenses from a Protestant standpoint—Various forms of the heresy—Persecution of all and sundry—The crusade under Innocent III.—Documentary evidence concerning points of Albigensian belief—The hostile evidence—On either assumption the Albigenses offer nothing to our purpose—The doctrine of transubstantiation—The speculations of Aroux—And those of the elder Rossetti—The argument from the Divine Comedy—Confusions on the subject of the Graal—Thesis concerning chivalry—An analogy from another controversy—General conclusion on the subject.* III. THE LATIN LITERATURE OF ALCHEMY AND THE HERMETIC SECRET IN THE LIGHT OF THE EUCHARISTIC MYSTERY.—*Development of two concurrent*

517

The Hidden Church of the Holy Graal

secret schools at the period of the Graal—*The claim of alchemy on the surface—The subsurface claim developed in later times—Declared object of the present research—Analogies of the arch-natural Eucharist—Correspondence with the notion of a voided House of Doctrine—Position of alchemy in respect of the first instance and of Kabalism in respect of the second—The period of transition in Hermetic literature—Byzantine Alchemy—Difficulties of the subject—The two schools of the Art—Their modern representatives—The terminology common to both—The one vessel—The alchemical matter—The Three Principles—Correspondences with the Holy Eucharist—Further concerning the alchemical matter—The Art as a Mystery of the Soul—Of purgations in Alchemy—Their correspondence in the experience of conversion—The Hermetic Stone—The Elixir—Of man as the whole Subject of the Art—Schedule of the chief process—Further concerning Eucharistic analogies—Distinctions in the order of symbolism—Summary of the catholic interpretation.* IV. THE KABALISTIC ACADEMIES. *—Of the Secret Language—The Mystery of Loss—The early schools of Kabalism—Its Theosophical Scheme—Of that which was taken from the Sanctuary of Israel—Analogies with Graal legend—The Holy Name—Accidental analogies between Graal and Kabalistic legend—Absence of all communication between the school of theosophy and the school of romance—Of Jewry in Spain and Southern France during the Middle Ages—Practical independence of all the coincident schools—The mind of Kabalism.* V. THE CLAIM IN RESPECT OF TEMPLAR INFLUENCE.— *An illustration of the romance of history—The Templars and the Latin Church—After what manner the Temple has been brought within the chain of the Secret Tradition—The Graal and Templarism—Nature of one hypothesis—*

The Argument

BOOK IX

I

PRELIMINARY TO THE WHOLE SUBJECT

THOUGHT in the Middle Ages moved, like external science, through a world of mystery, and the Christ-light moved through the mist-light filling the bounds of sense with the shapes and symbols of vision. It follows, and this naturally, that most things seemed possible at a period when all things were dubious in respect of knowledge and apart from the power of religion, which tinged life itself with the lesser elements of ecstasy, there was the kind of enchantment which dwells always about the precincts of unknown vistas. Apart also from the shapes of imagination, there were the extravagances of minds seeking emancipation from law and authority, more especially in the matters of faith. The Books of the Holy Graal do not belong to the last category, but after their own manner they are like echoes from far away, because even as the secrets of the Greater Mysteries have not been written, and the Holy Assemblies do not issue proceedings, so the higher life of sanctity and the experiment towards that term, whether manifested in books of mystical theology or in books of romance, reach only a partial expression. The value of the Graal legends is like the value of other legends—I mean, in the mind of the mystic at this day : it is resident in the suggestions and the lights

521

which it can afford us for the maintenance of the great, implied concordat which constitutes the Divine Alliance. Having found that we are dealing with a body of writing which puts forth the rumour of strange claims and suggests concealed meanings, having found also that it is a literature which was acquired as if almost with a conscious intention to develop these particular interests, and being desirous of knowing the kind of intervention and the particular motives which were at work, if this indeed be possible, we are naturally disposed to ask whether there were other concealed literatures at the same period, and what light—if any—they cast upon these questions. The great school of Christian mystic thought within the official church was concerned wholly with a mystery of sanctity, the term of which was identical with the object that I have sought to put forward as the term of the Graal quest; but it had no secret claim and no concealed motive. We cannot, therefore, explain the one in a complete simplicity by the other, though we know in a general sense that it was from the other that the one issued. There were, however, independent schools of literature belonging to the same period which do give us certain lights, because, in the last resource, they did come, one and all, out of the same sanctuary; and it is obviously reasonable to suppose that so far as there are difficulties in the one path we may receive help from the collateral paths and thus attain some better understanding of the whole. If a particular spirit or secret mind, school or sodality, took over the old folk-lore legends, infusing a new motive therein, which motive is akin to the purpose discernible in coincident literatures, that which intervened in the one case was probably in relation with the others. I propose, therefore, to consider these extrinsic schools shortly, and to show that throughout a number of centuries we can trace successively the same implicits, it being understood that they are always put forward in a different way. In this manner we shall come to see that there have been several interventions, but taking place under such circumstances that those who intervened may have been always the same secret school, on the understanding that this school does not correspond to a corporate institution and never spoke officially. It is necessary, however, to deal in the first place with one attempt to account for the Graal literature which has been already put forward, because there are certain directions in which it is idle to look and it is well to know concerning them. Prior to the settlement of this preliminary question in the section that next follows, there is a specific point that demands our attention at the moment, and it can be stated in a few words. On the assumption that there has been a Secret Tradition perpetuated through Christian times, the place of which is in the West, it seems desirable to understand what part of it matters vitally in respect of our own subject. There are several schools of secret literature, and each of them, under its proper veil, has perpetuated something belonging to its particular order. There are, for example, the schools of magic, and it is these precisely that embody nothing to our purpose ; they constitute heresies of occult practice which find their strict correlation in the external heresies of doctrine, wherein also there is no light, as we shall see immediately. If the resolution has not been made already, and that definitely, it is time—and it is high time—that the whole domain of phenomenal occultism should be transferred to the care of psychological science, with the hope that it will pursue that path of research into the nature of man and his environment which less accredited investigations of the past have proved productive. They are no part of the mystic work and, having regard to the extent of our preoccupations, it is fortunate that neither approximately nor remotely do they enter into the subject of those schools of thought, the remains of which may cast a certain light upon the greater implicits of the Graal literature.

II

SOME ALLEGED SECRET SCHOOLS OF THE MIDDLE AGES

Perhaps no Christian sect has been the subject of more foolish misapprehension than the Albigenses, and this on all sides, but more especially on the part of writers who represent the borderland of mystic thought. Against the iniquity of Albigensian persecution in the past, we have later the folly, not unmixed with dishonesty, of the Protestant apologists ; but worse perhaps than the rest is that folly which has attempted to connect the sect and its exponents in the twelfth and thirteenth centuries with the literature of the Holy Graal. The initial impulse in this direction is found in speculations, criticisms and modes of interpretation with which France made us familiar about the middle of the nineteenth century, and this leading has been followed by a few writers in England who scarcely know their subject, and offer reflections of opinion which has risen up in obscure and unaccepted places. For the purpose of this investigation I care nothing whether the Albigenses were pure Christians, as pure Christianity is understood according to sectarian canons, or whether they were Manichæans. The all-important question is the light under which they presented Eucharistic doctrine, and from this standpoint it is certain that they could have had no connection with the development of the Graal cycle. If they were Manichæans, they had a voided and tinkered Eucharist, from which nothing follows in connection with that mystery. If, on the other hand, they were the Protestants of their period, they would as such deny most of the sacraments, and in respect of doctrine, at least, they would have tampered doubtless with the Eucharist. Setting aside for a moment some

French speculations which have nothing to tell us regarding Albigensian teachings, and deal only, as we shall see later, with a particular construction of a great body of romantic literature, it may be said—and is necessary to note in order to clear the issues—that the Protestant standpoint in all matters of this kind has been naturally one of opposition to the Latin Church, and to the Church theory that the Albigensians, including the Paulicians, who were their predecessors, were Manichæans, while the connected sect of Waldenses, or disciples of Peter Valdo, were originally Donatists. With these questions in themselves we have no concern, nor yet with the old egregious contention that there was a line of succession in perpetuity from Apostolic times through the Waldensians. There is no reason to suppose that the hypothesis was true, and it matters little if it was. I place in the same category one not less preposterous supposition—that the Vaudois had been located in the Cottian Alps since the times of the Apostles, and that their system had never varied from the tenets and practices of primitive Christianity. It is not of necessity a seal or mark of favour if these facts are undoubted ; actually, they are questionable enough, like the apologetical *pièce de résistance* which accounts for the smallness of the Vaudois community by inferring from the Apocalypse that the Church during a certain disastrous period would be reduced within very narrow limits, and that for this reason—among reasons not less logical— Vaudois, Waldenses and Albigenses constituted during such period the sole and truly Catholic Church. If majorities are usually in the wrong, it is not less true that some minorities are foolish and wild in their notions, as expressed by those who are their mouthpiece. Another contention connects the so-called Waldensian Church with the Church Primitive through the Albigenses, and if the last sect had really the Paulicians for their ancestors they date back to a considerable antiquity, while, as regards distribution, it is said that the earlier heresy had its conventicles established all the way from Thrace to Gascony. They came from the East originally, or this is their legend, but their traces have disappeared, supposing that the story is true outside the imagination of apologists. However this may be, the Paulicians, so far as history is concerned, arose in Armenia, where they were founded by one Constantine about the middle of the seventh century. They were mixed up with the Milesians, who made common cause with Constantine, but they were proscribed by the Emperors of Byzantium and the heretic was himself put to death. The same Paulicians have been identified with the Cathari, and these are said to have been in union with the Waldenses, whose first stronghold was among the Alpine valleys of Pied-mont. On the other hand, the Paterins, whose chain of dissemination is affirmed to have extended from Bulgaria through Lombardy to the Atlantic, have been represented as a variety of the Albigensian sect, if not identical therewith. These views constitute a cloud upon the dubious sanctuary, in respect of its origin. Other accounts say that they appeared in Italy during the first years of the eleventh century, with which may be compared the counter-suggestion that their most probable founder was Peter of Lyons more than a hundred years later. Persecution may well have joined distinct elements of sect till they became merged in one another; it caused them also to move, like the Graal, westward, and thus they entered Southern France, where those who had pre-existed under more than one name received the title of Albigenses—as it is thought, from their headquarters at Albi. Here also they fell under proscription, and because at that period men believed—and never more strongly—that they were doing God's work by annihilating those who worshipped Him under another code of doctrine, we learn of St. Dominic fighting the heresy with other weapons than the Sword of the Spirit—in the belief that there also might be either the Word of God, or its convenient substitute. This was under Innocent III., who proclaimed the first crusade against the Albigenses, its leader being Simon, Count of Montfort. The crusade began about 1213, and Folquet—the troubadour Bishop of Marseilles—was one of its most violent partisans. It was in the course of this villainous business that the Castle of Montseques—or Mont Ségur—which a few zealous, indiscriminating minds have sought to identify with Mont Salvatch—was stormed and burnt with many of the Perfect Brethren, including the Lady Esclairmonde. So do official churches illustrate their construction of the mystic paradox concerning the Prince of Peace, who came with a sword. That the gates of hell do not prevail against the true Church seems without prejudice to the counter-fact that there are times and seasons when perdition itself rises up, as one might say, in the external sanctuary itself, and God knows that if ever there was a period when the mystery of all iniquity came from the deeps in its power, the time was the thirteenth century, and the places were Provence and Languedoc.

If we set aside every thesis of apologists, it is possible to obtain from documents a certain first-hand impression concerning Albigensian beliefs. On the basis of their own confessions they denied Manichæan connections and principles, claiming to follow primitive Christian teaching as they constructed it from the New Testament or certain parts thereof, since it does not appear that they accepted all the epistles. It is possible, however, that their real views were concealed even in their confessions, and though to us the question does not signify in either alternative, it is out of this view that the counter-hypothesis arises, which is that of the accusing voice testifying in the church that destroyed them. A Dominican missionary and inquisitor, who recounted, in a poem which has survived, his controversy with an Albigensian theologian, accuses the sect (1) of denying baptism and regarding Satan as the creator of this world ;

(2) of rejecting confession and teaching that those who had sons and daughters were outside the pale of salvation ; (3) of claiming inspiration from the Holy Spirit and making a traffic therein amongst its disciples ; (4) of denying the resurrection and affirming that the souls of the redeemed would assume a new body, having a certain resemblance to the old and yet differing therefrom ; and in fine (5) of maintaining that the souls of men are those of lost angels—the difficulty about this, in the mind of the Dominican, being apparently that we have no recollection of our past. The importance of this text is that although it embodies accusations included in the proscription of the sect it may also have reflected current fluidic opinions in orthodox circles at the period. Other accusations affirm (*a*) that the Baptism which was recognised by the Albigenses was that of Fire or of the Spirit, recalling the mysterious office of the Paraclete which is often a subject of reference in the Graal literature ; (*b*) that the wandering preachers of the sect distributed nourishment for the body as well as the Bread of Angels—here recalling the twofold ministry of the Graal ; (*c*) that they rejected the books of Moses ; (*d*) that they regarded this sublunary world as the only hell ; (*e*) that their subsurface working was that of a new and secret priesthood which was to dispossess and succeed the papal hierarchy, as if here also there was a special succession from the apostles having kinship with the super-apostolical succession of the Graal priesthood.

Such fantastic analogies notwithstanding, it is clear that the sects of Southern France—as presented by either hypothesis—offer nothing to our purpose. From eclectic Gnosticism, which took over from Christianity that which coincided with its purpose, to Vaudois and Lollards, there is not one which sought to develop or exalt the sacramental teaching of the ancient Church. I know that, on the authority of Origen, the Marcionites taught the communication to the soul of man of a

Divine and Sanctifying Spirit added by the Redeemer, Who imparted it in the Eucharist, and if this meant the descent of the Paraclete, the perpetuation of such a doctrine might help us to understand why the Voice of the Graal was that of the Holy Ghost and yet in some mysterious way was that also of Christ. But of such perpetuation there is no trace whatever. As regards the Albigenses, it is certain historically that they denied transubstantiation, though they accepted some qualified sacramental teaching concerning the Lord's Supper, which they commemorated in the woods and forests on a cloth spread upon the ground. It is worse than idle to suppose that they had any connection with the Graal cycle, and this would remain substantially true if, by a wild supposition, we elected to suppose that Guiot, with his Provençal connections, was a member of their sect, and—going still further—if we suggested that his poem conveyed, after some hidden manner, a part of Albigensian teaching. That it did nothing of the kind is clear on the evidence of Wolfram. The poem is lost, or at least withdrawn for a period, like the Graal itself, and though we cannot speak certainly on most matters which concern it, on this one matter there does not seem room for doubt.

For the rest, the Albigenses were a sect without a literature, except in so far as that of the Troubadours at the period may have been—and this is likely enough —an occasional spokesman among them. Contemporary chroniclers estimated that all the principal minstrels, except two, were on the side of the sect ; these exceptions were Izarn and Fulke. The conquest of Toulouse extinguished the literature and even the language of Southern France, as also its chivalry.

I should now be justified in regarding the whole matter as determined in the negative sense, but a word must be said to dispose of that other claim to which I adverted at the beginning. It took, as I have hinted, all chivalrous romance for its province, and it claimed to have demonstrated that a vast European literature had been written by Albigenses for the edification of Albigenses and to put forth in a veiled manner Albigensian doctrine. There are certain precursors who do not prepare the way, but they open up issues which end either in a *cul de sac* or take the seeker through by-paths which can be followed interminably without leading to a true goal. The author of this demonstration was E. Aroux, who published in 1858 the *Mysteries of Chivalry and of Platonic Love in the Middle Ages*. Its inspiration in chief was derived from Gabriele Rossetti and particularly from the *Antipapal Spirit which preceded the Reformation*. Both works have exercised an influence on certain schools of occult thought in England; but Rossetti does not speak of the Graal, and hence there is no call that here I should speak of him. The monument of M. Aroux was preceded by other of his works designed to show that Dante was (*a*) heretical, revolutionary and socialistic; (*b*) connected with an alleged fusion between the Albigenses, Templars and Ghibellines for the creation of Freemasonry; (*c*) himself so far implicated in Freemasonry that the *Divine Comedy* is really Masonic in its purpose. In further support of these views Aroux had translated the whole *Commedia* into literal French verse and had commented on it " according to the spirit." Finally, he had instituted comparisons between Dante and the writers of the Graal cycle. It thus came about that the products of this cycle were included by his general ingarnering, but he shows little familiarity with his subject, and he wrote at a period when the literature was still practically unprinted. He affirms, absurdly enough, that the Holy Graal was a mysterious association and that the mission of its initiates was " to recover the vessel of truth with luminous characters wherein was received the Precious Blood of the Saviour." According to his peculiar canon of criticism this signified the design of " leading back the Christian Church to apostolic times and the faithful observation of the Gospel precepts." M. Aroux wrote as a defender of the Roman Church, and, after all that has been said and done upon the whole subject, it has not occurred to any one—perhaps least of all to him—that the true mission of the Church may have been to get away from apostolic times and to put aside, like St. Paul, in its maturity the things which belong to the child. For the rest, M. Aroux confused in a grotesque manner the Graal knights with those of the Round Table, and appeared to suppose that the *Parsifal* and *Titurel* are representative of the entire literature.

As regards chivalry, his thesis can be stated shortly : The actual, historical, feudal chivalry was an institution more or less savage, and the chivalry set forth in the romances had no existence on earth. This is equivalent to saying that the heroes and heroines of Mrs. Radcliffe, the modes and manners which she depicts, the spirit which characterises her episodes, perhaps even the scenes which she describes so graphically at hearsay, are never found in real life, though sentimentalism is always sentimentalism, mountains are always mountains, and as regards the Pyrenees in particular they are situated indubitably between France and Spain. The thing goes without saying in each case, for the romance, one would say, is—well, precisely a romance. But on the basis of this transparent fact, M. Aroux builds his theory that the books of chivalry were the *corpus doctrinale* and literary body-politic of the Protestantism of its period, reduced to this resource because of the intolerant powers that were. And this is just what appears to be so highly ridiculous, not because a literature cannot have concealed motives, or that of the Graal among them, but because it could be shown in a still more conclusive manner that the *Confessional of the Black Penitents* was the final rescript of the followers of Manes. And this seems to be intolerable.

Speaking generally as to the canon of criticism, it is

in all respects like that of the late Mrs. Henry Pott in the Bacon and Shakespeare controversy : he, as she, proves far too much for his own credit. If the canons of Mrs. Pott demonstrate that Bacon was the concealed author of the disputed plays, then the same canons show that he must have written the works of Marlowe, Massinger, Ford, and nearly all Elizabethan literature. In the same way, the evidences adduced by M. Aroux are either insufficient to prove his point, or alternatively a similar scheme has given us the *Nights* of Straparola, the *Nibelungen Sagas*, the *Romance of the Rose*, and the entire literature of the Troubadours, to say nothing of the Welsh *Mabinogion*, *Reynard the Fox*, and things innumerable of the German Minnesingers. This is indeed the express thesis of M. Aroux, and the only reason that he omitted the Latin literature of alchemy is because he had not come across it. There is no need to outline the nature of his evidences, but, to speak generally concerning it, the same canons might be applied with the same success to Mrs. Radcliffe's *Romance of the Forest* and to the *Mysteries of Udolpho*. The principle, in other words, repeats itself.

I should not have dealt with these fantastic matters except for the interest which they once raised in schools which draw from my own and because in the last resource they are an attempt, after their own manner, to show the hand of supposed secret schools in the development of the Graal literature. I now conclude as follows : (*a*) That the chivalry of all the romances was an ideal conception, corresponding as much and as little to the subject-matter of any other cycle of romance ; and (*b*) that the historical chivalry of the period corresponded to the idea which we obtain of the period by reading old chronicles, like those of Froissart. For the rest, M. Aroux's canon of interpretation is simple exceedingly : (*a*) any heroine of the romances signifies the Albigensian pseudo-church ; (*b*) any hero signifies one of its apostles or teachers ; (*c*) the enemies of both are the dominant, opposing Church ; (*d*) the Holy Vase of the Graal is its divine and hidden doctrine.   I can imagine, in byways of literature, the stories of Captain Macheath, Claude Duval and Richard Turpin interpreted along analogous lines—for example, as the records of a secret attempt to re-establish the Roman hierarchy in England.

III

THE LATIN LITERATURE OF ALCHEMY AND THE HERMETIC SECRET IN THE LIGHT OF THE EUCHARISTIC MYSTERY

It will be understood that the sects of Southern France, holding various offices of protestation, testified by act and word that the gates of hell had prevailed against the Latin Church and that the efficacious doctrines, the plenary rights, were in their hands.   In other words, they had a special office in religion, and, I must add, the fatality of a superior process—all which instructs us precisely and fully why the Mystery of the Holy Graal was beyond their horizon and why they form no part of the Secret Tradition in Christian times.   Their exponents—it is all as you please—were kings or rebels in warfare ;   they were unaccredited and disputatious doctors ;   they were errant preachers of a new-fangled scheme for the improved spiritual housing of priest-ridden classes.   They trafficked—if you please otherwise —in Brummagem wares of apostolic Christianity ;   they were pedlars, and they carried no licence ;   their goods were either contraband or they were put forward under false marks.   But if you prefer an alternative—since nothing in respect of them carries the least consequence —they handed down, diluted or otherwise, the remanents of some earlier heresy, gnosis, or occult confection of dogma, and if in respect thereof they concealed their real beliefs, nothing which signifies in respect of our proper concern reposes behind the evasion. If I have any view on the subject—and honestly I have next to none—they were perhaps the Protestants of their period, dealing in poisonous nostrums of pure doctrine, simple faith, Bible Christianity, and they circulated uncorrupted interpretations of the Word of God—all horrors of that spurious simplicity which takes the wayfaring man into the first pit. We who know that *omnia exeunt in mysterium* have recited long since our *Asperge* and have turned aside from such blasphemous follies.

Outside these sects, there were two great concurrent schools of secret thought which were developing in Europe at the period of the Graal ; there was the wonder and the rumour of alchemy and there was the great sacred mystery of Kabalistic Jewry. The first was scattered all over the western countries, and its reflection at the period in England was Roger Bacon, though, as it so happens, he signifies nothing for our purpose. The chief seat of the other was in Spain, but it had important academies coming into being in the South of France. I shall take my first illustration from Alchemy, and it must be understood that on the surface it claims to put forward the mystery of a material operation, behind which we discern—but this is not invariably —another subject and another intention. Speaking generally, the evidences of a Secret Tradition are very strong in alchemy and they are strong also in other schools of thought which will remain subsequently for our consideration. But seeing that it may strike the unversed student as not less than fantastic that I should choose the old and dubious science of metallic transmutation to cast light upon the Eucharistic side of the Graal Mystery, I must in the first place explain that two governing motives will actuate the whole inquest which follows hereafter : (1) To ascertain whether the concurrent or succeeding schools of secret thought, which appeared in Europe before or after the canon of the Graal was closed, offered any analogies to the notion of an arch-national Eucharist, or—in other words—to the existence, prosecution and success of the Great Experiment; and (2) whether they offered anything which corresponds with the alternative notion of a voided House of Doctrine. The concurrence or competition which may subsist between the two theses will be mentioned at the term of the research. It is obvious, meanwhile, that we shall not expect to find secret words of consecration or some concealed form of the Mass, because we are investigating the analogies of intention which may be imbedded in distinct literatures. If we came across, for example—as we might, if we cared to seek—an occult requiem for the soul of a dead alchemist, we should set it aside simply as impertinent rather than relative. It will prove—and quite naturally—that such literatures will contain many secret verbal formulæ but not those which we should require if our zeal went before our discretion and we sought after secret words—as, for example, a super-efficacious version of the *Epiclesis* clause. The same counsels of prudence will teach us not to expect in the other schools a replicated claim regarding super-apostolical succession; it is sufficient—and it does not concern us either—that the epopts of these imbedded Christian and cognate mysteries were ordained specially and strangely in the paths which they followed for the proper term thereof—but this is of election to the mysteries. Lastly, we shall not look to find a plainer expression than we have met with already in the rumours of the Graal sanctuary, but though we are dealing in some cases with the most cryptic of all literatures and in others with elusive forms of initiation, we shall find as a fact that there is less room for misconception than —all things considered—might be expected. I premise, therefore, that the great Eucharistic experiment, concealed under the supposition of a secret consecration formula, has its strict analogy in the second sense attributed to the doctrines and processes of alchemical transmutation; while the loss of the Graal—or its counterpart, the loss of the gracious and piteous words —has its analogy in the loss of the word in Kabalism and in the symbolical science of Masonry. We have seen already that the analogies of the Graal Quest are in the annals of sanctity and the present researches are the other side of the same annals. It follows that there is a super-incession between all the schools, but it is of the ideological order only and of the experience thereto belonging, and not of successive derivation. Perhaps I ought to add that the true interpretation of alchemy depends upon a construction of symbolism which has not entered previously into the heart of criticism.

At the period of the Holy Graal the books of the Hermetic Adepts were in a state of transition, or alternatively they corresponded to the elements of folklore before the Great Christian Hallow reigned in the Kingdom of Romance. In other words, the Secret School of alchemy began in an experimental operation pursued on material things, but the school was taken over subsequently, though at a time when the Graal literature was only a sacred memory. It is this mystery which was the next witness in the world.

Alchemy may not have originated much further East than Alexandria, or, alternatively, it may have travelled from China when the port of Byzantium was opened to the commerce of the world. In either case its first development, in the forms with which we are acquainted, is connected with the name of Byzantium, and the earliest alchemists of whom we have any particulars and any remains in literature constitute a class by themselves under the name of Byzantine alchemists. The records of their processes went further eastward, into Syria and Arabia, where they assumed a new mode, which bore, however, all necessary evidence of its origin. In this form the texts do not appear to have had a specific influence upon the *corpus doctrinale* of later days. The records were also taken West, like other mysteries of varying importance, and when they began to assume a place in western history this was chiefly in France, Germany and England. In other words, there arose the cycle of Latin alchemy, passing at a later date, by the way of translation, into the vernaculars of the respective countries, until finally, but much later, we have original documents in various almost modern languages. It follows—but has not been noticed so far—that the entire literature is a product of Christian times and has Christianity as its motive, whether subconsciously or otherwise. This statement applies to the Latin Geber and even the tracts which are ascribed to Morien and Rhasis. The dubious and the certain exceptions which prove the rule are the colloquy of the *Turba Philosophorum*—about which it is difficult to speculate in respect of its source—and the Kabalistic *Æsh Mezareph*—which we know only by fragments included in the great collection of Rosenroth. I suppose that there is no labyrinth which it is quite so difficult to thread as that of the *Theatrum Chemicum*. It is beset on every side with pitfalls, and its clues, though not destroyed actually, have been buried beneath the ground. Expositors of the subject have gone astray over the generic purpose of the art, because some have believed it to be (*a*) the transmutation of metals, and that only, while others have interpreted it as (*b*) a veiled method of delineating the secrets of the soul on its way through the world within, and besides this nothing. We have on our part to realise that (*a*) there were two schools making use of the same language in a distinct sense, the one branch seeking the transmutation of metals and the art of prolonging life, the other branch investigating the mysteries of arch-natural life ; and that (*b*) more than one text-book of physical alchemy would seem to have been re-edited in this more recent, exotic interest. It is to the latter that I refer when I speak of an intervention in alchemy by which it was assumed, and—while preserving the same veils of language—was transformed in respect of its purpose. I deal therefore with the *corpora spiritualia* of the mystic school; we can leave to the physical alchemists those things of Cæsar which belong to them, retaining the things which concern the mysteries of divine symbolism.

The true philosophers of each school are believed to have taught the same thing, with due allowance for the generic difference of their term, and seeing that they used—as I have said—the same language, it would seem that, given a criterion of distinction in respect of the term, this should make the body of cryptogram comparatively easy to disentangle. But as one of the chief problems is held to reside in the fact that many text-books do not begin at the same point of the process, this advantage of uniformity is cancelled largely. There are affirmed to be experimental schools still existing in Europe which have carried the physical work much further than it is ever likely to be taken by an isolated student ; but this must be accepted under some notable reserves, or I can at least say that, having better occasions than most people of knowing the schools and their development, I have so far found no evidence. But there are known otherwise to be—and I speak here with the certainty of first-hand acquaintance—other schools, also experimental, also existing in Europe, which claim to possess the master-key of the mystical work. How far they have been successful in using that key, and whether it opens all locks, I am not in a position to say, for reasons which those who are concerned will regard as obvious. It so happens, however, that the mystery of the process is one thing and that which lies on the surface, or more immediately beneath the externals of concealed language, is fortunately another thing. And, as in this case it occurs for our salvation, the enlightening correspondences are offering their marks and seals, if not at our very doors, at least in the official churches. Among all those places that are holy there is no holy place in which they do not abide, *a mane usque ad vesper-*

tinum, and the name of this correspondence is the Holy Eucharist.

Before entering further into this matter, I propose to tabulate certain palmary points of terminology which are common to all the adepts—including both schools indifferently, though we are dealing here, and this is understood fully, with the process of one school. By the significance of these terms we shall see to what extent the symbolism of the Higher Alchemy is in conformity with mystic symbolism and with the repose of the life of the Church in God. We shall see further in respect of the operations that some are in correspondence with that High Mass which was once said in Corbenic. It should be realised, however, that there is nothing so hard and so thankless as to elucidate one symbolism in the words of another, and this notwithstanding the identity which may be indicated as the term of each. It should be understood further, and accepted, that all alchemists, outside the distinctions of their schools, were actuated by an express determination to veil their mystery, and that seemingly they had recourse for this purpose to every kind of subterfuge.

At the same time they tell us that the whole art is contained, manifested and set forth by means of a single vessel which, amidst all manner of minor variations, is described with essential uniformity throughout the multitude of texts. This statement constitutes a certain lesser key to the art ; but as on the one hand the alchemists veil their *vas insigne* by reference, in spite of their assurance, to many pretended vessels, so has the key itself a certain aspect of subterfuge, since the alleged unity is in respect only of the term final of the process in the unity of the recipient. This unity is the last reduction of a triad, because, according to these aspects of Hermetic philosophy, man in the course of his attainment is at first three—body, soul and spirit— that is, when he sets out on the Great Quest ; he is two at a certain stage—when the soul has conceived Christ, for the spirit has then descended and the body is for the time being outside the Divine alliance ; but he is in fine one—that is to say, when the whole man has died in Christ—which is the term of his evolution. So in the Graal Mystery there are three seekers who attain after their own measure—Perceval, Bors and Galahad— who are distinguished from the hereditary incapacity of Gawain, from the particular inhibition of Lancelot, and from the external election of the King.

The black state of the alchemical matter, on which the process of the art is engaged, is the body of this death—" the dedeley flesshe "—from which the adepts have asked to be detached. It is more especially our natural life. The white state of the Stone, the confection of which is desired as a chief term of the art, is the vesture of that immortality with which the epopts are clothed upon.

The Salt of the Philosophers is that savour of life without which the material earth can neither be salted nor cleansed. The Sulphur of the Philosophers is the inward substance by which some souls are saved, yet so as by fire. The Mercury of the Sages is that which must be fixed and volatilised—naturally it is fluidic and wandering—but except under this name, or by some analogous substitute, it must not be described literally outside the particular circles of secret knowledge. It is nearer than hands and feet.

Now, the perfect correspondence of these things in the symbolism of official Christianity, and the great mystery of perfect sanctification, is set forth in the great churches under the sacramentalism of the Holy Eucharist, behind which we see in the liturgies and ritual of the Graal a high rendering of the same subject under the same terms, as if there were secret wardens who were aware of certain insufficiencies and of the way in which they might be rectified. The same exalted mystery which lies behind the symbols of Bread and Wine, behind the undeclared priesthood which is according to the Order of Melchisedech, was expressed by the alchemists under the guise of transmutation ; but it is understood that I refer here to the secret school of adeptship which had taken over in another and transcendent interest the terminology and processes of occult metallurgy. The confusion of distinct symbolisms signifying the same thing makes for no illumination ; but because of the identity in the term, because both schools deal with the same thing, and because the same thing is everywhere, the natural analogy of these symbolisms, distinct as they are, can, by maintaining their distinction—that is, without mutation of the accidents—be made to elucidate each other. In the last resource, therefore, the physician heals himself ; but I am speaking here of that which wise men have termed the Medicine.

The vessel is consequently one, but the matter thereto adapted is not designated especially, or at least after an uniform manner ; it is said to be clay by those who speak at times more openly in order that they may be understood the less, as if they also were singing in their strange chorus :

> " Let us be open as the day
> That we may deeper hide ourselves."

It is most commonly described as metallic because on the surface of the literature there is the declared mystery of all metals, and the concealed purpose is to show that in the roots and essence of these things there is a certain similarity or analogy. The reason is that the epopt who has been translated again finds his body after many days, but under a great transmutation, as if in another sense the *panis quotidianus* had been changed into the *panis vivus et vitalis*, but—as I have just said—without mutation of the accidents. The reason is also that in normal states the body is—here and now—not without the soul, nor can we separate readily, by any intellectual process, the soul from the spirit which broods thereover, to fertilise it in a due season. There is, however, one vessel, and this makes for simplicity ; though it is not by such simplicity that the art is testified to be a *ludus puerorum*. The contradistinction hereto is that it is hard to be a Christian, which is the comment of the man born blind upon the light that he cannot see. It is the triumphant affirmation of the mystical counterposition, that to sin is hard indeed for the man who knows truly. The formula of this is that man is born for the heights rather than the deeps, and its verbal paradox is : *facilis ascensus superno*. The process of the art is without haste or violence by the mediation of a graduated fire, and the seat of this fire is in the soul. It is a mystery of the soul's love, and for this reason she is called " undaunted daughter of desire." The sense of the gradation is that love is set free from the impetuosity and violence of passion, and has become a constant and incorruptible flame. The formula of this is that the place of unity is a centre wherein there is no exaggeration. That which the fire consumes is certain materials or elements which are called *recrementa*, the grosser parts, the superfluities ; and it should be observed that there are two purgations, of which the first is the gross and the second the subtle. The first is the normal process of conversion, by which there is such a separation of components seemingly external that what remains is as a new creature, and may be said to be reborn. The second is the exalted conversion, by which that which has been purified is so raised that it enters into a new region, or a certain heaven comes down and abides therein.

It is not my design in this place to exhaust the sources of interpretation, because such a scheme would be impossible in this sub-section, and I can allude therefore but scantily to the many forms of the parables which are concerned with the process up to this point. The ostensible object—which was material in the alternative school—was the confection of a certain Stone or Powder, which is that of projection, and the symbolical theorem is that this powder, when added to a base metal, performs the wonder of transmutation into pure silver or gold, better than those of the mines. The Stone transmutes what is base, but in its own elements it has undergone transmutation itself, from what is base to what is perfect. In another form it prolongs life and renews youth in the adept philosopher and lover of learning. In this case it is spoken of usually as an elixir, but the transmuting powder and the renewing draught are really one thing with the spiritual alchemists. As it is certain that under any light of interpretation the Stone of the Graal is not actually and literally a stone—nor found in the nest of the phœnix—it may be held to follow as a reasonable inference that the Cup or Chalice is not a cup actually or literally, much less a vessel which contains blood, *sang réal* or otherwise. In like manner, if there is one thing which appears than another more clearly in the books of the Philosophers, it is that the Stone of alchemy is not a stone at all, and that the Elixir of alchemy is not a brew or an essence which can be communicated in ewers or basins. The Stone, on one side of its symbolism, represents more especially the visible sign of the mystery, and it is spoken of as offering two phases—of which one is white and the other red.

It must be affirmed further that in virtue of a very high mysticism there is an unity in the trinity of the stone—or powder—the metal and the vase. The vase is also the alchemist, for none of the instruments, the materials, the fires, the producer and the thing produced are external to the one subject. At the same time the inward man is distinguished from the outward man ; we may say that the one is the alchemist and the other the vessel ; it is in this sense that the art is termed both physical and spiritual. But the symbolism is many times enfolded, and the gross matter which is placed within the vessel is the untransmuted life of reason, motive, concupiscence, self-interest and all that which constitutes the intelligent creature on the normal plane of manifestation. Hereof is the natural man enclosed in an animal body, as the metal is placed in the vessel, and from this point of view the alchemist is he who is sometimes termed arrogantly the super-man. But because there is only one vessel it must be understood that herein the Stone is confected and the base metal is converted. The alchemist is himself finally the Stone, and because many zealous aspirants to the Art have not understood this they have failed in the Great Work on the spiritual side.

The schedule which now follows may elucidate this hard subject somewhat more fully, if not indeed more plainly : There are (*a*) the natural, external man, whose equivalent is the one vessel ; (*b*) the body of desire which answers to the gross matter ; (*c*) the aspiration, the consciousness, the will of the supernatural life ; (*d*) the process of the will working on the body of desire within the external vessel ; (*e*) the psychic and transcendental conversion thus effected ; (*f*) the re-action of the purified body of desire on the essential will, so that the one supports the other, the will is again exalted, and therefrom follows this further change—that the spirit of a man puts on a new quality of life, becoming an instrument which is at once feeding and itself fed ; (*g*) herein is the symbol of the Stone and the Great Elixir ; (*h*) the spirit is nourished from above by the analogies of Eucharistic ministry—that is to say, the Dove descends from Heaven carrying the arch-natural Host to renew the virtues of the Stone ; (*i*) the spirit nourishes the soul, as by Bread and Wine—that is, the Bread is taken from the Graal ; (*k*) the soul effects the higher conversion in the body of desire ; (*l*) it comes about thus that the essence which dissolves everything is still contained in a vessel, or alternatively that God abides in man.

This process, thus delineated exhaustively in the parables of alchemy, is put with almost naked simplicity by Eucharistic doctrine—which says that material lips receive the super-substantial Bread and Wine, that the soul is nourished and that Christ enters the soul.

The Eucharistic Bread signifies the super-substantial sustenance, and the Wine is arch-natural life. It is for this reason that the Alchemical Stone at the red has a higher tingeing and transmuting power than the Stone at the white. The first matters of the alchemical work, to make use of another language of subterfuge, are Sulphur, Mercury and Salt; but these are the elements of the Philosophers and not those of the ordinary kind. In other words, common Sulphur and Mercury correspond to the Bread and Wine before consecration, and the philosophical elements are those which have been transubstantiated by the power of the secret words. That which is produced is called *Panis Vivus et Vitalis* and *Vinum Mirabile*, instead of the daily meat and drink by which we ask to be sustained in the Lord's Prayer. The Salt is that which is called the formula of consecration; it is that which salts and transmutes the natural earth. When Christ said : " If the Salt lose its savour, wherewith shall it be salted ? "— this can be understood of the super-excellent and extra-valid consecration; the removal of the Graal signifies that of a certain arch-natural salting, yet the salt of sufficing grace remains, like that of nature, and in its way also it communicates. Christ further said : " You are the salt of the earth "—and this is the true priesthood.

That which the text-books have agreed from time immemorial to term a Stone is that also which we find in greater Gospel books, where it is described as a Stone not made with hands, and the transmutation performed thereby is the work of inward conversion, resulting in the condition which one of the adepts recommends to his disciples when he exclaims : " *Transmutemini, trans-mutemini à lapidibus mortuis in lapides vivos philosophicos.*" The possession of the Stone is, in other words, the possession of the tingeing Christ.

It should be understood, therefore, that the First Matter in transcendence—that is, in the state of the Stone—must be taken to signify the elements after conversion has been operated by the secret words of consecration. But the words signify here the Divine Life, and the process which really takes place is represented by the most sacramental of all words : *Et verbum caro factum est* (And the Word was made flesh). In this new light of alchemy we may continue, if we please, to regard the elements of the Graal as the communication of the Eucharist in exaltation, of which our own Eucharist is only a shadow and substitute ; or we can do what is the same thing and is preferable in respect of finality, that is, we can transfer the entire symbolism to man who is the recipient of the Eucharist, the vessel of reception, the subject of conversion, the container which in the outward order is less than the thing contained, the life which receives the life above all life that is manifest and known. Without man the conversion and transmutation of elements would be void of all office, since there would be no *terminus ad quem*.

Prior to the efficacious consecration we may assume that the simple elements are those substances, or, if we prefer it, are that one substance variously manifested, which, as the alchemists tell us so expressly, may be found everywhere. It is of no account till the Wise have introduced their mystical ferment therein. Having concealed it under a thousand names, they say in their strange manner that it is known by these ; and so also some of them have declared in their derision, as against all the untutored material operations which involve a prodigal outlay, that he who spends upon the Great Work more than thirty thalers—not including the cost of personal maintenance—has already passed aside from the whole truth of the process. It follows from these elucidations that the higher understanding of the Eucharist and the mystic side of alchemy are concerned with the same subject, that is to say, with man, his conversion and transfiguration : the implicits are therefore the same, and of these things alchemy was the next witness in the world after the epoch of the Holy Graal.

But though it seems therefore within all reason and all truth to testify that the *panis vivus et vitalis* is even as the transmuting Stone and that the Chalice of the New and Eternal Testament is as the renewing Elixir, the witness is subject to the reserve of my previous indication ; the closer the analogies between distinct systems of symbolism the more urgent is that prudence which counsels us not to confound them by an interchangeable use. The priest as priest neither dealt in the symbolism of alchemy nor assumed its external offices ; the alchemist as alchemist did not celebrate Mass. It is true notwithstanding that all Christian mysticism—whatever its vestures—came out of the Mass-Book, and it is true that it returns therein. But the Mass-Book in the first instance came out of the heart mystic which had unfolded in Christendom. The nucleus of truth in the Missal is : *Dominus prope est.* The Mass shows that the Great Work is in the first sense a work of the hands of man, because it is he, officiating as a priest in his own temple, who offers the sacrifice which he has purified ; but the elements of that sacrifice are taken over by an intervention from another Order, and that which follows is transfusion.

Re-expressing all this now in a closer summary, the apparatus of mystical alchemy is indeed, comparatively speaking, simple. The first matter is myrionymous and is yet one, corresponding to the unity of the natural will and the unlimited complexity of its motives, dispositions, desires, passions and distractions—on all of which the work of wisdom must operate. The vessel is also one, for this is the normal man complete in his own degree. The process has the seal of Nature's directness ; it is the graduation and increasing maintenance of a particular fire. The initial work is a change in the substance of will, aspiration and desire, which is the first conversion—or transmutation in the elementary sense. But it is identical, even to the end, with the term proposed by the Eucharist, which is the modification of the noumenal man by the communication of Divine Substance. Here is the *lapis qui non lapis, lapis tingens, lapis angularis, lapis qui multiplicatur, lapis per quem justus ædificabit domum Domini, et jam valde ædificatur et terram possidebit per omnia,* &c. When it is said that the Stone is multiplied, even to a thousand-fold, we know that this is true of all seed which is sown upon good soil.

So, therefore, the Stone transmutes and the Eucharist transmutes also ; the philosophical elements on the physical side go to the making of the Stone, which is also physical, and the sacramental elements to the generation of a new life in the soul. He who says *Lapis Philosophorum* says also : My beloved to me and I to him. Christ is therefore the Stone, and the Stone in adept humanity is the Union realised, while the Great Secret is that Christ must be manifested within.

Now, it seems to me that it has not served less than an useful purpose to establish after a new manner the intimate resemblance between the higher understanding of one part of the Secret Tradition and the fuller interpretation of one Sacrament of the Church. We are not dealing in either case with the question of attainment. The analogy would remain if Spiritual Alchemy and Christian Sacramentalism abode in the intellectual order as theorems only which have been never carried into experience. And further it is not affirmed that the Hermetic symbolism has attained a grade of perfection. When Christian symbolism took over the old legends and created out of them the literature of the Holy Graal, the work was not done perfectly, and it is the same with alchemical books. It remains that the doctrine of sanctity offered a Divine Experience, to those who entered the pathway of sanctity, as a foretaste in this life of the union which is consummated in eternity, or of that end beyond which there is nothing whatever that is conceivable. We know from the old books that " it hath not entered into the heart of man," but the heart which has put away the things of sense may at least conceive it by representations and types. This is the great tradition of that which the early alchemists term Truth in the Art ; the experience is representation after its own kind rather than felicity, but the representation is of that grade which begins in ecstasy and ends in absorption. Let no man say therefore that he loses himself in experiences of this order, for perchance it is then only that he finds himself, even in that way which suggests that after many paths of activity he is at length coming into his own.

The alchemical maxim which might be inscribed on the gate of the *palais espiriteus* or any Castle of the Graal should be :

" Est in Mercurio quicquid quærunt sapientes."

The Eucharistic maxim which might be written over the laboratory of the alchemist, in addition to *Laborare est orare*, is :

> *" Et antiquum documentum*
> *Novo cedat ritui :*
> *Præstet fides supplementum*
> *Sensuum defectui."*

The maxim which might be written over the temples of the official churches is *Corporis Mysterium*—that the mystery of the body might lead them more fully into the higher mystery of the soul. And in fine the maxim which might and would be inscribed over the one Temple of the truly Catholic Religion when the faiths of this wes ern world have been united in the higher consciousness—that is assuredly *Mysterium Fidei*—the mystery which endures for ever and for ever passes into experience.

Within the domain of the Secret Tradition the initiations are many and so are the schools of thought, but those which are true schools and those which are high orders issue from one root. *Est una sola res*, and they whose heart of contemplation is fixed upon this one thing may differ but can never be far apart. Personally I do not believe—and this has the ring of a commonplace—that they will be found to differ widely. I know not what systems of the æons may intervene between that which is imperishable within us and the union wherein the universe will in fine repose at the centre. But I know that the great systems—aye, even the great processes—of the times that are gone, as of those which now encompass us, do not pass away, because that which was from the beginning is now and ever shall be—is one motive, one aspiration, one term of thought remaining, as if in the stillness of an everlasting present. We really understand one another, and our terms are terms over which our collective aspirations are united world without end.

IV

THE KABALISTIC ACADEMIES

We have now dealt with the testimony of the chief witness to the perpetuity and perfection of the Great Experiment, and if it be necessary—as it is at times and seasons—to conceal or re-express things in an artificial and evasive language, I do not know of a more convincing substituted terminology than that of transmutation by alchemy as a high analogy of God's work in the soul. Other analogies there are, but for the most part unrealised, as, for example, the sublime clause of the Apostle's Creed : "*Et expecto resurrectionem mortuorum et vitam venturi sæculi*," which, as it stands, is a testimony to the prospect and not the attainment. The motives which lead to the adoption of artificial language and the circumstances which may help to justify it belong to the term of our inquiry, of which this is the penultimate stage only. We have now finished for the present with the Mystery of Attainment —or why it was necessary to seek and find the Holy Graal in order that the spiritual knight might in fine be assumed into Heaven, carrying the Palladium with him into those stars whence it first descended ; and we have next to determine whether there are other traces which may help us to understand better the Mystery of Loss, or the meaning of the Voided Sanctuary. It is admitted out of hand that the first indications are placed here in respect of the order of time, and that they are introductory and subsidiary only—a place of sidelights and incidental correspondences. The reason is that, although the root-matters must be identical when the term in finality is one, we are dealing in respect of the Graal with a manifestation in Christendom but here with a manifestation in Israel.

The schools of Kabalism can scarcely be said to have done more than emerge partly into public existence when the canon of the Graal literature had already closed ; in these schools there were great masters of mystic thought, though more especially on the intellectual side. Now, in its own way, the theosophical scheme of Jewry in exile is a story of loss like the Graal, though it is one which ends in expectation—or, as I should say, in certainty. The loss in external history and in national life was counterpoised by a loss in the sanctuary, as if the arch-natural Eucharist, the Graal which is of all things holy, had been taken therefrom. It was that which of old was written not only in one galaxy of stars but by the power of which the worlds themselves were made. The substitution which, according to the Graal legends, was left with the Christian Church in place of the living sanctities is paralleled closely by that other legend which tells how the stress and inhibition of Israel is because the Divine Word has been withdrawn from the Holy Place, and instead of the true Tetragram, the voice of the priest only pronounces now the name

Adonai. But the Eucharist, as I have said, is still the Eucharist, the House from which the Graal has departed is still the Holy House, and all sanctity attaches in like manner to the substituted sacred Name and to the cortex of those letters which now represent the Tetragram—יהוה. There was a time when this name in its true form was pronounced by the High Priest once annually in the sanctuary; it restored the people of God and maintained the Inmost Shrine, keeping open the channels of grace, even as the heavenly dove, descending on Good Friday, renewed the virtue of the Graal. Afterwards, as I have indicated, there came another time when disaster fell upon Israel, with the result that the essential elements of the Name, in which its true pronunciation was involved, became lost even to the sanctuary.

It should be scarcely necessary to say that I am not putting forward the hypothesis of a channel of communication by which something was derived into romance literature from implicits which about the same time or subsequently were developed into Zoharic books. I know that behind the Graal Castle—according to the *Longer Prose Perceval*—there was the Earthly Paradise, and that the House of the Holy Vessel was also the Castle of Souls. I know that, according to the *Zohar*, the Garden of Eden is placed in a position which corresponds to that of the Graal itself. I know that both were removed—the Graal into the heavenly regions and the Garden of Eden into that which is no longer manifest. The latter place was connected nearly in Kabalism with the Great Sanctuary—truly a Castle of Souls—wherein all those who are to come await incarnation in turn, for, according to Jewish theosophy, the creation of souls is not successive, or dependent on earthly generation, but eternal in the heavens. I know that there is nothing in literature so like the departure of Galahad as that of R. Simeon ben Jochai; and in spite of great divergences, of distinctions in the root-matter, the Mystery of the Holy Graal has its sub-surface analogy with the Mystery of the *Lesser Holy Assembly.* I know that the *Greater* and *Lesser Sanhedrim* sound like oracular voices speaking in an unknown tongue concerning the Holy House, and we feel that behind the outward offices of religion there was an Inner Church of Israel. I know that, according to the involved scheme of the *Sephiroth*, the Waters of Life are in Knowledge, which is also the place of the Cup, and this is reserved always for those who are athirst. But these things, with others and many others, do not constitute the lightest shadow of transmission. No French poet could be expected to know thereof; no exponent of Christian legend, even when interpreted mystically, ever looked to Israel for light and leading in those internecine days—however much the name of Provence may suggest a certain difference in mind from the prevalent orthodoxy of the age. That there may be no mistake on this subject among those whom I address more especially, I note further that the peculiar presentation of Graal symbolism which is connected with the name of the reputed Provençal Guiot—who of all only might confess to some curious memories from a course of study at Toledo—is precisely that presentation in which the sanctuary is not voided and the Graal is not taken away.

It is a matter of common knowledge that at the period in question Spain was one place in the world where the Jews were not merely free from raging perse-cution but where worldly positions of importance were open to their competition. We know further that a great light of Moslem learning shone forth in some Spanish academies. We know finally or may learn that another light had kindled therein among the chosen people themselves. Palestine and the East generally thereabouts may have contributed its portion, and did indeed do so, but the heart and marrow of Kabalism was in Spain. The Jews of Cordova, the Jews of Toledo

and of other places in the Peninsula look great figures
in the literature, and so also do certain academies of
Southern France, though there the Jews did not find
the same peace in their abodes. For them the asylum
was Spain, and that indeed must have been little less
than a Terrestrial Paradise realised. And as between
the South of France and Spain the channels of communication stood wide open, as Provence is the legendary
place of the first Graal quest, as the Ideal Castle, the
Holy Place, Mont Salvatch, had its abode unapproachable
in the Pyrenees, so the imaginative mind may perhaps
incline to say that behind the strange legend of the
Jew of Toledo there is something undemonstrable of
a lost Graal connection; yet this is the stuff only of
which dreams are made, and it is well for my own case.
The analogy between all the schools in succession is
the testimony which they bear in common, and if after
other manners they reflected one into another the
witness would be weaker in proportion. There is no
concert, there is no debt in literature, there is no result
in fine, as by a course of development from cycle to
cycle of books. The scheme of theosophical Kabalism
is distinct, and absolutely, from that of metaphysical
alchemy; it is the evidence of two schools which did
not know one another, and, although at the root their
evidence is of the same kind, the relation between them
is that of the pairs of opposites. So also when another
and no less noteworthy voice began to speak within the
body-legendary of symbolical Masonry, it said what
Kabalism had said, but it was not Kabalism speaking
behind a later mask. As I must look to be challenged
in the gate over the thesis of this book, I assume at this
point so much harness as will suffice to dissuade the
gentlemen of the counter-guard from considering that
I am open to attack as one who seeks to explain that
generic literature A is the concealed father of generic
literature B, though I speak more seriously as a counsel
to some of the confraternities with which I am affiliated

in thought and the pursuit of a term in common. When it is said that God so loved the world, the counterpart in Kabalism is that the *Kingdom* is in no sense apart from the *Crown*, and that the progression from *Aleph* to *Tau* is complete without break or intermission ; but St. Paul is not for that reason a precursor of the *Zohar*. So also when the Arabian Academies of Spain became the resort of Christian scholars—" men of curious inquiry," as one has said concerning them—it does not mean that from such schools they brought back Sufic mysticism and translated it into romance. It does not mean that there also they met with the *corpus materiale* of the Kabalah, a final receptacle of the *débris* and drift of all the old theogonies, theosophies and occult knowledge of many places and periods, or that learning there how the Daughter of the Voice was withdrawn from the sanctuary of Israel, they told in another tongue how, after the departure of the Graal, the dwelling of King Fisherman " began to fall," though the chapel thereto belonging never " wasted nor decayed." The voices say one thing, but they do not speak in concert. We know only and realise that Israel is waiting by the waters of Babylon, and it has come to pass that, though we draw from far other places, we are also beside her, remembering, perhaps more dimly and yet with deeper yearning, the glory that once was in Zion.

Of such was the mind of Kabalism, its appanage, its baggage and its quest.

V

THE CLAIM IN RESPECT OF TEMPLAR INFLUENCE

I suppose that there is no one at this day, even on the outermost fringes of the wide world of books, who will need to be acquainted with the fact that the old chivalry of the Temple was instituted as a protection to the Christian pilgrims who visited the Holy Places of Jerusalem in the first quarter of the twelfth century. It was a military and religious organisation *ab origine symboli*, differing as such from the Hospital of St. John, which at its incorporation was a healing fraternity, and only assumed arms following the example of the *Militia Crucifera Evangelica* which had arisen suddenly at its side. Templar history is a great storehouse of enchanting hypothesis and also of unreclaimed speculation repeated from writer to writer. I know no greater sea on which ships of imagination and fantasy have launched more boldly; if they have reached no final harbour, they have paused to take in further stores at innumerable " summer isles " of an imaginary Eden " lying in dark purple spheres of sea," and if in some undemonstrable way they have slipped their cables and eluded sporadic hostile vessels, this has been because the equipment of the latter has not been better than their own, white as regards credentials the letter of marque carried by the unwelcome visitor would often not bear much closer inspection than their own unchartered licence. Now, an Order which was established in the East for a specific Christian purpose, which embodied ideas of devotion that were ecclesiastical as well as religious, which accepted monastic vows—even those counsels of perfection that qualified for the Quest of the Graal—yet, in spite of these, which became wealthy in the corporate sense beyond the dreams of avarice, insolent and haughty beyond the prerogatives of feudal royalty, and had darker charges looming against it, does assuredly offer a picture to research the possibilities of which are likely to be exploited in all directions. The story of the brotherhood and the things implied therein have been therefore approached from many points of view, enforced by many considerations and by much which passes for evidence. I speak—as it will be understood—here of the things recognised or divined beneath its external surface, for on that side there is nothing more direct and more simple. We know that the Latin Church has a heavy account to balance in respect of the Order, and by the characteristics of the charges preferred it is also responsible for having brought it—whether warrantably or otherwise, but at least all unwittingly—within the dubious circle of the Secret Tradition in Christian times, for a considerable proportion of those who recognise the fact of the Tradition. It remains, however, that from this standpoint the story has never been told at all by any one who spoke with knowledge on so involved a subject. Here there is no place to attempt it, but the Mystery of the Temple in a minor degree interpenetrated the Mystery of the Graal, and something must be said concerning it in this connection. There is at the present time in England (*a*) an extending disposition to appreciate remotely and dimly an imbedded evidence that the romance-literature did somehow shadow forth an initiatory process—but this I have hinted previously; and (*b*) that in some manner not yet understood the Knights Templars and the Graal legend grew up together, and will answer with strange voices if set to question one another across the void which intervenes between an externalised chivalry in fact and an ideal knighthood in books. In a word, the literature has been held sometimes to represent, within clouds and under curious veils, something of the imputed Templar subsurface design, or alternatively certain Graal texts do at least indubitably reflect in their own manner, on their own authority, the Knighthood of the Morning and of Palestine raised from the world of reflections into the world of the archetype. The *Longer Prose Perceval* is not only a work with an allegorical and also a mystic motive; it is not only the story of a suppressed word, of the sorrow and suffering which were wrought by that suppression, and the joy and deliverance which followed the recovery of the word; it is not only the prototypical correlative of the legend of the Royal Arch and the eighteenth degree in a form not less clear because it can be traced only by a specialist; but—at least in adventitious ways—it has ever-recurring characters of Templar symbolism. But that which wears herein—and so through the French cycle—little more than the aspect of accident, passes in the *Parsifal* of Wolfram into the appearance of a preconceived plan. Herein is the story of a confraternity, partly military but in part also religious, connecting by the legend of its lineage with a kind of secret history in Christendom written under the guise of knight-errantry; it is the romance of an Order of the Holy Graal whose members are chosen out of thousands, dedicated, set apart, and sometimes terrible in power, almost "like Cedron in flood." I do not wonder that before the face of this picture the criticism of the Graal literature has been haunted here and there with the dream of Templar intervention, and the only question which concerns us is the extent to which such an hypothesis can be justified. Even in the least illuminated circles the possibility is regarded with increasing respect, and apart from any claims on its own basis it would be difficult for this reason to pass it over entirely. The imputed fact, or the likelihood, that the literature was a vehicle, officially or otherwise, of some mystical tradition, without depending for any one on the merits of this hypothesis, would in certain minds be enhanced substantially thereby. But it is desirable to note, in the first place, that it is now an old speculation; secondly, that recent years have not brought to light, that I am aware, any new facts on the subject; and, lastly, that in so far as the contention is put freshly there is a disposition to dwell on the *Templeisen* depicted in the *Parsifal* as not only a militant body but also a governing theocracy, and one which above all things was not ecclesiastical. It is just this which impresses me as perhaps a little exaggerated in tone: I do not know that Amfortas and his chivalry can be called a governing power any more than the company over-ruled by King Pelles of Lytenoys, of whose warfare we hear in the *Vulgate Merlin.* If Mont Salvatch was anything of the kind, it was obviously a secret kingdom, and as much might be said of Corbenic and the realm to which it belonged. Seeing also that the keepers of the Graal and the cohort of their ministers had at no time a sacerdotal aspect—some express claims notwithstanding as to their geniture and their ministers— the ecclesiastical note therein is wanting through all the cycles ; the distinction in chief between the *Templeisen* and the other knights of the Graal is that in Wolfram the former are elaborately organised, while the latter are either an inchoate gathering or they are merely the retinue which would be attached to a feudal castle. In one case, which is that of the *Didot Perceval*, the House Mystic is perhaps a simple tower, which, from all that we learn by the context, might be little more than a hermit's hold.

It is obviously one thing to say that Wolfram modelled his chivalry on the prototype of the Knights Templars— which is an interesting fact without consequence—and another that the modelling was inspired by a familiarity with Templar secret intention, and it is on this point, which is obviously the hypothesis in its motive, that reasonable evidence is wanted. The next step is to recognise *tendances suspectes* in the poem of Wolfram, to predicate them of Guiot, his precursor, and to regard the Templar design—whatever otherwise it was—as anti-Catholic in its spirit. With the first ascription I have dealt in discussing the German cycle in general ; of the second we can divine little, and then but darkly ; while in respect of the third I recur to that canon of criticism which has served me well already : in so far as the Templar Order is held to be anti-Catholic, it is antecedently and proportionately unlikely that any evidence will connect it with the Graal literature. Whatever the origin of that literature, as we now have it, in one and all its forms, it is not merely a Catholic legend, but it seems so to have issued from the heart and centre of Catholicity that it is almost in the likeness of an exotic, as if from some sanctuary behind the external and visible sanctuary of the universal Church. If this is the heart of romance going out in its yearning towards God, there was never a heart in Christendom " which warmer beat and stronger." It is like the voice of that ideal city, the first city, the spiritual city, of which Wagner spoke, and it is seldom heard on earth ; it seems to speak from the pictured home of the soul, the place of pre-existence, with all the mystery and wonder of enchanted Hud and of Irêm in the Land of the Morning. And in the melody of that voice, within the verbal message thereof, we know that the country deep in Asia is not to be found in any Highlands beyond the Himalayas, or in the fabled Sarras. Again, it is the country of the soul and of the soul's legend ; it is the Kabalistic place of the palaces at the centre of the dimensions, sustaining all things. We know also that we shall look vainly for Corbenic on the wild coast of Wales, and for the local habitation of the Graal Castle of Mont Salvatch at any of the grand passes of the Pyrenees into Spain ; for this also is like the Rosicrucian mountain of Abiegnus and the mystic Fir-Cone, a mystery enfolded within and without by many meanings.

But if such is the position in respect of the Holy Graal, and if it follows therefrom that in some hands it has rested under a serious cloud of misapprehension, there is something to be said on the same subject, though not in the same sense, in respect of the Knights Templars. The eye which has turned from the Graal literature to the records of the great chivalry has been drawn in that direction because of the charge of heresy which was preferred of old against it. I am not designing to suggest that the side of criticism which is prominent in the open day is interested—or much less concerned seriously—in heresy as such, though I confess—if it be fitting to say so—that next to the truth which is of God and the deeps therein, whereof simple minds dream nothing, I am conscious of few things more fascinating than the story of the bad old doctrines and of those who loved, followed and honoured them. It draws the mind for ever with vague and preposterous hopes ; and seeing further that I am on the side of the orthodox faith only in so far as the old mule which carries the mysteries can be shown to be on God's side—as the *High History* testifies—I do not doubt that many are the *choses suspectes* which might be gleaned from this book, and many there may still be who could wish to include its writer in the annals carried forward of Smithfield or Tyburn and those who went thither in the days of Mary or Elizabeth.

Here is cleansing confession ; but scholarship, as I have intimated, is detached, subject to its inoculation by the notion of pagan faiths perpetuated through Christian centuries—the stilettos of which virus have pierced me also in both arms. But I believe, apart from such images, that I carry a lamp which enlightens these obscure ways, and much as I may love their crookedness, they do not deceive me. It is on this account precisely that the heresy of the Temple, so far as it concerns the Graal, can be dealt with shortly here, for which purpose I will go back as early as my knowledge of the criticism extends along these lines.

The summary of the particulars in chief may be grouped together as follows : (1) In the year 1825, Von Hammer, an orientalist of the period, identified certain baptismal fonts or vases—which he included among antique memorials of the Templars—as examples of the true San Graal vessels, and as he connected Templar secret doctrine with that of the Gnostics, he remembered that, according to Epiphanius, the Marcosians made use of three large vases in their celebration of the Eucharist. These were filled with white wine, which was supposed to undergo a transformation of colour and other magical changes. (2) In the year 1828, the Abbé Grégoire expressed a conviction that Christ transmitted to St. John the Evangelist a secret doctrine which descended ultimately to the Templars. (3) In the year 1834 Gabriele Rossetti affirmed that the Templars belonged to secret societies, and that they professed doctrines inimical to Rome ; but though much has been hazarded concerning their opinions, nothing has been ascertained conclusively. He held further that they were of Egyptian derivation and that from them the Albigenses emanated. Here I am reminded of a rumour regarding a manuscript said to be in the Louvre, but of which I know nothing, either as to title or claims ; it is reported to state that the Templars originated from a more ancient Order, called the Magian Brothers. (4) In the year 1854 it was sustained by Eugène Aroux that all the archaic romances of the Holy Graal were written to glorify the Order of the Temple and to present its doctrine in the form of romance. (5) In the year 1858 the same writer went further and suggested that the Templars were parties to a concealed programme for the creation at Jerusalem of a religious and military rival of the power and orthodoxy at Rome. (6) In the year 1842 Dr. K. Simrock expressed an opinion that the doctrine and tradition of the Templars were based on the tradition of the Graal ; that Christ had been instructed by the Essenes ; that he confided a secret knowledge to some of his disciples ; and that this was imparted subsequently to the priests of the Temple chivalry. (7) In 1844, writing on the influence of Welsh tradition, it was hazarded by A. Schulze that the symbols and doctrines of the Templars might have been borrowed from the Graal. (8) In 1865 Louis Moland in his *Origines Littéraires* considered that the Graal legend and the Templar Order were expressions in literature and life of the same ideal, being the union of knighthood with sanctity, and he further stated (a) that there was a strange Templar reflection in a literature which was unquestionably and closely related with the principles of that Order ; (*b*) that the Roman Curia interdicted the Graal romances coincidently with the suppression of the knightly Order. It will be seen that the root of this thesis is identical with that of Schulze.

The summary above has of necessity omitted many allocations and many hazards of hypothesis which might have been collected from other sources. Our next step is to ascertain from the charges against the Templars in the course of the processes instituted by the ecclesiastical Courts of France, and elsewhere, what were the heresies of doctrine and practice imputed to the chivalry. Setting aside those which constituted infringements of the Decalogue and sins crying to heaven for vengeance, the major accusations were two—that candidates for reception into the Order were required to deny Christ and offer a ceremonial outrage to the Cross, as the symbol of his Passion. The minor accusations were many, but after disentangling the alleged cultus of the Baphometic head and some other things which I rule outside our concern, they are reducible also to two, being (1) the secular absolution from sin which was said to be given by the Grand Master in open chapter, or alternatively, I believe, by the preceptors of local commanderies and encampments ; (2) a practice in respect of the Eucharist which did not involve exactly a denial in doctrine, but exhibited hostility thereto. The first is important because in a qualified form it was the only charge which was held proven against the Templars as a result of the examinations in England ; but it is on the second that the whole thesis with which we are concerned breaks down. The accusation was that in consecrating the Blessed Sacrament, the necessary and efficacious words were omitted. The evidence adduced on this question included that of an English priest who had once officiated for the Templars and who was forbidden to recite the Clause of Institution.

I do not propose to report upon the validity of the

charges in whole or in detail ; those who are concerned must be referred—if they can summons such patience for their aid—to the Latin process of the trial, which was published many years since in France. The Templars have been accused by learned people of Gnosticism, Manichæanism, Albigensianism, on the authority of those memorials ; but there is no evidence for such charges ; it is wanting also for the other speculations which are included in my summary above ; and, in fine, there is none also for the suggested Graal connections, though I confess that my researches were begun in an expectation of the kind. The Templars, if guilty, as affirmed of old on the worst of all possible authority, were in the position of the heresies in Southern France ; they reduced, denied, derided, or stood in fear of the Eucharist, and therefore the abyss intervenes between them and a literature which existed to exalt it. As regards the German *Parsifal*, it possesses the putative *tendances suspectes* to which I have referred in more than one connection. It may be said that the Host which came from heaven was a designed antithesis to the Host consecrated on earth, but I believe that this is fantasy, because to hear an ordinary Mass was as much a duty of knighthood according to Wolfram, as we find it in the *Quest of Galahad*, the *Longer Prose Perceval* and any of the other romances. I believe in my heart that the instituted analogy between the *Templeisen* of Mont Salvatch and the great Order of Chivalry was natural and irresistible in the mind of the poet who conceived it—whether Wolfram or Guiot ; I believe that it is the only connection and, as I have said, that nothing follows therefrom. I believe that the sole Eucharistic privilege enjoyed by the Templars was a decree which permitted them to celebrate one Mass annually in places under interdict ; that they were militantly papal ; that there were next to no instances in which they renounced their faith, much as they may have dishonoured it by their lives ; and that their foundation under the patronage of *la doce mère de Dieu* represented their ecclesiastical ideal. I believe in fine that their first principles were expressed on their behalf in the Epistle of St. Bernard *ad Milites Templi*. It was written at the instance of Hugo, the first Commander, and this fact is all that need be derived from the prologue. The text itself exhorts the new institution to strive with intrepid souls against the enemies of the Cross of Christ, because those to whom death is a reward and life is Christ need fear nothing. Let them stand for Christ therefore, rather desiring to be dissolved, that they may be with Him. Let them live in good fellowship, having neither wives nor children. A later section concerns that external Temple from which their particular title was taken, and it compares the glories of the House built by Solomon with the inward grace of that to which the Order was attached in the spirit. In other words, this was for St. Bernard a house not made with hands, since the chivalry was itself a Temple, and, like that of Masonry, the edifice was erected in the heart. The brethren are in fact described as a Holy City ; they are connected with the idea of the Church itself ; and the enumerated details of the Holy Place are used for spiritual exhortation addressed to the knighthood. The promise to Zion that its wilderness shall become an abode of all delights, its solitude a garden of the Lord echoing with joy and gladness, with thanksgiving and the voice of praise, is said to be the heritage of the Order, and to watch over their heavenly treasure should be their chief care—so acting that in all things He should be pleased Who guides their arms to the battle and their hands to the warfare.

Whether it profits to add more I question, but this I will say at least—that I am sacrificing all my predilections and making my task in the next book much harder by throwing over the Templar hypothesis, not alone in its connection with the Graal on the historical side, but as one of the channels through which the Secret Tradition may have passed in Christian times. I cannot say even that I speak under correction, for I question that correction is possible. I have searched many of these byways with an anxious eye for the evidence, and I have been haunted with the dreams of those who went before me in the way, but I have returned so far with hands empty. I can therefore say only : *magis amica veritas.*

VI

THE GRAAL FORMULA IN THE LIGHT OF OTHER GLEANINGS FROM THE CATHOLIC SACRAMENTARY

The Secret Orders illustrate the realised life of sanctity on the plane of symbolism, but if it were tolerable to suppose that the literature of alchemy was put forward by an instituted confraternity, then that would be the one association which *per doctrinam sanctam* had gone apparently beyond symbolism and reached the catholic heart of all experience. On the question of fact, I believe that the Hermetic adepts had a *via secretissima* which was communicated from one to another under self-enforcing covenants—because it was *Sacramentum Regis*—and that at least the best among them were not incorporated formally. The adepts of the physical work had successive fellowships—and so also had the seekers thereafter—which we can trace at different periods ; but these do not concern us. The others exchanged the watchwords of the Night and the vision of Aurora breaking in the soul ; they left their memorials in books as guides one to another, saying what they best could about that which was never expressed openly and caring little, except under God's will, whether there were any listeners, since it could not fail that the light should remain somehow in the world. Outside the wisdom of the very Church itself, they are the greatest witnesses in the age of Christ to the truth of its greatest experiment. The literature of the Holy Graal—in some of its aspects—is also a witness, and chiefly to the depth and wonders of the Catholic Mass. After all the worlds of language have been exhausted, I conceive that we have approximated only to those wonders and have sounded, here and there, only with short lines and unadapted plummets those immeasurable deeps. The keyword of the whole Mystery is *sacramentum mirabile*. O *mirabile* indeed and *sacramentum* in all truth, but because of the words that fail us, we must perforce fill the great intervening breaks even with the little books of popular devotion; and when the dark sayings of Paracelsus in *De Cœna Domini* have failed to satisfy us, we must even see whether the learned Dr. Ralph Cudworth on *The Lord's Supper*—demonstrating many follies—may not have a chance word there or here in his pages which will open, outside all knowledge of his own, some gate that we had passed without thinking! Here therefore are a few gleanings from the Catholic Sacramentary as further sidelights on the most catholic of all experiments—the Quest of the Graal.

If ever there was a verbal formula of Eucharistic consecration concealed by some school in the Church—if ever a time came when there was something missing from any Mass, Celtic or another—I believe that God has filled the vacant space with channels of sufficing grace, and that grace efficacious is not so very far away from any illuminated heart. The fact however remains that it is not ready to our hands, and that though we say *Introibo* we do not enter and go in, except into the outer sanctuary. For this reason we feel a divine and loving envy when we hear what Galahad and Perceval saw after the material visions had passed away, when there was no longer any doctrine of transubstantiation made sensible, but only *les esperitueus choses*. So also the gracious and piteous legend haunts us for ever, and we are aware that we have dwelt overlong in Logres and know the loss thereof.

The Hidden Church of the Holy Graal

It has been said, I believe, by a certain school of interpretation, which has not so far satisfied the other schools in respect of its titles, that the Graal vessel is that which contains the universe. There is unfortunately some disposition to put forward suppositions on the basis of research in other fields, and without specific acquaintance with the field covered by the speculation taken thus lightly in hand. The statement in question is not true in the sense that is intended, though it is exhaustive in its accuracy from another standpoint, and this in a dual manner : (*a*) because those who receive that Eucharist of which it is the symbol, in the highest grade and manner of reception, do behold the beginning and the end; and (*b*) because man in this manner enters into the consciousness of himself as being actually the vessel of reflection which testifies of everything without to the *centrum concentratum* within. In such sense we may all pray that the time shall come when man will reflect in his universal glass of vision that truth which is within the universe and not only its external impressions. When this comes to pass it can be said of him, as it was said once of Perceval : *Et li seintimes Gréax ne s'aperra plus çà dedanz ; mès vos sauroiz bien trusqu'à brief là où il ièra*—And the most Holy Graal shall appear herein no more, but in a brief space shall you know well the place where it shall be.

The age which saw the production of the Graal literature was, in all the public places, far from this goal like ourselves ; the communication of Him who is *Alpha* and *Omega*, who brings with Him the knowledge of the beginning and the end, took place in the symbol, not in the life essential, and the first-hand revelation of Mysteries was therefore wanting. That which doctrine and ordinary devotional practice contrived to impress upon men's memories and to impose on their faith offered an exercise to their intelligence, but in the activity intelligence was baffled. The sword of the spirit broke upon the ineffable mystery of the Kingdom of Heaven, as the symbolic sword of Perceval broke upon the gate of entrance to the Earthly Paradise. The hermit-priest who tells his wonderful story at the inception of the *Book of the Holy Graal* is in labour with the problem of the Trinity, and when his praying and longing have carried him to the Third Heaven, it is this secret of the Eternal Sanctity which is unveiled before the eyes of his soul. Many noble and learned clerks, hermits and anchoresses innumerable, did not toil less hard, but without reaping so high a reward. They also who wrote of these wonders in the best sense thereof had their limitations, and keenly defined enough. It is so that we must account for certain grave confusions in respect of the Divine Personality of Christ, and perhaps not differently for those vague traces of doctrine belonging to a very early period and abandoned as the mind of the Church grew clearer in the comprehension of her own dogmas.

It is so also that I account personally for the material side of the Graal wonders ; to say that they have come over from folk-lore is a statement of fact simply, and does not explain their toleration not only by side and by side therewith but as a part of the Mystery of Faith. Yet there was also a superincession of the gross old pagan myth and the recognised implicit of Eucharistic doctrine that the nourishment of the soul has a reflex action by which it contributes to physical welfare. The man who attends Mass, prepared suitably thereto, profits in all degrees, and for him who communicates in the higher state of grace it must be remembered that the consecrated symbols of Bread and Wine, through which the Divine is conveyed to the man within, pass through the mouth and the reins and may, as tradition and experience have testified, convey to the natural humanity some part and reflection of that grace which is declared abundantly in the other side of his being. It is in this sense that the body as well as the soul can testify at the altar rails that it is good to be here. A very subtle point is developed in this connection by the mystic and theologian Görres, who affirms that in ordinary nourishment he who eats being superior to that which is eaten assimilates the elements which he receives, but in the Eucharist the transmuted nourishment is more potent than is he who partakes, and instead of being assimilated by him, it is the nutriment which assimilates the man and raises him to a superior sphere. Because of the solidarity between body, soul and spirit, I say therefore that the *salus, honor, virtus quoque* which descend upon our higher part have also their operation below. The food-giving powers of the Graal are not therefore a reflection of the *epulum ex oblatis* but a *reductio ad fabulam* of the spiritual truth that Grace sustains Nature, and a guarantee in perpetuity that the Quest of the Kingdom of God will never fail for the want of external taverns carrying a full licence at all points of the way. The Dish of Plenty is therefore the simulacrum of *Manna abscondita*, and the priest who says Mass in his chapel carefully and recollectedly, and with illumination, by word and by word, turning at the due time to utter his *sursum corda* in the right sense, is doing more in the fellowship of humanity than all the corporal works of mercy pressed down and overflowing. He will be assuredly inspired in his reason to organise charity, so that his people shall be fitly prepared to receive the Eucharist worthily, that he may give it freely with open and venerable hands. As regards the lesser and material side of charity, the broken meats and the garlic, with the tokens of Cæsar, he will probably adopt some rule of relaxed observance, as it is good enough in these minima for God to find out His own, and He will give anywhere.

In respect further of the Manna itself, the *Longer Prose Perceval* gets, sacramentally speaking, nearest of all to the Mystery when it indicates the exaltation of the recipient by five in the five manifested changes. The text indeed is like a prolonged *Hosannah* or a *Gloria in excelsis* chanted from scene to scene in a great cycle of questing. The same note runs through all the legends, and its last echo is heard faintly in the late Lohengrin romance. In this Swan story, the chain of one of the Swans was made into two chalices, and, Mass being said therein, the bird was restored to his proper and human form. This is an Eucharistic allegory concerning the deligation of the body by Divine Substance communicated to the soul, putting a period to the enchantments and sorceries of the five senses.

I conclude therefore with St. Dionysius that the Eucharist is the first of the Divine Mysteries which now are; with the *Paraphrase* of St. Maximus, that it is the consummation of all other sacraments; and with official doctrine in the Latin Church, that it operates by intrinsic efficacity, *ex opere operato*, in virtue of its institution by Christ.

VII

THE LAPIS EXILIS

According to Wolfram von Eschenbach, the Graal was the crown of desire understood on the material plane, but it would also respond to the title which was given by Heinrich to his independent version of the legend, for it was certainly the crown of adventure, and on more planes than one. It was borne aloft on a green cushion by the maid who was chosen for the office, and this suggests that the object was, speaking comparatively, small—that is to say, portable. There is nothing in the whole poem to make us connect it with a jewel in the conventional sense, and it is nowhere described actually : it is simply that object of wonder to which the name of Graal is given. It was light as wool, as we have seen, in the hands of its licensed bearer, but an unprepared person could not move it from the place of its repose.

This is rather, however, a question of magic than of variation in specific gravity. *Ex hypothesi*, it was large enough on one specific occasion to hold a considerable inscription on its surface—that is to say, when the King's healing was promised as the reward of the mystic question. At the same time its possible dimensions were restricted by the counter fact that it could and did repose in the nest of a bird which tradition describes as about the size of an eagle. Indeed, the stone which renewed the phœnix recalls the *Lapis Aquilæ*, which, according to another tradition, was sought by the eagle and used to assist the hatching of its eggs.

This enumeration is made to preface some reflections upon the Latin term which Wolfram applied to his talisman. What he wrote—or his scribe rather—we have to divine as we can from the choice of impossibilities which are offered by the extant manuscripts, and that which has received most countenance among the guess-work readings is *Lapis exilis*, meaning the slender stone. The *scholia* of lexicographers on the second of these words indicate some difference of opinion among the learned on the question of its philology—*de etymo mire se torquent viri docti*—and as an additional quota of confusion one of them has placed the significance of slender upon the word exile as it is used in English. I do not know of such an adjective in our language and still less of one bearing this interpretation; but this apart it would seem that the slender stone connecting with the conception of the Graal is even more disconcerting than any philological difficulty. Further, the word *exilis* suffers the meaning of leanness, and this in connection with a stone of plenty which paints in the *Parsifal* an eternal larder, *à parte ante et à parte post*, is not less than hopeless. It may be said that Wolfram's intention was to specify by *Lapis exilis* that his talisman was least among stones in dimension yet great in its efficacy, even as the Scriptures tell us that the mustard seed is least among grains and yet becomes a great tree.

There is a certain plausibility in this, and students of another school will know that *Lapis exilis* is a term which corresponds wholly to the great talisman of metallic transmutation, for no adept experienced any difficulty when he carried the powder of projection—which, as we have seen, was in fact the Stone—in his wallet, or even his girdle, yet this was also great in its efficacy, as there is no need to insist. The explanation is shallow notwithstanding, when we know that the true description of the Graal Stone on the historical side, or rather the accurate statement of fact, would be *è cœlo veniens*. But it is understood of course that this does not enter the lists as a construction of the chaotic readings found in the manuscripts. Their only possible rendering to preserve the verbal similarity with a reasonable consonance in the root-idea of the subject is *Lapis exilii* = the Stone of Exile, or *Lapis exsulis* = the Exile's Stone. The correspondence is here twofold, for in the first place there is the exile of Lucifer, who—if the jewel was once in his crown—lost it on expulsion from heaven, and in the second place there is the exile of humanity, which is *ex hypothesi* a derivation from the fall of the angels. It was given to men as a palladium—perhaps even as a gage of their final exaltation to the thrones vacated above. It so happens that there are some curious lights of symbolism which illustrate a reading that I put forward under every reserve and tentatively. No one will believe at first sight that the Graal Stone and the Graal Chalice can have any affinity between them, unless indeed the cup was hewn—let us say—out of jasper or chalcedony. This notwithstanding, we shall find the analogy rather in unlooked-for places. Let us recur for a moment to the *Lesser Holy Graal* and its comparison of the Mystic Vessel to the Stone in which Christ was laid—an imputed analogy which is put into the mouth of the Master when He discourses to Joseph of Arimathæa, delineating the purport and perfection of the whole mystery. It seems assuredly the most extraordinary analogy which it is

573

possible to institute, and I do not pretend that it assists us to understand the substitution of a Stone for a Chalice in Wolfram's version of the legend, which is devoid of any connection between the Graal and the Passion of Christ—almost as if the Repairer had returned to the heights after the institution of the Eucharist and henceforward Himself—as *Pontifex futurorum bonorum*—sent down the efficacious sacrament for the sustenance of his chosen people. In the ordinary Eucharistic Rite one would tolerate the comparison in respect of the Pyx, though the elucidation of things which *ex hypothesi* are alive by means of things which are dead is scarcely in the order of enlightenment. One thing at least seems to follow from all the texts, and this is that the sacramental Chalice in the Graal Mass was rather the receptacle of the Consecrated Bread than of the Consecrated Wine. The Chalice, which corresponds to a Stone, and this Stone the Rock in which Christ was laid, must symbolise the Vessel of the Bread. In the *Book of the Holy Graal* and in the *Quest of Galahad*, Hosts were taken from the Chalice; in the *Parsifal*, Bread in the first instance was taken from the Talismanic Stone; in Heinrich, that Reliquary which was itself the Graal had a Host reposing therein; Chrétien is vague enough, but his undeclared Warden in prostration seems to have been nourished after the same manner as Mordrains and Heinrich's ghostly Keeper.

The analogy of these things, by which we are helped to their understanding at least up to a certain point, is Scriptural, as we should expect it to be; it connects with that other Stone which followed the people of Israel during forty years in the wilderness, and the interpretation is given by St. Paul. "Our fathers . . . did all eat the same spiritual meat; and did all drink the same spiritual drink : for they drank of that spiritual Rock that followed them : and that Rock was Christ." It will be inferred that the root-idea of the story is based upon the natural fact that torrents or streams flow occasionally through rocky ground, but the masters in Israel knew of the deeper meaning, or divined it at least in their subtlety, seeing that their whole concern was with a spiritual pilgrimage. It is said in the Zoharic tract entitled *The Faithful Shepherd*, that a Stone or Rock is given, and yet another Stone is given, the Name of which is the Name of Tetragrammaton. Now, this is a reference to the Prophecy of Daniel which says that the Stone which struck the statue became like a mountain and filled the whole earth. It is applied to Messias and his Kingdom by the preface to the *Zohar*, which says further that the Israelites, during their exile in Egypt, had lost the Mystery of the Holy Name. When, however, Moses appeared, he recalled this Name to their minds. It follows herefrom that we are dealing with another legend of the Lost Word, and of course if Christ was the Rock or Stone which supplied sustenance to the Jews, we can understand in a vague manner not only the correspondence between the Graal and a Mystic Stone but also the manner—otherwise of all so discounselling—in which the cycle ascribes to its Great Palladium, whether Stone or Cup, a marvellous power of nourishment. The allusion is therefore to the Corner Stone, which is Christ and which became the head of the building. It is the old Talmudic and Kabalistic tradition that the *Lapis fundamentalis* was set in the Temple of Jerusalem under the Ark of the Covenant, even as the Rock of Calvary, by another legend, is called the centre of the world. All these stones in the final exhaustion of symbolism are one Stone, which does not differ from the white cubic stone which the elect receive in the *Apocalypse* together with the New and Secret Name written thereon. This stone in its symbolic form would no doubt be the least possible in cubic measurement— that is to say, in the correspondence between things within and without, even as that which is given, strangely inscribed within, to the recipient in one of the most deeply symbolic of the Masonic High Grades.

Analogies are subtle and analogies are also precarious, but those which I have traced here are at least more in consonance with the spirit of the Graal literature than (1) The Sacred Stone, called the Mother of the Gods, which is mentioned by Ovid and of which Arnobius tells us that it was small and could be carried easily by a single man; (2) the Roman *Lapis manalis*, which brought rain in drought, as it might have brought food in famine; (3) the *Bœtilus* or Oracular Stone which gave oracles to its bearer, speaking with a still small voice.

VIII

THE ANALOGIES OF MASONRY

§ *A*. THE ASSUMPTION OF THE BUILDING GUILD

The interpretation of doctrine is good, but the thing which is essential is life, and thereafter those measures of experience which are proper to the degree of life. In like manner, there is the study of the symbolism which is outside doctrine but gives evidence of its inward sense; herein, as I believe, there are the keys of many sanctuaries, or at least of many gates leading to the holy places; but again it is a certain quality of life—and this only—which sheds light upon symbolism, or by which there is an entrance effected beyond the threshold or artificial and corporate part of secret knowledge and much more therefore into the Holy of Holies. It is in this sense that it is said in the old Scriptures: " He is not the God of the dead but of the living."

As regards the keys and the secrets, it is necessary also that we should distinguish between life and its records. The latter remain as examples, as traces, as evidences, and no one should presume to affirm that they are not of high value. It is, however, after their own manner, and although the bodies of the dead may be embalmed, though they may be laid under all consecrations in the places of rest, and though there is a certain very true and very high manner in which we should look for their glorious resurrection, they remain dead bodies until the Word shall pass above them, crying : "Let these bones live."

It is especially over the place and importance of certain literatures which contain a hidden meaning, and over certain unmanifested confraternities which communicate mysteries other than political in their complexion, that the memorials of the past sometimes prove to be as lavender laid among linen—fragrant, as it may perhaps be, but dead as the past which has buried them. So long, for example, as our great, authorised scholarship—holding, though it does, all warrants of textual research—has recourse only to pre-Christian Celtic records for an explanation of the Graal and its literature, so long it will have nothing to give us but the dry bones of things antecedent in semi-savage folk-lore, and not the essence which is alive. Again, while other experts in research seek among the trade guilds of the Middle Ages for the sources of that which is termed Masonry, they will find nothing that will communicate to them either life or the life of life. Of the latter it should be added that scholarship is not in search, and at its sudden manifestation the old students might be perplexed, and that certainly. I am writing, however, for those who in literature and in secret association would look indifferently for some signs of that quest which they are themselves pursuing—I mean, the Divine Quest. To these I can say plainly that out of the mere things of genealogy there is nothing that can rise again. It is only under high light and guidance that the gift of interpretation, acknowledging all antecedents which have been demonstrated in the historical order, can relegate them to their proper sphere, and can say at need to others, as they have said long since to themselves :

"Seek not the living among the dead; this has risen; it is not here."

I have bracketed for the moment the external history of the Holy Graal with that of Freemasonry, because although the analogy between them is of one kind only it is an analogy of great importance. As a time came when the old Celtic folk-tales were taken over in a Christian and indeed in a mystic interest, as it is only subsequently to this acquisition that the literature of the Holy Graal can be said properly to exist, so also came that hour when the mystery—such as it was—of the old building guild was assumed by another mystery, as a consequence of which it was re-expressed with a different intention, and it is thus, and so only, that, as a shadow of things beyond it, there came into being the association which we understand as symbolical Masonry. So far as we can regard it under the aspect of a succeeding or co-incident witness, the epoch of Kabalism was prolonged by the scholiasts of the *Zohar*, until that period when the next witness was beginning to emerge. After this manner I return to my initial statement that the gift of interpretation is good, but that which is essential is life. It is only the spirit of life which can account, in whatever form it was manifested, for the assumption either of the romance-literature or the particular craft. Without it we have indeed interpretations, as we have also hypotheses of origin, but they are devoid of true roots. As a species of extra-illustration in the first case, there have been various hypotheses put forward which are neither countenanced by the records of the past nor characterised by a gift of understanding; while in the second case we have had simply the romance of archæology or that alternative gift which fills gaps in history by arbitrary suppositions masqued thinly in the guise of fact. Official authorities may be sometimes short of sight, as they are, outside their horizon, but these un-accredited intermediaries have brought their subjects into something approaching disdain, though a sense of justice inclines me to add that creators of wild hypothesis, with all their distracted material, sometimes make shots in the dark which come nearer to the true goal than the more sober skill which aims only in one direction, but at what happens to be a false object.

The historical side of Masonry has at this day its expositors and students who are characterised by the same patient and untiring spirit which supports other branches of research. They have done valuable work in the past and again will do so in the future, but at present all zeal is held in suspension by the exhaustion of materials—I speak here of the things which are or would be of living and high importance, not of those which are subsidiary or accidental. These too serve their purpose, but they have little or no office in the larger issues ; they keep green the spirit of inquiry, which takes into its field the things that signify little and so keeps its hands on the plough. It is better for that spirit to investigate at need the memorials of local lodges than to perish of enforced inanition. It is excusable also, and in a sense it is even good, to exaggerate in one's mind the importance of such tasks, to make much of the little till the great comes in our way, and then to make more of that. But some things—and these vital—which exceed the sphere understood as that of research, pass out of sight in this manner, because, excepting for very gifted, very keen—may I say ?—illuminated minds, a dry stick in the hand, though it has no probability of blooming like Aaron's rod, is for some practical purposes more convenient than a live sapling at the top of an inaccessible hill. This is rather the position of those things out of sight which I have at the moment mentioned ; the lesser memorials and their aspects tend to keep them where they are—in remote and unnoticed distances. It is not my design to impeach the historical sense—to which all exaltations and crowns !—but there is a dual difficulty in the path of the perfect term, for the heart of imagination—and those orders—is inhibited by this sense, while imagination, in the excess of its enthusiasm, takes the heart out of history and sets in its place I know not what spirit of fantasy. Between these gulfs on either side of the prudent way, to be an historian is hard.

For myself—if I may be permitted to say so—I present the first consideration of the Holy Graal from a mystic standpoint, which, so far as I am aware, is founded on the requisite knowledge of every existing text. It is such knowledge or its result that enables me to take the *via prudentiæ* which I have mentioned, and to find that, accepting most statements made by official scholarship with any show of evidence, all the important points remain in my hands unaffected. In exactly the same way we can afford—and that gladly—to let the Masonic authorities prosecute their search for still earlier records of the building guilds, while in the absence of fresh materials we can sympathise with their sorrow and aspiration. If things much more archaic than have been so far found should in fine reward their vigilance, it will be all honour to their industry, but it will be also small concern of ours. Let us make a ceremonial obeisance before anything of this kind which may yet transpire, as we do—and also gladly—before the records of Mary's Chapel. I know beforehand the best that can be said about those which are possibly to come, as I know of those which are among us. They will be, as these others are, excellent and valuable within their own degree, but they will not signify beyond it, and they will not serve any purpose which I can claim to cherish in common with those to whom my appeal is made herein. The Elohim may have formed Adam of the dust of the earth, but it is useless to question that dust concerning man who was created male and female, as the sign of life and its perpetuity. It is useless equally to question the old craft guild concerning symbolical Masonry, since it was not by a natural development that the one was transformed into the other ; the seeds of the transformation were brought from very far away, or, to express it more correctly, the craft, as we have it, is not an example of growth after the ordinary kind but of an exceedingly curious grafting. The ground of contention is not that things of handicraft could never have developed by possibility into allegory and symbolism, but that they could not, as the result of that process, have produced the synthesis and summary of all past initiation which we find in the symbolical degrees. Now, it is at the point of grafting, or taking over, and this because of the results which I have just specified, that we, as transcendentalists or mystics, become concerned— and then only—in Masonry.

For the better illustration of my purpose let me now make a short distinction concerning three classes : (1) There are those who have a love for the *minima* of instituted mystery ; who, if they are carefully sifted, would be found to attach some importance to the possession in common with B and C of certain titles, signs and passwords which are unknown to X and Y ; (2) there are those who believe, and this in all honesty, that morality is enhanced when expressed, let us say, in parables ; when materialised by analogical representation ; when decorated by a ceremonial pageant ; (3) there are, in fine, those who are looking for the real things, among whom we ask to be inscribed—at least as the lovers of truth, if we cannot with the same boldness demand to be classed among those who love God. This lesser—or is it an equivalent ?—nomenclature we require on the faith that our certain criteria enable us at least to know in what directions, and under what circumstances, it is useless to go in search of real things.

It will be agreed that the first class does not call for our serious attention ; they are children, with full licence to take all joy in their play. The second class is entitled to a measure of our respect, for they are at least on the side of the natural goodness, and they re-cognise in their own mode that it is not exactly in a position to stand alone. At the same time they mistake a means for an end, and they do not know where to turn for the only efficacious consecrations; so that these also signify only in the lesser degree. I have indicated already that it is to the third class that all my thesis is addressed; its members are in a position to appreciate the historical aspects at their proper value, giving to this natural Cæsar all that belongs to Cæsar, yet confessing to some great reservations, which are not less than the things that concern God.

Speaking therefore in the interests of this class, and in terms which they will understand, there is a sharp alternative as follows: Masonry is either consanguineous by the root-meaning of its symbols and legends with schools of real experience; either it shows forth the one thing about which we have been in labour from the beginning, or it returns in the last resource into the category of the Worshipful Company of Vintners, of Cardmakers, of Fishmongers, and so forth. These are admirable institutions, and to be free of them, which is not easy, is no less than a civic distinction. So also are the friendly societies, in their way, excellent, including that Order of Buffaloes which, perhaps because it is late in its series, is termed antediluvian; but if we are incorporated by these it is for much the same reason that we may be members of a Ratepayers' Association, namely, for benefit and protection in common. These are good reasons, but it is not on account of eternal life that they move us in a given direction.

Eternal Life—initiates, companions and brethren of all the sodalities!—I know well that from the mere reference there will follow the irresistible question: What is there in Masonry, or in any of the allied Orders, which can justify us in suggesting that they might or could be taken up in conjunction with a quest after eternal life? Now, the most pertinent questions are those which have replied to themselves already in the mind of the speaker, and, in this case, the persons who would ask might answer : Masonry is obviously the remanent of a trade guild, which once had its trade secrets and covenanted those whom it received to divulge nothing in respect of its mystery to any who were outside the particular craft of building. They would not conclude at this point, but we may intervene for a moment with an observation on our own part. Assume that, so far as it has proceeded, this is a correct answer, and what then follows ? It is not now a building guild ; it has no longer any trade secrets ; there is perhaps no class of society which would be more utterly discounselled by the suggestion that it should design edifices, or should even dig foundations and lay bricks. To this extent therefore, as the inheritors of a building guild, the Order is apparently stultified. It has as little part in its antecedents and precursors as had the Christ of the fourth gospel in the coming Prince of this world. The proper answer of symbolical Freemasonry as to the operative art might well be : In me it hath not anything.

Those even who are acquainted merely with the rituals of craft Masonry—and they may be numerous enough outside the ranks of the brotherhood—will here intervene and say, in continuation of that answer which I have so far given in part : That is true, or at least in a certain sense ; but the old craft guild became symbolised, and its instruments, and ritual procedure, were taken over—since you emphasise the term—by the genius of allegory, so that things which were originally physical were exalted into the moral order, and thus they remain till to-day, as the rites, teachings and documents prove indubitably. This is estimable and convincing in its way ; it so happens, however, that an appeal of the kind is going to prove too much ; and yet it is by such a clear issue that we shall reach one term of our subject.

§ *B*. MASONRY AND MORAL SCIENCE

I must put my first point somewhat roughly and crudely, with an apology for the frankness which it involves ; decoration is here impossible, and on account of so much that will yet remain to say after, I believe that I shall be exonerated in the end. The ethical position is then, so far as Masonry is concerned, a sincere attempt—and this simply—to effect a sanctification of things which of necessity and essentially are obvious in moral teachings. No one challenges these teachings, and in the world about us no one cares anything. It cannot be less than regrettable if any person should join either one or another confraternity with the idea of improving his ethical position, not because the design is anything except highly laudable, but because his most proper incentives are in himself and his daily life. No association has anything to tell him which he does not know already, and this from his earliest childhood. If I may speak my whole mind, after having followed many highways and byways, I should say that his best and only necessary guides are the official religions, the gate of which is morality, as I have striven to make plain elsewhere. It is they that provide the spirit and reason which—unless he is called to go further, and that journey will be further within them—should actuate his conduct, just as the laws of his country take charge of the letter thereof, and see that it shall be constructed after their manner and not according to his own.

From this view it is impossible to derogate, and it is difficult, in respect of it, to qualify ; but there is one matter over which misconception may be avoided. Let it be understood therefore that I do not take exception to the ethical value of Masonic or the other laws—in those matters which belong to the conduct of life—because it is so obviously identical with the written or unwritten law of all civilised conscience ; but I affirm that a knowledge which is possessed independently by all, which is mainly derived from unassisted lights of Nature, which no one disputes seriously, which is withal so simple that there is no difficulty in teaching it directly, which in fine has been taught us in our catechisms, even at the knees of our mothers—I affirm that this knowledge does not require an allegorical and ceremonial system of considerable complexity to explain or enforce it. There is above all no evident warrant for secrecy and mystery in the plain basis of individual and social morality. It must be added that, on the evidence of their own history, the associations included by my category have not succeeded in developing a more perfect moral man than has any other system of ethical discipline which is now at work in the world. They do not therefore possess a more powerful instrument than are other instruments with which we may be acquainted independently. When it is said that a Mason, for example, who abides scrupulously by the rule of his Order, cannot fail to be a good man, such a statement may be accepted without reserve ; but since the laws of Masonry are simply the expression of an universal ethical standard, as much may be declared of any person, initiated or not initiated, who elects to guide his life by the recognised code of morality and goodwill, more especially as the element of *esprit de corps* scarcely enters into questions of this nature.

A certain severity will be read into these strictures, more especially as the majority of Masons have never supposed that their association could offer a higher light than that of good conduct in exaltation, and I ought therefore to add that if this were really the limit of its horizon, so far as they are concerned, the craft as such is—in one sense—amply justified. That which is desirable for them, that which for them is the term and aim of goodness may not only be their strong incentive but a necessity in the lesser degree. Moreover, on broader grounds it is no matter of pretence, for it has never, except in some spurious high grades, which are its burden and not its possession, offered more than it can give. It is not, therefore, as it was described by De Quincey, the great imposture of the modern world; and if it be an error of enthusiasm to put forward an ideal of natural goodness in the guise of a mystery of knowledge, one can only wish that the effect had been to make that ideal an actuality over the whole world.

All this notwithstanding, its success or failure along these lines could be scarcely a special concern of ours, who know of ways as excellent after its own kind and of better ways beyond them. I return therefore to my previous proposition—that Masonry can interest us so far only as it enshrines something more than an ethical doctrine and instruction. This other thing is not, however, by way of *additamentum*, but by way of essence. The recognition of such an essence will enable us to understand more clearly some of the lesser processes, or at least to tolerate them more patiently, as first stages in a history of development which have also the heights as their term. I may alienate the sympathies of some of my readers, seeing that there are so many listeners, but the explanation of this last point lies to my mind in the fact that the *raison d'être* of all natural goodness must be sought in the law of grace. So also it remains that the churches are still the accredited guides because grace has its channels therein, or so at least till we transmute the official beliefs into direct experience and thus enter not into that which is apart from them, but that which is their wider consciousness. In the meantime, all that is innocent, all that is blameless, all that is of fair repute makes in fine for goodness; and if that goodness is natural in the first degree, it has also a mode of dissolution into the goodness which transcends Nature. If therefore the laws of brotherly love are maintained and promoted in a lodge of Masons, as they certainly are, it is all honour to Masonry, and so much towards the reign of peace on earth. But it is not less true that it is easy, and very easy, to reach those limits beyond which it has scarcely entered into the heart of Masonry to conceive—by which I mean as it is so far understood in the lodges ; as it is to be judged by its literature ; and as, outside all personal initiation, we may know it in the life of its members. It is at this point that some who are on higher quests than those of conduct must part with it, leaving their benedictions behind them ; or that they must find therein, after all the horizon of ethics has been at last traversed, some region beyond the ordinary ken which may prove the land of their desire. Beyond the seven bands which comprise the spectrum of the corporal works of mercy, there are other rays of light, and in Masonry also there are rays beyond the violet. We may glean something concerning them from its history, but we must seek above all in its symbolism and in the proper meaning of its legends. To conclude as to this part, Masonry either belongs to the secret tradition or it is for us made void.

§ C. A Theory of Hermetic Interference

Having given an example of the manner in which symbolical Masonry explains, as if almost on its own part, how the old craft guild was taken over and transformed, and—although it is by no means suggested that Mary's Chapel and Canongate Kilwinning should burn their earliest records—having seen that the surface explanation is characterised by great insufficiency, I will now show another side of the same subject, prior to which it is assumed that even if craft Masonry may be subject to certain errors of enthusiasm, it has always good faith on its side. On the other hand, outside its records and their inferences, and shipped upon the great sea of speculation, I have seldom met with any subject which has produced more explicit falsehood in the manufacture of historical materials than has the question of the origins of Masonry. There is no need to specify the mendacious legends of some of the high degrees, for they carry their proper seals and marks upon their mere surface. Let us rather take for our illustration one great name in the literature of the craft, for I suppose that there is none more respected in its own country than is that of J. M. Ragon among the Masons of France. I believe that, on questions of historical fact, his authority has been regarded as almost final. He appears indeed as a sober and careful recorder, though it is obvious that he had several strong pre-judgments interleaving his notes of researches, and these would, in any case, make his impartiality doubtful. It must, however, be said that between his materials, some of which must have come to him already tinkered, and his peculiar construction of facts, it is almost pure incautiousness to take anything that he says unverified. He is at the same time the one writer in modern times—that is to say, in and about the year 1853—who has spoken with the most unhesitating voice on the origin of symbolical Masonry outside any natural development of the old craft mystery. In order that I may do no unconscious injustice, I will put his thesis as nearly as possible in his own words.

"Philosophical Masonry," he says, "which neither in fact nor in name had any existence previously, was conceived and embodied in three rituals, in the year 1646, by Elias Ashmole, who rediscovered antique initiation, as Mesmer rediscovered magnetism" (*Orthodoxie Maconnique*, p. 5). "It is from this primitive source that the Masonic world has drawn that light which illuminates its labours" (*ib.*). In the same year, being that which saw the reception of Ashmole into the old building guild, a society of Rosicrucians, formed on the plan of Bacon's *New Atlantis*, assembled at Freemason's Hall, London. Ashmole and the other brethren of the Rose-Cross, seeing that speculative Masons already exceeded the diminishing remnant of operative members, concluded that the time had come to abrogate the old form of reception and to substitute a written method of initiation, based upon the Ancient Mysteries, and especially those of Egypt and Greece. "The first grade was composed, substantially as we now have it" (p. 29). It received the approbation of the initiates, and the grade of Fellow-Craft was devised in 1648, being followed by the Grade of Master a short time subsequently. The specific object of Ashmole was to regenerate, under the veil of architecture, the mysteries of ancient Indian and Egyptian initiation and to provide the new association with a bond of union, fraternity, perfection, equality and science, grounded upon the laws of Nature and the love of humanity (*ib.*, p. 99). The learned alchemist codified all the oral traditions; they assumed a form and body; and this was the true and proper beginning of Freemasonry, as we now have it (*ib.*, p. 292).

It will be seen that I have not overestimated the force and finality of these statements; it would appear almost incredible that they could be a pure invention of Ragon, or a mere fable which he took over from some earlier source that cannot now be identified; yet this is the case actually, and outside the bare fact that Ashmole was received into the old craft guild, as he records in a few cold and detached lines of his private diary, there is no particle of evidence to support it. That it were otherwise I could well desire, for I have said that the craft was acquired, and that which took it over knew well enough the purport of the Ancient Mysteries, or, under all its veils and subterfuges, we could never have had the legend of the Chief Degree, nor the equally memorable closing which is attached thereto. But the bodies of tradition, which may coincide, and that closely—which may reflect on one another—which may independently testify to each other—are not derived from one another, and the Alchemists, as such, did not invent Masonry. I do not propose to go over the ground which I have traversed in some previous writings and in particular to recite the conclusions of my *Studies in Mysticism* as to spiritual rebirth in connection with Masonic Doctrine and Symbolism. That herein lies the true understanding of the Craft Degrees, I am entirely certain, and it is to this point that the grades lead up from the beginning. That the mysteries which we call ancient—though I think that in some form they are always in the world—were concerned with no other subject, I am not less certain. Outside all offices of Masonry there are derivations of the Rosy Cross which, although at a great distance, testify concerning the same doctrine and the same high experience; the old records of the brotherhood also testify; and as there is at least one school of alchemical literature which has inwritten the secret life of the soul under the veil of metallic transmutation, there would be no cause for surprise if we could trace the interference of one or other of the Hermetic fraternities in the transformation of the building guild into symbolical Freemasonry. But the evidence of fact is wanting, either by the way of record or otherwise; while as regards the change in itself, this is much too general in its character to show the hand of an individual school. We must be content therefore with the voice of the grades themselves, with the legends and the symbolism which they involve.

§ *D.* One Key to the Sanctuary

It should be understood that I am speaking at the present moment only of the craft degrees. I have every reason to know that the high grades do not deserve the unqualified condemnation with which they have been set aside by writers like Ragon and by certain expositors of the German school of Masonic thought. Several of them are great rites which embody important mystic teaching, and without some of them I regard the craft degrees as offering, mystically speaking, an unfinished experience. Those, however, who are familiar with the craft rituals—about which I do not intend to speak otherwise than by assuming such knowledge—will be in a position to realise how far they can be said to embody an ethical doctrine, except as side-issues of their mystery. There is, of course, a very plain inculcation of certain obvious virtues, but it is all so slight, and it is all so obvious, that to speak of it as an ethical system seems to magnify the subject out of all due proportion. On the other hand, we do find certain provinces of knowledge recommended to the study of the candidate at one stage of his advancement. We find also certain illustrations of a great mystery of building, certain references to a secret which has been lost, and a great legend concerning the destruction of a master of knowledge who took away with him that secret, and except under very deep veils, outside all craft Masonry, it has not been since recovered. As I have quoted Ragon in a connection which was necessarily unfavourable, let me now cite him in a different sense. He has said that when we find in Masonry and in some other secret ways of the past a reference to building—whether of temples, palaces, or towns—what is intended is that there was a manifestation of doctrine ; in other words, there was an ordered communication of mysteries. As to the great majority of instances, I believe in this as little as I believe that Troy town was a solar mythos ; but in respect of craft Masonry it is the one note of illumination in Ragon's great wild of speculation and discursion on the degrees, high and otherwise, of the fraternity. We may be quite certain that those who transformed the building guild did not intend to put forward an historical thesis. The change which took place pre-supposes such a spiritualisation of the traditional temple that it passes into the world of symbolism, becoming itself a House of Doctrine. If, apart from the question of mystical death and rebirth, which I have set aside from consideration in this paper, we are to look anywhere for another clue, it is in the amazing inference which follows from the craft legend concerning the stultification of the House of Doctrine before its erection was finished. Those who are familiar with the rituals will understand exactly what I mean, and I give this as the key by which any one who is properly qualified, and who chooses, may really open one of the secret sanctuaries. We know that the Master was asked one little question, and that for one little answer which he declined to make the traditional founder of doctrine came to an end of violence ; the mysteries which he reserved perished in his person, and although it has never been noticed so far by any Masonic writer in the living world, it follows therefrom that the Great Symbolical Temple was not finished according to the original plans. It is for this reason that symbolically, if not actually, the True Temple still remains to be erected. Meanwhile, in Masonry, as in other institutions, we rest content as we can with certain conventional proxies in which we suppose, by a precarious hypothesis, which has, however, a profound meaning imbedded, that some analogy inheres. It is understood that two kings who represented at one time the royal houses of official Grace and Nature knew the canonical answer to the question, supposing that this had been put under the due warrants, but it is to be inferred that it was the verbal formula and not the ground-plan of the mystic building. In any case it remained *Sacramentum Regis*, the Secret of the King, and it follows, still speaking symbolically, that all Masonry derives not from a lodge of Masters but from that of an inferior grade. The missing formula was a word of life, and the *locum tenens*, by a contradistinctive analogy, is a word of death. It is for this reason that the whole corporate fraternity undertakes a Quest which is in rigid correspondence with that of the Round Table, but they move in the opposite direction to that in which the Mysteries repose. It is the most mystical of all inquests, for it is the history of our human life. But there is an Orient from on high which in fine rises on the soul ; the soul turns in that light and moves thenceforward in the true and one direction.

It is possible to express what follows from these facts in terms of comparative simplicity, for even as Moses came down from the mountain of God with a veil upon the face of him, so have I been speaking thus far to the mixed assembly of my readers under the veil of a careful reservation, because these things are not to be discussed in public without changing the voice. Let me say now more openly, since this is permitted, that the ideal of the True Temple is in our hearts, and it is there that we rebuild it. We do this daily by all the aspirations of our nature, but for want of the lost designs we have not been able to externalise it. No doubt we have not led the life which entitles us to know of the doctrine ; we feel that it is implied and latent in all the roots of our being ; and we seem to die with it on our lips. It speaks in our dreams but it uses an unknown language, and if heart utters it to heart, it is only in oracles. But we have conceived enough regarding it to be aware that the Spiritual Temple is a House not made with hands. And so neither Masonry nor any other one of the great instituted Mysteries has designed a rebuilding of material holy places. The rites of initiation may deal—as they do certainly—in parables and in allegories ; they may present—and they do also—their particular forms of thought in the guise of a legend of yesterday, but they are really the legends of to-morrow, the expressed heart of expectation and not a retrospective review. But if this be the case—as it is indeed beyond challenge—what part have we otherwise in Masonry, seeing that we have come out of Jewry as others came out of Egypt ? If this, I say, be the case, what manner of House was that which was planned of old in wisdom and was afterwards finished as it best could be, because treason fell upon the keeper, because, in the absence of preparation and title, there had been an attempt to take the Kingdom of

Heaven by violence ? Let us seek our first illustrative answer from an episode of the Law which was once promulgated in Israel. Moses the prophet came down in his glory from Mount Sinai bringing with him the Tables of the Law, but he found his rebellious people unqualified for the high knowledge, and before the face of them he broke those tables. Afterwards he gave them indeed certain commandments, but I do not doubt that they were the shadows of the others only—the code of unruly children, not of the elected truly. The world was not worthy. And the second example is that which we know already—that the Graal was taken away, that something was missing thereafter from the House of Quest, that again the world was not worthy. The three stories are therefore one story, and the same thing is everywhere. It is so much everywhere that the knowledge which remained with Moses was not withdrawn utterly by him—according to the tradition of Israel—when he went up the mountain in fine, when no man living followed him, when he did not return ever more. It has been held always in Jewry that there were certain elders who received the secret deposit and transmitted it in their turn in secret, so that it was perpetuated from generation to generation till it became known to the world at large, but only in an imperfect form, about the middle period of the Christian centuries. The original *Zohar* is reported by a paradox to have been a sufficient load for twelve camels, and the extant *Zohar* is on its own showing a substitute. The correspondence in Graal literature is the disparting of the Hallows among certain holy hermits and the removal of the Sacred Vessel to that place of which Perceval should know surely and with all speed.

That which was made void, according to the great craft legend, was a non-Christian House of Doctrine. The step beyond this is to show that there is a parallel in Masonry concerning Christian doctrine, but it is found in high degrees and in those which are militantly

Christian. If I were asked to speak frankly, I should call it a concealed legend of Templar vengeance. It is an old story in the high grades that the murder of Jacques de Molai was destined to be avenged heavily, and one section of criticism has concluded that this was effected ultimately by the decapitation of Louis XVI.; but this is romance of Faerie. Whether the supposed vengeance came otherwise to anything I am not prepared to say, but I can show that the secret plan was more deeply laid, though it may have been actuated by far different motives than inhere usually in the idea of vengeance. The plan is not illustrated by any legend of murder or by anything that, remotely or approximately, can suggest a *vendetta ;* but in one Masonic grade which, by the hypothesis, is the last transformation of the Templars, the fact is shown forth by the silent eloquence of symbolism. As in the craft degrees we learn how the vital secret was taken away, so here the rite sets before us a picture of all Christendom, personified by the flower of its chivalry, standing guard, amidst the adjuncts of pomp and ceremony, over a vacant sepulchre—the shrine from which a God has departed. Could anything signify more profoundly the bereavement and widowhood of the Christian House of Doctrine ? Could anything indicate more pregnantly the presence of a sub-surface design among the old Knights Templars, supposing that this grade were really, at some far distance, descended therefrom ? Would it not seem like a challenge by the way of evasion, saying to the modern world : "Do you suppose, in your fondness, that about those hallows of the past our intention was ever centralised except to conceal it ? "

Our next step takes us to a grade which is, comparatively speaking, obscure, though it is still worked in England. It is one the position and claim of which is a little difficult to determine, whether as to origin or history. On the surface its similarity to the eighteenth degree of Rose Croix has caused many persons to repudiate it as a mere copy. The better view is, however, to infer that both rites originated from a common prototype, and I may mention here that there are not only several variants of the eighteenth degree incorporated by other systems, but there have also been Rosicrucian degrees current from time to time in Masonry which have very slight correspondence with the grade supereminent of the Ancient and Accepted Scottish Rite. This question apart, the particular chivalrous and Masonic Order is rendered important to our present purpose because it gives the symbolical counterpart by alternative of that intimation which is conveyed in the analogous grade. The latter represents a particular state of the assumed case at the period of the Crusades, the former at an epoch which—on account of several historical confusions, having an appearance of design —is scarcely possible to determine. In any event it dissolves at a certain stage into yet another degree, and between the successive points of the two rituals the candidate is brought to a period when all earthly Houses of Doctrine have given place to the high spiritual House of Eternal Wisdom. As a preliminary to this, the externalised House of Doctrine, represented by the Holy Sepulchre, is made subject to a simple visitation, with the result that it is found empty, and those who look therein are told in a veiled manner that in such a place it is useless to go in quest of lost secrets, because the Divine Warden thereof has risen and gone away. As the candidate—and this of necessity—is left always in the position of Satan after his lectures at Salamanca, that is to say, with the shadow instead of the substance, so here the chivalry of the sepulchre has to be content with what it has—with the rumour of the resurrection constructed into glad tidings, though it remains that the place of the Hallows is now an empty place.

Our last step takes us again to the literature of the Holy Graal, which depicts a House of Doctrine, like the temples, towns and palaces of which we have been speaking previously. It shows how that House was in the first place visited by sin and sorrow ; how secondly it was made void, the secret things thereto belonging being transferred therefrom. Symbolism has sometimes the way of sparing nothing, and probably the makers of the legend intended only—as some expressly say—to show how the realm of Logres had become unworthy of the most holy things ; but the House of the Doctrine is involved in the common ruin.

The question which now supervenes is one which will occur spontaneously to all those who have followed this account. Is it intended to suggest—shall I say ?— that the secret of Masonry is anti-Jewish and anti-Christian, or, to put it better, that the interests which took over the building guild had either never entered into those holy places of the past or had come forth therefrom ? The answer is a decisive negative. It follows from all the legends, all the symbolism, or that part at least which is other than accidental, and in fine from all the rituals of Masonry, that those who set forth the widowhood of the House of Doctrine spoke not from without it but from within ; that they looked for the return of that which, for the time, had been taken away ; that when they speak to us of what was lost to Jewry, they were never more assured of the wisdom which once dwelt in Israel ; that when they mourn over the Holy Sepulchre, they were never more certain that what has been removed is alive ; and as all the degrees end in a substituted restoration it is also certain that thither where the truth and beauty had been taken they looked also to go. In other words, it is the intimation of the secret schools that somewhere in time and the world there is that which can confer upon the candidate a real as well as a symbolical experience. And this is the identical message of the Graal literature ; it speaks too from within the official House of Christian Doctrine concerning that which once inhered therein and is now in the state of withdrawal or profound latency; but it offers all honour and devotion to the substituted sanctuary which remains, as Masonry offers it in the higher understanding both to Jew and Christian. Here therefore is no enemy setting to at the work of destruction, but here rather are the rumours and voices as if of Unknown Superiors, like a power—which makes for righteousness—between the seat of Peter and the seat of the chief Patriarch, as if something were guiding and consoling all the keepers of the keys, but dissuading them at the same time from the opening of certain doors till that which has been lost is at length restored to the sanctuaries. It is in this sense only that we shall ever get to understand the inner Mystery of the Holy Graal, the Mystery of the Craft Degrees, and of the great, disordered cohort of things from near and far—reflections, rumours, replicæ and morganatic descents from older Mysteries—which make up the cloud of witnesses in the high degrees. The work, not indeed of the same hands but of many at the same work, is therefore everywhere, the traces of the same high intention, the evidence—not less strong because it is not declared openly—of masters, who are also our brothers, watching haply over the quests of humanity and shaping them, at proper seasons, to the true ends.

I conclude therefore (1) that Masonry is herein referred to its true place and is saved otherwise from the category of vain observances that are consecrated by good intention, because it leads us back, after many travellings, to the one subject; (2) that it is an index-finger pointing to other rites, to pure and exalted ceremonies, which—somewhat shadowy, somewhat dubious, yet distinguishable as to their purpose—remain among the records of the past, not without suggestions that, even at this day, the Mysteries have not died utterly.

I have made it plain already that in so far as there is mystic purpose or hidden doctrine in the Graal literature it is at most an echo from afar—a rumour, a legend which had fallen into the hands of romancers. It is as if Sir Walter Montbeliard, the patron of Robert de Borron, being by the hypothesis a Templar, had told a strange story to the poet of things which he also had heard from afar concerning the Sons of the Valley ; it is as if Guiot de Provence, having seen a transcript from Toledo, had compared it with some Templar records belonging to the house of Anjou. These are not the directions of research, but they stand for more likely ways, and I put forward as so many materials of assistance, so many traces of the same implicits perpetuated through several centuries—(*a*) the Sacramental Mystery of Alchemy as corresponding to the Eucharistic Mystery of the Holy Graal ; (*b*) the mystical pageant of Kabalism as analogical to the Graal pageant ; (*c*) certain quests in Masonry as synonymous with the Graal Quest. The conclusion is that from the middle of the twelfth century, and so forward, there has been always a witness in the world that the greatest and the highest among the holy things have been represented by a certain substitution within the official churches. The churches have not been made void ; they are still " those holy fields " ; but they bear the same relation to the sacred mystery behind them that Sinai and Horeb, Tabor and Carmel, Gethsemane and Calvary, bear to the official churches. Remember that the highest office in no sense makes void the second best among any offices that are inferior. The Supernatural Graal is without prejudice to the instituted sacrament, even as the transliterations and complexities of Kabalistic interpretation reduce nothing in the literal word.

IX

THE HALLOWS OF THE GRAAL MYSTERY RE-DISCOVERED IN THE TALISMANS OF THE TAROT

To restate the fact that the canonical Hallows of the Graal legend are the Cup, the Lance, the Sword and the Dish will seem almost impertinent at this stage; the least versed of my readers will regard it as a weary re-iteration, for he and they all are in plenary possession of whatever need be said upon the subject. I must specify the bare fact, this notwithstanding, because of what follows hereafter. And it may seem to arise from the repetition if, further, I recall to their minds—and my own memory—one experience which comes to us all, and startles us when it does come, revealing the fund of unobservance to which we must confess by necessity. When any of us have been studying exhaustively—as we think—a given subject and are surfeited in our familiarity therewith, it may happen that we alight unawares on something which had escaped us utterly. It may be through the random remark of a stranger, through an apparently detached sentence in a forgotten or unknown book, but the well of other waters is opened and we see the whole thing under a new aspect. On the surface this illustrates the difficulty with which we notice anything that is ever so little outside our special groove; but there are times when it seems to have a deeper root, and we realise in our hearts that anything may serve as a pretext to open another horizon—" a flower, a leaf, the ocean " may touch and kindle " the electric chain wherewith we are darkly bound." So falls the " spark from heaven." Now, as an example to the purpose in hand, I wonder how many critical works have been written on the Holy Graal, and yet it has occurred to no one that its Hallows, under a slight modification, may be somewhere else in the world than in those old books of romance. I might have shown that their bases are in modern high grades of Masonry, but I can understand how this has been missed, and my default means that I have not attached undue importance to the fact. But they are to be found also in the most unexpected of all places, outside the grades of literature, and they have existed there from what would be termed masonically time immemorial. They are in the antecedents of our playing-cards—that is to say, in the old Talismans of the Tarot. These are things which, in a sense, are almost of world-wide knowledge, which have interested innumerable people, which still constitute, as they have constituted for generations and centuries, the most prolific form of divination and the vagrant art of fortune-telling. We know nothing concerning their origin and of their distribution little enough. I trust that I am least disposed of any one to assume the antiquity of doubtful documents or to predate traditions on the basis of their uncertain origin. I leave to those whom it may concern the history of playing-cards and their precedents, this so-called *Book of Thoth*, nor do I need to recite, even shortly, what has been assumed regarding it, because one class of scholarship which has dealt more particularly with the question of historical antiquity in these matters is that precisely which lies under most suspicion on the ground of its enthusiasm. In particular the measures on the side of speculation are pressed down and running over with every kind of folly and extravagance. The uttermost of all hazards is expressed in the language of certitude, even as J. M. Ragon expressed the hazard of a root-connection between Elias Ashmole and the institution of speculative Masonry. There is another order of learning which has confined itself to the simple archæology of the subject with sober and valuable results ; by such people I shall be challenged scarcely if I say that there are traces of the Tarot cards in the fourteenth century, prior to which they are not of necessity non-existent because, like the Graal itself, they are lost to sight.

Archæology is, however, its own term, so that usually there is nothing beyond it; and therefore, having so far distinguished between two schools, I must say that there is yet another side which might rivet attention generally if it were possible to speak fully concerning it. I record in the first place (*a*) that the correspondence of certain Tarot symbols with those of the Holy Graal stands rather in the light of a discovery without a consequence which I can pretend to develop here; and (*b*) the reason will, I think, be evident because this side which I have mentioned reposes in certain secret schools now existing in Europe. In these the Talismans of the Tarot have been pressed into the service of a logical, constructed system of symbolism with results that are very curious. It might or might not be useless to speak about the system in public, supposing that this were possible, but I think that there are considerations involved which would be almost an unknown language to people who have not had their training in a particular school of thought. Those who know regard the results as important, yet those who see the importance have not in most cases any idea of the term. As I must now say that this term belongs under one of its aspects to the domain of occultism, it should be understood that my strictures on wild Tarot speculations ought to carry a certain weight because those speculations are of the occult order. If any of my readers should wish to look a little further into a strange and problematical subject, they may be recommended to consult one book called *Le Tarot des Bohémiens*, issued by the French school of philosophical Martinism. I can tell them for their consolation that from root to branch it is a tissue of errors, because this school has not the true reading, while specific alternative readings in other academies are also wrong. Except in purely archæological aspects, the inquirer can, however, get nothing better than the content of this work, and if he misses the major sacraments he will find a limited quantity of fortune-telling rubbish therein which is altogether diverting and may be mastered with a little trouble.

It must be explained that the old sheaf of oracles consists of seventy-eight cards, of which fifty-six are the equivalents of ordinary playing-cards, plus four knights; and the remaining twenty-two are pictorial keys, the symbolical nature of which is seen on their surface, though it must be understood that hereon all of them are conventional and many are grotesque, as if they were coarse allegories. The keys are allocated by interpretation in various orders to the letters of the Hebrew alphabet, and herefrom as a root many instituted analogies with Kabalism have been devised by the divergent schools which have devoted their attention to the pictures. The Sephirotic attributions which have been obtained in this way are especially remarkable. I offer my assurance, as one who has more to lose than to gain by making the statement, that certain secret schools have developed their scheme of symbolic interpretation to a very high point by the allocation of these cards according to a system which is not known outside them.

Having made this explanation, my next point is to state that the four palmary symbols of the Tarot are—

1. The Cup, corresponding to Hearts in the common signs of cards.
2. The Wand, corresponding to Diamonds in the common signs of cards.
3. The Sword, corresponding to Spades in the common signs of cards.
4. The Pentacle, corresponding to Clubs in the common signs of cards.

The Wand is alternately a sceptre in the Tarot descriptions, but its proper alternative in the symbolism is a spear or lance, the misdescribed Diamond in the modern suit being obviously the head of the weapon. In respect of the Pentacle that which is depicted under this name answers to a dish, usually after the outline of a four-leaved shamrock, or alternatively of a circle. In either case the emblem is also misdescribed under the term Pentacle, which must have five angles or flanges. With these modifications, which are in no sense of an arbitrary kind, the Tarot suits are actually the Graal Hallows.

And now, to move one step forward, being the last point to which I can take the subject : The place of the Cup in the extension of the symbolism under the light of all its analogies, corresponds to the place of spiritual life ; to the rest of knowledge ; to the receptacle of the graces which are above and to the channel of their communication to things which are below ; but this is the equivalent *ex hypothesi* of the arch-natural Eucharist. In a word, it is the world not manifested, and this is the world of adeptship, attained by sanctity. In so far therefore as it can be said in the open day, hereof is the message of the Secret Tradition in Christian times—as it remains among the guardians thereof—on the subject of the Graal Mystery. So also under a certain transfiguration does the Graal still appear in the Hidden Sanctuaries.

But now in conclusion generally as to all the schools of symbolism, successive or coincident : it follows from the considerations which I have developed in what approaches an exhaustive manner that we are confronted by two theses, from the first of which it follows that the Mystery of Divine Attainment is of that order which passes into experience, while dubiously and elusively its traces are met with even in the modern world, though it does not say " Come quickly " to the majority of aspirants. From the second it follows that the great secret—at least so far as its specific declaration and visible existence are concerned—has passed into abeyance in the external sanctuaries. I can scarcely conceive of a clearer issue established by way of contrast. Several accredited scholars have recognised the evidences of secret doctrine in the Graal literature, more especially in respect of the Eucharist, but some of them have been disposed to account for its presence by a familiarity with obscure apocryphal gospels. This is a source in legend, and of sources in the experiences of sanctity or of perpetuated secret doctrine they knew little enough. In particular they did not dream that such perpetuation could have taken place except in heretical schools. They appreciated the concealment of sects which carried their lives in danger, but not the concealment of the sanctuary. There is, however, the vision of the Third Heaven, about which it is not lawful to speak, the reason being that it exceeds expression, and utterance is therefore only by way of similitude and approximation. The secret school for which I look and of which I recognise the existence did not differ in doctrine from the external ways of salvation, but it opened out the infinite world which lies behind the manifest life of teaching—that world which was recognised by St. Augustine when he said—as we have seen —that the definition of Three Persons subsisting in one God was not an expression which satisfied the mind, but that some kind of expression is necessary. This school never came forward with improvements on doctrine, with proposals to reduce doctrine, or with new opinions on the Eucharist. It carried the implicits of religious teaching to their final issue ; the implicits were Catholic and the issue was also Catholic.

Therefore so it remains to this day, while we in our spiritual isolation are conscious of loss everywhere.

The great rites are celebrated, the high offices continue, the moving liturgical formulæ are recited from day to day and year after year ; we pass hurriedly through the crowded streets, over the quiet countrysides ; we pause by solitary seas. The veiled voices signify the Presence, yet the Master is taken away, and we know not where they have laid Him. The great legends tell us that He has been assumed into Heaven because of the evil times, or that He is in a place of concealment, or that He is not seen so openly. Prohibited, spoliated and extirpated with fire and sword, the memory of the dead sects of Southern France can offer us at their highest only the lips of the noble lady Esclairmonde communicating the *osculum fraternitatis—consolamentum* of all things saddest—through the flames of the *auto-da-fé*. One Masonic chivalry consents to protect us from the insidious attacks of the infidel if we visit the holy fields, but it is confessed that the sepulchre is empty and we know that the worst danger is from the infidel who is within. A later and more obscure chivalry, with a vainer office of observance, keeps ritual guard over the shadow of a sacred legend, we asking the daughters of Zion whether there is any greater desolation. It pledges us to maintain the Sepulchre when it is agreed that the Master is not there, and we continue to say with our lips : *Et unam sanctam catholicam et apostolicam ecclesiam*, with a certain unconscious relief that the word *Credo* stands far away in the symbol. Saddest and proudest of all, the great craft legends of Masonry tell us that until that which from time immemorial has been lost in the secret places is at length restored to the mysteries, the true temple can only be built in the heart. The Kabalistic sages are also waiting for the word, that there may be mercy on every side, and the stress and terror of the centuries is because Adonai has been substituted for Jehovah in the true form thereof. It is only the higher side of alchemy which, without faltering, has continued to point the path of attainment, speaking of no change, no substitution therein—telling us of the one matter, the one vessel, the one way of perfection, yet also saying that except the Divine Guidance lead us in the path of illumination, no man shall acquire the most hidden of all secrets without a Master, which is another mode of expressing the same thing. I suppose that there is no more unvarying witness continued through the ages, amidst all which we have felt, as we still feel, that only a small change in the axis of inclination would transform the world of greatest inhibition into that of the greatest grace. It is as if we were in the position of Perceval, according to the High History—as if we had failed only on account of " óne little question." But we do not know what it is, or rather we know it only in its external and substituted forms. We go on, therefore, sadly enough and slowly, yet in a sense we are haunted men, with a voice saying ever and again in our ears : " Ask, and ye shall receive " ; search your heart, for the true question is within and the answer thereof.—A sad and strange enchantment has fallen even over the animal world, and all the gentle creatures with kind eyes are waiting with us for the close of the adventurous times, the term of enchantment in Logres, and the unspelling quest. Of these three things, two are of the Order of Mercy and one is of the High Order of the Union. All this is not to say that the high offices fail, that the great conventions are abrogated, that the glorious sense of chivalry towards our second mother in those sodalities which are external—but yet in that order are some intellectual and some also spiritual—that this sense is not of the highest counsel. But a time comes when the " glory to God in the highest," having been declared sufficiently without, is expressed more perfectly within, and we know in fine that this glory is to be revealed.

The same story of loss is therefore everywhere, but it is never told twice in the same way. Now it is a despoiled sanctuary ; now a withdrawn sacramental mystery ; now the abandonment of a great military and religious order ; now the age-long frustration of the greatest building plan which was ever conceived ; now the Lost Word of Kabalism ; now the vacancy of the most holy of all sepulchres. But the sanctuary is sacred, the king is to return, the Order of Chivalry has not really died ; at some undeclared time, and under some unknown circumstances, the Word which gives the key to some treasure-house of the building plan will be restored in full, and meanwhile the quest is continued for ever; the true Word will also be restored to Israel, and so from age to age goes on the great story of divine expectation. Meanwhile the Christian mystics say : " Take no thought for the morrow, because it is here and now " ; and to this grand antiphon the response of the Hermetic Mystery is : " Even so, in the place of wisdom there is still the Stone of the Wise."

BOOK X

THE SECRET CHURCH

THE ARGUMENT

The Hidden Church of the Holy Graal

schools of the Secret Tradition—Further concerning spiritual alchemy—The Quest of the Graal—Of Kabalism and Masonry—The proper understanding of a doctrine of loss in the Church—The Church as the House of Souls—Orthodoxy of the Graal literature—Its branches from this point of view —That its rumours and implicits are not the voice of a rival Christian conclave working in the hidden places—The same is to be said of Kabalism and Masonry—The position of Alchemy—Removal of a certain interdict on speech and thought—Councillor Karl von Eckartshausen—The Cloud on the Sanctuary—Loupoukine—His Characteristics of the Interior Church—The conception of a Holy Assembly— The sodality of a consciousness in common—The rise of a more express witness—A confusion in respect of the evidence —An illustration from the natural world—The Visible Church in connection with the doctrine of a Holy Assembly —Comparison of the Secret Church to a School of the Prophets—Inferences from secret fraternities—Testimony of the Sons of the Valley—Specific claim put forward by The Cloud on the Sanctuary—Its reduction into a complete schedule—The similar evidence of Loupoukine— Errors of expression in both witnesses—That the Secret Church is an arbitrary name—Definition of the mystic life—Of certain elements in the hands of the Graal romancers—That the Secret Church recognises the external Church—The consensus of sanctity—That the Secret Church is not an instituted Assembly—Of Mass in the Secret Church—Of certain limits to expression—The Graal literature as a rumour of Sanctuary Doctrine—Mystery concerning the rumour—How the official Sanctuary is made void. IV. THE MYSTERY WHICH IS WITHIN.—The Secret Church as an hypothesis, an implicit and a truth—Condi-

The Argument

tions of its membership—That it has not issued manifestoes —In what sense the evidence is misleading concerning it— The silence of its work—Its chief mystery as that of Divine Communication—Its connection with the Eucharist—The Secret Church as an integration of believers in the higher consciousness. V. THE SECLUDED AND UNKNOWN SANCTUARY.—An alternative for the romances of the Graal—A further summary concerning the Secret Tradition—The mystery of love and the world of grace—Another reconsideration of the literature—A new comparison from alchemy— The Graal romances as an implied impeachment of Rome— Whether the Graal Church stood for official Christianity— The Rich Fisherman from this point of view—Difficulties of this assumption—Conclusion that the Hidden Sanctuary could not represent the Visible Church of Rome—Evidence of the literature itself on this subject—Whether the literature was, in some other sense, hostile to Rome—Assumption that the Graal sanctuary was really the Celtic Church— Evidence of the literature from this standpoint—The claim of the Lesser Chronicles is in conflict with the assumption— The Greater Chronicles are in some respects militantly Roman—One text only may be concerned with the aggrandisement of British Christianity—A note on the German cycle—Of certain plain stories told by the Graal texts— The mystery of the Graal Sanctuary—The makers of the literature did not dream of a pan-Britannic Church— Clearness of its concern at the highest—A lesson of these considerations—Its various counsels of caution—The true Question of the Graal—The literature as a witness of the Church—Of experience in transcendence—The harmony of all quests and histories outside the terms of romance—The Hidden Church of the Holy Graal—The hope of Western

The Hidden Church of the Holy Graal

Mysticism—The Secret Tradition in Catholic Experience. VI. THE TRADITION OF ST. JOHN THE DIVINE.—*That the Secret Tradition in Christian times was never put into official language as by one instituted school which stood for the whole—Eckartshausen approximated only—Loupoukine expressed probably a strong intellectual sentiment—Were there no traces in the annals of the Church itself?—The* Disciplina Arcani—*Whether this was imbedded in the tradition of St. John the Divine—The Eucharist and the beloved disciple—Traditions concerning St. John—The rumour of his secret knowledge—In what manner he was assumed by the physical alchemists—The search after heresy—Some previous speculations—One suggested alternative—Of so-called Johannine Christians—Traditions concerning St. John—Traces of a higher Gnosis—An unfinished Quest.* VII. THE CONCLUSION OF THIS HOLY QUEST.—*Of certain unfulfilled covenants—Preliminary remarks—The Veil of the Eucharist—The French and German Percivals—Collectanea Mystica—The Lost Book—The Great Experiment—The Inner House of Doctrine—The world of attainment—Of the highest symbols as pretexts—The Mystic Quest—A praise of scholarship—But of that also which remains after—And this as a Spiritual Sun—The monastic Graal—Of that which may be superadded to the official consciousness of the Church—The many voices of tradition—The one testimony—An end of these pleadings—The colophon.*

BOOK X

THE SECRET CHURCH

I

THE HERMENEUTICS OF THE HOLY GRAAL

Two things follow from the considerations of the ninth book : (*a*) That there are or there have been custodians of secret knowledge in Christian times, but I express only my personal view if I say that they remain to this day ; (*b*) that the term of their purpose does not differ in kind from that of the external Churches ; but (*c*) by their claim they had carried the Great Experiment further. Their testimony offers therefore (1) deeper intimations of Church doctrine ; (2) a contribution in concealment to the annals of the life of sanctity ; (3) by the remembrance—in perpetuity of dedication—that there is one thing needful; (4) and this is to partake, if it be possible, of Divine Substance—that is, spirit and life—of which the impermanent consubstantiation with Divine Humanity in the official Eucharist is the vestige in symbolism only. The way of attainment must have had its doctrinal correspondence in the Descent of the Paraclete. It does not follow that the custodians celebrated what we understand by a Mass, but it is impossible to delineate their process by a stricter analogy. After exhausting all other considerations we can speak of it only in this manner. I suggest that it was said in the heart, and that Christ came down into the heart. It follows that for those unseen masters, as for us also, the *Mysterium Fidei* was the Eucharist. The Greek

Epiclesis clause may pass, therefore, among official things as the nearest approach to a rite above all things valid, that is, manifesting supernaturally. Its history is one of the most interesting in the wild garden of liturgical formulæ. It should be understood, in this connection, that during the earlier days of the Church there was not a method of consecration which prevailed everywhere ; the Latin rite held, with certain variations, to the canonical words of institution, as I have shown in a previous section ; but there are traces of instances in which it was performed by the recitation of an *Oratio Dominica*—possibly the *Pater noster* over the elements, thus by the hypothesis converting the daily bread into heavenly manna. By the hypothesis also, the *Epiclesis* clause brought down upon the elements the influence and even the presence of the Holy Ghost, and it must be admitted that this contains, ritually speaking, a very high suggestion. At the Council of Florence the Latins required the Greeks to expunge the *Epiclesis*, with all forms of invocation, and there can be no doubt that they were doctrinally and technically correct, within the convention of their own order, because it was admitted on all hands that the words of institution produced a valid Eucharist, and the principle of invocation was to give the officiating priest within the range of the convention an express and personal part in the mystery of consecrating, which, by the same hypothesis, must be regarded as superfluous, though we can—on our own part—discern a deeper reason. The clause remains to this day in the Greek Church, and for those who lay stress on its efficacy that Church has therefore the words but not seemingly more than the outward sign of that life which should be resident therein.

If it be said that in these considerations the Churches are impeached collectively, and because the literature of the Graal creates exactly the same contrast in the same manner exactly, that it therefore concurs in the impeachment, the conclusion on the surface may seem almost irresistible, but that it is untrue is my whole contention. The facts which here follow must be held to silence any voices of dissent. We have seen that there are three literatures which testify concerning the voided House of Doctrine. (*a*) The first is the Graal literature, and in no uncertain way does it bear witness that the official Church has the efficacious means. (*b*) The second is Zoharic Kabalism, with all its connections, but while it tells of the cloud on the official sanctuary of Israel, this also bears witness (1) that Israel is of God; (2) that the Church in Israel contains the Words of the Mystery, with the reflection at least of the cohabiting glory, and (3) that the way of salvation is that Law by which the world was made in Mercy. (*c*) The third is Masonry, and in the dual schools thereof —which are the Craft and High Degrees—it bears the same witness: (1) that the Symbolic Temple is the Holy Place, but the Spiritual Temple is to come; (2) that the Lord has risen truly, and though at the present time we do not know certainly where we shall find Him, we are on the Quest which does not fail. I say therefore again that there has been no more faithful testimony throughout the centuries. It does not concern a competitive orthodoxy or a distinct process, but the development of the same doctrine and the extension of the same process to what is called in Masonry the *ne plus ultra* degree. It is not that anything exists outside the Church, but that more subsists within it than is comprehended by the lower grades. The equivalent is that the Law of Nature reflects the Law of Grace, and the perfect paradox that Nature imitates Grace.

The external Church is therefore, and so it remains, that body in which the first work of regeneration takes place—and this, as one may say, of necessity; it is the reflection of life everlasting projected on the perishable plane. It is in this sense the condign and legitimate governor of all holy external places. The Church is the good husbandman who prepares the ground and tills the earth of humanity. It fertilises that earth after various manners, as, for example, by the laws of moral conduct, by the great literatures, by the high consecration of the seven sacraments, by the water, the oils and the wine. In all these ways it sows with a generous hand the seeds of secret life. But the earth is hard and the earth is also unresponsive. The seed will germinate in many directions, and the earth will therefore be irradiated by a certain undeclared presence of the secret life ; but it issues above the ground only in a few cases, and then the individual enters into the manifested life of sanctity. It is a question thereafter of the particular quality of the earth and the environment of the life. Generally the growth is stunted and too weak to put forth its powers. It is only on rare occasions that they spring up into the high light and the clear air, lifting the radiant glory of a perfect head amidst their peers.

The hidden life of the soul is well known to the doctors of the soul, and the Church has also its hidden life, wherein it communicates with all things nearest to the Divine in the higher consciousness. Official doctrine is, however, in the same position as normal consciousness ; it covers a part of the field only. There is therefore, on both sides, a certain sense of the incommensurate, and assuredly it is for this reason that the Churches are desolate ; such desolation is, however, on account of that which is in hiding, not of that which is withdrawn. The offices are not abrogated and the sacraments are still administered, being also efficacious up to a determined point. Perhaps indeed the desolation is not less especially in ourselves, so that it is we who individually and collectively have helped to make void the House of Doctrine. The fact that the external Church is from this point of view in widowhood makes its desertion a grave offence against the high unwritten code of chivalry, just as a dereliction of masonic good conduct is implied in forsaking one's mother lodge. At the same time the great work can sometimes be done from without as well as from within, but in this case that work is an approximation towards a higher side of the Church.

It follows that the official Church can act only up to the extent of its consciousness, and the side on which it has derogated has been the side of policy and conduct. We can account in this manner for all its imperfections, for that which we term its abuses, but there will remain the glories of its doctrine as things which, in their proper understanding, emerge apart and unaffected. These are the treasures which it was instituted to preserve, and if it has added some things to the jewel-house which are of secondary or even dubious value, our part is to wait for its wakening in the higher mind. The Greek Rite has slept over-long therein, and the Roman Rite has had nightmares, but the happy Prince, who is a true Son of the House, will arrive one of these days and will ask the unspelling question. Meanwhile, the individual man must be appraised at his highest only, so far as that highest has been indicated, and it is the same with the Church. The lower standards are deceptive, and it is for this reason that conduct—as we understand it conventionally—is comparatively of less importance ; it is that which maintains the world and not that which renews it. There is also the irrefutable consideration of all those unhappy sects which exist for the dissemination of a contracted symbolism under the guise of pure doctrine, thinking that the situation can be ameliorated by taking in their fairyland. The undue multiplication of symbols tends, of necessity, to attenuate their force by spreading it over too large a surface, but it is not to be compared with the malefic dismemberment of symbolism, which produces its paralysis, for the loss of so many limbs causes the body to decay and puts an end to the office of the Wardens.

II

THE GOOD HUSBANDMAN

At the risk of some repetition on a subject of all so vital, I will put the position thus from another standpoint. The value of the Graal legends resides in their suggestions and lights towards a concordat of Divine Alliance, while the Graal Castle is the House of Alliance and of the doctrine thereto belonging. The same description applies to the Sanctuaries of the other schools, on the understanding that in the last resource all the Sanctuaries are one. They do not differ from the external Houses of Doctrine into which we were born and wherein we were first nourished by the food of souls. Here also—if we set apart innumerable temples of the fantastic spirit—the House of Doctrine is one, and the official does not differ from the mystical; but in the one House there are many chambers, being those of the soul's advancement, and the soul in response to its election proceeds by stage and by stage on the ascent upward—or beyond and further beyond into that more secret place which lies behind the sanctuary of the Visible Church. The correspondence in identity hereto is the oratory of the spiritual alchemist, who testifies by first-hand experience at the Fountain of Nature and Grace that nothing has been lost, that he has himself recovered the working process in which the Trinity is manifested and the plan of redemption is exhibited.

The Graal literature was the spiritual emotion of the Church expressed in romance. The texts which do not correspond to this description are of no importance as mystic texts of the legend. I set apart, however, the lost poem of Guiot, which will be considered in another section. The high texts of all are products of monasticism, and—as they are extant among us—the vision which is the true Graal came out of cells and scriptoria. We must not go further for that which is ready to our hand in the nearest places. The monks conceived the high miracle of sanctity and connected it with a wonderful and pious legend. They knew so much that they knew also the void in the heart of the age and the maiming of the outer Church. The efficacious Graal —that which alone profits us—came out of their fasts, watches and prayers. They did not invent the Secret Words and the super-apostolical priesthood, but they knew of these rumours ; they knew that many strange quests were pursued about them ; they dreamed of mysteries of sanctity which they had not fathomed, and we can well understand that the story of Prester John re-expressed the dream after a manner of parable in their yearning minds. When they left the House of Doctrine void in respect of its chief Hallow, they meant only that the Church shared on its manifest side the inhibition of the age ; they felt all that was wanting thereto. But the first makers of texts had heard of those things more plainly—that is, of a priesthood within the priesthood, of a Mass behind the Mass, or rather the equivalents of these by the pursuit of an experiment which was identical with that of the Church carried— as I have said—to an advanced degree. The putative letter of Prester John was perhaps invented expressly to put this claim forward in a singularly evasive manner, but one certain to attract universal interest and attention.

The experiment had been pursued everywhere, the aphorism which ruled it being *omnia exeunt in mysterium,* the pursuit of that Mystery to which St. Augustine alluded when he said that Christianity had been always in the world—to which the New Testament itself alluded when speaking of the Lamb slain from the foundation of the cosmic order. It follows that any one who suggests that the experiment or the school became Christian at a certain epoch is in error over the elements of that subject to which must be attributed in a superlative sense the *locus communis* of the ecclesiastical test : *Quod semper, quod ubique, quod ab omnibus*. We should remember that things which concur with one another do of necessity find one another at a certain point of their extension ; the one Quest adopts many veils, but without diminution of identity. It has been disguised very often under the old formula concerning words of power, but though this is a necessary illustration, it carries a suggestion of fatality, because in no instance did the sign survive the idea—and so lapse into superstition—more frequently or with greater facility. In its proper understanding it corresponds to the idea of an union between the expressed consciousness of the soul and the Word of God—the *verbum caro factum*, declaring itself in the world and in the heart of man. Robert de Borron heard or read of the rumour in some such form and he combined it with secret words of Christ. He knew so little of its horizon that he left it an open question whether the words were Eucharistic or not. Those who converted his work into prose concluded that they could have no other office, and so allocated them accordingly. The author of the *Book of the Holy Graal*, having certain materials, including those which were incorporated in his prologue, put forward the rumour in the guise of a sacerdotal mystery and followed those who had preceded him in developing the conversion legend. Guiot de Provence represented the secret custodians as an autonomous chivalry after the model of the Knights Templars, bringing into it materials from oriental sources. Other traditions had already presented Joseph of Arimathæa as the Grand Master of an instituted knighthood. The authors of the *Longer Prose Perceval* and the *Quest of Galahad* saw that the whole subject belonged to the Church, and they connected it with Eucharistic transubstantiation as the most approximate gate through which supernatural faith could follow those things which issue in mystery. They were glad enough when their symbolism had served its purpose to allow its dissolution, as I have shown, and it has been in no sense my design to suggest that they had overcome all burdens of their period by an excess of wisdom ; the glass through which they looked was clouded and scoriated enough, and in manifesting the doctrine as they did I suppose that its intolerable sense had never occurred to them. It is sufficient for our purpose that they discerned something of the secrets which lay beyond, to do which they must have travelled far. I am sure also that in common with the independent schools of concealment they distinguished between the Church as the custodian of Rite, Symbol and Doctrine and the seat of government at Rome. In this connection it is wholesome to remember, among many other points that might be enumerated : (1) That before 1000 A.D. Claudius, Archbishop of Turin, characterised the censure pronounced on his anti-papal writings as the voice of the members of Satan ; (2) that Arnulph, the Bishop of Orleans, at the Council of Rheims pointed to the Roman Pontiff, saying : " Who is that seated upon a high throne and radiant with purple and gold ? . . . If he thus follow uncharitableness, . . . he must be Antichrist sitting in the Temple of God ; (3) that Everard, Bishop of Salzburg, said much later : " He who is the *servus servorum Dei* desires to be lord of lords ; he profanes, he pillages, he defrauds, he robs, he murders, and he is the lost man who is called Antichrist ; (4) that Cardinal Benno, speaking of Sylvester II., said that by God's permission he rose from the abyss ; (5) that the same pope was described at the Council of Brixen as the false monk and the prince of abomination. These were the accusations of prelates and with them may be compared the opinion of Figueiras the troubadour, who described Rome as an immoral and faithless city, having its seat fixed in the depths of hell ; that of Petrarch, who called Avignon the western Babylon, and—as a comparison by way of antithesis with the Rich Fisherman—exclaimed :

" Here reigns a proud race of fishermen who are poor no longer ; " and that of the same poet who described the papal court as a people who follow the example of Judas Iscariot—in other words, selling God for money, like the King of Castle Mortal. So also St. Bridget termed Rome the whirlpool of hell and the house of mammon, wherein the devil barters the patrimony of Christ.

I think it has been indicated abundantly in the course of this work, but more especially in the present sections, that the high truth is in all Church doctrine, and therefore in citing these instances I also am far from expressing the spirit of impeachment ; but on the side of policy, apart from that of teaching, there is evidence enough that the yoke was no longer easy nor the burden light. It is conceivable that the symbol of the voided House of Doctrine was an appeal against the Church in so far as it had been unfaithful to itself, a protest against the spirit of the world which had invaded the sanctuary. The admission of these facts does not derogate from the claim that the Church had all the means. Even in new definitions and altered practice there may have been a guiding hand. It will be suggested, I know, that at the period of the Graal literature two unhappy ferments were working in the Western branch : (1) The denial of the chalice ; (2) the various doctrinal tendencies which resulted in the definition of transubstantiation. From this point of view the wound of the Latin Church would be that it misconstrued the *Mysterium Fidei ;* that it had, in fact, five wounds corresponding to the five changes of the Graal. Of these changes the last only seemed to be a chalice, for at that time it is said that there was no chalice, and the mystic reason of this is that the *Dominus qui non pars est sed totum* is not contained in a chalice though the Lord is *Pars hereditatis meæ et calicis mei.* The Latin Church cannot be accused of having failed to discern the Body of the Lord, but it may be advanced that its discernment, like that of the Greek orthodoxy, was apart from the life which their own scriptures tell them is resident in the blood—that is to say, it is the symbolical seat thereof. And yet on the basis of transubstantiation it is difficult to reject the Roman plea, that he who receives the Body receives also the Blood, because that which is communicated in the Eucharist is the living Christ made Flesh. To this it may be rejoined that the implicit of the symbolism is really in the contrary sense, that the elements are dual to show how the flesh of itself profits nothing, while the spirit and the truth are in the communication of Divine Life. By those who regard transubstantiation as the burden of the Church which defined it, there is a disposition to consider the Latin Eucharist as only a dismembered sacrament; by those who look upon it simply as a memorial, all subtleties notwithstanding, there is a feeling that the memory is broken and that the isolated sign does not signify fully. On the other hand, that view which belongs more especially to the Mystics, namely, that the covenant of Christ to his followers concerns what I have called so frequently the communication of Divine Substance, will, I think, be aware that the accidents of such a communication are not of vital consequence; that perhaps the official Church was even more subtle than it knew, because it is certain that transposition or substitution in the external signs cannot occasion even the shadow of vicissitude in the mystery which is imparted. In fine, to extinguish these questions, those who speak of Christ's spiritual presence say well, but the mystery of abiding redemption is the perpetuity of the incarnation in that Church to which Christ came in flesh.

In conclusion, I do not confess that it would be putting the case truly if it were said that at the period of the Graal literature the highest minds of the Church had grown weary of the Vatican and all its ways. I think that for long, and for very long indeed, there had existed an uncompetitive stream of tendency which raised no voice, but pursued its path unobtrusively towards a very high term. It had no remedies to offer on the practical side of things and it was too wise to denounce abuses which it was powerless to remedy—even as I who write, supposing that I had attained the term of the Great Experiment, should not for that reason be qualified to purify the commercial houses of exchange. That term belongs to a region about which it is idle to speak in connection with schemes of amelioration or the raising of the masses. So far as those who have pursued or do now follow it have led or to-day lead the life of the world, it is implied in their calling that they should do what to do is given them, but in respect of the Experiment itself, those who attain can lead others on the way, but they do not bring back helping hands for the furtherance and welfare of the body politic. So much for the stream of tendency in the earlier times. At a later period I do think that the unknown mystics who wrote upon spiritual alchemy had got to see not only where the path of sanctity led, but that the Church as a whole had lost the power of leading. They were made circumspect by the anxiety of their position, and they spoke only in parables.

III

THE CATHOLIC SECRET OF THE LITERATURE

But if there were custodians of a Secret Tradition at any time during the Christian centuries there arises the inevitable question : Who were these mysterious Wardens and also where were they ? Can we learn anything about them ? What was this strange power or influence working within the Church ? Well, in the first place, it was not a power at all in any acting, governing, or intervening sense. When I speak about the region of a higher consciousness behind the manifest mind of the Catholic Church, it is equivalent to saying that in the uttermost degrees of sanctity, the *consensus omnium sanctorum* does by a certain participation become the *sensus Spiritus Sancti*. It is, again, as if within the Church Militant there had been always a little body which had pursued a peculiar path and had travelled a great distance, making no obvious sign. We are faced, however, by the apparent problem of two schools which seem to bear testimony in conflict, and there is the witness to both in the Graal literature. The first is that of spiritual alchemy, which knows not the voice of faltering concerning the *terra viventium* and the *Bona Domini* therein. Its correspondence in the Graal literature is the grace and secret knowledge behind the Eucharist, when the sensible veils of bread and wine and the ultra-sensible veils of thaumaturgic transubstantiation have utterly dissolved, and God is revealed in Christ. The second is the testimony of Kabalism and Masonry to the glory departed from the Sanctuary, and hereof the Graal correspondence is the dispartition of the Hallows, the removal of the Sacred Vessel and the voiding of the Holy House. Looking, it will be said, on either side ; on the experiment of alchemy, than which nothing seems lost more obviously at this late day ; on the Quest of the Graal, over which the chivalry of Logres—except for twelve knights—broke and went to pieces utterly ; on the theosophy of Israel, all dead and all forgotten ; on the sad confession—*ab origine symboli*—of loss and dereliction in Masonry ; how is there any choice to be taken between either school ? If " green's forsaken and yellow's forsworn," in virtue of what melancholy persuasion can we exercise a preference among them ? Surely beneath the title of this book there should be written the word *Ichabod*, "the glory has departed." On the contrary I have written : *Vel sanctum invenit, vel sanctum facit*, for the implicits of the Graal literature are the shadowed secrets of a Holy School, or rather their inexpress formulation. I confess that in either school it may seem difficult on the surface to suppose another construction than that of a treasure which there was but a treasure which is now withdrawn. And, as if to accentuate the position, I have said on my own part that the official sanctuary has closed down on its higher consciousness. But in so recording I have testified in the same terms that everything remains. The house is not less mine because I have locked its doors on the outer side ; the ancestral heirlooms are still in my keeping, though I have not opened the secret chambers for so many moons or years that I have forgotten the fact of the keys still hanging, with many others, from my girdle. The Church, in like manner, is still the House of Souls ; the Castle behind which there is the Earthly Paradise and Eden ; the Temple with a Sanctuary on the other side of which there is the Ark of the New Covenant—the Hidden Altar of Repose, wherein is the Sacred Vessel. It is obvious therefore that no other House of God is possible in this age, and that if I or another were to institute a Church of the Holy Graal, dedicated to the Quest of the Sacred Vessel, and in hope of the grace thereof, I should have my pains for my recompense and I should communicate nothing therein. Our part is therefore one of watching and prayer until such time as the Church herself unfolds from within and all the doors are opened.

In harmony herewith, the characteristic of the Graal literature is its great ostensible orthodoxy, and that which is ostensible I regard also as implied and involved within. Here and there we discern a dubious hint which might signify a subdued hostility towards Rome ; but its sacraments are still the sacraments ; its doctrines are true doctrines, and its practices are the code of spiritual life. The metrical romance of De Borron is a Catholic poem, and if the *Early Merlin* and the *Didot Perceval* are scarcely religious works, there is no tincture of dissent from either institution or dogma ; there are only the Secret Words and what is signified therein. The *Book of the Holy Graal* is a religious romance, and its one questionable element is the meaning of the Super-Apostolical Succession. The zeal of the Graal has eaten up the later *Merlin* in both the texts thereof. The *Longer Prose Perceval* is the Church of chivalry spiritualised. The *Romance of Lancelot* is the ideal spirit in the exile of a morganatic marriage, but still remembering Zion. The *Quest of Galahad* is of him who came forth from Jerusalem and returned thereto ; he was born in the place of the Great Mystery, but it was necessary that he should be put outside the gates thereof and should win his way back ; he is the only seeker who belonged to the House from his beginning.

There is another point which is not of less importance, and I hope that this also will be seen to follow with clearness from what has been said previously. The rumours and implicits of the Graal literature being in no sense the voice of any Christian conclave speaking on its own authority from the hidden places ; and Kabalism —though it bears the same testimony—being a confession of insufficiency on the part of a cognate but non-Christian school, and therefore only an accessory deponent ; it should be understood further that the voice of Masonry is also not the authoritative voice of such a conclave ; it is the testimony of those who knew, who derived their symbolism from the old mysteries of spiritual rebirth, and, for the rest, on their own warrants made an experiment on the mind of their age. The one voice which we can and must recognise as the most approximate echo or replica of the Unknown Voice is that of alchemy—which only adored and exemplified in respect of Church doctrine. It is understood that I do not put forward the literature of spiritual alchemy as the *corpus doctrinale* of those who in Christian times were the Wardens of the Secret Tradition. Masonry, Kabalism, the root-matter of a few Graal books are all in their special manner and under their particular reserves the independent channels of the doctrine. Deeply imbedded in the higher side of the Hermetic works I believe that we get nearest to the Secret Tradition. A time came when the bare possibility of speaking more openly led to more open speaking, and so in the eighteenth century and the first flush of the age which followed thereafter, we have two or three text-books wherein are put forth the most express intimations on the subject which have so far transpired in the world. I will speak only of two, which were at once independent and concurrent—Eckartshausen's *Cloud on the Sanctuary* and *Characteristics of the Interior Church*, attributed to a Russian named Lopoukine and said to be translated from the Russian. The dates of these works are respectively 1800 and 1801.

Such as are acquainted with the literature of the mystic life will not be unfamiliar with the conception of a Holy Assembly in the hands of which the guidance of the Christian Church is thought to have rested during the ages of Christendom. It is not, by the claim put forward, more especially a corporate union than the life of humanity at large on this earth is also a corporate union. It will not have occurred of necessity to my colleagues in thought, but they will understand what is meant when I say that the hypothetical Holy Assembly should perhaps be described as the sodality of a consciousness in common, and as I have spoken already of a consciousness behind the Church as of a region now untrodden, it will be understood that on the present supposition this region is not vacant. As we have inferred further from the researches of the ninth book that there are in specific literatures the records of a Secret Tradition in Christian times, the written veils of which are actually those literatures, so in the Doctrine of the Holy Assembly we find a late, sporadic, but unusually definite witness which, after an entirely new manner, is saying the same thing. I believe that the mode in which this claim has been advanced, though in one sense it is the most temperate and moderate of all, does tend towards a certain confusion because two streams of influence are identified therein—one being the holy, exalted and saving mind of the official Church at its own highest in the manifest, and the other that of the Hidden School itself as this is presented in the claim. The inference, moreover, seems to be that the Holy Assembly is a kind of head in concealment, and this I reject because of the misconception which it tends to induce of necessity. If we could suppose for a moment that man is the last development and issue from the anthropoid ape— much as one might agree to regard the story of the princess who came out of the water as a little chronicle of fact—that point—and whatever that point might be—at which the animal consciousness passed into the human consciousness would represent the analogical kind of transition by which the members of the mystical body enter—if they do enter—into the consciousness of the Holy Assembly. But the human being is not leading the anthropoid ape, nor are the adepts who devised symbolical Masonry ruling the Craft from a specific, unseen centre. The worst of all illustrations would be, in like manner, to say that the Visible Church is the body and the Secret Church is the head. The Visible Church has been described most truly as the mystical body of Christ, and the Real Presence in the Eucharist is the mystical communication in perpetuity of Christ's life to that body ; but this is on the understanding that the body is the incorporation of souls in sanctity. In respect of the Holy Assembly a similar description may obtain, but also on the understanding that it is a generic union of illuminated spirits in Christ— making use of the term spirit in that sense which attributes to man the possession of a higher soul. The head is Christ in both cases indifferently, but in the case of the Secret Church that Divine Union, which here is of faith or imputation, has been established there under the sun of consciousness.

Perhaps, within the more familiar forms of expression, the idea of the Secret Church corresponds most closely with that which is understood by a school of the prophets, though the term describes an advanced spiritual state by one only of the gifts which belong thereto. The gift itself has little connection with the external meaning of prophecy ; it is not especially the power of seeing forward, but rather of sight within. In subjects of this kind, as in other subjects, the greater includes the lesser—it being of minor importance to discern, for example, the coming of Christ in a glass of vision than to realise, either before or after, the deep significance of that coming. So also the interpretation of doctrine is not manifested so much by the exhibition of meaning behind meaning as of truth understanding truth.

I suppose that it would be almost impossible to undertake a more arduous task than that which is imposed on me in these sections of this last book. My experience in the secret fraternities is that those which work under any warrants, and with any shadow of tradition behind them, suggest, in spite of their divergences, a single root of all, and this is so patent that even in exoteric circles the hand of the Hermetic brotherhoods has been surmised in Craft Masonry ; of the Rosicrucians in the high grades ; of so-called Magian adepts in Knight Templary—and hence onward and onward. The root fact at the back of all these dreams is the actuality of an experiment which has always existed in the world, which has never changed, which has been pursued unceasingly by a few, the rumours of which are everywhere, which has many literatures, and all these literatures are veils. When the German poet Werner produced his wonderful legend concerning the Sons of the Valley as the guiding hand behind the old Order of the Temple ; when he told how it was afterwards withdrawn, so that they were left to their fate in the power of the French King and the miserable pontiff ; he—Werner—was dreaming of this Experiment and those who pursued it. In after-days he struck out this hypothesis and all element of life from his two strange plays; but apart from any Templar hypothesis he knew that he was on the right track, in the light of which knowledge he took the path of Lancelot and died as a priest of the Latin Church, having sung Mass for I know not how many moons. When Eckartshausen, who had been born in the sanctuary and was filled with the spirit of the sanctuary, made an end of composing little books of popular devotion which took Germany and France by storm, he saw that the Great Experiment and its great tradition were in truth the secret of the sanctuary and the heritage thereof. People who did not understand him said: " This is Deism "— but it was the higher mystery of the Eucharist in the adyta of a conceived Holy Assembly, and he it was— as I have hinted—who, on the intellectual side, drew nearest of all to the heart of truth within.

The scheme of his interpretation of those Mysteries of Compassion which summarise God's providence towards man for the fulfilment of our return into union may be divided into a part of preamble and a part of definition. The preamble announces the conditions by which an entrance is hypothetically possible into the communion of saints. The requisite faculty is the interior sense of the transcendental world, and the opening of this sense is the beginning of Regeneration, understood as the eradication of that virus which entered into man at the Fall. Rebirth has three stages—that of the intelligence, that of the heart and will, but that in fine which—seeing that it embraces the entire being—is called corporeal rebirth, because the beast is also saved together with the man, and the Great Quintessence by which the soul is converted transmutes the body as well. It is held to follow herefrom that union with God is possible in this life in the opening of the world within us by a triple gradation through the moral, metaphysical and plenary worlds, wherein is the Kingdom of the Spirit. This is the process of Regeneration expressed in other terms. So far as regards the preamble, but the dogmatic part affirms : (1) that an advanced school has existed from the beginning of our history, deriving directly from Christ, as He in Whom there dwells substantially the whole plenitude of God ; (2) that this is the enlightened community of the interior Church, disseminated throughout the world and governed therein by one spirit ; (3) that it is the most hidden of sodalities ; (4) that the outer school, which is the visible Church, is founded thereon, and by its symbols and ceremonies it gives an external utterance to the truth which abides in the Hidden Sanctuary ; (5) that the work of the Interior Church has been the building of a Spiritual Temple of regenerated souls ; (6) that it possesses the direct knowledge of those means by which man is restored to his first estate ; (7) that the external Church became a subsequent necessity by the frailty of man as a whole ; (8) that the external worship fell away automatically from the service within ; (9) that the Church which was founded in Abraham was raised to perfection in Christ ; (10) that the Inmost Sanctuary is without change or shadow of vicissitude ; (11) that it is the union of those who have received the light and share in the communion of saints ; (12) that it unites the science of the old, external Covenant with that of the new and interior Covenant ; (13) that it has three degrees corresponding to the stages of Regeneration ; (14) that herein repose the mysteries of all true knowledge ; (15) that it resembles no secret society, for all external forms have passed utterly away ; (16) that the path thereto is Wisdom and the way is Love ; (17) that although the Inner Sanctuary has been separated from the Temple, they are destined for reunion ; (18) that the Way which is Wisdom and Love is also Christ ; (19) that the Mystery of the Incarnation is the deep Mystery of re-union with God ; (20) that man in his first estate was the Temple of Divinity, and God in His wisdom has projected the rebuilding of this Temple ; (21) that the plans of His scheme are in the Holy

Mysteries and constitute the secret of Regeneration, which is the royal and sacerdotal science; (22) that man approximates to Regeneration, and does in fine attain it, by the discernment of the Body and Blood of Christ, or, as I have myself expressed it continually throughout this work, by the Mystery of the Eucharist.

The same testimony was given independently at the same time by the Chevalier Loupoukine in his little tract on the *Characteristics of the Interior Church*. He defined the higher spiritual mind as that of consciousness in grace only, by which those who participate therein become that which Christ is by His nature. Here also the Great Work is that of Regeneration, which is accomplished in Christ, and the Church within has the keys of the process. The testimony is also identical as to the sanctity and indefectible character of the external Church, which is the means of entrance into the Church of Christ unseen. The way, again, is Love, as the essence of the Body of Christ; by Regeneration that Body is reborn in us; and so the whole process—though in neither case is the truth stated expressly—becomes the arch-natural Mystery of the Eucharist.

There are errors of expression in both these works, and, as I have said, there is a certain confusion; they are not to be taken by themselves or in connection simply with one another; but it will be evident that, after their own manner, they bear the same testimony as the schools of tradition in Christian time and as the higher literature of the Graal.

It will be seen otherwise that the Secret Church is an arbitrary name adopted to describe the penetralia of the tradition in secret; the idea itself does not correspond to any titular description, and in adopting of necessity some distinguishing name, I have chosen one which in several respects is perhaps the most arbitrary of all; but it serves to particularise the school as essentially Christian. Whether in the East or the

West, I believe that there are still custodians in the world, for the hidden truth does not perish. It is not a sectarian school, and I think that it has even abandoned all those Houses of Initiation, the fact of which has transpired in the outer world. Its reflections, however, remain imbedded therein. For those secret fraternities at the present day which confess to two incorporated orders and to have recipients in both, it corresponds to that third Order from which they claim to hold—though how they do not know. For those Masonic Rites of the past which were, by their own imputation, under the obedience of Unknown Superiors, whom they never saw probably, these Superiors would answer to the Holy School. It is the Holy Assembly of Eckartshausen and the Interior Church of Loupoukine; it is the Crowned Masters of Alchemy; it is the Unknown Philosopher of early Martinism, but for Martinism this Leader was the Repairer Himself, who is certainly the first-fruits of the Great Transfiguration. I believe that if any member of this school were authorised to manifest, he would come—and this I shall reiterate—like Melchisedech out of Salem, carrying Bread and Wine. Meanwhile, their old rumours are everywhere, and it is not curious that they are in the Graal literature; having regard to its subject-matter, it would be more curious if they were not. The mystic life is the way of the Secret Sanctuary; it is the way of the opening of consciousness towards the things that are Divine. The makers of the Graal books found certain elements to their hands, and they incorporated them as they best could. The literature expresses after several manners its absolute belief in the truth of doctrinal Christianity, but also that behind all doctrine there was something great and undemonstrable, the direct knowledge of which had departed because the world was unworthy. Like the Graal literature, the Secret Church recognises fully the external Church and presents something from within it. I conclude that a valid Mass has always been said in Rome and the other assemblies, but unfortunately at the present time it is a memorial rather than a realisation. Transubstantiation and reservation are the nearest approaches to the idea of the arch-natural Eucharist. There is also in the Christian Church generally a consensus of sanctity at the height, and it is the reflected glory of a greater height beyond. But this is only an affirmation on the testimony of all the saints, after every deduction has been made for the decorative renunciations and denials of the self-abnegating mind.

By summary, therefore, the term of research in the doctrine of the Secret Church is no instituted Assembly —not even an orthodoxy in ascension. It does not mean that another Mass is said than that which is celebrated daily at any high altar in Christendom ; it does not mean that other elements are used or that the words of consecration differ in kind or genus. The Secret Church is our own Church when it has entered into the deeper understanding of its proper implicits. In so far as it can be said that external forms may remain at all, I conceive that it uses the same forms, but in virtue of interior organs which receive more fully from the immanence of the Divine Will, so that the priest who begins by reciting *Introibo ad altare Dei* has the direct experience that God is truly at His altar, and thus he ascends the steps, discerning the Presence with his eyes in the spiritual part of his nature, rather than with faith. I would that it were here and now given me to say how this condition is reached in the term of sanctity ; but I think that it is by the imagination raised in ecstasy. In the normal sense there is imagination, but it is not a pure and constant fire ; there is also ecstasy in many stages, and some of these are experienced in the devout life apart from any shaping spirit. I put it forward tentatively as a high speculation that the union of which I have spoken is consummated in the higher consciousness, so that the priest prepared thereto enters and attains. What he celebrates there is a Mass of the Beatific Vision; but this is the Mass of the Graal. At that *Veni Creator* the Lord Christ comes, and the Comforter. I believe further that these things are done in the sanctuary of a man's own spirit, as in an Ark of the Graal.

It is obvious that this is the limit of things at which expression suffers a complete paralysis. If I say with Elias Ashmole that of what is beyond I know enough to hold my tongue but not enough to speak, even then it is obvious that I exceed my narrow measures: "I know not, God knoweth." It is useless, in any case, to pursue the evidential questions further than I have taken them up to this point. I might have begun by saying that what I proposed to present was an hypothesis only; the true evidences of the Secret Tradition are in the Secret Schools, and of these it is idle to think that one can produce more than the rumour in the open day. I have left nothing unstated that it has been in any sense possible to adduce; those of my own tradition will understand what remains over and what is indeed involved. I put forward no claims; that day has passed long since when one man could be so much as desired to believe on the authority of another where things vital are involved. I invite no verdict; I care utterly nothing for the impression which the considerations of this book may occasion in the academies of external thought, and in the words of one who has preceded me carrying no warrants but those of his own genius: in any case whatsoever, I shall not on my own part be "the less convinced or the more discouraged." The rumours of Graal literature are a part of sanctuary doctrine. I do not know how they transpired; I am not certain that the question is much of my concern; no doubt in the historical sense I could desire that I did know. I am certain that the spiritual alchemists were men after the heart of Christ; I am not less certain that those who created symbolical Masonry were the members of a lower grade; and when the Quest of Galahad takes that high prince and king among all anointed through the veils of transubstantiation into the Divine Vision, I know that the sanctuary is made void for him who has so achieved, the curtains are parted, and it is given him to depart hence, for there is nothing left to detain him.

IV

THE MYSTERY WHICH IS WITHIN

On the historical side the Secret Church is then the shadow of an hypothesis at best; on the spiritual side of the intellect it is an implicit, but it is that irresistibly; mystically it is a truth which is not less than obvious, but it should be understood—and I repeat therefore— that it is apart from all forms, conventions and instituted existence. When in our highest moments we conceive with least unworthiness of the Church on the ideal plane, we approximate, but still under the reserves of our own insufficiency, to the Holy Assembly. It is the unity of arch-natural minds. It is that in which, by the mediation of the creeds, we confess our beliefs daily—the communion of saints. If we like to express it in such words—and they are excellent apart from their unhappy associations—it is the choir invisible. It is even like the priesthood of the Graal sanctuary, as we judge by the romances concerning it; it does not ordain or teach; it fulfils its office sufficiently because, speaking symbolically, it is " in the foremost files of time." It is like Saint-Martin—its feet are on earth and its head is in Heaven.

The Secret Church has said therefore: "*Introibo ad altare Dei*," and it has entered and gone in. When it comes out, in the person of one of its members, it carries bread and wine, like Melchisedech. The conditions of its membership correspond to the conditions of finding the Holy Graal, as described in the German *Parsifal.* If it were possible to regard it as an Order, it might be said that its device is : " Behold, I am with you always, even unto the consummation of the world." It is the place in which Mary conceived in her heart before she conceived in her body. As already indicated, it has not issued manifestoes, or we should be in a better position to judge regarding it ; it has not had its documents abstracted, or we should not have had the Graal romances extant in their present form. But things have transpired concerning it, and thus we have the *Characteristics of the Interior Church* by Loupoukine, the *Cloud upon the Sanctuary* by Eckartshausen, Werner's *Sons of the Valley*, the Eucharistic side of Alchemy and the rumour of the Holy Quest. It gives to those who can receive it a full answer to the question : " Art thou He that is to come, or do we look for another ? " In a word, the natural Graal is everywhere but the supernatural Graal is in the Secret Church.

So far as there has been any evidence offered on the hypothesis concerning it, this has gone entirely astray, because it has assumed that we are concerned with some corporate and organised body, whereas we are concerned only with the course of experience in the higher consciousness. Now, if there is no such experience, the claim of the official Church is at once voided.

The presence of the Secret Church is like that of angels unawares. In the outer courts are those who are prepared for regeneration, and in the *adyta* are those who have attained it : these are the Holy Assembly. It is the place of those who, after the birth of flesh, which is the birth of the will of man, have come to be born of God. It is in the persons of those who are regenerate that the gates of hell cannot prevail against the Church. The place of the Holy Assembly is the place of Eden and Paradise ; it is that whence man came and whither he returns. It is also that place from which the Spirit and the Bride say " Come " ;

or it is the place of the Waters of Life, with power to take freely. It is like the still, small voice ; it is heard only in the midst of the heart's silence, and there is no written word to show us how its rite is celebrated. Its work upon things without is a work of harmony, wherein is neither haste nor violence. There are no admissions—at least of the ceremonial kind—to the Holy Assembly, but in the last instance the candidate inducts himself. There is no sodality, no institution, no order which throughout the Christian centuries has worked in such silence. It is for this reason that it remains an implicit in mystic literature rather than a formal revelation ; it is not a revelation but an inference ; when it is not an inference it is an attainment. It is neither an interference nor a guidance actually ; it is better described as an influence. It does not come down ; more correctly it draws up, but it also inheres. It is the place of those who have become transmuted and tingeing stones.

The mystery in chief of the Secret Church is that of Divine communication, of which it has the sanctifying sacraments ; but, once more, so far as these are typified symbolically it can have no more efficient and unspotted outward signs than the bread and wine for oblation. It is in this sense that it connects more especially with the Eucharist. Christian temples are oriented to show that there is a light behind, and by all previous considerations churches with open doors are the thresholds of the Church which is not entered by doors because it has not been built with hands. The Secret Church is the manifest Church glorified and installed in the spiritual kingdom, as this was first set over the kingdom of the visible world. It is therefore the withdrawn spirit of the outward Holy Assembly, and it would be unreasonable for those who acknowledge the visible body to deny that which transcends it. But to speak of a spirit which thus transcends a body is still to say that, because the lesser is contained by the greater, the latter is until now not exactly without the former nor apart therefrom, and its mode of manifestation, in so far as it can be said to manifest, is not otherwise than from within. There is no separate incorporation. It has no ambassadors nor *chargés d'affaires* at any court of the hierarchies, nor does it send out visible physicians and healers, for it has no conventional offices either in the interests of things above or even of those below. If some have spoken of it as leading the official Church, there is here an imperfection of expression, because it is speaking after a formal manner concerning modes which are apart from all whatsoever that we understand by convention. Without in any sense representing and much less exhausting the process, I have indicated that it draws rather than leads, and if I may attempt one further definition, as the synthesis of all my statements—echoing and reflecting all—I would describe the Secret Church as the integration of believers in the higher consciousness.

V

THE SECLUDED AND UNKNOWN SANCTUARY

It is obvious that the romances of the Graal are either legendary histories of religion on the external side, and as such are concerned with the quest of conversion—that is, Christianity colonising—or they are spiritual histories with a strong individual element but a wide field of application on the universal side, corresponding to the province of mysticism—such as the legend of the Church in the world and the soul in its progress. The first class would include the metrical *Joseph of Arimathæa* and the *Book of the Holy Graal*, while the most notable examples of the second class are the *Longer Prose Perceval* and the *Quest of Galahad*. The idea of their secret meaning must be held to reside, as regards the first class, in the claims which they put forward, and, as regards the second, in the special application of the stories. In our consideration of certain successive literatures which came into existence during the Christian centuries, we have seen tha the books of the Graal do enter into a particular scheme, and they are the first in time therein. They tell us—now that the secret words, which were of the essence of the Mystery of Faith, had passed out of all common knowledge ; now that the true succession from Christ had been resumed into Heaven ; again that the sacred mysteries were reserved in an inaccessible mountain from all but the highest sanctity, or alternatively that the House of Doctrine stood vacant as a testimony to the external world. There was also the literature of alchemy, saying that He is truly here but that the way of His attainment comes only by the revelation which He gives, and for all else there are only the age-long processes of Nature. There was further the literature of Israel in exile, saying : " By the Waters of Babylon " —yet also to those who could hear it : " Enter into the nuptial joys of Rabbi Simeon." There was, lastly, as there is also, the great witness of Masonry, saying : " Not yet, in quiet lie "—to every heart of aspiration seeking to build the temple otherwise than in the heart. And so from age to age the story of substitution continues, but with a hint everywhere that still there is known somewhere that which the sign signifies. The Wardens are withdrawn, but they are alive. There is a cloud upon the Sanctuary, but the Sanctuary is within the Church, and other rumours distinguishable throughout the centuries speak of a Holy Place which is behind the manifest Altar, of a deeper mystery of love behind the world of grace—a rumour, a legend, a voice, an unknown witness testifying concerning a more Holy Assembly and an Interior and more Secret Church.

So far therefore an attempt has been made to justify the hypothesis that there were rumours abroad in the world which entered into houses of romance and account for the implicits which have been traced in the Graal literature. All that which lay behind the rumour—an undeclared region, giving forth strange portents under a cloud of mystery—was apart, and that utterly, from the connections of romance, and the story-tellers, working under their proper warrants, went their own way, incorporating, as we have seen, from all quarters. We get in this manner the three schools which I mentioned at the beginning : (*a*) the school of transition from folk-lore ; (*b*) the school of Guiot de Provence ; and (*c*) the monastic school. The end of these considerations is now upon the very threshold, but before I take the closing it is desirable to set out briefly some possible hypotheses in divergence and decide how far they have any claim on our attention. When the alchemists of old intended more than usually to confuse their various issues in unversed minds, and to distract the curiosity-monger regarding that Mystery which has been termed throughout all Hermetic times the First Matter of the Philosopher, they had recourse to concealment by application thereto of almost opprobrious epithets. It was a vile and unclean matter, a thing of no account and despised, an object that was found everywhere and trodden under the feet of the wayfarer. The uninitiated went astray accordingly in foolish and revolting processes. I do not know whether a similar subtlety might have commended itself to the writers of Graal romances—supposing that there had been a common understanding between them for the attainment of a specific end—but having regard to the enormous machinery which was put in operation to determine the enchantments of Britain, "the desolation which fell upon Logres" and the adventurous times, it is natural to look about for a causation in proportion thereto—for instance, some event in history ; but nothing emerges in response except a possible conspiracy in matters of religion. We will therefore begin by assuming that for what purpose soever the literature concealed in part but in part also put forward an attack upon the Roman Church.

The first observation to make in this connection is that those who were concerned with the movement out of which the impeachment originated must have accepted the sacraments and the body of ecclesiastical procedure. This is therefore assumed tacitly, as there would be otherwise no working agreement possible.

Now, seeing that in one case the keeper of the Graal is supposed to have fallen from righteousness, and that —obscurely enough in respect of logic in the scheme— he could only look for healing outside his own House of Doctrine, one might be disposed at first sight to conclude that the Graal Church may stand for Latin Christianity and the Rich Fisherman for its central seat of authority. He is the Keeper of the Divine Mysteries, the possessor of the valid forms, but he and his environment have been laid waste by the spirit of the world. Alternatively, it might be a confession of apparent failure in respect of God's work in the world. From either point of view the literature would be concerned with the amelioration of the Latin Church by recalling it to its higher part. The position, however, becomes involved curiously, and that at once, for the presence of the Hallows may preserve the king alive, but otherwise they cannot help him. No recitation of the putative, all-powerful words can ever relieve his sickness, and the House of God is therefore—as it long remains—in mourning. Here also the difficulty of the unasked question—of that question which seems exclusive in symbolism—intervenes for our further confusion. What purpose, in this connection, could it serve the Hereditary Keeper of the Graal, that an apparent stranger should visit him and ask the meaning of the Graal and its pageant? We remember the question in Masonry which is one of violence, doing outrage to the law and the order and voiding the erection of a true temple: there it is simple in symbolism, and thus transparent in meaning; but here is a question which is necessary in some utterly mystical manner, belonging to the law and the order, and one by which the Warden is restored : it is less intelligible on this hypothesis than are darker corners of thought. It follows, however this may be, that there is a heavy cloud on the Sanctuary, and if the symbolism belongs simply to the official Church, it has the Words of Life, but is still, after some manner, inhibited ; it must be challenged before it can speak and it must communicate before it can be healed. The Quests are so far external that they involve transit from place to place, as a pageant passes through a temple ; but the question is an intellectual research. The heroes of research offer no light on the subject, because Perceval at his highest does not ask in the end and the romance of Galahad confesses to no question. The *Didot Perceval* leaves the new Keeper, with all to him belonging, in final seclusion, where the evidence of things not seen is put away from the eyes of all, and it is impossible therefore that the Hidden Sanctuary should represent an official Church. To express it in another way, the Son of the Doctrine was received into the House of the Doctrine and had the great secret imparted to him. Faintly and far away the *Didot Perceval* shows how the æonian Keeper has waited in the castle of the soul till the natural man, who is the scion of his house, comes in and asks the question of the union. The natural man understands nothing and does not ask till he is driven, but he is driven at last. As faintly and still further away, the *Conte del Graal* tells the same symbolical story, with many variations ; but as it reaches no term till a later period in time, when it is simply a reflection of other texts, and has hence no independent implicits, there is no call to examine it in this connection. It may be noted, however, that the prologue, which is regarded as its latest part, tells of things which exceed experience —that is to say, evidence—of sins against spiritual life and of return to the House of the Father, as aspiration returns to its source. But it is difficult to connect it with any sanctuary doctrine. The German *Parsifal* tells how the House is always in the world, but that it is only attainable by great sanctity, which is sufficient to show that it does not symbolise the institutes of external religion. It has, however, a strange sacramental side, which seems to indicate that the Eucharist in its highest efficacy comes down from Heaven direct. It therefore incorporates not indeed a distinct motive but the terms of another school. To conclude concerning it, it is obvious from the beginning that the Keepers of Mont Salvatch were a secret order of chivalry, after the manner of the Templars. The *Titurel* recites the building of the Spiritual House in beauty as a Palace of Art; and its meaning is that the Mystery of Knowledge was in the custody of a special election, though there is nothing to suggest that it was opposed to the official Church. The *Longer Prose Perceval* lifts up a different corner of the veil, telling how one Keeper died unhealed and that the last Warden of the Mysteries was taken away, though the Holy Things remained. We have now only the great and paramount Quest left for consideration, which is that of Galahad, and it tells how the Warden of the Mysteries, together with the Holy Things, was removed once and for all, as if the House of Doctrine were itself nothing and the term of research everything. The Great Quest was written with the highest sanctity as its actuating motive, and we can do no otherwise than accept it as an instance of the literature at its greatest. It forms with the *Longer Prose Perceval* the consummation of the cycle. These quests are mirrors of spiritual chivalry, mirrors of perfection, pageants of the mystic life, and it does not matter what the legend was prior to their appearance. They are the teaching of the Church spiritualised, if I may be pardoned such a term, and they offer in romance form a presentation of the soul's chronicle.

So far therefore from the Graal sanctuary representing the Latin or any other external Church, we find that the mystery of the sanctuary within is written through all the romances, though it is in the words of the sanctuary without and the savour of the external incense is more noticeable in some quests than in others.

In this light we shall still find the *Didot Perceval* a little wanting in meaning and the *Conte del Graal* too composite to reflect a full light of intention. As regards the German cycle, it shows how the great mystery descends and abides in us. The *High History* empties the House of Doctrine and leaves it as a vacant sign before the face of the world. The Galahad Quest says that the world was not worthy. Yet in a sense all this is comparative, constituting the several presentations and various aspects of that which is one at the root, for the Secret Church does indeed say : *Mysterium Fidei*, and the official Church says : *Corpus Domini;* but these two are one.

It will be agreed on these considerations that we can only contemplate the Church of the Holy Graal as a mystery of secrecy, but it can be assumed that in this sense it may either have been hostile to Rome or at peace in its mind concerning it. In connection with the first alternative, let us imagine for a moment that the Welsh or some other Celtic Church was making through the medium of the romances a last bid for recognition. If the prevalence of the Roman Rite constituted the enchantment and desolation ; if the questioning of the Wardens of the Mystery, on the Mystery itself manifested, signified the illumination of the elect concerning the faith once delivered to the Celtic saints and now in danger of extinction ; we should have a design adequate to the machinery, and should be able to understand the magnitude of the claims in conjunction with the follies which abound in the form of its expression, for it seems difficult to say that, for example, the Sanctuary in Wales had a wise church built about it. It was chaotic rather than in confusion, and in respect of its working was almost a prolonged abuse. The suggestion is otherwise preposterous ; but British Christianity generally, and its desire for independence, centralised, by example, in the crown at the period of Henry II., may be said to account for a certain complexion sometimes discerned in the literature in respect of Rome, and to explain why, this notwithstanding, it is otherwise so catholic at heart. The speculation at the present time has a certain presumption in its favour because a section of scholarship is inclined thereto, but a slight study of the texts must, I think, dispose of it, once and for all.

The short recension, comprised in the Lesser Chronicles, tells how a warranted company came westward ; how it abode for many centuries in a Veiled Sanctuary ; how the Quest for this Sanctuary was instituted ; how it failed in the first instance, but was achieved subsequently ; how the secrets of the Sanctuary were learned ; how he who learned them remained within the Sanctuary, and there is no story afterwards. The metrical romance of De Borron and the *Lesser Holy Graal* are not a legend concerning the conversion of England, but the prolegomena thereto. They leave the real intention doubtful outside the bare fact that something would be brought into Britain which was unknown to the Church at large, for the canonical apostles were not present when his great mission was conferred on Joseph by Christ. There is nothing on the mere surface to show that any priesthood followed the possession of the Graal Vessel or the knowledge of the Secret Words. Yet these are Eucharistic ; according to the *Lesser Holy Graal* they are a formula of consecration ; and in a sense Joseph must have been ordained, because it is obvious that at need he could recite the words effectually. It is certain, moreover, that Joseph and his company carried no official priests westward. A great lacuna follows, and then comes the *Early Merlin*, showing that the Secret Sanctuary is in Britain, that a firebrand prophet is going about in the land, carrying the warrants of the Graal, and is bent upon fulfilling prophecy by instituting the Third Table for the completion of the Graal Trinity. There are no claims put forward regarding the sanctuary, and the same statement holds for the *Didot Perceval*. It remains that the Lesser Chronicles generally intimate the existence of a particular Eucharistic knowledge, but not of a Church demanding recognition thereon. As secrecy is the primary seal, it is obvious that the Graal Church is not the Church in Britain, nor do the texts contain any counter-picture, object, or character which might by possibility correspond to the official Church apart from that notion of enchantment which, in the absence of any warrant, it is arbitrary to explain along these lines. For example, it would be madness to suggest that Moses, who was interned in secrecy, represents the Latin Church in apostasy or rejection. It is obvious, in fine, that Robert de Borron was acquainted with no tradition which connected Joseph of Arimathæa with Glastonbury or even with Britain. In the poem, he remains where he was or returns to Syria, as Moses the Law-giver went up the holy mountain.

The Greater Chronicles bear the same witness, but the evidence of transubstantiation and other matters of doctrine indicate that the major texts are typically and militantly Roman. The long recension tells how the same company, strangely extended, arrived in Britain and there established, in the person of Joseph II., the beginnings of a supreme orthodoxy, so that nothing which came after in the name of the Gospel could abide in competition therewith; how the prophet and enchanter Merlin carried a strange warrant to connect his work with the Mystery of the Holy Graal; how he possessed from the beginning of his symbol the power to promise Blaise that he should be united with the secret assembly; how the Castle of the Graal, though not altogether hidden from the world, was encompassed with perils and difficulties, which notwithstanding there were wars or the rumour of wars about it. The

The Secret Church

Book of the Holy Graal narrates the conversion of Britain by those who carried the license of super-apostolical succession, the design of which may have been pan-Britannic, or conceivably the implicit of a plan of campaign against papal claims over Britain. It is at least the legend *par excellence* which, if any, would be regarded as devised in this interest ; and it would stand alone as such among the Anglo-Norman texts. The colonisation, whatever its design, conquered all Britain in all publicity. When however the later *Merlin* texts enter the field, everything has passed into seclusion, and the prophet's personation of the character of messenger does not carry public knowledge concerning the Graal further than an echoing rumour. Outside the sacro-saintly character of ordinary Church-practice, the texts offer no ecclesiastical element but the implications which are resident in the notion of the adventurous times and the preparation at the royal court for the Quest of the Sacred Vessel, the term of which is to break up the Round Table. The intermediate prose *Lancelot* follows the *Merlin* texts, working for the same end, and we are already at a far distance from the letter and spirit of the *Book of the Holy Graal*. In the *Longer Prose Perceval* the term is to strip the sanctuary, but it remains a consecrated place, and those who enter therein become thereafter men of holy lives and saints of the official Church. The *Quest of Galahad* offers in the term thereof the instance of a Keeper who is dispossessed without any intimation of his end. It may be said that he is treated with something almost approaching contumely. There is an apparent equivalent of an expulsion of the profane in that command for those to withdraw who are not in the Quest of the Graal. But behind this and behind the unnamed yet acknowledged warrant of the Knights from Gaul, Ireland and Denmark, there is some mystery concealed deeply ; the latter took away from their high experience the memory of a glorious vision which could well serve as the basis of a tradition thereafter in various parts of the world ; but they had not received communication of the last secrets. The hidden life of the Holy Graal during the Arthurian period seems next after one the most wonderful of all hidden lives. What could King Pelles, with whom the Graal had abode for years, and it may be for centuries, whose daughter had also borne it through all the secret rites from her childhood, what could he learn from the Quest ?

I conclude therefore as regards the Greater Chronicles that they offer in one text, which is one of the latest, a certain aggrandisement of British ecclesiastical tradition by the incorporation of a rumour which belonged in its root-matter to a different concern totally ; but the remaining branches have little part in the scheme. The Graal Church is held in secrecy and mystery, and when the *Quest of Galahad* certifies that a certain Joseph, not otherwise particularised, was the first bishop of Christendom, there is no longer any consequence involved in the ecclesiastical order.

In the German cycle the Graal has nothing to do with any conversion legend and nothing to do with Britain ; that country is not entered at all in the *Parsifal*. The assumption of a particular concern in the aspirations or ambitions of the House of Anjou is an irresistible inference from that portion which contains the Angevin elements ; but it is accidental and not essential to the design of the poem, and is not its inspiration but its burden. The poem is to be judged wholly by other standards.

It must, I think, be concluded from this brief and literal schedule that, except by a bare possibility in a single sporadic instance, we are not dealing in the Graal literature with an ecclesiastical conspiracy for the furtherance of any independence in matters of religion ; the scheme of the whole mystery is opposed to such a supposition. It seems impossible to affirm that the Graal writers were working a similar scheme under a common agreement, as if all were imbued by a pan-Britannic fever, or were the concealed disciples of an obscure sect in religion. There are few consecutive documents which offer so little trace of a concerted effort. Some writers manifest a very high purpose and some no purpose at all, beyond the true intent which is all for our delight in story-telling. Otherwise than by simple predilection, we shall never understand why these chose for their subject a Mystery like that of the Graal. But the rumours and implicits run through all the texts, as an echo perpetuated, and in their several degrees the stories are plain concerning them. Even the *Conte del Graal* enshrines them after its own manner, in spite of a piecemeal tradition. Apart from this text, the *Didot Perceval* tells a plain story by interning the Warden-in-chief, with the Hallows, in that place which it never names; but it knows nothing of the House made void. The German *Parsifal* tells a plain story by leaving the great chivalry in the great Temple, all things completed and all things as they were at the beginning. Again there is nothing made void. The removal of the Mystery in the *Titurel* and the transport of the Sacred House cannot signify more than a change of imputed location and a further withdrawal. The *Longer Prose Perceval* tells a plain story, but it leaves the voided Castle as a public sign to the nations, taking the Keeper and the Hallows into that great distance which is not in time or place. The *Quest of Galahad*, in fine, tells a plain story also of the voided House and its vacated offices, but it has byways of allusion from which the infinite opens.

Now, the mystery which covers the sanctuary is never drawn away in the Lesser Chronicles. We know only that the weight of many centuries presses heavily upon the Keeper. We infer that the hermit, Blaise, was taken into the choirs of heaven according to the promise of Merlin, and is, therefore, in *la joie perdurable*. But we know not of any messenger who has relieved Perceval;

so, therefore, in eternal virginity and in utter loneliness
he is waiting till the world shall be worthy. His place
is not known; he does not come out therefrom; and
there is none that goes in.

But in the Greater Chronicles there is another version
of his legend which says very surely, although by implication only, that the *Didot Perceval* is not the whole
story, and therein indeed Perceval is taken away, for
the Red Cross ship carries him, as the dark barge bears
King Arthur. This story stands apart almost from
everything and is very difficult to account for, since all
things fail therein. The king dies, the question is not
asked, the Hallows are parted from one another, the
Castle of Souls and the Gate of Paradise are left utterly
vacant, as a sign of wrath to the centuries, and the hands
of Perceval are empty as he passes into the unseen. We
learn only that he goes through a golden distance and
that he knows that which awaits him.

I have said that there are wars and rumours of wars
about Corbenic in the Galahad Quest, yet is it found
by grace only, or special license, and it is a house of
terrors and of marvels. Under these reserves, it is a
house of many visitations, nor is it therefore so utterly
unknown as is that of the Lesser Chronicles. Its building is described at large, as is that of the Temple in the
Titurel, and if its location remains a mystery we are
not without some materials for reconstructing its broad
environment.

We have now made a circuitous journey and we
return to our starting-point, being the evidences of
a concealed claim, presupposing its proper custodians
working within the Church and in no sort setting it
aside. We have found—as I at least should have expected
to find antecedently—the rationale of that Mystery of
Faith which tells us that the Lamb was slain from the
foundation of the world. The makers of the Anglo-
Norman Graal cycle had heard in some undeclared
manner of the secret tradition, and they were so far

properly informed that they allocated it to the Holy
Eucharist, some of them reflecting it as secret words
used in consecrating the elements. They knew also
that it was a mystery of orthodox tradition and therefore
some others perhaps reflected it as super-apostolical
succession, but this particular rumour fell speedily out of
sight. The writers did not register their remembrance
of the *Epiclesis* clause in a Celtic liturgy ; they never
dreamed of a pan-Britannic Church, though one text
may have reflected hostility to the executive of Rome.
Nothing could be less in correspondence with such
an ambition than their conception of a Mystery of
Grace which was at no time intended to prevail
in public. Notwithstanding a certain quasi-publicity
during the adventurous times, to the end it remained
a mystery. There is no suggestion that any sect,
company, or institution was intended to replace some
public institution, church, company, or sect. Amidst
all the diadems and emblazonments of the great, wonderful literature, its concern at the highest emerges
in the uttermost clearness, being a tradition of the
panis vivus in its deeper understanding. The Mass
went on for ever in the lands and the islands ; but
in a place apart and out of all declaration there was
a Secret Ark of Alliance, and those who could be
present at its service beheld, in a heart of revelation,
how Christ was manifested in the heart and administered
His own Eucharist, as He did at the Last Supper. There
is no other message put forward by the still more secret
literatures, for these testify that he who desires to be
dissolved shall be actually with Christ—but whether in
passing through literal or mystical death is a great
question. Every document comprised in the Lesser
and Greater Chronicles may be regarded as beginning
in sanctity and culminating in greater sanctity, which
term is to be understood in the sense of the Catholic
Church. In the last resource, even Secret Words and
super-apostolical succession mean only the mind of the

Church entering into its higher part, and all the companies of epopts are joined therein in a common act of experience. The official Church at its greatest is not apart really from the Secret Church, and the one is wounded in the other, nor will they be disjoined in their healing. The Graal is the sacred legend of the Eucharist, but as behind its Castle of Souls there was a hidden Paradise, so, as a Graal which is behind the Holy Graal, there is an inward or transcendent sense of the entire Mystery.

The first lesson which we must put to heart from these considerations is one of great caution in applying the actual or possible implicits of the Graal literature. We may suggest in the exercise of our ingenuity that Logres stands for the colonies of Christianity, as the lesser stands for the greater, but we shall not be counselled wisely if we think that the enchantment of Logres was the prevalence of the official Churches, whether these were Roman or Welsh. We may say that the King's wounding sometimes signified the dereliction of the Great Experiment in the isolation of its concealment ; but the King's healing—when it happens that he is healed—was not a dream of some triumph of doctrine over other doctrines in the world at large. We may say that the supersanctified Mystery of Faith located in the House of Doctrine is like the Supernal *Sephiroth* of Kabalism separated from the *Sephiroth* below by the serpent spirit of the world ; but if we chance to be Kabalists we shall remember that *Daath* remains as a channel of indirect communication without break or intermission. We must not say that the removal of the Great Palladium signifies the complete denudation of the official Church, but we may " remember of this unstable world " and the spirit thereof. When we say that the House of Doctrine is voided, we must not mean that the official Church has ceased to be holy in its teaching, or that the King of Castle Mortal is the Judas spirit of Rome. Seeing that the Graal Castle is the House of the Great Experiment and that King Fisherman is the custodian of the hidden knowledge concerning it, we may, however, regard the higher Perceval as the mystic spirit and the chivalry of sanctity. The question that he ought to have asked concerned the Greater Office of the Eucharist. This would have caused the Mystery to manifest. His failure brought the House of Sanctity into desolation, because there was no heir found to carry on the great tradition. But when the Keeper of the Hallows perished and the Holy Place fell to the enemies thereof, the tradition did not die, and in the end it was restored thereto. The supplement to these things is the complete agreement in the romances with all church doctrine and practice, from the least even to the greatest. They have, at the same time, their own insufficiencies, and it is for this reason that they lend themselves readily to misconstruction. When rumours came into the hands, let us say, of some mere neophyte, as it might be Guiot de Provence, we can understand his misconception and confusion, including why he went further, as, for example, to the Chronicles of Anjou; in other words, to the events of the outside world for the explanation of that which happened only in the secret world of initiation. He was in the position of some who at this day go to " those holy fields " for living evidence concerning Him "who brought life and immortality to light." We can understand also that various successive translators and independent tellers of the legend did also, after their own fashion, go further astray, losing all touch with the centre, till the official Church, at once jealous and zealous, stepped in and took over the dismembered body of the legend, putting it to its own use. It discerned something which belonged properly to itself, collected it accordingly out of the débris of romance-literature and put it again into romance. Of such is the *Quest of Galahad* and of such is the *Longer Prose Perceval*. The Mystery, *qua* Mystery of Experience

2 T

in transcendence, was reflected from scoriated glass to scoriated glass, giving us indeed here and there high intimations of the original, but not a true likeness, so that we are constrained, like Guiot, to look elsewhere for a fuller explanation, not indeed in Chronicles of Anjou, but in unofficial, fragmentary and elusive traces of the true legitimacy in religion which can be excavated by those who seek them from the tombs of other dead literatures.

It is after this manner that we reach by insensible stages that point at which the imperfect testimonies of romance are transferred altogether in our minds, by the light shining from those higher fields of consciousness in the mystery of religion ; and allowing them to dissolve for a moment, but in consequence setting aside the literature on its romantic side, there emerge the grades of the Graal subject in the harmony of all quests equally with all histories. The inward man, as I have said, is the wounded Keeper, and he is indeed in the Castle of Souls, which is the Graal Castle, as it is also Eden, Paradise and the Body of Man. That is to say, it is the Earthly Paradise, but behind it there is another Eden. The Keeper has been (*a*) wounded for immemorial sin ; (*b*) he is infirm by reason of his long exile ; (*c*) he has become maimed for some obscure profanation of the mysteries, in the unsanctified warfare of this world ; or (*d*) he suffers from the failure to ask one little question. This question is : Who is served of the Graal ?—as of those who attain the Divine Life even in the body of them. What part is the Lord ? Art thou He that is to come ? Who goeth into the Mountain of the Lord ? The answer to this last is : The innocent of hands and clean of heart. The Keeper is in fine healed and set free by those who come from without—by Perceval and Galahad, who lay down their arms in a state of purity. Gawain cannot help him, because he is the natural man unconverted, and the day of Sir Bors is not yet. After the former Keeper's healing, he sometimes remains with the new Keeper, his successor, whom he has incorporated into the mysteries, and this represents one stage of the progress; in others he passes away and is forgotten. The explanation in either case is that the bondage, the desolation, the lapse of the immortal spirit into earthly life is here shadowed forth, in which state he can only be helped from without—that is to say, by his mortal half, his external nature; and his great deliverance is in such a transfiguration that the one is succeeded by the other or the two are joined henceforth. Hereof is the tradition of a secret sanctuary, and its application may be found by those who will take out the details, seeing that it prevails through all the quests. There will be no need to say, even to the unversed student, that in the wilderness of this mortal life that which maintains the spirit is that which is involved by the higher understanding of the Holy Graal. But at the same time it is also a Feeding Dish, a Dish of Plenty, because the life of the body comes from the same source. When the natural man undertakes the great quest, all the high kingdoms of this world, which cannot as such have any part therein, look for the ends of everything. It is the quest for that which is real, wherein enchantments dissolve and the times of adventure are also set over. The enchantments are in the natural world, and so again are the adventures, but the unspelling quest is in the world of soul. The witness of this doctrine has been always in the world and therein it has been always secret. The realisation of it is the Shekinah restored to the Sanctuary; when it is overshadowed there is a Cloud on the Sanctuary. It is the story of the individual man passing into the concealment of the interior and secret life, but carrying with him his warrants and his high insignia. In a word, it is that doctrine the realisation of which in the consciousness I have called, under all reserves and for want of a better term, the Secret Church, even the Holy Assembly—I should say rather, the cohort of just men made perfect.

The Hidden Church of the Holy Graal

The Graal literature is not only one of growth, with a great mixture of elements from the standpoint of folk-lore and official scholarship, but it is such also from the ecclesiastical and mystical standpoint. Many lights of the past thereon have proved illusory—as, for example, the western manifestation of Manichæan elements ; but the Hidden Church of the Holy Graal is the reasonable deduction drawn out of certain implied claims which are supported by identical inferences from independent evidence, and they do not signify that the rumours with which we are now so familiar were more than rumours or the romances more than romances, except in so far as some of them embody the high life of sanctity manifested in that vehicle. We have seen that the Secret Church is a term of exaggeration, but it is difficult to characterise exactly by any formal title the Holy School which perpetuated the mystery of the Great Experiment. In that Experiment lies the hope of Western Mysticism, but it does not follow from this statement that I hold a brief for Eckartshausen or for others who in the past have put forward on their own basis the claim of a Secret Church up to the point that they have conceived thereof. The shadows of the Great Experiment which are found in the Graal literature bear witness to that Quest, to the Mystery of Initiation and advancement contained therein, but we know otherwise concerning it. It is in this sense that against all the wonders of a world no longer realised, the lost legends of folk-lore, the putative liturgies which have vanished, the implicits in the villainous transactions of Henry II., the power—possibly unscrupulous—behind the fidelity to death of St. Thomas à Becket, the sectarian ravings concerning Protestant succession from apostolic times, the great dream of undemonstrable archaic heresy behind the Knights Templars, and the other visions *per omnia sæcula sæculorum*, I set the reasonable and veridic intimation of a secret tradition in Catholic experience, the equivalents of which are the super-valid Eucharistic Rite and the direct succession from Christ. If in fine it be said that I have "sat and played with similes," my rejoinder is that they have not been "loose types of things in all degrees," but rather consanguinities of the spirit in the following of one quest—we also—unto this last—seeking *le moyen de parvenir*.

VI

THE TRADITION OF ST. JOHN THE DIVINE AND OTHER TRACES OF A HIGHER MIND OF THE CHURCH

I have set aside in succession every school of tradition in Christian times as an exclusive mouthpiece of the tradition in its root-matter ; the most catholic of all is the literature of spiritual alchemy, and it occupies a very high place, being especially a strong contrast to the scheme of symbolical Masonry, which is a legend of loss only. I think that the alchemists had the matter of the whole work, by which I mean the Scriptural Mystery of being born again of water and the Holy Spirit, and the fact—if I am right in the fact—that they did not give under their particular veils an accredited exposition of the Great Experiment, according to the canons of the Art and the tradition which reposed in its Wardens, is positive proof to myself that it was never put into official language. I am not less certain that Eckartshausen approximated only, and that if he had been fully qualified he would have dwelt more expressly upon the Eucharist. Loupoukine at his highest is an interesting and beloved ghost expressing a remote annunciation dictated perhaps by a strong sentiment rather than a certain knowledge in the heart or even in the head. We remain therefore with all the counters in our hands, and perhaps some day they will be rearranged in yet another manner as the time approaches when *nihil tam*

occultum erit quod non revelabitur. Meanwhile, it seems
not unreasonable to suppose that several minds will
have raised already the question whether there are no
traces in the annals of the Church itself. On the
assurance that the Great Experiment does not set the
Church aside, surely outside the official records and
first-hand memorials of sanctity there may be some
vestiges of the secret school in the East or the West.
When Origen denied in all truth and sincerity that
Christian doctrine was a secret system, he made haste
to determine the subsistence of an esoteric part which
was not declared to the multitude, and he justified it not
only by a reference to the more secret side of Pytha-
gorean teaching, but by the secrecy attaching to all
the Mysteries. The question therefore arises whether
the *disciplina arcani,* which is usually referred to the
Eucharist, because to all else it must be foreign, may
not be imbedded in that tradition of St. John the
Divine of which we have traces certainly. I set aside
without any hesitation the obvious objection that the
Fourth Gospel has no Eucharistic memorial, and its
inference, that for St. John less than for the other
evangelists did the flesh profit anything. The great
contention of the Gospel is that the Word became flesh,
and if it fails to recite the high office and ceremonial
of the Last Supper, it announces in the words of the
Master (*a*) that this is a " meat which endureth unto
everlasting life; " (*b*) that Christ is " the living bread
which came down from heaven; " and (*c*) that " he that
eateth thereof shall live for ever." In other words,
the doctrine concerning the communication of Divine
Substance is taught more explicitly by St. John than
by the rest of the evangelists.

The traditions concerning the beloved disciple are
numerous in the Christian Church, and on the thaumaturgic side they issue from the evasive intimation of
his gospel that he was to remain on earth until the
Second Coming of the Saviour. From his ordeal of

martyrdom he therefore came forth alive, according to his legend, and so he remained, in the opinion of St. Augustine, resting as one asleep in his grave at Ephesus. St. Cyril also testifies that he never died. But it is Ephrem, I believe, who offers an explicit account of St. John's interment by his own will at the hands of his disciple, after giving them the last instructions on the mysteries of faith. The grave was dug in his presence; he entered therein; it was sealed by the disciples, who returned as commanded on the day following, opened the sepulchre and found only the grave-clothes. This story represents an alternative legend of St. John's translation to heaven in the flesh of his body. From the place where he had rested so briefly an oil or manna was collected and was used for healing diseases.

That which did actually survive was the tradition of his secret knowledge, the implicit of which is that he who reposed on the breast of his Master did not arise and go forth without an intimate participation in the Mysteries of the Sacred Heart. Again, the tradition has many forms; and seeing that St. Isidore of Seville in the sixth century tells how St. John not only broke and rejoined certain precious stones but converted the branches of a tree into golden boughs and changed pebbles into jewels, reconverting both at the end; seeing also that Adam de St. Victor commemorated one of these miracles in a prose of his period:

> " Cum gemmarum partes fractas
> Solidasset," &c.—

it is not surprising that alchemists who had heard of these things adopted the belief that he was a great master of metallic transmutation—by which I speak of the material side and not of the spiritual work.

There is no need to say that this is fantasy of its period, and it is cited only as such. The legends and inventions —but it should be understood that there are many others—are the mere rumours, and so being are less even than intimations, concerning a traditional influence exercised by St. John, of which, as I have said, there are traces. But it has proved impossible in the past for researches into a concealed side of Christian doctrine to be actuated by another expectation than the discovery of obscure heresy, and it is important that we on our part should again make it plain to ourselves that there is nothing to our purpose in any devious ways of doctrinal thought, nor do those who pursue them, under the banner of the Graal and its quest, carry any antecedent warrant in the likelihood of things. It is said, for example, that there is a chain of evidence passing through Spain and the Knights Templars to St. John the Divine, so onward to the Essenes, after whom there is the further East. This is the pleasing fable of a few who look to India as the asylum-in-chief of all the veridic mysteries; but it has been found more convenient to state the fact of the evidence than to produce it. Much further back in the past the Abbé Grégoire affirmed that our Saviour placed His disciples under the authority of St. John, who never quitted the East and from whom certain secret teachings were handed on to his successors, the Johannine Christians, leading after many centuries to the institution of the Templars. Again, the evidence is wanting in respect of the last statement. The general hypothesis has found some favour with the critics of the Graal literature, and Simrock in particular, as we have seen, put forward the tradition of the Sacred Vessel as the root-matter of alleged Templar secrets. He also suggested a connection between the chivalry and the Essenes as the repositories of a concealed science confided by Jesus to His disciples and, in fine, by them communicated to Templar priests.

We hear otherwise of another unbroken chain of tradition hallowed by age, an esoteric oral tradition, revealing " the sacred lore of primæval times," intimations concerning which are to be found in the Johannine Apocalypse.

Some have referred it to the antecedents of the Antichrist myth, to which allusions are supposed in one of St. Paul's epistles ; but there is a wider horizon within which the whole subject calls to be regarded anew. Several of the speculative directions in which light has been sought thereon are difficult and—so long as we do not exaggerate the evidential possibilities—unnecessary to set aside. The Essenian consanguinities suggest themselves in connection with that which could have been only a contemplative school, the possible repository of the mystic experience which in early times lay behind external Christianity. Thebaid solitaries, children of the valley, so-called penitents of the desert, Eckartshausen, Lopoukine, sons of the Resurrection, and others too many for simple recitation here, are offered to the mind in their order as a possible channel of tradition from age into age. We can only say in our restraint that as there were so many sects with variations in doctrine, it is not unreasonable to suppose that there may have been one in seclusion having a difference, by the way of extension, concerning that spiritual practice which is called the science of the saints.

When I have spoken of the Johannine tradition in previous sections, I must not be understood as referring to a specific external community, such as that which has been popularly described in the past as Johannine Christians. The information concerning them, and reproduced by one writer from another, is based upon exceedingly imperfect research, but among some of my readers, who have not entered these paths, it may remain in some vague sense. It supposed an obscure sect which we are enabled to separate at once from all that we should ourselves understand by a connection with the disciple whom Jesus loved. Their patriarchs or pontiffs are said to have assumed the title of Christ, as Parsifal, with a higher warrant, took that of *Presbyter Johannes ;* but the Christ of their spurious legend is neither King nor Lord, and with an irony all unconscious he is disqualified from the beginning by their own tinkered gospel, which substitutes simple illegitimacy for the virginal and supernatural conception of the Holy Canon. Virus of this kind suggests inoculation from the *Sepher Toldosh Jeshu* rather than from any Christian—as, for example, a Gnostic—sect.

It must be confessed that the traditional sources concerning St. John are chiefly the apocryphal texts, and they lie, one and all, under the suspicion of heresy. Leucius— sometimes called pseudo-Luke—who is said to have been a disciple of Marcion, wrote, among other apocrypha, the *Acts of John*, the particulars of which claim to be drawn from the apostle himself. Now there is, I suppose, no question that *fabulatores famosi* of this kind were not unlike Master Blihis ; if for some things they depended on their invention, they drew much more from floating tradition, and it is obvious on every consideration that round no evangelist and no apostle were legends so likely to collect as the apocalyptic seer of Patmos. We shall therefore deal cautiously with the criticism which suggests that fathers of the Church like Tertullian drew their mythical accounts of St. John from heretical texts, for it is equally and more likely that the two schools drew from a source in common. The perpetual virginity of St. John, which entitled his body to translation or assumption, on the ground that virginity is not subject to death, is a case in point. The Catholic Church did not derive the counsels of perfection from Encratites or Manichees, and St. Jerome, who tells this story, would not owe it to pseudo-Luke, though Abdias —a very different narrator—in all probability did.

Speaking generally of the Johannine traditions, these represent the apostle as a saint of contemplation who transmitted directly from Christ, and as it is clear from his own gospel that he regarded the Eucharist, interpreted after a spiritual manner, as the condition of Divine Vision, we shall be antecedently prepared for the fact that there is an Eucharistic tradition concerning him. It is said that when preparing for translation he took bread, blessed, broke it and gave it to his disciples, exactly after the manner of his Master, but what he asked with uplifted eyes was that each of the brethren might be worthy of the Eucharist of the Lord and that, in such case, his portion might be also with theirs. It does not signify that, according to orthodox canons, this comes from a dubious source in doctrine ; the Eucharistic connection was not devised by that source, and—though it scarcely signifies for my purpose—I suppose—and it is interesting to note—that herein is the first recorded instance of communion in one kind.

The last asylum of St. John was Ephesus, which was a great house of theosophical speculations, and though the pivot and centre of the fourth gospel is that the Word was made flesh, that composite and wonderful text bears all the marks of being written in a Gnostic atmosphere. From that which it was intended to denounce, it has been thought to derive something in the higher part of the old eclectic dream, and as the personal influence of the writer must have been great, so also it is reasonable to think that it did not pass with him utterly away. The notion that he communicated something, and that this something remained, is so recurring, and amidst so many divided interests, that it is hard to reject it as a fiction ; it is hard even to say that no Knight Templar sojourning in the East did never, in late centuries, hear strange tidings. Apart from this last, too curious dream, it will be seen that here is slender ground on which to affirm that the Secret Tradition connected more closely with the Church side of Christianity at a Johannine point of contact ; but it is good to remember that not only has the last word not been said on the subject, but that we have listened here and there only to a strange rumour. I conclude that he who reported the deepest and most sacramental words which are on record from the mouth of Christ : " My flesh is meat indeed and my blood is drink indeed " is our first historical witness to the Eucharistic side of the Secret Tradition in Christian times. There are strange indications of sources behind the *Gospel according to St. John.* Behind the memorials of the *Gnosis* there are also indications of a stage when there was no separation as yet of orthodox and heretical schools, but rather an union in the highest direct experience, as if mysteries were celebrated, and at a stage of these there was the presence of the Master. But the presence of the Master was the term of experience in the Graal. I leave therefore the Johannine tradition, its possible perpetuation all secretly within the Church and its possible westward transition, as a quest so far unfinished for want of materials.

VII

THE CONCLUSION OF THIS HOLY QUEST

And now, seeing that the end of all is upon the very threshold, that the keepers of the paths of quest have sounded the horns for our retirement, and that the hour has also struck when we must turn down the glass of vision, it remains as a last duty to gather up certain threads which have been left under a covenant to recur, and these in their turn involve other considerations which must be treated shortly. The result of necessity is an attempt to codify things which, for the most part, are detached and even disjointed, yet some of them will be found to overlap under any mode of grouping.

Preliminary and General.—Setting aside its sacramental part, the literature, as literature, is Celtic in its elements and atmosphere ; but this is the body and the environment in which the spirit of the mystery reposes. The Graal itself is in the root a reliquary legend. This legend was taken over and connected with rumours of secret doctrine concerning the Eucharist and the priesthood, being part of a tradition handed down within the

Church, but unconsciously to the Church at large. It passed into romance and incorporated many folk-lore elements which seemed adaptable to its purpose. They are naturally its hindrance. In the hands of the Northern French writers, it got further away from the Celtic element as it drew towards its term. We cannot therefore explain the French cycles and much less the German Graal literature by means of the Celtic Church. The secret doctrine reflected into the literature abode in a secret school. Out of this school—but not in an official sense—there developed at later periods spiritual alchemy, symbolical craft Masonry, certain Rosicrucian institutions and certain Christian high grades of Masonic complexion, as successive veils. It was a school of Christian mystics, and it was Latin for a long time on its external side. It is of necessity catholic at heart. The doctrine concerning it is that there are High Princes of the Spirit whose experiences surpass not only those of devout souls but of many of the great saints. Their time was not " about half-an-hour," but an experience in perpetuity. The school said that the way of the Church was the true way and not a good one only, but also that the heights are still the heights. It comes about thus that the message of the Secret Words and the Super-Apostolical Succession is that until we enter the paths of sanctity and reach a defined term therein, we have only the shadow of the real things ; but that shadow is a sacred reflection. On the surface the claim concerning them sounds like a word written against the Church, but it is really a call to go forward. Those who are satisfied with the literal sense of sacred things are not defrauded thereby, but receive ministry therein. Yet the second sense remains, which is brought from very far away, because it draws from the sanctuary of the soul. Where there is no consciousness of this sense, and of the deep implicits of doctrine, the Graal is said to be removed, yet all things remain and are waiting to manifest. The mystery which the school celebrated corresponded, as I have said, to a Mass of the Beatific Vision. It is obvious that this was celebrated by the Hermit in the *Book of the Holy Graal*. He carried its signs on his person ; but they were not the badge, symbol, or token of an instituted Order. The prologue to this book is the nearest that we are likely to get to the expressed side of the mystery. The event in history which is parallel to the removal of the Graal is the entrance of the spirit of the world into the instituted House of Doctrine. The Mass of the Graal is recoverable, but it is understood that it is celebrated only in the Secret Church and that Church is within. When the priest enters the Sanctuary he returns into himself by contemplation and approaches the altar which is within. He says : *Introibo.* When he utters the words which are spirit and life, the Lord Christ comes down and communicates to him in the heart ; or, alternatively, he is taken up into the Third Heaven and enjoys the dilucid contemplation. But I do not put it in this way because I am satisfied with the expression : only we must have some expression.

The Veil of the Eucharist.—It has been said that, as the supreme mystery of the Christian Church, the Eucharist was the last ceremony of initiation and constituted the final enlightenment of the neophyte. The terms of expression may here be exaggerated, but those who were stewards of the Christian Mystery had in many cases received the Mysteries of the Gentiles and may have adapted some of their procedure. The rumour which came into romance—and this in the natural manner that official religion permeated romance everywhere—was a mystery of the Eucharist, and in the minds of external piety it translated itself into memorials of the Divine Body and the Precious Blood. It would be idle to suggest that any higher school of religion was concerned with the veneration of relics. The desire was to behold in the Eucharist that which the faithful believed to repose in the Eucharist. Beyond the knowledge of the outside world there is another knowledge, but it abides in concealed sources which are outside all reach of the senses, and in simple Eucharistic terms it is called the communication of Christ. In the deeper speculation behind the *Epiclesis* clause, it is the Descent of the Comforter within. The missing events and motives behind Super-Apostolical Succession are the Great Event and the Divine Reason. He who has performed the one rigorously scientific experiment and has opened the Holy Place does go in and celebrate his Mass in virtue of a warrant which is not necessarily that of the official priesthood, but it does not set it aside or compete therewith. I say that this interpretation remains *donec de medio fiat*, but it will not be taken out of the way. Herein is the experiment which I believe to be performed even now in the world, because the great mysteries of experience do not die. I have found that the Graal romances in their proper understanding—but chiefly because of their implicits—are a great introduction to the whole great subject. They testify after many ways. The Graal is a guide of the distressed in the Lesser Chronicles. They represent that Mystery which is implied in the Hidden Voice of Christ and of the Holy Spirit. Their Secret Words were words of power, because that which rules above rules also below. As such the Lesser Chronicles did not derive from Fécamp, which — like the Greater Chronicles — put forward the wonder-side of transubstantiation. But the *Book of the Holy Graal*, which cuts short the discourse between Christ and Joseph in the tower and so suppresses all reference to the communication of Secret Words, can derive no more than a reflection from this source, and even that little may be, alternatively, drawn from general tradition. I should state in this connection that the insufficiency of transubstantiation is on the external side mainly ; on the spiritual side the arch-natural body is communicated to the human body and the Divine Life to the human spiritual part. This is the deeper aspect not only of the Blessed Sacrament but of the Bowl of Plenty. Every text of the French cycles is confused and discounselled by this extraneous element, for which reason I have called it foreign, for example, to the *Romance of Lancelot*. I do not mean that the feeding properties are never introduced therein, but that the writer was dubious as to their proper place and ministry. The meats and the spicery now follow the dove—as in the case of Lancelot's visit to the Castle and that of Sir Bors—but now follow the Vessel—as in that of Gawain. The *Longer Prose Perceval* hints, as we have seen, at a secret of the sacrament which was held in utter reserve. It tells us by inference that it was the revelation of Christ in His own person, behind which there is another mystery. Only in the texts of transubstantiation do we find these deep allusions. The *Conte del Graal* has not heard of them; the *Didot Perceval* is aware of an undeclared mystery, but has no license to speak; the German *Parsifal* has chiefly an office of concealed mercy amidst suffering, and hereof is Heinrich a shadow. Yet all of them, in their several manners, are haunted from far away : Joseph II. began in priesthood and therein ends the Perceval of Manessier, as if he too discerned that those who attained the Great Mystery were thereby *Pontifices maximi*. I think also that the Fish in the *Metrical Joseph* has curious sacramental intimations; it is the sign of spiritual sustenance, of Christ's presence among His faithful, and hence of the Eucharist. In the *Book of the Holy Graal* it only duplicates one part of a canonical miracle. The master-key of the Mystery is most surely provided by the *Quest of Galahad*, where, after the magical marriage of High Art and Nature has taken place in transubstantiation, the questing knight bows his head, utters his *consummatum est*, and is dissolved. I conclude that the Christian and Graal Mystery of the Eucharist was a veil which could at need be parted by warranted hands, and that behind it there was then found the path which leads to the Union. The knowledge of that path arose within the Church but led behind it, the Church remaining the gate by which man enters into salvation. The romance-literature of the Graal worked towards the consciousness of the path, reaching its term in the last texts of quest.

The French and German Percevals.—The notion of an exalted hero is given in the *Longer Prose Perceval*, but he does not attain the highest vision, as Galahad does. The return of the Graal to the Castle after his induction is only like the return of a Reliquary. By the evidence of the text itself, he saw less than Arthur. Wolfram's *Parsifal* is indeed a dream of Eden, for that which is likened to the glory of the celestial height is truly of the supernal Paradise. It is to be understood—without exhausting the subject—that the poet's religious claim depends from the genealogy of the Stone, which is that whereby we are enabled to make the best of both worlds through a participation in the world which signifies in the absolute degree. I have said that Wolfram, Chrétien and Heinrich are agreed over the most important of their concerns, for the wonders of the Feeding Dish in the *Parsifal* are only a gross exaggeration of miraculous sustenance by the Host. The point which remains for our solution is after what manner did Wolfram and his source draw from the Secret Tradition. The answer is that their Graal is the Stone of Knowledge, and the hidden meaning behind the non-removal of the Graal is the perpetuity of the Secret Tradition somewhere in the world. The Mystic Question itself is only, and can be, the search after knowledge. The Keeper is in travail therewith—he must communicate, but he must be asked. The sense is that, in the order of human prudence, the tradition is in danger of perishing, and the Keeper must remain, like the Master of a Craft Lodge, till his successor is appointed. The same idea may lie behind the *Questiones Druidicæ*, or tests of proficiency which were put by the Druids to the Bards. The key to the meaning of the Stone of Knowledge—that testimony of main importance which we know to have existed in Guiot—is that the Graal was written in the heavens and remains therein ; for I do not doubt that the stars tell the same story. In allegories of this kind the hindrance to attainment inheres in its necessary conditions. The keeper in Heinrich must press Gawain to drink, and the brother of the Rich Fisher must persuade Perceval not to ask questions.

Collectanea Mystica.—(*a*) The Lesser Hallows.—The Lance renewed the Graal in some of the legends, but the places of the Hallows are in certain symbolical worlds which are known to the Secret Tradition. The Dish, which, as I have said, signifies little in the romances, has, for the above reason, aspects of importance in the Tarot. It was never pretended in any Church legend that the Sacred Lance was in England. The Sword of St. John the Baptist was not a relic of the Celtic or indeed of another Church. The subsidiary Hallows of the Lesser Chronicles therefore arrived later than the Graal in Britain, but we do not know how or why. In the Greater Chronicles many sacred relics were displayed at the ordination of Joseph II., and they were evidently brought over in the Ark of the Graal. (*b*) The Implicits.—Those of the Graal Keepers are of inheritance by genealogical legitimacy, in or out of marriage. This is simply the succession of initiation. Masonry recites the order in the same manner with the same kind of variations. There are three keepers in the Lesser Chronicles, and there are three archetypal Craft Lodges. There are nine keepers in the Greater Chronicles and there are nine Masonic Wardens who preserved the Secret Tradition. (2) Merlin is the sorcery of the sensitive life, which—because of its mixed nature—is of the serpent on one side and of Eve on the other, who is a virgin. The admixture makes therefore for righteousness, and the true son, after having been nurtured therein, is called out of its Egypt ; but it makes also for delusion, and when the spirit of the world intervenes all is withdrawn. (3) Moses is the intrusion of heretical Christianity into the Holy Place on the ground that it has the signs. His redemption is promised, but this does not take place, because it is found afterwards that " the end is everywhere," and the Church itself is not spared. (4) As regards the destruction of the Round Table, with all its chivalry and kinghood, I must register, with some reluctance, that it seems to convey chiefly a very simple and also obvious lesson, being that of the fatality of trespass and the poison instilled into those who partake of the evil fruit ; but in so far as in some of the texts it appears predetermined by Merlin, it is not accounted for so simply. I think that it may be left at this point, because we have no criterion for distinction between the enchanter's prophetic foresight and his formal intent. We should remember, however, (5) that the meaning of the enchantments and adventures is identified by the *Quest of Galahad* with the prevalence of an evil time and forgetfulness of the great things. It was for much the same reason that, according to the *Vulgate Merlin*, the Round Table was removed to the Kingdom of Leodegan prior to the coming of Arthur. (6) Sarras was the place of exit on the outward journey, and was thus the point at which the holy things began to manifest in the world ; but it was this also on the return journey, when they issued forth *in mysterium*. The transit westward is here of the soul outward. (7) It must be admitted that the Lesser Chronicles are in some sense a failure : they seem to hold up only an imperfect and a partial glass of vision. But they are full testimony to the secrecy of the whole experiment ; they are also the most wonderful cycle by way of intimation. Their especial key-phrase is my oft-quoted *exeunt in mysterium*. How profited the Secret Words to the interned Perceval ? It is the most ghostly of all suggestions concerning that which is done in the heart.

The Lost Book.—I have said that Chrétien must have

followed some book which had strange materials. I do not mean that it was an authorised text of Secret Tradition, but that there were many rumours oral and written, and that this was one of the latter. The speculation concerning it is like the warrant of the nine knights—that is to say, we can speculate, but we cannot find out. The alleged document which went before the tradition at large may have been the rumour of the tradition itself. We have seen that the *Huth Merlin* speaks of a *Book of the Sanctuary*, as of records continued henceforward, like a Calendar of the Saints ; but it is to be understood that this is romance and not a dark allusion. If I must admit speculation on my own part and suppose that there was any written legend of the Graal *per se* in 1100, *vel circa*, I should say that this was a Mass-Book and there is a hypothetical possibility of such a document ; but I do not think in my heart that it ever existed. If it did, I have indicated that it was concerned with such a Mass as might have been assumed to follow the Last Supper—when Christ gave Himself visibly, and the priest served like the altar-boy. I conclude that, in or out of such a text, the epochs of the literature are those of origin, manifestation and removal in respect of the Graal. As to the first, it was part of the mystery of the Incarnation ; as to the second, there was a manifestation intended, but it did not take place because the world was not worthy ; so the third epoch supervened, and the Graal was said to be removed. This is the secret intention, exhibited but not declared.

The Great Experiment.—To those who have studied the secret literatures with something of the spirit in themselves by which those literatures are informed, it becomes a matter of assurance that the signs of the Stewards of the Mysteries have never been wanting in the world. The Masonic High Grades suggest that they became Christian, but this is an error of expression : it was the Official Mysteries that became Christian : the Stewards had always known that their Redeemer liveth. Again, therefore, it is not surprising that a time came—and it was in many ways a remarkable time— when the rumours passed into romance. I speak here of the encompassing circle of wisdom which stands round the Great Experiment and not of the things which lie too deep for words. The memorials of that which has never been uttered because it is entombed in manifestation are about us in all our ways, and for ever and ever goes out the yearning of the heart in the presence of these silent witnesses. The genius of romance drew all things from all quarters to serve its purpose, and there is no question that the *Longer Prose Perceval* and the *Quest of Galahad* incorporated some of this yearning ; but I refer more especially to the rumours of the Holy Threshold. In this connection it is most important to understand that their makers neither were nor could be the spokesmen of a secret school. They had heard only, and it was but dimly that they grasped what they heard. Otherwise, they would have scarcely put forward the arch-natural side of relics. The office of minstrelsy and romance was to collect traditions, to express the current motive and sentiment. They became the mirror of their period and had therefore their religious side, which was accentuated sometimes, as when abbeys like Fécamp kept a court of song attached to them. A time came, however, when the consciousness of express intention intervened ; it is prominent in the Graal cycles, and it accounts for the great process of editing, harmonising and allegorising upon earlier texts. The normal limits of the horizon in romance were not, however, broken up except by the latest quests. These had also their restrictions, as I have tried to show previously, and the complexity of their symbolic machinery has tempted me to add that alchemy—sealed house of darkness as it is—seems in a manner more simple. The vessel, the matter and the fire are the three which give testimony therein on the physical side, and these are one on the spiritual. Its literature had also restrictions, more especially in its use of artificial language to conceal the real sense. It is high commonplace to say that the device is justified when it is dangerous to speak openly because the rulers of the Church or the world are jealous, or when the things which exceed common understanding are proscribed thereby. I say therefore that conceal-ment is justified when it is to hide the Secret of the King.

The Inner House of Doctrine.—I have promised to show whether there is commerce or competition between the theory of the Great Experiment and that of the Voided House, but I believe that it has been made clear abundantly in much that has preceded. The position is indeed simple, for the Great Experiment exists, but it is not remembered in the world at large : it is in this sense that the House is made void. It may well be that those who said it in romance had imagined an instituted House, while those others who said in effect : " Lift up your eyes, for your salvation is both there and here," were aware that the roots of the House are not in this world. The explanation is that the location of the Secret Church is in that ineffable region which lies, behind dogma, in glorious sanctuaries. It is not a repository of relics, and the reliquary is the husk only of the Holy Graal, which is a mystery of the Eucharist in its essence and not a legend of the preservation of the Precious Blood. The location of that Church and the places of the Hallows therein will be understood by saying that it is entered sometimes in an ecstasy through the eastern side of the plainest external sanctuary. It may be thought that on the evidence of the romances it is the Secret Church which itself is made void. But after the departure of the Supreme Mystery, what remains is the official Church. This does not mean that the Graal Castle or Temple signifies the official Church during an age of perfection. It is the inward mystery of doctrine. So long as it remained there, however hard of entrance, there was a way in—as Pausanias tells us that there was a way into the Garden of Venus. It died, however, in the consciousness except of a few faithful witnesses who knew after what manner it was still and is ever possible to lie, like St. John, on the breast of the Master.

The remembrance of the one thing needful is starred over all the secret literatures. Their maxim is not so much that God encompasses as that God is within ; and in virtue hereof they could say in their hearts what they said with their lips so often : *Absque nube pro nobis.* I affirm on the authority of research and on other authority and on that which I have seen of the Mysteries and on the high intimations which are communicated to those who seek, that the Great Experiment subsists, that those exist who have pursued it, and that behind the Secret Orders which are good and just and holy, we discern many traces of the Veiled Masters. The term of quest in those orders is the term of the Graal Quest, and the sacraments of procedure are not otherwise therein. The path of the instituted Mysteries, it should be understood, is in no sense the only path, but it is one of the nearest, because the mind is trained therein, firstly, in the sense of possibility, and, secondly, in the direction of consciousness, so that it may be overflowed by the experience of the experiment. It was carried on in the secret schools ; but at this day the great instituted Rites are like the Rich King Fisherman, either wounded or in a condition of languishment, and it is either for the same symbolic reason—namely, that few are prepared to come forward and ask the required question—the equivalent of which is to beget Galahad on the daughter of King Pelles—or the consciousness of the Great Experiment has closed down upon the Wardens of the Rites and they stand guard over its memorials only. It has been pursued also in the official Churches, which are permanent witnesses to its root-matter in the world. The two constitute together a great, holy, catholic and apostolic Church, which is empowered to say : *Signatum est super nos lumen vultus tui.* But seeing that it is more than all *signatum*, we have to look in the deep places for its hidden virtue. The key which we must take in our hands is that God is everywhere and that He recompenses those who seek Him out. But we do not look to find Him more especially in the Master's chair of a Craft Lodge or the pulpit of a popular preacher, and hence those who are on the quest of the Veiled Masters will do well to release themselves from the notion of any corporate fellowship as a *sine quâ non*. I say now truly and utterly that the Veiled Master is in the heart of each one of us and the path to his throne is the path to the Secret Church. Some say that the Pearl without Price is here, some that it is there, some that it has been taken into hiding, and some that it is withdrawn into heaven; which things are true and without let or hindrance of my own testimony; wherefore I add that if any one can exclaim truly : *Nunc dimittis, Domine, servum tuum secundum verbum tuum in pace*, it is, and this only, *quoniam vidit oculus meus salutare tuum*, and he then also has seen the Graal.

If I have not spoken my whole mind on certain aspects and memorials of the Secret Tradition which do now repose in the instituted but veiled sanctuaries, it is because I am conscious of several inherent difficulties, and I remember many covenants. If, therefore, recognising this, some voice in the cloud of listeners should intervene and say : " But again, where are they—the Stewards ? "—I should answer, as I could answer only : " I have brought back from a long and long journey those few typical memorials which I have interwoven in this book for the encouragement of some of my kinship, that where I have been they may enter also in their time—supposing that they are called in truth. If they see at the end only the trail of the garments of some who elude them at a distant angle of the vista, they may at least confess with me that Titans have gone before and have cast their shadows behind. To whatever such quest might lead in one case or another, be it understood, and this clearly, that in assuming the legends of the Holy Graal as a sacred and beautiful opportunity to speak of the Eucharist and other divine things connected with and arising therefrom, I have put forward no personal claim. If I have dwelt in the secret places it has not been to return and testify that no others can enter ; and I, least of all, am the authorised spokesman of Stewards behind the veil. But that which it has been given me to do, I have done faithfully, within the measure of my knowledge : I have indicated the stages of reception, or the golden links of the chain, from Christian High Grades of Masonry to the Craft Grades, from the Rosy Cross to the spiritual alchemists, and from these to the Graal literature. Behind all this I should look assuredly to the East, in the direction of that pure catholic gnosticism which lies like a pearl of great price within the glistening shell of external Christianity, which is not of Marcion or Valentinus, of Cerinthus and all their cohorts, but is the unexpressed mystery of experience in deep wells whence issues no strife of sects.

We know that in its higher grades the spirit of imagination moves through a world not manifest, and this is the world of mystery ; it is that also in which many are initiated who are called but not chosen utterly ; yet it is that in which the epopt is at last enthroned— that world in which the Graal Castle, Corbenic or Mont Salvatch, the most holy temple and secret sanctuary, are attainable at any point, all points being out of time and place. It is the world of Quest, which is also the world of Attainment. There in fine, at the striking of a certain mystic hour, that translation takes place in which the soul is removed, with the Graal thereto belonging, and it is idle for any one to say that it is shown henceforth so openly. It is there that the offices of all the high degrees meet in the term of their unity, and the great systems also, at which height we understand vitally what now we realise intellectually— that the great translation of alchemy, the passage from kingdom to crown in Kabalism, the journey through Hades to Elysium in the Greek Mysteries and in Dante as their last spokesman, and lastly the great *Quest of Galahad*, are the various aspects and symbolical presentations of one subject.

At this stage of the interpretation I shall not need to point out that in the final adjustments even the highest symbols are merely pretexts ; they are tokens, " lest we forget " ; and this is for the same reason that neither chalice nor paten really impart anything. They are among the great conventions to which the soul confesses on the upward path of its progress, but within their proper offices they are not to be set aside. The explanation is less that they impart as that through them the high graces communicate in proportion to the powers of reception. The soul which has opened up the heights of the undeclared consciousness within partakes as a great vessel of election, while another soul, which is still under seals, may receive nothing.

Independently of corporate connections, the Mystic Quest is the highest of all adventures, the mirror of all knighthood, all institutes of chivalry. And this Quest is also that of the Graal, but written after another manner. The makers of the mighty chronicles said more than they knew that they were saying, but they knew in part and they saw through a glass darkly. We are " full of sad and strange experience," though we have not come to our rest, and for this reason we are in a better position to understand the old books than when they were first drawn into language. Better than they who wrote them in their far past do we now know after what manner the highest things go forth into mystery ; but of the gate they knew and of the way also. Chivalry was a mystery of idealism and the Graal a mystery of transfiguration, but when it was removed from this world it was not any further away.

We have, on these considerations, and many others, every cause to be thankful to those learned persons who have gone before us, taking such lamps as they have been licensed to carry ; but in the last resource the term of learning is attained, after which there is only the great light which can be made to enlighten every man who comes into this world. It is that sun which shines in Mont Salvatch, in Sarras, the spiritual city, and in the place of rest which is Avalon. It exhibits the abiding necessity of the sacraments as well as their suspension ; it exhibits that priesthood which comes rather by inward grace than by apostolical succession, albeit those who deny the succession are usually far from the grace.

The monks sat in their cells and stalls and scriptoria during the great adventurous times when the rumour of the Holy Graal moved through the world of literature ; they dreamed of a chivalry spiritualised and a church of sanctity exalted : so came into being the *Longer Prose Perceval*, the *Quest of Galahad* and the *Parsifal* of Wolfram. Whether in the normal consciousness I know not or in the subconsciousness I know not —God knoweth—that dream of theirs was of the super-concealed sanctuary behind the known chancel and the visible altar. This is the sense of all that which I understand concerning the traces of the Secret Church in the Graal literature. As before, I am not speaking of formal institutions, of esoteric brotherhoods, or incorporations of any kind ; it is a question of the direction of consciousness and of its growth in that direction. A man does not leave the external church because he enters into the spiritual Church ; Ruysbroeck does not cease to say Mass because he has been in those heights and across those seas of which we hear in his *Adornment of the Spiritual Marriage*. At the same time his language is not exactly that of the official Church in its earliest or latest encyclical ; it is not like that of St. Irenæus writing against heresies or Pius X. denouncing the spirit of modernism. It is something the same as, if one may say it, in the brotherhood of Masonry. The craft degrees are the whole summary of Masonry, but there

is a certain distinction between him who has taken these
only and him who has added thereto the eighteenth
degree of Rose Croix, or the still more exalted and now
almost secret grade of Knights Beneficent of the Holy
City of Jerusalem. Yet the one is a Mason and the other
is not more than a Mason, but there are or at least
there may be degrees of consciousness in the Mysteries.
So also the lay member of any one among the official
Churches whose instruction has scarcely exceeded the
catechisms of Christian doctrine is not—or need not
be at least—less a Christian than he who has studied
Summa, but again there are degrees of consciousness in
the mystery of the faith.

Now the Secret Tradition in Christian times is the
rumour of the Secret Sanctuary, and this tradition has
many voices. The voice of spiritual alchemy, succeeding
that of the Graal, is the voice of the Graal literature
under another veil, but it says that He is there ; and
after its departure it is known and recorded that many
earnest and holy persons beheld the Vessel of Singular
Devotion : yet there is something wanting in the
official sanctuaries. The voice of the Temple, reflected
in its later revival, says that He is risen and gone away.
The voice of Masonry says that the old Temple was not
built according to the true and original plan. The
voice of the Rosy Cross says that in places withdrawn
He, being dead, yet testifies. The voice of St. John on
Patmos says that he was given a book to eat, and that
in his mouth it was sweet but in his belly it was bitter—
because thenceforward he was in travail with the Secret
Doctrine. The witness of the Graal literature heard
something at a very great distance, and to decorate
what they had heard the artists of the literature gathered
from the four quarters of romance and legend and
folk-lore. As such their reflection is a failure. The
witness of alchemical books chose a worse medium, but
they made it serve their purpose more expressly. The
voice of Masonry created a great legend to commemorate

684

an universal loss, and testified that the Quest would never end till the speculative Masons found that which was once among them. The Voice of the Rosy Cross said that, having found the body of the Master, the brethren again closed the sepulchre and set their seals thereon, though they also looked for a great resurrection. The voice of St. John reflected the last message of the Master: "Behold, I come quickly." And all Christendom has resounded since with the anthem: "Amen, even so, come, Lord Jesus." The Hidden Voice of Christ is in the Secret Literature, and I have therefore written this book as the text-book of a Great Initiation. Meanwhile, the Churches are not made void, but they are in widowhood and desolation, during which time our place is with them, that we may offer them comfort in their sorrow, without being deceived by their distractions. It is certain also that His reflections abide with them. Chrétien may have drawn from an episodic romance of adventure in the possession of the Count of Flanders. Master Blihis, the great maker of fables, may have recited things, with or without consequence, concerning *Sanctum Graal*. Neither these nor others that could be mentioned are the books concerning the Secret Words of the Eucharist or the text of Secret Ordination. The legends of Welsh saints may tell us of Sacred Hosts coming down from heaven, but the *Epiclesis* clause, if the Welsh had it, in their book of the Mass, is not the Lost Word which we seek like the Mason. They may tell us also of holy personages who were consecrated by Christ, and the fables may be famous indeed, but they want the motive which fills the Greater Chronicles of the Holy Graal with meaning and suggestions of meaning. Therefore I still hear and listen with all my ears while the voices of many traditions say the same things differently. The Holy Sepulchre is empty; the Tomb of C. R. C. in the House of the Holy Spirit is sealed up; the Word of Masonry is lost; the Zelator of alchemy now looks in vain for a Master. The traditional book of the Graal, by whatever name of convention we may choose to term it—*Liber Gradalis* or *Sanctum Graal*—is not only as much lost as that which was eaten by St. John, though it might not be so difficult to conjecture the elements in the one as in the other case.

And now to make an end of these pleadings : I have chosen to give some account of the Holy Graal as it was and as it is, that I could lead up to what it might be, that is to say, how it could be realised in high literature, because in other respects some things which might be in the ideal order are those also which are—and God redeems the future as well as the past. As regards therefore the true theory of this mystery, with others of the mystic school, we may hope in the Lord continually, even as one who believes that he will not be confounded unto eternity. Reason has many palaces, but the sovereign peace rules in a single place. Dilated in the mystery of cloud and moisture and moonlight, the Graal appears even now, and that suddenly. It abides in the memory for those who can live in its light, and it is elevated in the light for those who can so keep it in the high spirit of recollection that it has become their guide and their nourishment. For myself it is in virtue of many related dedications that I have allocated a great experiment in literature to a great consanguineous experiment in spiritual life. I have not so much demonstrated the value of a pure hypothesis as elucidated after what manner those who are concerned with the one subject do from all points return triumphantly thereto. As a seeker after the high mysteries, at this last I testify that whosoever shall in any subject offer me daily bread, I will say to him : "But what of the *Panis vivus et vitalis?* What of the supersubstantial bread?" And if there be any one who deals therein, under what rules soever of any houses of exchange, I will have him know that if he sells in the open market, even I am a buyer. So therefore the author of this book gives thanks that he has written concerning the romance-pageants and sanctity as of the catholic and eternal secrets of religion. *Quod erat demonstrandum :* it is written for those alone who in the silence of the heart and in a sacred suspension of the senses have heard the voice of the Graal.

In the great desolation of Logres I hear also—I hear and I hear—the penitent Knight Lancelot singing his twelve-month Mass. So also till he turns at the Altar saying : *Ite, Missa est,* because the King himself is coming in the morning tide, I will respect all the findings of scholarship concerning quests which are not of the Graal and Cups which contain no sacrament, but I am on the quest of the Graal and, Master of True Life, after all and all and all, it is not so far to Thee. And even Gwalchmai saw it.

The colophon of this book wishes Godspeed to all whom it may concern on the Great Quest.

APPENDIX

A BRIEF METHODISED BIBLIOGRAPHY OF

THE HOLY GRAAL

IN LITERATURE AND CRITICISM

Comprising a Key to the Study of the Texts and the Several Schools of Interpretation

PART I

THE TEXTS

IT is desirable in fairness to myself, but more especially out of justice to my readers, that the limitations of these sections should be made plain from the beginning. A complete bibliography of the Holy Graal in literature and criticism should assuredly include, so far as the texts are concerned, at least a sufficient study of the chief manuscripts; and in respect of the critical works it should embrace a survey of continental periodical literature—chiefly French and German—wherein a very important part is, and will remain, imbedded. The large knowledge which is necessary in one of these cases, the opportunity in the other, and the space in regard to both, would—I must confess—fail me, were so ambitious a research called for; but it exceeds the scope of my purpose, as it would have little or no appeal to those whom I address. I have confined myself, therefore, to particulars of the printed texts, to the most important of the critical works, and to a few characteristic essays towards interpretation along independent lines, because these—whatever their value—will be of interest to mystic students, if only as counsels of caution. As regards the intermediate group, I have sought in a few words to indicate, where possible, certain points of correspondence with my own thesis. If, therefore, it be inferred that this section is written in the spirit and exists in the interests of a partisan, I shall neither dissuade nor protest; but rather—that I may do all things sincerely within my particular field—I will begin by assuming that the matter of my own research, having to be judged by unusual canons, would be unlikely, in any case, to receive the *imprimatur* of the existing schools. In so far as my book

has been done zealously and truly, I believe that it will engage
their interest, at whatever cost of disagreement, and my debt of
gratitude to their great, patient and productive research may be a
little reduced should any of them here and there feel that a new
vista has been opened. They also know that although the Graal
literature began in folk-lore it did not end therein; and if its
consanguinities—actual, but yet remote—with secret ways of
thought and strange schools of experience should be naturally outside their sphere, it may even be that the end which I descry is not
so foreign after all but that they have almost caught at it in dreams.

A. EARLY EPOCHS OF THE QUEST, being documents that
embody materials which have been elsewhere incorporated into
the Graal legends, but do not themselves refer to the Holy
Vessel; in their extant form these texts are much later than
the rest of the literature.

1. *Peredur the son of Evrawc,* first printed, with the Welsh
text, translation and notes, in the *Mabinogion,* by Lady Charlotte
E. Guest, 3 vols., 1849; a second edition, without the text and
with abridged notes, appeared in 1877. The collection has
since been reissued in many forms, and is available in the
Temple Classics and another popular series. The edition of
Mr. Alfred Nutt, first published in 1902, with notes by the editor,
has an appeal to scholars. The *Mabinogion* have been also translated into French and German.

2. *The Romance of Syr Percyvelle of Galles,* included in *The
Thornton Romances,* edited by J. O. Halliwell, and published by
the Camden Society in 1844. The manuscript is preserved in
the Library of Lincoln Cathedral, and Robert Thornton, its
scribe, is thought to have compiled the collection about 1440.
The year mentioned is speculative in two ways: (*a*) because the
Thornton volume can only be dated approximately, and (*b*)
because the poem with which we are concerned is almost unquestionably a transcript from an unknown original. By the
evidence of language and style it is thought, however, to belong
to the approximate period of its transcription. *Syr Percyvelle* is
a rhymed poem of 2228 lines.

B. LE CONTE DEL GRAAL.—·I. *Le Poème de* CHRÉTIEN DE
TROYES *et de ses continuateurs d'après le manuscrit de* MONS, being
vols. 2 to 6 of *Perceval le Gallois, ou le Conte du Graal—vide infra*
for the first volume, containing the romance in prose. This is
so far the only printed edition, and it was produced under the
auspices of C. Potvin for the *Société des Bibliophiles Belges.* It
appeared from 1866 to 1871, and copies are exceedingly rare.
The text is that of a manuscript in the *Bibliothèque Communale*

de MONS, and it is considered unfavourably by scholarship. The equipment of the editor has been also regarded as insufficient, but the pains which made the poem available deserve our highest thanks, and the gift has been priceless. I believe that a new edition is promised in Germany. It may be useful to mention that the work of Chrétien is held to have ended at line 10,601; that of Gautier—but here opinions differ—at line 34,934; while the conclusion of Manessier extends the work to 45,379 lines, not including the fragment of Gerbert, which exceeds 15,000 lines. The *excursus* which M. Potvin appended to his last volume is still pleasant reading, but it represents no special research and at need is now almost negligible. It seems to look favourably on the dream of a Latin primordial Graal text; it affirms that the *Conte* was called the *Bible du démon* by Gallic monks of old, and that *Lancelot of the Lake* was placed on the Index by Innocent III.

II. *The Berne Perceval.* Our chief knowledge of this un-printed text is due to Alfred Rochat, who gave extracts therefrom in *Ueber einen bisher unbekannten Percheval li Gallois* (Zurich, 1855). It has variations which are important for textual purposes, but the conclusion only is of moment to ourselves. In the first place, it is an attempt to complete the Quest of Perceval prac-tically within the limits of Gautier's extension, which it does, in a summary manner, by recounting how the Fisher King dies within three days of Perceval's second visit and how the latter becomes Keeper of the Graal. The version follows the historical matter of the Lesser Chronicles, which is of interest in view of my remarks on pp. 207 and 235. The Fisher King is Brons; he is the father of Alain le Gros; and his wife is sister to Joseph of Arimathæa. It will be noted that this is the succession of the *Didot Perceval*, the Keepership not passing to Alain.

III. *Trèsplaisante et Recreative Hystoire du trèspreulx et vaillant chevallier Perceval le Galloys . . . lequel acheva les adventures du Sainct Graal, &c.*—Paris, 1530. This is the prose version of the *Conte del Graal*, the summaries of which are given among the marginal notes of Potvin's text of the poem. It includes, in certain copies, the important *Elucidation*, which was long thought to exist only in this form. The object which actuated the edition is stated very simply—namely, to place a work which had long become archaic in an available form. As such, it might appeal to some readers who would be hindered by the difficulties of th original, but it is available only in a few great libraries.

The *Conte del Graal* is said to have been translated into Spanish and published at Seville in 1526. We may assume, in this case, that it is in prose, and the interesting point concerning it would then be that it anteceded the French prose version. I do not think that its existence detracts from my general conclusion that the Quest of Perceval had little appeal, during that period when the literature of chivalry reigned, in Spain and Portugal. The full title is *Historia de Perceval de Gaula, Caballero de la Tabla Rotonda*, but at a later period it has been suggested alternatively that it is really a Spanish version of the *Longer Prose Perceval*. No one seems to have seen it. A Flemish and an Icelandic version remain unprinted.

C. THE LESSER CHRONICLES.—It is understood that I have adopted this title as comprehensive and suitable for my purpose, but there is no collection of manuscripts which bears the name.

I. *Le Roman du Saint Graal, publié pour la première fois d'après un manuscrit de la Bibliothèque Royale, par* FRANCISQUE MICHEL, Bordeaux, 1841. The manuscript in question is unique and the poem which is now under consideration consists of 3514 lines. There is a lacuna between lines 2752 and 2753, being at and about that point when destruction overwhelms the false Moses in the prose version. The metrical romance was reprinted in the *Dictionnaire des Légendes*, forming part of Migne's *Troisième . . . Encyclopédie Théologique*, and in this form is still, I believe, available. It was also included by Dr. Furnivall in his edition of the *Seynt Graal or the Sank Ryal*, printed for the Roxburgh Club, 2 vols., 1861–63.

It seems desirable to couple with this text certain archaic English versions of the Joseph legend : (*a*) The alliterative poem of *Joseph of Aramathie*, otherwise, the *Romance of the Seint Graal*, known only by the Vernon MS. at Oxford, which belongs to the middle of the fourteenth century. It is a summary of the *Book of the Holy Graal*, beginning with the release of Joseph from the tower and ending with the departure from Sarras. It is imperfect at the inception, and, of course, breaks off far from the term. (*b*) *The Lyfe of Joseph of Armathy*, printed by Wynkyn de Worde and corresponding to the account given by Capgrave in his *Nova Legenda Angliæ*. It pretends to be founded on a book discovered by the Emperor Theodosius at Jerusalem. It is evident, however, that this is really the *Book of the Holy Graal*, though the account of Joseph's imprisonment follows the Apocryphal Gospel of Nicodemus and there is no reference to the Holy Vessel. (*c*) *The Lyfe of Joseph of Armathia*, believed to have been written about the year 1502, and first printed in 1520. The authorship is entirely unknown and so are manuscripts prior to publication. It is, of course, much too late to possess any historical importance. It is exceedingly curious, and, in spite of its rude verse and chaotic manner, is not without a certain pictorial sense and vividness. In place of the Sacred Vessel of Reception there are two cruets substituted in which the blood of Christ was collected by Joseph. These fragments are all included by the Rev. W. W. Skeat in his *Joseph of Arimathie*, published for the Early English Text Society, 1871.

II. *The Lesser Holy Graal*, i.e. *Le Petit Saint Graal, ou Joseph d'Arimathie*, is known by a number of MSS., one of which is called *Cangé*; it belongs to the thirteenth century and is preserved in the Bibliothèque Nationale at Paris. Two codices, together with a version in modern French, are included in the first volume of *Le Saint Graal*, published by Eugène Hucher, 3 vols., Paris, 1874. This text was regarded by the editor as De Borron's original work, from which the metrical version was composed later on by an unknown hand.

III. *The Early Prose Merlin.* We have seen that the metrical Romance of Joseph concludes at line 3514, after which the unique MS. proceeds, without any break, to the life of Merlin, reaching an abrupt term at line 4018, all being missing thereafter. This fragment is included in the text of Michel. The complete prose version forms the first part of the *Vulgate* and the second of the *Huth Merlin*, the bibliographical particulars of which are given later. It follows from one, and apparently one only, of the *Early Merlin* codices that Robert de Borron proposed as his next branch to take the life of Alain, and in so stating he, or his personator, uses some of the words which occur in the colophon of his *Joseph* poem. It appears further that the Alain branch was intended to show how the enchantments fell upon Britain.

IV. *The Didot Perceval*, i.e. *Perceval, ou la Quête du Saint Graal, par* Robert de Borron. This text is included in the first volume of Hucher's collection, with a summary prefixed thereto. The date borne by the MS. is 1301. The root-matter of the romance is, of course, the non-Graal myth of Perceval, the existence of which is posited on such excellent grounds by scholarship. Critical opinion is perhaps equally divided on the question whether the *Didot Perceval* does or does not represent the third part of De Borron's metrical trilogy. The name of Gaston Paris must be ranged on the affirmative side, and on the negative that of Mr. Alfred Nutt.

D. THE GREATER CHRONICLES.—It is again understood that this title is merely a matter of convenience in connection with my particular classification of texts.

I. *The Book of the Holy Graal*, i.e. *Le Saint Graal ou Joseph d'Arimathie*. There are several MSS., among which may be mentioned that of the *Bibliothèque de la Ville de Mans*, which is referred to the middle of the thirteenth century. Other codices are at Cambridge and in the British Museum. It was first edited by Furnivall (*op. cit.*), from the MSS. preserved in England, and subsequently by Hucher, forming vols. 2 and 3 of his collection, as described previously. Dr. Furnivall also included the English rendering called *The Seynt Graal* or *Sank Ryal*, known by a single MS. attributed to the middle of the fifteenth century. The work is in conventional verse of very poor quality, the author being Henry Lovelich or Lonelich, described as a skinner, but of whom no particulars are forthcoming. It is a rendering by way of summary extending to nearly 24,000 lines, with several extensive lacunæ. Outside the testimony of its existence to the interest in the Graal literature, as illustrated by the pains of translation at a length so great, it has no importance for our subject. It was again edited by Dr. Furnivall (1874–78) for the Early English Text Society, but after thirty-four years it remains incomplete, no titles or a satisfactory introduction to the text having been produced.

II. *The Vulgate Merlin*, i.e. *Le Roman de Merlin*, or the *Early History of King Arthur*. The available French text is that which was edited, in 1884, by Professor H. Oskar Sommer from the Add. MS. 10292 in the British Museum. It is ascribed to the beginning of the fourteenth century. The prose version of Robert de Borron's substantially lost poem is brought to its term in this edition at the end of Chapter V. With this the reader may compare, and is likely to use at his pleasure, *Merlin, or the Early History of King Arthur*, edited for the Early English Text Society by Mr. Henry B. Wheatley, 1865–99, which during another modest period of thirty-four years has certainly produced a satisfactory and valuable edition of the anonymous rendering of the *Vulgate Merlin* preserved in the unique MS. of the University Library, Cambridge. This text is allocated to A.D. 1450–60, and as a translation it is fairly representative of the French original. A metrical rendering has been edited from an Auchinleck MS. by Professor E. Koelling in his *Arthour and Merlin*, Leipsic, 1890.

I have spoken of *Les Prophéties de Merlin*, which appeared with no date at Rouen, but probably in 1520 or thereabouts. It claims to be translated from the Latin, and contains episodes of Merlin's history which are unlike anything in the canonical texts. A few points may be enumerated as follows : (*a*) In place of the faithful Blaise of the other chronicles, there is a long list of the scribes employed by Merlin to record his prophecies, being (1) Master Tholomes, who subsequently became a bishop ; (2) Master

Anthony ; (3) Meliadus, the brother of Sir Tristram and paramour of the Lady of the Lake ; (4) the sage clerk, Raymon ; (5) Rubers, the chaplain. (*b*) The prophet in this curious romance is unbridled in his amours. (*c*) The account of his internment by the Lady of the Lake recalls the parallel story in the *Huth Merlin*, but differs also therefrom. (*d*) There is a full portrayal of Morgan le Fay, her early life and her transition from beauty to ugliness through evil arts of magic. (*e*) The sin and suffering of Moses are also recounted. (*f*) The Siege Perilous at the Third Table is said to have been occupied, with disastrous results, by a knight named Rogier le Bruns. (*g*) There is a summary of the circumstances under which Joseph of Arimathæa and his son Joseph II. came to Britain for its conversion. (*h*) But perhaps the most remarkable episode is that of the meeting between King Arthur and a damosel in the church of St. Stephen. She came sailing over the land in that ship which afterwards carried Arthur to Avalon.

The early printed editions of the *Vulgate Merlin*, which appeared at Paris from 1498 and onward, have variations from the *textus receptus*, representing the ingenuities of successive editors. An Italian *Merlin* was issued at Venice and again at Florence towards the end of the fifteenth century. I shall speak later of texts printed in Spain.

III. *The Huth Merlin*, i.e. *Merlin—Roman en prose du XIIIe siècle, publié avec la mise en prose du poème de Merlin de Robert de Boron, d'après le manuscrit appartenant à* M. Alfred H. Huth, *par* Gaston Paris *et* Jacob Ulrich. 2 vols., Paris, 1886. The position and content of this romance have been dealt with so fully in the text that, although much rests to be said in a complete analysis, it will be sufficient for my purpose to enumerate three casual points : (*a*) The unique portion—which is the great bulk of the story—is believed to have been composed after the *Lancelot* ; (*b*) it is perhaps for this reason that it shares responsibility for the unfavourable portraiture of Gawain which characterises most of the Greater Chronicles ; (*c*) in some undecided way the death of a lady who killed herself over the body of a knight, slain by Balyn in self-defence, is said by Merlin to involve the latter in dealing "the stroke most dolourous that ever man stroke, except the stroke of our Lord."

IV. *The Great Prose Lancelot.* The importance of this romance is fully recognised by scholarship, and the careful collation of the numerous manuscripts is desired, but so far it remains a counsel of perfection. No text has been edited in modern days, and though the reissue of one of the old printed versions, on account of their great extent, was unlikely under any circumstances, it is singular that not even a satisfactory modernised rendering has been so far produced. In 1488 the *Lancelot* appeared at Paris in three folio volumes, and as there were other editions it is only necessary to mention that of 1533, which bears the imprint of Philippe le Noir, because great stress has been laid thereon. In his *Studies on the Sources* of Malory's *Morte d'Arthur*, Dr. Sommer has taken as his basis the edition of 1513, but without expressing preference. It appears from this text (*a*) that Galahad was acquainted with his paternity even in his childhood, and (*b*) that he was sent to the abbey of white nuns by King Pelles, his grandfather. The omission of these details by Malory enhances the sacred mystery of the story.

V. *The Longer Prose Perceval.* This text constitutes the first volume of Potvin's *Conte del Graal*, as described in section *B.* Of its translation by Dr. Sebastian Evans under its proper title of *The High History of the Holy Graal*, I have said sufficient to indicate the gratitude which is due to a new sacrament in literature from those who are in the grace of the sacraments. The original is known in textual criticism as *Perceval li Gallois* and *Perlesvaux*. The date of composition is referred by its first editor to the end of the twelfth century, but later authorities assign it to a period not much prior to 1225. The manuscript itself is allocated broadly to the thirteenth century, and is preserved in the Bibliothèque de Bourgogne at Brussels. The second of the Hengwrt Graal texts, of which we shall hear shortly, is a Welsh version of the *Longer Prose Perceval* and is a short recension which abounds in mistranslations, but at the same time it supplies a missing portion of the manuscript to which we owe the story in its printed form. If some of its variations were important, they might lie under a certain suspicion on account of the translator's defects, but I do not know that there is anything which need detain us concerning it. I will add only that a Berne MS. contains two fragments, some account of which has been given by Potvin and Dr. Evans. It should be noted, however, that since the edition of Potvin appeared in 1866, several other codices have come to light, but it has not been suggested that they offer important variations. A French text is also supposed to have been printed in 1521.

VI. *The Quest of Galahad*, otherwise *La Queste del Saint Graal*, the head and crown of the legend, is, in the early printed texts, either incorporated with the prose *Lancelot*, as in the edition of 1513, already mentioned, or with the *Book of the Holy Graal*, as in the Paris edition of 1516, which is called: *L'hystoire du sainct Greaal, qui est le premier livre de la Table Ronde.* . . . .

Appendix

Ensemble la Queste dudict sainct Greaal, ffaicte par Lancelot, Galaad, Boors et Perceval qui est le dernier livre de la Table Ronde, &c. But that which is available more readily to students who desire to consult the original is *La Queste del Saint Graal*: Edited by F. J. Furnivall, M.A., for the Roxburghe Club, London, 1864. Every one is, however, aware that the great prose *Quest* was rendered almost bodily into the *Morte d'Arthur* of Sir Thomas Malory, first printed by Caxton in the year 1485, as the colophon of the last book sets forth. The full title is worth reproducing from the edition of Robert Southey, as follows : *The Byrth, Lyf, and Actes of Kyng Arthur ; of his Noble Knyghtes of the Rounde Table, theyr merveyllous enquestes and aduentures, thachyeuyng of the Sanc Greal ; and in the end* LE MORTE DARTHUR, *with the Dolourous Deth and departyng out of thys worlde of them all.* Dr. H. Oskar Sommer has of recent years (1889 91) faithfully reprinted the Caxton Malory in three volumes of text, introduction and studies on the sources. This constitutes the *textus receptus.* Other editions, abridgments and modern versions are too numerous for mention.

VII. *The Welsh Quest*, i.e. *Y Seint Greal, being the Adventures of King Arthur's Knights of the Round Table, in the Quest of the Holy Greal, and on other occasions.* Edited with a Translation and Glossary, by the Rev. Robert Williams, M.A., London, 1876. This is the first volume of *Selections from the Hengwrt MSS.*, the second appearing in 1892 and containing the *Gests of Charlemagne*, with other texts outside our particular subject. *The Welsh Quest* is entitled simply *The Holy Greal* and is divided into two parts, of which the first concerns Galahad and his peers, the second being that recension of *The Longer Prose Perceval* to which reference has been made above.

E. THE GERMAN CYCLE.—As the French legends of the Holy Graal are reducible in the last resource to the *Quest of Galahad*, so are those of Germany summed up in the epic poem with which we are now so well acquainted and which here follows in my list.

I. The *Parsifal* of Wolfram von Eschenbach was written some time within the period which intervened between 1200 and 1215, the poet dying, as it is believed, about 1220, while towards the close of his life he was occupied with another long composition, this time on the life of William of Orange. I conceive that in respect of the German Cycle I shall have no occasion to speak of early printed editions, so I will name only (*a*) The critical edition based on various manuscripts, by Karl Lachmann, a fourth issue of which appeared at Berlin in 1879 ;

(*b*) the text edited by Karl Bartsch and published in *Deutsche Classiker des Mittelalters*, vols. ix.-xi., 1875-9 ; (*c*) the metrical rendering in modern German, published from 1839 to 1841 by A. Schulz, under the name of *San Marte ;* (*d*) the modern version by Simrock, 1842 ; (*e*) that of Dr. Bötticher in rhymeless measures, 1880 ; (*f*) and in fine the translation into English of *Parzival : a Knightly Epic,* by Miss Jessie L. Weston, 2 vols., London, 1894.

II. The poem of Heinrich von dem Türlin, entitled *Diu Crône.* Of this text there was a servicable edition published at Stuttgart in 1852, under the editorship of G. H. F. Scholl, who prefixed a full introduction. The work forms the twenty-seventh volume of the *Bibliothek des Litterarischen Vereins.* It was again edited in 1879.

III. The *Titurel* of Albrecht von Scharfenberg—i.e. *Der Jüngere Titurel*—was edited in 1842 for the *Bibliothek der Deutschen National Litteratur* by K. A. Hahn. It was also edited by E. Droyran in 1872 under the title *Der Tempel des Heiligen Graal.* In my account of this poem—but presumably because the particular legend is scarcely within my subject—I have omitted to mention that the history of Lohengrin is given in a more extended form than that of Wolfram, and the catastrophe—which is also different—involves the destruction of the Swan Knight.

IV. *The Dutch Lancelot.* Seeing that the extant text of this compilation exceeds 90,000 lines, it will be understood that the task of editing and carrying it through the press was not likely to be attempted on more than a single occasion, the heroic scholar being M. Jonckbloet. The *Morien* section was subsequently treated separately by M. T. Winkel. The few to whom it is accessible assign to the whole poem a place of importance as a reflection in part of materials which are not otherwise extant. There was also a German *Lanzelet,* by Ulrich von Zatzikhofen, whose work is usually ascribed to the end of the twelfth or the beginning of the thirteenth century : in this case he preceded Wolfram, which theory recent criticism is, however, inclined to question. Ulrich followed a French model.

F. THE SPANISH AND PORTUGUESE CYCLES.—Among the more popular historians of Spanish literature, it is customary to pass over the texts of romantic chivalry with the citation of a few typical examples, such as *Amadis of Gaul, Palmerin of England* and *Don Belianis of Greece.* I speak under all reserves, having no special knowledge of the subject, but as a comprehensive analysis of the vast printed literature does not appear to have been attempted, except in Spanish, so it seems reasonable to speculate that there may be many texts in manuscript still practically entombed in public and monastic libraries, and their discovery might extend our scanty knowledge concerning Spanish books of the Graal. The same observation may apply also to Portugal ; but in the absence of all research we must be content with the little which has been gleaned from the common sources of knowledge.

I. *El Baladro del Sabio Merlin con sus Proficias*, printed at Burgos in 1498, of which there is a single extant copy, preserved in a private library at Madrid. The analysis of contents furnished to Gaston Paris shows it to contain : (*a*) The *Early Prose Merlin* of Robert de Borron : (*b*) the continuation of the *Huth Merlin*, so far as the recital of the marriage of Arthur and Guinevere, or a few pages further ; and (*c*) three final chapters which are unknown in the extant *Merlin* texts, but are thought to be derived from the lost *Conte du Brait* of the so-called Hélie de Borron.

II. *Merlin y demanda del Santo Grial*, Seville, 1500. But of this text I find no copy in English public libraries, and there are few particulars available. It is mentioned by Leandro Fernandez de Moratin in his *Origines del Teatro Español*, Madrid, 1830. I suggest, however, that it may have been reprinted in

III. *La Demanda del Sancto Grial : con los marvillosos fechos de Lancarote y de Galas su hijo*, Toledo, 1515. This is now in the British Museum, but was once in the collection of Heber, who had heard of no other copy. It is divided into two parts, being respectively the *Romance of Merlin* and a version of the *Quest of Galahad*. The first part corresponds to the Burgos *El Baladro*, as we know this by the analysis of its contents, and I believe the texts to be substantially identical, though that of Toledo is much longer and is divided into numbered paragraphs, or short sections, instead of into forty chapters. But the reference to *El Baladro* in the *Libros de Caballerias* by Pascual de Gayangos, Madrid, 1857, seems to show that these chapters were subdivided into sections or paragraphs. The first part is therefore based on the *Huth Merlin*, and the second seems to represent the lost Quest attached thereto. It is indeed nearly identical with

IV. *El Historia dos Cavalleiros da Mesa Redonda e da Demanda do Santo Graal*, which is the Portuguese Quest of Galahad, partly printed from a Viennese manuscript by Carl von Reinhardstoellner in *Handschrift* No. 2594 *der K. K. Hofbibliothek zu Wien*, 1887. The points concerning it are (*a*) that it is attributed to Robert de Borron ; (*b*) that it contains things missing from the extant French Quest ; (*c*) that it mentions the promised wounding of Gawain because he attempted to draw from the block of marble that sword which was intended for Galahad alone ; (*d*) that it narrates the murder of Bademagus by Gawain ; and (*e*) that generally it seems to correspond with the indications concerning the missing *Quest* which were gleaned from various sources by Gaston Paris, and included in his Introduction to the *Huth Merlin*, § v., *La Quête du Saint Graal*, vol. i. pp. l–lxii.

G. ADDITAMENTA.—The following brief particulars may interest some of my readers. (1) As regards the *Saone de Nausay*, this Northern French poem of 21,321 lines was edited by Moritz Goldschmid, and forms the 216th publication *Der Litterarischen Vereins in Stuttgart.* Saone, or Sone, who is the hero, received the communication of the mystery of the Holy Graal, and was the means of saving Norway with the help of a sword which once belonged to Joseph of Arimathæa. He married the king's daughter, and reigned after him. The Holy Palladium is described as *li vaisseau . . . qui jadis fu grëalz nommés.* (2) As Sir Tristram went in search of the Graal, according to some of the French romances, those who are disposed to go further into this side-issue may consult the extended analysis of the *Roman de Tristan*, which forms *Fascicule* 82 of the Bibliothèque de l'École des Hautes Études, Paris, 1890-91. He will there find Galahad among the other peers of the Quest, but he is no longer more than a shadow of the perfect Knight. (3) The nearest approach to the Perceval question is in the sense of its antithesis, and perhaps the most express form hereof is in the old Provençal metrical romance which has been translated into modern French by Mary Lapon as *Les Aventures du Chevalier Jaufre et de la Belle Brunissende*, Paris, 1856. Violence and contumely befall the hero every time that he asks a specific question, being why at a certain period of the day every inhabitant of a given district, from peasant to peer, falls into loud lamentation. A fatality leads him, however, to go on asking, just as another fatality prevents the Graal question. The explanation in the present case is that a knight has been wounded, and that whenever the hurt heals it is reopened by the cruelty of his enemy. Sir Jaufre, or Geoffrey, is the son of Dovon, and he is known in the French cycle of Arthurian romance.

PART II

SOME CRITICAL WORKS

It should be understood that the editors of the various texts mentioned in Part I. have prefixed or appended thereto introductory matter of a less or more elaborate kind, and that they are

Appendix

therefore, within their measure, to be regarded as critical editions. To these introductions I do not propose to refer in the present section, nor do I lay any claim either to analysis of contents or exhaustive bibliographical enumeration. The list will be useful for those who desire to carry their studies further, more especially along textual lines, and it has no higher pretension. As it follows, within certain limits, a chronological arrangement, it will help to indicate the growth of the criticism.

Joseph Görres : *Lohengrin, ein alt Deutsche Gedicht*, &c., 1813.
> The introduction is sympathetic and interesting as an early study of the Graal literature. The text is a Vatican MS. It may be mentioned that, according to Görres, Mont Salvatch stands in Salvatierra, in Arragonia, at the entrance into Spain, close to the Valley of Ronceval.

Le Roux de Lincy : *Analyse critique et littéraire du Roman de Garin*, &c., 1835. And *Essai historique et littéraire sur l'abbaye de Fécamp*, 1840.
> This author also was a student of the subject, and his later work is still our authority for the Fécamp legend.

Paulin Paris : *Les Manuscrits françois de la Bibliothèque du Roi*, 7 vols., 1836–48, and *Les Romans de la Table Ronde*, 5 vols., 1868–1877.
> In the first work is contained what I believe to be the earliest account of certain unprinted Graal texts. The second has modernised versions of *The Metrical Joseph, The Book of the Holy Graal, The Early Prose Merlin, The Vulgate Merlin* and the romance of *Lancelot of the Lake*. The long introduction is still interesting and valuable reading. Paulin Paris considered that *The Metrical Joseph* was founded on a Breton Gospel-legend, and that the original Graal text was a Latin Gradual.

Francisque Michel and Thomas Wright : *Vie de Merlin, attribuée à Geoffroy de Monmouth*, 1837.
> The elaborate introduction is useful for Merlin literature and for allusions to the prophet in other poems and romances.

San Marte, *i.e.* A. Schulz, *Der Mythus van Heiligen Graal*, 1837, regarded at one time as the best survey of the subject; the *Parzival* of Wolfram von Eschenbach, in modern German, 1836–1842 ; *Die Arthur-Sage und die Mährchen des rothen Buchs von Hergest*, 1841 ; *Die Sagen von Merlin*, 1853 ; with other works and numerous contributions to periodical literature.
> San Marte considered : (*a*) that the *Lapis Exilis* was the

Stone of the Lord, which at the beginning of all things was with God ; (*b*) that the passage of the Graal to the Kingdom of Prester John was itself a suggestion of heresy, interior Asia being filled with numerous Christian sects ; (*c*) that Wolfram depicted a Christian Brotherhood, or Kingdom of the Faithful, apart from pope and priesthood ; (*d*) that the Graal was not a Christian relic ; and (*e*) that Wolfram's Provençal Kyot may have been Guiot de Provins, that monk of Clairvaux who wrote the *Bible Guiot* and had himself visited Jerusalem.

Karl Simrock : The *Parzival* of Wolfram von Eschenbach translated into modern German, 1842, immediately after the completion of San Marte's enterprise and traversing his most important veiws ; *Parzival und Titurel*, 1857.

This writer maintained : (*a*) That the original Graal Legend was connected with St. John Baptist, whose head was enshrined at Constantinople and was used to maintain the life of a dying emperor in the eleventh century ; (*b*) that the Templar connections of the *Parsifal* were a mere reflection ; (*c*) that the *Templeisen* were the Knights of San Salvador de Mont Réal—founded in 1120 ; and (*d*) that the Graal and its veneration suggest the Gnostic body called Christians of St. John.

T. H. de la Villemarqué : *Les Romans de la Table Ronde et les contes des anciens Bretons*, 1842 ; *Contes Populaires de la Bretagne*, 2 vols., 1846 (fourth edition) ; *Myrdhinn ou l'Enchanteur Merlin* (new edition), 1861.

In the last work Merlin is treated as a mythological, historical, legendary and romantic character. It is entertaining, but largely fantastic, and at the present day it is difficult to accept anything advanced by this writer without careful verification. He considered that a pagan tradition was received from the bards and, in combination with a particular presentation of the Eucharistic mystery, was passed on to the romancers of northern France. The Graal is Celtic, and the word signifies a basin.

Reichel : *Studien zu Parzival*, 1856.

This work was written in opposition to San Marte, and it denied that the theology of the twelfth century should be applied to the interpretation of the poem.

Louis Moland : *Origines littéraires de la France*, 1862.

(*a*) The old history, the high history, was contained in a Latin book ; (*b*) it embodied that chivalrous ideal which it was sought to realise in the Temple ; (*c*) this was con-

Appendix

nected with another idea, namely, that of communion apart ; (*d*) the vast cycle formed a systematic allegory ; (*e*) but folk-lore intervened and a strange admixture followed ; (*f*) it is doubtful whether the books of the Holy Graal can rank as orthodox ; (*g*) beneath the allegory there are *tendances suspectes ;* (*h*) the errors diffused among the Templars may have been reflected into works which evidently embody their principles.

S. Baring-Gould : *Curious Myths of the Middle Ages,* 1867.
At the period of its publication the essay on the *Sangreal,* contained herein, provided a certain knowledge in a populai form, but at this day it is without office or appeal.

F. G. Bergmann : *The San Grĕal,* 1870.
I think that this account was the first to offer in English an outline of the *Later Titurel,* by A. von Scharfenberg. The two sources of all Graal romances are the Quest-poem of Guyot and a Graal-history written in Latin by Walter Map. The tract is translated from the French, but the fact is not specified.

Gustav Oppert : *Der Presbyter Johannes in Sage und Geschichte,* 1870.
An interesting summary of the known facts concerning this mythical personage.

Zarncke : *Zur Geschichte der Gralsage,* 1876.
So far from being Provençal or Celtic, Graal literature has its source in the legends concerning Joseph of Arimathæa. The metrical romance of De Borron is the earliest in point of time and Chrétien drew therefrom, but also from the *Quest of Galahad,* which itself was preceded by some form of *The Book of the Holy Graal.* Guiot was an invention of Wolfram.

A. Birch-Hirschfeld : *Die Sage, vom Gral,* 1877 ; *Ueber die den provenzalischen Troubadours des xii. und xiii. Jahrunderts,* 1878. The first work created a strong impression, and exercised great influence at its period. The history of Robert de Borron preceded Chrétien, who drew from De Borron's *Per-ceval-Quest,* on which Gautier also depended. *The Longer Prose Perceval* drew from the *Quest of Galahad* and *The Book of the Holy Graal.* The Graal is not Celtic, and Robert de Borron followed the *Vindicta Salvatoris* and the *Gesta Pilati.* His Sacred Vessel is one of sacramental grace. There is a powerful defence of the *Didot Perceval,* in which De Borron ingarnered Breton legends. The source of Wolfram was Chrétien, and him only.

E. Martin : The decisive findings of Birch-Hirschfeld were opposed by this writer in a German *Journal of Archæology,* 1878, and in *Zur Gralsage, Unterschungen*, 1880. He maintained the Celtic origin of the legend, the possibility of a Latin version, the unlikelihood that the *Didot Perceval* belongs to the De Borron trilogy, and that the derivation of Wolfram was from a source other than Chrétien.

C. Domanig : *Parzival-Studien* (Two Parts), 1878–80.

A defence of Wolfram as an adherent of the Catholic faith.

G. Bötticher : *Die Wolfram Literatur seit Lachmann*, 1880.

A consideration of the argument for and against the in-debtedness of Wolfram to no source but that of Chrétien and tending to the conclusion that another source is probable.

J. Van Santen : *Zur Beurtheilung Wolfram von Eschenbach*, 1882.

A hostile criticism of the poet's ethical position, founded, however, not on the limitations of the *Parsifal*, but on Wolfram's general concessions to the morality of his time.

W. Hertz : *Sage vom Parzival und dem Gral*, 1882.

The motive of the legends must be sought in the anti-Papal spirit of the British Church, within which it was, for this and other reasons, developed.

Paul Steinbach : *Vber dem Einfluss des Crestien de Troies auf die altenglische Literatur*, 1885.

An exhaustive study of the debt due to Chrétien and Breton tradition by the Thornton *Syr Percyvelle*.

M. Gaster : *Jewish Sources of and Parallels to the Early English Metrical Legends of King Arthur and Merlin*, 1887.

The contention is that the commerce between women and demons has its authority in the Talmud, to which I might add that the legendary orgies of the mediæval Black Sabbath have some of their roots therein. I do not think that comparisons of this kind serve much purpose.

Gaston Paris : *La Littérature française au moyen-age*, 1888 ; *Histoire Littéraire de la France*, vol. xxx., 1888.

I cite two instances only from the long literary record of this excellent and charming scholar. It is impossible in a brief note to speak of his whole achievement. I will specify only one point with which I have just made acquaintance, and this is that, in his opinion, as independently in my own, the beginning and the end of Gerbert's alternative sequel to the *Conte del Graal* may have suffered alteration.

Alfred Nutt : *Studies on the Legend of the Holy Graal*, 1888.

The sub-title adds—" with special reference to the hypothesis of its Celtic origin." It was this work which paved a way for the criticism of the Graal literature in England, and I am certain that no more welcome offering could be made to

Appendix

scholars everywhere than the issue of a new edition, with such extension and revision as would be warranted by the present state of our knowledge.   Mr. Nutt has done more than any one in this country to promote the acceptance of the Celtic source in legend, but he has the gift of treating all the competitive hypotheses on every side of the subject with moderation and fairness.   He regards the De Borron story as the starting-point of Christian transformation, and of late years he has shown some disposition to accept the possibility of Templar influence on the development of the literature.   In 1902 Mr. Nutt published a pamphlet on the *Legends of the Holy Graal* which offers a serviceable summary.

Professor Rhys : *Studies in the Arthurian Legend,* 1891.

A development of Welsh analogies, a theory of Celtic origins, tinctured with the old dream of solar myths at the root of many of the stories.

Richard Heinzel : *Ueber die franzoezischen Gralromane,* 1891.

An elaborate and careful examination.   The *Longer Prose Perceval* is said to depend from Gerbert, and the priority of the Quest is rejected.

G. M. Harper : *The Legend of the Holy Graal,* 1893.

Though it can be scarcely regarded as a work of original research there is here an useful resumption of results obtained by scholarship, showing an acquaintance with the original documents of the literature.   The Graal, as typifying the Eucharist, was the beginning, middle and end of all the cycles.   "It is as if a Divine hand had been holding the hands of all the writers of these books."

Miss Jessie L. Weston : I have mentioned already the English translation of the *Parsifal,* which has only one disadvantage, being its unfortunate metrical form.   Since the period of its publication, Miss Weston has written : (1) *The Legend of Gawain,* 1897 ; (2) *The Legend of Sir Lancelot du Lac,* 1900 ; (3) *The Three Days' Tournament,* 1902 ; (4) *The Legend of Perceval,* vol. i., 1906.   These are individual monographs, and the two last are of particular and high importance.   Miss Weston has also translated several Arthurian texts not included in the great collection of Malory, and among these I will mention (5) the episode of *Morien,* 1901, derived from the *Dutch Lancelot,* and (6) *Sir Gawain at the Grail Castle,* 1903, being extracts from the *Conte del Graal, Diu Crône,* by Heinrich, and the prose *Lancelot.*   The others are not of our concern exactly.

Among English writers, Miss Weston is our foremost textual

scholar in respect of the literature of the Holy Graal. In the *Legend of Sir Lancelot* she has dwelt upon the necessity of collating the numerous manuscripts of this vast romance with a view to the production of a sound text. Whether she herself projects this undertaking there is no means of knowing; perhaps it would be possible only to a concerted effort, but there is no single student who is better fitted for the task. In the *Legend of Perceval* she has made an important first-hand study of texts now extant of the *Conte del Graal*, and the results are with us. It is to her that we owe the discovery of the Fécamp reference in Manessier. The place of that abbey in the reliquary-history of the Precious Blood has been known, of course, to students since the collection of documents included by Leroux de Lincy in his account of the ancient religious foundation.

Dr. Sebastian Evans : *In Quest of the Holy Graal*, 1898.

An amazing dream, which identifies Innocent III. with the Rich Fisherman, the Emperor with the King of Castle Mortal, St. Dominic with Perceval, the Interdict of 1208 with the languishment and enchantments of Britain, and the question which should have been asked, but was not, with an omission of St. Dominic to secure the exemption of the Cistercians from certain effects of the Interdict. Lancelot is the elder Simon de Montfort ; Gawain is Fulke of Marseilles ; Alain le Gros is Alanus de Insulis, the universal Doctor ; Yglais, the mother of Perceval, is Holy Church. The Graal is, of course, the Eucharist, which is denied to Logres. The speculation is founded on the *Longer Prose Perceval*, so that no distraction is caused by the presence of Blanchefleur, but as all French texts of quest speak of the removal or internment of the Sacred Vessel, it is a pity that the ingenuity which has woven this wonderful web should have passed such a point in silence. I fear that in all truth Dr. Evans has not succeeded in creating more conviction than, I suppose, has Dr. Vercoutre; but he has gifts in literature, gifts of entertainment and gifts of subtlety which are wanting to his French *confrère*.

Dr. Wendelin Foerster—who projected a complete edition of the works of Chrétien de Troyes—has published several texts, including (1) *Erec und Énid*, 1896; (2) *Cligés*, 1901; (3) *Yvain*, 1902.

As regards the *Conte del Graal*, he considered that its confessed prototype, the book belonging to Count Philip of Flanders, was not a quest of the Sacred Vessel but a prose account of the Palladium.

Appendix

Paul Hagan : *Der Graal*, 1900.

This study has been welcomed warmly by scholars; it is valuable in many respects, but more particularly for the. German cycle, Guiot de Provence and his eastern elements Dr. Hagan suggests a Persian origin for the name Flegitanis = Felek thâni = *sphæra altera*.

Dr. A. T. Vercoutre : *Origine et Genèse de la Légende du Saint Graal*, 1901.

This tract claims to offer the solution of a literary problem. The legend of the Graal is based upon an error of translation. The supposed Vessel, or *Vas*, is the Celtic *Vasso*, and the romances really commemorate the Gaulish Temple of Puy de Dôme, mentioned by Gregory of Tours. It was originally Gaulish and dedicated to Lug, but it was Roman subsequently, and was then sacred to Mercury. It was a place of initiation and as such hidden from the world, like the Graal. The Temple was unearthed in 1873. This appears to be a frantic hypothesis.

W. A. Nitze : *The Old French Graal Romance*, 1902.

Here is an attempt to determine more fully the relation of the *Longer Prose Perceval* to Chrétien and his continuators. Mr. Nitze agrees that we have no certain knowledge as to the original form of Gerbert's poem.

C. Macdonald : *Origin of the Legend of the Holy Graal*, 1903.

This is, unfortunately, an introduction only to a large projected work, but the death of the author intervened. There is an interesting account of early apocryphal and later traditions concerning Joseph, Nicodemus, Pilate, Veronica, &c. The intention was—at the term of a full inquiry into the documentary sources—to consider whether the Graal tradition at its core was known under another form before it was adapted to Christian symbolism, "having been borrowed from a system of which it was a legitimate and undoubted growth and which presented many points in common with the hagiology and ritual of both eastern and western churches."

Dorothy Kempe : *Legend of the Holy Graal*, 1905.

This pamphlet was written to accompany the *History of the Holy Graal* of Lovelich or Lonelich. The prospectus of the *Early English Text Society* describes it as a capital summary. It is a reflection of previous English authorities.

PART III

PHASES OF INTERPRETATION

The few works which will be included in this section lie outside the ordinary range of scholarship, and for this reason—whatever their merits or defects—I have placed them under a sub-title which is designed to mark their particular distinction of motive.

I. Eugène Aroux : (a) *Dante, Hérétique, Révolutionnaire, et Socialiste : Révélations d'un Catholique sur le Moyen Age*, 1854 ; (b) *Les Mystères de la Chevalerie et de l'Amour Platonique au Moyen Age*, 1858.

There are others, but these will suffice, and I have dealt with the author's standpoint sufficiently in the text of the present work. As instances of criticism moving under heavy spells of sorcery, as phenomena of reverie in research, I know few things so profoundly entertaining. The section entitled *La Massénie du Saint Graal* in the later work deserves and would receive a crown in any Academy of Fantasy.

II. F. Naelf : *Opinions Religieuses des Templiers*, 1890.

The Graal is the symbol of mystic wisdom and of the communion between God and Man. It is affirmed that the Templars perpetuated a secret doctrine which did not perish with them, if they indeed perished ; it passed afterwards through Masonry and is there still embedded. The position of the Johannine sect is considered in the same connection. On our own part, we have already appreciated and set aside these interesting views.

III. Émile Burnouf : *Le Vase Sacré et ce qu'il contient*, 1896.

The legend of the Holy Graal contains certain essential elements of the universal *cultus* which prevailed among the Aryan peoples—which elements are identical with those of India, Persia and Greece. The romances are not important for the religious history of the Sacred Vessel ; for that in its Christian aspects we must have recourse to the liturgical texts and ceremonies of the Catholic Church. The true legend of the Graal goes back, however, through Christian times, and thence through the great faiths of the East, to the Vedic Hymns, wherein its explanation is found—otherwise, in that vase which contains *Agni* under the appearance of *Soma*.

708

Appendix

IV. Isabel Cooper-Oakley : *Traces of a Hidden Tradition in Masonry and Mediæval Mysticism,* 1900.

Mrs. Cooper-Oakley's chief authorities are Gabriele Rossetti and Eugène Aroux. This is in respect of her views on Masonic tradition, but unfortunately neither of these writers was acquainted at first-hand with the subject, seeing that neither were Masons. As regards the literature of the Holy Graal, a considerable acquaintance is shown with the German cycle, though the writer prefers to depend on her somewhat doubtful precursors rather than on her own impressions. In this way she reflects the opinions of Burnouf as expressed in *Le Vase Sacré.* She has written some interesting papers, but they do not carry us further than the pre-occupations of those whom she cites. She is right on the fact that there is assuredly a tradition in Masonry and a tradition in the literature of the Holy Graal, but on the nature of that tradition she is of necessity far from the goal because those are far whom she follows.

A. L. Cleather and Basil Crump : *Parsifal, Lohengrin and the Legend of the Holy Graal,* 1904.

We have here a summary of Wagner's two operatic dramas from the standpoint of Wagner himself, or, as the sub-title says, "described and interpreted" in accordance with his own writings. The Graal in Wagner is like the Arthurian chronicles in Tennyson, a high and uplifting ceremonial, but not more faithful to the matter of the German cycle than is the English poet to Malory whom he followed. In their account of the sacramental legend, apart from Wagner, Miss Cleather and her collaborator have been guided in part by accepted critics of the literature, like Nutt and Simrock, whose views they have combined with those of Mrs. Cooper-Oakley and her sources. It is said that, according to tradition, the abode of the Holy Graal is on a lofty mountain of India—being, I suppose, a reference to the realm of Prester John. It came also originally from the East, probably from the Himalayas. It connects with Johannine tradition and Templar chivalry.

It should be added that I published in seven successive issues of Mr. Ralph Shirley's monthly magazine, *The Occult Review,* some articles on the Graal and its literature which constituted a first draft or summary of the present work. They appeared from March to September 1907. Two of these issues also contain some particulars concerning an alleged discovery of the Holy Graal at Glastonbury, with remarks upon the claim and its value.

INDEX

Index

Index

Index

Index

Printed in the United States
51553LVS00004B/1